THE POETICAL WORKS OF EDMUND SPENSER

IN THREE VOLUMES

VOLUME II

SPENSER'S
FAERIE QUEENE

EDITED BY

J. C. SMITH

VOLUME I: BOOKS I–III

OXFORD
AT THE CLARENDON PRESS

Oxford University Press, Amen House, London E.C.4

GLASGOW   NEW YORK   TORONTO   MELBOURNE   WELLINGTON
BOMBAY   CALCUTTA   MADRAS   KARACHI   LAHORE   DACCA
CAPE TOWN   SALISBURY   NAIROBI   IBADAN   ACCRA
KUALA LUMPUR   HONG KONG

FIRST PUBLISHED 1909
REPRINTED LITHOGRAPHICALLY IN GREAT BRITAIN
AT THE UNIVERSITY PRESS, OXFORD
FROM SHEETS OF THE FIRST IMPRESSION
1961, 1964

INTRODUCTION.

I.

IN these volumes I seek to present a true text of the *Faerie Queene*, founded upon a fresh collation of the Quartos of 1590 and 1596 and the Folio of 1609. I shall call these editions by their dates for short.

The fragmentary Seventh Book appeared first in 1609 : for the rest the text is based on 1596. Some typographical peculiarities — long s, &, ŏ, and superscribed m and n (e.g. frŏ, whē)—have not been reproduced, but noted only where they first occur. With these exceptions, the readings of 1596 if not adopted in the text are recorded in the notes ; so that text and notes together amount, in effect, to a complete reprint of 1596. No such completeness has been attempted in recording variants from 1590 and 1609. But all verbal differences are recorded, and all differences of punctuation that imply a different view of the meaning. Mere changes of spelling that answer to no change of pronunciation are, as a rule, ignored ; but I have recorded such differences of spelling as seemed likely to interest students of Elizabethan phonology, grammar, and usage. The evidence of these variants must be used with caution in view of Spenser's deliberate archaism. Yet I believe that they have some value. I give one instance in each kind :—

1. A fluid *e*-sound is indicated by the variants 'seeldome' 1590, 'seldome' 1596, 'sildom' 1609, at I. iv. 23, l. 5.

2. Syllabic -*es* in possessives and plurals, which still lingered in the early fifteen-nineties, has grown quite strange to the editor of 1609. To this point I shall return.

3. The conjunctions 'since' and 'sith' are used indifferently in 1590 and 1596, choice of one or other form being determined by euphony alone. But 1609 makes a deliberate, though not quite consistent, attempt to appropriate 'since' to the temporal, 'sith' to the causal sense. The attempt unfortunately did not avail to save the more primitive form.

I have departed from the punctuation of 1596 only where it seemed likely to puzzle or mislead a modern reader. These departures, which are all recorded, are not very numerous. Spenser's punctuation, though by no means sacrosanct, is less arbitrary than might at first appear; but, as Mr. Gregory Smith says of the punctuation of Addison, it has a rhetorical rather than a logical value. We feel its force best when we read the poem aloud. Two peculiarities are so common that the reader may be warned of them here. One is the absence of punctuation with vocatives: the other is the single comma after qualifying phrases. With this warning I leave these peculiarities, as a rule, unchanged.

In the treatment of capitals and in the distribution of roman and italic type I have followed the same principle of adhering, wherever possible, to the original text.

I have regularized the spelling of proper names wherever the variation seemed to be due to the printer rather than the poet. And this is generally the case with double letters. But for many variations in proper names Spenser was himself responsible. He varied them sometimes for the sake of the metre, as *Serena, Serene*; or of the rhyme, as *Florimell, Florimele*. In two instances he seems actually to have wavered or changed his mind. *Braggadocchio's* name is generally spelt thus in Book II; in Books III and IV it varies; in V. iii it is regularly *Braggadochio*. So we generally find *Arthegall* in Book III, but *Artegall* regularly in Book V; 1609, however, returns to *Arthegall*.

II.

Aiming not at a reprint but a true text, I have not hesitated to depart from 1596 wherever I believed it to be in error and the error the printer's.   But it is no part of an editor's duty to correct, though he may indicate, mistakes made by the author himself.   There are many such in the *Faerie Queene.*

(1) There are mistakes of fact, of literary allusion, of quantity in classical names, hardly to be avoided by a poet writing far from libraries.

(2) There are confusions of personages, or of names of personages, within the poem itself.   Sir *Guyon* is confused with the *Redcrosse Knight* in III. ii. 4, and with Prince *Arthur* in II. viii. 48 (but not in 1609); *Æmylia* with *Pœana* in IV. ix. Arg.; *Calepine* with *Calidore* in VI. vi. 17; while over *Serena* Spenser's confusion becomes comical—he calls her *Crispina* in VI. iii. 23,[1] and *Matilda* in VI. v. Arg.

(3) Some lines are hypermetrical; some are short by a foot; and there are two or three broken lines.   One of these last (III. iv. 39, l. 7) is certainly intentional, and all may be so; the supposed example of Virgil may have influenced Spenser in this.

(4) Imperfect rhymes and concords are numerous, especially in Books IV, V, and VI.

(5) There is one form of imperfect rhyme so singular as to deserve a fuller discussion.   Its nature will be best seen in an example :—

'Like two faire marble pillours they were seene,
    Which doe the temple of the Gods support, (2)
Whom all the people decke with girlands greene,
    And honour in their festiuall resort; (4)

---

[1] But this was corrected as the sheet passed through the press.   See note *ad loc.* in the Critical Appendix.

Those same with stately grace, and princely port (5)
She taught to tread, when she her selfe would grace,
But with the wooddie Nymphes when she did play, (7)
Or when the flying Libbard she did chace,
She could them nimbly moue, and after fly apace.'

(II. iii. 28.)

Here 'play' in l. 7 is rhymed to 'support', 'resort', 'port': 'sport' is the obvious correction. There are, in all, nine instances of this singularity in the *Faerie Queene*. I subjoin them all, citing the rhyme-words only: the number following each word shows the line that it ends:—

1. day (2), dismay (4), way (5), chace (7) (II. ii. 7)
2. make (6), bold (8), told (9) (II. ii. 42)
3. support (2), resort (4), port (5), play (7) (II. iii. 28)
4. leaue (2), cleaue (4), bereaue (5), vpreare (7)
(II. viii. 29)
5. spyde (6), law (8), draw (9) (III. vi. 40)
6. enclose (2), plaine (4), Maine (5), complaine (7)
(III. vii. 34)
7. times (6), equipage (8), parentage (9) (IV. xi. 17)
8. place (2), aread (4), dread (5), read (7) (V. Proem 11)
9. desyre (2), entyre (4), yre (5), meed (7) (V. xi. 61)

In every case the correction is obvious: 'chace' should be 'pray' (i.e. prey); 'make', 'hold'; 'play', 'sport'; 'vpreare', 'vpheaue'; 'spyde', 'saw'; 'enclose', 'containe'; 'times', 'age'; 'place', 'stead' (as in 1609); 'meed', 'hyre'. The phenomenon may now be described in general terms: in these nine places Spenser substitutes for a rhyming word a metrically equivalent synonym which does not rhyme. Our analysis shows further that, the rhyme-scheme of the Spenserian stanza being *ababbcbcc*, this substitution occurs only in the first or last of the *b*-group, or in the first of the *c*-group. It seems as if, borne along on the swell of his metre and the easy flow of his imagination, two words identical in sense and metre but different in sound rose to the poet's mind almost simultaneously; and the one which he meant to reject slipped nevertheless from his pen, having been (we infer) the first to occur. This explains why this phenomenon always occurs either in the first word of a rhyme-group, where the rhyme is still undetermined; or, if in the last, then only in the last of the *b*-group, where the ear has already been satisfied with as many as three rhymes; and why it never occurs in the *a*-group, where two rhymeless endings would at once have alarmed the ear. I have dwelt on this phenomenon at some length because it is, so far as I know, peculiar to Spenser.[1]

(6) I must glance at another, though a rare, source of error. Our sage and serious Spenser was a thoughtful, even a philosophic writer; but his thought is large, simple, contemplative, not acute and analytic. When he has to deal with a subtle or complex situation he sometimes involves himself inextricably. If any lover of Spenser resent this judgement, let him apply his devotion to explain or emend II. v. 12, ll. 8 and 9; V. vi. 5, ll. 6 and 7; V. vi. 26, ll. 5 and 6: to me these passages appear incorrigible.

III.

The first mention of the *Faerie Queene* occurs in a letter of Spenser's to Gabriel Harvey, dated *Quarto Nonas Aprilis* 1580. 'I wil in hande forthwith,' he writes, 'with my *Faery Queene*, whyche I praye you hartily send me with al expedition : and your frendly Letters, and long expected

---

[1] The peculiarity consists not in the occasional occurrence of a rhymeless line—a thing that can easily be paralleled from Shelley or any poet of equal fluency—but in the fact that the right word is in every case so obvious that we cannot but believe it to have been in Spenser's mind.

Judgement wythal.' 'I haue nowe sent hir home at the laste,' writes Harvey in reply. These phrases show that the parcel of the *Faerie Queene* had been in Harvey's hands for some considerable time. The poem must therefore have been begun not later than 1579. Now in 1579 Spenser was an inmate of Leicester House, and the constant associate of Sir Philip Sidney. There is therefore no reason to doubt the assertion of W. L. in his commendatory verses that by Sidney the poem was originally inspired.

Harvey's long-expected judgement, when it came, was far from favourable. But the poet was not discouraged, and doubtless took the manuscript with him when he went to Ireland with Lord Grey in August, 1580. Though he afterwards spoke of the poem as 'wilde fruit which salvage soyl hath bred', there is some reason to think that he had actually written as much as a book and a half before he left England. For though allusions to Ireland are not rare in the *Faerie Queene*, the first of them occurs in II. ix. 16.[1] Moreover, the industry of commentators has discovered in Book I only one imitation of Tasso's *Gierusalemme Liberata*,

---

[1] This argument loses some of its weight from the likelihood that Spenser had been in Ireland before 1580. In his *View of the Present State of Ireland*, Irenæus, who is Spenser's mouthpiece, speaks of himself as an eyewitness of the execution of Murrogh O'Brien, which took place at Limerick in July, 1577. The statement, of course, is not conclusive, as it would be if made in Spenser's own person. Yet Spenser's account of this hideous incident has the stamp of personal observation, and, taken with the evidence of Phillips's *Theatrum Poetarum Anglicorum*, points to the conclusion that in 1577 Spenser had been sent to Ireland by Leicester with letters to Sir Henry Sidney. His visit, however, must have been brief, and may well have left no trace in his poetry.

Upton believed that the *Ruddymane* episode in II. ii referred to the O'Neills, whose badge was a bloody hand (*v.* the *View of the Present State of Ireland*). If there be anything in this, it makes against the view that a book and a half had been written by August, 1580; for Spenser is not likely to have known the O'Neill 'badge' till he settled in Ireland.

and that doubtful [1] (I. vii. 31); undoubted imitations begin
to appear in II. v, vi, vii, viii, and II. xii blazes with spoils
from the Garden of Armida.   Now the *Gierusalemme Liberata*
was published in 1581 ; an imperfect edition had been issued
surreptitiously in 1580.

Our next glimpse of the *Faerie Queene* we owe to
Lodovick Bryskett, whose *Discourse of Civill Life*, though not
published till 1606, purports to record a conversation held
in his cottage near Dublin as early, it would seem, as the
spring of 1583.   Spenser is one of the interlocutors.   He
is made to say that he has already undertaken a work 'which
is in *heroical verse* under the title of a *Faerie Queene*'; which
work he has 'already well entered into'.   The company
express an 'extreme longing' after this *Faerie Queene*,
'whereof some parcels had been by some of them seene'.

Parcels of the *Faerie Queene* had been seen, it appears, not
only by Spenser's friends in Dublin, but by his literary
contemporaries in London.   I. v. 2 is imitated in Peele's
David and Bethsabe (date unknown, but probably before
1590).   I. vii. 32 and I. viii. 11 are imitated in Act IV,
Sc. 4 and Act IV, Sc. 3 respectively of the second part of
Marlowe's *Tamburlaine* (published 1590, but acted some years
earlier).   Finally, Abraham Fraunce in his *Arcadian Rhetorike*
(1588) quotes Spenser 'in his *Fairie Queene*, 2 booke,
cant. 4'.   Fraunce's quotation is the more interesting in-
asmuch as it shows that by 1588 [2] the *F. Q.* had not only
been composed, but disposed into its present arrangement of

---

[1] The passage in Tasso (*G. L.* ix. 25) is itself an imitation of Virgil, *Aen.*
vii. 785.   Yet the 'greedie pawes' and 'golden wings' of Spenser's picture
seem due to Tasso's 'Sù le zampe s'inalza, e l'ali spande.'

Both these arguments, then, are indecisive; and in the absence of decisive
proof I find it hard to believe that Harvey, who though a pedant was no fool,
can have seen anything like the whole of Book I without recognizing its
superlative merits.

[2] Fraunce's book was licensed on June 11.

books and cantos so far at least as II. iv. It is worth
remarking that all these imitations of and quotations from
F. Q. before it was published are from that part of the
poem which we have seen some reason to think was written
before Spenser left England. Allusions in the poem shed
no certain light on the progress of its composition.

There is no reason to suppose that Spenser composed
the whole of the *F. Q.* in the order in which he gave
it to the world. It is more likely that he worked up
many incidents and episodes as they occurred to him, and
afterwards placed them in the poem. We know that the
Wedding of Thames and Medway, which now forms IV. xi, is
a redaction of an *Epithalamium Thamesis* which he originally
undertook as an experiment in quantitative metre before
April, 1580. And it seems probable that the *Legendes* and
Court of Cupid mentioned by E. K. in his preface to the
Shepheards Calender, as well as the *Pageaunts*[1] mentioned in
the Glosse on *June*, were similarly worked over and incor-
porated in the *F. Q.*

Combining these pieces of evidence, we receive the
impression that for some time after he came to Ireland
Spenser worked but intermittently on the *F. Q.*, resuming
the regular composition and arrangement of the poem about
the time when he ceased to reside in Dublin.[2] By 1588—
the date of Fraunce's quotation—he may have already been
settled at Kilcolman. There, at least, Raleigh found him
in 1589, and was shown the poem; with the result that in
the autumn of that year Spenser accompanied Raleigh to
London, and set about the publication of Books I-III.

---

[1] From these *Pageaunts* E. K. quotes a line:
'An hundred Graces on her eyelidde sate,'
which appears, slightly altered, in *F. Q.* II. iii. 25.

[2] The 'fennes of Allan' (II. ix. 16) would be near New Abbey in Co.
Kildare, where Spenser seems to have occasionally resided in the years 1582-4.

The volume was licensed to William Ponsonbye on Dec. 1, 1589. Spenser's explanatory letter to Raleigh bears date Jan. 23, 1589 (i. e. 1590 N. S.). In the course of 1590, but not before March 25, the volume was published. The printing shows some signs of haste; there is a long list of errata or 'Faults Escaped in the Print'. This list, though not itself faultless, is of paramount authority in determining the text of Books I–III; it is cited in the notes as *F. E.*

In 1591 Spenser returned to Ireland, a disappointed man. I fear that Burleigh had taken occasion of the Milesian tone of certain episodes in Book III to stir the ashes of an old resentment: the second part of *F. Q.* begins and ends with complaints of misconstruction by that 'mighty Pere'. But once back at Kilcolman he resumed his task. At first the stream of poetry flows languidly. The fable rambles, dispersing its force in many channels, like a river choked with sand; the verse flags; the play of alliteration is fitful; and Spenser essays a new, but to my ear an unhappy, variation in the form of a feminine ending.[1] But presently he gathers strength again under some new influence, which one would fain associate with his courtship of Elizabeth Boyle. The treatment of *Britomart* in Book V has strong, dramatic touches beyond anything in the earlier books; and in the lovely pastoral episodes of Book VI the poet lives once more in Arcadia. But positive indications of date are very rare. Book V Canto xi must be later than July 25, 1593, when Henri IV heard that mass which was the price of Paris : the singular dislocation of the Argument to Canto xii—half of which refers to the incidents of Canto xi—suggests that this *Burbon* episode was an afterthought; that it was inserted after Book V had been disposed into Cantos ; and that Spenser meant it to form part of Canto xii. On the ordinary interpretation

---

[1] In the whole of Books I–III there is only one feminine ending. viz. in II. ix. 47. In Books IV–VI such endings abound.

of the *Amoretti*,[1] all these books were finished before, but not long before, his wedding on June 11, 1594 (*v. Sonnet* 80); and on any interpretation they must have been finished by 1595, when Sir Robert Needham brought the manuscript of the *Amoretti* to London. Yet Spenser may have added and retouched up to the date of publication. For, in spite of *Sonnet* 80, I have fancied that when he wrote certain descriptions in Books V and VI Spenser was not only a husband but a father. See especially V. v. 53 (simile of the nurse and infant); V. vi. 14 (the child crying in the night) ; VI. iv. 18, 23, 24 (*Calepine's* treatment of the foundling, which should be compared with *Guyon's* behaviour in a similar situation, II. ii. 1); also VI. iv. 37, particularly line 8. Now Spenser's eldest child was born in 1595. This may be fanciful. What is certain is that towards the close of 1595 Spenser followed Needham to London with the manuscript of the second part of *F. Q.* It was licensed to Ponsonbye on Jan. 20, 1596, and published by autumn of that year. James VI took offence at the treatment of *Duessa*, and had to be appeased by the English Ambassador, whose letter detailing the incident is dated Nov. 12, 1596. The new edition was in two volumes, the first being a reprint, with alterations, of 1590.

Late in 1596, or early in 1597, Spenser returned to Ireland. In 1598 Tyrone's rebellion broke out. In October the rebels attacked and burned Kilcolman Castle. Spenser fled to Cork, whence in December he made his way to London; and there, on Jan. 16, 1599, he died. Ten years after his death a folio edition of *F. Q.* was published by Mathew Lownes, which added to the six books already published two Cantos of *Mutabilitie*, 'which, both for Forme

---

[1] ' On the ordinary interpretation,' I say ; for an attempt has recently been made (*Mod. Lang. Rev.* 1908) to prove that the lady of the *Amoretti* and the ' countrey lasse' of *F. Q.* VI was not Elizabeth Boyle, but Lady Elizabeth Carey.

and Matter, appear to be parcell of some following Booke of the *Faerie Queene*, vnder the Legend of *Constancie*.' These two cantos, with two stanzas of a third, are all that remain of the third part of *F. Q.* Whether Spenser wrote more is unknown. But the fact that the two cantos are numbered vi and vii makes it fairly certain that he had at least sketched the whole Seventh Book. I cannot accept the view that these two cantos are an independent poem, in the sense that they were not designed to form part of *F. Q.* The lines (VII. vi. 37)—

'And, were it not ill fitting for this file,

To sing of hilles and woods, mongst warres and Knights '—

show clearly that they were so designed. That they may have been written independently, in the sense in which the *Wedding of Thames and Medway* was written independently, I am not concerned to deny. The view that these cantos are spurious is unworthy of serious discussion. If they are spurious, there must have been living in 1609 an unknown poet who could write the Spenserian style and stanza as well as Spenser at his best. For there is nothing of its kind in *F. Q.* superior to the pageant [1] of the months and seasons; and no one who really knows Spenser can doubt that the two stanzas which alone remain of the 'vnperfite' eighth canto came from his heart.

IV.

The chief critical problem that confronts an editor of *F. Q.* concerns the text of Books I–III. Should the text of these books be based on 1590 or on 1596? I have chosen the latter. And I have done so, in the main, for a quite general

---

[1] The occurrence of feminine endings makes it very unlikely that this was among the *Pageaunts* mentioned by E. K. The greater part of the *Mutabilitie* cantos was certainly written in Ireland, probably in 1597–8.

reason. 1596 was produced under Spenser's eye and by his authority. That authority must be held to cover both volumes, not the second only. Behind this we cannot go. The case is quite different with the later quartos of the *Shepheards Calender*, which were produced in Spenser's absence.

This general position is confirmed by a minute comparison of 1590 and 1596. To take the more massive changes first: in 1596 Spenser completely remodelled the conclusion of Book III. Instead of bringing *Scudamour* and *Amoret* together, as in 1590, he left them still parted, hoping thus to prolong the interest of their story into Book IV, and so to form a link between the two volumes, which he desired to be read as one continuous poem. For this he sacrificed five glorious stanzas, one of them the most rapturous that he ever wrote. The three stanzas which he substituted are far inferior, as he must have known; but they served his purpose. He also added a new stanza at I. xi. 3. He rewrote single lines, in the interests of sound or sense; he altered single words or phrases; and he made—what is even more significant—several minute changes of order designed to improve the rhythm. Let me add that most of these changes are more happily inspired than the second-thoughts of poets have sometimes been.

I hasten to make two admissions. The first volume of 1596 was not reset afresh from Spenser's manuscript. It was printed from a copy of 1590. In the nature of the case, while it escapes some of the blunders of its original, it reproduces others, and perpetrates some new. Nor did Spenser do more than glance at the proof. The 1596 volumes, as we have seen, were printed rapidly; the poet was busy,[1] and such time as he had for proof-reading was

[1] The scene of the dialogue on the *Present State of Ireland* is laid in England; so that, unless this is a mere literary device, the tract must have been written, or at least begun, during this visit in 1596.

given to the new books. I infer that the alterations which he made in 1590 were made not on the proof, but on the copy. In no other way can we account for that combination of author's corrections with printer's errors which marks the first volume of 1596. And this conclusion is strengthened by another consideration. It is one of the worst faults of 1596 that it so often ignores *F. E.* But the significance of the fault has been overlooked. Making corrections on the copy, Spenser did not trouble himself about errors that he had already noted in *F. E.*; had he made his corrections on the proof, they could not have escaped him.

I believe this to be a true account of the relations of these two texts. But when all is said there remain many places where we cannot pronounce on mere inspection whether an alteration is the author's or the printer's, but must be guided by a calculation of probabilities, inclining (e. g.) to the author where there is clear evidence of his hand in the neighbourhood of the vexed passage, to the printer where the *ductus litterarum* in both readings is suspiciously alike. The most important of these places are discussed in the Critical Appendix to Vol. III.

Has 1609 any independent authority? In the main a reprint of 1596, it is certainly a respectable piece of work, in punctuation especially far more logical and consistent than either of the quartos: the editor seldom fails to show exactly how he understands his text. Our respect for 1609 would be enhanced if we could believe that the editor was Gabriel Harvey, as Todd at one time fancied. But that notion is untenable, and Todd himself abandoned it. We may go further: the editor of 1609 did not belong to the generation of Harvey and Spenser. For this conclusion I will adduce only one piece of evidence, but it is decisive. In the last decade of the sixteenth century syllabic *-es* in possessives and plurals still lingered even in verse not deliberately archaic. But it was strange to the editor of 1609. Sometimes he remarks it, and signalizes his discovery by printing it -*ez*, as 'woundez', 'beastez', 'clothez'. Sometimes he fails to remark it, and fills up the syllable by conjecture : thus '*Nightes* children' becomes '*Nights* drad children' (I. v. 23); 'th'Earthes gloomy shade' becomes 'the Earthes gloomy shade' (III. x. 46). He seems, moreover, to have made little or no use of 1590. When, as sometimes happens, a word has been dropped in 1596, he emends by conjecture: thus at I. ii. 29 :—

'For the coole shade him thither hastly got' 1590;

'For the coole shade thither hastly got' 1596;

'For the coole shadow thither hast'ly got' 1609.

Cf. also III. ix. 13, l. 9, III. xi. 26, l. 7, &c. The few instances in which 1590 and 1609 agree as against 1596 may fairly be set down to coincidence.

Yet I am disposed to assign some independent authority to 1609.[1] The grounds for this view are slight, and may be stated in full :—

(1) At I. x. 20, l. 5, 1609 adds the missing line, 'Dry-shod to passe, she parts the flouds in tway.'

(2) At II. viii. 48, l. 8, it corrects 'Sir *Guyon*' to 'Prince *Arthur*'.

(3) At III. iii. 50, l. 9, it completes the imperfect Alexandrine by adding 'as earst'.

(4) At III. vi. 45, l. 4, it adds a broken line, 'And dearest loue,' to an eight-line stanza.

(5) At IV. xii. 13, ll. 1, 2, 1596 reads:—

'Thus whilst his stony heart with tender ruth

Was toucht, and mighty courage mollifide';

---

[1] No such authority, I think, belongs to the 'Second Folio', though it sometimes corrects printer's errors. In the Critical Appendix I have cited some of its characteristic variants in support of this view.

1609 reads:—

> 'Thus whilst his stony heart was toucht with tender ruth,
>   And mighty courage something mollifide.'

(6) At V. Proem 11, l. 2, it reads 'stead' for the non-rhyming 'place'.

Of these changes, (2) and (3) are not beyond the capacity of an ordinary editor; yet it is worth noting that 1609 does not correct other confusions of names almost as obvious as (2). Even the missing line (1), Spenserian as it sounds, might conceivably be editorial. But to add a *broken* line, like (4), seems to me a touch beyond an editor. And (5) is most easily explained by supposing that Spenser altered the text, meaning to omit 'tender', but left that word standing. (6) is an instance of a phenomenon that has already been discussed. The significant point is that this is the only instance of that phenomenon which is corrected in 1609. An editor who corrected one of these mistakes might be expected to correct others; but the author who perpetrated these non-rhymes would more easily overlook them.

The addition of the *Mutabilitie* cantos in 1609 must be allowed to create a prejudice in favour of the view for which I argue. The editor who recovered so much of Spenser's manuscript may have recovered more: parcels of *F. Q.*, as we have seen, were handed about in London in Spenser's absence. Or—and the form of the variants at IV. xii. 13 makes this the more probable hypothesis—the editor of 1609 may have had a copy of 1596 with some corrections by the author. Finally, it is not impossible that these corrections were actually embodied in exemplars of 1596 which no longer survive. Elizabethan writers were in the habit of correcting sheets as they passed through the press: in *F. Q.* itself I have noted more than a score of places in which the readings of the copies used for this edition differ from those of other copies in the Bodleian or the British Museum, or of copies used by previous editors; and the notes of Church, Upton, and Todd show that they had seen copies which differ in minute points from any now available. As the sheets were probably bound indiscriminately, it is possible that no two exemplars exactly correspond. The charges of careless collation freely bandied among Spenser's editors are sometimes due to this cause.

It remains for me to acknowledge with gratitude the unwearied help that I have received in preparing this edition, first, from my wife, who read 1609 with me twice; next, from my friend Dr. Soutar, of University College, Dundee, who revised the difficult proofs of Books I-III; last, from an unknown coadjutor, Mr. Ostler of the Clarendon Press, to whose skill and vigilance above all I owe whatever measure of accuracy has been secured. An edition like this has little claim to any higher virtue; yet perfect accuracy, even, is too much to hope for in the reproduction, by ordinary typography, of the original spelling and punctuation of a poem which runs to more than 35,000 lines. In the Critical Appendix I have called attention to one or two places in which I have noted what now seem to me to be errors, or on which I have changed my mind since the sheets were printed.

I have also to thank Sir James Murray, Dr. Bradley, and Dr. Craigie for information on points of lexicography; and Mr. Charles Cannan for the protracted loan of his copy of the first folio.

J. C. SMITH.

ST. ANDREWS,
  September, 1909.

BIBLIOGRAPHICAL NOTE.

Of the copies collated for this edition, three are in the Bodleian, viz. :—

(1) Malone 615, Books I–III, 1590.

(2) Malone 616, Books IV–VI, 1596.

(3) 4° Art. Seld. S. 22, Books I–VI, 1596 (collated for Books I–III).

For 1609 I have used (4) a copy belonging to Mr. Charles Cannan.

The following copies, though not collated *verbatim*, have been examined for variants :—

(5) Malone 7, 1609 ⎫

(6) M. 4. 5 Art. { Books I–III, 1611 / Books IV–VII, 1612 ⎬ in the Bodleian.

(7) Douce S. 817 { Books I–III, 1609 / Books IV–VII, 1613 ⎭

(8) G. 11535, 6 { Books I–III, 1590 / Books IV–VI, 1596

(9) C. 12. h. 17, 18 { Books I–III, 1590 / Books IV–VI, 1596

(10) 686 g. 21, 22, 1596

(11) G. 11537, 1596 ⎬ in the British Museum.

(12) C. 57. f. 6, 1609

(13) 78 g 13 { Books I–III, 1609 / Books IV–VII, 1613

(14) 79 h. 23 { Books I–III, 1611 / Books IV–VII, 1613

The bibliographical note on Spenser in the *Dictionary of National Biography* appears to ignore 4° Art. Seld. S. 22.

The 1590, 1596, 1609 editions of *F. Q.* have been described already. In 1611 Lownes (the publisher of the 1609 *F. Q.*) set about a complete edition of Spenser's poems. But having on hand unsold copies of 1609, he incorporated parts of these under the new title-page.[1] This has happened to (6), the first part of which is identical with 1609, except for the title-page and dedication. The genuine 1611 edition of *F. Q.* I–III is represented by

---

[1] From a MS. note of Malone's I learn that Ponsonbye had played the same trick in 1596; and even of the 1617 folio Church avers that some copies are made up with sheets of the old 1611.

the first part of (14). The second part of (6), bearing date 1612, has been reset: it is identical with the second parts of (7), (13), (14), which bear date 1613. No 1611 edition of *F. Q.* IV–VII is known to me. But in the footnotes I have followed the custom of citing this 'Second Folio' as 1611, except where readings not found by me in editions prior to 1612–13 have been attributed to 1609 by previous editors, misled perhaps by the omission from the British Museum catalogue of the second title to (13). In the Critical Appendix on Books IV–VII I cite this Second Folio (for these Books) as 16(11)–12–13.

Subsequent editions of Spenser's works:—The folios of 1617, 1679 (the latter said to have been overseen by Dryden); ed. J. Hughes, 1715; H. J. Todd, 1805; F. J. Child, 1855; J. P. Collier, 1862; R. Morris, 1869; A. B. Grosart, 1882–4.

Separate editions of *Faerie Queene*:—ed. J. Upton, 1758; R. Church, 1758–9; Kate M. Warren, 1897–1900.

Commentaries:— *Remarks on Spenser's Poems*, by J. Jortin, 1734.

Observations on the Faerie Queene, by T. Warton, 1754.

[For the matter of this note I am largely indebted to Mr. Ostler and Mr. Percy Simpson.]

CONTENTS.

THE FAERIE QVEENE.

THE FAERIE QVEENE.

Difposed into twelue bookes,

Fashioning

XII. Morall vertues.

LONDON

Printed for VVilliam Ponfonbie.

1 5 9 6.

TO
THE MOST HIGH,
MIGHTIE
And
MAGNIFICENT
EMPRESSE RENOVV-
MED FOR PIETIE, VER-
TVE, AND ALL GRATIOVS
GOVERNMENT ELIZABETH BY
THE GRACE OF GOD QVEENE
OF ENGLAND FRAVNCE AND
IRELAND AND OF VIRGI-
NIA, DEFENDOVR OF THE
FAITH, &c. HER MOST
HVMBLE SERVAVNT
EDMVND SPENSER
DOTH IN ALL HV-
MILITIE DEDI-
CATE, PRE-
SENT
AND CONSECRATE THESE
HIS LABOVRS TO LIVE
VVITH THE ETERNI-
TIE OF HER
FAME.

THE FIRST
BOOKE OF THE
FAERIE QVEENE.

Contayning

THE LEGENDE OF THE
KNIGHT OF THE RED CROSSE,

OR

OF HOLINESSE.

LO I the man, whose Muse whilome did maske, i
 As time her taught, in lowly Shepheards weeds,
 Am now enforst a far vnfitter taske,
 For trumpets sterne to chaunge mine Oaten reeds,
 And sing of Knights and Ladies gentle deeds ;
 Whose prayses hauing slept in silence long,
 Me, all too meane, the sacred Muse areeds
 To blazon broad emongst her learned throng :
Fierce warres and faithfull loues shall moralize my song.

Helpe then, O holy Virgin chiefe of nine, ii
 Thy weaker Nouice to performe thy will,
 Lay forth out of thine euerlasting scryne
 The antique rolles, which there lye hidden still,
 Of Faerie knights and fairest *Tanaquill*,
 Whom that most noble Briton Prince so long
 Sought through the world, and suffered so much ill,
 That I must rue his vndeserued wrong :
O helpe thou my weake wit, and sharpen my dull tong.

i 2 taught *1596* 8 'broad, amongst *1609* ii 1 O] ô *1596, 1609 passim*

And thou most dreaded impe of highest *Ioue*,   iii
  Faire *Venus* sonne, that with thy cruell dart
  At that good knight so cunningly didst roue,
  That glorious fire it kindled in his hart,
  Lay now thy deadly Heben bow apart,
  And with thy mother milde come to mine ayde :
  Come both, and with you bring triumphant *Mart*,
  In loues and gentle iollities arrayd,
After his murdrous spoiles and bloudy rage allayd.

And with them eke, O Goddesse heauenly bright,   iv
  Mirrour of grace and Maiestie diuine,
  Great Lady of the greatest Isle, whose light
  Like *Phœbus* lampe throughout the world doth shine,
  Shed thy faire beames into my feeble eyne,
  And raise my thoughts too humble and too vile,
  To thinke of that true glorious type of thine,
  The argument of mine afflicted stile :
The which to heare, vouchsafe, O dearest dred a-while.

iv 5 my] mine 1590

Canto I.

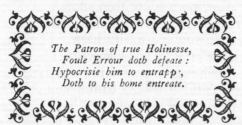

The Patron of true Holinesse,
Foule Errour doth defeate :
Hypocrisie him to entrappe,
Doth to his home entreate.

A Gentle Knight was pricking on the plaine,   i
Y cladd in mightie armes and siluer shielde,
Wherein old dints of deepe wounds did remaine,
The cruell markes of many' a bloudy fielde ;
Yet armes till that time did he neuer wield :
His angry steede did chide his foming bitt,
As much disdayning to the curbe to yield :
Full iolly knight he seemd, and faire did sitt,
As one for knightly giusts and fierce encounters fitt.

But on his brest a bloudie Crosse he bore,   ii
The deare remembrance of his dying Lord,
For whose sweete sake that glorious badge he wore,
And dead as liuing euer him ador'd :
Vpon his shield the like was also scor'd,
For soueraine hope, which in his helpe he had :
Right faithfull true he was in deede and word,
But of his cheere did seeme too solemne sad ;
Yet nothing did he dread, but euer was ydrad.

Vpon a great aduenture he was bond,   iii
That greatest *Gloriana* to him gaue,
That greatest Glorious Queene of *Faerie* lond,
To winne him worship, and her grace to haue,
Which of all earthly things he most did craue ;
And euer as he rode, his hart did earne
To proue his puissance in battell braue
Vpon his foe, and his new force to learne ;
Vpon his foe, a Dragon horrible and stearne.

Arg. 3 *entrape 1596 : entrap 1609*   i 4 bloody *1590 passim*
ii 1 But] And *1590*

A louely Ladie rode him faire beside, iv
   Vpon a lowly Asse more white then snow,
   Yet she much whiter, but the same did hide
   Vnder a vele, that wimpled was full low,
   And ouer all a blacke stole she did throw,
   As one that inly mournd: so was she sad,
   And heauie sat vpon her palfrey slow :
   Seemed in heart some hidden care she had,
And by her in a line a milke white lambe she lad.

So pure an innocent, as that same lambe, v
   She was in life and euery vertuous lore,
   And by descent from Royall lynage came
   Of ancient Kings and Queenes, that had of yore
   Their scepters stretcht from East to Westerne shore,
   And all the world in their subiection held ;
   Till that infernall feend with foule vprore
   Forwasted all their land, and them expeld:
Whom to auenge, she had this Knight from far compeld.

Behind her farre away a Dwarfe did lag, vi
   That lasie seemd in being euer last,
   Or wearied with bearing of her bag
   Of needments at his backe. Thus as they past,
   The day with cloudes was suddeine ouercast,
   And angry *Ioue* an hideous storme of raine
   Did poure into his Lemans lap so fast,
   That euery wight to shrowd it did constrain,
And this faire couple eke to shroud themselues were fain.

Enforst to seeke some couert nigh at hand, vii
   A shadie groue not far away they spide,
   That promist ayde the tempest to withstand:
   Whose loftie trees yclad with sommers pride,
   Did spred so broad, that heauens light did hide,
   Not perceable with power of any starre :
   And all within were pathes and alleies wide,
   With footing worne, and leading inward farre :
Faire harbour that them seemes ; so in they entred arre.

   iv 7 sat] sate *1590*   v 1 and innocent *1590* : an Innocent *1609*
9 cõpeld *1590, 1596 passim*

And foorth they passe, with pleasure forward led,   viii
    Ioying to heare the birdes sweete harmony,
    Which therein shrouded from the tempest dred,
    Seemd in their song to scorne the cruell sky.
    Much can they prayse the trees so straight and hy,
    The sayling Pine, the Cedar proud and tall,
    The vine-prop Elme, the Poplar neuer dry,
    The builder Oake, sole king of forrests all,
The Aspine good for staues, the Cypresse funerall.

The Laurell, mecd of mightie Conquerours   ix
    And Poets sage, the Firre that weepeth still,
    The Willow worne of forlorne Paramours,
    The Eugh obedient to the benders will,
    The Birch for shaftes, the Sallow for the mill,
    The Mirrhe sweete bleeding in the bitter wound,
    The warlike Beech, the Ash for nothing ill,
    The fruitfull Oliue, and the Platane round,
The caruer Holme, the Maple seeldom inward sound.

Led with delight, they thus beguile the way,   x
    Vntill the blustring storme is ouerblowne ;
    When weening to returne, whence they did stray,
    They cannot finde that path, which first was showne,
    But wander too and fro in wayes vnknowne,
    Furthest from end then, when they neerest weene,
    That makes them doubt, their wits be not their owne :
    So many pathes, so many turnings seene,
That which of them to take, in diuerse doubt they been.

At last resoluing forward still to fare,   xi
    Till that some end they finde or in or out,
    That path they take, that beaten seemd most bare,
    And like to lead the labyrinth about ;
    Which when by tract they hunted had throughout,
    At length it brought them to a hollow caue,
    Amid the thickest woods.   The Champion stout
    Eftsoones dismounted from his courser braue,
And to the Dwarfe a while his needlesse spere he gaue.

viii 3 tempests *1609*   ix 6 sweet, *1609*   9 sildom *1609 passim*
x 4 They] The *1596*

Be well aware, quoth then that Ladie milde,   xii
    Least suddaine mischiefe ye too rash prouoke:
    The danger hid, the place vnknowne and wilde,
    Breedes dreadfull doubts: Oft fire is without smoke,
    And perill without show: therefore your stroke
    Sir knight with-hold, till further triall made.
    Ah Ladie (said he) shame were to reuoke
    The forward footing for an hidden shade:
Vertue giues her selfe light, through darkenesse for to wade.

Yea but (quoth she) the perill of this place   xiii
    I better wot then you, though now too late
    To wish you backe returne with foule disgrace,
    Yet wisedome warnes, whilest foot is in the gate,
    To stay the steppe, ere forced to retrate.
    This is the wandring wood, this *Errours den*,
    A monster vile, whom God and man does hate :
    Therefore I read beware.   Fly fly (quoth then
The fearefull Dwarfe :) this is no place for liuing men.

But full of fire and greedy hardiment,   xiv
    The youthfull knight could not for ought be staide,
    But forth vnto the darksome hole he went,
    And looked in: his glistring armor made
    A litle glooming light, much like a shade,
    By which he saw the vgly monster plaine,
    Halfe like a serpent horribly displaide,
    But th'other halfe did womans shape retaine,
Most lothsom, filthie, foule, and full of vile disdaine.

And as she lay vpon the durtie ground,   xv
    Her huge long taile her den all ouerspred,
    Yet was in knots and many boughtes vpwound,
    Pointed with mortall sting.   Of her there bred
    A thousand yong ones, which she dayly fed,
    Sucking vpon her poisonous dugs, eachone
    Of sundry shapes, yet all ill fauored :
    Soone as that vncouth light vpon them shone,
Into her mouth they crept, and suddain all were gone.

xii 5 your hardy stroke *1590 &c.*: *corr. F. E.*   xiii 2 late, *1596*
                    xv 6 poisnous *1590*

Their dam vpstart, out of her den effraide,　　　　xvi
　And rushed forth, hurling her hideous taile
　About her cursed head, whose folds displaid
　Were stretcht now forth at length without entraile.
　She lookt about, and seeing one in mayle
　Armed to point, sought backe to turne againe;
　For light she hated as the deadly bale,
　Ay wont in desert darknesse to remaine,
Where plaine none might her see, nor she see any plaine.

Which when the valiant Elfe perceiu'd, he lept　　　xvii
　As Lyon fierce vpon the flying pray,
　And with his trenchand blade her boldly kept
　From turning backe, and forced her to stay:
　Therewith enrag'd she loudly gan to bray,
　And turning fierce, her speckled taile aduaunst,
　Threatning her angry sting, him to dismay:
　Who nought aghast, his mightie hand enhaunst:
The stroke down from her head vnto her shoulder glaunst.

Much daunted with that dint, her sence was dazd,　　xviii
　Yet kindling rage, her selfe she gathered round,
　And all attonce her beastly body raizd
　With doubled forces high aboue the ground:
　Tho wrapping vp her wrethed sterne arownd,
　Lept fierce vpon his shield, and her huge traine
　All suddenly about his body wound,
　That hand or foot to stirre he stroue in vaine:
God helpe the man so wrapt in *Errours* endlesse traine.

His Lady sad to see his sore constraint,　　　　xix
　Cride out, Now now Sir knight, shew what ye bee,
　Add faith vnto your force, and be not faint:
　Strangle her, else she sure will strangle thee.
　That when he heard, in great perplexitie,
　His gall did grate for griefe and high disdaine,
　And knitting all his force got one hand free,
　Wherewith he grypt her gorge with so great paine,
That soone to loose her wicked bands did her constraine.

　　　xvii 1 perceiu'ed *1596*　　　　xix 2 ye] you *1609*

Therewith she spewd out of her filthy maw   xx
  A floud of poyson horrible and blacke,
  Full of great lumpes of flesh and gobbets raw,
  Which stunck so vildly, that it forst him slacke
  His grasping hold, and from her turne him backe :
  Her vomit full of bookes and papers was,
  With loathly frogs and toades, which eyes did lacke,
  And creeping sought way in the weedy gras :
Her filthy parbreake all the place defiled has.

As when old father *Nilus* gins to swell   xxi
  With timely pride aboue the *Aegyptian* vale,
  His fattie waues do fertile slime outwell,
  And ouerflow each plaine and lowly dale :
  But when his later spring gins to auale,
  Huge heapes of mudd he leaues, wherein there breed
  Ten thousand kindes of creatures, partly male
  And partly female of his fruitfull seed ;
Such vgly monstrous shapes elswhere may no man reed.

The same so sore annoyed has the knight,   xxii
  That welnigh choked with the deadly stinke,
  His forces faile, ne can no longer fight.
  Whose corage when the feend perceiu'd to shrinke,
  She poured forth out of her hellish sinke
  Her fruitfull cursed spawne of serpents small,
  Deformed monsters, fowle, and blacke as inke,
  Which swarming all about his legs did crall,
And him encombred sore, but could not hurt at all.

As gentle Shepheard in sweete euen-tide,   xxiii
  When ruddy *Phœbus* gins to welke in west,
  High on an hill, his flocke to vewen wide,
  Markes which do byte their hasty supper best ;
  A cloud of combrous gnattes do him molest,
  All striuing to infixe their feeble stings,
  That from their noyance he no where can rest,
  But with his clownish hands their tender wings
He brusheth oft, and oft doth mar their murmurings.

xx 4 vilely *1609*   xxi 5 spring] ebbe *1590 &c.: corr. F. E.*   t'auale
1590: corr F. E.   xxii 3 lenger *1590*   xxiii 2 *Phebus 1590*   5 cumbrous
1590

Thus ill bestedd, and fearefull more of shame,   xxiv
    Then of the certaine perill he stood in,
    Halfe furious vnto his foe he came,
    Resolv'd in minde all suddenly to win,
    Or soone to lose, before he once would lin ;
    And strooke at her with more then manly force,
    That from her body full of filthie sin
    He raft her hatefull head without remorse ;
A streame of cole black bloud forth gushed from her corse.

Her scattred brood, soone as their Parent deare   xxv
    They saw so rudely falling to the ground,
    Groning full deadly, all with troublous feare,
    Gathred themselues about her body round,
    Weening their wonted entrance to haue found
    At her wide mouth : but being there withstood
    They flocked all about her bleeding wound,
    And sucked vp their dying mothers blood,
Making her death their life, and eke her hurt their good.

That detestable sight him much amazde,   xxvi
    To see th'vnkindly Impes of heauen accurst,
    Deuoure their dam ; on whom while so he gazd,
    Hauing all satisfide their bloudy thurst,
    Their bellies swolne he saw with fulnesse burst,
    And bowels gushing forth : well worthy end
    Of such as drunke her life, the which them nurst ;
    Now needeth him no lenger labour spend,
His foes haue slaine themselues, with whom he should contend.

His Ladie seeing all, that chaunst, from farre   xxvii
    Approcht in hast to greet his victorie,
    And said, Faire knight, borne vnder happy starre,
    Who see your vanquisht foes before you lye :
    Well worthy be you of that Armorie,
    Wherein ye haue great glory wonne this day,
    And proou'd your strength on a strong enimie,
    Your first aduenture : many such I pray,
And henceforth euer wish, that like succeed it may.

xxiv 6 stroke *1590*   8 reft *1609*   xxv 7 wound. *1596*
    xxvi 8 longer *1609*   xxvii 2 haste *1609*

Then mounted he vpon his Steede againe,   xxviii
   And with the Lady backward sought to wend ;
   That path he kept, which beaten was most plaine,
   Ne euer would to any by-way bend,
   But still did follow one vnto the end,
   The which at last out of the wood them brought.
   So forward on his way (with God to frend)
   He passed forth, and new aduenture sought ;
Long way he trauelled, before he heard of ought.

At length they chaunst to meet vpon the way   xxix
   An aged Sire, in long blacke weedes yclad,
   His feete all bare, his beard all hoarie gray,
   And by his belt his booke he hanging had ;
   Sober he seemde, and very sagely sad,
   And to the ground his eyes were lowly bent,
   Simple in shew, and voyde of malice bad,
   And all the way he prayed, as he went,
And often knockt his brest, as one that did repent.

He faire the knight saluted, louting low,   xxx
   Who faire him quited, as that courteous was :
   And after asked him, if he did know
   Of straunge aduentures, which abroad did pas.
   Ah my deare Sonne (quoth he) how should, alas,
   Silly old man, that liues in hidden cell,
   Bidding his beades all day for his trespas,
   Tydings of warre and worldly trouble tell ?
With holy father sits not with such things to mell.

But if of daunger which hereby doth dwell,   xxxi
   And homebred euill ye desire to heare,
   Of a straunge man I can you tidings tell,
   That wasteth all this countrey farre and neare.
   Of such (said he) I chiefly do inquere,
   And shall you well reward to shew the place,
   In which that wicked wight his dayes doth weare :
   For to all knighthood it is foule disgrace,
That such a cursed creature liues so long a space.

   xxviii 8 passeth *1596, 1609*   xxx 9 fits *1609*   xxxi 1 danger *1609*
2 euill *bis 1596*   3 strange *1609*   6 you] thee *1590*

Far hence (quoth he) in wastfull wildernesse   xxxii
   His dwelling is, by which no liuing wight
   May euer passe, but thorough great distresse.
   Now (sayd the Lady) draweth toward night,
   And well I wote, that of your later fight
   Ye all forwearied be : for what so strong,
   But wanting rest will also want of might ?
   The Sunne that measures heauen all day long,
At night doth baite his steedes the *Ocean* waues emong.

Then with the Sunne take Sir, your timely rest,   xxxiii
   And with new day new worke at once begin :
   Vntroubled night they say giues counsell best.
   Right well Sir knight ye haue aduised bin,
   (Quoth then that aged man ;) the way to win
   Is wisely to aduise : now day is spent ;
   Therefore with me ye may take vp your In
   For this same night.   The knight was well content :
So with that godly father to his home they went.

A little lowly Hermitage it was,   xxxiv
   Downe in a dale, hard by a forests side,
   Far from resort of people, that did pas
   In trauell to and froe : a little wyde
   There was an holy Chappell edifyde,
   Wherein the Hermite dewly wont to say
   His holy things each morne and euentyde :
   Thereby a Christall streame did gently play,
Which from a sacred fountaine welled forth alway.

Arriued there, the little house they fill,   xxxv
   Ne looke for entertainement, where none was :
   Rest is their feast, and all things at their will ;
   The noblest mind the best contentment has.
   With faire discourse the euening so they pas :
   For that old man of pleasing wordes had store,
   And well could file his tongue as smooth as glas ;
   He told of Saintes and Popes, and euermore
He strowd an *Aue-Mary* after and before.

     xxxii 6 for wearied *1596*   xxxv 8 euemore *1596*

The drouping Night thus creepeth on them fast,   xxxvi
    And the sad humour loading their eye liddes,
As messenger of *Morpheus* on them cast
Sweet slombring deaw, the which to sleepe them biddes.
Vnto their lodgings then his guestes he riddes:
Where when all drownd in deadly sleepe he findes,
He to his study goes, and there amiddes
His Magick bookes and artes of sundry kindes,
He seekes out mighty charmes, to trouble sleepy mindes.

Then choosing out few wordes most horrible,   xxxvii
    (Let none them read) thereof did verses frame,
With which and other spelles like terrible,
He bad awake blacke *Plutoes* griesly Dame,
And cursed heauen, and spake reprochfull shame
Of highest God, the Lord of life and light ;
A bold bad man, that dar'd to call by name
Great *Gorgon*, Prince of darknesse and dead night,
At which *Cocytus* quakes, and *Styx* is put to flight.

And forth he cald out of deepe darknesse dred   xxxviii
    Legions of Sprights, the which like little flyes
Fluttring about his euer damned hed,
A-waite whereto their seruice he applyes,
To aide his friends, or fray his enimies :
Of those he chose out two, the falsest twoo,
And fittest for to forge true-seeming lyes;
The one of them he gaue a message too,
The other by him selfe staide other worke to doo.

He making speedy way through spersed ayre,   xxxix
    And through the world of waters wide and deepe,
To *Morpheus* house doth hastily repaire.
Amid the bowels of the earth full steepe,
And low, where dawning day doth neuer peepe,
His dwelling is; there *Tethys* his wet bed
Doth euer wash, and *Cynthia* still doth steepe
In siluer deaw his euer-drouping hed,
Whiles sad Night ouer him her mantle black doth spred.

Whose double gates he findeth locked fast,   xl
  The one faire fram'd of burnisht Yuory,
  The other all with siluer ouercast ;
  And wakefull dogges before them farre do lye,
  Watching to banish Care their enimy,
  Who oft is wont to trouble gentle Sleepe.
  By them the Sprite doth passe in quietly,
  And vnto *Morpheus* comes, whom drowned deepe
In drowsie fit he findes : of nothing he takes keepe.

And more, to lulle him in his slumber soft,   xli
  A trickling streame from high rocke tumbling downe
  And euer-drizling raine vpon the loft,
  Mixt with a murmuring winde, much like the sowne
  Of swarming Bees, did cast him in a swowne :
  No other noyse, nor peoples troublous cryes,
  As still are wont t'annoy the walled towne,
  Might there be heard : but carelesse Quiet lyes,
Wrapt in eternall silence farre from enemyes.

The messenger approching to him spake,   xlii
  But his wast wordes returnd to him in vaine :
  So sound he slept, that nought mought him awake.
  Then rudely he him thrust, and pusht with paine,
  Whereat he gan to stretch : but he againe
  Shooke him so hard, that forced him to speake.
  As one then in a dreame, whose dryer braine
  Is tost with troubled sights and fancies weake,
He mumbled soft, but would not all his silence breake.

The Sprite then gan more boldly him to wake,   xliii
  And threatned vnto him the dreaded name
  Of *Hecate* : whereat he gan to quake,
  And lifting vp his lumpish head, with blame
  Halfe angry asked him, for what he came.
  Hither (quoth he) me *Archimago* sent,
  He that the stubborne Sprites can wisely tame,
  He bids thee to him send for his intent
A fit false dreame, that can delude the sleepers sent.

xl 6 sleepe *1596* : sleep *1609*   xli 3 euer] euery *1590* : *corr. F. E.*
xlii 2 waste *1590, 1609*   retournd *1590*   4 thrust] trust *1596*   8 sights]
sighes *1590* : *corr. F. E.*   xliii 4 lompish *1590*   6 Hether *1590*

The God obayde, and calling forth straight way   xliv
   A diuerse dreame out of his prison darke,
   Deliuered it to him, and downe did lay
   His heauie head, deuoide of carefull carke,
   Whose sences all were straight benumbd and starke.
   He backe returning by the Yuorie dore,
   Remounted vp as light as chearefull Larke,
   And on his litle winges the dreame he bore
In hast vnto his Lord, where he him left afore.

Who all this while with charmes and hidden artes,   xlv
   Had made a Lady of that other Spright,
   And fram'd of liquid ayre her tender partes
   So liuely, and so like in all mens sight,
   That weaker sence it could haue rauisht quight :
   The maker selfe for all his wondrous witt,
   Was nigh beguiled with so goodly sight :
   Her all in white he clad, and ouer it
Cast a blacke stole, most like to seeme for *Vna* fit.

Now when that ydle dreame was to him brought,   xlvi
   Vnto that Elfin knight he bad him fly,
   Where he slept soundly void of euill thought,
   And with false shewes abuse his fantasy,
   In sort as he him schooled priuily :
   And that new creature borne without her dew,
   Full of the makers guile, with vsage sly
   He taught to imitate that Lady trew,
Whose semblance she did carrie vnder feigned hew.

Thus well instructed, to their worke they hast,   xlvii
   And comming where the knight in slomber lay,
   The one vpon his hardy head him plast,
   And made him dreame of loues and lustfull play,
   That nigh his manly hart did melt away,
   Bathed in wanton blis and wicked ioy :
   Then seemed him his Lady by him lay,
   And to him playnd, how that false winged boy
Her chast hart had subdewd, to learne Dame pleasures toy.

xlvi 7 vsage] visage *1609*   xlvii 8 boy, *1590, 1596*

And she her selfe of beautie soueraigne Queene,   xlviii
   Faire *Venus* seemde vnto his bed to bring
   Her, whom he waking euermore did weene
   To be the chastest flowre, that ay did spring
   On earthly braunch, the daughter of a king,
   Now a loose Leman to vile seruice bound :
   And eke the *Graces* seemed all to sing,
   Hymen iö Hymen, dauncing all around,
Whilst freshest *Flora* her with Yuie girlond crownd.

In this great passion of vnwonted lust,   xl:x
   Or wonted feare of doing ought amis,
   He started vp, as seeming to mistrust
   Some secret ill, or hidden foe of his :
   Lo there before his face his Lady is,
   Vnder blake stole hyding her bayted hooke,
   And as halfe blushing offred him to kis,
   With gentle blandishment and louely looke,
Most like that virgin true, which for her knight him took.

All cleane dismayd to see so vncouth sight,   l
   And halfe enraged at her shamelesse guise,
   He thought haue slaine her in his fierce despight :
   But hasty heat tempring with sufferance wise,
   He stayde his hand, and gan himselfe aduise
   To proue his sense, and tempt her faigned truth.
   Wringing her hands in wemens pitteous wise,
   Tho can she weepe, to stirre vp gentle ruth,
Both for her noble bloud, and for her tender youth.

And said, Ah Sir, my liege Lord and my loue,   li
   Shall I accuse the hidden cruell fate,
   And mightie causes wrought in heauen aboue,
   Or the blind God, that doth me thus amate,
   For hoped loue to winne me certaine hate ?
   Yet thus perforce he bids me do, or die.
   Die is my dew : yet rew my wretched state
   You, whom my hard auenging destinie
Hath made iudge of my life or death indifferently.

xlviii 3 weene, *1590, 1596*   9 with *om. 1596, 1609*   xlix 3 starteth
1590   mistrust, *1590, 1596*   l 3 t'haue *1609*   7 womens *1609*
SPENSER II   C

Your owne deare sake forst me at first to leaue   lii
  My Fathers kingdome, There she stopt with teares;
  Her swollen hart her speach seemd to bereaue,
  And then againe.begun, My weaker yeares
  Captiu'd to fortune and frayle worldly feares,
  Fly to your faith for succour and sure ayde:
  Let me not dye in languor and long teares.
  Why Dame (quoth he) what hath ye thus dismayd?
What frayes ye, that were wont to comfort me affrayd?

Loue of your selfe, she said, and deare constraint   liii
  Lets me not sleepe, but wast the wearie night
  In secret anguish and vnpittied plaint,
  Whiles you in carelesse sleepe are drowned quight.
  Her doubtfull words made that redoubted knight
  Suspect her truth : yet since no'vntruth he knew,
  Her fawning loue with foule disdainefull spight
  He would not shend, but said, Deare dame I rew,
That for my sake vnknowne such griefe vnto you grew.

Assure your selfe, it fell not all to ground;   liv
  For all so deare as life is to my hart,
  I deeme your loue, and hold me to you bound ;
  Ne let vaine feares procure your needlesse smart,
  Where cause is none, but to your rest depart.
  Not all content, yet seemd she to appease
  Her mournefull plaintes, beguiled of her art,
  And fed with words, that could not chuse but please,
So slyding softly forth, she turnd as to her ease.

Long after lay he musing at her mood,   lv
  Much grieu'd to thinke that gentle Dame so light,
  For whose defence he was to shed his blood.
  At last dull wearinesse of former fight
  Hauing yrockt a sleepe his irkesome spright,
  That troublous dreame gan freshly tosse his braine,
  With bowres, and beds, and Ladies deare delight :
  But when he saw his labour all was vaine,
With that misformed spright he backe returnd againe.

lii 4 begonne *1590*   liii 6 sith n'vntruth *1609*   liv 8 chose *1590*

Cant. II.

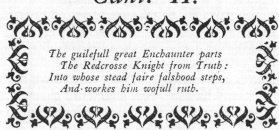

The guilefull great Enchaunter parts
The Redcrosse Knight from Truth:
Into whose stead faire falshood steps,
And·workes him wofull ruth.

B Y this the Northerne wagoner had set   i
His seuenfold teme behind the stedfast starre,
That was in Ocean waues yet neuer wet,
But firme is fixt, and sendeth light from farre
To all, that in the wide deepe wandring arre:
And chearefull Chaunticlere with his note shrill
Had warned once, that *Phœbus* fiery carre
In hast was climbing vp the Easterne hill,
Full enuious that night so long his roome did fill.

When those accursed messengers of hell,   ii
That feigning dreame, and that faire-forged Spright
Came to their wicked maister, and gan tell
Their bootelesse paines, and ill succeeding night:
Who all in rage to see his skilfull might
Deluded so, gan threaten hellish paine
And sad *Proserpines* wrath, them to affright.
But when he saw his threatning was but vaine,
He cast about, and searcht his balefull bookes againe.

Eftsoones he tooke that miscreated faire,   iii
And that false other Spright, on whom he spred
A seeming body of the subtile aire,
Like a young Squire, in loues and lusty-hed
His wanton dayes that euer loosely led,
Without regard of armes and dreaded fight:
Those two he tooke, and in a secret bed,
Couered with darknesse and misdeeming night,
Them both together laid, to ioy in vaine delight.

Arg. 3 *stead*] *steps 1590: corr. F. E.*   iii 4 lusty-hed. *1596*
c 2

Forthwith he runnes with feigned faithfull hast   iv
  Vnto his guest, who after troublous sights
  And dreames, gan now to take more sound repast,
  Whom suddenly he wakes with fearefull frights,
  As one aghast with feends or damned sprights,
  And to him cals, Rise rise vnhappy Swaine,
  That here wex old in sleepe, whiles wicked wights
  Haue knit themselues in *Venus* shamefull chaine ;
Come see, where your false Lady doth her honour staine.

All in amaze he suddenly vp start   v
  With sword in hand, and with the old man went ;
  Who soone him brought into a secret part,
  Where that false couple were full closely ment
  In wanton lust and lewd embracement :
  Which when he saw, he burnt with gealous fire,
  The eye of reason was with rage yblent,
  And would haue slaine them in his furious ire,
But hardly was restreined of that aged sire.

Returning to his bed in torment great,   vi
  And bitter anguish of his guiltie sight,
  He could not rest, but did his stout heart eat,
  And wast his inward gall with deepe despight,
  Yrkesome of life, and too long lingring night.
  At last faire *Hesperus* in highest skie
  Had spent his lampe, and brought forth dawning light,
  Then vp he rose, and clad him hastily ;
The Dwarfe him brought his steed : so both away do fly.

Now when the rosy-fingred Morning faire,   vii
  Weary of aged *Tithones* saffron bed,
  Had spred her purple robe through deawy aire,
  And the high hils *Titan* discouered,
  The royall virgin shooke off drowsy-hed,
  And rising forth out of her baser bowre,
  Lookt for her knight, who far away was fled,
  And for her Dwarfe, that wont to wait each houre ;
Then gan she waile and weepe, to see that woefull stowre.

And after him she rode with so much speede   viii
   As her slow beast could make ; but all in vaine :
   For him so far had borne his light-foot steede,
   Pricked with wrath and fiery fierce disdaine,
   That him to follow was but fruitlesse paine;
   Yet she her weary limbes would neuer rest,
   But euery hill and dale, each wood and plaine
   Did search, sore grieued in her gentle brest,
He so vngently left her, whom she loued best.

But subtill *Archimago*, when his guests   ix
   He saw diuided into double parts,
   And *Vna* wandring in woods and forrests,
   Th'end of his drift, he praisd his diuelish arts,
   That had such might ouer true meaning harts ;
   Yet rests not so, but other meanes doth make,
   How he may worke vnto her further smarts :
   For her he hated as the hissing snake,
And in her many troubles did most pleasure take.

He then deuisde himselfe how to disguise;   x
   For by his mightie science he could take
   As many formes and shapes in seeming wise,
   As euer *Proteus* to himselfe could make :
   Sometime a fowle, sometime a fish in lake,
   Now like a foxe, now like a dragon fell,
   That of himselfe he oft for feare would quake,
   And oft would flie away.   O who can tell
The hidden power of herbes, and might of Magicke spell ?

But now seemde best, the person to put on   xi
   Of that good knight, his late beguiled guest :
   In mighty armes he was yclad anon,
   And siluer shield : vpon his coward brest
   A bloudy crosse, and on his crauen crest
   A bounch of haires discolourd diuersly :
   Full iolly knight he seemde, and well addrest,
   And when he sate vpon his courser free,
Saint George himself ye would haue deemed him to be.

viii 9 louest *1596*   xi 3 anon: *1590, 1596*   4 shield, *1590, 1596*
6 heares *1590*

But he the knight, whose semblaunt he did beare,   xii
    The true *Saint George* was wandred far away,
    Still flying from his thoughts and gealous feare ;
    Will was his guide, and griefe led him astray.
    At last him chaunst to meete vpon the way
    A faithlesse Sarazin all arm'd to point,
    In whose great shield was writ with letters gay
    Sans foy : full large of limbe and euery ioint
He was, and cared not for God or man a point.

He had a faire companion of his way,   x'ii
    A goodly Lady clad in scarlot red,
    Purfled with gold and pearle of rich assay,
    And like a *Persian* mitre on her hed
    She wore, with crownes and owches garnished,
    The which her lauish louers to her gaue ;
    Her wanton palfrey all was ouerspred
    With tinsell trappings, wouen like a waue,
Whose bridle rung with golden bels and bosses braue.

With faire disport and courting dalliaunce   xiv
    She intertainde her louer all the way :
    But when she saw the knight his speare aduaunce,
    She soone left off her mirth and wanton play,
    And bad her knight addresse him to the fray :
    His foe was nigh at hand.   He prickt with pride
    And hope to winne his Ladies heart that day,
    Forth spurred fast : adowne his coursers side
The red bloud trickling staind the way, as he did ride.

The knight of the *Redcrosse* when him he spide,   xv
    Spurring so hote with rage dispiteous,
    Gan fairely couch his speare, and towards ride :
    Soone meete they both, both fell and furious,
    That daunted with their forces hideous,
    Their steeds do stagger, and amazed stand,
    And eke themselues too rudely rigorous,
    Astonied with the stroke of their owne hand,
Do backe rebut, and each to other yeeldeth land.

xiv 4 off] of *1590 passim*   xv 2 dispighteous *1609*

As when two rams stird with ambitious pride,　　xvi
　　Fight for the rule of the rich fleeced flocke,
　　Their horned fronts so fierce on either side
　　Do meete, that with the terrour of the shocke
　　Astonied both, stand sencelesse as a blocke,
　　Forgetfull of the hanging victory :
　　So stood these twaine, vnmoued as a rocke,
　　Both staring fierce, and holding idely
The broken reliques of their former cruelty.

The *Sarazin* sore daunted with the buffe　　xvii
　　Snatcheth his sword, and fiercely to him flies ;
　　Who well it wards, and quyteth cuff with cuff :
　　Each others equall puissaunce enuies,
　　And through their iron sides with cruell spies
　　Does seeke to perce: repining courage yields
　　No foote to foe.　The flashing fier flies
　　As from a forge out of their burning shields,
And streames of purple bloud new dies the verdant fields.

Curse on that Crosse (quoth then the *Sarazin*)　　xviii
　　That keepes thy body from the bitter fit ;
　　Dead long ygoe I wote thou haddest bin,
　　Had not that charme from thee forwarned it :
　　But yet I warne thee now assured sitt,
　　And hide thy head.　Therewith vpon his crest
　　With rigour so outrageous he smitt,
　　That a large share it hewd out of the rest,
And glauncing downe his shield, from blame him fairely blest.

Who thereat wondrous wroth, the sleeping spark　　xix
　　Of natiue vertue gan eftsoones reuiue,
　　And at his haughtie helmet making mark,
　　So hugely stroke, that it the steele did riue,
　　And cleft his head.　He tumbling downe aliue,
　　With bloudy mouth his mother earth did kis,
　　Greeting his graue : his grudging ghost did striue
　　With the fraile flesh ; at last it flitted is,
Whither the soules do fly of men, that liue amis.

　　xvi 4 terror *1590*　　5 stands fencelesse *1590*: *corr. F. E.*　　8 idely,
1590, 1596: idlely *1609*　　xvii 5 cruelties *1590 &c.*: *corr. F. E.*　　9 die
1609　　xviii 1 quoth] qd. *1590 passim*　7 rigor *1590*　　xix 4 strooke,
1609　　9 Whether *1590 passim*

The Lady when she saw her champion fall,   xx
    Like the old ruines of a broken towre,
    Staid not to waile his woefull funerall,
    But from him fled away with all her powre ;
    Who after her as hastily gan scowre,
    Bidding the Dwarfe with him to bring away
    The *Sarazins* shield, signe of the conqueroure.
    Her soone he ouertooke, and bad to stay,
For present cause was none of dread her to dismay.

She turning backe with ruefull countenaunce,   xxi
    Cride, Mercy mercy Sir vouchsafe to show
    On silly Dame, subiect to hard mischaunce,
    And to your mighty will.   Her humblesse low
    In so ritch weedes and seeming glorious show,
    Did much emmoue his stout heroïcke heart,
    And said, Deare dame, your suddein ouerthrow
    Much rueth me ; but now put feare apart,
And tell, both who ye be, and who that tooke your part.

Melting in teares, then gan she thus lament ;   xxii
    The wretched woman, whom vnhappy howre
    Hath now made thrall to your commandement,
    Before that angry heauens list to lowre,
    And fortune false betraide me to your powre,
    Was, (O what now auaileth that I was !)
    Borne the sole daughter of an Emperour,
    He that the wide West vnder his rule has,
    And high hath set his throne, where *Tiberis* doth pas.

He in the first flowre of my freshest age,   xxiii
    Betrothed me vnto the onely haire
    Of a most mighty king, most rich and sage ;
    Was neuer Prince so faithfull and so faire,
    Was neuer Prince so meeke and debonaire ;
    But ere my hoped day of spousall shone,
    My dearest Lord fell from high honours staire,
    Into the hands of his accursed fone,
And cruelly was slaine, that shall I euer mone.

    xxii 2 wreched *1590*   5 your] thy *1590*   6 I was? *1590*

His blessed body spoild of liuely breath,   xxiv
   Was afterward, I know not how, conuaid
   And fro me hid: of whose most innocent death
   When tidings came to me vnhappy maid,
   O how great sorrow my sad soule assaid.
   Then forth I went his woefull corse to find,
   And many yeares throughout the world I straid,
   A virgin widow, whose deepe wounded mind
With loue, long time did languish as the striken hind.

At last it chaunced this proud *Sarazin*   xxv
   To meete me wandring, who perforce me led
   With him away, but yet could neuer win
   The Fort, that Ladies hold in soueraigne dread.
   There lies he now with foule dishonour dead,
   Who whiles he liu'de, was called proud *Sans foy*,
   The eldest of three brethren, all three bred
   Of one bad sire, whose youngest is *Sans ioy*,
And twixt them both was borne the bloudy bold *Sans loy*.

In this sad plight, friendlesse, vnfortunate,   xxvi
   Now miserable I *Fidessa* dwell,
   Crauing of you in pitty of my state,
   To do none ill, if please ye not do well.
   He in great passion all this while did dwell,
   More busying his quicke eyes, her face to view,
   Then his dull eares, to heare what she did tell;
   And said, Faire Lady hart of flint would rew
The vndeserued woes and sorrowes, which ye shew.

Henceforth in safe assuraunce may ye rest,   xxvii
   Hauing both found a new friend you to aid,
   And lost an old foe, that did you molest:
   Better new friend then an old foe is said.
   With chaunge of cheare the seeming simple maid
   Let fall her eyen, as shamefast to the earth,
   And yeelding soft, in that she nought gain-said,
   So forth they rode, he feining seemely merth,
And she coy lookes: so dainty they say maketh derth.

xxv 1 *Sarazin, 1590, 1596*   xxvi 8 faire *1590, 1596*
xxvii 9 so, Dainty *1609*

Long time they thus together traueiled,   xxviii
   Till weary of their way, they came at last,
   Where grew two goodly trees, that faire did spred
   Their armes abroad, with gray mosse ouercast,
   And their greene leaues trembling with euery blast,
   Made a calme shadow far in compasse round:
   The fearefull Shepheard often there aghast
   Vnder them neuer sat, ne wont there sound
His mery oaten pipe, but shund th'vnlucky ground.

But this good knight soone as he them can spie,   xxix
   For the coole shade him thither hastly got:
   For golden *Phœbus* now ymounted hie,
   From fiery wheeles of his faire chariot
   Hurled his beame so scorching cruell hot,
   That liuing creature mote it not abide ;
   And his new Lady it endured not.
   There they alight, in hope themselues to hide
From the fierce heat, and rest their weary limbs a tide.

Faire seemely pleasaunce each to other makes,   xxx
   With goodly purposes there as they sit:
   And in his falsed fancy he her takes
   To be the fairest wight, that liued yit;
   Which to expresse, he bends his gentle wit,
   And thinking of those braunches greene to frame
   A girlond for her dainty forehead fit,
   He pluckt a bough ; out of whose rift there came
Small drops of gory bloud, that trickled downe the same.

Therewith a piteous yelling voyce was heard,   xxxi
   Crying, O spare with guilty hands to teare
   My tender sides in this rough rynd embard,
   But fly, ah fly far hence away, for feare
   Least to you hap, that happened to me heare,
   And to this wretched Lady, my deare loue,
   O too deare loue, loue bought with death too deare.
   Astond he stood, and vp his haire did houe,
And with that suddein horror could no member moue.

    xxix 2 shade him] shade *1596*:   shadow *1609*   3 ymounted] that
mounted *1590 &c.*: *corr. F. E.*   xxxi 6 this] his *1609*

At last whenas the dreadfull passion   xxxii
  Was ouerpast, and manhood well awake,
  Yet musing at the straunge occasion,
  And doubting much his sence, he thus bespake;
  What voyce of damned Ghost from *Limbo* lake,
  Or guilefull spright wandring in empty aire,
  Both which fraile men do oftentimes mistake,
  Sends to my doubtfull eares these speaches rare,
And ruefull plaints, me bidding guiltlesse bloud to spare ?

Then groning deepe, Nor damned Ghost, (quoth he,)   xxxiii
  Nor guilefull sprite to thee these wordes doth speake,
  But once a man *Fradubio*, now a tree,
  Wretched man, wretched tree ; whose nature weake,
  A cruell witch her cursed will to wreake,
  Hath thus transformd, and plast in open plaines,
  Where *Boreas* doth blow full bitter bleake,
  And scorching Sunne does dry my secret vaines:
For though a tree I seeme, yet cold and heat me paines.

Say on *Fradubio* then, or man, or tree,   xxxiv
  Quoth then the knight, by whose mischieuous arts
  Art thou misshaped thus, as now I see ?
  He oft finds med'cine, who his griefe imparts ;
  But double griefs afflict concealing harts,
  As raging flames who striueth to suppresse.
  The author then (said he) of all my smarts,
  Is one *Duessa* a false sorceresse,
That many errant knights hath brought to wretchednesse.

In prime of youthly yeares, when corage hot   xxxv
  The fire of loue and ioy of cheualree
  First kindled in my brest, it was my lot
  To loue this gentle Lady, whom ye see,
  Now not a Lady, but a seeming tree ;
  With whom as once I rode accompanyde,
  Me chaunced of a knight encountred bee,
  That had a like faire Lady by his syde,
Like a faire Lady, but did fowle *Duessa* hyde.

  xxxii 9 tuefull *1590*: *corr. F. E.*   plants *1590*   guitlesse *1596*

Whose forged beauty he did take in hand,   xxxvi
    All other Dames to haue exceeded farre;
    I in defence of mine did likewise stand,
    Mine, that did then shine as the Morning starre :
    So both to battell fierce arraunged arre,
    In which his harder fortune was to fall
    Vnder my speare : such is the dye of warre :
    His Lady left as a prise martiall,
Did yield her comely person, to be at my call.

So doubly lou'd of Ladies vnlike faire,   xxxvii
    Th'one seeming such, the other such indeede,
    One day in doubt I cast for to compare,
    Whether in beauties glorie did exceede ;
    A Rosy girlond was the victors meede :
    Both seemde to win, and both seemde won to bee,
    So hard the discord was to be agreede.
    Frælissa was as faire, as faire mote bee,
And euer false *Duessa* seemde as faire as shee.

The wicked witch now seeing all this while   xxxviii
    The doubtfull ballaunce equally to sway,
    What not by right, she cast to win by guile,
    And by her hellish science raisd streight way
    A foggy mist, that ouercast the day,
    And a dull blast, that breathing on her face,
    Dimmed her former beauties shining ray,
    And with foule vgly forme did her disgrace :
Then was she faire alone, when none was faire in place.

Then cride she out, Fye, fye, deformed wight,   xxxix
    Whose borrowed beautie now appeareth plaine
    To haue before bewitched all mens sight ;
    O leaue her soone, or let her soone be slaine.
    Her loathly visage viewing with disdaine,
    Eftsoones I thought her such, as she me told,
    And would haue kild her ; but with faigned paine,
    The false witch did my wrathfull hand with-hold ;
So left her, where she now is turnd to treen mould.

      xxxvi 5 batteill *1590 passim*   xxxix 1 fye *1590, 1596*

Thens forth I tooke *Duessa* for my Dame,   xl
  And in the witch vnweeting ioyd long time,
  Ne euer wist, but that she was the same,
  Till on a day (that day is euery Prime,
  When Witches wont do penance for their crime)
  I chaunst to see her in her proper hew,
  Bathing her selfe in origane and thyme:
  A filthy foule old woman I did vew,
That euer to haue toucht her, I did deadly rew.

Her neather partes misshapen, monstruous,   xli
  Were hidd in water, that I could not see,
  But they did seeme more foule and hideous,
  Then womans shape man would beleeue to bee.
  Thens forth from her most beastly companie
  I gan refraine, in minde to slip away,
  Soone as appeard safe opportunitie:
  For danger great, if not assur'd decay
I saw before mine eyes, if I were knowne to stray.

The diuelish hag by chaunges of my cheare   xlii
  Perceiu'd my thought, and drownd in sleepie night,
  With wicked herbes and ointments did besmeare
  My bodie all, through charmes and magicke might,
  That all my senses were bereaued quight:
  Then brought she me into this desert waste,
  And by my wretched louers side me pight,
  Where now enclosd in wooden wals full faste,
Banisht from liuing wights, our wearie dayes we waste.

But how long time, said then the Elfin knight,   xliii
  Are you in this misformed house to dwell?
  We may not chaunge (quoth he) this euil plight,
  Till we be bathed in a liuing well;
  That is the terme prescribed by the spell.
  O how, said he, mote I that well out find,
  That may restore you to your wonted well?
  Time and suffised fates to former kynd
Shall vs restore, none else from hence may vs vnbynd.

xl 1, xli 5 Then forth *1590, 1596*: *corr. F. E.*: Thenceforth *1609*
xli 7 oportunitie *1596*

The false *Duessa*, now *Fidessa* hight,   xliv
    Heard how in vaine *Fradubio* did lament,
    And knew well all was true.   But the good knight
    Full of sad feare and ghastly dreriment,
    When all this speech the liuing tree had spent,
    The bleeding bough did thrust into the ground,
    That from the bloud he might be innocent,
    And with fresh clay did close the wooden wound:
Then turning to his Lady, dead with feare her found.

Her seeming dead he found with feigned feare,   xlv
    As all vnweeting of that well she knew,
    And paynd himselfe with busie care to reare
    Her out of carelesse swowne.   Her eylids blew
    And dimmed sight with pale and deadly hew
    At last she vp gan lift : with trembling cheare
    Her vp he tooke, too simple and too trew,
    And oft her kist.   At length all passed feare,
He set her on her steede, and forward forth did beare.

Cant. III.

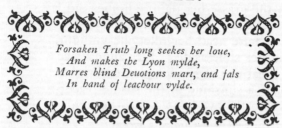

Forsaken Truth long seekes her loue,
And makes the Lyon mylde,
Marres blind Deuotions mart, and fals
In hand of leachour vylde.

N Ought is there vnder heau'ns wide hollownesse,   i
    That moues more deare compassion of mind,
  Then beautie brought t'vnworthy wretchednesse
  Through enuies snares or fortunes freakes vnkind:
  I, whether lately through her brightnesse blind,
  Or through alleageance and fast fealtie,
  Which I do owe vnto all woman kind,
  Feele my heart perst with so great agonie,
When such I see, that all for pittie I could die.

And now it is empassioned so deepe,   ii
  For fairest *Vnaes* sake, of whom I sing,
  That my fraile eyes these lines with teares do steepe,
  To thinke how she through guilefull handeling,
  Though true as touch, though daughter of a king,
  Though faire as euer liuing wight was faire,
  Though nor in word nor deede ill meriting,
  Is from her knight diuorced in despaire
And her due loues deriu'd to that vile witches share.

Yet she most faithfull Ladie all this while   iii
  Forsaken, wofull, solitarie mayd
  Farre from all peoples prease, as in exile,
  In wildernesse and wastfull deserts strayd,
  To seeke her knight; who subtilly betrayd
  Through that late vision, which th'Enchaunter wrought,
  Had her abandond. She of nought affrayd,
  Through woods and wastnesse wide him daily sought;
Yet wished tydings none of him vnto her brought.

    i 5 brightne *1590*: brightnes *F. E.*   iii 6 wrought *1590*

One day nigh wearie of the yrkesome way,   iv
  From her vnhastie beast she did alight,
  And on the grasse her daintie limbes did lay
  In secret shadow, farre from all mens sight:
  From her faire head her fillet she vndight,
  And laid her stole aside. Her angels face
  As the great eye of heauen shyned bright,
  And made a sunshine in the shadie place;
Did neuer mortall eye behold such heauenly grace.

It fortuned out of the thickest wood   v
  A ramping Lyon rushed suddainly,
  Hunting full greedie after saluage blood;
  Soone as the royall virgin he did spy,
  With gaping mouth at her ran greedily,
  To haue attonce deuour'd her tender corse:
  But to the pray when as he drew more ny,
  His bloudie rage asswaged with remorse,
And with the sight amazd, forgat his furious forse.

In stead thereof he kist her wearie feet,   vi
  And lickt her lilly hands with fawning tong,
  As he her wronged innocence did weet.
  O how can beautie maister the most strong,
  And simple truth subdue auenging wrong?
  Whose yeelded pride and proud submission,
  Still dreading death, when she had marked long,
  Her hart gan melt in great compassion,
And drizling teares did shed for pure affection.

The Lyon Lord of euerie beast in field,   vii
  Quoth she, his princely puissance doth abate,
  And mightie proud to humble weake does yield,
  Forgetfull of the hungry rage, which late
  Him prickt, in pittie of my sad estate:
  But he my Lyon, and my noble Lord,
  How does he find in cruell hart to hate
  Her that him lou'd, and euer most adord,
As the God of my life? why hath he me abhord?

vii 1 field *1590, 1596*   6 Lord *1590, 1596*

Redounding teares did choke th'end of her plaint,   viii
  Which softly ecchoed from the neighbour wood;
  And sad to see her sorrowfull constraint
  The kingly beast vpon her gazing stood;
  With pittie calmd, downe fell his angry mood.
  At last in close hart shutting vp her paine,
  Arose the virgin borne of heauenly brood,
  And to her snowy Palfrey got againe,
To seeke her strayed Champion, if she might attaine.

The Lyon would not leaue her desolate,   ix
  But with her went along, as a strong gard
  Of her chast person, and a faithfull mate
  Of her sad troubles and misfortunes hard:
  Still when she slept, he kept both watch and ward,
  And when she wakt, he waited diligent,
  With humble seruice to her will prepard:
  From her faire eyes he tooke commaundement,
And euer by her lookes conceiued her intent.

Long she thus traueiled through deserts wyde,   x
  By which she thought her wandring knight shold pas,
  Yet neuer shew of liuing wight espyde;
  Till that at length she found the troden gras,
  In which the tract of peoples footing was,
  Vnder the steepe foot of a mountaine hore;
  The same she followes, till at last she has
  A damzell spyde slow footing her before,
That on her shoulders sad a pot of water bore.

To whom approching she to her gan call,   xi
  To weet, if dwelling place were nigh at hand;
  But the rude wench her answer'd nought at all,
  She could not heare, nor speake, nor vnderstand;
  Till seeing by her side the Lyon stand,
  With suddaine feare her pitcher downe she threw,
  And fled away: for neuer in that land
  Face of faire Ladie she before did vew,
And that dread Lyons looke her cast in deadly hew.

        xi 1 Whom *1596*   9 dredd *1590*

Full fast she fled, ne euer lookt behynd,   xii
  As if her life vpon the wager lay,
  And home she came, whereas her mother blynd
  Sate in eternall night : nought could she say,
  But suddaine catching hold, did her dismay
  With quaking hands, and other signes of feare :
  Who full of ghastly fright and cold affray,
  Gan shut the dore. By this arriued there
Dame *Vna*, wearie Dame, and entrance did requere.

Which when none yeelded, her vnruly Page   xiii
  With his rude clawes the wicket open rent,
  And let her in ; where of his cruell rage
  Nigh dead with feare, and faint astonishment,
  She found them both in darkesome corner pent ;
  Where that old woman day and night did pray
  Vpon her beades deuoutly penitent ;
  Nine hundred *Pater nosters* euery day,
And thrise nine hundred *Aues* she was wont to say.

And to augment her painefull pennance more,   xiv
  Thrise euery weeke in ashes she did sit,
  And next her wrinkled skin rough sackcloth wore,
  And thrise three times did fast from any bit :
  But now for feare her beads she did forget.
  Whose needlesse dread for to remoue away,
  Faire *Vna* framed words and count'nance fit :
  Which hardly doen, at length she gan them pray,
That in their cotage small, that night she rest her may.

The day is spent, and commeth drowsie night,   xv
  When euery creature shrowded is in sleepe ;
  Sad *Vna* downe her laies in wearie plight,
  And at her feet the Lyon watch doth keepe :
  In stead of rest, she does lament, and weepe
  For the late losse of her deare loued knight,
  And sighes, and grones, and euermore does steepe
  Her tender brest in bitter teares all night,
All night she thinks too long, and often lookes for light.

xiv 1 penaunce *1590*

Now when *Aldeboran* was mounted hie   xvi
  Aboue the shynie *Cassiopeias* chaire,
  And all in deadly sleepe did drowned lie,
  One knocked at the dore, and in would fare;
  He knocked fast, and often curst, and sware,
  That readie entrance was not at his call:
  For on his backe a heauy load he bare
  Of nightly stelths and pillage seuerall,
Which he had got abroad by purchase criminall.

He was to weete a stout and sturdie thiefe,   xvii
  Wont to robbe Churches of their ornaments,
  And poore mens boxes of their due reliefe,
  Which giuen was to them for good intents;
  The holy Saints of their rich vestiments
  He did disrobe, when all men carelesse slept,
  And spoild the Priests of their habiliments,
  Whiles none the holy things in safety kept;
Then he by cunning sleights in at the window crept.

And all that he by right or wrong could find,   xviii
  Vnto this house he brought, and did bestow
  Vpon the daughter of this woman blind,
  Abessa daughter of *Corceca* slow,
  With whom he whoredome vsd, that few did know,
  And fed her fat with feast of offerings,
  And plentie, which in all the land did grow;
  Ne spared he to giue her gold and rings:
And now he to her brought part of his stolen things.

Thus long the dore with rage and threats he bet,   xix
  Yet of those fearefull women none durst rize,
  The Lyon frayed them, him in to let:
  He would no longer stay him to aduize,
  But open breakes the dore in furious wize,
  And entring is; when that disdainfull beast
  Encountring fierce, him suddaine doth surprize,
  And seizing cruell clawes on trembling brest,
Vnder his Lordly foot him proudly hath supprest.

    xvi 9 purchas *1590*   xvii 9 conning *1590*

Him booteth not resist, nor succour call,   xx
  His bleeding hart is in the vengers hand,
  Who streight him rent in thousand peeces small,
  And quite dismembred hath: the thirstie land
  Drunke vp his life; his corse left on the strand.
  His fearefull friends weare out the wofull night,
  Ne dare to weepe, nor seeme to vnderstand
  The heauie hap, which on them is alight,
Affraid, least to themselues the like mishappen might.

Now when broad day the world discouered has,   xxi
  Vp *Vna* rose, vp rose the Lyon eke,
  And on their former iourney forward pas,
  In wayes vnknowne, her wandring knight to seeke,
  With paines farre passing that long wandring *Greeke*,
  That for his loue refused deitie;
  Such were the labours of this Lady meeke,
  Still seeking him, that from her still did flie,
Then furthest from her hope, when most she weened nie.

Soone as she parted thence, the fearefull twaine,   xxii
  That blind old woman and her daughter deare
  Came forth, and finding *Kirkrapine* there slaine,
  For anguish great they gan to rend their heare,
  And beat their brests, and naked flesh to teare.
  And when they both had wept and wayld their fill,
  Then forth they ranne like two amazed deare,
  Halfe mad through malice, and reuenging will,
To follow her, that was the causer of their ill.

Whom ouertaking, they gan loudly bray,   xxiii
  With hollow howling, and lamenting cry,
  Shamefully at her rayling all the way,
  And her accusing of dishonesty,
  That was the flowre of faith and chastity;
  And still amidst her rayling, she did pray,
  That plagues, and mischiefs, and long misery
  Might fall on her, and follow all the way,
And that in endlesse error she might euer stray.

But when she saw her prayers nought preuaile,　　_{xxiv}
　She backe returned with some labour lost;
　And in the way as she did weepe and waile,
　A knight her met in mighty armes embost,
　Yet knight was not for all his bragging bost,
　But subtill *Archimag*, that *Vna* sought
　By traynes into new troubles to haue tost:
　Of that old woman tydings he besought,
If that of such a Ladie she could tellen ought.

Therewith she gan her passion to renew,　　_{xxv}
　And cry, and curse, and raile, and rend her heare,
　Saying, that harlot she too lately knew,
　That causd her shed so many a bitter teare,
　And so forth told the story of her feare:
　Much seemed he to mone her haplesse chaunce,
　And after for that Ladie did inquere;
　Which being taught, he forward gan aduaunce
His fair enchaunted steed, and eke his charmed launce.

Ere long he came, where *Vna* traueild slow,　　_{xxvi}
　And that wilde Champion wayting her besyde:
　Whom seeing such, for dread he durst not show
　Himselfe too nigh at hand, but turned wyde
　Vnto an hill; from whence when she him spyde,
　By his like seeming shield, her knight by name
　She weend it was, and towards him gan ryde:
　Approching nigh, she wist it was the same,
And with faire fearefull humblesse towards him shee came.

And weeping said, Ah my long lacked Lord,　　_{xxvii}
　Where haue ye bene thus long out of my sight?
　Much feared I to haue bene quite abhord,
　Or ought haue done, that ye displeasen might,
　That should as death vnto my deare hart light:
　For since mine eye your ioyous sight did mis,
　My chearefull day is turnd to chearelesse night,
　And eke my night of death the shadow is;
But welcome now my light, and shining lampe of blis.

xxv 7 inquire *1596*

He thereto meeting said, My dearest Dame,   xxviii
    Farre be it from your thought, and fro my will,
    To thinke that knighthood I so much should shame,
    As you to leaue, that haue me loued still,
    And chose in Faery court of meere goodwill,
    Where noblest knights were to be found on earth :
    The earth shall sooner leaue her kindly skill
    To bring forth fruit, and make eternall derth,
Then I leaue you, my liefe, yborne of heauenly berth.

And sooth to say, why I left you so long,   xxix
    Was for to seeke aduenture in strange place,
    Where *Archimago* said a felon strong
    To many knights did daily worke disgrace ;
    But knight he now shall neuer more deface :
    Good cause of mine excuse ; that mote ye please
    Well to accept, and euermore embrace
    My faithfull seruice, that by land and seas
Haue vowd you to defend, now then your plaint appease.

His louely words her seemd due recompence   xxx
    Of all her passed paines : one louing howre
    For many yeares of sorrow can dispence :
    A dram of sweet is worth a pound of sowre :
    She has forgot, how many a wofull stowre
    For him she late endur'd ; she speakes no more
    Of past : true is, that true loue hath no powre
    To looken backe ; his eyes be fixt before.
Before her stands her knight, for whom she toyld so sore.

Much like, as when the beaten marinere,   xxxi
    That long hath wandred in the *Ocean* wide,
    Oft soust in swelling *Tethys* saltish teare,
    And long time hauing tand his tawney hide
    With blustring breath of heauen, that none can bide,
    And scorching flames of fierce *Orions* hound,
    Soone as the port from farre he has espide,
    His chearefull whistle merrily doth sound,
And *Nereus* crownes with cups ; his mates him pledg around.

Such ioy made *Vna*, when her knight she found ;   xxxii
  And eke th'enchaunter ioyous seemd no lesse,
  Then the glad marchant, that does vew from ground
  His ship farre come from watrie wildernesse,
  He hurles out vowes, and *Neptune* oft doth blesse :
  So forth they past, and all the way they spent
  Discoursing of her dreadfull late distresse,
  In which he askt her, what the Lyon ment :
† Who told her all that fell in iourney as she went.

They had not ridden farre, when they might see   xxxiii
  One pricking towards them with hastie heat,
  Full strongly armd, and on a courser free,
  That through his fiercenesse fomed all with sweat,
  And the sharpe yron did for anger eat,
  When his hot ryder spurd his chauffed side ;
  His looke was sterne, and seemed still to threat
  Cruell reuenge, which he in hart did hyde,
And on his shield *Sans loy* in bloudie lines was dyde.

When nigh he drew vnto this gentle payre   xxxiv
  And saw the Red-crosse, which the knight did beare,
  He burnt in fire, and gan eftsoones prepare
  Himselfe to battell with his couched speare.
  Loth was that other, and did faint through feare,
  To taste th'vntryed dint of deadly steele ;
  But yet his Lady did so well him cheare,
  That hope of new good hap he gan to feele ;
So bent his speare, and spurnd his horse with yron heele.

But that proud Paynim forward came so fierce,   xxxv
  And full of wrath, that with his sharp-head speare
  Through vainely crossed shield he quite did pierce,
  And had his staggering steede not shrunke for feare,
  Through shield and bodie eke he should him beare :
  Yet so great was the puissance of his push,
  That from his saddle quite he did him beare :
  He tombling rudely downe to ground did rush,
And from his gored wound a well of bloud did gush.

  xxxii 9 told, *1609*   all that her fell *sugg. ed.*   xxxiv 5 feare,]
fea, *1596*   9 spurd *1590*   xxxv 1 ferce *1590*   3 perce *1590*
4 shronke *1590*

Dismounting lightly from his loftie steed,   xxxvi
  He to him lept, in mind to reaue his life,
  And proudly said, Lo there the worthie meed
  Of him, that slew *Sansfoy* with bloudie knife ;
  Henceforth his ghost freed from repining strife,
  In peace may passen ouer *Lethe* lake,
  When morning altars purgd with enemies life,
  The blacke infernall *Furies* doen aslake :
Life from *Sansfoy* thou tookst, *Sansloy* shall from thee take.

Therewith in haste his helmet gan vnlace,   xxxvii
  Till *Vna* cride, O hold that heauie hand,
  Deare Sir, what euer that thou be in place :
  Enough is, that thy foe doth vanquisht stand
  Now at thy mercy : Mercie not withstand :
  For he is one the truest knight aliue,
  Though conquered now he lie on lowly land,
  And whilest him fortune fauourd, faire did thriue
In bloudie field : therefore of life him not depriue.

Her piteous words might not abate his rage,   xxxviii
  But rudely rending vp his helmet, would
  Haue slaine him straight : but when he sees his age,
  And hoarie head of *Archimago* old,
  His hastie hand he doth amazed hold,
  And halfe ashamed, wondred at the sight :
  For the old man well knew he, though vntold,
  In charmes and magicke to haue wondrous might,
Ne euer wont in field, ne in round lists to fight.

And said, Why *Archimago*, lucklesse syre,   xxxix
  What doe I see ? what hard mishap is this,
  That hath thee hither brought to taste mine yre ?
  Or thine the fault, or mine the error is,
  In stead of foe to wound my friend amis ?
  He answered nought, but in a traunce still lay,
  And on those guilefull dazed eyes of his
  The cloud of death did sit. Which doen away,
He left him lying so, ne would no lenger stay.

    xxxvi 7 mourning *1590*   xxxviii 3 streight *1590*   7 the] that
    F. E. referring probably to this line

But to the virgin comes, who all this while   xl
  Amased stands, her selfe so mockt to see
  By him, who has the guerdon of his guile,
  For so misfeigning her true knight to bee :
  Yet is she now in more perplexitie,
  Left in the hand of that same Paynim bold,
  From whom her booteth not at all to flie;
  Who by her cleanly garment catching hold,
Her from her Palfrey pluckt, her visage to behold.

But her fierce seruant full of kingly awe   xli
  And high disdaine, whenas his soueraine Dame
  So rudely handled by her foe he sawe,
  With gaping iawes full greedy at him came,
  And ramping on his shield, did weene the same
  Haue reft away with his sharpe rending clawes:
  But he was stout, and lust did now inflame
  His corage more, that from his griping pawes
He hath his shield redeem'd, and foorth his swerd he drawes.

O then too weake and feeble was the forse   xlii
  Of saluage beast, his puissance to withstand:
  For he was strong, and of so mightie corse,
  As euer wielded speare in warlike hand,
  And feates of armes did wisely vnderstand.
  Eftsoones he perced through his chaufed chest
  With thrilling point of deadly yron brand,
  And launcht his Lordly hart : with death opprest
He roar'd aloud, whiles life forsooke his stubborne brest.

Who now is left to keepe the forlorne maid   xliii
  From raging spoile of lawlesse victors will?
  Her faithfull gard remou'd, her hope dismaid,
  Her selfe a yeelded pray to saue or spill.
  He now Lord of the field, his pride to fill,
  With foule reproches, and disdainfull spight
  Her vildly entertaines, and will or nill,
  Beares her away vpon his courser light :
Her prayers nought preuaile, his rage is more of might.

        xli 9 forth *1590*   xliii 5 fled *1596*

And all the way, with great lamenting paine,   xliv
  And piteous plaints she filleth his dull eares,
  That stony hart could riuen haue in twaine,
  And all the way she wets with flowing teares:
  But he enrag'd with rancor, nothing heares.
  Her seruile beast yet would not leaue her so,
  But followes her farre off, ne ought he feares,
  To be partaker of her wandring woe,
More mild in beastly kind, then that her beastly foe.

Cant. IIII.

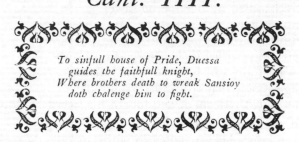

To sinfull house of Pride, Duessa
guides the faithfull knight,
Where brothers death to wreak Sansioy
doth chalenge him to fight.

Young knight, what euer that dost armes professe,   i
  And through long labours huntest after fame,
  Beware of fraud, beware of ficklenesse,
  In choice, and change of thy deare loued Dame,
  Least thou of her beleeue too lightly blame,
  And rash misweening doe thy hart remoue:
  For vnto knight there is no greater shame,
  Then lightnesse and inconstancie in loue;
That doth this *Redcrosse* knights ensample plainly proue.

Who after that he had faire *Vna* lorne,   ii
  Through light misdeeming of her loialtie,
  And false *Duessa* in her sted had borne,
  Called *Fidess'*, and so supposd to bee ;
  Long with her traueild, till at last they see
  A goodly building, brauely garnished,
  The house of mightie Prince it seemd to bee :
  And towards it a broad high way that led,
All bare through peoples feet, which thither traueiled.

Great troupes of people traueild thitherward   iii
    Both day and night, of each degree and place,
    But few returned, hauing scaped hard,
    With balefull beggerie, or foule disgrace,
    Which euer after in most wretched case,
    Like loathsome lazars, by the hedges lay.
    Thither *Duessa* bad him bend his pace :
    For she is wearie of the toilesome way,
And also nigh consumed is the lingring day.

A stately Pallace built of squared bricke,   iv
    Which cunningly was without morter laid,
    Whose wals were high, but nothing strong, nor thick,
    And golden foile all ouer them displaid,
    That purest skye with brightnesse they dismaid :
    High lifted vp were many loftie towres,
    And goodly galleries farre ouer laid,
    Full of faire windowes, and delightfull bowres ;
And on the top a Diall told the timely howres.

It was a goodly heape for to behould,   v
    And spake the praises of the workmans wit ;
    But full great pittie, that so faire a mould
    Did on so weake foundation euer sit.
    For on a sandie hill, that still did flit,
    And fall away, it mounted was full hie,
    That euery breath of heauen shaked it :
    And all the hinder parts, that few could spie,
Were ruinous and old, but painted cunningly.

Arriued there they passed in forth right ;   vi
    For still to all the gates stood open wide,
    Yet charge of them was to a Porter hight
    Cald *Maluenù*, who entrance none denide :
    Thence to the hall, which was on euery side
    With rich array and costly arras dight :
    Infinite sorts of people did abide
    There waiting long, to win the wished sight
Of her, that was the Lady of that Pallace bright.

       iii 5 case] care *1590* : *corr. F. E.*

By them they passe, all gazing on them round,   vii
    And to the Presence mount; whose glorious vew
    Their frayle amazed senses did confound:
    In liuing Princes court none euer knew
    Such endlesse richesse, and so sumptuous shew;
    Ne *Persia* selfe, the nourse of pompous pride
    Like euer saw. And there a noble crew
    Of Lordes and Ladies stood on euery side,
Which with their presence faire, the place much beautifide.

High aboue all a cloth of State was spred,   viii
    And a rich throne, as bright as sunny day,
    On which there sate most braue embellished
    With royall robes and gorgeous array,
    A mayden Queene, that shone as *Titans* ray,
    In glistring gold, and peerelesse pretious stone:
    Yet her bright blazing beautie did assay
    To dim the brightnesse of her glorious throne,
As enuying her selfe, that too exceeding shone.

Exceeding shone, like *Phœbus* fairest childe,   ix
    That did presume his fathers firie wayne,
    And flaming mouthes of steedes vnwonted wilde
    Through highest heauen with weaker hand to rayne;
    Proud of such glory and aduancement vaine,
    While flashing beames do daze his feeble eyen,
    He leaues the welkin way most beaten plaine,
    And rapt with whirling wheeles, inflames the skyen,
With fire not made to burne, but fairely for to shyne.

So proud she shyned in her Princely state,   x
    Looking to heauen ; for earth she did disdayne,
    And sitting high ; for lowly she did hate:
    Lo vnderneath her scornefull feete, was layne
    A dreadfull Dragon with an hideous trayne,
    And in her hand she held a mirrhour bright,
    Wherein her face she often vewed fayne,
    And in her selfe-lou'd semblance tooke delight;
For she was wondrous faire, as any liuing wight.

Of griesly *Pluto* she the daughter was,   xi
  And sad *Proserpina* the Queene of hell ;
  Yet did she thinke her pearelesse worth to pas
  That parentage, with pride so did she swell,
  And thundring *Ioue*, that high in heauen doth dwell,
  And wield the world, she claymed for her syre,
  Or if that any else did *Ioue* excell :
  For to the highest she did still aspyre,
Or if ought higher were then that, did it desyre.

And proud *Lucifera* men did her call,   xii
  That made her selfe a Queene, and crownd to be,
  Yet rightfull kingdome she had none at all,
  Ne heritage of natiue soueraintie,
  But did vsurpe with wrong and tyrannie
  Vpon the scepter, which she now did hold :
  Ne ruld her Realmes with lawes, but pollicie,
  And strong aduizement of six wisards old,
That with their counsels bad her kingdome did vphold.

Soone as the Elfin knight in presence came,   xiii
  And false *Duessa* seeming Lady faire,
  A gentle Husher, *Vanitie* by name
  Made rowme, and passage for them did prepaire :
  So goodly brought them to the lowest staire
  Of her high throne, where they on humble knee
  Making obeyssance, did the cause declare,
  Why they were come, her royall state to see,
To proue the wide report of her great Maiestee.

With loftie eyes, halfe loth to looke so low,   xiv
  She thanked them in her disdainefull wise,
  Ne other grace vouchsafed them to show
  Of Princesse worthy, scarse them bad arise.
  Her Lordes and Ladies all this while deuise
  Themselues to setten forth to straungers sight :
  Some frounce their curled haire in courtly guise,
  Some prancke their ruffes, and others trimly dight
Their gay attire : each others greater pride does spight.

  xi 3 wroth *1596*   xii 2 a *om. 1596*   7 Realme *1590*
    xiii 1 Elfing *1596*   7 obeysaunce *1590* : obeisance *1609*

Goodly they all that knight do entertaine, xv
  Right glad with him to haue increast their crew:
  But to *Duess'* each one himselfe did paine
  All kindnesse and faire courtesie to shew ;
  For in that court whylome her well they knew :
  Yet the stout Faerie mongst the middest crowd
  Thought all their glorie vaine in knightly vew,
  And that great Princesse too exceeding prowd,
That to strange knight no better countenance allowd.

Suddein vpriseth from her stately place xvi
  The royall Dame, and for her coche doth call :
  All hurtlen forth, and she with Princely pace,
  As faire *Aurora* in her purple pall,
  Out of the East the dawning day doth call :
  So forth she comes : her brightnesse brode doth blaze ;
  The heapes of people thronging in the hall,
  Do ride each other, vpon her to gaze :
Her glorious glitterand light doth all mens eyes amaze.

So forth she comes, and to her coche does clyme, xvii
  Adorned all with gold, and girlonds gay,
  That seemd as fresh as *Flora* in her prime,
  And stroue to match, in royall rich array,
  Great *Iunoes* golden chaire, the which they say
  The Gods stand gazing on, when she does ride
  To *Ioues* high house through heauens bras-paued way
  Drawne of faire Pecocks, that excell in pride,
And full of *Argus* eyes their tailes dispredden wide.

But this was drawne of six vnequall beasts, xviii
  On which her six sage Counsellours did ryde,
  Taught to obay their bestiall beheasts,
  With like conditions to their kinds applyde :
  Of which the first, that all the rest did guyde,
  Was sluggish *Idlenesse* the nourse of sin ;
  Vpon a slouthfull Asse he chose to ryde,
  Arayd in habit blacke, and amis thin,
Like to an holy Monck, the seruice to begin.

xvi 3 hurtlen] hurlen *1609*   9 glitter and *1596, 1609*

And in his hand his Portesse still he bare,   xix
  That much was worne, but therein little red,
  For of deuotion he had little care,
  Still drownd in sleepe, and most of his dayes ded ;
  Scarse could he once vphold his heauie hed,
  To looken, whether it were night or day:
  May seeme the wayne was very euill led,
  When such an one had guiding of the way,
That knew not, whether right he went, or else astray.

From worldly cares himselfe he did esloyne,   xx
  And greatly shunned manly exercise,
  From euery worke he chalenged essoyne,
  For contemplation sake : yet otherwise,
  His life he led in lawlesse riotise ;
  By which he grew to grieuous malady ;
  For in his lustlesse limbs through euill guise
  A shaking feuer raignd continually :
Such one was *Idlenesse,* first of this company.

And by his side rode loathsome *Gluttony,*   xxi
  Deformed creature, on a filthie swyne,
  His belly was vp-blowne with luxury,
  And eke with fatnesse swollen were his eyne,
  And like a Crane his necke was long and fyne,
  With which he swallowd vp excessiue feast,
  For want whereof poore people oft did pyne ;
  And all the way, most like a brutish beast,
He spued vp his gorge, that all did him deteast.

In greene vine leaues he was right fitly clad ;   xxii
  For other clothes he could not weare for heat,
  And on his head an yuie girland had,
  From vnder which fast trickled downe the sweat:
  Still as he rode, he somewhat still did eat,
  And in his hand did beare a bouzing can,
  Of which he supt so oft, that on his seat
  His dronken corse he scarse vpholden can,
In shape and life more like a monster, then a man.

xx 3 For *1596, 1609*   xxii 8 corse] course *1590* : *corr. F. E.*

Vnfit he was for any worldly thing,
　　And eke vnhable once to stirre or go,
　　Not meet to be of counsell to a king,
　　Whose mind in meat and drinke was drowned so,
　　That from his friend he seldome knew his fo :
　　Full of diseases was his carcas blew,
　　And a dry dropsie through his flesh did flow :
　　Which by misdiet daily greater grew :
Such one was *Gluttony*, the second of that crew.

And next to him rode lustfull *Lechery*,
　　Vpon a bearded Goat, whose rugged haire,
　　And whally eyes (the signe of gelosy,)
　　Was like the person selfe, whom he did beare :
　　Who rough, and blacke, and filthy did appeare,
　　Vnseemely man to please faire Ladies eye ;
　　Yet he of Ladies oft was loued deare,
　　When fairer faces were bid standen by :
O who does know the bent of womens fantasy ?

In a greene gowne he clothed was full faire,
　　Which vnderneath did hide his filthinesse,
　　And in his hand a burning hart he bare,
　　Full of vaine follies, and new fanglenesse :
　　For he was false, and fraught with ficklenesse,
　　And learned had to loue with secret lookes,
　　And well could daunce, and sing with ruefulnesse,
　　And fortunes tell, and read in louing bookes,
And thousand other wayes, to bait his fleshly hookes.

Inconstant man, that loued all he saw,
　　And lusted after all, that he did loue,
　　Ne would his looser life be tide to law,
　　But ioyd weake wemens hearts to tempt and proue
　　If from their loyall loues he might then moue ;
　　Which lewdnesse fild him with reprochfull paine
　　Of that fowle euill, which all men reproue,
　　That rots the marrow, and consumes the braine :
Such one was *Lecherie*, the third of all this traine.

xxiii 1 wordly *1590*   2 vnable *1609*   5 seeldome *1590* : sildom *1609*
xxvi 4 tempt, *1590*

And greedy *Auarice* by him did ride,   xxvii
   Vpon a Camell loaden all with gold;
   Two iron coffers hong on either side,
   With precious mettall full, as they might hold,
   And in his lap an heape of coine he told;
   For of his wicked pelfe his God he made,
   And vnto hell him selfe for money sold;
   Accursed vsurie was all his trade,
And right and wrong ylike in equall ballaunce waide.

His life was nigh vnto deaths doore yplast,   xxviii
   And thred-bare cote, and cobled shoes he warc,
   Ne scarse good morsell all his life did tast,
   But both from backe and belly still did spare,
   To fill his bags, and richesse to compare;
   Yet chylde ne kinsman liuing had he none
   To leaue them to; but thorough daily care
   To get, and nightly feare to lose his owne,
He led a wretched life vnto him selfe vnknowne.

Most wretched wight, whom nothing might suffise,   xxix
   Whose greedy lust did lacke in greatest store,
   Whose need had end, but no end couetise,
   Whose wealth was want, whose plenty made him pore,
   Who had enough, yet wished euer more;
   A vile disease, and eke in foote and hand
   A grieuous gout tormented him full sore,
   That well he could not touch, nor go, nor stand:
Such one was *Auarice*, the fourth of this faire band.

And next to him malicious *Enuie* rode,   xxx
   Vpon a rauenous wolfe, and still did chaw
   Betweene his cankred teeth a venemous tode,
   That all the poison ran about his chaw;
   But inwardly he chawed his owne maw
   At neighbours wealth, that made him euer sad;
   For death it was, when any good he saw,
   And wept, that cause of weeping none he had,
But when he heard of harme, he wexed wondrous glad.

xxvii 3 coffets *1590*   6 pelfe] pelpe *1590*: *corr. F. E.*   xxix 5 euermore
1609   9 fourth] forth *1590*   xxx 4 chaw] jaw *1609*   6 neibors *1590*

All in a kirtle of discolourd say   xxxi
  He clothed was, ypainted full of eyes ;
  And in his bosome secretly there lay
  An hatefull Snake, the which his taile vptyes
  In many folds, and mortall sting implyes.
  Still as he rode, he gnasht his teeth, to see
  Those heapes of gold with griple Couetyse,
  And grudged at the great felicitie
Of proud *Lucifera*, and his owne companie.

He hated all good workes and vertuous deeds,   xxxii
  And him no lesse, that any like did vse,
  And who with gracious bread the hungry feeds,
  His almes for want of faith he doth accuse ;
  So euery good to bad he doth abuse :
  And eke the verse of famous Poets witt
  He does backebite, and spightfull poison spues
  From leprous mouth on all, that euer writt :
Such one vile *Enuie* was, that fifte in row did sitt.

And him beside rides fierce reuenging *Wrath*,   xxxiii
  Vpon a Lion, loth for to be led ;
  And in his hand a burning brond he hath,
  The which he brandisheth about his hed ;
  His eyes did hurle forth sparkles fiery red,
  And stared sterne on all, that him beheld,
  As ashes pale of hew and seeming ded ;
  And on his dagger still his hand he held,
Trembling through hasty rage, when choler in him sweld.

His ruffin raiment all was staind with blood,   xxxiv
  Which he had spilt, and all to rags yrent,
  Through vnaduized rashnesse woxen wood ;
  For of his hands he had no gouernement,
  Ne car'd for bloud in his auengement :
  But when the furious fit was ouerpast,
  His cruell facts he often would repent ;
  Yet wilfull man he neuer would forecast,
How many mischieues should ensue his heedlesse hast.

Full many mischiefes follow cruell *Wrath*;   xxxv
  Abhorred bloudshed, and tumultuous strife,
  Vnmanly murder, and vnthrifty scath,
  Bitter despight, with rancours rusty knife,
  And fretting griefe the enemy of life ;
  All these, and many euils moe haunt ire,
  The swelling Splene, and Frenzy raging rife,
  The shaking Palsey, and Saint *Fraunces* fire:
Such one was *Wrath*, the last of this vngodly tire.

And after all, vpon the wagon beame   xxxvi
  Rode *Sathan*, with a smarting whip in hand,
  With which he forward lasht the laesie teme,
  So oft as *Slowth* still in the mire did stand.
  Huge routs of people did about them band,
  Showting for ioy, and still before their way
  A foggy mist had couered all the land;
  And vnderneath their feet, all scattered lay
Dead sculs and bones of men, whose life had gone astray.

So forth they marchen in this goodly sort,   xxxvii
  To take the solace of the open aire,
  And in fresh flowring fields themselues to sport;
  Emongst the rest rode that false Lady faire,
  The fowle *Duessa*, next vnto the chaire
  Of proud *Lucifera*, as one of the traine:
  But that good knight would not so nigh repaire,
  Him selfe estraunging from their ioyaunce vaine,
Whose fellowship seemd far vnfit for warlike swaine.

So hauing solaced themselues a space   xxxviii
  With pleasaunce of the breathing fields yfed,
  They backe returned to the Princely Place;
  Whereas an errant knight in armes ycled,
  And heathnish shield, wherein with letters red
  Was writ *Sans ioy*, they new arriued find:
  Enflam'd with fury and fiers hardy-hed,
  He seemd in hart to harbour thoughts vnkind,
And nourish bloudy vengeaunce in his bitter mind.

      xxxvi 2 *Satan 1609*   xxxvii 6 *Lucifer' 1590*

Who when the shamed shield of slaine *Sans foy*   xxxix
  He spide with that same Faery champions page,
  Bewraying him, that did of late destroy
  His eldest brother, burning all with rage
  He to him leapt, and that same enuious gage
  Of victors glory from him snatcht away:
  But th'Elfin knight, which ought that warlike wage,
  Disdaind to loose the meed he wonne in fray,
And him rencountring fierce, reskewd the noble pray.

Therewith they gan to hurtlen greedily,   xl
  Redoubted battaile ready to darrayne,
  And clash their shields, and shake their swords on hy,
  That with their sturre they troubled all the traine;
  Till that great Queene vpon eternall paine
  Of high displeasure, that ensewen might,
  Commaunded them their fury to refraine,
  And if that either to that shield had right,
In equall lists they should the morrow next it fight.

Ah dearest Dame, (quoth then the Paynim bold,)   xli
  Pardon the errour of enraged wight,
  Whom great griefe made forget the raines to hold
  Of reasons rule, to see this recreant knight,
  No knight, but treachour full of false despight
  And shamefull treason, who through guile hath slayn
  The prowest knight, that euer field did fight,
  Euen stout *Sans foy* (O who can then refrayn?)
Whose shield he beares renuerst, the more to heape disdayn.

And to augment the glorie of his guile,   xlii
  His dearest loue the faire *Fidessa* loe
  Is there possessed of the traytour vile,
  Who reapes the haruest sowen by his foe,
  Sowen in bloudy field, and bought with woe:
  That brothers hand shall dearely well requight
  So be, O Queene, you equall fauour showe.
  Him litle answerd th'angry Elfin knight;
He neuer meant with words, but swords to plead his right.

But threw his gauntlet as a sacred pledge,   _{xliii}
  His cause in combat the next day to try:
  So been they parted both, with harts on edge,
  To be aueng'd each on his enimy.
  That night they pas in ioy and iollity,
  Feasting and courting both in bowre and hall;
  For Steward was excessiue *Gluttonie*,
  That of his plenty poured forth to all;
Which doen, the Chamberlain *Slowth* did to rest them call.

Now whenas darkesome night had all displayd   _{xliv}
  Her coleblacke curtein ouer brightest skye,
  The warlike youthes on dayntie couches layd,
  Did chace away sweet sleepe from sluggish eye,
  To muse on meanes of hoped victory.
  But whenas *Morpheus* had with leaden mace
  Arrested all that courtly company,
  Vp-rose *Duessa* from her resting place,
And to the Paynims lodging comes with silent pace.

Whom broad awake she finds, in troublous fit,   _{xlv}
  Forecasting, how his foe he might annoy,
  And him amoues with speaches seeming fit:
  Ah deare *Sans ioy*, next dearest to *Sans foy*,
  Cause of my new griefe, cause of my new ioy,
  Ioyous, to see his ymage in mine eye,
  And greeu'd, to thinke how foe did him destroy,
  That was the flowre of grace and cheualrye;
Lo his *Fidessa* to thy secret faith I flye.

With gentle wordes he can her fairely greet,   _{xlvi}
  And bad say on the secret of her hart.
  Then sighing soft, I learne that litle sweet
  Oft tempred is (quoth she) with muchell smart:
  For since my brest was launcht with louely dart
  Of deare *Sansfoy*, I neuer ioyed howre,
  But in eternall woes my weaker hart
  Haue wasted, louing him with all my powre,
And for his sake haue felt full many an heauie stowre.

xliii 1 pledg *1590*   3 edg *1590*   xlv 4 *Sans ioy*] *Sans foy 1590*
5 cause of new ioy, *1590, 1596*: *corr. F. E.*   xlvi 2 secrete *1590*

At last when perils all I weened past,   xlvii
  And hop'd to reape the crop of all my care,
  Into new woes vnweeting I was cast,
  By this false faytor, who vnworthy ware
  His worthy shield, whom he with guilefull snare
  Entrapped slew, and brought to shamefull graue.
  Me silly maid away with him he bare,
  And euer since hath kept in darksome caue,
For that I would not yeeld, that to *Sans-foy* I gaue.

But since faire Sunne hath sperst that lowring clowd,   xlviii
  And to my loathed life now shewes some light,
  Vnder your beames I will me safely shrowd,
  From dreaded storme of his disdainfull spight:
  To you th'inheritance belongs by right
  Of brothers prayse, to you eke longs his loue.
  Let not his loue, let not his restlesse spright
  Be vnreueng'd, that calles to you aboue
From wandring *Stygian* shores, where it doth endlesse moue.

Thereto said he, Faire Dame be nought dismaid   xlix
  For sorrowes past; their griefe is with them gone:
  Ne yet of present perill be affraid;
  For needlesse feare did neuer vantage none,
  And helplesse hap it booteth not to mone.
  Dead is *Sans-foy*, his vitall paines are past,
  Though greeued ghost for vengeance deepe do grone:
  He liues, that shall him pay his dewties last,
And guiltie Elfin bloud shall sacrifice in hast.

O but I feare the fickle freakes (quoth shee)   l
  Of fortune false, and oddes of armes in field.
  Why dame (quoth he) what oddes can euer bee,
  Where both do fight alike, to win or yield?
  Yea but (quoth she) he beares a charmed shield,
  And eke enchaunted armes, that none can perce,
  Ne none can wound the man, that does them wield.
  Charmd or enchaunted (answerd he then ferce)
I no whit reck, ne you the like need to reherce.

xlix 1 faire *1590 &c.*

But faire *Fidessa*, sithens fortunes guile,   11
   Or enimies powre hath now captiued you,
   Returne from whence ye came, and rest a while
   Till morrow next, that I the Elfe subdew,
   And with *Sans-foyes* dead dowry you endew.
   Ay me, that is a double death (she said)
   With proud foes sight my sorrow to renew:
   Where euer yet I be, my secrete aid
Shall follow you.   So passing forth she him obaid.

Cant. V.

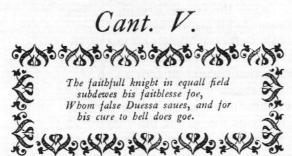

     The faithfull knight in equall field
     subdewes his faithlesse foe,
     Whom false Duessa saues, and for
     his cure to hell does goe.

THe noble hart, that harbours vertuous thought,   1
   And is with child of glorious great intent,
   Can neuer rest, vntill it forth haue brought
   Th'eternall brood of glorie excellent:
   Such restlesse passion did all night torment
   The flaming corage of that Faery knight,
   Deuizing, how that doughtie turnament
   With greatest honour he atchieuen might;
Still did he wake, and still did watch for dawning light.

At last the golden Orientall gate   11
   Of greatest heauen gan to open faire,
   And *Phœbus* fresh, as bridegrome to his mate,
   Came dauncing forth, shaking his deawie haire :
   And hurld his glistring beames through gloomy aire.
   Which when the wakeful Elfe perceiu'd, streight way
   He started vp, and did him selfe prepaire,
   In sun-bright armes, and battailous array :
For with that Pagan proud he combat will that day.

   i 9 he *om. 1596*   ii 1 gate, *1590, 1596*   5 hurld] hurls *1590, 1596* :
hurles *1609* : *corr. F. E.*

And forth he comes into the commune hall,   iii
   Where earely waite him many a gazing eye,
   To weet what end to straunger knights may fall.
   There many Minstrales maken melody,
   To driue away the dull melancholy,
   And many Bardes, that to the trembling chord
   Can tune their timely voyces cunningly,
   And many Chroniclers, that can record
Old loues, and warres for Ladies doen by many a Lord.

Soone after comes the cruell Sarazin,   iv
   In wouen maile all armed warily,
   And sternly lookes at him, who not a pin
   Does care for looke of liuing creatures eye.
   They bring them wines of *Greece* and *Araby*,
   And daintie spices fetcht from furthest *Ynd*,
   To kindle heat of corage priuily:
   And in the wine a solemne oth they bynd
T'obserue the sacred lawes of armes, that are assynd.

At last forth comes that far renowmed Queene,   v
   With royall pomp and Princely maiestie;
   She is ybrought vnto a paled greene,
   And placed vnder stately canapee,
   The warlike feates of both those knights to see.
   On th'other side in all mens open vew
   Duessa placed is, and on a tree
   Sans-foy his shield is hangd with bloudy hew:
Both those the lawrell girlonds to the victor dew.

A shrilling trompet sownded from on hye,   vi
   And vnto battaill bad them selues addresse:
   Their shining shieldes about their wrestes they tye,
   And burning blades about their heads do blesse,
   The instruments of wrath and heauinesse:
   With greedy force each other doth assayle,
   And strike so fiercely, that they do impresse
   Deepe dinted furrowes in the battred mayle;
The yron walles to ward their blowes are weake and fraile.

iii 1 common *1609*   vi 3 wrists *1609*

The Sarazin was stout, and wondrous strong,   vii
  And heaped blowes like yron hammers great:
  For after bloud and vengeance he did long.
  The knight was fiers, and full of youthly heat:
  And doubled strokes, like dreaded thunders threat:
  For all for prayse and honour he did fight.
  Both stricken strike, and beaten both do beat,
  That from their shields forth flyeth firie light,
And helmets hewen deepe, shew marks of eithers might.

[So th'one for wrong, the other striues for right: viii
  As when a Gryfon seized of his pray,
  A Dragon fiers encountreth in his flight,
  Through widest ayre making his ydle way,
  That would his rightfull rauine rend away:
  With hideous horrour both together smight,
  And souce so sore, that they the heauens affray:
  The wise Southsayer seeing so sad sight,
Th'amazed vulgar tels of warres and mortall fight.

So th'one for wrong, the other striues for right,   ix
  And each to deadly shame would driue his foe:
  The cruell steele so greedily doth bight
  In tender flesh, that streames of bloud down flow,
  With which the armes, that earst so bright did show,
  Into a pure vermillion now are dyde:
  Great ruth in all the gazers harts did grow,
  Seeing the gored woundes to gape so wyde,
That victory they dare not wish to either side.]

[At last the Paynim chaunst to cast his eye,   x
  His suddein eye, flaming with wrathfull fyre,
  Vpon his brothers shield, which hong thereby:
  Therewith redoubled was his raging yre,
  And said, Ah wretched sonne of wofull syre,
  Doest thou sit wayling by black *Stygian* lake,
  Whilest here thy shield is hangd for victors hyre,
  And sluggish german doest thy forces slake,
To after-send his foe, that him may ouertake?

vii 9 hewen helmets *1590*   ix 5 show *1590, 1596*: showe *1609*
    x 6 Doost *1609 passim*

Goe caytiue Elfe, him quickly ouertake,   xi
    And soone redeeme from his long wandring woe;
    Goe guiltie ghost, to him my message make,
    That I his shield haue quit from dying foe.
    Therewith vpon his crest he stroke him so,
    That twise he reeled, readie twise to fall;
    End of the doubtfull battell deemed tho
    The lookers on, and lowd to him gan call
The false *Duessa*, Thine the shield, and I, and all. ⌉

Soone as the Faerie heard his Ladie speake,   xii
    Out of his swowning dreame he gan awake,
    And quickning faith, that earst was woxen weake,
    The creeping deadly cold away did shake:
    Tho mou'd with wrath, and shame, and Ladies sake,
    Of all attonce he cast auengd to bee,
    And with so'exceeding furie at him strake,
    That forced him to stoupe vpon his knee;
Had he not stouped so, he should haue clouen bee.

And to him said, Goe now proud Miscreant,   xiii
    Thy selfe thy message doe to german deare,
    Alone he wandring thee too long doth want:
    Goe say, his foe thy shield with his doth beare.
    Therewith his heauie hand he high gan reare,
    Him to haue slaine; when loe a darkesome clowd
    Vpon him fell: he no where doth appeare,
    But vanisht is.   The Elfe him cals alowd,
But answer none receiues: the darknes him does shrowd.

In haste *Duessa* from her place arose,   xiv
    And to him running said, O prowest knight,
    That euer Ladie to her loue did chose,
    Let now abate the terror of your might,
    And quench the flame of furious despight,
    And bloudie vengeance; lo th'infernall powres
    Couering your foe with cloud of deadly night,
    Haue borne him hence to *Plutoes* balefull bowres.
The conquest yours, I yours, the shield, and glory yours.

xi 7 battaile *1590 passim*   xii 8 stoupe *1609*   xiv 4 terrour *1590*

Not all so satisfide, with greedie eye   xv
  He sought all round about, his thirstie blade
  To bath in bloud of faithlesse enemy;
  Who all that while lay hid in secret shade:
  He standes amazed, how he thence should fade.
  At last the trumpets Triumph sound on hie,
  And running Heralds humble homage made,
  Greeting him goodly with new victorie,
And to him brought the shield, the cause of enmitie.

Wherewith he goeth to that soueraine Queene,   xvi
  And falling her before on lowly knee,
  To her makes present of his seruice seene:
  Which she accepts, with thankes, and goodly gree,
  Greatly aduauncing his gay cheualree.
  So marcheth home, and by her takes the knight,
  Whom all the people follow with great glee,
  Shouting, and clapping all their hands on hight,
That all the aire it fils, and flyes to heauen bright.

Home is he brought, and laid in sumptuous bed: xvii
  Where many skilfull leaches him abide,
  To salue his hurts, that yet still freshly bled.
  In wine and oyle they wash his woundes wide,
  And softly can embalme on euery side.
  And all the while, most heauenly melody
  About the bed sweet musicke did diuide,
  Him to beguile of griefe and agony:
And all the while *Duessa* wept full bitterly.

As when a wearie traueller that strayes   xviii
  By muddy shore of broad seuen-mouthed *Nile*,
  Vnweeting of the perillous wandring wayes,
  Doth meet a cruell craftie Crocodile,
  Which in false griefe hyding his harmefull guile,
  Doth weepe full sore, and sheddeth tender teares:
  The foolish man, that pitties all this while
  His mournefull plight, is swallowd vp vnwares,
Forgetfull of his owne, that mindes anothers cares.

xv 2 thristy *1590*   3 bathe *1590, 1609*   6 trumpets, *1596, 1609*
    xvii 5 can] gan *1590*   xviii 1 traueiler *1590*

So wept *Duessa* vntill euentide,   xix
    That shyning lampes in *Ioues* high house were light:
    Then forth she rose, ne lenger would abide,
    But comes vnto the place, where th'Hethen knight
    In slombring swownd nigh voyd of vitall spright,
    Lay couer'd with inchaunted cloud all day:
    Whom when she found, as she him left in plight,
    To wayle his woefull case she would not stay,
But to the easterne coast of heauen makes speedy way.

Where griesly *Night*, with visage deadly sad,   xx
    That *Phœbus* chearefull face durst neuer vew,
    And in a foule blacke pitchie mantle clad,
    She findes forth comming from her darkesome mew,
    Where she all day did hide her hated hew.
    Before the dore her yron charet stood,
    Alreadie harnessed for iourney new;
    And coleblacke steedes yborne of hellish brood,
That on their rustie bits did champ, as they were wood.

Who when she saw *Duessa* sunny bright,   xxi
    Adornd with gold and iewels shining cleare,
    She greatly grew amazed at the sight,
    And th'vnacquainted light began to feare:
    For neuer did such brightnesse there appeare,
    And would haue backe retyred to her caue,
    Vntill the witches speech she gan to heare,
    Saying, Yet O thou dreaded Dame, I craue
Abide, till I haue told the message, which I haue.

She stayd, and foorth *Duessa* gan proceede,   xxii
    O thou most auncient Grandmother of all,
    More old then *Ioue*, whom thou at first didst breede,
    Or that great house of Gods cælestiall,
    Which wast begot in *Dæmogorgons* hall,
    And sawst the secrets of the world vnmade,
    Why suffredst thou thy Nephewes deare to fall
    With Elfin sword, most shamefully betrade?
Lo where the stout *Sansioy* doth sleepe in deadly shade.

        xix 5 swoune *1609*   xxi 8 yet *1590 &c.*

And him before, I saw with bitter eyes   xxiii
   The bold *Sansfoy* shrinke vnderneath his speare;
And now the pray of fowles in field he lyes,
Nor wayld of friends, nor laid on groning beare,
That whylome was to me too dearely deare.
O what of Gods then boots it to be borne,
If old *Aveugles* sonnes so euill heare?
Or who shall not great *Nightes* children scorne,
When two of three her Nephews are so fowle forlorne.

Vp then, vp dreary Dame, of darknesse Queene,   xxiv
   Go gather vp the reliques of thy race,
Or else goe them auenge, and let be scene,
That dreaded *Night* in brightest day hath place,
And can the children of faire light deface.
Her feeling speeches some compassion moued
In hart, and chaunge in that great mothers face:
Yet pittie in her hart was neuer proued
Till then: for euermore she hated, neuer loued.

And said, Deare daughter rightly may I rew   xxv
   The fall of famous children borne of mee,
And good successes, which their foes ensew:
But who can turne the streame of destinee,
Or breake the chayne of strong necessitee,
Which fast is tyde to *Ioues* eternall seat?
The sonnes of Day he fauoureth, I see,
And by my ruines thinkes to make them great:
To make one great by others losse, is bad excheat.

Yet shall they not escape so freely all;   xxvi
   For some shall pay the price of others guilt:
And he the man that made *Sansfoy* to fall,
Shall with his owne bloud price that he hath spilt.
But what art thou, that telst of Nephews kilt?
I that do seeme not I, *Duessa* am,
(Quoth she) how euer now in garments gilt,
And gorgeous gold arayd I to thee came;
Duessa I, the daughter of Deceipt and Shame.

       xxiii 8 *Nightes*] *Nights* drad *1609*
  xxiv 9 for] and *1596, 1609*   xxvi 6 ame *1590*

Then bowing downe her aged backe, she kist   xxvii
  The wicked witch, saying; In that faire face
  The false resemblance of Deceipt, I wist
  Did closely lurke; yet so true-seeming grace
  It carried, that I scarse in darkesome place
  Could it discerne, though I the mother bee
  Of falshood, and root of *Duessaes* race.
  O welcome child, whom I haue longd to see,
And now haue seene vnwares.   Lo now I go with thee.

Then to her yron wagon she betakes,   xxviii
  And with her beares the fowle welfauourd witch:
  Through mirkesome aire her readie way she makes.
  Her twyfold Teme, of which two blacke as pitch,
  And two were browne, yet each to each vnlich,
  Did softly swim away, ne euer stampe,
  Vnlesse she chaunst their stubborne mouths to twitch;
  Then foming tarre, their bridles they would champe,
And trampling the fine element, would fiercely rampe.

So well they sped, that they be come at length   xxix
  Vnto the place, whereas the Paynim lay,
  Deuoid of outward sense, and natiue strength,
  Couerd with charmed cloud from vew of day,
  And sight of men, since his late luckelesse fray.
  His cruell wounds with cruddy bloud congealed,
  They binden vp so wisely, as they may,
  And handle softly, till they can be healed:
So lay him in her charet, close in night concealed.

And all the while she stood vpon the ground,   xxx
  The wakefull dogs did neuer cease to bay,
  As giuing warning of th'vnwonted sound,
  With which her yron wheeles did them affray,
  And her darke griesly looke them much dismay;
  The messenger of death, the ghastly Owle
  With drearie shriekes did also her bewray;
  And hungry Wolues continually did howle,
At her abhorred face, so filthy and so fowle.

xxvii 7 fashood 1590

Thence turning backe in silence soft they stole,   xxxi
  And brought the heauie corse with easie pace
  To yawning gulfe of deepe *Auernus* hole.
  By that same hole an entrance darke and bace
  With smoake and sulphure hiding all the place,
  Descends to hell: there creature neuer past,
  That backe returned without heauenly grace;
  But dreadfull *Furies,* which their chaines haue brast,
And damned sprights sent forth to make ill men aghast.

By that same way the direfull dames doe driue   xxxii
  Their mournefull charet, fild with rusty blood,
  And downe to *Plutoes* house are come biliue:
  Which passing through, on euery side them stood
  The trembling ghosts with sad amazed mood,
  Chattring their yron teeth, and staring wide
  With stonie eyes; and all the hellish brood
  Of feends infernall flockt on euery side,
To gaze on earthly wight, that with the Night durst ride.

They pas the bitter waues of *Acheron,*   xxxiii
  Where many soules sit wailing woefully,
  And come to fiery flood of *Phlegeton,*
  Whereas the damned ghosts in torments fry,
  And with sharpe shrilling shriekes doe bootlesse cry,
  Cursing high *Ioue,* the which them thither sent.
  The house of endlesse paine is built thereby,
  In which ten thousand sorts of punishment
The cursed creatures doe eternally torment.

Before the threshold dreadfull *Cerberus*   xxxiv
  His three deformed heads did lay along,
  Curled with thousand adders venemous,
  And lilled forth his bloudie flaming tong:
  At them he gan to reare his bristles strong,
  And felly gnarre, vntill dayes enemy
  Did him appease; then downe his taile he hong
  And suffered them to passen quietly:
For she in hell and heauen had power equally.

There was *Ixion* turned on a wheele,   xxxv
　　For daring tempt the Queene of heauen to sin;
　　And *Sisyphus* an huge round stone did reele
　　Against an hill, ne might from labour lin;
　　There thirstie *Tantalus* hong by the chin;
　　And *Tityus* fed a vulture on his maw;
　　Typhœus ioynts were stretched on a gin,
　　Theseus condemned to endlesse slouth by law,
And fifty sisters water in leake vessels draw.

They all beholding worldly wights in place,   xxxvi
　　Leaue off their worke, vnmindfull of their smart,
　　To gaze on them; who forth by them doe pace,
　　Till they be come vnto the furthest part:
　　Where was a Caue ywrought by wondrous art,
　　Deepe, darke, vneasie, dolefull, comfortlesse,
　　In which sad *Æsculapius* farre a part
　　Emprisond was in chaines remedilesse,
For that *Hippolytus* rent corse he did redresse.

Hippolytus a iolly huntsman was,   xxxvii
　　That wont in charet chace the foming Bore;
　　He all his Peeres in beautie did surpas,
　　But Ladies loue as losse of time forbore:
　　His wanton stepdame loued him the more,
　　But when she saw her offred sweets refused
　　Her loue she turnd to hate, and him before
　　His father fierce of treason false accused,
And with her gealous termes his open eares abused.

Who ail in rage his Sea-god syre besought,   xxxviii
　　Some cursed vengeance on his sonne to cast:
　　From surging gulf two monsters straight were brought,
　　With dread whereof his chasing steedes aghast,
　　Both charet swift and huntsman ouercast,
　　His goodly corps on ragged cliffs yrent,
　　Was quite dismembred, and his members chast
　　Scattered on euery mountaine, as he went,
That of *Hippolytus* was left no moniment.

His cruell stepdame seeing what was donne,   xxxix
  Her wicked dayes with wretched knife did end,
  In death auowing th'innocence of her sonne.
  Which hearing his rash Syre, began to rend
  His haire, and hastie tongue, that did offend:
  Tho gathering vp the relicks of his smart
  By *Dianes* meanes, who was *Hippolyts* frend,
  Them brought to *Æsculape*, that by his art
Did heale them all againe, and ioyned euery part.

Such wondrous science in mans wit to raine   xl
  When *Ioue* auizd, that could the dead reuiue,
  And fates expired could renew againe,
  Of endlesse life he might him not depriue,
  But vnto hell did thrust him downe aliue,
  With flashing thunderbolt ywounded sore:
  Where long remaining, he did alwaies striue
  Himselfe with salues to health for to restore,
And slake the heauenly fire, that raged euermore.

There auncient Night arriuing, did alight   xli
  From her nigh wearie waine, and in her armes
  To *Æsculapius* brought the wounded knight:
  Whom hauing softly disarayd of armes,
  Tho gan to him discouer all his harmes,
  Beseeching him with prayer, and with praise,
  If either salues, or oyles, or herbes, or charmes
  A fordonne wight from dore of death mote raise,
He would at her request prolong her nephews daies.

Ah Dame (quoth he) thou temptest me in vaine,   xlii
  To dare the thing, which daily yet I rew,
  And the old cause of my continued paine
  With like attempt to like end to renew.
  Is not enough, that thrust from heauen dew
  Here endlesse penance for one fault I pay,
  But that redoubled crime with vengeance new
  Thou biddest me to eeke?   Can Night defray
The wrath of thundring *Ioue*, that rules both night and day?

xxxix 6 reliques *1609*   xl 9 fire] sire *1590*: *corr. F. E.*
xli 2 nigh] high *1596, 1609*

Not so (quoth she) but sith that heauens king   xliii
  From hope of heauen hath thee excluded quight,
  Why fearest thou, that canst not hope for thing,
  And fearest not, that more thee hurten might,
  Now in the powre of euerlasting Night?
  Goe to then, O thou farre renowmed sonne
  Of great *Apollo*, shew thy famous might
  In medicine, that else hath to thee wonne
Great paines, and greater praise, both neuer to be donne.

Her words preuaild: And then the learned leach   xliv
  His cunning hand gan to his wounds to lay,
  And all things else, the which his art did teach:
  Which hauing seene, from thence arose away
  The mother of dread darknesse, and let stay
  Aueugles sonne there in the leaches cure,
  And backe returning tooke her wonted way,
  To runne her timely race, whilst *Phœbus* pure
In westerne waues his wearie wagon did recure.

The false *Duessa* leauing noyous Night,   xlv
  Returnd to stately pallace of dame Pride;
  Where when she came, she found the Faery knight
  Departed thence, albe his woundes wide
  Not throughly heald, vnreadie were to ride.
  Good cause he had to hasten thence away;
  For on a day his wary Dwarfe had spide,
  Where in a dongeon deepe huge numbers lay
Of caytiue wretched thrals, that wayled night and day.

A ruefull sight, as could be seene with eie;   xlvi
  Of whom he learned had in secret wise
  The hidden cause of their captiuitie,
  How mortgaging their liues to *Couetise*,
  Through wastfull Pride, and wanton Riotise,
  They were by law of that proud Tyrannesse
  Prouokt with *Wrath*, and *Enuies* false surmise,
  Condemned to that Dongeon mercilesse,
Where they should liue in woe, and die in wretchednesse.

There was that great proud king of *Babylon*, xlvii
  That would compell all nations to adore,
  And him as onely God to call vpon,
  Till through celestiall doome throwne out of dore,
  Into an Oxe he was transform'd of yore:
  There also was king *Cræsus*, that enhaunst
  His heart too high through his great riches store;
  And proud *Antiochus*, the which aduaunst
His cursed hand gainst God, and on his altars daunst.

And them long time before, great *Nimrod* was, xlviii
  That first the world with sword and fire warrayd;
  And after him old *Ninus* farre did pas
  In princely pompe, of all the world obayd;
  There also was that mightie Monarch layd
  Low vnder all, yet aboue all in pride,
  That name of natiue syre did fowle vpbrayd,
  And would as *Ammons* sonne be magnifide,
Till scornd of God and man a shamefull death he dide.

All these together in one heape were throwne, xlix
  Like carkases of beasts in butchers stall.
  And in another corner wide were strowne
  The antique ruines of the *Romaines* fall:
  Great *Romulus* the Grandsyre of them all,
  Proud *Tarquin*, and too lordly *Lentulus*,
  Stout *Scipio*, and stubborne *Hanniball*,
  Ambitious *Sylla*, and sterne *Marius*,
High *Cæsar*, great *Pompey*, and fierce *Antonius*.

Amongst these mighty men were wemen mixt, l
  Proud wemen, vaine, forgetfull of their yoke:
  The bold *Semiramis*, whose sides transfixt
  With sonnes owne blade, her fowle reproches spoke;
  Faire *Sthenobœa*, that her selfe did choke
  With wilfull cord, for wanting of her will;
  High minded *Cleopatra*, that with stroke
  Of Aspes sting her selfe did stoutly kill:
And thousands moe the like, that did that dongeon fill.

      xlvii 9 altares *1590*   l 6 chord *1590*

Besides the endlesse routs of wretched thralles,   li
  Which thither were assembled day by day,
  From all the world after their wofull falles,
  Through wicked pride, and wasted wealthes decay.
  But most of all, which in that Dongeon lay
  Fell from high Princes courts, or Ladies bowres,
  Where they in idle pompe, or wanton play,
  Consumed had their goods, and thriftlesse howres,
And lastly throwne themselues into these heauy stowres.

Whose case when as the carefull Dwarfe had tould,   lii
  And made ensample of their mournefull sight
  Vnto his maister, he no lenger would
  There dwell in perill of like painefull plight,
  But early rose, and ere that dawning light
  Discouered had the world to heauen wyde,
  He by a priuie Posterne tooke his flight,
  That of no enuious eyes he mote be spyde:
For doubtlesse death ensewd, if any him descryde.

Scarse could he footing find in that fowle way,   liii
  For many corses, like a great Lay-stall
  Of murdred men which therein strowed lay,
  Without remorse, or decent funerall:
  Which all through that great Princesse pride did fall
  And came to shamefull end. And them beside
  Forth ryding vnderneath the castell wall,
  A donghill of dead carkases he spide,
The dreadfull spectacle of that sad house of *Pride*.

li 5 that] the *1590* &c.: *corr. F. E.*

Cant. VI.

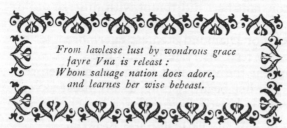

From lawlesse lust by wondrous grace
fayre Vna is releast :
Whom saluage nation does adore,
and learnes her wise beheast.

A S when a ship, that flyes faire vnder saile,   i
  An hidden rocke escaped hath vnwares,
That lay in waite her wrack for to bewaile,
The Marriner yet halfe amazed stares
At perill past, and yet in doubt ne dares
To ioy at his foole-happie ouersight :
So doubly is distrest twixt ioy and cares
  The dreadlesse courage of this Elfin knight,
Hauing escapt so sad ensamples in his sight.

Yet sad he was that his too hastic speed   ii
  The faire *Duess'* had forst him leaue behind ;
And yet more sad, that *Vna* his deare dreed
Her truth had staind with treason so vnkind ;
Yet crime in her could neuer creature find,
But for his loue, and for her owne selfe sake,
She wandred had from one to other *Ynd*,
  Him for to seeke, ne euer would forsake,
Till her vnwares the fierce *Sansloy* did ouertake.

Who after *Archimagoes* fowle defeat,   iii
  Led her away into a forrest wilde,
And turning wrathfull fire to lustfull heat,
With beastly sin thought her to haue defilde,
And made the vassall of his pleasures vilde.
Yet first he cast by treatie, and by traynes,
Her to perswade, that stubborne fort to yilde :
  For greater conquest of hard loue he gaynes,
That workes it to his will, then he that it constraines.

     i 5 in] it *1590 &c.*: *corr. F. E.*   8 corage *1590*

With fawning wordes he courted her a while,   iv
  And looking louely, and oft sighing sore,
  Her constant hart did tempt with diuerse guile:
  But wordes, and lookes, and sighes she did abhore,
  As rocke of Diamond stedfast euermore.
  Yet for to feed his fyrie lustfull eye,
  He snatcht the vele, that hong her face before;
  Then gan her beautie shine, as brightest skye,
And burnt his beastly hart t'efforce her chastitye.

So when he saw his flatt'ring arts to fayle,   v
  And subtile engines bet from batteree,
  With greedy force he gan the fort assayle,
  Whereof he weend possessed soone to bee,
  And win rich spoile of ransackt chastetee.
  Ah heauens, that do this hideous act behold,
  And heauenly virgin thus outraged see,
  How can ye vengeance iust so long withhold,
And hurle not flashing flames vpon that Paynim bold?

The pitteous maiden carefull comfortlesse,   vi
  Does throw out thrilling shriekes, and shrieking cryes,
  The last vaine helpe of womens great distresse,
  And with loud plaints importuneth the skyes,
  That molten starres do drop like weeping eyes;
  And *Phœbus* flying so most shamefull sight,
  His blushing face in foggy cloud implyes,
  And hides for shame. What wit of mortall wight
Can now deuise to quit a thrall from such a plight?

Eternall prouidence exceeding thought,   vii
  Where none appeares can make her selfe a way:
  A wondrous way it for this Lady wrought,
  From Lyons clawes to pluck the griped pray.
  Her shrill outcryes and shriekes so loud did bray,
  That all the woodes and forestes did resownd;
  A troupe of *Faunes* and *Satyres* far away
  Within the wood were dauncing in a rownd,
Whiles old *Syluanus* slept in shady arber sownd.

Who when they heard that pitteous strained voice,   viii
    In hast forsooke their rurall meriment,
    And ran towards the far rebownded noyce,
    To weet, what wight so loudly did lament.
    Vnto the place they come incontinent:
    Whom when the raging Sarazin espide,
    A rude, misshapen, monstrous rablement,
    Whose like he neuer saw, he durst not bide,
But got his ready steed, and fast away gan ride.

The wyld woodgods arriued in the place,   ix
    There find the virgin dolefull desolate,
    With ruffled rayments, and faire blubbred face,
    As her outrageous foe had left her late,
    And trembling yet through feare of former hate;
    All stand amazed at so vncouth sight,
    And gin to pittie her vnhappie state,
    All stand astonied at her beautie bright,
In their rude eyes vnworthie of so wofull plight.

She more amaz'd, in double dread doth dwell;   x
    And euery tender part for feare does shake:
    As when a greedie Wolfe through hunger fell
    A seely Lambe farre from the flocke does take,
    Of whom he meanes his bloudie feast to make,
    A Lyon spyes fast running towards him,
    The innocent pray in hast he does forsake,
    Which quit from death yet quakes in euery lim
With chaunge of feare, to see the Lyon looke so grim.

Such fearefull fit assaid her trembling hart,   xi
    Ne word to speake, ne ioynt to moue she had:
    The saluage nation feele her secret smart,
    And read her sorrow in her count'nance sad;
    Their frowning forheads with rough hornes yclad,
    And rusticke horror all a side doe lay,
    And gently grenning, shew a semblance glad
    To comfort her, and feare to put away,
Their backward bent knees teach her humbly to obay.

viii 7 mishappen *1590* : mishapen *1596*   ix 2 doolfull *1590*
            x 3 honger *1590*

The doubtfull Damzell dare not yet commit   xii
   Her single person to their barbarous truth,
   But still twixt feare and hope amazd does sit,
   Late learnd what harme to hastie trust ensu'th,
   They in compassion of her tender youth,
   And wonder of her beautie soueraine,
   Are wonne with pitty and vnwonted ruth,
   And all prostrate vpon the lowly plaine,
Do kisse her feete, and fawne on her with count'nance faine.

Their harts she ghesseth by their humble guise,   xiii
   And yieldes her to extremitie of time;
   So from the ground she fearelesse doth arise,
   And walketh forth without suspect of crime:
   They all as glad, as birdes of ioyous Prime,
   Thence lead her forth, about her dauncing round,
   Shouting, and singing all a shepheards ryme,
   And with greene braunches strowing all the ground,
Do worship her, as Queene, with oliue girlond cround.

And all the way their merry pipes they sound,   xiv
   That all the woods with doubled Eccho ring,
   And with their horned feet do weare the ground,
   Leaping like wanton kids in pleasant Spring.
   So towards old *Syluanus* they her bring;
   Who with the noyse awaked, commeth out,
   To weet the cause, his weake steps gouerning,
   And aged limbs on Cypresse stadle stout,
And with an yuie twyne his wast is girt about.

Far off he wonders, what them makes so glad,   xv
   Or *Bacchus* merry fruit they did inuent,
   Or *Cybeles* franticke rites haue made them mad;
   They drawing nigh, vnto their God present
   That flowre of faith and beautie excellent.
   The God himselfe vewing that mirrhour rare,
   Stood long amazd, and burnt in his intent;
   His owne faire *Dryope* now he thinkes not faire,
And *Pholoe* fowle, when her to this he doth compaire.

xiv 2 double *1609*   9 waste *1590, 1609*
   xv 2 Or] Of *1596, 1609* : If *conj. Hughes*

The woodborne people fall before her flat,   xvi
 And worship her as Goddesse of the wood;
 And old *Syluanus* selfe bethinkes not, what
 To thinke of wight so faire, but gazing stood,
 In doubt to deeme her borne of earthly brood;
 Sometimes Dame *Venus* selfe he seemes to see,
 But *Venus* neuer had so sober mood;
 Sometimes *Diana* he her takes to bee,
But misseth bow, and shaftes, and buskins to her knee.

By vew of her he ginneth to reuiue   xvii
 His ancient loue, and dearest *Cyparisse*,
 And calles to mind his pourtraiture aliue,
 How faire he was, and yet not faire to this,
 And how he slew with glauncing dart amisse
 A gentle Hynd, the which the louely boy
 Did loue as life, aboue all worldly blisse;
 For griefe whereof the lad n'ould after ioy,
But pynd away in anguish and selfe-wild annoy.

The wooddy Nymphes, faire *Hamadryades*   xviii
 Her to behold do thither runne apace,
 And all the troupe of light-foot *Naiades*,
 Flocke all about to see her louely face:
 But when they vewed haue her heauenly grace,
 They enuie her in their malitious mind,
 And fly away for feare of fowle disgrace:
 But all the *Satyres* scorne their woody kind,
And henceforth nothing faire, but her on earth they find.

Glad of such lucke, the luckelesse lucky maid,   xix
 Did her content to please their feeble eyes,
 And long time with that saluage people staid,
 To gather breath in many miseries.
 During which time her gentle wit she plyes,
 To teach them truth, which worshipt her in vaine,
 And made her th'Image of Idolatryes;
 But when their bootlesse zeale she did restraine
From her own worship, they her Asse would worship fayn.

It fortuned a noble warlike knight   xx
  By iust occasion to that forrest came,
  To seeke his kindred, and the lignage right,
  From whence he tooke his well deserued name:
  He had in armes abroad wonne muchell fame,
  And fild far landes with glorie of his might,
  Plaine, faithfull, true, and enimy of shame,
  And euer lou'd to fight for Ladies right,
But in vaine glorious frayes he litle did delight.

A Satyres sonne yborne in forrest wyld,   xxi
  By straunge aduenture as it did betyde,
  And there begotten of a Lady myld,
  Faire *Thyamis* the daughter of *Labryde*,
  That was in sacred bands of wedlocke tyde
  To *Therion*, a loose vnruly swayne;
  Who had more ioy to raunge the forrest wyde,
  And chase the saluage beast with busie payne,
Then serue his Ladies loue, and wast in pleasures vayne.

The forlorne mayd did with loues longing burne,   xxii
  And could not lacke her louers company,
  But to the wood she goes, to serue her turne,
  And seeke her spouse, that from her still does fly,
  And followes other game and venery:
  A Satyre chaunst her wandring for to find,
  And kindling coles of lust in brutish eye,
  The loyall links of wedlocke did vnbind,
And made her person thrall vnto his beastly kind.

So long in secret cabin there he held   xxiii
  Her captiue to his sensuall desire,
  Till that with timely fruit her belly sweld,
  And bore a boy vnto that saluage sire:
  Then home he suffred her for to retire,
  For ransome leauing him the late borne childe;
  Whom till to ryper yeares he gan aspire,
  He noursled vp in life and manners wilde,
Emongst wild beasts and woods, from lawes of men exilde.

xxiii 8 nousled *1590*

For all he taught the tender ymp, was but　　xxiv
　To banish cowardize and bastard feare;
　His trembling hand he would him force to put
　Vpon the Lyon and the rugged Beare,
　And from the she Beares teats her whelps to teare;
　And eke wyld roring Buls he would him make
　To tame, and ryde their backes not made to beare;
　And the Robuckes in flight to ouertake,
That euery beast for feare of him did fly and quake.

Thereby so fearelesse, and so fell he grew,　　xxv
　That his owne sire and maister of his guise
　Did often tremble at his horrid vew,
　And oft for dread of hurt would him aduise,
　The angry beasts not rashly to despise,
　Nor too much to prouoke; for he would learne
　The Lyon stoup to him in lowly wise,
　(A lesson hard) and make the Libbard sterne
Leaue roaring, when in rage he for reuenge did earne.

And for to make his powre approued more,　　xxvi
　Wyld beasts in yron yokes he would compell;
　The spotted Panther, and the tusked Bore,
　The Pardale swift, and the Tigre cruell;
　The Antelope, and Wolfe both fierce and fell;
　And them constraine in equall teme to draw.
　Such ioy he had, their stubborne harts to quell,
　And sturdie courage tame with dreadfull aw,
That his beheast they feared, as a tyrans law.

His louing mother came vpon a day　　xxvii
　Vnto the woods, to see her little sonne;
　And chaunst vnwares to meet him in the way,
　After his sportes, and cruell pastime donne,
　When after him a Lyonesse did runne,
　That roaring all with rage, did lowd requere
　Her children deare, whom he away had wonne:
　The Lyon whelpes she saw how he did beare,
And lull in rugged armes, withouten childish feare.

xxvi 5 fierce and fell] swifte and cruell *1590*: corr. *F. E.*　　9 a *om.*
1596: proud *1609*

The fearefull Dame all quaked at the sight,   xxviii
  And turning backe, gan fast to fly away,
  Vntill with loue reuokt from vaine affright,
  She hardly yet perswaded was to stay,
  And then to him these womanish words gan say;
  Ah *Satyrane,* my dearling, and my ioy,
  For loue of me leaue off this dreadfull play;
  To dally thus with death, is no fit toy,
Go find some other play-fellowes, mine own sweet boy.

In these and like delights of bloudy game   xxix
  He trayned was, till ryper yeares he raught,
  And there abode, whilst any beast of name
  Walkt in that forest, whom he had not taught
  To feare his force : and then his courage haught
  Desird of forreine foemen to be knowne,
  And far abroad for straunge aduentures sought :
  In which his might was neuer ouerthrowne,
But through all Faery lond his famous worth was blown.

Yet euermore it was his manner faire,   xxx
  After long labours and aduentures spent,
  Vnto those natiue woods for to repaire,
  To see his sire and ofspring auncient.
  And now he thither came for like intent;
  Where he vnwares the fairest *Vna* found,
  Straunge Lady, in so straunge habiliment,
  Teaching the Satyres, which her sat around,
Trew sacred lore, which from her sweet lips did redound.

He wondred at her wisedome heauenly rare,   xxxi
  Whose like in womens wit he neuer knew;
  And when her curteous deeds he did compare,
  Gan her admire, and her sad sorrowes rew,
  Blaming of Fortune, which such troubles threw,
  And ioyd to make proofe of her crueltie
  On gentle Dame, so hurtlesse, and so trew :
  Thenceforth he kept her goodly company,
And learnd her discipline of faith and veritie.

But she all vowd vnto the *Redcrosse* knight,   xxxii
   His wandring perill closely did lament,
   Ne in this new acquaintaunce could delight,
   But her deare heart with anguish did torment,
   And all her wit in secret counsels spent,
   How to escape. At last in priuie wise
   To *Satyrane* she shewed her intent;
   Who glad to gain such fauour, gan deuise,
How with that pensiue Maid he best might thence arise.

So on a day when Satyres all were gone,   xxxiii
   To do their seruice to *Syluanus* old,
   The gentle virgin left behind alone
   He led away with courage stout and bold.
   Too late it was, to Satyres to be told,
   Or euer hope recouer her againe:
   In vaine he seekes that hauing cannot hold.
   So fast he carried her with carefull paine,
That they the woods are past, and come now to the plaine.

The better part now of the lingring day,   xxxiv
   They traueild had, when as they farre espide
   A wearie wight forwandring by the way,
   And towards him they gan in hast to ride,
   To weet of newes, that did abroad betide,
   Or tydings of her knight of the *Redcrosse.*
   But he them spying, gan to turne aside,
   For feare as seemd, or for some feigned losse ;
More greedy they of newes, fast towards him do crosse.

A silly man, in simple weedes forworne,   xxxv
   And soild with dust of the long dried way ;
   His sandales were with toilesome trauell torne,
   And face all tand with scorching sunny ray,
   As he had traueild many a sommers day,
   Through boyling sands of *Arabie* and *Ynde*;
   And in his hand a *Iacobs* staffe, to stay
   His wearie limbes vpon: and eke behind,
His scrip did hang, in which his needments he did bind.

xxxiii 9   woods] wods *1590*

The knight approching nigh, of him inquerd   xxxvi
 Tydings of warre, and of aduentures new;
 But warres, nor new aduentures none he herd.
 Then *Vna* gan to aske, if ought he knew,
 Or heard abroad of that her champion trew,
 That in his armour bare a croslet red.
 Aye me, Deare dame (quoth he) well may I rew
 To tell the sad sight, which mine eies haue red:
These eyes did see that knight both liuing and eke ded.

That cruell word her tender hart so thrild,   xxxvii
 That suddein cold did runne through euery vaine,
 And stony horrour all her sences fild
 With dying fit, that downe she fell for paine.
 The knight her lightly reared vp againe,
 And comforted with curteous kind reliefe:
 Then wonne from death, she bad him tellen plaine
 The further processe of her hidden griefe;
The lesser pangs can beare, who hath endur'd the chiefe.

Then gan the Pilgrim thus, I chaunst this day,   xxxviii
 This fatall day, that shall I euer rew,
 To see two knights in trauell on my way
 (A sory sight) arraung'd in battell new,
 Both breathing vengeaunce, both of wrathfull hew:
 My fearefull flesh did tremble at their strife,
 To see their blades so greedily imbrew,
 That drunke with bloud, yet thristed after life:
What more? the *Redcrosse* knight was slaine with Paynim knife.

Ah dearest Lord (quoth she) how might that bee,   xxxix
 And he the stoutest knight, that euer wonne?
 Ah dearest dame (quoth he) how might I see
 The thing, that might not be, and yet was donne?
 Where is (said *Satyrane*) that Paynims sonne,
 That him of life, and vs of ioy hath reft?
 Not far away (quoth he) he hence doth wonne
 Foreby a fountaine, where I late him left
Washing his bloudy wounds, that through the steele were cleft.

Therewith the knight thence marched forth in hast,   xl
  Whiles *Vna* with huge heauinesse opprest,
  Could not for sorrow follow him so fast;
  And soone he came, as he the place had ghest,
  Whereas that *Pagan* proud him selfe did rest,
  In secret shadow by a fountaine side:
  Euen he it was, that earst would haue supprest
  Faire *Vna*: whom when *Satyrane* espide,
With fowle reprochfull words he boldly him defide.

And said, Arise thou cursed Miscreaunt,   xli
  That hast with knightlesse guile and trecherous train
  Faire knighthood fowly shamed, and doest vaunt
  That good knight of the *Redcrosse* to haue slain:
  Arise, and with like treason now maintain
  Thy guilty wrong, or else thee guilty yield.
  The Sarazin this hearing, rose amain,
  And catching vp in hast his three square shield,
And shining helmet, soone him buckled to the field.

And drawing nigh him said, Ah misborne Elfe,   xlii
  In euill houre thy foes thee hither sent,
  Anothers wrongs to wreake vpon thy selfe:
  Yet ill thou blamest me, for hauing blent
  My name with guile and traiterous intent;
  That *Redcrosse* knight, perdie, I neuer slew,
  But had he beene, where earst his armes were lent,
  Th'enchaunter vaine his errour should not rew:
But thou his errour shalt, I hope now prouen trew.

Therewith they gan, both furious and fell,   xliii
  To thunder blowes, and fiersly to assaile
  Each other bent his enimy to quell,
  That with their force they perst both plate and maile,
  And made wide furrowes in their fleshes fraile,
  That it would pitty any liuing eie.
  Large floods of bloud adowne their sides did raile;
  But floods of bloud could not them satisfie:
Both hungred after death: both chose to win, or die.

So long they fight, and fell reuenge pursue,   xliv
   That fainting each, themselues to breathen let,
   And oft refreshed, battell oft renue:
   As when two Bores with rancling malice met,
   Their gory sides fresh bleeding fiercely fret,
   Til breathlesse both them selues aside retire,
   Where foming wrath, their cruell tuskes they whet,
   And trample th'earth, the whiles they may respire;
Then backe to fight againe, new breathed and entire.

So fiersly, when these knights had breathed once,   xlv
   They gan to fight returne, increasing more
   Their puissant force, and cruell rage attonce,
   With heaped strokes more hugely, then before,
   That with their drerie wounds and bloudy gore
   They both deformed, scarsely could be known.
   By this sad *Vna* fraught with anguish sore,
   Led with their noise, which through the aire was thrown,
Arriu'd, where they in erth their fruitles bloud had sown.

Whom all so soone as that proud Sarazin   xlvi
   Espide, he gan reuiue the memory
   Of his lewd lusts, and late attempted sin,
   And left the doubtfull battell hastily,
   To catch her, newly offred to his eie:
   But *Satyrane* with strokes him turning, staid,
   And sternely bad him other businesse plie,
   Then hunt the steps of pure vnspotted Maid:
Wherewith he all enrag'd, these bitter speaches said.

O foolish faeries sonne, what furie mad   xlvii
   Hath thee incenst, to hast thy dolefull fate?
   Were it not better, I that Lady had,
   Then that thou hadst repented it too late?
   Most sencelesse man he, that himselfe doth hate,
   To loue another.   Lo then for thine ayd
   Here take thy louers token on thy pate.
   So they to fight; the whiles the royall Mayd
Fled farre away, of that proud Paynim sore afrayd.

xliv 1 fell] full *1590*   xlv 8 thrown: *1590, 1596*
    xlvii 2 fete *1596*   8 to] two *1596, 1609*

But that false *Pilgrim*, which that leasing told,   xlviii
   Being in deed old *Archimage*, did stay
   In secret shadow, all this to behold,
   And much reioyced in their bloudy fray:
   But when he saw the Damsell passe away
   He left his stond, and her pursewd apace,
   In hope to bring her to her last decay.
   But for to tell her lamentable cace,
And eke this battels end, will need another place.

Cant. VII.

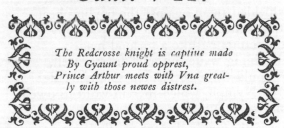

The Redcrosse knight is captiue made
By Gyaunt proud opprest,
Prince Arthur meets with Vna great-
ly with those newes distrest.

WHat man so wise, what earthly wit so ware,   i
   As to descry the crafty cunning traine,
   By which deceipt doth maske in visour faire,
   And cast her colours dyed deepe in graine,
   To seeme like Truth, whose shape she well can faine,
   And fitting gestures to her purpose frame,
   The guiltlesse man with guile to entertaine?
   Great maistresse of her art was that false Dame,
The false *Duessa*, cloked with *Fidessaes* name.

Who when returning from the drery *Night*,   ii
   She fownd not in that perilous house of *Pryde*,
   Where she had left, the noble *Redcrosse* knight,
   Her hoped pray, she would no lenger bide,
   But forth she went, to seeke him far and wide.
   Ere long she fownd, whereas he wearie sate,
   To rest him selfe, foreby a fountaine side,
   Disarmed all of yron-coted Plate,
And by his side his steed the grassy forage ate.

    i 6 frame ; *1590, 1596*   ii 4 pray ; *1590 &c.*

He feedes vpon the cooling shade, and bayes   iii
　　His sweatie forehead in the breathing wind,
　　Which through the trembling leaues full gently playes
　　Wherein the cherefull birds of sundry kind
　　Do chaunt sweet musick, to delight his mind:
　　The Witch approching gan him fairely greet,
　　And with reproch of carelesnesse vnkind
　　Vpbrayd, for leauing her in place vnmeet,
With fowle words tempring faire, soure gall with hony sweet.

Vnkindnesse past, they gan of solace treat,   iv
　　And bathe in pleasaunce of the ioyous shade,
　　Which shielded them against the boyling heat,
　　And with greene boughes decking a gloomy glade,
　　About the fountaine like a girlond made;
　　Whose bubbling waue did euer freshly well,
　　Ne euer would through feruent sommer fade:
　　The sacred Nymph, which therein wont to dwell,
Was out of *Dianes* fauour, as it then befell.

The cause was this: one day when *Phœbe* fayre   v
　　With all her band was following the chace,
　　This Nymph, quite tyr'd with heat of scorching ayre
　　Sat downe to rest in middest of the race:
　　The goddesse wroth gan fowly her disgrace,
　　And bad the waters, which from her did flow,
　　Be such as she her selfe was then in place.
　　Thenceforth her waters waxed dull and slow,
And all that drunke thereof, did faint and feeble grow.

Hereof this gentle knight vnweeting was,   vi
　　And lying downe vpon the sandie graile,
　　Drunke of the streame, as cleare as cristall glas;
　　Eftsoones his manly forces gan to faile,
　　And mightie strong was turnd to feeble fraile.
　　His chaunged powres at first them selues not felt,
　　Till crudled cold his corage gan assaile,
　　And chearefull bloud in faintnesse chill did melt,
Which like a feuer fit through all his body swelt.

　　v 5 her] he *1596*   8 wexed *1590*   9 did] do *1590*
　　　　vi 3 glas, *1596*

Yet goodly court he made still to his Dame,   vii
  Pourd out in loosnesse on the grassy grownd,
  Both carelesse of his health, and of his fame:
  Till at the last he heard a dreadfull sownd,
  Which through the wood loud bellowing, did rebownd,
  That all the earth for terrour seemd to shake,
  And trees did tremble. Th'Elfe therewith astownd,
  Vpstarted lightly from his looser make,
And his vnready weapons gan in hand to take.

But ere he could his armour on him dight,   viii
  Or get his shield, his monstrous enimy
  With sturdie steps came stalking in his sight,
  An hideous Geant horrible and hye,
  That with his talnesse seemd to threat the skye,
  The ground eke groned vnder him for dreed ;
  His liuing like saw neuer liuing eye,
  Ne durst behold: his stature did exceed
The hight of three the tallest sonnes of mortall seed.

The greatest Earth his vncouth mother was,   ix
  And blustring *Æolus* his boasted sire,
  Who with his breath, which through the world doth pas,
  Her hollow womb did secretly inspire,
  And fild her hidden caues with stormie yre,
  That she conceiu'd ; and trebling the dew time,
  In which the wombes of women do expire,
  Brought forth this monstrous masse of earthly slime,
Puft vp with emptie wind, and fild with sinfull crime.

So growen great through arrogant delight   x
  Of th'high descent, whereof he was yborne,
  And through presumption of his matchlesse might,
  All other powres and knighthood he did scorne.
  Such now he marcheth to this man forlorne,
  And left to losse: his stalking steps are stayde
  Vpon a snaggy Oke, which he had torne
  Out of his mothers bowelles, and it made
His mortall mace, wherewith his foemen he dismayde.

ix 7 women] wemen *1590*

G 2

That when the knight he spide, he gan aduance   xi
  With huge force and insupportable mayne,
  And towardes him with dreadfull fury praunce;
  Who haplesse, and eke hopelesse, all in vaine
  Did to him pace, sad battaile to darrayne,
  Disarmd, disgrast, and inwardly dismayde,
  And eke so faint in euery ioynt and vaine,
  Through that fraile fountaine, which him feeble made,
That scarsely could he weeld his bootlesse single blade.

The Geaunt strooke so maynly mercilesse,   xii
  That could haue ouerthrowne a stony towre,
  And were not heauenly grace, that him did blesse,
  He had beene pouldred all, as thin as flowre:
  But he was wary of that deadly stowre,
  And lightly lept from vnderneath the blow:
  Yet so exceeding was the villeins powre,
  That with the wind it did him ouerthrow,
And all his sences stound, that still he lay full low.

As when that diuelish yron Engin wrought   xiii
  In deepest Hell, and framd by *Furies* skill,
  With windy Nitre and quick Sulphur fraught,
  And ramd with bullet round, ordaind to kill,
  Conceiueth fire, the heauens it doth fill
  With thundring noyse, and all the ayre doth choke,
  That none can breath, nor see, nor heare at will,
  Through smouldry cloud of duskish stincking smoke,
That th'onely breath him daunts, who hath escapt the stroke.

So daunted when the Geaunt saw the knight,   xiv
  His heauie hand he heaued vp on hye,
  And him to dust thought to haue battred quight,
  Vntill *Duessa* loud to him gan crye;
  O great *Orgoglio*, greatest vnder skye,
  O hold thy mortall hand for Ladies sake,
  Hold for my sake, and do him not to dye,
  But vanquisht thine eternall bondslaue make,
And me thy worthy meed vnto thy Leman take.

    xi 4 hopelesse; *1590, 1596*   xii 9 stoond *1590*
  xiii 4 bollet *1590*   8 smok *1590*   xiv 1 knight *1596*

He hearkned, and did stay from further harmes, xv
  To gayne so goodly guerdon, as she spake:
  So willingly she came into his armes,
  Who her as willingly to grace did take,
  And was possessed of his new found make.
  Then vp he tooke the slombred sencelesse corse,
  And ere he could out of his swowne awake,
  Him to his castle brought with hastie forse,
And in a Dongeon deepe him threw without remorse.

From that day forth *Duessa* was his deare, xvi
  And highly honourd in his haughtie eye,
  He gaue her gold and purple pall to weare,
  And triple crowne set on her head full hye,
  And her endowd with royall maiestye:
  Then for to make her dreaded more of men,
  And peoples harts with awfull terrour tye,
  A monstrous beast ybred in filthy fen
He chose, which he had kept long time in darksome den.

Such one it was, as that renowmed Snake xvii
  Which great *Alcides* in *Stremona* slew,
  Long fostred in the filth of *Lerna* lake,
  Whose many heads out budding euer new,
  Did breed him endlesse labour to subdew:
  But this same Monster much more vgly was;
  For seuen great heads out of his body grew,
  An yron brest, and backe of scaly bras,
And all embrewd in bloud, his eyes did shine as glas.

His tayle was stretched out in wondrous length, xviii
  That to the house of heauenly gods it raught,
  And with extorted powre, and borrow'd strength,
  The euer-burning lamps from thence it brought,
  And prowdly threw to ground, as things of nought;
  And vnderneath his filthy feet did tread
  The sacred things, and holy heasts foretaught.
  Vpon this dreadfull Beast with seuenfold head
He set the false *Duessa*, for more aw and dread.

xviii 4, 5 braught, naught *1590*

The wofull Dwarfe, which saw his maisters fall,   xix
  Whiles he had keeping of his grasing steed,
  And valiant knight become a caytiue thrall,
  When all was past, tooke vp his forlorne weed,
  His mightie armour, missing most at need;
  His siluer shield, now idle maisterlesse;
  His poynant speare, that many made to bleed,
  The ruefull moniments of heauinesse,
And with them all departes, to tell his great distresse.

He had not trauaild long, when on the way   xx
  He wofull Ladie, wofull *Vna* met,
  Fast flying from the Paynims greedy pray,
  Whilest *Satyrane* him from pursuit did let:
  Who when her eyes she on the Dwarfe had set,
  And saw the signes, that deadly tydings spake,
  She fell to ground for sorrowfull regret,
  And liuely breath her sad brest did forsake,
Yet might her pitteous hart be seene to pant and quake.

The messenger of so vnhappie newes   xxi
  Would faine haue dyde: dead was his hart within,
  Yet outwardly some little comfort shewes:
  At last recouering hart, he does begin
  To rub her temples, and to chaufe her chin,
  And euery tender part does tosse and turne:
  So hardly he the flitted life does win,
  Vnto her natiue prison to retourne:
Then gins her grieued ghost thus to lament and mourne.

Ye dreary instruments of dolefull sight,   xxii
  That doe this deadly spectacle behold,
  Why do ye lenger feed on loathed light,
  Or liking find to gaze on earthly mould,
  Sith cruell fates the carefull threeds vnfould,
  The which my life and loue together tyde?
  Now let the stony dart of senselesse cold
  Perce to my hart, and pas through euery side,
And let eternall night so sad sight fro me hide.

        xx 3 the] that *1590*   xxi 1 newes, *1590 &c.*
              xxii 9 sight *om. 1590*

O lightsome day, the lampe of highest *Ioue*,
  First made by him, mens wandring wayes to guyde,
  When darknesse he in deepest dongeon droue,
  Henceforth thy hated face for euer hyde,
  And shut vp heauens windowes shyning wyde:
  For earthly sight can nought but sorrow breed,
  And late repentance, which shall long abyde.
  Mine eyes no more on vanitie shall feed,
But seeled vp with death, shall haue their deadly meed.

Then downe againe she fell vnto the ground;   xxiv
  But he her quickly reared vp againe:
  Thrise did she sinke adowne in deadly swownd,
  And thrise he her reviu'd with busie paine:
  At last when life recouer'd had the raine,
  And ouer-wrestled his strong enemie,
  With foltring tong, and trembling euery vaine,
  Tell on (quoth she) the wofull Tragedie,
The which these reliques sad present vnto mine eie.

Tempestuous fortune hath spent all her spight,   xxv
  And thrilling sorrow throwne his vtmost dart;
  Thy sad tongue cannot tell more heauy plight,
  Then that I feele, and harbour in mine hart:
  Who hath endur'd the whole, can beare each part.
  If death it be, it is not the first wound,
  That launched hath my brest with bleeding smart.
  Begin, and end the bitter balefull stound;
If lesse, then that I feare, more fauour I haue found.

Then gan the Dwarfe the whole discourse declare,   xxvi
  The subtill traines of *Archimago* old;
  The wanton loues of false *Fidessa* faire,
  Bought with the bloud of vanquisht Paynim bold:
  The wretched payre transform'd to treen mould;
  The house of Pride, and perils round about;
  The combat, which he with *Sansioy* did hould;
  The lucklesse conflict with the Gyant stout,
Wherein captiu'd, of life or death he stood in doubt.

She heard with patience all vnto the end,   xxvii
   And stroue to maister sorrowfull assay,
   Which greater grew, the more she did contend,
   And almost rent her tender hart in tway;
   And loue fresh coles vnto her fire did lay:
   For greater loue, the greater is the losse.
   Was neuer Ladie loued dearer day,
   Then she did loue the knight of the *Redcrosse*;
For whose deare sake so many troubles her did tosse.

At last when feruent sorrow slaked was,   xxviii
   She vp arose, resoluing him to find
   A liue or dead: and forward forth doth pas,
   All as the Dwarfe the way to her assynd:
   And euermore in constant carefull mind
   She fed her wound with fresh renewed bale;
   Long tost with stormes, and bet with bitter wind,
   High ouer hils, and low adowne the dale,
She wandred many a wood, and measurd many a vale.

At last she chaunced by good hap to meet   xxix
   A goodly knight, faire marching by the way
   Together with his Squire, arayed meet:
   His glitterand armour shined farre away,
   Like glauncing light of *Phœbus* brightest ray;
   From top to toe no place appeared bare,
   That deadly dint of steele endanger may:
   Athwart his brest a bauldrick braue he ware,
That shynd, like twinkling stars, with stons most pretious rare.

And in the midst thereof one pretious stone   xxx
   Of wondrous worth, and eke of wondrous mights,
   Shapt like a Ladies head, exceeding shone,
   Like *Hesperus* emongst the lesser lights,
   And stroue for to amaze the weaker sights;
   Thereby his mortall blade full comely hong
   In yuory sheath, ycaru'd with curious slights;
   Whose hilts were burnisht gold, and handle strong
Of mother pearle, and buckled with a golden tong.

His haughtie helmet, horrid all with gold,   xxxi
  Both glorious brightnesse, and great terrour bred;
  For all the crest a Dragon did enfold
  With greedie pawes, and ouer all did spred
  His golden wings: his dreadfull hideous hed
  Close couched on the beuer, seem'd to throw
  From flaming mouth bright sparkles fierie red,
  That suddeine horror to faint harts did show;
And scaly tayle was stretcht adowne his backe full low.

Vpon the top of all his loftie crest,   xxxii
  A bunch of haires discolourd diuersly,
  With sprincled pearle, and gold full richly drest,
  Did shake, and seem'd to daunce for iollity,
  Like to an Almond tree ymounted hye
  On top of greene *Selinis* all alone,
  With blossomes braue bedecked daintily;
  Whose tender locks do tremble euery one
At euery little breath, that vnder heauen is blowne.

His warlike shield all closely couer'd was,   xxxiii
  Ne might of mortall eye be euer seene;
  Not made of steele, nor of enduring bras,
  Such earthly mettals soone consumed bene:
  But all of Diamond perfect pure and cleene
  It framed was, one massie entire mould,
  Hewen out of Adamant rocke with engines keene,
  That point of speare it neuer percen could,
Ne dint of direfull sword diuide the substance would.

The same to wight he neuer wont disclose,   xxxiv
  But when as monsters huge he would dismay,
  Or daunt vnequall armies of his foes,
  Or when the flying heauens he would affray;
  For so exceeding shone his glistring ray,
  That *Phœbus* golden face it did attaint,
  As when a cloud his beames doth ouer-lay;
  And siluer *Cynthia* wexed pale and faint, •
As when her face is staynd with magicke arts constraint.

xxxii 2 bounch *1590*   6 Selinis *1596*   8 Whose] Her *1590*
xxxiii 3 steeld *1590*: corr. F. E.

No magicke arts hereof had any might,   xxxv
  Nor bloudie wordes of bold Enchaunters call,
  But all that was not such, as seemd in sight,
  Before that shield did fade, and suddeine fall:
  And when him list the raskall routes appall,
  Men into stones therewith he could transmew,
  And stones to dust, and dust to nought at all;
  And when him list the prouder lookes subdew,
He would them gazing blind, or turne to other hew.

Ne let it seeme, that credence this exceedes,   xxxvi
  For he that made the same, was knowne right well
  To haue done much more admirable deedes.
  It *Merlin* was, which whylome did excell
  All liuing wightes in might of magicke spell:
  Both shield, and sword, and armour all he wrought
  For this young Prince, when first to armes he fell;
  But when he dyde, the Faerie Queene it brought
To Faerie lond, where yet it may be seene, if sought.

A gentle youth, his dearely loued Squire   xxxvii
  His speare of heben wood behind him bare,
  Whose harmefull head, thrice heated in the fire,
  Had riuen many a brest with pikehead square;
  A goodly person, and could menage faire
  His stubborne steed with curbed canon bit,
  Who vnder him did trample as the aire,
  And chauft, that any on his backe should sit;
The yron rowels into frothy fome he bit.

When as this knight nigh to the Ladie drew,   xxxviii
  With louely court he gan her entertaine;
  But when he heard her answeres loth, he knew
  Some secret sorrow did her heart distraine:
  Which to allay, and calme her storming paine,
  Faire feeling words he wisely gan display,
  And for her humour fitting purpose faine,
  To tempt the cause it selfe for to bewray;
Wherewith emmou'd, these bleeding words she gan to say.

xxxvi 1 seeme] seene *1590*: *corr. F. E.*   xxxvii 5 faire, *1590, 1596*
7 trample] amble *1590*   8 chauft] chanst *1590*: *corr. F. E.*   xxxviii 9
enmoud *1590*

What worlds delight, or ioy of liuing speech   xxxix
  Can heart, so plung'd in sea of sorrowes deepe,
  And heaped with so huge misfortunes, reach?
  The carefull cold beginneth for to creepe,
  And in my heart his yron arrow steepe,
  Soone as I thinke vpon my bitter bale:
  Such helplesse harmes yts better hidden keepe,
  Then rip vp griefe, where it may not auaile,
My last left comfort is, my woes to weepe and waile.

Ah Ladie deare, quoth then the gentle knight,   xl
  Well may I weene, your griefe is wondrous great;
  For wondrous great griefe groneth in my spright,
  Whiles thus I heare you of your sorrowes treat.
  But wofull Ladie let me you intrete,
  For to vnfold the anguish of your hart:
  Mishaps are maistred by aduice discrete,
  And counsell mittigates the greatest smart;
Found neuer helpe, who neuer would his hurts impart.

O but (quoth she) great griefe will not be tould,   xli
  And can more easily be thought, then said.
  Right so; (quoth he) but he, that neuer would,
  Could neuer: will to might giues greatest aid.
  But griefe (quoth she) does greater grow displaid,
  If then it find not helpe, and breedes despaire.
  Despaire breedes not (quoth he) where faith is staid.
  No faith so faot (quoth she) but flesh does paire.
Flesh may empaire (quoth he) but reason can repaire.

His goodly reason, and well guided speach   xlii
  So deepe did settle in her gratious thought,
  That her perswaded to disclose the breach,
  Which loue and fortune in her heart had wrought,
  And said; Faire Sir, I hope good hap hath brought
  You to inquire the secrets of my griefe,
  Or that your wisedome will direct my thought,
  Or that your prowesse can me yield reliefe:
Then heare the storie sad, which I shall tell you briefe.

    xlii 5 faire *1590, 1596*   6 inquere *1590*

The forlorne Maiden, whom your eyes haue seene   xliii
  The laughing stocke of fortunes mockeries,
  Am th'only daughter of a King and Queene,
  Whose parents deare, whilest equall destinies
  Did runne about, and their felicities
  The fauourable heauens did not enuy,
  Did spread their rule through all the territories,
  Which *Phison* and *Euphrates* floweth by,
And *Gehons* golden waues doe wash continually.

Till that their cruell cursed enemy,   xliv
  An huge great Dragon horrible in sight,
  Bred in the loathly lakes of *Tartary*,
  With murdrous rauine, and deuouring might
  Their kingdome spoild, and countrey wasted quight:
  Themselues, for feare into his iawes to fall,
  He forst to castle strong to take their flight,
  Where fast embard in mightie brasen wall,
He has them now foure yeres besiegd to make them thrall.

Full many knights aduenturous and stout   xlv
  Haue enterprizd that Monster to subdew;
  From euery coast that heauen walks about,
  Haue thither come the noble Martiall crew,
  That famous hard atchieuements still pursew,
  Yet neuer any could that girlond win,
  But all still shronke, and still he greater grew:
  All they for want of faith, or guilt of sin,
The pitteous pray of his fierce crueltie haue bin.

At last yledd with farre reported praise,   xlvi
  Which flying fame throughout the world had spred,
  Of doughtie knights, whom Faery land did raise,
  That noble order hight of Maidenhed,
  Forthwith to court of *Gloriane* I sped,
  Of *Gloriane* great Queene of glory bright,
  Whose kingdomes seat *Cleopolis* is red,
  There to obtaine some such redoubted knight,
That Parents deare from tyrants powre deliuer might.

  xliii 4 whiles *1590*   5 runne] come *1590*: ronne *F. E.*   9 *Gebons*
1596, 1609

It was my chance (my chance was faire and good)   xlvii
  There for to find a fresh vnproued knight,
  Whose manly hands imbrew'd in guiltie blood
  Had neuer bene, ne euer by his might
  Had throwne to ground the vnregarded right:
  Yet of his prowesse proofe he since hath made
  (I witnesse am) in many a cruell fight;
  The groning ghosts of many one dismaide
Haue felt the bitter dint of his auenging blade.

And ye the forlorne reliques of his powre,   xlviii
  His byting sword, and his deuouring speare,
  Which haue endured many a dreadfull stowre,
  Can speake his prowesse, that did earst you beare,
  And well could rule: now he hath left you heare,
  To be the record of his ruefull losse,
  And of my dolefull disauenturous deare:
  O heauie record of the good *Redcrosse*,
Where haue you left your Lord, that could so well you tosse?

Well hoped I, and faire beginnings had,   xlix
  That he my captiue langour should redeeme,
  Till all vnweeting, an Enchaunter bad
  His sence abusd, and made him to misdeeme
  My loyalty, not such as it did seeme;
  That rather death desire, then such despight.
  Be iudge ye heauens, that all things right esteeme,
  How I him lou'd, and loue with all my might,
So thought I eke of him, and thinke I thought aright.

Thenceforth me desolate he quite forsooke,   l
  To wander, where wilde fortune would me lead,
  And other bywaies he himselfe betooke,
  Where neuer foot of liuing wight did tread,
  That brought not backe the balefull body dead;
  In which him chaunced false *Duessa* meete,
  Mine onely foe, mine onely deadly dread,
  Who with her witchcraft and misseeming sweete,
Inueigled him to follow her desires vnmeete.

xlvii 3 hand *1590*: *corr. F. E.*
xlviii 9 haue you] haue yee *1590*   xlix 2 languor *1590*

At last by subtill sleights she him betraid   li
   Vnto his foe, a Gyant huge and tall,
   Who him disarmed, dissolute, dismaid,
   Vnwares surprised, and with mightie mall
   The monster mercilesse him made to fall,
   Whose fall did neuer foe before behold;
   And now in darkesome dungeon, wretched thrall,
   Remedilesse, for aie he doth him hold;
This is my cause of griefe, more great, then may be told.

Ere she had ended all, she gan to faint: lii
   But he her comforted and faire bespake,
   Certes, Madame, ye haue great cause of plaint,
   That stoutest heart, I weene, could cause to quake.
   But be of cheare, and comfort to you take:
   For till I haue acquit your captiue knight,
   Assure your selfe, I will you not forsake.
   His chearefull words reuiu'd her chearelesse spright,
So forth they went, the Dwarfe them guiding euer right.

Cant. VIII.

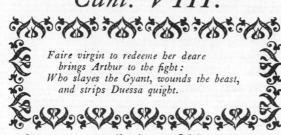

*Faire virgin to redeeme her deare
brings Arthur to the fight:
Who slayes the Gyant, wounds the beast,
and strips Duessa quight.*

AY me, how many perils doe enfold　　　　　i
The righteous man, to make him daily fall?
Were not, that heauenly grace doth him vphold,
And stedfast truth acquite him out of all.
Her loue is firme, her care continuall,
So oft as he through his owne foolish pride,
Or weaknesse is to sinfull bands made thrall:
Else should this *Redcrosse* knight in bands haue dyde,
For whose deliuerance she this Prince doth thither guide.

They sadly traueild thus, vntill they came　　　　ii
Nigh to a castle builded strong and hie:
Then cryde the Dwarfe, lo yonder is the same,
In which my Lord my liege doth lucklesse lie,
Thrall to that Gyants hatefull tyrannie:
Therefore, deare Sir, your mightie powres assay.
The noble knight alighted by and by
From loftie steede, and had the Ladie stay;
To see what end of fight should him befall that day.

So with the Squire, th'admirer of his might,　　　iii
He marched forth towards that castle wall;
Whose gates he found fast shut, ne liuing wight
To ward the same, nor answere commers call.
Then tooke that Squire an horne of bugle small,
Which hong adowne his side in twisted gold,
And tassels gay.　Wyde wonders ouer all
Of that same hornes great vertues weren told,
Which had approued bene in vses manifold.　·

Arg. 3 *the Gyant*] *that Gyaunt 1590 &c.*: *corr. F. E.*
i 6 through] *thorough 1590*　　iii 1 the] *his 1590*

Was neuer wight, that heard that shrilling sound,   iv
    But trembling feare did feele in euery vaine;
    Three miles it might be easie heard around,
    And Ecchoes three answerd it selfe againe :
    No false enchauntment, nor deceiptfull traine
    Might once abide the terror of that blast,
    But presently was voide and wholly vaine:
    No gate so strong, no locke so firme and fast,
But with that percing noise flew open quite, or brast.

The same before the Geants gate he blew,   v
    That all the castle quaked from the ground,
    And euery dore of freewill open flew.
    The Gyant selfe dismaied with that sownd,
    Where he with his *Duessa* dalliance fownd,
    In hast came rushing forth from inner bowre,
    With staring countenance sterne, as one astownd,
    And staggering steps, to weet, what suddein stowre
Had wrought that horror strange, and dar'd his dreaded powre.

And after him the proud *Duessa* came,   vi
    High mounted on her manyheaded beast,
    And euery head with fyrie tongue did flame,
    And euery head was crowned on his creast,
    And bloudie mouthed with late cruell feast.
    That when the knight beheld, his mightie shild
    Vpon his manly arme he soone addrest,
    And at him fiercely flew, with courage fild,
And eger greedinesse through euery member thrild.

Therewith the Gyant buckled him to fight,   vii
    Inflam'd with scornefull wrath and high disdaine,
    And lifting vp his dreadfull club on hight,
    All arm'd with ragged snubbes and knottie graine,
    Him thought at first encounter to haue slaine.
    But wise and warie was that noble Pere,
    And lightly leaping from so monstrous maine,
    Did faire auoide the violence him nere;
It booted nought, to thinke, such thunderbolts to beare.

    v 8 stowre, *1590, 1596*   vii 6 wise] wist *1590* : *corr. F. E.*

Ne shame he thought to shunne so hideous might: viii
 The idle stroke, enforcing furious way,
 Missing the marke of his misaymed sight
 Did fall to ground, and with his heauie sway
 So deepely dinted in the driuen clay,
 That three yardes deepe a furrow vp did throw:
 The sad earth wounded with so sore assay,
 Did grone full grieuous vnderneath the blow,
And trembling with strange feare, did like an earthquake show.

As when almightie *Ioue* in wrathfull mood,   ix
 To wreake the guilt of mortall sins is bent,
 Hurles forth his thundring dart with deadly food,
 Enrold in flames, and smouldring dreriment,
 Through riuen cloudes and molten firmament;
 The fierce threeforked engin making way,
 Both loftie towres and highest trees hath rent,
 And all that might his angrie passage stay,
And shooting in the earth, casts vp a mount of clay.

His boystrous club, so buried in the ground,   x
 He could not rearen vp againe so light,
 But that the knight him at auantage found,
 And whiles he stroue his combred clubbe to quight
 Out of the earth, with blade all burning bright
 He smote off his left arme, which like a blocke
 Did fall to ground, depriu'd of natiue might;
 Large streames of bloud out of the truncked stocke
Forth gushed, like fresh water streame from riuen rocke.

Dismaied with so desperate deadly wound,   xi
 And eke impatient of vnwonted paine,
 He loudly brayd with beastly yelling sound,
 That all the fields rebellowed againe;
 As great a noyse, as when in Cymbrian plaine
 An heard of Bulles, whom kindly rage doth sting,
 Do for the milkie mothers want complaine,
 And fill the fields with troublous bellowing,
The neighbour woods around with hollow murmur ring.

  viii 1 shonne *1590* x 3 aduantage *1590*
  xi 9 murmur ring] murmuring *1590 &c.: corr. F. E.*
SPENSER II   H

That when his deare *Duessa* heard, and saw   xii
  The euill stownd, that daungerd her estate,
  Vnto his aide she hastily did draw
  Her dreadfull beast, who swolne with bloud of late
  Came ramping forth with proud presumpteous gate,
  And threatned all his heads like flaming brands.
  But him the Squire made quickly to retrate,
  Encountring fierce with single sword in hand,
And twixt him and his Lord did like a bulwarke stand.

The proud *Duessa* full of wrathfull spight,   xiii
  And fierce disdaine, to be affronted so,
  Enforst her purple beast with all her might
  That stop out of the way to ouerthroe,
  Scorning the let of so vnequall foe:
  But nathemore would that courageous swayne
  To her yeeld passage, gainst his Lord to goe,
  But with outrageous strokes did him restraine,
And with his bodie bard the way atwixt them twaine.

Then tooke the angrie witch her golden cup,   xiv
  Which still she bore, replete with magick artes;
  Death and despeyre did many thereof sup,
  And secret poyson through their inner parts,
  Th'eternall bale of heauie wounded harts;
  Which after charmes and some enchauntments said,
  She lightly sprinkled on his weaker parts;
  Therewith his sturdie courage soone was quayd,
And all his senses were with suddeine dread dismayd.

So downe he fell before the cruell beast,   xv
  Who on his necke his bloudie clawes did seize,
  That life nigh crusht out of his panting brest:
  No powre he had to stirre, nor will to rize.
  That when the carefull knight gan well auise,
  He lightly left the foe, with whom he fought,
  And to the beast gan turne his enterprise;
  For wondrous anguish in his hart it wrought,
To see his loued Squire into such thraldome brought.

And high aduauncing his bloud-thirstie blade,   xvi
  Stroke one of those deformed heads so sore,
  That of his puissance proud ensample made;
  His monstrous scalpe downe to his teeth it tore,
  And that misformed shape mis-shaped more:
  A sea of bloud gusht from the gaping wound,
  That her gay garments staynd with filthy gore,
  And ouerflowed all the field around;
That ouer shoes in bloud he waded on the ground.

Thereat he roared for exceeding paine,   xvii
  That to haue heard, great horror would haue bred,
  And scourging th'emptie ayre with his long traine,
  Through great impatience of his grieued hed
  His gorgeous ryder from her loftie sted
  Would haue cast downe, and trod in durtie myre,
  Had not the Gyant soone her succoured;
  Who all enrag'd with smart and franticke yre,
Came hurtling in full fierce, and forst the knight retyre.

The force, which wont in two to be disperst,   xviii
  In one alone left hand he now vnites,
  Which is through rage more strong then both were erst;
  With which his hideous club aloft he dites,
  And at his foe with furious rigour smites,
  That strongest Oake might seeme to ouerthrow:
  The stroke vpon his shield so heauie lites,
  That to the ground it doubleth him full low:
What mortall wight could euer beare so monstrous blow?

And in his fall his shield, that couered was,   xix
  Did loose his vele by chaunce, and open flew:
  The light whereof, that heauens light did pas,
  Such blazing brightnesse through the aier threw,
  That eye mote not the same endure to vew.
  Which when the Gyaunt spyde with staring eye,
  He downe let fall his arme, and soft withdrew
  His weapon huge, that heaued was on hye
For to haue slaine the man, that on the ground did lye.

xviii 8 low *1590, 1596*: lowe, *1609*

H 2

And eke the fruitfull-headed beast, amaz'd   xx
  At flashing beames of that sunshiny shield,
  Became starke blind, and all his senses daz'd,
  That downe he tumbled on the durtie field,
  And seem'd himselfe as conquered to yield.
  Whom when his maistresse proud perceiu'd to fall,
  Whiles yet his feeble feet for faintnesse reeld,
  Vnto the Gyant loudly she gan call,
O helpe *Orgoglio*, helpe, or else we perish all.

At her so pitteous cry was much amoou'd   xxi
  Her champion stout, and for to ayde his frend,
  Againe his wonted angry weapon proou'd:
  But all in vaine: for he has read his end
  In that bright shield, and all their forces spend
  Themselues in vaine: for since that glauncing sight,
  He hath no powre to hurt, nor to defend;
  As where th'Almighties lightning brond does light,
It dimmes the dazed eyen, and daunts the senses quight.

Whom when the Prince, to battell new addrest,   xxii
  And threatning high his dreadfull stroke did see,
  His sparkling blade about his head he blest,
  And smote off quite his right leg by the knee,
  That downe he tombled; as an aged tree,
  High growing on the top of rocky clift,
  Whose hartstrings with keene steele nigh hewen be,
  The mightie trunck halfe rent, with ragged rift
Doth roll adowne the rocks, and fall with fearefull drift.

Or as a Castle reared high and round,   xxiii
  By subtile engins and malitious slight
  Is vndermined from the lowest ground,
  And her foundation forst, and feebled quight,
  At last downe falles, and with her heaped hight
  Her hastie ruine does more heauie make,
  And yields it selfe vnto the victours might;
  Such was this Gyaunts fall, that seemd to shake
The stedfast globe of earth, as it for feare did quake.

The knight then lightly leaping to the pray,   xxiv
  With mortall steele him smot againe so sore,
  That headlesse his vnweldy bodie lay,
  All wallowd in his owne fowle bloudy gore,
  Which flowed from his wounds in wondrous store.
  But soone as breath out of his breast did pas,
  That huge great body, which the Gyaunt bore,
  Was vanisht quite, and of that monstrous mas
Was nothing left, but like an emptie bladder was.

Whose grieuous fall, when false *Duessa* spide,   xxv
  Her golden cup she cast vnto the ground,
  And crowned mitre rudely threw aside;
  Such percing griefe her stubborne hart did wound,
  That she could not endure that dolefull stound,
  But leauing all behind her, fled away:
  The light-foot Squire her quickly turnd around,
  And by hard meanes enforcing her to stay,
So brought vnto his Lord, as his deserued pray.

The royall Virgin, which beheld from farre,   xxvi
  In pensiue plight, and sad perplexitie,
  The whole atchieuement of this doubtfull warre,
  Came running fast to greet his victorie,
  With sober gladnesse, and myld modestie,
  And with sweet ioyous cheare him thus bespake;
  Faire braunch of noblesse, flowre of cheualrie,
  That with your worth the world amazed make,
How shall I quite the paines, ye suffer for my sake?

And you fresh bud of vertue springing fast,   xxvii
  Whom these sad eyes saw nigh vnto deaths dore,
  What hath poore Virgin for such perill past,
  Wherewith you to reward? Accept therefore
  My simple selfe, and seruice euermore;
  And he that high does sit, and all things see
  With equall eyes, their merites to restore,
  Behold what ye this day haue done for mee,
And what I cannot quite, requite with vsuree.

xxiv 5 store, *1596*: store: *1609*   6 his] her *1590*   xxvii 7 eye *1590*

But sith the heauens, and your faire handeling   xxviii
  Haue made you maister of the field this day,
  Your fortune maister eke with gouerning,
  And well begun end all so well, I pray,
  Ne let that wicked woman scape away;
  For she it is, that did my Lord bethrall,
  My dearest Lord, and deepe in dongeon lay,
  Where he his better dayes hath wasted all.
O heare, how piteous he to you for ayd does call.

Forthwith he gaue in charge vnto his Squire,   xxix
  That scarlot whore to keepen carefully;
  Whiles he himselfe with greedie great desire
  Into the Castle entred forcibly,
  Where liuing creature none he did espye;
  Then gan he lowdly through the house to call:
  But no man car'd to answere to his crye.
  There raignd a solemne silence ouer all,
Nor voice was heard, nor wight was seene in bowre or hall.

At last with creeping crooked pace forth came   xxx
  An old old man, with beard as white as snow,
  That on a staffe his feeble steps did frame,
  And guide his wearie gate both too and fro:
  For his eye sight him failed long ygo,
  And on his arme a bounch of keyes he bore,
  The which vnused rust did ouergrow:
  Those were the keyes of euery inner dore,
But he could not them vse, but kept them still in store.

But very vncouth sight was to behold,   xxxi
  How he did fashion his vntoward pace,
  For as he forward moou'd his footing old,
  So backward still was turnd his wrincled face,
  Vnlike to men, who euer as they trace,
  Both feet and face one way are wont to lead.
  This was the auncient keeper of that place,
  And foster father of the Gyant dead;
His name *Ignaro* did his nature right aread.

xxviii 1 handling *1609*   2 maister] master *1590*
xxix 4 forcibly. *1596*   xxx 2 An] And *1596*

His reuerend haires and holy grauitie
  The knight much honord, as beseemed well,
  And gently askt, where all the people bee,
  Which in that stately building wont to dwell.
  Who answerd him full soft, he could not tell.
  Againe he askt, where that same knight was layd,
  Whom great *Orgoglio* with his puissaunce fell
  Had made his caytiue thrall; againe he sayde,
He could not tell: ne euer other answere made.

Then asked he, which way he in might pas:
  He could not tell, againe he answered.
  Thereat the curteous knight displeased was,
  And said, Old sire, it seemes thou hast not red
  How ill it sits with that same siluer hed
  In vaine to mocke, or mockt in vaine to bee:
  But if thou be, as thou art pourtrahed
  With natures pen, in ages graue degree,
Aread in grauer wise, what I demaund of thee.

His answere likewise was, he could not tell.
  Whose sencelesse speach, and doted ignorance
  When as the noble Prince had marked well,
  He ghest his nature by his countenance,
  And calmd his wrath with goodly temperance.
  Then to him stepping, from his arme did reach
  Those keyes, and made himselfe free enterance.
  Each dore he opened without any breach;
There was no barre to stop, nor foe him to empeach.

There all within full rich arayd he found,
  With royall arras and resplendent gold.
  And did with store of euery thing abound,
  That greatest Princes presence might behold.
  But all the floore (too filthy to be told)
  With bloud of guiltlesse babes, and innocents trew,
  Which there were slaine, as sheepe out of the fold,
  Defiled was, that dreadfull was to vew,
And sacred ashes ouer it was strowed new.

xxxii 8 thrall, *1596*   xxxiii 3 courteous *1590*   5 sits] fits *1596, 1609*

And there beside of marble stone was built   xxxvi
    An Altare, caru'd with cunning imagery,
    On which true Christians bloud was often spilt,
    And holy Martyrs often doen to dye,
    With cruell malice and strong tyranny:
    Whose blessed sprites from vnderneath the stone
    To God for vengeance cryde continually,
    And with great griefe were often heard to grone,
That hardest heart would bleede, to heare their piteous mone.

Through euery rowme he sought, and euery bowr,   xxxvii
    But no where could he find that wofull thrall:
    At last he came vnto an yron doore,
    That fast was lockt, but key found not at all
    Emongst that bounch, to open it withall;
    But in the same a little grate was pight,
    Through which he sent his voyce, and lowd did call
    With all his powre, to weet, if liuing wight
Were housed therewithin, whom he enlargen might.

Therewith an hollow, dreary, murmuring voyce   xxxviii
    These piteous plaints and dolours did resound;
    O who is that, which brings me happy choyce
    Of death, that here lye dying euery stound,
    Yet liue perforce in balefull darkenesse bound?
    For now three Moones haue changed thrice their hew,
    And haue beene thrice hid vnderneath the ground,
    Since I the heauens chearefull face did vew,
O welcome thou, that doest of death bring tydings trew.

Which when that Champion heard, with percing point   xxxix
    Of pitty deare his hart was thrilled sore,
    And trembling horrour ran through euery ioynt,
    For ruth of gentle knight so fowle forlore:
    Which shaking off, he rent that yron dore,
    With furious force, and indignation fell;
    Where entred in, his foot could find no flore,
    But all a deepe descent, as darke as hell,
That breathed euer forth a filthie banefull smell.

But neither darkenesse fowle, nor filthy bands,   xl
   Nor noyous smell his purpose could withhold,
   (Entire affection hateth nicer hands)
   But that with constant zeale, and courage bold,
   After long paines and labours manifold,
   He found the meanes that Prisoner vp to reare;
   Whose feeble thighes, vnhable to vphold
   His pined corse, him scarse to light could beare,
A uefull spectacle of death and ghastly drere.

His sad dull eyes deepe sunck in hollow pits,   xli
   Could not endure th'vnwonted sunne to view;
   IIis bare thin cheekes for want of better bits,
   And empty sides decciued of their dew,
   Could make a stony hart his hap to rew;
   His rawbone armes, whose mighty brawned bowrs
   Were wont to riue steele plates, and helmets hew,
   Were cleane consum'd, and all his vitall powres
Decayd, and all his flesh shronk vp like withered flowres.

Whom when his Lady saw, to him she ran   xlii
   With hasty ioy: to see him made her glad,
   And sad to view his visage pale and wan,
   Who earst in flowres of freshest youth was clad.
   Tho when her well of teares she wasted had,
   She said, Ah dearest Lord, what euill starre
   On you hath fround, and pourd his influence bad,
   That of your selfe ye thus berobbed arre,
And this misoceming hew your manly looks doth marre ?

But welcome now my Lord, in wele or woe,   xliii
   Whose presence 1 haue lackt too long a day;
   And fie on Fortune mine auowed foe,
   Whose wrathfull wreakes them selues do now alay.
   And for these wrongs shall treble penaunce pay
   Of treble good: good growes of euils priefe.
   The chearelesse man, whom sorrow did dismay,
   Had no delight to treaten of his griefe;
His long endured famine needed more reliefe.

      xli 7 and *om. 1596*   xliii 3 fie] sie *1590* : fye *F. E.*

Faire Lady, then said that victorious knight,   xliv
   The things, that grieuous were to do, or beare,
   Them to renew, I wote, breeds no delight;
   Best musicke breeds †delight in loathing eare:
   But th'onely good, that growes of passed feare,
   Is to be wise, and ware of like agein.
   This dayes ensample hath this lesson deare
   Deepe written in my heart with yron pen,
That blisse may not abide in state of mortall men.

Henceforth sir knight, take to you wonted strength,   xlv
   And maister these mishaps with patient might;
   Loe where your foe lyes stretcht in monstrous length,
   And loe that wicked woman in your sight,
   The roote of all your care, and wretched plight,
   Now in your powre, to let her liue, or dye.
   To do her dye (quoth *Vna*) were despight,
   And shame t'auenge so weake an enimy;
But spoile her of her scarlot robe, and let her fly.

So as she bad, that witch they disaraid,   xlvi
   And robd of royall robes, and purple pall,
   And ornaments that richly were displaid;
   Ne spared they to strip her naked all.
   Then when they had despoild her tire and call,
   Such as she was, their eyes might her behold,
   That her misshaped parts did them appall,
   A loathly, wrinckled hag, ill fauoured, old,
Whose secret filth good manners biddeth not be told.

Her craftie head was altogether bald,   xlvii
   And as in hate of honorable eld,
   Was ouergrowne with scurfe and filthy scald;
   Her teeth out of her rotten gummes were feld,
   And her sowre breath abhominably smeld;
   Her dried dugs, like bladders lacking wind,
   Hong downe, and filthy matter from them weld;
   Her wrizled skin as rough, as maple rind,
So scabby was, that would haue loathd all womankind.

    xliv 4 delight] dislike *conj. J. Jortin*   xlvi 7 mishaped *1596*

Her neather parts, the shame of all her kind,   xlviii
  My chaster Muse for shame doth blush to write;
  But at her rompe she growing had behind
  A foxes taile, with dong all fowly dight;
  And eke her feete most monstrous were in sight;
  For one of them was like an Eagles claw,
  With griping talaunts armd to greedy fight,
  The other like a Beares vneuen paw:
More vgly shape yet neuer liuing creature saw.

Which when the knights beheld, amazd they were,   xlix
  And wondred at so fowle deformed wight.
  Such then (said *Vna*) as she seemeth here,
  Such is the face of falshood, such the sight
  Of fowle *Duessa*, when her borrowed light
  Is laid away, and counterfesaunce knowne.
  Thus when they had the witch disrobed quight,
  And all her filthy feature open showne,
They let her goe at will, and wander wayes vnknowne.

She flying fast from heauens hated face,   l
  And from the world that her discouered wide,
  Fled to the wastfull wildernesse apace,
  From liuing eyes her open shame to hide,
  And lurkt in rocks and caues long vncspide.
  But that faire crew of knights, and *Vna* faire
  Did in that castle afterwards abide,
  To rest them selues, and weary powres repaire,
Where store they found of all, that dainty was and rare.

          xlviii 2 write *1596*   l 5 lurket *1596*

Cant. IX.

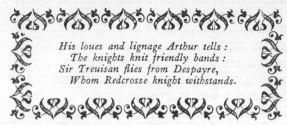

O Goodly golden chaine, wherewith yfere   i
  The vertues linked are in louely wize :
And noble minds of yore allyed were,
In braue poursuit of cheualrous emprize,
That none did others safety despize,
Nor aid enuy to him, in need that stands,
But friendly each did others prayse deuize
How to aduaunce with fauourable hands,
As this good Prince redeemd the *Redcrosse* knight from bands.

Who when their powres, empaird through labour long,   ii
  With dew repast they had recured well,
And that weake captiue wight now wexed strong,
Them list no lenger there at leasure dwell,
But forward fare, as their aduentures fell,
But ere they parted, *Vna* faire besought
That straunger knight his name and nation tell ;
Least so great good, as he for her had wrought,
Should die vnknown, and buried be in thanklesse thought.

Faire virgin (said the Prince) ye me require   iii
  A thing without the compas of my wit :
For both the lignage and the certain Sire,
From which I sprong, from me are hidden yit.
For all so soone as life did me admit
Into this world, and shewed heauens light,
From mothers pap I taken was vnfit :
And streight deliuered to a Faery knight,
To be vpbrought in gentle thewes and martiall might.

Arg. 1 *tells 1596*   2 *bands*] *hands 1590 : corr. F. E.*
i 7 deuize, *1590, 1596*   ii 1 powres *1590, 1596*

Vnto old *Timon* he me brought byliue,
  Old *Timon*, who in youthly yeares hath beene
  In warlike feates th'expertest man aliue,
  And is the wisest now on earth I weene;
  His dwelling is low in a valley greene,
  Vnder the foot of *Rauran* mossy hore,
  From whence the riuer *Dee* as siluer cleene
  His tombling billowes rolls with gentle rore:
There all my dayes he traind me vp in vertuous lore.

Thither the great Magicien *Merlin* came,   v
  As was his vse, ofttimes to visit me:
  For he had charge my discipline to frame,
  And Tutours nouriture to ouersee.
  Him oft and oft I askt in priuitie,
  Of what loines and what lignage I did spring:
  Whose aunswere bad me still assured bee,
  That I was sonne and heire vnto a king,
As time in her iust terme the truth to light should bring.

Well worthy impe, said then the Lady gent,   vi
  And Pupill fit for such a Tutours hand.
  But what aduenture, or what high intent
  Hath brought you hither into Faery land,
  Aread Prince *Arthur*, crowne of Martiall band?
  Full hard it is (quoth he) to read aright
  The course of heauenly cause, or vnderstand
  The secret meaning of th'eternall might,
That rules mens wayes, and rules the thoughts of liuing wight.

For whither he through fatall deepe foresight   vii
  Me hither sent, for cause to me vnghest,
  Or that fresh bleeding wound, which day and night
  Whilome doth rancle in my riuen brest,
  With forced fury following his behest,
  Me hither brought by wayes yet neuer found,
  You to haue helpt I hold my selfe yet blest.
  Ah curteous knight (quoth she) what secret wound
Could euer find, to grieue the gentlest hart on ground?

Deare Dame (quoth he) you sleeping sparkes awake,   viii
    Which troubled once, into huge flames will grow,
    Ne euer will their feruent fury slake,
    Till liuing moysture into smoke do flow,
    And wasted life do lye in ashes low.
    Yet sithens silence lesseneth not my fire,
    But told it flames, and hidden it does glow,
    I will reuele, what ye so much desire:
Ah Loue, lay downe thy bow, the whiles I may respire.

It was in freshest flowre of youthly yeares,   ix
    When courage first does creepe in manly chest,
    Then first the coale of kindly heat appeares
    To kindle loue in euery liuing brest;
    But me had warnd old *Timons* wise behest,
    Those creeping flames by reason to subdew,
    Before their rage grew to so great vnrest,
    As miserable louers vse to rew,
Which still wex old in woe, whiles woe still wexeth new.

That idle name of loue, and louers life,   x
    As losse of time, and vertues enimy
    I euer scornd, and ioyd to stirre vp strife,
    In middest of their mournfull Tragedy,
    Ay wont to laugh, when them I heard to cry,
    And blow the fire, which them to ashes brent:
    Their God himselfe, grieu'd at my libertie,
    Shot many a dart at me with fiers intent,
But I them warded all with wary gouernment.

But all in vaine: no fort can be so strong,   xi
    Ne fleshly brest can armed be so sound,
    But will at last be wonne with battrie long,
    Or vnawares at disauantage found;
    Nothing is sure, that growes on earthly ground:
    And who most trustes in arme of fleshly might,
    And boasts, in beauties chaine not to be bound,
    Doth soonest fall in disauentrous fight,
And yeeldes his caytiue neck to victours most despight.

viii 9 the] that *1590*: *corr. F. E.*   ix 3 the] that *1590*   5 *Timons*]
Cleons 1590: *corr. F. E.*   xi 4 vnawares *1596*

Ensample make of him your haplesse ioy, xii
  And of my selfe now mated, as ye see;
  Whose prouder vaunt that proud auenging boy
  Did soone pluck downe, and curbd my libertie.
  For on a day prickt forth with iollitie
  Of looser life, and heat of hardiment,
  Raunging the forest wide on courser free,
  The fields, the floods, the heauens with one consent
Did seeme to laugh on me, and fauour mine intent.

For-wearied with my sports, I did alight xiii
  From loftie steed, and downe to sleepe me layd;
  The verdant gras my couch did goodly dight,
  And pillow was my helmet faire displayd:
  Whiles euery sence the humour sweet embayd,
  And slombring soft my hart did steale away,
  Me seemed, by my side a royall Mayd
  Her daintie limbes full softly down did lay:
So faire a creature yet saw neuer sunny day.

Most goodly glee and louely blandishment xiv
  She to me made, and bad me loue her deare,
  For dearely sure her loue was to me bent,
  As when iust time expired should appeare.
  But whether dreames delude, or true it were,
  Was neuer hart so rauisht with delight,
  Ne liuing man like words did euer heare,
  As she to me deliuered all that night;
And at her parting said, She Queene of Faeries hight.

When I awoke, and found her place deuoyd, xv
  And nought but pressed gras, where she had lyen,
  I sorrowed all so much, as earst I ioyd,
  And washed all her place with watry eyen.
  From that day forth I lou'd that face diuine;
  From that day forth I cast in carefull mind,
  To seeke her out with labour, and long tyne,
  And neuer vow to rest, till her I find,
Nine monethes I seeke in vaine yet ni'll that vow vnbind.

xii 9 on] at *1590, 1596*: *corr. F. E. & 1609*   xv 8 vowd *1590*

Thus as he spake, his visage wexed pale,   xvi
  And chaunge of hew great passion did bewray;
  Yet still he stroue to cloke his inward bale,
  And hide the smoke, that did his fire display,
  Till gentle *Vna* thus to him gan say;
  O happy Queene of Faeries, that hast found
  Mongst many, one that with his prowesse may
  Defend thine honour, and thy foes confound:
True Loues are often sown, but seldom grow on ground.

Thine, O then, said the gentle *Redcrosse* knight,   xvii
  Next to that Ladies loue, shalbe the place,
  O fairest virgin, full of heauenly light,
  Whose wondrous faith, exceeding earthly race,
  Was firmest fixt in mine extremest case.
  And you, my Lord, the Patrone of my life,
  Of that great Queene may well gaine worthy grace:
  For onely worthy you through prowes priefe
Yf liuing man mote worthy be, to be her liefe.

So diuersly discoursing of their loues,   xviii
  The golden Sunne his glistring head gan şhew,
  And sad remembraunce now the Prince amoues,
  With fresh desire his voyage to pursew:
  Als *Vna* earnd her traueill to renew.
  Then those two knights, fast friendship for to bynd,
  And loue establish each to other trew,
  Gaue goodly gifts, the signes of gratefull mynd,
And eke as pledges firme, right hands together ioynd.

Prince *Arthur* gaue a boxe of Diamond sure,   xix
  Embowd with gold and gorgeous ornament,
  Wherein were closd few drops of liquor pure,
  Of wondrous worth, and vertue excellent,
  That any wound could heale incontinent:
  Which to requite, the *Redcrosse* knight him gaue
  A booke, wherein his Saueours testament
  Was writ with golden letters rich and braue;
A worke of wondrous grace, and able soules to saue.

  xviii 9 as] the *1596, 1609*   xix 7 his] this *1590*: *corr. F. E.*
9 hable *1590*

Thus beene they parted, *Arthur* on his way   xx
  To seeke his loue, and th'other for to fight
  With *Vnaes* foe, that all her realme did pray.
  But she now weighing the decayed plight,
  And shrunken synewes of her chosen knight,
  Would not a while her forward course pursew,
  Ne bring him forth in face of dreadfull fight,
  Till he recouered had his former hew:
For him to be yet weake and wearie well she knew.

So as they traueild, lo they gan espy   xxi
  An armed knight towards them gallop fast,
  That seemed from some feared foe to fly,
  Or other griesly thing, that him agast.
  Still as he fled, his eye was backward cast,
  As if his feare still followed him behind;
  Als flew his steed, as he his bands had brast,
  And with his winged heeles did tread the wind,
As he had beene a fole of *Pegasus* his kind.

Nigh as he drew, they might perceiue his head   xxii
  To be vnarmd, and curld vncombed heares
  Vpstaring stiffe, dismayd with vncouth dread;
  Nor drop of bloud in all his face appeares
  Nor life in limbe: and to increase his feares,
  In fowle reproch of knighthoods faire degree,
  About his neck an hempen rope he weares,
  That with his glistring armes does ill agree;
But he of rope or armes has now no memoree.

The *Redcrosse* knight toward him crossed fast,   xxiii
  To weet, what mister wight was so dismayd:
  There him he finds all sencelesse and aghast,
  That of him selfe he seemd to be afrayd;
  Whom hardly he from flying forward stayd,
  Till he these wordes to him deliuer might;
  Sir knight, aread who hath ye thus arayd,
  And eke from whom make ye this hasty flight:
For neuer knight I saw in such misseeming plight.

He answerd nought at all, but adding new   xxiv
   Feare to his first amazment, staring wide
   With stony eyes, and hartlesse hollow hew,
   Astonisht stood, as one that had aspide
   Infernall furies, with their chaines vntide.
   Him yet againe, and yet againe bespake
   The gentle knight; who nought to him replide,
   But trembling euery ioynt did inly quake,
And foltring tongue at last these words seemd forth to shake.

For Gods deare loue, Sir knight, do me not stay;   xxv
   For loe he comes, he comes fast after mee.
   Eft looking backe would faine haue runne away;
   But he him forst to stay, and tellen free
   The secret cause of his perplexitie:
   Yet nathemore by his bold hartie speach,
   Could his bloud-frosen hart emboldned bee,
   But through his boldnesse rather feare did reach,
Yet forst, at last he made through silence suddein breach.

And am I now in safetie sure (quoth he)   xxvi
   From him, that would haue forced me to dye?
   And is the point of death now turnd fro mee,
   That I may tell this haplesse history?
   Feare nought: (quoth he) no daunger now is nye.
   Then shall I you recount a ruefull cace,
   (Said he) the which with this vnlucky eye
   I late beheld, and had not greater grace
Me reft from it, had bene partaker of the place.

I lately chaunst (Would I had neuer chaunst)   xxvii
   With a faire knight to keepen companee,
   Sir *Terwin* hight, that well himselfe aduaunst
   In all affaires, and was both bold and free,
   But not so happie as mote happie bee:
   He lou'd, as was his lot, a Ladie gent,
   That him againe lou'd in the least degree:
   For she was proud, and of too high intent,
And ioyd to see her louer languish and lament.

xxiv 4 espide *1609*   xxvi 5 nye? *1590* &c.

From whom returning sad and comfortlesse,
  As on the way together we did fare,
  We met that villen (God from him me blesse)
  That cursed wight, from whom I scapt whyleare,
  A man of hell, that cals himselfe *Despaire*:
  Who first vs greets, and after faire areedes
  Of tydings strange, and of aduentures rare:
  So creeping close, as Snake in hidden weedes,
Inquireth of our states, and of our knightly deedes.

Which when he knew, and felt our feeble harts
  Embost with bale, and bitter byting griefe,
  Which loue had launched with his deadly darts,
  With wounding words and termes of foule repriefe
  He pluckt from vs all hope of due reliefe,
  That earst vs held in loue of lingring life;
  Then hopelesse hartlesse, gan the cunning thiefe
  Perswade vs die, to stint all further strife:
To me he lent this rope, to him a rustie knife.

With which sad instrument of hastie death,
  That wofull louer, loathing lenger light,
  A wide way made to let forth liuing breath.
  But I more fearefull, or more luckie wight,
  Dismayd with that deformed disinall sight,
  Fled fast away, halfe dead with dying feare:
  Ne yet assur'd of life by you, Sir knight,
  Whose like infirmitie like chaunce may beare:
But God you neuer let his charmed speeches heare.

How may a man (said he) with idle speach
  Be wonne, to spoyle the Castle of his health?
  I wote (quoth he) whom triall late did teach,
  That like would not for all this worldes wealth:
  His subtill tongue, like dropping honny, mealt'th
  Into the hart, and searcheth euery vaine,
  That ere one be aware, by secret stealth
  His powre is reft, and weaknesse doth remaine.
O neuer Sir desire to try his guilefull traine.

       xxix 3 launced *1609*   4 repriefe, *1590 &c.*
   xxxi 5 mealt'h *1590 &c.*   *But cf.* Bk. II, Cant. II iv 5

Certes (said he) hence shall I neuer rest,   xxxii
  Till I that treachours art haue heard and tride;
  And you Sir knight, whose name mote I request,
  Of grace do me vnto his cabin guide.
  I that hight *Treuisan* (quoth he) will ride
  Against my liking backe, to doe you grace:
  But nor for gold nor glee will I abide
  By you, when ye arriue in that same place;
For leuer had I die, then see his deadly face.

Ere long they come, where that same wicked wight   xxxiii
  His dwelling has, low in an hollow caue,
  Farre vnderneath a craggie clift ypight,
  Darke, dolefull, drearie, like a greedie graue,
  That still for carrion carcases doth craue:
  On top whereof aye dwelt the ghastly Owle,
  Shrieking his balefull note, which euer draue
  Farre from that haunt all other chearefull fowle;
And all about it wandring ghostes did waile and howle.

And all about old stockes and stubs of trees,   xxxiv
  Whereon nor fruit, nor leafe was euer seene,
  Did hang vpon the ragged rocky knees;
  On which had many wretches hanged beene,
  Whose carcases were scattered on the greene,
  And throwne about the cliffs. Arriued there,
  That bare-head knight for dread and dolefull teene,
  Would faine haue fled, ne durst approchen neare,
But th'other forst him stay, and comforted in feare.

That darkesome caue they enter, where they find   xxxv
  That cursed man, low sitting on the ground,
  Musing full sadly in his sullein mind;
  His griesie lockes, long growen, and vnbound,
  Disordred hong about his shoulders round,
  And hid his face; through which his hollow eyne
  Lookt deadly dull, and stared as astound;
  His raw-bone cheekes through penurie and pine,
Were shronke into his iawes, as he did neuer dine.

His garment nought but many ragged clouts,   xxxvi
   With thornes together pind and patched was,
   The which his naked sides he wrapt abouts;
   And him beside there lay vpon the gras
   A drearie corse, whose life away did pas,
   All wallowd in his owne yet luke-warme blood,
   That from his wound yet welled fresh alas;
   In which a rustie knife fast fixed stood,
And made an open passage for the gushing flood.

Which piteous spectacle, approuing trew   xxxvii
   The wofull tale that *Treuisan* had told,
   When as the gentle *Redcrosse* knight did vew,
   With firie zeale he burnt in courage bold,
   Him to auenge, before his bloud were cold,
   And to the villein said, Thou damned wight,
   The author of this fact, we here behold,
   What iustice can but iudge against thee right,
With thine owne bloud to price his bloud, here shed in sight?

What franticke fit (quoth he) hath thus distraught   xxxviii
   Thee, foolish man, so rash a doome to giue?
   What iustice euer other iudgement taught,
   But he should die, who merites not to liue?
   None else to death this man despayring driue,
   But his owne guiltie mind deseruing death.
   Is then vniust to each his due to giue?
   Or let him die, that loatheth liuing breath?
Or let him die at ease, that liueth here vneath?

Who trauels by the wearie wandring way,   xxxix
   To come vnto his wished home in haste,
   And meetes a flood, that doth his passage stay,
   Is not great grace to helpe him ouer past,
   Or free his feet, that in the myre sticke fast?
   Most enuious man, that grieues at neighbours good,
   And fond, that ioyest in the woe thou hast,
   Why wilt not let him passe, that long hath stood
Vpon the banke, yet wilt thy selfe not passe the flood?

      xxxvii 9 sight. *1590 &c.*   xxxix 1 trauailes *1590*

He there does now enioy eternall rest   xl
  And happie ease, which thou doest want and craue,
  And further from it daily wanderest:
  What if some litle paine the passage haue,
  That makes fraile flesh to feare the bitter waue?
  Is not short paine well borne, that brings long ease,
  And layes the soule to sleepe in quiet graue?
  Sleepe after toyle, port after stormie seas,
Ease after warre, death after life does greatly please.

The knight much wondred at his suddeine wit,   xli
  And said, The terme of life is limited,
  Ne may a man prolong, nor shorten it;
  The souldier may not moue from watchfull sted,
  Nor leaue his stand, vntill his Captaine bed.
  Who life did limit by almightie doome,
  (Quoth he) knowes best the termes established;
  And he, that points the Centonell his roome,
Doth license him depart at sound of morning droome.

Is not his deed, what euer thing is donne,   xlii
  In heauen and earth? did not he all create
  To die againe? all ends that was begonne.
  Their times in his eternall booke of fate
  Are written sure, and haue their certaine date.
  Who then can striue with strong necessitie,
  That holds the world in his still chaunging state,
  Or shunne the death ordaynd by destinie?
When houre of death is come, let none aske whence, nor why.

The lenger life, I wote the greater sin,   xliii
  The greater sin, the greater punishment:
  All those great battels, which thou boasts to win,
  Through strife, and bloud-shed, and auengement,
  Now praysd, hereafter deare thou shalt repent:
  For life must life, and bloud must bloud repay.
  Is not enough thy euill life forespent?
  For he, that once hath missed the right way,
The further he doth goe, the further he doth stray.

Then do no further goe, no further stray,   xliv
  But here lie downe, and to thy rest betake,
  Th'ill to preuent, that life ensewen may.
  For what hath life, that may it loued make,
  And giues not rather cause it to forsake?
  Feare, sicknesse, age, losse, labour, sorrow, strife,
  Paine, hunger, cold, that makes the hart to quake;
  And euer fickle fortune rageth rife,
All which, and thousands mo do make a loathsome life.

Thou wretched man, of death hast greatest need,   xlv
  If in true ballance thou wilt weigh thy state:
  For neuer knight, that dared warlike deede,
  More lucklesse disauentures did amate:
  Witnesse the dongeon deepe, wherein of late
  Thy life shut vp, for death so oft did call;
  And though good lucke prolonged hath thy date,
  Yet death then, would the like mishaps forestall,
Into the which hereafter thou maiest happen fall.

Why then doest thou, O man of sin, desire   xlvi
  To draw thy dayes forth to their last degree?
  Is not the measure of thy sinfull hire
  High heaped vp with huge iniquitie,
  Against the day of wrath, to burden thee?
  Is not enough, that to this Ladie milde
  Thou falsed hast thy faith with periurie,
  And sold thy selfe to serue *Duessa* vilde,
With whom in all abuse thou hast thy selfe defilde?

Is not he iust, that all this doth behold   xlvii
  From highest heauen, and beares an equall eye?
  Shall he thy sins vp in his knowledge fold,
  And guiltie be of thine impietie?
  Is not his law, Let euery sinner die:
  Die shall all flesh? what then must needs be donne,
  Is it not better to doe willinglie,
  Then linger, till the glasse be all out ronne?
Death is the end of woes: die soone, O faeries sonne.

xlvi 7 falsest 1590

The knight was much enmoued with his speach,   xlviii
    That as a swords point through his hart did perse,
    And in his conscience made a secret breach,
    Well knowing true all, that he did reherse,
    And to his fresh remembrance did reuerse
    The vgly vew of his deformed crimes,
    That all his manly powres it did disperse,
    As he were charmed with inchaunted rimes,
That oftentimes he quakt, and fainted oftentimes.

In which amazement, when the Miscreant   xlix
    Perceiued him to wauer weake and fraile,
    Whiles trembling horror did his conscience dant,
    And hellish anguish did his soule assaile,
    To driue him to despaire, and quite to quaile,
    He shew'd him painted in a table plaine,
    The damned ghosts, that doe in torments waile,
    And thousand feends that doe them endlesse paine
With fire and brimstone, which for euer shall remaine.

The sight whereof so throughly him dismaid,   l
    That nought but death before his eyes he saw,
    And euer burning wrath before him laid,
    By righteous sentence of th'Almighties law:
    Then gan the villein him to ouercraw,
    And brought vnto him swords, ropes, poison, fire,
    And all that might him to perdition draw;
    And bad him choose, what death he would desire:
For death was due to him, that had prouokt Gods ire.

But when as none of them he saw him take,   li
    He to him raught a dagger sharpe and keene,
    And gaue it him in hand: his hand did quake,
    And tremble like a leafe of Aspin greene,
    And troubled bloud through his pale face was seene
    To come, and goe with tydings from the hart,
    As it a running messenger had beene.
    At last resolu'd to worke his finall smart,
He lifted vp his hand, that backe againe did start.

Which when as *Vna* saw, through euery vaine   lii
    The crudled cold ran to her well of life,
    As in a swowne: but soone reliu'd againe,
    Out of his hand she snatcht the cursed knife,
    And threw it to the ground, enraged rife,
    And to him said, Fie, fie, faint harted knight,
    What meanest thou by this reprochfull strife?
    Is this the battell, which thou vauntst to fight
With that fire-mouthed Dragon, horrible and bright?

Come, come away, fraile, feeble, fleshly wight,   liii
    Ne let vaine words bewitch thy manly hart,
    Ne diuelish thoughts dismay thy constant spright.
    In heauenly mercies hast thou not a part?
    Why shouldst thou then despeire, that chosen art?
    Where iustice growes, there grows eke greater grace,
    The which doth quench the brond of hellish smart,
    And that accurst hand-writing doth deface.
Arise, Sir knight arise, and leaue this cursed place.

So vp he rose, and thence amounted streight.   liv
    Which when the carle beheld, and saw his guest
    Would safe depart, for all his subtill sleight,
    He chose an halter from among the rest,
    And with it hung himselfe, vnbid vnblest.
    But death he could not worke himselfe therehy;
    For thousand times he so himselfe had drest,
    Yet nathelesse it could not doe him die,
Till he should die his last, that is eternally.

    lii 1 saw] heard *1590*   3 reliev'd *1609*   liii 1 feeble] seely *1596*:
silly *1609*.   *But cf.* Cant. VII vi 5, xi 8   8 deface, *1596*: deface: *1609*

Cant. X.

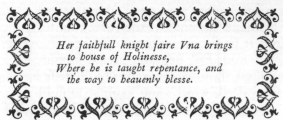

Her faithfull knight faire Vna brings
to house of Holinesse,
Where he is taught repentance, and
the way to heauenly blesse.

WHat man is he, that boasts of fleshly might,   i
    And vaine assurance of mortality,
Which all so soone, as it doth come to fight,
Against spirituall foes, yeelds by and by,
Or from the field most cowardly doth fly?
Ne let the man ascribe it to his skill,
That thorough grace hath gained victory.
If any strength we haue, it is to ill,
But all the good is Gods, both power and eke will.

By that, which lately hapned, *Vna* saw,   ii
    That this her knight was feeble, and too faint;
And all his sinews woxen weake and raw,
Through long enprisonment, and hard constraint,
Which he endured in his late restraint,
That yet he was vnfit for bloudie fight:
Therefore to cherish him with diets daint,
She cast to bring him, where he chearen might,
Till he recouered had his late decayed plight.

There was an auntient house not farre away,   iii
    Renowmd throughout the world for sacred lore,
And pure vnspotted life: so well they say
It gouernd was, and guided euermore,
Through wisedome of a matrone graue and hore;
Whose onely ioy was to relieue the needes
Of wretched soules, and helpe the helpelesse pore:
All night she spent in bidding of her bedes,
And all the day in doing good and godly deedes.

ii 4 imprisonment *1609*

Dame *Cælia* men did her call, as thought   iv
  From heauen to come, or thither to arise,
  The mother of three daughters, well vpbrought
  In goodly thewes, and godly exercise:
  The eldest two most sober, chast, and wise,
  Fidelia and *Speranza* virgins were,
  Though spousd, yet wanting wedlocks solemnize;
  But faire *Charissa* to a louely fere
Was lincked, and by him had many pledges dere.

Arriued there, the dore they find fast lockt;   v
  For it was warely watched night and day,
  For feare of many foes: but when they knockt,
  The Porter opened vnto them streight way :
  He was an aged syre, all hory gray,
  With lookes full lowly cast, and gate full slow,
  Wont on a staffe his feeble steps to stay,
  Hight *Humiltá*. They passe in stouping low;
For streight and narrow was the way, which he did show.

Each goodly thing is hardest to begin,   vi
  But entred in a spacious court they see,
  Both plaine, and pleasant to be walked in,
  Where them does meete a francklin faire and free,
  And entertaines with comely courteous glee,
  His name was *Zele*, that him right well became,
  For in his speeches and behauiour hee
  Did labour liuely to expresse the same,
And gladly did them guide, till to the Hall they came.

There fairely them receiues a gentle Squire,   vii
  Of milde demeanure, and rare courtesie,
  Right cleanly clad in comely sad attire;
  In word and deede that shew'd great modestie,
  And knew his good to all of each degree,
  Hight *Reuerence*. He them with speeches meet
  Does faire entreat; no courting nicetie,
  But simple true, and eke vnfained sweet,
As might become a Squire so great persons to greet.

And afterwards them to his Dame he leades,   viii
 That aged Dame, the Ladie of the place:
 Who all this while was busie at her beades:
 Which doen, she vp arose with seemely grace,
 And toward them full matronely did pace.
 Where when that fairest *Vna* she beheld,
 Whom well she knew to spring from heauenly race,
 Her hart with ioy vnwonted inly sweld,
As feeling wondrous comfort in her weaker eld.

And her embracing said, O happie earth,   ix
 Whereon thy innocent feet doe euer tread,
 Most vertuous virgin borne of heauenly berth,
 That to redeeme thy woefull parents head,
 From tyrans rage, and euer-dying dread,
 Hast wandred through the world now long a day;
 Yet ceasest not thy wearie soles to lead,
 What grace hath thee now hither brought this way?
Or doen thy feeble feet vnweeting hither stray?

Strange thing it is an errant knight to see   x
 Here in this place, or any other wight,
 That hither turnes his steps. So few there bee,
 That chose the narrow path, or seeke the right:
 All keepe the broad high way, and take delight
 With many rather for to go astray,
 And be partakers of their euill plight,
 Then with a few to walke the rightest way;
O foolish men, why haste ye to your owne decay?

Thy selfe to see, and tyred limbs to rest,   xi
 O matrone sage (quoth she) I hither came,
 And this good knight his way with me addrest,
 Led with thy prayses and broad-blazed fame,
 That vp to heauen is blowne. The auncient Dame
 Him goodly greeted in her modest guise,
 And entertaynd them both, as best became,
 With all the court'sies, that she could deuise,
Ne wanted ought, to shew her bounteous or wise.

   x 4 chuse *1609*   xi 5 Dame, *1590 &c.*

Thus as they gan of sundry things deuise,   xii
   Loe two most goodly virgins came in place,
   Ylinked arme in arme in louely wise,
   With countenance demure, and modest grace,
   They numbred euen steps and equall pace:
   Of which the eldest, that *Fidelia* hight,
   Like sunny beames threw from her Christall face,
   That could haue dazd the rash beholders sight,
And round about her head did shine like heauens light.

She was araied all in lilly white,   xiii
   And in her right hand bore a cup of gold,
   With wine and water fild vp to the hight,
   In which a Serpent did himselfe enfold,
   That horrour made to all, that did behold;
   But she no whit did chaunge her constant mood:
   And in her other hand she fast did hold
   A booke, that was both signd and seald with blood,
Wherein darke things were writ, hard to be vnderstood.

Her younger sister, that *Speranza* hight,   xiv
   Was clad in blew, that her beseemed well;
   Not all so chearefull seemed she of sight,
   As was her sister; whether dread did dwell,
   Or anguish in her hart, is hard to tell:
   Vpon her arme a siluer anchor lay,
   Whereon she leaned euer, as befell :
   And euer vp to heauen, as she did pray,
Her stedfast eyes were bent, ne swarued other way.

They seeing *Vna*, towards her gan wend,   xv
   Who them encounters with like courtesie;
   Many kind speeches they betwene them spend,
   And greatly ioy each other well to see:
   Then to the knight with shamefast modestie
   They turne themselues, at *Vnaes* meeke request,
   And him salute with well beseeming glee;
   Who faire them quites, as him beseemed best,
And goodly gan discourse of many a noble gest.

xv 4 well] for *1590*   9 gan] can *1609*

Then *Vna* thus ; But she your sister deare;   xvi
  The deare *Charissa* where is she become?
  Or wants she health, or busie is elsewhere?
  Ah no, said they, but forth she may not come :
  For she of late is lightned of her wombe,
  And hath encreast the world with one sonne more,
  That her to see should be but troublesome.
  Indeede (quoth she) that should her trouble sore,
But thankt be God, and her encrease so euermore.

Then said the aged *Cælia*, Deare dame,   xvii
  And you good Sir, I wote that of your toyle,
  And labours long, through which ye hither came,
  Ye both forwearied be: therefore a whyle
  I read you rest, and to your bowres recoyle.
  Then called she a Groome, that forth him led
  Into a goodly lodge, and gan despoile
  Of puissant armes, and laid in easie bed;
His name was meeke *Obedience* rightfully ared.

Now when their wearie limbes with kindly rest,   xviii
  And bodies were refresht with due repast,
  Faire *Vna* gan *Fidelia* faire request,
  To haue her knight into her schoolehouse plaste,
  That of her heauenly learning he might taste,
  And heare the wisedome of her words diuine.
  She graunted, and that knight so much agraste,
  That she him taught celestiall discipline,
And opened his dull eyes, that light mote in them shine.

And that her sacred Booke, with bloud ywrit,   xix
  That none could read, except she did them teach,
  She vnto him disclosed euery whit,
  And heauenly documents thereout did preach,
  That weaker wit of man could neuer reach,
  Of God, of grace, of iustice, of free will,
  That wonder was to heare her goodly speach :
  For she was able, with her words to kill,
And raise againe to life the hart, that she did thrill.

And when she list poure out her larger spright,   xx
  She would commaund the hastie Sunne to stay,
  Or backward turne his course from heauens hight;
  Sometimes great hostes of men she could dismay,
  Dry-shod to passe, she parts the flouds in tway;
  And eke huge mountaines from their natiue seat
  She would commaund, themselues to beare away,
  And throw in raging sea with roaring threat.
Almightie God her gaue such powre, and puissance great.

The faithfull knight now grew in litle space,   xxi
  By hearing her, and by her sisters lore,
  To such perfection of all heauenly grace,
  That wretched world he gan for to abhore,
  And mortall life gan loath, as thing forlore,
  Greeu'd with remembrance of his wicked wayes,
  And prickt with anguish of his sinnes so sore,
  That he desirde to end his wretched dayes:
So much the dart of sinfull guilt the soule dismayes.

But wise *Speranza* gaue him comfort sweet,   xxii
  And taught him how to take assured hold
  Vpon her siluer anchor, as was meet;
  Else had his sinnes so great, and manifold
  Made him forget all that *Fidelia* told.
  In this distressed doubtfull agonie,
  When him his dearest *Vna* did behold,
  Disdeining life, desiring leaue to die,
She found her selfe assayld with great perplexitie.

And came to *Cælia* to declare her smart,   xxiii
  Who well acquainted with that commune plight,
  Which sinfull horror workes in wounded hart,
  Her wisely comforted all that she might,
  With goodly counsell and aduisement right;
  And streightway sent with carefull diligence,
  To fetch a Leach, the which had great insight
  In that disease of grieued conscience,
And well could cure the same; His name was *Patience*.

xx 5 *om. 1590, 1596: add. 1609*   xxi 8 desirde, *1590, 1596.*

Who comming to that soule-diseased knight,   xxiv
 Could hardly him intreat, to tell his griefe:
 Which knowne, and all that noyd his heauie spright
 Well searcht, eftsoones he gan apply reliefe
 Of salues and med'cines, which had passing priefe,
 And thereto added words of wondrous might:
 By which to ease he him recured briefe,
 And much asswag'd the passion of his plight,
That he his paine endur'd, as seeming now more light.

But yet the cause and root of all his ill,   xxv
 Inward corruption, and infected sin,
 Not purg'd nor heald, behind remained still,
 And festring sore did rankle yet within,
 Close creeping twixt the marrow and the skin.
 Which to extirpe, he laid him priuily
 Downe in a darkesome lowly place farre in,
 Whereas he meant his corrosiues to apply,
And with streight diet tame his stubborne malady.

In ashes and sackcloth he did array   xxvi
 His daintie corse, proud humors to abate,
 And dieted with fasting euery day,
 The swelling of his wounds to mitigate,
 And made him pray both earely and eke late:
 And euer as superfluous flesh did rot
 Amendment readie still at hand did wayt,
 To pluck it out with pincers firie whot,
That soone in him was left no one corrupted iot.

And bitter *Penance* with an yron whip,   xxvii
 Was wont him once to disple euery day:
 And sharpe *Remorse* his hart did pricke and nip,
 That drops of bloud thence like a well did play;
 And sad *Repentance* vsed to embay
 His bodie in salt water smarting sore,
 The filthy blots of sinne to wash away.
 So in short space they did to health restore
The man that would not liue, but earst lay at deathes dore.

xxiv 3 spright, *1590 &c.*   4 relief, *1590*: reliefe, *1596*   xxv 9 streight]
streict *1609*   xxvii 5 embay, *1590 &c.*   6 His blamefull body in salt
water sore, *1590*

In which his torment often was so great,   xxviii
    That like a Lyon he would cry and rore,
    And rend his flesh, and his owne synewes eat.
    His owne deare *Vna* hearing euermore
    His ruefull shriekes and gronings, often tore
    Her guiltlesse garments, and her golden heare,
    For pitty of his paine and anguish sore;
    Yet all with patience wisely she did beare;
For well she wist, his crime could else be neuer cleare.

Whom thus recouer'd by wise Patience,   xxix
    And trew *Repentance* they to *Vna* brought :
    Who ioyous of his cured conscience,
    Him dearely kist, and fairely eke besought
    Himselfe to chearish, and consuming thought
    To put away out of his carefull brest.
    By this *Charissa*, late in child-bed brought,
    Was woxen strong, and left her fruitfull nest ;
To her faire *Vna* brought this vnacquainted guest.

She was a woman in her freshest age,   xxx
    Of wondrous beauty, and of bountie rare,
    With goodly grace and comely personage,
    That was on earth not easie to compare;
    Full of great loue, but *Cupids* wanton snare
    As hell she hated, chast in worke and will ;
    Her necke and breasts were euer open bare,
    That ay thereof her babes might sucke their fill ;
The rest was all in yellow robes arayed still.

A multitude of babes about her hong,   xxxi
    Playing their sports, that ioyd her to behold,
    Whom still she fed, whiles they were weake and young,
    But thrust them forth still, as they wexed old :
    And on her head she wore a tyre of gold,
    Adornd with gemmes and owches wondrous faire,
    Whose passing price vneath was to be told ;
    And by her side there sate a gentle paire
Of turtle doues, she sitting in an yuorie chaire.

        xxxi 6 faire. *1596*

The knight and *Vna* entring, faire her greet,   xxxii
  And bid her ioy of that her happie brood ;
  Who them requites with court'sies seeming meet,
  And entertaines with friendly chearefull mood.
  Then *Vna* her besought, to be so good,
  As in her vertuous rules to schoole her knight,
  Now after all his torment well withstood,
  In that sad house of *Penaunce*, where his spright
Had past the paines of hell, and long enduring night.

She was right ioyous of her iust request,   xxxiii
  And taking by the hand that Faeries sonne,
  Gan him instruct in euery good behest,
  Of loue, and righteousnesse, and well to donne,
  And wrath, and hatred warely to shonne,
  That drew on men Gods hatred, and his wrath,
  And many soules in dolours had fordonne:
  In which when him she well instructed hath,
From thence to heauen she teacheth him the ready path.

Wherein his weaker wandring steps to guide,   xxxiv
  An auncient matrone she to her does call,
  Whose sober lookes her wisedome well describe:
  Her name was *Mercie*, well knowne ouer all,
  To be both gratious, and eke liberall:
  To whom the carefull charge of him she gaue,
  To lead aright, that he should neuer fall
  In all his wayes through this wide worldes waue,
That Mercy in the end his righteous soule might saue.

The godly Matrone by the hand him beares   xxxv
  Forth from her presence, by a narrow way,
  Scattred with bushy thornes, and ragged breares,
  Which still before him she remou'd away,
  That nothing might his ready passage stay :
  And euer when his feet encombred were,
  Or gan to shrinke, or from the right to stray,
  She held him fast, and firmely did vpbeare,
As carefull Nourse her child from falling oft does reare.

xxxiv 8 worlds *1609*

Eftsoones vnto an holy Hospitall,   xxxvi
    That was fore by the way, she did him bring,
    In which seuen Bead-men that had vowed all
    Their life to seruice of high heauens king
    Did spend their dayes in doing godly thing :
    Their gates to all were open euermore,
    That by the wearie way were traueiling,
    And one sate wayting euer them before,
To call in commers-by, that needy were and pore.

The first of them that eldest was, and best,   xxxvii
    Of all the house had charge and gouernement,
    As Guardian and Steward of the rest :
    His office was to giue entertainement
    And lodging, vnto all that came, and went :
    Not vnto such, as could him feast againe,
    And double quite, for that he on them spent,
    But such, as want of harbour did constraine :
Those for Gods sake his dewty was to entertaine.

The second was as Almner of the place,   xxxviii
    His office was, the hungry for to feed,
    And thristy giue to drinke, a worke of grace :
    He feard not once him selfe to be in need,
    Ne car'd to hoord for those, whom he did breede :
    The grace of God he layd vp still in store,
    Which as a stocke he left vnto his seede ;
    He had enough, what need him care for more ?
And had he lesse, yet some he would giue to the pore.

The third had of their wardrobe custodie,   xxxix
    In which were not rich tyres, nor garments gay,
    The plumes of pride, and wings of vanitie,
    But clothes meet to keepe keene could away,
    And naked nature seemely to aray ;
    With which bare wretched wights he dayly clad,
    The images of God in earthly clay ;
    And if that no spare cloths to giue he had,
His owne coate he would cut, and it distribute glad.

xxxvi 6 Their *1609* : There *1590, 1596*   9 in-commers by *1590, 1596*
xxxviii 1 as] an *1609*   xxxix 4 clothez *1609*   8 clothes *1590, 1609*

K 2

The fourth appointed by his office was,   xl
  Poore prisoners to relieue with gratious ayd,
  And captiues to redeeme with price of bras,
  From Turkes and Sarazins, which them had stayd;
  And though they faultie were, yet well he wayd,
  That God to vs forgiueth euery howre
  Much more then that, why they in bands were layd,
  And he that harrowd hell with heauie stowre,
The faultie soules from thence brought to his heauenly bowre.

The fift had charge sicke persons to attend,   xli
  And comfort those, in point of death which lay;
  For them most needeth comfort in the end,
  When sin, and hell, and death do most dismay
  The feeble soule departing hence away.
  All is but lost, that liuing we bestow,
  If not well ended at our dying day.
  O man haue mind of that last bitter throw;
For as the tree does fall, so lyes it euer low.

The sixt had charge of them now being dead,   xlii
  In seemely sort their corses to engraue,
  And deck with dainty flowres their bridall bed,
  That to their heauenly spouse both sweet and braue
  They might appeare, when he their soules shall saue.
  The wondrous workemanship of Gods owne mould,
  Whose face he made, all beasts to feare, and gaue
  All in his hand, euen dead we honour should.
Ah dearest God me graunt, I dead be not defould.

The seuenth now after death and buriall done,   xliii
  Had charge the tender Orphans of the dead
  And widowes ayd, least they should be vndone:
  In face of iudgement he their right would plead,
  Ne ought the powre of mighty men did dread
  In their defence, nor would for gold or fee
  Be wonne their rightfull causes downe to tread:
  And when they stood in most necessitee,
He did supply their want, and gaue them euer free.

There when the Elfin knight arriued was,   xliv
   The first and chiefest of the seuen, whose care
   Was guests to welcome, towardes him did pas:
   Where seeing *Mercie*, that his steps vp bare,
   And alwayes led, to her with reuerence rare
   He humbly louted in meeke lowlinesse,
   And seemely welcome for her did prepare:
   For of their order she was Patronesse,
Albe *Charissa* were their chiefest founderesse.

There she awhile him stayes, him selfe to rest,   xlv
   That to the rest more able he might bee:
   During which time, in euery good behest
   And godly worke of Almes and charitee
   She him instructed with great industree;
   Shortly therein so perfect he became,
   That from the first vnto the last degree,
   His mortall life he learned had to frame
In holy righteousnesse, without rebuke or blame.

Thence forward by that painfull way they pas,   xlvi
   Forth to an hill, that was both steepe and hy;
   On top whereof a sacred chappell was,
   And eke a litle Hermitage thereby,
   Wherein an aged holy man did lye,
   That day and night said his deuotion,
   Ne other worldly busines did apply;
   His name was heauenly *Contemplation*;
Of God and goodnesse was his meditation.

Great grace that old man to him giuen had;   xlvii
   For God he often saw from heauens hight,
   All were his earthly eyen both blunt and bad,
   And through great age had lost their kindly sight,
   Yet wondrous quick and persant was his spright,
   As Eagles eye, that can behold the Sunne:
   That hill they scale with all their powre and might,
   That his frayle thighes nigh wearie and fordonne
Gan faile, but by her helpe the top at last he wonne.

There they do finde that godly aged Sire,   xlviii
  With snowy lockes adowne his shoulders shed,
  As hoarie frost with spangles doth attire
  The mossy braunches of an Oke halfe ded.
  Each bone might through his body well be red,
  And euery sinew seene through his long fast:
  For nought he car'd his carcas long vnfed;
  His mind was full of spirituall repast,
And pyn'd his flesh, to keepe his body low and chast.

Who when these two approching he aspide,   xlix
  At their first presence grew agrieued sore,
  That forst him lay his heauenly thoughts aside;
  And had he not that Dame respected more,
  Whom highly he did reuerence and adore,
  He would not once haue moued for the knight.
  They him saluted standing far afore;
  Who well them greeting, humbly did requight,
And asked, to what end they clomb that tedious height.

What end (quoth she) should cause vs take such paine,   l
  But that same end, which euery liuing wight
  Should make his marke, high heauen to attaine?
  Is not from hence the way, that leadeth right
  To that most glorious house, that glistreth bright
  With burning starres, and euerliuing fire,
  Whereof the keyes are to thy hand behight
  By wise *Fidelia*? she doth thee require,
To shew it to this knight, according his desire.

Thrise happy man, said then the father graue,   li
  Whose staggering steps thy steady hand doth lead,
  And shewes the way, his sinfull soule to saue.
  Who better can the way to heauen aread,
  Then thou thy selfe, that was both borne and bred
  In heauenly throne, where thousand Angels shine?
  Thou doest the prayers of the righteous sead
  Present before the maiestie diuine,
And his auenging wrath to clemencie incline.

l 1 she] he *1596*

Yet since thou bidst, thy pleasure shalbe donne.   lii
    Then come thou man of earth, and see the way,
    That neuer yet was seene of Faeries sonne,
    That neuer leads the traueiler astray,
    But after labours long, and sad delay,
    Brings them to ioyous rest and endlesse blis.
    But first thou must a season fast and pray,
    Till from her bands the spright assoiled is,
And haue her strength recur'd from fraile infirmitis.

That done, he leads him to the highest Mount;   liii
    Such one, as that same mighty man of God,
    That bloud-red billowes like a walled front
    On either side disparted with his rod,
    Till that his army dry-foot through them yod,
    Dwelt fortie dayes vpon ; where writ in stone
    With bloudy letters by the hand of God,
    The bitter doome of death and balefull mone
He did receiue, whiles flashing fire about him shone.

Or like that sacred hill, whose head full hie,   liv
    Adornd with fruitfull Oliues all arownd,
    Is, as it were for endlesse memory
    Of that deare Lord, who oft thereon was fownd,
    For euer with a flowring girlond crownd:
    Or like that pleasaunt Mount, that is for ay
    Through famous Poets verse each where renownd,
    On which the thrise three learned Ladies play
Their heauenly notes, and make full many a louely lay.

From thence, far off he vnto him did shew   lv
    A litle path, that was both steepe and long,
    Which to a goodly Citie led his vew;
    Whose wals and towres were builded high and strong
    Of perle and precious stone, that earthly tong
    Cannot describe, nor wit of man can tell;
    Too high a ditty for my simple song;
    The Citie of the great king hight it well,
Wherein eternall peace and happinesse doth dwell.

    lii 1 since] sith *1609*   6 Brings] Bring *1590, 1596*

As he thereon stood gazing, he might see   lvi
  The blessed Angels to and fro descend
  From highest heauen, in gladsome companee,
  And with great ioy into that Citie wend,
  As commonly as friend does with his frend.
  Whereat he wondred much, and gan enquere,
  What stately building durst so high extend
  Her loftie towres vnto the starry sphere,
And what vnknowen nation there empeopled were.

Faire knight (quoth he) *Hierusalem* that is,   lvii
  The new *Hierusalem*, that God has built
  For those to dwell in, that are chosen his,
  His chosen people purg'd from sinfull guilt,
  With pretious bloud, which cruelly was spilt
  On cursed tree, of that vnspotted lam,
  That for the sinnes of all the world was kilt:
  Now are they Saints all in that Citie sam,
More deare vnto their God, then younglings to their dam.

Till now, said then the knight, I weened well,   lviii
  That great *Cleopolis*, where I haue beene,
  In which that fairest *Faerie Queene* doth dwell,
  The fairest Citie was, that might be seene;
  And that bright towre all built of christall cleene,
  Panthea, seemd the brightest thing, that was:
  But now by proofe all otherwise I weene;
  For this great Citie that does far surpas,
And this bright Angels towre quite dims that towre of glas.

Most trew, then said the holy aged man;   lix
  Yet is *Cleopolis* for earthly frame,
  The fairest peece, that eye beholden can:
  And well beseemes all knights of noble name,
  That couet in th'immortall booke of fame
  To be eternized, that same to haunt,
  And doen their seruice to that soueraigne Dame,
  That glorie does to them for guerdon graunt:
For she is heauenly borne, and heauen may iustly vaunt.

lvii 5 pretious] piteous *1590 &c.* : *corr. F. E.*
lviii 3 dwell *1590 &c.*   lix 2 frame] fame *1590 &c.* : *corr. F. E.*

And thou faire ymp, sprong out from English race,   lx
   How euer now accompted Elfins sonne,
   Well worthy doest thy seruice for her grace,
   To aide a virgin desolate foredonne.
   But when thou famous victorie hast wonne,
   And high emongst all knights hast hong thy shield,
   Thenceforth the suit of earthly conquest shonne,
   And wash thy hands from guilt of bloudy field:
For bloud can nought but sin, and wars but sorrowes yield.

Then seeke this path, that I to thee presage,   lxi
   Which after all to heauen shall thee send ;
   Then peaceably thy painefull pilgrimage
   To yonder same *Hierusalem* do bend,
   Where is for thee ordaind a blessed end:
   For thou emongst those Saints, whom thou doest see,
   Shalt be a Saint, and thine owne nations frend
   And Patrone: thou Saint *George* shalt called bee,
Saint *George* of mery England, the signe of victoree.

Vnworthy wretch (quoth he) of so great grace,   lxii
   How dare I thinke such glory to attaine?
   These that haue it attaind, were in like cace
   (Quoth he) as wretched, and liu'd in like paine.
   But deeds of armes must I at last be faine,
   And Ladies loue to leaue so dearely bought?
   What need of armes, where peace doth ay remaine,
   (Said he) and battailes none are to be fought?
As for loose loues are vaine, and vanish into nought.

O let me not (quoth he) then turne againe   lxiii
   Backe to the world, whose ioyes so fruitlesse are ;
   But let me here for aye in peace remaine,
   Or streight way on that last long voyage fare,
   That nothing may my present hope empare.
   That may not be (said he) ne maist thou yit
   Forgo that royall maides bequeathed care,
   Who did her cause into thy hand commit,
Till from her cursed foe thou haue her freely quit.

   lx 2 accounted *1609*   lxi 3 to thy *1596*   lxii 4 As wretched
men, and liued in like paine. *1590*   8 and bitter battailes all are fought?
1590   9 they are vaine, *1590*   lxiii 1 then turne] returne *1609*

Then shall I soone, (quoth he) so God me grace,   lxiv
  Abet that virgins cause disconsolate,
  And shortly backe returne vnto this place,
  To walke this way in Pilgrims poore estate.
  But now aread, old father, why of late
  Didst thou behight me borne of English blood,
  Whom all a Faeries sonne doen nominate?
  That word shall I (said he) auouchen good,
Sith to thee is vnknowne the cradle of thy brood.

For well I wote, thou springst from ancient race   lxv
  Of *Saxon* kings, that haue with mightie hand
  And many bloudie battailes fought in place
  High reard their royall throne in *Britane* land,
  And vanquisht them, vnable to withstand:
  From thence a Faerie thee vnweeting reft,
  There as thou slepst in tender swadling band,
  And her base Elfin brood there for thee left.
Such men do Chaungelings call, so chaungd by Faeries theft.

Thence she thee brought into this Faerie lond,   lxvi
  And in an heaped furrow did thee hyde,
  Where thee a Ploughman all vnweeting fond,
  As he his toylesome teme that way did guyde,
  And brought thee vp in ploughmans state to byde,
  Whereof *Georgos* he thee gaue to name;
  Till prickt with courage, and thy forces pryde,
  To Faery court thou cam'st to seeke for fame,
And proue thy puissaunt armes, as seemes thee best became.

O holy Sire (quoth he) how shall I quight   lxvii
  The many fauours I with thee haue found,
  That hast my name and nation red aright,
  And taught the way that does to heauen bound?
  This said, adowne he looked to the ground,
  To haue returnd, but dazed were his eyne,
  Through passing brightnesse, which did quite confound
  His feeble sence, and too exceeding shyne.
So darke are earthly things compard to things diuine.

lxiv 7 doen then nominate? *1596*
lxv 3 place] face *1590*   4 *Britans 1590*

At last whenas himselfe he gan to find,   lxviii
  To *Vna* back he cast him to retire;
  Who him awaited still with pensiue mind.
  Great thankes and goodly meed to that good syre,
  He thence departing gaue for his paines hyre.
  So came to *Vna*, who him ioyd to see,
  And after litle rest, gan him desire,
  Of her aduenture mindfull for to bee.
So leaue they take of *Cælia*, and her daughters three.

Cant. XI.

The knight with that old Dragon fights
two dayes incessantly:
The third him ouerthrowes, and gayns
most glorious victory.

Igh time now gan it wex for *Vna* faire,   i
  To thinke of those her captiue Parents deare,
  And their forwasted kingdome to repaire:
  Whereto whenas they now approched neare,
  With hartie words her knight she gan to cheare,
  And in her modest manner thus bespake;
  Deare knight, as deare, as euer knight was deare,
  That all these sorrowes suffer for my sake,
High heauen behold the tedious toyle, ye for me take.

Now are we come vnto my natiue soyle,   ii
  And to the place, where all our perils dwell;
  Here haunts that feend, and does his dayly spoyle,
  Therefore henceforth be at your keeping well,
  And euer ready for your foeman fell.
  The sparke of noble courage now awake,
  And striue your excellent selfe to excell;
  That shall ye euermore renowmed make,
Aboue all knights on earth, that batteill vndertake.

    i 1 faire] *fayre 1590: faire 1596*   ii 4 at] *it 1590: corr. F. E.*

And pointing forth, lo yonder is (said she)   iii
 The brasen towre in which my parents deare
 For dread of that huge feend emprisond be,
 Whom I from far see on the walles appeare,
 Whose sight my feeble soule doth greatly cheare :
 And on the top of all I do espye
 The watchman wayting tydings glad to heare,
 That O my parents might I happily
Vnto you bring, to ease you of your misery.

With that they heard a roaring hideous sound,   iv
 That all the ayre with terrour filled wide,
 And seemd vneath to shake the stedfast ground.
 Eftsoones that dreadfull Dragon they espide,
 Where stretcht he lay vpon the sunny side
 Of a great hill, himselfe like a great hill.
 But all so soone, as he from far descride
 Those glistring armes, that heauen with light did fill,
He rousd himselfe full blith, and hastned them vntill.

Then bad the knight his Lady yede aloofe,   v
 And to an hill her selfe with draw aside,
 From whence she might behold that battailles proof
 And eke be safe from daunger far descryde:
 She him obayd, and turnd a little wyde.
 Now O thou sacred Muse, most learned Dame,
 Faire ympe of *Phœbus*, and his aged bride,
 The Nourse of time, and euerlasting fame,
That warlike hands ennoblest with immortall name ;

O gently come into my feeble brest,   vi
 Come gently, but not with that mighty rage,
 Wherewith the martiall troupes thou doest infest,
 And harts of great Heroës doest enrage,
 That nought their kindled courage may aswage,
 Soone as thy dreadfull trompe begins to sownd ;
 The God of warre with his fiers equipage
 Thou doest awake, sleepe neuer he so sownd,
And scared nations doest with horrour sterne astownd.

iii *om. 1590*   3 be *1596*   4 far, appeare *1596*   iv 5 stretcht]
stretch *1596*   side, *1590, 1596*   v 1 his] this *1590 &c.*: corr. *F. E.*
vi 5 assuage ; *1609*   6 sound, *1609*   9 scared] feared *1590 &c.*:
corr. *F. E.*

Faire Goddesse lay that furious fit aside, vii
  Till I of warres and bloudy *Mars* do sing,
  And Briton fields with Sarazin bloud bedyde,
  Twixt that great faery Queene and Paynim king,
  That with their horrour heauen and earth did ring,
  A worke of labour long, and endlesse prayse:
  But now a while let downe that haughtie string,
  And to my tunes thy second tenor rayse,
That I this man of God his godly armes may blaze.

By this the dreadfull Beast drew nigh to hand, viii
  Halfe flying, and halfe footing in his hast,
  That with his largenesse measured much land,
  And made wide shadow vnder his huge wast;
  As mountaine doth the valley ouercast.
  Approching nigh, he reared high afore
  His body monstrous, horrible, and vast,
  Which to increase his wondrous greatnesse more,
Was swolne with wrath, and poyson, and with bloudy gore.

And ouer, all with brasen scales was armd, ix
  Like plated coate of steele, so couched neare,
  That nought mote perce, ne might his corse be harmd
  With dint of sword, nor push of pointed speare;
  Which as an Eagle, seeing pray appeare,
  His aery plumes doth rouze, full rudely dight,
  So shaked he, that horrour was to heare,
  For as the clashing of an Armour bright,
Such noyse his rouzed scales did send vnto the knight.

His flaggy wings when forth he did display, x
  Were like two sayles, in which the hollow wynd
  Is gathered full, and worketh speedy way:
  And eke the pennes, that did his pineons bynd,
  Were like mayne-yards, with flying canuas lynd,
  With which whenas him list the ayre to beat,
  And there by force vnwonted passage find,
  The cloudes before him fled for terrour great,
And all the heauens stood still amazed with his threat.

    viii 7 vaste *1590* : wast *1596*   ix 4 swerd *1590*
      x 4 bynd *1596*   5 lynd] kynd *1590*

His huge long tayle wound vp in hundred foldes,   xi
  Does ouerspred his long bras-scaly backe,
  Whose wreathed boughts when euer he vnfoldes,
  And thicke entangled knots adown does slacke,
  Bespotted as with shields of red and blacke,
  It sweepeth all the land behind him farre,
  And of three furlongs does but litle lacke;
  And at the point two stings in-fixed arre,
Both deadly sharpe, that sharpest steele exceeden farre.

But stings and sharpest steele did far exceed   xii
  The sharpnesse of his cruell rending clawes;
  Dead was it sure, as sure as death in deed,
  What euer thing does touch his rauenous pawes,
  Or what within his reach he euer drawes.
  But his most hideous head my toung to tell
  Does tremble : for his deepe deuouring iawes
  Wide gaped, like the griesly mouth of hell,
Through which into his darke abisse all rauin fell.

And that more wondrous was, in either iaw   xiii
  Three ranckes of yron teeth enraunged were,
  In which yet trickling bloud and gobbets raw
  Of late deuoured bodies did appeare,
  That sight thereof bred cold congealed feare:
  Which to increase, and all atonce to kill,
  A cloud of smoothering smoke and sulphur seare
  Out of his stinking gorge forth steemed still,
That all the ayre about with smoke and stench did fill.

His blazing eyes, like two bright shining shields,   xiv
  Did burne with wrath, and sparkled liuing fyre;
  As two broad Beacons, set in open fields,
  Send forth their flames farre off to euery shyre,
  And warning giue, that enemies conspyre,
  With fire and sword the region to inuade;
  So flam'd his eyne with rage and rancorous yre:
  But farre within, as in a hollow glade,
Those glaring lampes were set, that made a dreadfull shade.

    xi 4 slack. *1590* : slacke. *1596* : slack; *1609*   5 as] all *1590 &c.* :
corr. F. E.   xii 6 tell, *1590, 1596*

So dreadfully he towards him did pas,   xv
  Forelifting vp aloft his speckled brest,
  And often bounding on the brused gras,
  As for great ioyance of his newcome guest.
  Eftsoones he gan aduance his haughtie crest,
  As chauffed Bore his bristles doth vpreare,
  And shoke his scales to battell readie drest;
  That made the *Redcrosse* knight nigh quake for feare,
As bidding bold defiance to his foeman neare.

The knight gan fairely couch his steadie speare,   xvi
  And fiercely ran at him with rigorous might:
  The pointed steele arriuing rudely theare,
  His harder hide would neither perce, nor bight,
  But glauncing by forth passed forward right;
  Yet sore amoued with so puissant push,
  The wrathfull beast about him turned light,
  And him so rudely passing by, did brush
With his long tayle, that horse and man to ground did rush.

Both horse and man vp lightly rose againe,   xvii
  And fresh encounter towards him addrest:
  But th'idle stroke yet backe recoyld in vaine,
  And found no place his deadly point to rest.
  Exceeding rage enflam'd the furious beast,
  To be auenged of so great despight;
  For neuer felt his imperceable brest
  So wondrous force, from hand of liuing wight;
Yet had he prou'd the powre of many a puissant knight.

Then with his wauing wings displayed wyde,   xviii
  Himselfe vp high he lifted from the ground,
  And with strong flight did forcibly diuide
  The yielding aire, which nigh too feeble found
  Her flitting partes, and element vnsound,
  To beare so great a weight: he cutting way
  With his broad sayles, about him soared round:
  At last low stouping with vnweldie sway,
Snatcht vp both horse and man, to beare them quite away.

Long he them bore aboue the subiect plaine,   xix
    So farre as Ewghen bow a shaft may send,
    Till struggling strong did him at last constraine,
    To let them downe before his flightes end:
    As hagard hauke presuming to contend
    With hardie fowle, aboue his hable might,
    His wearie pounces all in vaine doth spend,
    To trusse the pray too heauie for his flight;
Which comming downe to ground, does free it selfe by fight.

He so disseized of his gryping grosse,   xx
    The knight his thrillant speare againe assayd
    In his bras-plated body to embosse,
    And three mens strength vnto the stroke he layd;
    Wherewith the stiffe beame quaked, as affrayd,
    And glauncing from his scaly necke, did glyde
    Close vnder his left wing, then broad displayd.
    The percing steele there wrought a wound full wyde,
That with the vncouth smart the Monster lowdly cryde.

He cryde, as raging seas are wont to rore,   xxi
    When wintry storme his wrathfull wreck does threat,
    The rolling billowes beat the ragged shore,
    As they the earth would shoulder from her seat,
    And greedie gulfe does gape, as he would eat
    His neighbour element in his reuenge:
    Then gin the blustring brethren boldly threat,
    To moue the world from off his stedfast henge,
And boystrous battell make, each other to auenge.

The steely head stucke fast still in his flesh,   xxii
    Till with his cruell clawes he snatcht the wood,
    And quite a sunder broke.   Forth flowed fresh
    A gushing riuer of blacke goarie blood,
    That drowned all the land, whereon he stood;
    The streame thereof would driue a water-mill.
    Trebly augmented was his furious mood
    With bitter sense of his deepe rooted ill,
That flames of fire he threw forth from his large nosethrill.

His hideous tayle then hurled he about,　　　　　　xxiii
　　And therewith all enwrapt the nimble thyes
　　Of his froth-fomy steed, whose courage stout
　　Striuing to loose the knot, that fast him tyes,
　　Himselfe in streighter bandes too rash implyes,
　　That to the ground he is perforce constraynd
　　To throw his rider : who can quickly ryse
　　From off the earth, with durty bloud distaynd,
For that reprochfull fall right fowly he disdaynd.

And fiercely tooke his trenchand blade in hand,　　xxiv
　　With which he stroke so furious and so fell,
　　That nothing seemd the puissance could withstand :
　　Vpon his crest the hardned yron fell,
　　But his more hardned crest was armd so well,
　　That deeper dint therein it would not make ;
　　Yet so extremely did the buffe him quell,
　　That from thenceforth he shund the like to take,
But when he saw them come, he did them still forsake.

The knight was wrath to see his stroke beguyld,　　xxv
　　And smote againe with more outrageous might ;
　　But backe againe the sparckling steele recoyld,
　　And left not any marke, where it did light ;
　　As if in Adamant rocke it had bene pight.
　　The beast impatient of his smarting wound,
　　And of so fierce and forcible despight,
　　Thought with his wings to stye aboue the ground,
But his late wounded wing vnseruiceable found.

Then full of griefe and anguish vehement,　　　　　xxvi
　　He lowdly brayd, that like was neuer heard,
　　And from his wide deuouring ouen sent
　　A flake of fire, that flashing in his beard,
　　Him all amazd, and almost made affeard :
　　The scorching flame sore swinged all his face,
　　And through his armour all his bodie seard,
　　That he could not endure so cruell cace,
But thought his armes to leaue, and helmet to vnlace.

　　　　xxiii 8 off] of *1590*　　　xxv 1 wroth *1590, 1609*
　　　　　　xxvi 6 swinged] singed *1609*

Not that great Champion of the antique world,   xxvii
   Whom famous Poetes verse so much doth vaunt,
   And hath for twelue huge labours high extold,
   So many furies and sharpe fits did haunt,
   When him the poysoned garment did enchaunt
   With *Centaures* bloud, and bloudie verses charm'd,
   As did this knight twelue thousand dolours daunt,
   Whom fyrie steele now burnt, that earst him arm'd,
That erst him goodly arm'd, now most of all him harm'd.

Faint, wearie, sore, emboyled, grieued, brent   xxviii
   With heat, toyle, wounds, armes, smart, and inward fire
   That neuer man such mischiefes did torment;
   Death better were, death did he oft desire,
   But death will neuer come, when needes require.
   Whom so dismayd when that his foe beheld,
   He cast to suffer him no more respire,
   But gan his sturdie sterne about to weld,
And him so strongly stroke, that to the ground him feld.

It fortuned (as faire it then befell)   xxix
   Behind his backe vnweeting, where he stood,
   Of auncient time there was a springing well,
   From which fast trickled forth a siluer flood,
   Full of great vertues, and for med'cine good.
   Whylome, before that cursed Dragon got
   That happie land, and all with innocent blood
   Defyld those sacred waues, it rightly hot
The well of life, ne yet his vertues had forgot.

For vnto life the dead it could restore,   xxx
   And guilt of sinfull crimes cleane wash away,
   Those that with sicknesse were infected sore,
   It could recure, and aged long decay
   Renew, as one were borne that very day.
   Both *Silo* this, and *Iordan* did excell,
   And th'English *Bath*, and eke the german *Spau*,
   Ne can *Cephise*, nor *Hebrus* match this well:
Into the same the knight backe ouerthrowen, fell.

xxvii 2 vaunt] daunt *1596, 1609*   xxx 5 one] it *1590 &c.*: *corr. F. E.*

Now gan the golden *Phœbus* for to steepe   xxxi
  His fierie face in billowes of the west,
  And his faint steedes watred in Ocean deepe,
  Whiles from their iournall labours they did rest,
  When that infernall Monster, hauing kest
  His wearie foe into that liuing well,
  Can high aduance his broad discoloured brest,
  Aboue his wonted pitch, with countenance fell,
And clapt his yron wings, as victor he did dwell.

Which when his pensiue Ladie saw from farre,   xxxii
  Great woe and sorrow did her soule assay,
  As weening that the sad end of the warre,
  And gan to highest God entirely pray,
  That feared chance from her to turne away;
  With folded hands and knees full lowly bent
  All night she watcht, ne once adowne would lay
  Her daintie limbs in her sad dreriment,
But praying still did wake, and waking did lament.

The morrow next gan early to appeare,   xxxiii
  That *Titan* rose to runne his daily race;
  But early ere the morrow next gan reare
  Out of the sea faire *Titans* deawy face,
  Vp rose the gentle virgin from her place,
  And looked all about, if she might spy
  Her loued knight to moue his manly pace:
  For she had great doubt of his safety,
Since late she saw him fall before his enemy.

At last she saw, where he vpstarted braue   xxxiv
  Out of the well, wherein he drenched lay;
  As Eagle fresh out of the Ocean waue,
  Where he hath left his plumes all hoary gray,
  And deckt himselfe with feathers youthly gay,
  Like Eyas hauke vp mounts vnto the skies,
  His newly budded pineons to assay,
  And marueiles at himselfe, still as he flies:
So new this new-borne knight to battell new did rise.

xxxiv 8 merueiles *1590*

L 2

Whom when the damned feend so fresh did spy,   xxxv
   No wonder if he wondred at the sight,
   And doubted, whether his late enemy
   It were, or other new supplied knight.
   He, now to proue his late renewed might,
   High brandishing his bright deaw-burning blade,
   Vpon his crested scalpe so sore did smite,
   That to the scull a yawning wound it made:
The deadly dint his dulled senses all dismaid.

I wote not, whether the reuenging steele   xxxvi
   Were hardned with that holy water dew,
   Wherein he fell, or sharper edge did feele,
   Or his baptized hands now greater grew;
   Or other secret vertue did ensew;
   Else neuer could the force of fleshly arme,
   Ne molten mettall in his bloud embrew:
   For till that stownd could neuer wight him harme,
By subtilty, nor slight, nor might, nor mighty charme.

The cruell wound enraged him so sore,   xxxvii
   That loud he yelded for exceeding paine;
   As hundred ramping Lyons seem'd to rore,
   Whom rauenous hunger did thereto constraine:
   Then gan he tosse aloft his stretched traine,
   And therewith scourge the buxome aire so sore,
   That to his force to yeelden it was faine;
   Ne ought his sturdie strokes might stand afore,
That high trees ouerthrew, and rocks in peeces tore.

The same aduauncing high aboue his head,   xxxviii
   With sharpe intended sting so rude him smot,
   That to the earth him droue, as stricken dead,
   Ne liuing wight would haue him life behot:
   The mortall sting his angry needle shot
   Quite through his shield, and in his shoulder seasd,
   Where fast it stucke, ne would there out be got:
   The griefe thereof him wondrous sore diseasd,
Ne might his ranckling paine with patience be appeasd.

xxxvii 2 yelded] yelled *1609*

But yet more mindfull of his honour deare,   xxxix
  Then of the grieuous smart, which him did wring,
  From loathed soile he can him lightly reare,
  And stroue to loose the farre infixed sting :
  Which when in vaine he tryde with struggeling,
  Inflam'd with wrath, his raging blade he heft,
  And strooke so strongly, that the knotty string
  Of his huge taile he quite a sunder cleft,
Fiue ioynts thereof he hewd, and but the stump him left.

Hart cannot thinke, what outrage, and what cryes,   xl
  With foule enfouldred smoake and flashing fire,
  The hell-bred beast threw forth vnto the skyes,
  That all was couered with darknesse dire :
  Then fraught with rancour, and engorged ire,
  He cast at once him to auenge for all,
  And gathering vp himselfe out of the mire,
  With his vneuen wings did fiercely fall
Vpon his sunne-bright shield, and gript it fast withall.

Much was the man encombred with his hold,   xli
  In feare to lose his weapon in his paw,
  Ne wist yet, how his talants to vnfold ;
  Nor harder was from *Cerberus* greedie iaw
  To plucke a bone, then from his cruell claw
  To reaue by strength the griped gage away :
  Thrise he assayd it from his foot to draw,
  And thrise in vaine to draw it did assay,
It booted nought to thinke, to robbe him of his pray

Tho when he saw no power might preuaile,   xlii
  His trustie sword he cald to his last aid,
  Wherewith he fiercely did his foe assaile,
  And double blowes about him stoutly laid,
  That glauncing fire out of the yron plaid ;
  As sparckles from the Anduile vse to fly,
  When heauie hammers on the wedge are swaid ;
  Therewith at last he forst him to vnty
One of his grasping feete, him to defend thereby.

xxxix 4 sting] string *1596, 1609*   7 string] sting *1596, 1609*   8 in
sunder *1609*   xl 8 fall, *1590, 1596*   xli 4 Nor *1609* : For *1590, 1596*
6 strength, *1590, 1596*

The other foot, fast fixed on his shield,   xliii
    Whenas no strength, nor stroks mote him constraine
    To loose, ne yet the warlike pledge to yield,
    He smot thereat with all his might and maine,
    That nought so wondrous puissance might sustaine;
    Vpon the ioynt the lucky steele did light,
    And made such way, that hewd it quite in twaine;
    The paw yet missed not his minisht might,
But hong still on the shield, as it at first was pight.

For griefe thereof, and diuelish despight,   xliv
    From his infernall fournace forth he threw
    Huge flames, that dimmed all the heauens light,
    Enrold in duskish smoke and brimstone blew;
    As burning *Aetna* from his boyling stew
    Doth belch out flames, and rockes in peeces broke,
    And ragged ribs of mountaines molten new,
    Enwrapt in coleblacke clouds and filthy smoke,
That all the land with stench, and heauen with horror choke.

The heate whereof, and harmefull pestilence   xlv
    So sore him noyd, that forst him to retire
    A little backward for his best defence,
    To saue his bodie from the scorching fire,
    Which he from hellish entrailes did expire.
    It chaunst (eternall God that chaunce did guide)
    As he recoyled backward, in the mire
    His nigh forwearied feeble feet did slide,
And downe he fell, with dread of shame sore terrifide.

There grew a goodly tree him faire beside,   xlvi
    Loaden with fruit and apples rosie red,
    As they in pure vermilion had beene dide,
    Whereof great vertues ouer all were red:
    For happie life to all, which thereon fed,
    And life eke euerlasting did befall:
    Great God it planted in that blessed sted
    With his almightie hand, and did it call
The tree of life, the crime of our first fathers fall.

    xliii 1 shield *1590, 1596*   xlvi 9 The tree of life, *1590, 1596.*
But cf. xxix 9

In all the world like was not to be found,   xlvii
   Saue in that soile, where all good things did grow,
   And freely sprong out of the fruitfull ground,
   As incorrupted Nature did them sow,
   Till that dread Dragon all did ouerthrow.
   Another like faire tree eke grew thereby,
   Whereof who so did eat, eftsoones did know
   Both good and ill: O mornefull memory:
That tree through one mans fault hath doen vs all to dy.

From that first tree forth flowd, as from a well,   xlviii
   A trickling streame of Balme, most soueraine
   And daintie deare, which on the ground still fell,
   And ouerflowed all the fertill plaine,
   As it had deawed bene with timely raine:
   Life and long health that gratious ointment gaue,
   And deadly woundes could heale, and reare againe
   The senselesse corse appointed for the graue.
Into that same he fell: which did from death him saue.

For nigh thereto the euer damned beast   xlix
   Durst not approch, for he was deadly made,
   And all that life preserued, did detest:
   Yet he it oft aduentur'd to inuade.
   By this the drouping day-light gan to fade,
   And yeeld his roome to sad succeeding night,
   Who with her sable mantle gan to shade
   The face of earth, and wayes of liuing wight,
And high her burning torch set vp in heauen bright.

When gentle *Vna* saw the second fall   l
   Of her deare knight, who wearie of long fight,
   And faint through losse of bloud, mou'd not at all,
   But lay as in a dreame of deepe delight,
   Besmeard with pretious Balme, whose vertuous might
   Did heale his wounds, and scorching heat alay,
   Againe she stricken was with sore affright,
   And for his safetie gan deuoutly pray;
And watch the noyous night, and wait for ioyous day.

      xlviii 7 heale *1596*   xlix 6 rowme *1590*

The ioyous day gan early to appeare,   li
  And faire *Aurora* from the deawy bed
  Of aged *Tithone* gan her selfe to reare,
  With rosie cheekes, for shame as blushing red;
  Her golden lockes for haste were loosely shed
  About her eares, when *Vna* her did marke
  Clymbe to her charet, all with flowers spred,
  From heauen high to chase the chearelesse darke;
With merry note her loud salutes the mounting larke.

Then freshly vp arose the doughtie knight,   lii
  All healed of his hurts and woundes wide,
  And did himselfe to battell readie dight;
  Whose early foe awaiting him beside
  To haue deuourd, so soone as day he spyde,
  When now he saw himselfe so freshly reare,
  As if late fight had nought him damnifyde,
  He woxe dismayd, and gan his fate to feare;
Nathlesse with wonted rage he him aduaunced neare.

And in his first encounter, gaping wide,   liii
  He thought attonce him to haue swallowd quight,
  And rusht vpon him with outragious pride;
  Who him r'encountring fierce, as hauke in flight,
  Perforce rebutted backe. The weapon bright
  Taking aduantage of his open iaw,
  Ran through his mouth with so importune might,
  That deepe emperst his darksome hollow maw,
And back retyrd, his life bloud forth with all did draw.

So downe he fell, and forth his life did breath,   liv
  That vanisht into smoke and cloudes swift;
  So downe he fell, that th'earth him vnderneath
  Did grone, as feeble so great load to lift;
  So downe he fell, as an huge rockie clift,
  Whose false foundation waues haue washt away,
  With dreadfull poyse is from the mayneland rift,
  And rolling downe, great *Neptune* doth dismay;
So downe he fell, and like an heaped mountaine lay.

    li 2 the] her *1596, 1609*   7 spred; *1590 &c.*   8 darke, *1590 &c.*
                  lii 2 woundez *1609*

The knight himselfe euen trembled at his fall,   lv
   So huge and horrible a masse it seem'd;
   And his deare Ladie, that beheld it all,
   Durst not approch for dread, which she misdeem'd,
   But yet at last, when as the direfull feend
   She saw not stirre, off-shaking vaine affright,
   She nigher drew, and saw that ioyous end:
   Then God she praysd, and thankt her faithfull knight,
That had atchieu'd so great a conquest by his might.

Cant. XII.

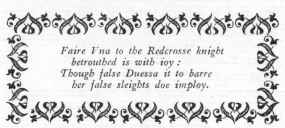

Faire Vna to the Redcrosse knight
betrouthed is with ioy:
Though false Duessa it to barre
her false sleights doe imploy.

BEhold I see the hauen nigh at hand,   i
   To which I meane my wearie course to bend;
   Vere the maine shete, and beare vp with the land,
   The which afore is fairely to be kend,
   And seemeth safe from stormes, that may offend;
   There this faire virgin wearie of her way
   Must landed be, now at her iourneyes end:
   There eke my feeble barke a while may stay,
Till merry wind and weather call her thence away.

Scarsely had *Phœbus* in the glooming East   ii
   Yet harnessed his firie-footed teeme,
   Ne reard aboue the earth his flaming creast,
   When the last deadly smoke aloft did steeme,
   That signe of last outbreathed life did seeme
   Vnto the watchman on the castle wall;
   Who thereby dead that balefull Beast did deeme,
   And to his Lord and Ladie lowd gan call,
To tell, how he had seene the Dragons fatall fall.

ii 5 seeme, *1590 &c.*　9 fall, *1590, 1596*

Vprose with hastie ioy, and feeble speed   iii
    That aged Sire, the Lord of all that land,
    And looked forth, to weet, if true indeede
    Those tydings were, as he did vnderstand,
    Which whenas true by tryall he out fond,
    He bad to open wyde his brazen gate,
    Which long time had bene shut, and out of hond
    Proclaymed ioy and peace through all his state;
For dead now was their foe, which them forrayed late.

Then gan triumphant Trompets sound on hie,   iv
    That sent to heauen the ecchoed report
    Of their new ioy, and happie victorie
    Gainst him, that had them long opprest with tort,
    And fast imprisoned in sieged fort.
    Then all the people, as in solemne feast,
    To him assembled with one full consort,
    Reioycing at the fall of that great beast,
From whose eternall bondage now they were releast.

Forth came that auncient Lord and aged Queene,   v
    Arayd in antique robes downe to the ground,
    And sad habiliments right well beseene;
    A noble crew about them waited round
    Of sage and sober Peres, all grauely gownd;
    Whom farre before did march a goodly band
    Of tall young men, all hable armes to sownd,
    But now they laurell braunches bore in hand;
Glad signe of victorie and peace in all their land.

Vnto that doughtie Conquerour they came,   vi
    And him before themselues prostrating low,
    Their Lord and Patrone loud did him proclame,
    And at his feet their laurell boughes did throw.
    Soone after them all dauncing on a row
    The comely virgins came, with girlands dight,
    As fresh as flowres in medow greene do grow,
    When morning deaw vpon their leaues doth light:
And in their hands sweet Timbrels all vpheld on hight.

iii 5 fond] found *1596, 1609*

And them before, the fry of children young   vii
   Their wanton sports and childish mirth did play,
   And to the Maydens sounding tymbrels sung
   In well attuned notes, a ioyous lay,
   And made delightfull musicke all the way,
   Vntill they came, where that faire virgin stood;
   As faire *Diana* in fresh sommers day
   Beholds her Nymphes, enraung'd in shadie wood,
Some wrestle, some do run, some bathe in christall flood.

So she beheld those maydens meriment   viii
   With chearefull vew; who when to her they came,
   Themselues to ground with gratious humblesse bent,
   And her ador'd by honorable name,
   Lifting to heauen her euerlasting fame:
   Then on her head they set a girland greene,
   And crowned her twixt earnest and twixt game;
   Who in her selfe-resemblance well beseene,
Did seeme such, as she was, a goodly maiden Queene.

And after, all the raskall many ran,   ix
   Heaped together in rude rablement,
   To see the face of that victorious man:
   Whom all admired, as from heauen sent,
   And gazd vpon with gaping wonderment.
   But when they came, where that dead Dragon lay,
   Stretcht on the ground in monstrous large extent,
   The sight with idle feare did them dismay,
Ne durst approch him nigh, to touch, or once assay.

Some feard, and fled; some feard and well it faynd;   x
   One that would wiser seeme, then all the rest,
   Warnd him not touch, for yet perhaps remaynd
   Some lingring life within his hollow brest,
   Or in his wombe might lurke some hidden nest
   Of many Dragonets, his fruitfull seed;
   Another said, that in his eyes did rest
   Yet sparckling fire, and bad thereof take heed;
Another said, he saw him moue his eyes indeed.

vii 3 tymbrel *1590*   7 day, *1590, 1596*
viii 3 gracious *1590 passim*   ix 1 after *1590*

One mother, when as her foolehardie chyld   xi
  Did come too neare, and with his talants play,
  Halfe dead through feare, her litle babe reuyld,
  And to her gossips gan in counsell say;
  How can I tell, but that his talants may
  Yet scratch my sonne, or rend his tender hand?
  So diuersly themselues in vaine they fray;
  Whiles some more bold, to measure him nigh stand,
To proue how many acres he did spread of land.

Thus flocked all the folke him round about,   xii
  The whiles that hoarie king, with all his traine,
  Being arriued, where that champion stout
  After his foes defeasance did remaine,
  Him goodly greetes, and faire does entertaine,
  With princely gifts of yuorie and gold,
  And thousand thankes him yeelds for all his paine.
  Then when his daughter deare he does behold,
Her dearely doth imbrace, and kisseth manifold.

And after to his Pallace he them brings,   xiii
  With shaumes, and trompets, and with Clarions sweet;
  And all the way the ioyous people sings,
  And with their garments strowes the paued street:
  Whence mounting vp, they find purueyance meet
  Of all, that royall Princes court became,
  And all the floore was vnderneath their feet
  Bespred with costly scarlot of great name,
On which they lowly sit, and fitting purpose frame.

What needs me tell their feast and goodly guize,   xiv
  In which was nothing riotous nor vaine?
  What needs of daintie dishes to deuize,
  Of comely seruices, or courtly trayne?
  My narrow leaues cannot in them containe
  The large discourse of royall Princes state.
  Yet was their manner then but bare and plaine:
  For th'antique world excesse and pride did hate;
Such proud luxurious pompe is swollen vp but late.

   xi 1 when as] whenas *1590*   2 too] to *1590*   4 gossibs *1590*
 5 talents *1590 &c.*: *corr. F. E.*   xiv 5 vntayne *1590*: *corr. F. E.*

Then when with meates and drinkes of euery kinde   xv
    Their feruent appetites they quenched had,
    That auncient Lord gan fit occasion finde,
    Of straunge aduentures, and of perils sad,
    Which in his trauell him befallen had,
    For to demaund of his renowmed guest:
    Who then with vtt'rance graue, and count'nance sad,
    From point to point, as is before exprest,
Discourst his voyage long, according his request.

Great pleasure mixt with pittifull regard,   xvi
    That godly King and Queene did passionate,
    Whiles they his pittifull aduentures heard,
    That oft they did lament his lucklesse state,
    And often blame the too importune fate,
    That heapd on him so many wrathfull wreakes:
    For neuer gentle knight, as he of late,
    So tossed was in fortunes cruell freakes;
And all the while salt teares bedeawd the hearers cheaks.

Then said that royall Pere in sober wise;   xvii
    Deare Sonne, great beene the euils, which ye bore
    From first to last in your late enterprise,
    That I note, whether prayse, or pitty more:
    For neuer liuing man, I weene, so sore
    In sea of deadly daungers was distrest;
    But since now safe ye seised haue the shore,
    And well arriued are, (high God be blest)
Let vs deuize of ease and euerlasting rest.

Ah dearest Lord, said then that doughty knight,   xviii
    Of ease or rest I may not yet deuize;
    For by the faith, which I to armes haue plight,
    I bounden am streight after this emprize,
    As that your daughter can ye well aduize,
    Backe to returne to that great Faerie Queene,
    And her to serue six yeares in warlike wize,
    Gainst that proud Paynim king, that workes her teene:
Therefore I ought craue pardon, till I there haue beene.

   xvi 1 pleasures *1596, 1609*   xvii 1 that] the *1596, 1609.*   7 since]
sith *1609*   xviii 8 Pynim *1596*

Vnhappie falles that hard necessitie,   xix
    (Quoth he) the troubler of my happie peace,
    And vowed foe of my felicitie;
    Ne I against the same can iustly preace:
    But since that band ye cannot now release,
    Nor doen vndo ; (for vowes may not be vaine)
    Soone as the terme of those six yeares shall cease,
    Ye then shall hither backe returne againe,
The marriage to accomplish vowd betwixt you twain.

Which for my part I couet to performe,   xx
    In sort as through the world I did proclame,
    That who so kild that monster most deforme,
    And him in hardy battaile ouercame,
    Should haue mine onely daughter to his Dame,
    And of my kingdome heire apparaunt bee:
    Therefore since now to thee perteines the same,
    By dew desert of noble cheualree,
    Both daughter and eke kingdome, lo I yield to thee.

Then forth he called that his daughter faire,   xxi
    The fairest *Vn'* his onely daughter deare,
    His onely daughter, and his onely heyre;
    Who forth proceeding with sad sober cheare,
    As bright as doth the morning starre appeare
    Out of the East, with flaming lockes bedight,
    To tell that dawning day is drawing neare,
    And to the world does bring long wished light;
So faire and fresh that Lady shewd her selfe in sight.

So faire and fresh, as freshest flowre in May;   xxii
    For she had layd her mournefull stole aside,
    And widow-like sad wimple throwne away,
    Wherewith her heauenly beautie she did hide,
    Whiles on her wearie iourney she did ride;
    And on her now a garment she did weare,
    All lilly white, withoutten spot, or pride,
    That seemd like silke and siluer wouen neare,
But neither silke nor siluer therein did appeare.

The blazing brightnesse of her beauties beame,   xxiii
  And glorious light of her sunshyny face
  To tell, were as to striue against the streame.
  My ragged rimes are all too rude and bace,
  Her heauenly lineaments for to enchace.
  Ne wonder; for her owne deare loued knight,
  All were she dayly with himselfe in place,
  Did wonder much at her celestiall sight:
Oft had he seene her faire, but neuer so faire dight.

So fairely dight, when she in presence came,   xxiv
  She to her Sire made humble reuerence,
  And bowed low, that her right well became,
  And added grace vnto her excellence:
  Who with great wisedome, and graue eloquence
  Thus gan to say. But eare he thus had said,
  With flying speede, and seeming great pretence,
  Came running in, much like a man dismaid,
A Messenger with letters, which his message said.

All in the open hall amazed stood,   xxv
  At suddeinnesse of that vnwarie sight,
  And wondred at his breathlesse hastie mood.
  But he for nought would stay his passage right,
  Till fast before the king he did alight;
  Where falling flat, great humblesse he did make,
  And kist the ground, whereon his foot was pight;
  Then to his hands that writ he did betake,
Which he disclosing, red thus, as the paper spake.

To thee, most mighty king of *Eden* faire,   xxvi
  Her greeting sends in these sad lines addrest,
  The wofull daughter, and forsaken heire
  Of that great Emperour of all the West;
  And bids thee be aduized for the best,
  Ere thou thy daughter linck in holy band
  Of wedlocke to that new vnknowen guest:
  For he already plighted his right hand
Vnto another loue, and to another land.

To me sad mayd, or rather widow sad,   <small>xxvii</small>
  He was affiaunced long time before,
  And sacred pledges he both gaue, and had,
  False erraunt knight, infamous, and forswore:
  Witnesse the burning Altars, which he swore,
  And guiltie heauens of his bold periury,
  Which though he hath polluted oft of yore,
  Yet I to them for iudgement iust do fly,
And them coniure t'auenge this shamefull iniury.

Therefore since mine he is, or free or bond,   <small>xxviii</small>
  Or false or trew, or liuing or else dead,
  Withhold, O soueraine Prince, your hasty hond
  From knitting league with him, I you aread;
  Ne weene my right with strength adowne to tread,
  Through weakenesse of my widowhed, or woe:
  For truth is strong, her rightfull cause to plead,
  And shall find friends, if need requireth soe,
So bids thee well to fare, Thy neither friend, nor foe,
                                    Fidessa.

When he these bitter byting words had red,   <small>xxix</small>
  The tydings straunge did him abashed make,
  That still he sate long time astonished
  As in great muse, ne word to creature spake.
  At last his solemne silence thus he brake,
  With doubtfull eyes fast fixed on his guest;
  Redoubted knight, that for mine onely sake
  Thy life and honour late aduenturest,
Let nought be hid from me, that ought to be exprest.

What meane these bloudy vowes, and idle threats,   <small>xxx</small>
  Throwne out from womanish impatient mind?
  What heauens? what altars? what enraged heates
  Here heaped vp with termes of loue vnkind,
  My conscience cleare with guilty bands would bind?
  High God be witnesse, that I guiltlesse ame.
  But if your selfe, Sir knight, ye faultie find,
  Or wrapped be in loues of former Dame,
With crime do not it couer, but disclose the same.

To whom the *Redcrosse* knight this answere sent,   xxxi
   My Lord, my King, be nought hereat dismayd,
   Till well ye wote by graue intendiment,
   What woman, and wherefore doth me vpbrayd
   With breach of loue, and loyalty betrayd.
   It was in my mishaps, as hitherward
   I lately traueild, that vnwares I strayd
   Out of my way, through perils straunge and hard;
That day should faile me, ere I had them all declard.

There did I find, or rather I was found   xxxii
   Of this false woman, that *Fidessa* hight,
   Fidessa hight the falsest Dame on ground,
   Most false *Duessa*, royall richly dight,
   That easie was t' inuegle weaker sight:
   Who by her wicked arts, and wylie skill,
   Too false and strong for earthly skill or might,
   Vnwares me wrought vnto her wicked will,
And to my foe betrayd, when least I feared ill.

Then stepped forth the goodly royall Mayd,   xxxiii
   And on the ground her selfe prostrating low,
   With sober countenaunce thus to him sayd;
   O pardon me, my soueraigne Lord, to show
   The secret treasons, which of late I know
   To haue bene wroght by that false sorceresse.
   She onely she it is, that earst did throw
   This gentle knight into so great distresse,
That death him did awaite in dayly wretchednesse.

And now it seemes, that she suborned hath   xxxiv
   This craftie messenger with letters vaine,
   To worke new woe and improuided scath,
   By breaking of the band betwixt vs twaine;
   Wherein she vsed hath the practicke paine
   Of this false footman, clokt with simplenesse,
   Whom if ye please for to discouer plaine,
   Ye shall him *Archimago* find, I ghesse,
The falsest man aliue ; who tries shall find no lesse.

xxxi 7 strayd] stayd *1590: corr. F.E.*   xxxii 5 t'] to *1590 &c.: corr. F.E.*
xxxiv 2 vaine] faine *1590: corr. F.E.*   9 who] wo *1590, 1596: corr. F.E.*

SPENSER II   M

The king was greatly moued at her speach,   xxxv
    And all with suddein indignation fraight,
    Bad on that Messenger rude hands to reach.
    Eftsoones the Gard, which on his state did wait,
    Attacht that faitor false, and bound him strait:
    Who seeming sorely chauffed at his band,
    As chained Beare, whom cruell dogs do bait,
    With idle force did faine them to withstand,
And often semblaunce made to scape out of their hand.

But they him layd full low in dungeon deepe,   xxxvi
    And bound him hand and foote with yron chains.
    And with continuall watch did warely keepe;
    Who then would thinke, that by his subtile trains
    He could escape fowle death or deadly paines?
    Thus when that Princes wrath was pacifide,
    He gan renew the late forbidden banes,
    And to the knight his daughter deare he tyde,
With sacred rites and vowes for euer to abyde.

His owne two hands the holy knots did knit,   xxxvii
    That none but death for euer can deuide;
    His owne two hands, for such a turne most fit,
    The housling fire did kindle and prouide,
    And holy water thereon sprinckled wide;
    At which the bushy Teade a groome did light,
    And sacred lampe in secret chamber hide,
    Where it should not be quenched day nor night,
For feare of euill fates, but burnen euer bright.

Then gan they sprinckle all the posts with wine,   xxxviii
    And made great feast to solemnize that day;
    They all perfumde with frankincense diuine,
    And precious odours fetcht from far away,
    That all the house did sweat with great aray:
    And all the while sweete Musicke did apply
    Her curious skill, the warbling notes to play,
    To driue away the dull Melancholy;
The whiles one sung a song of loue and iollity.

        xxxvii 6 the] a *1609*   xxxviii 3 frankencense *1596, 1609*

During the which there was an heauenly noise   xxxix
    Heard sound through all the Pallace pleasantly,
    Like as it had bene many an Angels voice,
    Singing before th'eternall maiesty,
    In their trinall triplicities on hye;
    Yet wist no creature, whence that heauenly sweet
    Proceeded, yet eachone felt secretly
    Himselfe thereby reft of his sences meet,
And rauished with rare impression in his sprite.

Great ioy was made that day of young and old,   xl
    And solemne feast proclaimd throughout the land,
    That their exceeding merth may not be told:
    Suffice it heare by signes to vnderstand
    The vsuall ioyes at knitting of loues band.
    Thrise happy man the knight himselfe did hold,
    Possessed of his Ladies hart and hand,
    And euer, when his eye did her behold,
His heart did seeme to melt in pleasures manifold.

Her ioyous presence and sweet company   xli
    In full content he there did long enioy,
    Ne wicked enuie, ne vile gealosy
    His deare delights were able to annoy:
    Yet swimming in that sea of blisfull ioy,
    He nought forgot, how he whilome had sworne,
    In case he could that monstrous beast destroy,
    Vnto his Farie Queene backe to returne:
The which he shortly did, and *Vna* left to mourne.

Now strike your sailes ye iolly Mariners,   xlii
    For we be come vnto a quiet rode,
    Where we must land some of our passengers,
    And light this wearie vessell of her lode.
    Here she a while may make her safe abode,
    Till she repaired haue her tackles spent,
    And wants supplide. And then againe abroad
    On the long voyage whereto she is bent:
Well may she speede and fairely finish her intent.

FINIS LIB. I.

xl 9 His] Her *1596, 1609*   xli 3 ne] nor *1609*

THE SECOND
BOOKE OF THE
FAERIE QVEENE.
Contayning,
THE LEGEND OF SIR GVYON,
OR
Of Temperaunce.

Ight well I wote most mighty Soueraine,　　　i
That all this famous antique history,
Of some th'aboundance of an idle braine
Will iudged be, and painted forgery,
Rather then matter of iust memory,
Sith none, that breatheth liuing aire, does know,
Where is that happy land of Faery,
Which I so much do vaunt, yet no where show,
But vouch antiquities, which no body can know.

But let that man with better sence aduize,　　　ii
That of the world least part to vs is red:
And dayly how through hardy enterprize,
Many great Regions are discouered,
Which to late age were neuer mentioned.
Who euer heard of th'Indian *Peru*?
Or who in venturous vessell measured
The *Amazons* huge riuer now found trew?
Or fruitfullest *Virginia* who did euer vew?

Proem. ii 8 *Amarons 1590*: *Amazon F. E.*

Yet all these were, when no man did them know;   iii
  Yet haue from wisest ages hidden beene:
  And later times things more vnknowne shall show.
  Why then should witlesse man so much misweene
  That nothing is, but that which he hath seene?
  What if within the Moones faire shining spheare?
  What if in euery other starre vnseene
  Of other worldes he happily should heare?
He wonder would much more: yet such to some appeare.

Of Faerie lond yet if he more inquire,   iv
  By certaine signes here set in sundry place
  He may it find; ne let him then admire,
  But yield his sence to be too blunt and bace,
  That no'te without an hound fine footing trace.
  And thou, O fairest Princesse vnder sky,
  In this faire mirrhour maist behold thy face,
  And thine owne realmes in lond of Faery,
And in this antique Image thy great auncestry.

The which O pardon me thus to enfold   v
  In couert vele, and wrap in shadowes light,
  That feeble eyes your glory may behold,
  Which else could not endure those beames bright,
  But would be dazled with exceeding light.
  O pardon, and vouchsafe with patient eare
  The braue aduentures of this Faery knight
  The good Sir *Guyon* gratiously to heare,
In whom great rule of Temp'raunce goodly doth appeare.

  iv 6 thou] then *1590*   v 4 else] elles *1590*   beamez *1609*

Cant. I.

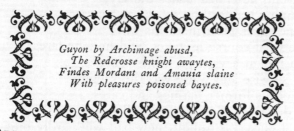

Guyon by Archimage abusd,
The Redcrosse knight awaytes,
Findes Mordant and Amauia slaine
With pleasures poisoned baytes.

THat cunning Architect of cancred guile,   i
  Whom Princes late displeasure left in bands,
For falsed letters and suborned wile,
Soone as the *Redcrosse* knight he vnderstands
To beene departed out of *Eden* lands,
To serue againe his soueraine Elfin Queene,
His artes he moues, and out of caytiues hands
Himselfe he frees by secret meanes vnseene;
His shackles emptic left, him selfe escaped cleene.

And forth he fares full of malicious mind,   ii
  To worken mischiefe and auenging woe,
Where euer he that godly knight may find,
His onely hart sore, and his onely foe,
Sith *Vna* now he algates must forgoe,
Whom his victorious hands did earst restore
To natiue crowne and kingdome late ygoe:
Where she enioyes sure peace for euermore,
As weather-beaten ship arriu'd on happie shore.

Him therefore now the obiect of his spight   iii
  And deadly food he makes: him to offend
By forged treason, or by open fight
He seekes, of all his drift the aymed end:
Thereto his subtile engins he does bend,
His practick wit, and his faire filed tong,
With thousand other sleights: for well he kend,
His credit now in doubtfull ballaunce hong;
For hardly could be hurt, who was already stong.

i 4 vnderstands, *1590 &c.*   7 caytiue *1609*   ii 7 natiues *1596, 1609*
  iii 2 food] feude *1609*   5 bend *1590, 1596*   9 be] he *1609*

Still as he went, he craftie stales did lay,   iv
  With cunning traines him to entrap vnwares,
  And priuie spials plast in all his way,
  To weete what course he takes, and how he fares;
  To ketch him at a vantage in his snares.
  But now so wise and warie was the knight
  By triall of his former harmes and cares,
  That he descride, and shonned still his slight:
The fish that once was caught, new bait will hardly bite.

Nath'lesse th'Enchaunter would not spare his paine,   v
  In hope to win occasion to his will;
  Which when he long awaited had in vaine,
  He chaungd his minde from one to other ill:
  For to all good he enimy was still.
  Vpon the way him fortuned to meet,
  Faire marching vnderneath a shady hill,
  A goodly knight, all armd in harnesse meete,
That from his head no place appeared to his feete.

His carriage was full comely and vpright,   vi
  His countenaunce demure and temperate,
  But yet so sterne and terrible in sight,
  That cheard his friends, and did his foes amate:
  He was an Elfin borne of noble state,
  And mickle worship in his natiue land;
  Well could he tourney and in lists debate,
  And knighthood tooke of good Sir *Huons* hand,
When with king *Oberon* he came to Faerie land.

Him als accompanyd vpon the way   vii
  A comely Palmer, clad in blacke attire,
  Of ripest yeares, and haires all hoarie gray,
  That with a staffe his feeble steps did stire,
  Least his long way his aged limbes should tire:
  And if by lookes one may the mind aread,
  He seemd to be a sage and sober sire,
  And euer with slow pace the knight did lead,
Who taught his trampling steed with equall steps to tread.

iv 1 lay. *1590, 1596*   5 avantage *1609*   6, 7 *transposed in 1596, 1606*

Such whenas *Archimago* them did view,　　viii
He weened well to worke some vncouth wile,
Eftsoones vntwisting his deceiptfull clew,
He gan to weaue a web of wicked guile,
And with faire countenance and flattring stile,
To them approching, thus the knight bespake:
Faire sonne of *Mars*, that seeke with warlike spoile,
And great atchieu'ments great your selfe to make,
Vouchsafe to stay your steed for humble misers sake.

He stayd his steed for humble misers sake,　　ix
And bad tell on the tenor of his plaint;
Who feigning then in euery limbe to quake,
Through inward feare, and seeming pale and faint
With piteous mone his percing speach gan paint;
Deare Lady how shall I declare thy cace,
Whom late I left in langourous constraint?
Would God thy selfe now present were in place,
To tell this ruefull tale; thy sight could win thee grace.

Or rather would, O would it so had chaunst,　　x
That you, most noble Sir, had present beene,
When that lewd ribauld with vile lust aduaunst
Layd first his filthy hands on virgin cleene,
To spoile her daintie corse so faire and sheene,
As on the earth, great mother of vs all,
With liuing eye more faire was neuer seene,
Of chastitie and honour virginall:
Witnesse ye heauens, whom she in vaine to helpe did call.

How may it be, (said then the knight halfe wroth,)　　xi
That knight should knighthood euer so haue shent?
None but that saw (quoth he) would weene for troth,
How shamefully that Maid he did torment.
Her looser golden lockes he rudely rent,
And drew her on the ground, and his sharpe sword
Against her snowy brest he fiercely bent,
And threatned death with many a bloudie word;
Toung hates to tell the rest, that eye to see abhord.

viii 5 with a faire *1596*　　7 spoile. *1596*　　ix 7 languorous *1590*
x 5 corps *1590*　　xi 6 sword, *1590 &c.*

Therewith amoued from his sober mood,   xii
  And liues he yet (said he) that wrought this act,
  And doen the heauens afford him vitall food?
  He liues, (quoth he) and boasteth of the fact,
  Ne yet hath any knight his courage crackt.
  Where may that treachour then (said he) be found,
  Or by what meanes may I his footing tract?
  That shall I shew (said he) as sure, as hound
The stricken Deare doth chalenge by the bleeding wound.

He staid not lenger talke, but with fierce ire   xiii
  And zealous hast away is quickly gone
  To seeke that knight, where him that craftie Squire
  Supposd to be.   They do arriue anone,
  Where sate a gentle Lady all alone,
  With garments rent, and haire discheueled,
  Wringing her hands, and making piteous mone;
  Her swollen eyes were much disfigured,
And her faire face with teares was fowly blubbered.

The knight approching nigh, thus to her said,   xiv
  Faire Ladie, through foule sorrow ill bedight,
  Great pittie is to see you thus dismaid,
  And marre the blossome of your beautie bright:
  For thy appease your griefe and heauie plight,
  And tell the cause of your conceiued paine.
  For if he liue, that hath you doen despight,
  He shall you doe due recompence againe,
Or else his wrong with greater puissance maintaine.

Which when she heard, as in despightfull wise,   xv
  She wilfully her sorrow did augment,
  And offred hope of comfort did despise:
  Her golden lockes most cruelly she rent,
  And scratcht her face with ghastly dreriment,
  Ne would she speake, ne see, ne yet be seene,
  But hid her visage, and her head downe bent,
  Either for grieuous shame, or for great teene,
As if her hart with sorrow had transfixed beene.

xiv 7 despight; *1596, 1609*

Till her that Squire bespake, Madame my liefe,   xvi
  For Gods deare loue be not so wilfull bent,
  But doe vouchsafe now to receiue reliefe,
  The which good fortune doth to you present.
  For what bootes it to weepe and to wayment,
  When ill is chaunst, but doth the ill increase,
  And the weake mind with double woe torment?
  When she her Squire heard speake, she gan appease
Her voluntarie paine, and feele some secret ease.

Eftsoone she said, Ah gentle trustie Squire,   xvii
  What comfort can I wofull wretch conceaue,
  Or why should euer I henceforth desire
  To see faire heauens face, and life not leaue,
  Sith that false Traytour did my honour reaue?
  False traytour certes (said the Faerie knight)
  I read the man, that euer would deceaue
  A gentle Ladie, or her wrong through might:
Death were too little paine for such a foule despight.

But now, faire Ladie, comfort to you make,   xviii
  And read, who hath ye wrought this shamefull plight;
  That short reuenge the man may ouertake,
  Where so he be, and soone vpon him light.
  Certes (saide she) I wote not how he hight,
  But vnder him a gray steede did he wield,
  Whose sides with dapled circles weren dight;
  Vpright he rode, and in his siluer shield
He bore a bloudie Crosse, that quartred all the field.

Now by my head (said *Guyon*) much I muse,   xix
  How that same knight should do so foule amis,
  Or euer gentle Damzell so abuse:
  For may I boldly say, he surely is
  A right good knight, and true of word ywis:
  I present was, and can it witnesse well,
  When armes he swore, and streight did enterpris
  Th'aduenture of the *Errant damozell*,
In which he hath great glorie wonne, as I heare tell.

    xvi 1 liefe] life *1590*   xvii 3 desyre, *1590* : desire, *1596*
      xviii 2 plight. *1590, 1596*   6 did he] he did *1590*

Nathlesse he shortly shall againe be tryde,   xx
  And fairely quite him of th'imputed blame,
  Else be ye sure he dearely shall abyde,
  Or make you good amendment for the same:
  All wrongs haue mends, but no amends of shame.
  Now therefore Ladie, rise out of your paine,
  And see the saluing of your blotted name.
  Full loth she seemd thereto, but yet did faine;
For she was inly glad her purpose so to gaine.

Her purpose was not such, as she did faine,   xxi
  Ne yet her person such, as it was seene,
  But vnder simple shew and semblant plaine
  Lurckt false *Duessa* secretly vnseene,
  As a chast Virgin, that had wronged beene:
  So had false *Archimago* her disguisd,
  To cloke her guile with sorrow and sad teene;
  And eke himselfe had craftily deuisd
To be her Squire, and do her seruice well aguisd.

Her late forlorne and naked he had found,   xxii
  Where she did wander in waste wildernesse,
  Lurking in rockes and caues farre vnder ground,
  And with greene mosse cou'ring her nakednesse,
  To hide her shame and loathly filthinesse;
  Sith her Prince *Arthur* of proud ornaments
  And borrow'd beautie spoyld.   Her nathelesse
  Th'enchaunter finding fit for his intents,
Did thus reuest, and deckt with due habiliments.

For all he did, was to deceiue good knights,   xxiii
  And draw them from pursuit of praise and fame,
  To slug in slouth and sensuall delights,
  And end their daies with irrenowmed shame.
  And now exceeding griefe him ouercame,
  To see the *Redcrosse* thus aduaunced hye;
  Therefore this craftie engine he did frame,
  Against his praise to stirre vp enmitye
Of such, as vertues like mote vnto him allye.

xx 2 quite] quit *1590*   7 blotting *1590*

So now he *Guyon* guides an vncouth way   xxiv
   Through woods and mountaines, till they came at last
   Into a pleasant dale, that lowly lay
   Betwixt two hils, whose high heads ouerplast,
   The valley did with coole shade ouercast,
   Through midst thereof a little riuer rold,
   By which there sate a knight with helme vnlast,
   Himselfe refreshing with the liquid cold,
After his trauell long, and labours manifold.

Loe yonder he, cryde *Archimage* alowd,   xxv
   That wrought the shamefull fact, which I did shew;
   And now he doth himselfe in secret shrowd,
 - To flie the vengeance for his outrage dew;
   But vaine: for ye shall dearely do him rew,
   So God ye speed, and send you good successe;
   Which we farre off will here abide to vew.
   So they him left, inflam'd with wrathfulnesse,
That streight against that knight his speare he did addresse.

Who seeing him from farre so fierce to pricke,   xxvi
   His warlike armes about him gan embrace,
   And in the rest his readie speare did sticke;
   Tho when as still he saw him towards pace,
   He gan rencounter him in equall race.
   They bene ymet, both readie to affrap,
   When suddenly that warriour gan abace
   His threatned speare, as if some new mishap
Had him betidde, or hidden daunger did entrap.

And cryde, Mercie Sir knight, and mercie Lord,   xxvii
   For mine offence and heedlesse hardiment,
   That had almost committed crime abhord,
   And with reprochfull shame mine honour shent,
   Whiles cursed steele against that badge I bent,
   The sacred badge of my Redeemers death,
   Which on your shield is set for ornament:
   But his fierce foe his steede could stay vneath,
Who prickt with courage kene, did cruell battell breath.

        xxvi 9 betidde] betide *1590*

But when he heard him speake, streight way he knew   xxviii
    His error, and himselfe inclyning sayd;
    Ah deare Sir *Guyon*, well becommeth you,
    But me behoueth rather to vpbrayd,
    Whose hastie hand so farre from reason strayd,
    That almost it did haynous violence
    On that faire image of that heauenly Mayd,
    That decks and armes your shield with faire defence:
Your court'sie takes on you anothers due offence.

So bene they both attone, and doen vpreare   xxix
    Their beuers bright, each other for to greete;
    Goodly comportance each to other beare,
    And entertaine themselues with court'sies meet.
    Then said the *Redcrosse* knight, Now mote I weet,
    Sir *Guyon*, why with so fierce saliaunce,
    And fell intent ye did at earst me meet;
    For sith I know your goodly gouernaunce,
Great cause, I weene, you guided, or some vncouth chaunce.

Certes (said he) well mote I shame to tell   xxx
    The fond encheason, that me hither led.
    A false infamous faitour late befell
    Me for to meet, that seemed ill bested,
    And playnd of grieuous outrage, which he red
    A knight had wrought against a Ladie gent;
    Which to auenge, he to this place me led,
    Where you he made the marke of his intent,
And now is fled; foule shame him follow, where he went.

So can he turne his earnest vnto game,   xxxi
    Through goodly handling and wise temperance.
    By this his aged guide in presence came;
    Who soone as on that knight his eye did glance,
    Eft soones of him had perfect cognizance,
    Sith him in Faerie court he late auizd;
    And said, Faire sonne, God giue you happie chance,
    And that deare Crosse vpon your shield deuizd,
Wherewith aboue all knights ye goodly seeme aguizd.

    xxix 1 attone] at one *1590*   xxxi 2 handling] handing *1596*   4 on]
one *1590*   7 fayre *1590* : faire *1596*

Ioy may you haue, and euerlasting fame,   xxxii
   Of late most hard atchieu'ment by you donne,
   For which enrolled is your glorious name
   In heauenly Registers aboue the Sunne,
   Where you a Saint with Saints your seat haue wonne:
   But wretched we, where ye haue left your marke,
   Must now anew begin, like race to runne;
   God guide thee, *Guyon*, well to end thy warke,
And to the wished hauen bring thy weary barke.

Palmer, (him answered the *Redcrosse* knight)   xxxiii
   His be the praise, that this atchieu'ment wrought,
   Who made my hand the organ of his might;
   More then goodwill to me attribute nought:
   For all I did, I did but as I ought.
   But you, faire Sir, whose pageant next ensewes,
   Well mote yee thee, as well can wish your thought,
   That home ye may report thrise happie newes;
For well ye worthie bene for worth and gentle thewes.

So courteous conge both did giue and take,   xxxiv
   With right hands plighted, pledges of good will.
   Then *Guyon* forward gan his voyage make,
   With his blacke Palmer, that him guided still.
   Still he him guided ouer dale and hill,
   And with his steedie staffe did point his way:
   His race with reason, and with words his will,
   From foule intemperance he oft did stay,
And suffred not in wrath his hastie steps to stray.

In this faire wize they traueild long yfere,   xxxv
   Through many hard assayes, which did betide;
   Of which he honour still away did beare,
   And spred his glorie through all countries wide.
   At last as chaunst them by a forest side
   To passe, for succour from the scorching ray,
   They heard a ruefull voice, that dearnly cride
   With percing shriekes, and many a dolefull lay;
Which to attend, a while their forward steps they stay.

xxxii 7 Must] Most *1590*   xxxiii 8 thrise] these *1590 &c.: corr. F. E.*
           xxxiv 6 steedy *1590*: steadie *1609*

But if that carelesse heauens (quoth she) despise   xxxvi
   The doome of iust reuenge, and take delight
   To see sad pageants of mens miseries,
   As bound by them to liue in liues despight,
   Yet can they not warne death from wretched wight.
   Come then, come soone, come sweetest death to mee,
   And take away this long lent loathed light:
   Sharpe be thy wounds, but sweet the medicines bee,
That long captiued soules from wearie thraldome free.

But thou, sweet Babe, whom frowning froward fate   xxxvii
   Hath made sad witnesse of thy fathers fall,
   Sith heauen thee deignes to hold in liuing state,
   Long maist thou liue, and better thriue withall,
   Then to thy lucklesse parents did befall:
   Liue thou, and to thy mother dead attest,
   That cleare she dide from blemish criminall;
   Thy litle hands embrewd in bleeding brest
Loe I for pledges leaue.   So giue me leaue to rest.

With that a deadly shrieke she forth did throw,   xxxviii
   That through the wood reecchoed againe,
   And after gaue a grone so deepe and low,
   That seemd her tender heart was rent in twaine,
   Or thrild with point of thorough piercing paine;
   As gentle Hynd, whose sides with cruell steele
   Through launched, forth her bleeding life does raine,
   Whiles the sad pang approching she does feele,
Brayes out her latest breath, and vp her eyes doth seele.

Which when that warriour heard, dismounting straict   xxxix
   From his tall steed, he rusht into the thicke,
   And soone arriued, where that sad pourtraict
   Of death and dolour lay, halfe dead, halfe quicke,
   In whose white alabaster brest did sticke
   A cruell knife, that made a griesly wound,
   From which forth gusht a streme of gorebloud thick,
   That all her goodly garments staind around,
And into a deepe sanguine dide the grassie ground.

xxxvi 4 liues] lifes *1609*   xxxviii 7 launced *1609*
xxxix 4 dolour] labour *1596, 1609*

Pittifull spectacle of deadly smart,   xl
   Beside a bubbling fountaine low she lay,
   Which she increased with her bleeding hart,
   And the cleane waues with purple gore did ray;
   Als in her lap a louely babe did play
   His cruell sport, in stead of sorrow dew;
   For in her streaming blood he did embay
   His litle hands, and tender ioynts embrew;
Pitifull spectacle, as euer eye did view.

Besides them both, vpon the soiled gras   xli
   The dead corse of an armed knight was spred,
   Whose armour all with bloud besprinckled was;
   His ruddie lips did smile, and rosy red
   Did paint his chearefull cheekes, yet being ded:
   Seemd to haue beene a goodly personage,
   Now in his freshest flowre of lustie hed,
   Fit to inflame faire Lady with loues rage,
But that fiers fate did crop the blossome of his age.

Whom when the good Sir *Guyon* did behold,   xlii
   His hart gan wexe as starke, as marble stone,
   And his fresh bloud did frieze with fearefull cold,
   That all his senses seemd bereft attonc:
   At last his mightie ghost gan deepe to grone,
   As Lyon grudging in his great disdaine,
   Mournes inwardly, and makes to himselfe mone;
   Till ruth and fraile affection did constraine
His stout courage to stoupe, and shew his inward paine.

Out of her gored wound the cruell steele   xliii
   He lightly snatcht, and did the floudgate stop
   With his faire garment: then gan softly feele
   Her feeble pulse, to proue if any drop
   Of liuing bloud yet in her veynes did hop;
   Which when he felt to moue, he hoped faire
   To call backe life to her forsaken shop;
   So well he did her deadly wounds repaire,
That at the last she gan to breath out liuing aire.

   xl 4 gore] gold *1596, 1609*   5 louely] little *1609*   xli 5 ded,
1590, 1596   xlii 4 attone, *1596*   8 constraine, *1590, 1596*   9 stout
courage] courage stout *1609*

Which he perceiuing greatly gan reioice,   xliv
    And goodly counsell, that for wounded hart
    Is meetest med'cine, tempred with sweet voice;
    Ay me, deare Lady, which the image art
    Of ruefull pitie, and impatient smart,
    What direfull chance, armd with reuenging fate,
    Or cursed hand hath plaid this cruell part,
    Thus fowle to hasten your vntimely date;
Speake, O deare Lady speake: help neuer comes too late.

Therewith her dim eie-lids she vp gan reare,   xlv
    On which the drery death did sit, as sad
    As lump of lead, and made darke clouds appeare;
    But when as him all in bright armour clad
    Before her standing she espied had,
    As one out of a deadly dreame affright,
    She weakely started, yet she nothing drad:
    Streight downe againe her selfe in great despight
She groueling threw to ground, as hating life and light.

The gentle knight her soone with carefull paine   xlvi
    Vplifted light, and softly did vphold:
    Thrise he her reard, and thrise she sunke againe,
    Till he his armes about her sides gan fold,
    And to her said; Yet if the stony cold
    Haue not all seized on your frozen hart,
    Let one word fall that may your griefe vnfold,
    And tell the secret of your mortall smart;
He oft finds present helpe, who does his griefe impart.

Then casting vp a deadly looke, full low   xlvii
    Shee sight from bottome of her wounded brest,
    And after, many bitter throbs did throw
    With lips full pale and foltring tongue opprest,
    These words she breathed forth from riuen chest;
    Leaue, ah leaue off, what euer wight thou bee,
    To let a wearie wretch from her dew rest,
    And trouble dying soules tranquilitee.
Take not away now got, which none would giue to me.

xliv 6 reuenging] auenging *1590*   xlv 8 despight. *1590*: despight,
1596, 1609   xlvii 1 low, *1596*   2 sigh't *1609*

Ah farre be it (said he) Deare dame fro mee,   xlviii
   To hinder soule from her desired rest,
   Or hold sad life in long captiuitee:
   For all I seeke, is but to haue redrest
   The bitter pangs, that doth your heart infest.
   Tell then, O Lady tell, what fatall priefe
   Hath with so huge misfortune you opprest?
   That I may cast to compasse your reliefe,
Or die with you in sorrow, and partake your griefe.

With feeble hands then stretched forth on hye,   xlix
   As heauen accusing guiltie of her death,
   And with dry drops congealed in her eye,
   In these sad words she spent her vtmost breath:
   Heare then, O man, the sorrowes that vneath
   My tongue can tell, so farre all sense they pas:
   Loe this dead corpse, that lies here vnderneath,
   The gentlest knight, that euer on greene gras
Gay steed with spurs did pricke, the good Sir *Mordant* was.

Was, (ay the while, that he is not so now)   l
   My Lord my loue; my deare Lord, my deare loue,
   So long as heauens iust with equall brow
   Vouchsafed to behold vs from aboue,
   One day when him high courage did emmoue,
   As wont ye knights to seeke aduentures wilde,
   He pricked forth, his puissant force to proue,
   Me then he left enwombed of this child,
This lucklesse child, whom thus ye see with bloud defild.

Him fortuned (hard fortune ye may ghesse)   li
   To come, where vile *Acrasia* does wonne,
   Acrasia a false enchaunteresse,
   That many errant knights hath foule fordonne:
   Within a wandring Island, that doth ronne
   And stray in perilous gulfe, her dwelling is;
   Faire Sir, if euer there ye trauell, shonne
   The cursed land where many wend amis,
And know it by the name; it hight the *Bowre of blis.*

xlix 9 Mortdant *1590, 1596*   l 3 brow, *1590, 1596*
li 6 is, *1590, 1596*

Her blisse is all in pleasure and delight,   lii
  Wherewith she makes her louers drunken mad,
  And then with words and weedes of wondrous might,
  On them she workes her will to vses bad:
  My lifest Lord she thus beguiled had;
  For he was flesh: (all flesh doth frailtie breed.)
  Whom when I heard to beene so ill bestad,
  Weake wretch I wrapt my selfe in Palmers weed,
And cast to seeke him forth through daunger and great dreed.

Now had faire *Cynthia* by euen tournes   liii
  Full measured three quarters of her yeare,
  And thrise three times had fild her crooked hornes,
  Whenas my wombe her burdein would forbeare,
  And bad me call *Lucina* to me neare.
  Lucina came: a manchild forth I brought:
  The woods, the Nymphes, my bowres, my midwiues weare,
  Hard helpe at need. So deare thee babe I bought,
Yet nought too deare I deemd, while so my dear I sought.

Him so I sought, and so at last I found,   liv
  Where him that witch had thralled to her will,
  In chaines of lust and lewd desires ybound,
  And so transformed from his former skill,
  That me he knew not, neither his owne ill;
  Till through wise handling and faire gouernance,
  I him recured to a better will,
  Purged from drugs of foule intemperance:
Then meanes I gan deuise for his deliuerance.

Which when the vile Enchaunteresse perceiu'd,   lv
  How that my Lord from her I would repriue,
  With cup thus charmd, him parting she deceiu'd;
  Sad verse, giue death to him that death does giue,
  And losse of loue, to her that loues to liue,
  So soone as Bacchus with the Nymphe does lincke:
  So parted we and on our iourney driue,
  Till comming to this well, he stoupt to drincke:
The charme fulfild, dead suddenly he downe did sincke.

      lii 5 liefest *1590*   lv 6 *lincke*, *1590*, *1596*

Which when I wretch, Not one word more she sayd   lvi
  But breaking off the end for want of breath,
  And slyding soft, as downe to sleepe her layd,
  And ended all her woe in quiet death.
  That seeing good Sir *Guyon*, could vneath
  From teares abstaine, for griefe his hart did grate,
  And from so heauie sight his head did wreath,
  Accusing fortune, and too cruell fate,
Which plunged had faire Ladie in so wretched state.

Then turning to his Palmer said, Old syre   lvii
  Behold the image of mortalitie,
  And feeble nature cloth'd with fleshly tyre,
  When raging passion with fierce tyrannie
  Robs reason of her due regalitie,
  And makes it seruant to her basest part:
  The strong it weakens with infirmitie,
  And with bold furie armes the weakest hart;   [smart.
The strong through pleasure soonest falles, the weake through

But temperance (said he) with golden squire   lviii
  Betwixt them both can measure out a meane,
  Neither to melt in pleasures whot desire,
  Nor fry in hartlesse griefe and dolefull teene.
  Thrise happie man, who fares them both atweene:
  But sith this wretched woman ouercome
  Of anguish, rather then of crime hath beene,
  Reserue her cause to her eternall doome,
And in the meane vouchsafe her honorable toombe.

Palmer (quoth he) death is an equall doome   lix
  To good and bad, the common Inne of rest;
  But after death the tryall is to come,
  When best shall be to them, that liued best:
  But both alike, when death hath both supprest,
  Religious reuerence doth buriall teene,
  Which who so wants, wants so much of his rest:
  For all so great shame after death I weene,
As selfe to dyen bad, vnburied bad to beene.

lvi 2 off] of, *1590* : off, *1596*   9 plonged *1590*   lvii 1 his] the *1609*
    lviii 3 whot] hot *1609 passim*   4 fry] fryze *sugg. Church*
        lix 1 equall] euill *1596, 1609*

So both agree their bodies to engraue;   lx
  The great earthes wombe they open to the sky,
  And with sad Cypresse seemely it embraue,
  Then couering with a clod their closed eye,
  They lay therein those corses tenderly,
  And bid them sleepe in euerlasting peace.
  But ere they did their vtmost obsequy,
  Sir *Guyon* more affection to increace,
Bynempt a sacred vow, which none should aye releace.

The dead knights sword out of his sheath he drew,   lxi
  With which he cut a locke of all their heare,
  Which medling with their bloud and earth, he threw
  Into the graue, and gan deuoutly sweare;
  Such and such euill God on *Guyon* reare,
  And worse and worse young Orphane be thy paine,
  If I or thou dew vengeance doe forbeare,
  Till guiltie bloud her guerdon doe obtaine:
So shedding many teares, they closd the earth againe.

Cant. II.

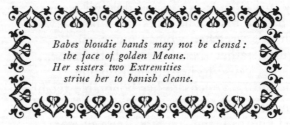

> *Babes bloudie hands may not be clensd:*
> *the face of golden Meane.*
> *Her sisters two Extremities*
> *striue her to banish cleane.*

THus when Sir *Guyon* with his faithfull guide   i
  Had with due rites and dolorous lament
  The end of their sad Tragedie vptyde,
  The litle babe vp in his armes he hent;
  Who with sweet pleasance and bold blandishment
  Gan smyle on them, that rather ought to weepe,
  As carelesse of his woe, or innocent
  Of that was doen, that ruth emperced deepe
In that knights heart, and wordes with bitter teares did steepe.

Arg. 1 *clensd,* 1590 &c.   3 *Extremities:* 1590 &c.

Ah lucklesse babe, borne vnder cruell starre,   ii
   And in dead parents balefull ashes bred,
   Full litle weenest thou, what sorrowes are
   Left thee for portion of thy liuelihed,
   Poore Orphane in the wide world scattered,
   As budding braunch rent from the natiue tree,
   And throwen forth, till it be withered:
   Such is the state of men : thus enter wee
Into this life with woe, and end with miseree.

Then soft himselfe inclyning on his knee   iii
   Downe to that well, did in the water weene
   (So loue does loath disdainfull nicitee)
   His guiltie hands from bloudie gore to cleene.
   He washt them oft and oft, yet nought they beene
   For all his washing cleaner. Still he stroue,
   Yet still the litle hands were bloudie seene;
   The which him into great amaz'ment droue,
And into diuerse doubt his wauering wonder cloue.

He wist not whether blot of foule offence   iv
   Might not be purgd with water nor with bath;
   Or that high God, in lieu of innocence,
   Imprinted had that token of his wrath,
   To shew how sore bloudguiltinesse he hat'th;
   Or that the charme and venim, which they druncke,
   Their bloud with secret filth infected hath,
   Being diffused through the senselesse truncke,
That through the great contagion direfull deadly stunck,

Whom thus at gaze, the Palmer gan to bord   v
   With goodly reason, and thus faire bespake;
   Ye bene right hard amated, gratious Lord,
   And of your ignorance great maruell make,
   Whiles cause not well conceiued ye mistake.
   But know, that secret vertues are infusd
   In euery fountaine, and in euery lake,
   Which who hath skill them rightly to haue chusd,
To proofe of passing wonders hath full often vsd.

iv 3 lieu] loue *sugg. Church*   5 hat'th] hat'h *1590*   v 3 hard] hart *1590*

Of those some were so from their sourse indewd   vi
  By great Dame Nature, from whose fruitfull pap
  Their welheads spring, and are with moisture deawd;
  Which feedes each liuing plant with liquid sap,
  And filles with flowres faire *Floraes* painted lap:
  But other some by gift of later grace,
  Or by good prayers, or by other hap,
  Had vertue pourd into their waters bace,
And thenceforth were renowmd, and sought from place to place.

Such is this well, wrought by occasion straunge,   vii
  Which to her Nymph befell. Vpon a day,
  As she the woods with bow and shafts did raunge,
  The hartlesse Hind and Robucke to dismay,
  Dan Faunus chaunst to meet her by the way,
  And kindling fire at her faire burning eye,
  Inflamed was to follow beauties chace,
  And chaced her, that fast from him did fly;
As Hind from her, so she fled from her enimy.

At last when fayling breath began to faint,   viii
  And saw no meanes to scape, of shame affrayd,
  She set her downe to weepe for sore constraint,
  And to *Diana* calling lowd for ayde,
  Her deare besought, to let her dye a mayd.
  The goddesse heard, and suddeine where she sate,
  Welling out streames of teares, and quite dismayd
  With stony feare of that rude rustick mate,
Transformd her to a stone from stedfast virgins state.

Lo now she is that stone, from whose two heads,   ix
  As from two weeping eyes, fresh streames do flow,
  Yet cold through feare, and old conceiued dreads;
  And yet the stone her semblance seemes to show,
  Shapt like a maid, that such ye may her know;
  And yet her vertues in her water byde:
  For it is chast and pure, as purest snow,
  Ne lets her waues with any filth be dyde,
But euer like her selfe vnstained hath beene tryde.

vi 9 to *om. 1590*: *corr. F. E.*
vii 7 chace] pray *sugg. Collier. Cf.* II ii 42, II iii 28 &c.
viii 3 set] sate *1609* ix 1 whose] those *1596, 1609* 8 be] he *1596*

From thence it comes, that this babes bloudy hand   x
  May not be clensd with water of this well:
  Ne certes Sir striue you it to withstand,
  But let them still be bloudy, as befell,
  That they his mothers innocence may tell,
  As she bequeathd in her last testament;
  That as a sacred Symbole it may dwell
  In her sonnes flesh, to minde reuengement,
And be for all chast Dames an endlesse moniment.

He hearkned to his reason, and the childe   xi
  Vptaking, to the Palmer gaue to beare;
  But his sad fathers armes with bloud defilde,
  An heauie load himselfe did lightly reare,
  And turning to that place, in which whyleare
  He left his loftie steed with golden sell,
  And goodly gorgeous barbes, him found not theare.
  By other accident that earst befell,
He is conuaide, but how or where, here fits not tell.

Which when Sir *Guyon* saw, all were he wroth,   xii
  Yet algates mote he soft himselfe appease,
  And fairely fare on foot, how euer loth;
  His double burden did him sore disease.
  So long they traueiled with litle ease,
  Till that at last they to a Castle came,
  Built on a rocke adioyning to the seas;
  It was an auncient worke of antique fame,
And wondrous strong by nature, and by skilfull frame.

Therein three sisters dwelt of sundry sort,   xiii
  The children of one sire by mothers three;
  Who dying whylome did diuide this fort
  To them by equall shares in equall fee:
  But strifull minde, and diuerse qualitee
  Drew them in parts, and each made others foe:
  Still did they striue, and dayly disagree;
  The eldest did against the youngest goe,
And both against the middest meant to worken woe.

  xii 7 seas, *1590, 1596*   8 fame] frame *1590*   xiii 5 strifefull *1609*

Where when the knight arriu'd, he was right well   xiv
  Receiu'd, as knight of so much worth became,
  Of second sister, who did far excell
  The other two; *Medina* was her name,
  A sober sad, and comely curteous Dame;
  Who rich arayd, and yet in modest guize,
  In goodly garments, that her well became,
  Faire marching forth in honorable wize,
Him at the threshold met, and well did enterprize.

She led him vp into a goodly bowre,   xv
  And comely courted with meet modestie,
  Ne in her speach, ne in her hauiour,
  Was lightnesse seene, or looser vanitie,
  But gratious womanhood, and grauitie,
  Aboue the reason of her youthly yeares:
  Her golden lockes she roundly did vptye
  In breaded tramels, that no looser heares
Did out of order stray about her daintie eares.

Whilest she her selfe thus busily did frame,   xvi
  Seemely to entertaine her new-come guest,
  Newes hereof to her other sisters came,
  Who all this while were at their wanton rest,
  Accourting each her friend with lauish fest:
  They were two knights of perelesse puissance,
  And famous far abroad for warlike gest,
  Which to these Ladies loue did countenaunce,
And to his mistresse each himselfe stroue to aduaunce.

He that made loue vnto the eldest Dame,   xvii
  Was hight Sir *Huddibras*, an hardy man;
  Yet not so good of deedes, as great of name,
  Which he by many rash aduentures wan,
  Since errant armes to sew he first began;
  More huge in strength, then wise in workes he was,
  And reason with foole-hardize ouer ran;
  Sterne melancholy did his courage pas,
And was for terrour more, all armd in shyning bras.

xv 8 brayded 1609

But he that lou'd the youngest, was *Sans-loy*,   xviii
   He that faire *Vna* late fowle outraged,
   The most vnruly, and the boldest boy,
   That euer warlike weapons menaged,
   And to all lawlesse lust encouraged,
   Through strong opinion of his matchlesse might:
   Ne ought he car'd, whom he endamaged
   By tortious wrong, or whom bereau'd of right.
He now this Ladies champion chose for loue to fight.

These two gay knights, vowd to so diuerse loues,   xix
   Each other does enuie with deadly hate,
   And dayly warre against his foeman moues,
   In hope to win more fauour with his mate,
   And th'others pleasing seruice to abate,
   To magnifie his owne. But when they heard,
   How in that place straunge knight arriued late,
   Both knights and Ladies forth right angry far'd,
And fiercely vnto battell sterne themselues prepar'd.

But ere they could proceede vnto the place,   xx
   Where he abode, themselues at discord fell,
   And cruell combat ioynd in middle space:
   With horrible assault, and furie fell,
   They heapt huge strokes, the scorned life to quell,
   That all on vprore from her settled seat
   The house was raysd, and all that in did dwell;
   Seemd that lowde thunder with amazement great
Did rend the ratling skyes with flames of fouldring heat.

The noyse thereof cald forth that straunger knight,   xxi
   To weet, what dreadfull thing was there in hand;
   Where when as two braue knights in bloudy fight
   With deadly rancour he enraunged fond,
   His sunbroad shield about his wrest he bond,
   And shyning blade vnsheathd, with which he ran
   Vnto that stead, their strife to vnderstond;
   And at his first arriuall, them began
With goodly meanes to pacifie, well as he can.

xx 6 seat, *1590 &c.*
xxi 1 cald] calth *1596, 1609*   2 hand] hond *1609*

But they him spying, both with greedy forse   xxii
    Attonce vpon him ran, and him beset
    With strokes of mortall steele without remorse,
    And on his shield like yron sledges bet:
    As when a Beare and Tygre being met
    In cruell fight on lybicke Ocean wide,
    Espye a traueiler with feet surbet,
    Whom they in equall pray hope to deuide,
They stint their strife, and him assaile on euery side.

But he, not like a wearie traueilere,   xxiii
    Their sharpe assault right boldly did rebut,
    And suffred not their blowes to byte him nere,
    But with redoubled buffes them backe did put:
    Whose grieued mindes, which choler did englut,
    Against themselues turning their wrathfull spight,
    Gan with new rage their shields to hew and cut;
    But still when *Guyon* came to part their fight,
With heauie load on him they freshly gan to smight.

As a tall ship tossed in troublous seas,   xxiv
    Whom raging windes threatning to make the pray
    Of the rough rockes, do diuersly disease,
    Meetes two contrary billowes by the way,
    That her on either side do sore assay,
    And boast to swallow her in greedy graue;
    She scorning both their spights, does make wide way,
    And with her brest breaking the fomy waue,
Does ride on both their backs, and faire her selfe doth saue.

So boldly he him beares, and rusheth forth   xxv
    Betweene them both, by conduct of his blade.
    Wondrous great prowesse and heroick worth
    He shewd that day, and rare ensample made,
    When two so mighty warriours he dismade:
    Attonce he wards and strikes, he takes and payes,
    Now forst to yield, now forcing to inuade,
    Before, behind, and round about him layes:
So double was his paines, so double be his prayse.

xxiii 2 boldly] bloudy 1596: boldy 1609

Straunge sort of fight, three valiaunt knights to see   xxvi
   Three combats ioyne in one, and to darraine
   A triple warre with triple enmitee,
   All for their Ladies froward loue to gaine,
   Which gotten was but hate. So loue does raine
   In stoutest minds, and maketh monstrous warre;
   He maketh warre, he maketh peace againe,
   And yet his peace is but continuall iarre:
O miserable men, that to him subiect arre.

Whilst thus they mingled were in furious armes,   xxvii
   The faire *Medina* with her tresses torne,
   And naked brest, in pitty of their harmes,
   Emongst them ran, and falling them beforne,
   Besought them by the womb, which them had borne,
   And by the loues, which were to them most deare,
   And by the knighthood, which they sure had sworne,
   Their deadly cruell discord to forbeare,
And to her iust conditions of faire peace to heare.

But her two other sisters standing by,   xxviii
   Her lowd gainsaid, and both their champions bad
   Pursew the end of their strong enmity,
   As euer of their loues they would be glad.
   Yet she with pitthy words and counsell sad,
   Still stroue their stubborne rages to reuoke,
   That at the last suppressing fury mad,
   They gan abstaine from dint of direfull stroke,
And hearken to the sober speaches, which she spoke.

Ah puissaunt Lords, what cursed euill Spright,   xxix
   Or fell *Erinnys*, in your noble harts
   Her hellish brond hath kindled with despight,
   And stird you vp to worke your wilfull smarts?
   Is this the ioy of armes? be these the parts
   Of glorious knighthood, after bloud to thrust,
   And not regard dew right and iust desarts?
   Vaine is the vaunt, and victory vniust,
That more to mighty hands, then rightfull cause doth trust.

xxviii **2** their] her *1590*   champion *1596, 1609*   xxix 2 *Erinnys*
in your noble harts, *1590, 1596*   6 thrust] thurst *1609*

And were there rightfull cause of difference,   xxx
 Yet were not better, faire it to accord,
 Then with bloud guiltinesse to heape offence,
 And mortall vengeaunce ioyne to crime abhord?
 O fly from wrath, fly, O my liefest Lord:
 Sad be the sights, and bitter fruits of warre,
 And thousand furies wait on wrathfull sword;
 Ne ought the prayse of prowesse more doth marre,
Then fowle reuenging rage, and base contentious iarre.

But louely concord, and most sacred peace   xxxi
 Doth nourish vertue, and fast friendship breeds;
 Weake she makes strong, and strong thing does increace,
 Till it the pitch of highest prayse exceeds:
 Braue be her warres, and honorable deeds,
 By which she triumphes ouer ire and pride,
 And winnes an Oliue girlond for her meeds:
 Be therefore, O my deare Lords, pacifide,
And this misseeming discord meekely lay aside.

Her gracious wordes their rancour did appall,   xxxii
 And suncke so deepe into their boyling brests,
 That downe they let their cruell weapons fall,
 And lowly did abase their loftie crests
 To her faire presence, and discrete behests.
 Then she began a treatie to procure,
 And stablish termes betwixt both their requests,
 That as a law for euer should endure;
Which to obserue in word of knights they did assure.

Which to confirme, and fast to bind their league,   xxxiii
 After their wearie sweat and bloudy toile,
 She them besought, during their quiet treague,
 Into her lodging to repaire a while,
 To rest themselues, and grace to reconcile.
 They soone consent: so forth with her they fare,
 Where they are well receiu'd, and made to spoile
 Themselues of soiled armes, and to prepare
Their minds to pleasure, and their mouthes to dainty fare.

 xxx 1 there] their *1590, 1596* 3 bloudguiltnesse *1590* : bloud guiltnesse
1596 xxxi 3 make *1590* : *corr. F. E.*

And those two froward sisters, their faire loues   xxxiv
   Came with them eke, all were they wondrous loth,
   And fained cheare, as for the time behoues,
   But could not colour yet so well the troth,
   But that their natures bad appeard in both :
   For both did at their second sister grutch,
   And inly grieue, as doth an hidden moth
   The inner garment fret, not th'vtter touch ;
One thought their cheare too litle, th'other thought too mutch.

Elissa (so the eldest hight) did deeme   xxxv
   Such entertainment base, ne ought would eat,
   Ne ought would speake, but euermore did seeme
   As discontent for want of merth or meat ;
   No solace could her Paramour intreat
   Her once to show, ne court, nor dalliance,
   But with bent lowring browes, as she would threat,
   She scould, and frownd with froward countenaunce,
Vnworthy of faire Ladies comely gouernaunce.

But young *Perissa* was of other mind,   xxxvi
   Full of disport, still laughing, loosely light,
   And quite contrary to her sisters kind ;
   No measure in her mood, no rule of right,
   But poured out in pleasure and delight ;
   In wine and meats she flowd aboue the bancke,
   And in excesse exceeded her owne might ;
   In sumptuous tire she ioyd her selfe to prancke,
But of her loue too lauish (litle haue she thancke.)

Fast by her side did sit the bold *Sans-loy*,   xxxvii
   Fit mate for such a mincing mineon,
   Who in her loosenesse tooke exceeding ioy ;
   Might not be found a franker franion,
   Of her lewd parts to make companion ;
   But *Huddibras*, more like a Malecontent,
   Did see and grieue at his bold fashion ;
   Hardly could he endure his hardiment,
Yet still he sat, and inly did him selfe torment.

      xxxiv 9 thought their] though ther *1590*
   xxxvii 1 Fast] First *1590 &c.: corr. F. E.*

Betwixt them both the faire *Medina* sate   xxxviii
   With sober grace, and goodly carriage:
   With equall measure she did moderate
   The strong extremities of their outrage;
   That forward paire she euer would asswage,
   When they would striue dew reason to exceed;
   But that same froward twaine would accourage,
   And of her plenty adde vnto their need:
So kept she them in order, and her selfe in heed.

Thus fairely she attempered her feast,   xxxix
   And pleasd them all with meete satietie,
   At last when lust of meat and drinke was ceast,
   She *Guyon* deare besought of curtesie,
   To tell from whence he came through ieopardie,
   And whither now on new aduenture bound.
   Who with bold grace, and comely grauitie,
   Drawing to him the eyes of all around,
From lofty siege began these words aloud to sound.

This thy demaund, O Lady, doth reuiue   xl
   Fresh memory in me of that great Queene,
   Great and most glorious virgin Queene aliue,
   That with her soueraigne powre, and scepter shene
   All Faery lond does peaceably sustene.
   In widest Ocean she her throne does reare,
   That ouer all the earth it may be seene;
   As morning Sunne her beames dispredden cleare,
And in her face faire peace, and mercy doth appeare.

In her the richesse of all heauenly grace   xli
   In chiefe degree are heaped vp on hye:
   And all that else this worlds enclosure bace
   Hath great or glorious in mortall eye,
   Adornes the person of her Maiestie;
   That men beholding so great excellence,
   And rare perfection in mortalitie,
   Do her adore with sacred reuerence,
As th'Idole of her makers great magnificence.

xl 5 peaceable *1596, 1609*
xli 1 grace, *1590, 1596*   3 bace, *1590, 1596*   4 eye. *1596*

To her I homage and my seruice owe,　　　　　　xlii
　　In number of the noblest knights on ground,
　　Mongst whom on me she deigned to bestowe
　　Order of *Maydenhead*, the most renownd,
　　That may this day in all the world be found:
　　An yearely solemne feast she wontes to make
　　The day that first doth lead the yeare around;
　　To which all knights of worth and courage bold
Resort, to heare of straunge aduentures to be told.

There this old Palmer shewed himselfe that day,　　xliii
　　And to that mighty Princesse did complaine
　　Of grieuous mischiefes, which a wicked Fay
　　Had wrought, and many whelmd in deadly paine,
　　Whereof he crau'd redresse.　My Soueraine,
　　Whose glory is in gracious deeds, and ioyes
　　Throughout the world her mercy to maintaine,
　　Eftsoones deuisd redresse for such annoyes;
Me all vnfit for so great purpose she employes.

Now hath faire *Phœbe* with her siluer face　　　xliv
　　Thrise seene the shadowes of the neather world,
　　Sith last I left that honorable place,
　　In which her royall presence is †introld;
　　Ne euer shall I rest in house nor hold,
　　Till I that false *Acrasia* haue wonne ;
　　Of whose fowle deedes, too hideous to be told,
　　I witnesse am, and this their wretched sonne,
Whose wofull parents she hath wickedly fordonne.

Tell on, faire Sir, said she, that dolefull tale,　　　xlv
　　From which sad ruth does seeme you to restraine,
　　That we may pitty such vnhappy bale,
　　And learne from pleasures poyson to abstaine :
　　Ill by ensample good doth often gayne.
　　Then forward he his purpose gan pursew,
　　And told the storie of the mortall payne,
　　Which *Mordant* and *Amauia* did rew;
As with lamenting eyes him selfe did lately vew.

xlii 5 found, *1590, 1596*　　　6 make] hold *conj. edd.*　　*Cf.* II ii 7, iii
28, &c.　　　xliv 4 introld] entrold *1590* : enrold *conj. edd.*　　7 told *1596*

Night was far spent, and now in *Ocean* deepe   xlvi
  Orion, flying fast from hissing snake,
  His flaming head did hasten for to steepe,
  When of his pitteous tale he end did make;
  Whilest with delight of that he wisely spake,
  Those guestes beguiled, did beguile their eyes
  Of kindly sleepe, that did them ouertake.
  At last when they had markt the chaunged skyes,
They wist their houre was spent; then each to rest him hyes.

Cant. III.

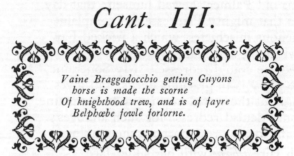

*Vaine Braggadocchio getting Guyons
horse is made the scorne
Of knighthood trew, and is of fayre
Belphœbe fowle forlorne.*

SOone as the morrow faire with purple beames   1
  Disperst the shadowes of the mistie night,
  And *Titan* playing on the eastern streames,
  Gan cleare the deawy ayre with springing light,
  Sir *Guyon* mindfull of his vow yplight,
  Vprose from drowsie couch, and him addrest
  Vnto the iourney which he had behight:
  His puissaunt armes about his noble brest,
And many-folded shield he bound about his wrest.

Then taking *Congé* of that virgin pure,   ii
  The bloudy-handed babe vnto her truth
  Did earnestly commit, and her coniure,
  In vertuous lore to traine his tender youth,
  And all that gentle noriture ensu'th:
  And that so soone as ryper yeares he raught,
  He might for memorie of that dayes ruth,
  Be called *Ruddymane,* and thereby taught,
T'auenge his Parents death on them, that had it wrought.

ii 6 raught] rought *1590*: *corr. F. E.*

So forth he far'd, as now befell, on foot,   iii
   Sith his good steed is lately from him gone;
   Patience perforce; helpelesse what may it boot
   To fret for anger, or for griefe to mone?
   His Palmer now shall foot no more alone:
   So fortune wrought, as vnder greene woods syde
   He lately heard that dying Lady grone,
   He left his steed without, and speare besyde,
And rushed in on foot to ayd her, ere she dyde.

The whiles a losell wandring by the way,   iv
   One that to bountie neuer cast his mind,
   Ne thought of honour euer did assay
   His baser brest, but in his kestrell kind
   A pleasing vaine of glory vaine did find,
   To which his flowing toung, and troublous spright
   Gaue him great ayd, and made him more inclind:
   He that braue steed there finding ready dight,
Purloynd both steed and speare, and ran away full light.

Now gan his hart all swell in iollitie,   v
   And of him selfe great hope and helpe conceiu'd,
   That puffed vp with smoke of vanitie,
   And with selfe-loued personage deceiu'd,
   He gan to hope, of men to be receiu'd
   For such, as he him thought, or faine would bee:
   But for in court gay portaunce he perceiu'd,
   And gallant show to be in greatest gree,
Eftsoones to court he cast t'auaunce his first degree.

And by the way he chaunced to espy   vi
   One sitting idle on a sunny bancke,
   To whom auaunting in great brauery,
   As Peacocke, that his painted plumes doth prancke,
   He smote his courser in the trembling flancke,
   And to him threatned his hart-thrilling speare:
   The seely man seeing him ryde so rancke,
   And ayme at him, fell flat to ground for feare,
And crying Mercy lowd, his pitious hands gan reare.

iv 5 glory vaine] glory he *1590*   v 9 aduaunce *1590*

Thereat the Scarcrow wexed wondrous prowd,   vii
  Through fortune of his first aduenture faire,
  And with big thundring voyce reuyld him lowd;
  Vile Caytiue, vassall of dread and despaire,
  Vnworthie of the commune breathed aire,
  Why liuest thou, dead dog, a lenger day,
  And doest not vnto death thy selfe prepare.
  Dye, or thy selfe my captiue yield for ay;
Great fauour I thee graunt, for aunswere thus to stay.

Hold, O deare Lord, hold your dead-doing hand,   viii
  Then loud he cryde, I am your humble thrall.
  Ah wretch (quoth he) thy destinies withstand
  My wrathfull will, and do for mercy call.
  I giue thee life: therefore prostrated fall,
  And kisse my stirrup; that thy homage bee.
  The Miser threw him selfe, as an Offall,
  Streight at his foot in base humilitee,
And cleeped him his liege, to hold of him in fee.

So happy peace they made and faire accord: .ix
  Eftsoones this liege-man gan to wexe more bold,
  And when he felt the folly of his Lord,
  In his owne kind he gan him selfe vnfold:
  For he was wylie witted, and growne old
  In cunning sleights and practick knauery.
  From that day forth he cast for to vphold
  His idle humour with fine flattery,
And blow the bellowes to his swelling vanity.

Trompart fit man for *Braggadocchio*,   x
  To serue at court in view of vaunting eye;
  Vaine-glorious man, when fluttring wind does blow
  In his light wings, is lifted vp to skye:
  The scorne of knighthood and trew cheualrye,
  To thinke without desert of gentle deed,
  And noble worth to be aduaunced hye:
  Such prayse is shame; but honour vertues meed
Doth beare the fairest flowre in honorable seed.

        vii 5 common *1609*   ix 7 From] For *1596*   8 slattery *1590*
                    x 1 *Braggadochio 1590 &c.*

So forth they pas, a well consorted paire,   xi
  Till that at length with *Archimage* they meet:
  Who seeing one that shone in armour faire,
  On goodly courser thundring with his feet,
  Eftsoones supposed him a person meet,
  Of his reuenge to make the instrument:
  For since the *Redcrosse* knight he earst did weet,
  To beene with *Guyon* knit in one consent,
The ill, which earst to him, he now to *Guyon* ment.

And comming close to *Trompart* gan inquere   xii
  Of him, what mighty warriour that mote bee,
  That rode in golden sell with single spere,
  But wanted sword to wreake his enmitee.
  He is a great aduenturer, (said he)
  That hath his sword through hard assay forgone,
  And now hath vowd, till he auenged bee,
  Of that despight, neuer to wearen none;
That speare is him enough to doen a thousand grone.

Th'enchaunter greatly ioyed in the vaunt,   xiii
  And weened well ere long his will to win,
  And both his foen with equall foyle to daunt.
  Tho to him louting lowly, did begin
  To plaine of wrongs, which had committed bin
  By *Guyon*, and by that false *Redcrosse* knight,
  Which two through treason and decciptfull gin,
  Had slaine Sir *Mordant*, and his Lady bright:
That mote him honour win, to wreake so foule despight.

Therewith all suddeinly he seemd enraged,   xiv
  And threatned death with dreadfull countenaunce,
  As if their liues had in his hand beene gaged;
  And with stiffe force shaking his mortall launce,
  To let him weet his doughtie valiaunce,
  Thus said; Old man, great sure shalbe thy meed,
  If where those knights for feare of dew vengeaunce
  Do lurke, thou certainly to me areed,
That I may wreake on them their hainous hatefull deed.

xi 4 courser] course *1590*

Certes, my Lord, (said he) that shall I soone,   xv
   And giue you eke good helpe to their decay,
   But mote I wisely you aduise to doon;
   Giue no ods to your foes, but do puruay
   Your selfe of sword before that bloudy day:
   For they be two the prowest knights on ground,
   And oft approu'd in many hard assay,
   And eke of surest steele, that may be found,
Do arme your selfe against that day, them to confound.

Dotard (said he) let be thy deepe aduise;   xvi
   Seemes that through many yeares thy wits thee faile,
   And that weake eld hath left thee nothing wise,
   Else neuer should thy iudgement be so fraile,
   To measure manhood by the sword or maile.
   Is not enough foure quarters of a man,
   Withouten sword or shield, an host to quaile?
   Thou little wotest, what this right hand can:
Speake they, which haue beheld the battailes, which it wan.

The man was much abashed at his boast;   xvii
   Yet well he wist, that who so would contend
   With either of those knights on euen coast,
   Should need of all his armes, him to defend;
   Yet feared least his boldnesse should offend,
   When *Braggadocchio* said, Once I did sweare,
   When with one sword seuen knights I brought to end,
   Thence forth in battell neuer sword to beare,
But it were that, which noblest knight on earth doth weare.

Perdie Sir knight, said then th'enchaunter bliue,   xviii
   That shall I shortly purchase to your hond:
   For now the best and noblest knight aliue
   Prince *Arthur* is, that wonnes in Faerie lond;
   He hath a sword, that flames like burning brond.
   The same by my deuice I vndertake
   Shall by to morrow by thy side be fond.
   At which bold word that boaster gan to quake,
And wondred in his mind, what mote that monster make.

He stayd not for more bidding, but away   xix
   Was suddein vanished out of his sight:
   The Northerne wind his wings did broad display
   At his commaund, and reared him vp light
   From off the earth to take his aerie flight.
   They lookt about, but no where could espie
   Tract of his foot: then dead through great affright
   They both nigh were, and each bad other flie:
Both fled attonce, ne euer backe returned eie.

Till that they come vnto a forrest greene,   xx
   In which they shrowd themselues from causelesse feare;
   Yet feare them followes still, where so they beene,
   Each trembling leafe, and whistling wind they heare,
   As ghastly bug their haire on end does reare:
   Yet both doe striue their fearfulnesse to faine.
   At last they heard a horne, that shrilled cleare
   Throughout the wood, that ecchoed againe,
And made the forrest ring, as it would riue in twaine.

Eft through the thicke they heard one rudely rush;   xxi
   With noyse whereof he from his loftie steed
   Downe fell to ground, and crept into a bush,
   To hide his coward head from dying dreed.
   But *Trompart* stoutly stayd to taken heed
   Of what might hap.   Eftsoone there stepped forth
   A goodly Ladie clad in hunters weed,
   That seemd to be a woman of great worth,
And by her stately portance, borne of heauenly birth.

Her face so faire as flesh it seemed not,   xxii
   But heauenly pourtraict of bright Angels hew,
   Cleare as the skie, withouten blame or blot,
   Through goodly mixture of complexions dew;
   And in her cheekes the vermeill red did shew
   Like roses in a bed of lillies shed,
   The which ambrosiall odours from them threw,
   And gazers sense with double pleasure fed,
Hable to heale the sicke, and to reuiue the ded.

   xx 5 does vnto them affeare *1590* : vnto *corr. to* greatly *in F. E.*
    xxi 5 heed, *1590, 1596*   xxii 9 Able *1609 passim*

In her faire eyes two liuing lamps did flame,   xxiii
    Kindled aboue at th'heauenly makers light,
    And darted fyrie beames out of the same,
    So passing persant, and so wondrous bright,
    That quite bereau'd the rash beholders sight:
    In them the blinded god his lustfull fire
    To kindle oft assayd, but had no might;
    For with dredd Maiestie, and awfull ire,
She broke his wanton darts, and quenched base desire.

Her iuorie forhead, full of bountie braue,   xxiv
    Like a broad table did it selfe dispred,
    For Loue his loftie triumphes to engraue,
    And write the battels of his great godhed:
    All good and honour might therein be red:
    For there their dwelling was. And when she spake,
    Sweet words, like dropping honny she did shed,
    And twixt the perles and rubins softly brake
A siluer sound, that heauenly musicke seemd to make.

Vpon her eyelids many Graces sate,   xxv
    Vnder the shadow of her euen browes,
    Working belgards, and amorous retrate,
    And euery one her with a grace endowes:
    And euery one with meekenesse to her bowes.
    So glorious mirrhour of celestiall grace,
    And soueraine moniment of mortall vowes,
    How shall fraile pen descriue her heauenly face,
For feare through want of skill her beautie to disgrace?

So faire, and thousand thousand times more faire   xxvi
    She seemd, when she presented was to sight,
    And was yclad, for heat of scorching aire,
    All in a silken Camus lylly whight,
    Purfled vpon with many a folded plight,
    Which all aboue besprinckled was throughout
    With golden aygulets, that glistred bright,
    Like twinckling starres, and all the skirt about
Was hemd with golden fringe

xxiii 4 pearceant *1609*   8 drad *1609*   xxvi 6 throughout, *1590 &c.*

Below her ham her weed did somewhat traine,   xxvii
  And her streight legs most brauely were embayld
  In gilden buskins of costly Cordwaine,
  All bard with golden bendes, which were entayld
  With curious antickes, and full faire aumayld:
  Before they fastned were vnder her knee
  In a rich Iewell, and therein entrayld
  The ends of all their knots, that none might see,
How they within their fouldings close enwrapped bee.

Like two faire marble pillours they were seene,   xxviii
  Which doe the temple of the Gods support,
  Whom all the people decke with girlands greene,
  And honour in their festiuall resort;
  Those same with stately grace, and princely port
  She taught to tread, when she her selfe would grace,
  But with the wooddie Nymphes when she did play,
  Or when the flying Libbard she did chace,
She could them nimbly moue, and after fly apace.

And in her hand a sharpe bore-speare she held,   xxix
  And at her backe a bow and quiuer gay,
  Stuft with steele-headed darts, wherewith she queld
  The saluage beastes in her victorious play,
  Knit with a golden bauldricke, which forelay
  Athwart her snowy brest, and did diuide
  Her daintie paps; which like young fruit in May
  Now little gan to swell, and being tide,
Through her thin weed their places only signifide.

Her yellow lockes crisped, like golden wyre,   xxx
  About her shoulders weren loosely shed,
  And when the winde emongst them did inspyre,
  They waued like a penon wide dispred,
  And low behinde her backe were scattered:
  And whether art it were, or heedlesse hap,
  As through the flouring forrest rash she fled,
  In her rude haires sweet flowres themselues did lap,
And flourishing fresh leaues and blossomes did enwrap.

xxvii 8 end *1609*   their] the *1590*   xxviii 1 were] did *1590*: *corr.*
F. E.   7 play] sport *conj. ed.* *Cf.* II ii 7, 42, &c.   xxx 4 disspred
1609

Such as *Diana* by the sandie shore   xxxi
   Of swift *Eurotas*, or on *Cynthus* greene,
   Where all the Nymphes haue her vnwares forlore,
   Wandreth alone with bow and arrowes keene,
   To seeke her game: Or as that famous Queene
   Of *Amazons*, whom *Pyrrhus* did destroy,
   The day that first of *Priame* she was seene,
   Did shew her selfe in great triumphant ioy,
To succour the weake state of sad afflicted *Troy*.

Such when as hartlesse *Trompart* her did vew,   xxxii
   He was dismayed in his coward mind,
   And doubted, whether he himselfe should shew,
   Or fly away, or bide alone behind:
   Both feare and hope he in her face did find,
   When she at last him spying thus bespake;
   Hayle Groome; didst not thou see a bleeding Hind,
   Whose right haunch earst my stedfast arrow strake?
If thou didst, tell me, that I may her ouertake.

Wherewith reviu'd, this answere forth he threw;   xxxiii
   O Goddesse, (for such I thee take to bee)
   For neither doth thy face terrestriall shew,
   Nor voyce sound mortall; I auow to thee,
   Such wounded beast, as that, I did not see,
   Sith earst into this forrest wild I came.
   But mote thy goodlyhed forgiue it mee,
   To weet, which of the Gods I shall thee name,
That vnto thee due worship I may rightly frame.

To whom she thus; but ere her words ensewed,   xxxiv
   Vnto the bush her eye did suddein glaunce,
   In which vaine *Braggadocchio* was mewed,
   And saw it stirre: she left her percing launce,
   And towards gan a deadly shaft aduaunce,
   In mind to marke the beast. At which sad stowre,
   Trompart forth stept, to stay the mortall chaunce,
   Out crying, O what euer heauenly powre,
Or earthly wight thou be, withhold this deadly howre.

O stay thy hand, for yonder is no game　　　　　xxxv
　　For thy fierce arrowes, them to exercize,
　　But loe my Lord, my liege, whose warlike name
　　Is farre renowmd through many bold emprize;
　　And now in shade he shrowded yonder lies.
　　She staid: with that he crauld out of his nest,
　　Forth creeping on his caitiue hands and thies,
　　And standing stoutly vp, his loftie crest
Did fiercely shake, and rowze, as comming late from rest.

As fearefull fowle, that long in secret caue　　　　xxxvi
　　For dread of soaring hauke her selfe hath hid,
　　Not caring how, her silly life to saue,
　　She her gay painted plumes disorderid,
　　Seeing at last her selfe from daunger rid,
　　Peepes foorth, and soone renewes her natiue pride;
　　She gins her feathers foule disfigured
　　Proudly to prune, and set on euery side,
So shakes off shame, ne thinks how erst she did her hide.

So when her goodly visage he beheld,　　　　　　xxxvii
　　He gan himselfe to vaunt: but when he vewed
　　Those deadly tooles, which in her hand she held,
　　Soone into other fits he was transmewed,
　　Till she to him her gratious speach renewed;
　　All haile, Sir knight, and well may thee befall,
　　As all the like, which honour haue pursewed
　　Through deedes of armes and prowesse martiall,
All vertue merits praise, but such the most of all.

To whom he thus; O fairest vnder skie,　·　　　xxxviii
　　True be thy words, and worthy of thy praise,
　　That warlike feats doest highest glorifie.
　　Therein haue I spent all my youthly daies,
　　And many battailes fought, and many fraies
　　Throughout the world, wher so they might be found,
　　Endeuouring my dreadded name to raise
　　Aboue the Moone, that fame may it resound
In her eternall trompe, with laurell girland cround.

But what art thou, O Ladie, which doest raunge   xxxix
  In this wilde forrest, where no pleasure is,
  And doest not it for ioyous court exchaunge,
  Emongst thine equall peres, where happie blis
  And all delight does raigne, much more then this?
  There thou maist loue, and dearely loued bee,
  And swim in pleasure, which thou here doest mis;
  There maist thou best be seene, and best maist see:
The wood is fit for beasts, the court is fit for thee.

Who so in pompe of proud estate (quoth she)   xl
  Does swim, and bathes himselfe in courtly blis,
  Does waste his dayes in darke obscuritee,
  And in obliuion euer buried is:
  Where ease abounds, yt's eath to doe amis;
  But who his limbs with labours, and his mind
  Behaues with cares, cannot so easie mis.
  Abroad in armes, at home in studious kind
Who seekes with painfull toile, shall honor soonest find.

In woods, in waues, in warres she wonts to dwell,   xli
  And will be found with perill and with paine;
  Ne can the man, that moulds in idle cell,
  Vnto her happie mansion attaine:
  Before her gate high God did Sweat ordaine,
  And wakefull watches euer to abide:
  But easie is the way, and passage plaine
  To pleasures pallace; it may soone be spide,
And day and night her dores to all stand open wide.

In Princes court, The rest she would haue said,   xlii
  But that the foolish man, fild with delight
  Of her sweet words, that all his sence dismaid,
  And with her wondrous beautie rauisht quight,
  Gan burne in filthy lust, and leaping light,
  Thought in his bastard armes her to embrace.
  With that she swaruing backe, her Iauelin bright
  Against him bent, and fiercely did menace:
So turned her about, and fled away apace.

Which when the Peasant saw, amazd he stood, xliii
    And grieued at her flight; yet durst he not
    Pursew her steps, through wild vnknowen wood;
    Besides he feard her wrath, and threatned shot
    Whiles in the bush he lay, not yet forgot:
    Ne car'd he greatly for her presence vaine,
    But turning said to *Trompart*, What foule blot
    Is this to knight, that Ladie should againe
Depart to woods vntoucht, and leaue so proud disdaine?

Perdie (said *Trompart*) let her passe at will, xliv
    Least by her presence daunger mote befall.
    For who can tell (and sure I feare it ill)
    But that she is some powre celestiall?
    For whiles she spake, her great words did apall
    My feeble courage, and my hart oppresse,
    That yet I quake and tremble ouer all.
    And I (said *Braggadocchio*) thought no lesse,
When first I heard her horne sound with such ghastlinesse.

For from my mothers wombe this grace I haue xlv
    Me giuen by eternall destinie,
    That earthly thing may not my courage braue
    Dismay with feare, or cause one foot to flie,
    But either hellish feends, or powres on hie:
    Which was the cause, when earst that horne I heard,
    Weening it had beene thunder in the skie,
    I hid my selfe from it, as one affeard;
But when I other knew, my selfe I boldly reard.

But now for feare of worse, that may betide, xlvi
    Let vs soone hence depart.   They soone agree;
    So to his steed he got, and gan to ride,
    As one vnfit therefore, that all might see
    He had not trayned bene in cheualree.
    Which well that valiant courser did discerne;
    For he despysd to tread in dew degree,
    But chaufd and fom'd, with courage fierce and sterne,
And to be easd of that base burden still did erne.

       xliii 2 greiued *1596*   xlv 4 one] on *1590, 1596*
             xlvi 9 yerne *1609*

Cant. IIII.

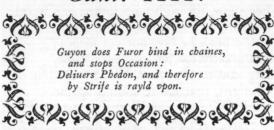

*Guyon does Furor bind in chaines,
and stops Occasion:
Deliuers Phedon, and therefore
by Strife is rayld vpon.*

IN braue pursuit of honorable deed,   i
There is I know not what great difference
Betweene the vulgar and the noble seed,
Which vnto things of valorous pretence
Seemes to be borne by natiue influence;
As feates of armes, and loue to entertaine,
But chiefly skill to ride, seemes a science
Proper to gentle bloud; some others faine
To menage steeds, as did this vaunter; but in vaine.

But he the rightfull owner of that steed,   ii
Who well could menage and subdew his pride,
The whiles on foot was forced for to yeed,
With that blacke Palmer, his most trusty guide;
Who suffred not his wandring feet to slide.
But when strong passion, or weake fleshlinesse
Would from the right way seeke to draw him wide,
He would through temperance and stedfastnesse,
Teach him the weake to strengthen, and the strong suppresse.

It fortuned forth faring on his way,   iii
He saw from farre, or seemed for to see
Some troublous vprore or contentious fray,
Whereto he drew in haste it to agree.
A mad man, or that feigned mad to bee,
Drew by the haire along vpon the ground,
A handsome stripling with great crueltee,
Whom sore he bett, and gor'd with many a wound,
That cheekes with teares, and sides with bloud did all abound.

Arg. 3 *Phedon*] *Phaon 1590*   4 *strife 1590, 1596*
i 2 (what) *1590*

And him behind, a wicked Hag did stalke,　　　iv
　In ragged robes, and filthy disaray,
　Her other leg was lame, that she no'te walke,
　But on a staffe her feeble steps did stay;
　Her lockes, that loathly were and hoarie gray,
　Grew all afore, and loosely hong vnrold,
　But all behind was bald, and worne away,
　That none thereof could euer taken hold,
And eke her face ill fauourd, full of wrinckles old.

And euer as she went, her tongue did walke　　　v
　In foule reproch, and termes of vile despight,
　Prouoking him by her outrageous talke,
　To heape more vengeance on that wretched wight;
　Sometimes she raught him stones, wherwith to smite,
　Sometimes her staffe, though it her one leg were,
　Withouten which she could not go vpright;
　Ne any euill meanes she did forbeare,
That might him moue to wrath, and indignation reare.

The noble *Guyon* mou'd with great remorse,　　　vi
　Approching, first the Hag did thrust away,
　And after adding more impetuous forse,
　His mightie hands did on the madman lay,
　And pluckt him backe; who all on fire streight way,
　Against him turning all his fell intent,
　With beastly brutish rage gan him assay,
　And smot, and hit, and kickt, and scratcht, and rent,
And did he wist not what in his auengement.

And sure he was a man of mickle might,　　　vii
　Had he had gouernance, it well to guide:
　But when the franticke fit inflamd his spright,
　His force was vaine, and strooke more often wide,
　Then at the aymed marke, which he had eide:
　And oft himselfe he chaunst to hurt vnwares,
　Whilst reason blent through passion, nought descride,
　But as a blindfold Bull at randon fares,　　[nought cares.
And where he hits, nought knowes, and whom he hurts,

iv 3 walke. *1590, 1596*

His rude assault and rugged handeling   viii
    Straunge seemed to the knight, that aye with foe
    In faire defence and goodly menaging
    Of armes was wont to fight, yet nathemoe
    Was he abashed now not fighting so,
    But more enfierced through his currish play,
    Him sternely grypt, and haling to and fro,
    To ouerthrow him strongly did assay,
But ouerthrew himselfe vnwares, and lower lay.

And being downe the villein sore did beat,   ix
    And bruze with clownish fistes his manly face:
    And eke the Hag with many a bitter threat,
    Still cald vpon to kill him in the place.
    With whose reproch and odious menace
    The knight emboyling in his haughtie hart,
    Knit all his forces, and gan soone vnbrace
    His grasping hold: so lightly did vpstart,
And drew his deadly weapon, to maintaine his part.

Which when the Palmer saw, he loudly cryde,   x
    Not so, O *Guyon,* neuer thinke that so
    That Monster can be maistred or destroyd:
    He is not, ah, he is not such a foe,
    As steele can wound, or strength can ouerthroe.
    That same is *Furor,* cursed cruell wight,
    That vnto knighthood workes much shame and woe;
    And that same Hag, his aged mother, hight
Occasion, the root of all wrath and despight.

With her, who so will raging *Furor* tame,   xi
    Must first begin, and well her amenage:
    First her restraine from her reprochfull blame,
    And euill meanes, with which she doth enrage
    Her franticke sonne, and kindles his courage,
    Then when she is withdrawen, or strong withstood,
    It's eath his idle furie to asswage,
    And calme the tempest of his passion wood;
The bankes are ouerflowen, when stopped is the flood.

x 4 He is not] He is no *1590 &c.* : *corr. F. E.*

Therewith Sir *Guyon* left his first emprise,   xii
  And turning to that woman, fast her hent
  By the hoare lockes, that hong before her eyes,
  And to the ground her threw: yet n'ould she stent
  Her bitter rayling and foule reuilement,
  But still prouokt her sonne to wreake her wrong;
  But nathelesse he did her still torment,
  And catching hold of her vngratious tong,
Thereon an yron lock did fasten firme and strong.

Then when as vse of speach was from her reft,   xiii
  With her two crooked handes she signes did make,
  And beckned him, the last helpe she had left:
  But he that last left helpe away did take,
  And both her hands fast bound vnto a stake,
  That she note stirre. Then gan her sonne to flie
  Full fast away, and did her quite forsake;
  But *Guyon* after him in haste did hie,
And soone him ouertooke in sad perplexitie.

In his strong armes he stiffely him embraste,   xiv
  Who him gainstriuing, nought at all preuaild:
  For all his power was vtterly defaste,
  And furious fits at earst quite weren quaild:
  Oft he re'nforst, and oft his forces fayld,
  Yet yield he would not, nor his rancour slacke.
  Then him to ground he cast, and rudely hayld,
  And both his hands fast bound behind his backe,
And both his feet in fetters to an yron racke.

With hundred yron chaines he did him bind,   xv
  And hundred knots that did him sore constraine:
  Yet his great yron teeth he still did grind,
  And grimly gnash, threatning reuenge in vaine;
  His burning eyen, whom bloudie strakes did staine,
  Stared full wide, and threw forth sparkes of fire,
  And more for ranck despight, then for great paine,
  Shakt his long lockes, colourd like copper-wire,
And bit his tawny beard to shew his raging ire.

             xii 8 tongue *1590*: tonge *F. E.*   9 lock, *1590, 1596*

Thus when as *Guyon Furor* had captiu'd,   xvi
    Turning about he saw that wretched Squire,
    Whom that mad man of life nigh late depriu'd,
    Lying on ground, all soild with bloud and mire:
    Whom when as he perceiued to respire,
    He gan to comfort, and his wounds to dresse.
    Being at last recured, he gan inquire,
    What hard mishap him brought to such distresse,
And made that caitiues thral, the thral of wretchednesse.

With hart then throbbing, and with watry eyes,   xvii
    Faire Sir (quoth he) what man can shun the hap,
    That hidden lyes vnwares him to surpryse?
    Misfortune waites aduantage to entrap
    The man most warie in her whelming lap.
    So me weake wretch, of many weakest one,
    Vnweeting, and vnware of such mishap,
    She brought to mischiefe through occasion,
Where this same wicked villein did me light vpon.

It was a faithlesse Squire, that was the sourse   xviii
    Of all my sorrow, and of these sad teares,
    With whom from tender dug of commune nourse,
    Attonce I was vpbrought, and eft when yeares
    More rype vs reason lent to chose our Peares,
    Our selues in league of vowed loue we knit:
    In which we long time without gealous feares,
    Or faultie thoughts continewd, as was fit;
And for my part I vow, dissembled not a whit.

It was my fortune commune to that age,   xix
    To loue a Ladie faire of great degree,
    The which was borne of noble parentage,
    And set in highest seat of dignitee,
    Yet seemd no lesse to loue, then loued to bee:
    Long I her seru'd, and found her faithfull still,
    Ne euer thing could cause vs disagree:
    Loue that two harts makes one, makes eke one will:
Each stroue to please, and others pleasure to fulfill.

    xvii 3 surpryse *1590, 1596*   6 one] wretch *1590*   8 occasion] her
guilful trech *1590*   9 light vpon] wandring ketch *1590*   xviii 8 Or]
Our *1609*   xix 8 one,] one ; *1596*

My friend, hight *Philemon,* I did partake   xx
    Of all my loue and all my priuitie;
    Who greatly ioyous seemed for my sake,
    And gratious to that Ladie, as to mee,
    Ne euer wight, that mote so welcome bee,
    As he to her, withouten blot or blame,
    Ne euer thing, that she could thinke or see,
    But vnto him she would impart the same:
O wretched man, that would abuse so gentle Dame.

At last such grace I found, and meanes I wrought,   xxi
    That I that Ladie to my spouse had wonne;
    Accord of friends, consent of parents oought,
    Affiance made, my happinesse begonne,
    There wanted nought but few rites to be donne,
    Which mariage make; that day too farre did seeme:
    Most ioyous man, on whom the shining Sunne
    Did shew his face, my selfe I did esteeme,
And that my falser friend did no lesse ioyous deeme.

But ere that wished day his beame disclosd,   xxii
    He either enuying my toward good,
    Or of himselfe to treason ill disposd,
    One day vnto me came in friendly mood,
    And told for secret how he vnderstood
    That Ladie whom I had to me assynd,
    Had both distaind her honorable blood,
    And eke the faith, which she to me did bynd;
And therfore wisht me stay, till I more truth should fynd.

The gnawing anguish and sharpe gelosy,   xxiii
    Which his sad speech infixed in my brest,
    Ranckled so sore, and festred inwardly,
    That my engreeued mind could find no rest,
    Till that the truth thereof I did outwrest,
    And him besought by that same sacred band
    Betwixt vs both, to counsell me the best.
    He then with solemne oath and plighted hand
Assur'd, ere long the truth to let me vnderstand.

     xx 1 partake, *1590, 1596*   xxi 7 Sunne, *1590, 1596*
       xxii 1 ere] ear *1590*   3 disposd *1590, 1596*

Ere long with like againe he boorded mee,   xxiv
  Saying, he now had boulted all the floure,
  And that it was a groome of base degree,
  Which of my loue was partner Paramoure:
  Who vsed in a darkesome inner bowre
  Her oft to meet: which better to approue,
  He promised to bring me at that howre,
  When I should see, that would me nearer moue,
And driue me to withdraw my blind abused loue.

This gracelesse man for furtherance of his guile,   xxv
  Did court the handmayd of my Lady deare,
  Who glad t'embosome his affection vile,
  Did all she might, more pleasing to appeare.
  One day to worke her to his will more neare,
  He woo'd her thus: *Pryene* (so she hight)
  What great despight doth fortune to thee beare,
  Thus lowly to abase thy beautie bright,
That it should not deface all others lesser light?

But if she had her least helpe to thee lent,   xxvi
  T'adorne thy forme according thy desart,
  Their blazing pride thou wouldest soone haue blent,
  And staynd their prayses with thy least good part;
  Ne should faire *Claribell* with all her art,
  Though she thy Lady be, approch thee neare:
  For proofe thereof, this euening, as thou art,
  Aray thy selfe in her most gorgeous geare,
That I may more delight in thy embracement deare.

The Maiden proud through prayse, and mad through loue xxvii
  Him hearkned to, and soone her selfe arayd,
  The whiles to me the treachour did remoue
  His craftie engin, and as he had sayd,
  Me leading, in a secret corner layd,
  The sad spectatour of my Tragedie;
  Where left, he went, and his owne false part playd,
  Disguised like that groome of base degree,
Whom he had feignd th'abuser of my loue to bee.

Eftsoones he came vnto th'appointed place,   xxviii
    And with him brought *Pryene*, rich arayd,
    In *Claribellaes* clothes.   Her proper face
    I not descerned in that darkesome shade,
    But weend it was my loue, with whom he playd.
    Ah God, what horrour and tormenting griefe
    My hart, my hands, mine eyes, and all assayd?
    Me liefer were ten thousand deathes priefe,
Then wound of gealous worme, and shame of such repriefe.

I home returning, fraught with fowle despight,   xxix
    And chawing vengeance all the way I went,
    Soone as my loathed loue appeard in sight,
    With wrathfull hand I slew her innocent;
    That after soone I dearely did lament:
    For when the cause of that outrageous deede
    Demaunded, I made plaine and euident,
    Her faultie Handmayd, which that bale did breede,
Confest, how *Philemon* her wrought to chaunge her weede.

Which when I heard, with horrible affright   xxx
    And hellish fury all enragd, I sought
    Vpon my selfe that vengeable despight
    To punish: yet it better first I thought,
    To wreake my wrath on him, that first it wrought.
    To *Philemon*, false faytour *Philemon*
    I cast to pay, that I so dearely bought;
    Of deadly drugs I gaue him drinke anon,
And washt away his guilt with guiltie potion.

Thus heaping crime on crime, and griefe on griefe,   xxxi
    To losse of loue adioyning losse of frend,
    I meant to purge both with a third mischiefe,
    And in my woes beginner it to end:
    That was *Pryene*; she did first offend,
    She last should smart: with which cruell intent,
    When I at her my murdrous blade did bend,
    She fled away with ghastly dreriment,
And I pursewing my fell purpose, after went.

    xxviii 2 *Priene, 1596*   4 discerned *1609*   8 deathez *1609*

Feare gaue her wings, and rage enforst my flight;   xxxii
   Through woods and plaines so long I did her chace,
   Till this mad man, whom your victorious might
   Hath now fast bound, me met in middle space,
   As I her, so he me pursewd apace,
   And shortly ouertooke: I, breathing yre,
   Sore chauffed at my stay in such a cace,
   And with my heat kindled his cruell fyre;
Which kindled once, his mother did more rage inspyre.

Betwixt them both, they haue me doen to dye,   xxxiii
   Through wounds, and strokes, and stubborne handeling,
   That death were better, then such agony,
   As griefe and furie vnto me did bring;
   Of which in me yet stickes the mortall sting,
   That during life will neuer be appeasd.
   When he thus ended had his sorrowing,
   Said *Guyon*, Squire, sore haue ye beene diseasd;
But all your hurts may soone through temperance be easd.

Then gan the Palmer thus, Most wretched man,   xxxiv
   That to affections does the bridle lend;
   In their beginning they are weake and wan,
   But soone through suff'rance grow to fearefull end;
   Whiles they are weake betimes with them contend:
   For when they once to perfect strength do grow,
   Strong warres they make, and cruell battry bend
   Gainst fort of Reason, it to ouerthrow:
Wrath, gelosie, griefe, loue this Squire haue layd thus low.

Wrath, gealosie, griefe, loue do thus expell: xxxv
   Wrath is a fire, and gealosie a weede,
   Griefe is a flood, and loue a monster fell;
   The fire of sparkes, the weede of little seede,
   The flood of drops, the Monster filth did breede:
   But sparks, seed, drops, and filth do thus delay;
   The sparks soone quench, the springing seed outweed,
   The drops dry vp, and filth wipe cleane away:
So shall wrath, gealosie, griefe, loue dye and decay.

xxxii 6 I,] I *1590, 1596*   xxxiv 1 most *1590, 1596*
xxxv 7 outweed *1590, 1596*

Vnlucky Squire (said *Guyon*) sith thou hast xxxvi
  Falne into mischiefe through intemperaunce,
  Henceforth take heede of that thou now hast past,
  And guide thy wayes with warie gouernaunce,
  Least worse betide thee by some later chaunce.
  But read how art thou nam'd, and of what kin.
  Phedon I hight (quoth he) and do aduaunce
  Mine auncestry from famous *Coradin,*
Who first to rayse our house to honour did begin.

Thus as he spake, lo far away they spyde xxxvii
  A varlet running towards hastily,
  Whose flying feet so fast their way applyde,
  That round about a cloud of dust did fly,
  Which mingled all with sweate, did dim his eye.
  He soone approched, panting, breathlesse, whot,
  And all so soyld, that none could him descry;
  His countenaunce was bold, and bashed not
For *Guyons* lookes, but scornefull eyglaunce at him shot.

Behind his backe he bore a brasen shield, xxxviii
  On which was drawen faire, in colours fit,
  A flaming fire in midst of bloudy field,
  And round about the wreath this word was writ,
  Burnt I do burne. Right well beseemed it,
  To be the shield of some redoubted knight;
  And in his hand two darts exceeding flit,
  And deadly sharpe he held, whose heads were dight
In poyson and in bloud, of malice and despight.

When he in presence came, to *Guyon* first xxxix
  He boldly spake, Sir knight, if knight thou bee,
  Abandon this forestalled place at erst,
  For feare of further harme, I counsell thee,
  Or bide the chaunce at thine owne ieoperdie.
  The knight at his great boldnesse wondered,
  And though he scornd his idle vanitie,
  Yet mildly him to purpose answered;
For not to grow of nought he it coniectured.

xxxvi 2 into] vnto *1596*   7 *Phedon*] *Phaon 1590*

Varlet, this place most dew to me I deeme,   xl
  Yielded by him, that held it forcibly.
  Butwhenceshouldcome that harme,which thou doest seeme
  To threat to him, that minds his chaunce t'abye?
  Perdy (said he) here comes, and is hard by
  A knight of wondrous powre, and great assay,
  That neuer yet encountred enemy,
  But did him deadly daunt, or fowle dismay;
Ne thou for better hope, if thou his presence stay.

How hight he then (said *Guyon*) and from whence?   xli
  Pyrochles is his name, renowmed farre
  For his bold feats and hardy confidence,
  Full oft approu'd in many a cruell warre,
  The brother of *Cymochles*, both which arre
  The sonnes of old *Acrates* and *Despight*,
  Acrates sonne of *Phlegeton* and *Iarre*;
  But *Phlegeton* is sonne of *Herebus* and *Night*;
But *Herebus* sonne of *Aeternitie* is hight.

So from immortall race he does proceede,   xlii
  That mortall hands may not withstand his might,
  Drad for his derring do, and bloudy deed;
  For all in bloud and spoile is his delight.
  His am I *Atin*, his in wrong and right,
  That matter make for him to worke vpon,
  And stirre him vp to strife and cruell fight.
  Fly therefore, fly this fearefull stead anon,
Least thy foolhardize worke thy sad confusion.

His be that care, whom most it doth concerne,   xliii
  (Said he) but whither with such hasty flight
  Art thou now bound? for well mote I discerne
  Great cause, that carries thee so swift and light.
  My Lord (quoth he) me sent, and streight behight
  To seeke *Occasion*, where so she bee:
  For he is all disposd to bloudy fight,
  And breathes out wrath and hainous crueltie;
Hard is his hap, that first fals in his ieopardie.

Madman (said then the Palmer) that does seeke   xliv
   Occasion to wrath, and cause of strife;
   She comes vnsought, and shonned followes eke.
   Happy, who can abstaine, when Rancour rife
   Kindles Reuenge, and threats his rusty knife;
   Woe neuer wants, where euery cause is caught,
   And rash *Occasion* makes vnquiet life.
   Then loe, where bound she sits, whom thou hast sought,
(Said *Guyon*,) let that message to thy Lord be brought.

That when the varlet heard and saw, streight way   xlv
   He wexed wondrous wroth, and said, Vile knight,
   That knights and knighthood doest with shame vpbray,
   And shewst th'ensample of thy childish might,
   With silly weake old woman thus to fight.
   Great glory and gay spoile sure hast thou got,
   And stoutly prou'd thy puissaunce here in sight;
   That shall *Pyrochles* well requite, I wot,
And with thy bloud abolish so reprochfull blot.

With that one of his thrillant darts he threw,   xlvi
   Headed with ire and vengeable despight;
   The quiuering steele his aymed end well knew,
   And to his brest it selfe intended right:
   But he was warie, and ere it empight
   In the meant marke, aduaunst his shield atweene,
   On which it seizing, no way enter might,
   But backe rebounding, left the forckhead keene;
Eftsoones he fled away, and might no where be seene.

xlv 5 thus to] that did 1590

Cant. V.

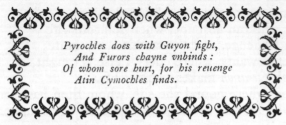

Ho euer doth to temperaunce apply
 His stedfast life, and all his actions frame,
Trust me, shall find no greater enimy,
Then stubborne perturbation, to the same;
To which right well the wise do giue that name,
For it the goodly peace of stayed mindes
Does ouerthrow, and troublous warre proclame:
His owne woes authour, who so bound it findes,
As did *Pyrochles,* and it wilfully vnbindes.

          i

After that varlets flight, it was not long,
 Ere on the plaine fast pricking *Guyon* spide
One in bright armes embatteiled full strong,
That as the Sunny beames do glaunce and glide
Vpon the trembling waue, so shined bright,
And round about him threw forth sparkling fire,
That seemd him to enflame on euery side:
His steed was bloudy red, and fomed ire,
When with the maistring spur he did him roughly stire.

          ii

Approching nigh, he neuer stayd to greete,
 Ne chaffar words, prowd courage to prouoke,
But prickt so fiers, that vnderneath his feete
The smouldring dust did round about him smoke,
Both horse and man nigh able for to choke;
And fairly couching his steele-headed speare,
Him first saluted with a sturdy stroke;
It booted nought Sir *Guyon* comming neare
To thinke, such hideous puissaunce on foot to beare.

          iii

  Arg. 2 *vnbinds :*] *vnbinds 1596 : vntyes, 1590* 3, 4 *as in 1596 (except*
Attin Gymochles 1596) : Who him sore wounds, whiles Atin to Gymochles for
ayd flyes. 1590 iii 2 chaffer *1609*

But lightly shunned it, and passing by, iv
  With his bright blade did smite at him so fell,
  That the sharpe steele arriuing forcibly
  On his broad shield, bit not, but glauncing fell
  On his horse necke before the quilted sell,
  And from the head the body sundred quight.
  So him dismounted low, he did compell
  On foot with him to matchen equall fight;
The truncked beast fast bleeding, did him fowly dight.

Sore bruzed with the fall, he slow vprose, v
  And all enraged, thus him loudly shent;
  Disleall knight, whose coward courage chose
  To wreake it selfe on beast all innocent,
  And shund the marke, at which it should be ment,
  Thereby thine armes seeme strong, but manhood fraile;
  So hast thou oft with guile thine honour blent;
  But litle may such guile thee now auaile,
If wonted force and fortune do not much me faile.

With that he drew his flaming sword, and strooke vi
  At him so fiercely, that the vpper marge
  Of his seuenfolded shield away it tooke,
  And glauncing on his helmet, made a large
  And open gash therein: were not his targe,
  That broke the violence of his intent,
  The weary soule from thence it would discharge;
  Nathelesse so sore a buff to him it lent,
That made him reele, and to his brest his beuer bent.

Exceeding wroth was *Guyon* at that blow, vii
  And much ashamd, that stroke of liuing arme
  Should him dismay, and make him stoup so low,
  Though otherwise it did him litle harme:
  Tho hurling high his yron braced arme,
  He smote so manly on his shoulder plate,
  That all his left side it did quite disarme;
  Yet there the steele stayd not, but inly bate
Deepe in his flesh, and opened wide a red floodgate.

iv 5 sell *1590, 1596*   v 9 doe me not much fayl *1590*

Deadly dismayd, with horrour of that dint   viii
  Pyrochles was, and grieued eke entyre;
  Yet nathemore did it his fury stint,
  But added flame vnto his former fire,
  That welnigh molt his hart in raging yre,
  Ne thenceforth his approued skill, to ward,
  Or strike, or hurtle round in warlike gyre,
  Remembred he, ne car'd for his saufgard,
But rudely rag'd, and like a cruell Tygre far'd.

He hewd, and lasht, and foynd, and thundred blowes,   ix
  And euery way did seeke into his life,
  Ne plate, ne male could ward so mighty throwes,
  But yielded passage to his cruell knife.
  But *Guyon*, in the heat of all his strife,
  Was warie wise, and closely did awayt
  Auauntage, whilest his foe did rage most rife;
  Sometimes a thwart, sometimes he strooke him strayt,
And falsed oft his blowes, t'illude him with such bayt.

Like as a Lyon, whose imperiall powre   x
  A prowd rebellious Vnicorne defies,
  T'auoide the rash assault and wrathfull stowre
  Of his fiers foe, him to a tree applies,
  And when him running in full course he spies,
  He slips aside; the whiles that furious beast
  His precious horne, sought of his enimies,
  Strikes in the stocke, ne thence can be releast,
But to the mighty victour yields a bounteous feast.

With such faire slight him *Guyon* often faild,   xi
  Till at the last all breathlesse, wearie, faint
  Him spying, with fresh onset he assaild,
  And kindling new his courage seeming queint,
  Strooke him so hugely, that through great constraint
  He made him stoup perforce vnto his knee,
  And do vnwilling worship to the Saint,
  That on his shield depainted he did see;
Such homage till that instant neuer learned hee.

    viii 7 hurtle] hurle, *1596* : hurlen *1609*   warlike] warelike *1596*
         x 7 enimye *1590* : enimies *1596*   8 relast *1596*

Whom *Guyon* seeing stoup, pursewed fast   xii
   The present offer of faire victory,
   And soone his dreadfull blade about he cast,
   Wherewith he smote his haughty crest so hye,
   That streight on ground made him full low to lye;
   Then on his brest his victour foote he thrust,
   With that he cryde, Mercy, do me not dye,
   Ne deeme thy force by fortunes doome vniust,
That hath (maugre her spight) thus low me laid in dust.

Eftsoones his cruell hand Sir *Guyon* stayd,   xiii
   Tempring the passion with aduizement slow,
   And maistring might on enimy dismayd:
   For th'equall dye of warre he well did know;
   Then to him said, Liue and allegaunce owe,
   To him that giues thee life and libertie,
   And henceforth by this dayes ensample trow,
   That hasty wroth, and heedlesse hazardrie
Do breede repentaunce late, and lasting infamie.

So vp he let him rise, who with grim looke   xiv
   And count'naunce sterne vpstanding, gan to grind
   His grated teeth for great disdeigne, and shooke
   His sandy lockes, long hanging downe behind,
   Knotted in bloud and dust, for griefe of mind,
   That he in ods of armes was conquered;
   Yet in himselfe some comfort he did find,
   That him so noble knight had maistered,
Whose bounty more then might, yet both he wondered.

Which *Guyon* marking said, Be nought agriev'd,   xv
   Sir knight, that thus ye now subdewed arre:
   Was neuer man, who most conquestes atchieu'd,
   But sometimes had the worse, and lost by warre,
   Yet shortly gaynd, that losse exceeded farre:
   Losse is no shame, nor to be lesse then foe,
   But to be lesser, then himselfe, doth marre
   Both loosers lot, and victours prayse alsoe.
Vaine others ouerthrowes, who selfe doth ouerthrowe.

   xii 8 by] but *conj. ed.*   xv 3 atchieu'd *1590 &c.*   9 who selfe] whose
selfe *1609*

Fly, O *Pyrochles*, fly the dreadfull warre, xvi
 That in thy selfe thy lesser parts do moue,
 Outrageous anger, and woe-working iarre,
 Direfull impatience, and hart murdring loue;
 Those, those thy foes, those warriours far remoue,
 Which thee to endlesse bale captiued lead.
 But sith in might thou didst my mercy proue,
 Of curtesie to me the cause aread,
That thee against me drew with so impetuous dread.

Dreadlesse (said he) that shall I soone declare: xvii
 It was complaind, that thou hadst done great tort
 Vnto an aged woman, poore and bare,
 And thralled her in chaines with strong effort,
 Voide of all succour and needfull comfort:
 That ill beseemes thee, such as I thee see,
 To worke such shame. Therefore I thee exhort,
 To chaunge thy will, and set *Occasion* free,
And to her captiue sonne yield his first libertee.

Thereat Sir *Guyon* smilde, And is that all xviii
 (Said he) that thee so sore displeased hath?
 Great mercy sure, for to enlarge a thrall,
 Whose freedome shall thee turne to greatest scath.
 Nath'lesse now quench thy whot emboyling wrath:
 Loe there they be; to thee I yield them free.
 Thereat he wondrous glad, out of the path
 Did lightly leape, where he them bound did see,
And gan to breake the bands of their captiuitee.

Soone as *Occasion* felt her selfe vntyde, xix
 Before her sonne could well assoyled bee,
 She to her vse returnd, and streight defyde
 Both *Guyon* and *Pyrochles*: th'one (said shee)
 Bycause he wonne; the other because hee
 Was wonne: So matter did she make of nought,
 To stirre vp strife, and do them disagree:
 But soone as *Furor* was enlargd, she sought
To kindle his quencht fire, and thousand causes wrought.

  xvi 8 a read, *1596* xvii 8 occasion *1590*: Occasion *1596* xviii 5
embayling *1590*: *corr. F. E.* xix 4 shee] hee *1590, 1596* 7 do]
garre *1590*

It was not long, ere she inflam'd him so,   xx
    That he would algates with *Pyrochles* fight,
    And his redeemer chalengd for his foe,
    Because he had not well mainteind his right,
    But yielded had to that same straunger knight:
    Now gan *Pyrochles* wex as wood, as hee,
    And him affronted with impatient might:
    So both together fiers engrasped bee,
Whiles *Guyon* standing by, their vncouth strife does see.

Him all that while *Occasion* did prouoke   xxi
    Against *Pyrochles,* and new matter framed
    Vpon the old, him stirring to be wroke
    Of his late wrongs, in which she oft him blamed
    For suffering such abuse, as knighthood shamed,
    And him dishabled quite.   But he was wise
    Ne would with vaine occasions be inflamed;
    Yet others she more vrgent did deuise:
Yet nothing could him to impatience entise.

Their fell contention still increased more,   xxii
    And more thereby increased *Furors* might,
    That he his foe has hurt, and wounded sore,
    And him in bloud and durt deformed quight.
    His mother eke, more to augment his spight,
    Now brought to him a flaming fire brond,
    Which she in *Stygian* lake, ay burning bright,
    Had kindled: that she gaue into his hond,
That armd with fire, more hardly he mote him withstond.

Tho gan that villein wex so fiers and strong,   xxiii
    That nothing might sustaine his furious forse;
    He cast him downe to ground, and all along
    Drew him through durt and myre without remorse,
    And fowly battered his comely corse,
    That *Guyon* much disdeignd so loathly sight.
    At last he was compeld to cry perforse,
    Helpe, O Sir *Guyon,* helpe most noble knight,
To rid a wretched man from hands of hellish wight.

    xxi 7 occasion *1609*   xxii 5 spight] spright *1609*   6 fyer *1590* :
fier *1609*   7 bright *1590, 1596*   xxiii 1 that] the *1609*

The knight was greatly moued at his plaint,   xxiv
    And gan him dight to succour his distresse,
    Till that the Palmer, by his graue restraint,
    Him stayd from yielding pitifull redresse;
    And said, Deare sonne, thy causelesse ruth represse,
    Ne 'let thy stout hart melt in pitty vayne:
    He that his sorrow sought through wilfulnesse,
    And his foe fettred would release agayne,
Deserues to tast his follies fruit, repented payne.

Guyon obayd; So him away he drew   xxv
    From needlesse trouble of renewing fight
    Already fought, his voyage to pursew.
    But rash *Pyrochles* varlet, *Atin* hight,
    When late he saw his Lord in heauy plight,
    Vnder Sir *Guyons* puissaunt stroke to fall,
    Him deeming dead, as then he seemd in sight,
    Fled fast away, to tell his funerall
Vnto his brother, whom *Cymochles* men did call.

He was a man of rare redoubted might,   xxvi
    Famous throughout the world for warlike prayse,
    And glorious spoiles, purchast in perilous fight:
    Full many doughtie knights he in his dayes
    Had doen to death, subdewde in equall frayes,
    Whose carkases, for terrour of his name,
    Of fowles and beastes he made the piteous prayes,
    And hong their conquered armes for more defame
On gallow trees, in honour of his dearest Dame.

His dearest Dame is that Enchaunteresse,   xxvii
    The vile *Acrasia,* that with vaine delightes,
    And idle pleasures in her *Bowre* of *Blisse,*
    Does charme her louers, and the feeble sprightes
    Can call out of the bodies of fraile wightes:
    Whom then she does transforme to monstrous hewes,
    And horribly misshapes with vgly sightes,
    Captiu'd eternally in yron mewes,
And darksom dens, where *Titan* his face neuer shewes.

                    xxiv 8 agayne. *1596*
        xxvii 3 her] his *1596*   6 trasforme *1590*

There *Atin* found *Cymochles* soiourning,   xxviii
  To serue his Lemans loue: for he, by kind,
  Was giuen all to lust and loose liuing,
  When euer his fiers hands he free mote find:
  And now he has pourd out his idle mind
  In daintie delices, and lauish ioyes,
  Hauing his warlike weapons cast behind,
  And flowes in pleasures, and vaine pleasing toyes,
Mingled emongst loose Ladies and lasciuious boyes.

And ouer him, art striuing to compaire   xxix
  With nature, did an Arber greene dispred,
  Framed of wanton Yuie, flouring faire,
  Through which the fragrant Eglantine did spred
  His pricking armes, entrayld with roses red,
  Which daintie odours round about them threw,
  And all within with flowres was garnished,
  That when myld *Zephyrus* emongst them blew,
Did breath out bounteous smels, and painted colors shew.

And fast beside, there trickled softly downe   xxx
  A gentle streame, whose murmuring waue did play
  Emongst the pumy stones, and made a sowne,
  To lull him soft a sleepe, that by it lay;
  The wearie Traueiler, wandring that way,
  Therein did often quench his thrioty heat,
  And then by it his wearie limbes display,
  Whiles creeping slumber made him to forget
His former paine, and wypt away his toylsom sweat.

And on the other side a pleasaunt groue   xxxi
  Was shot vp high, full of the stately tree,
  That dedicated is t'*Olympicke Ioue*,
  And to his sonne *Alcides*, whenas hee
  Gaynd in *Nemea* goodly victoree;
  Therein the mery birds of euery sort
  Chaunted alowd their chearefull harmonie:
  And made emongst them selues a sweet consort,
That quickned the dull spright with musicall comfort.

  xxviii 2 he,] he *1590, 1596*   xxix 5 pricking] prickling *1590*
   xxxi 5 Gaynd in *Nemea*] In *Netmus* gayned *1590* : *Nemus F. E.*

There he him found all carelesly displayd,   xxxii
   In secret shadow from the sunny ray,
   On a sweet bed of lillies softly layd,
   Amidst a flocke of Damzels fresh and gay,
   That round about him dissolute did play
   Their wanton follies, and light meriment;
   Euery of which did loosely disaray
   Her vpper parts of meet habiliments,
And shewd them naked, deckt with many ornaments.

And euery of them stroue, with most delights,   xxxiii
   Him to aggrate, and greatest pleasures shew;
   Some framd faire lookes, glancing like euening lights,
   Others sweet words, dropping like honny dew;
   Some bathed kisses, and did soft embrew
   The sugred licour through his melting lips:
   One boastes her beautie, and does yeeld to vew
   Her daintie limbes aboue her tender hips;
Another her out boastes, and all for tryall strips.

He, like an Adder, lurking in the weeds,   xxxiv
   His wandring thought in deepe desire does steepe,
   And his fraile eye with spoyle of beautie feedes;
   Sometimes he falsely faines himselfe to sleepe,
   Whiles through their lids his wanton eies do peepe,
   To steale a snatch of amorous conceipt,
   Whereby close fire into his heart does creepe:
   So, them deceiues, deceiu'd in his deceipt,
Made drunke with drugs of deare voluptuous receipt.

Atin arriuing there, when him he spide,   xxxv
   Thus in still waues of deepe delight to wade,
   Fiercely approching, to him lowdly cride,
   Cymochles; oh no, but *Cymochles* shade,
   In which that manly person late did fade,
   What is become of great *Acrates* sonne?
   Or where hath he hong vp his mortall blade,
   That hath so many haughtie conquests wonne?
Is all his force forlorne, and all his glory donne?

xxxiii 3 lights *1596*   xxxiv 6 conceit *1609*   8 So, he them *1590, 1596*

Then pricking him with his sharpe-pointed dart,   xxxvi
  He said; Vp, vp, thou womanish weake knight,
  That here in Ladies lap entombed art,
  Vnmindfull of thy praise and prowest might,
  And weetlesse eke of lately wrought despight,
  Whiles sad *Pyrochles* lies on senselesse ground,
  And groneth out his vtmost grudging spright,
  Through many a stroke, and many a streaming wound,
Calling thy helpe in vaine, that here in ioyes art dround.

Suddeinly out of his delightfull dreame   xxxvii
  The man awoke, and would haue questiond more;
  But he would not endure that wofull theame
  For to dilate at large, but vrged sore
  With percing words, and pittifull implore,
  Him hastie to arise. As one affright
  With hellish feends, or *Furies* mad vprore,
  He then vprose, inflam'd with fell despight,
And called for his armes; for he would algates fight.

They bene ybrought; he quickly does him dight,   xxxviii
  And lightly mounted, passeth on his way,
  Ne Ladies loues, ne sweete entreaties might
  Appease his heat, or hastie passage stay;
  For he has vowd, to beene aueng'd that day,
  (That day it selfe him seemed all too long:)
  On him, that did *Pyrochles* deare dismay;
  So proudly pricketh on his courser strong,
And *Atin* aie him pricks with spurs of shame and wrong.

xxxvi 2 Vp,] vp, *1590, 1596*

Q 2

Cant. VI.

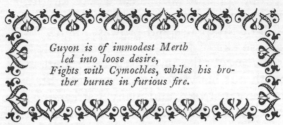

*Guyon is of immodest Merth
led into loose desire,
Fights with Cymochles, whiles his bro-
ther burnes in furious fire.*

A Harder lesson, to learne Continence　　　　　i
　In ioyous pleasure, then in grieuous paine:
For sweetnesse doth allure the weaker sence
So strongly, that vneathes it can refraine
From that, which feeble nature couets faine;
But griefe and wrath, that be her enemies,
And foes of life, she better can restraine;
　Yet vertue vauntes in both their victories,
And *Guyon* in them all shewes goodly maisteries.

Whom bold *Cymochles* trauelling to find,　　　　ii
　With cruell purpose bent to wreake on him
The wrath, which *Atin* kindled in his mind,
Came to a riuer, by whose vtmost brim
Wayting to passe, he saw whereas did swim
A long the shore, as swift as glaunce of eye,
A litle Gondelay, bedecked trim
　With boughes and arbours wouen cunningly,
That like a litle forrest seemed outwardly.

And therein sate a Ladie fresh and faire,　　　　iii
　Making sweet solace to her selfe alone;
Sometimes she sung, as loud as larke in aire,
Sometimes she laught, that nigh her breth was gone,
Yet was there not with her else any one,
That might to her moue cause of meriment:
Matter of merth enough, though there were none,
　She could deuise, and thousand waies inuent,
To feede her foolish humour, and vaine iolliment.

Arg. 1 *Merih, 1590, 1596*　　i 7 restraine] abstaine *1590*　　8 their] her
1590　　iii 4 that nigh her breth was gone,] as merry as Pope Io ne, *1590*
6 might to her] to her might *1590*　　7 none *1590 &c.*

Which when farre off *Cymochles* heard, and saw,
  He loudly cald to such, as were a bord,
  The little barke vnto the shore to draw,
  And him to ferrie ouer that deepe ford:
  The merry marriner vnto his word
  Soone hearkned, and her painted bote streightway
  Turnd to the shore, where that same warlike Lord
  She in receiu'd; but *Atin* by no way
She would admit, albe the knight her much did pray.

Eftsoones her shallow ship away did slide,
  More swift, then swallow sheres the liquid skie,
  Withouten oare or Pilot it to guide,
  Or winged canuas with the wind to flie,
  Only she turn'd a pin, and by and by
  It cut away vpon the yielding waue,
  Ne cared she her course for to apply:
  For it was taught the way, which she would haue,
And both from rocks and flats it selfe could wisely saue.

And all the way, the wanton Damzell found
  New merth, her passenger to entertaine:
  For she in pleasant purpose did abound,
  And greatly ioyed merry tales to faine,
  Of which a store-house did with her remaine,
  Yet seemed, nothing well they her became;
  For all her words she drownd with laughter vaine,
  And wanted grace in vtt'ring of the same,
That turned all her pleasance to a scoffing game.

And other whiles vaine toyes she would deuize
  As her fantasticke wit did most delight,
  Sometimes her head she fondly would aguize
  With gaudie girlonds, or fresh flowrets dight
  About her necke, or rings of rushes plight;
  Sometimes to doe him laugh, she would assay
  To laugh at shaking of the leaues light,
  Or to behold the water worke, and play
About her litle frigot, therein making way.

vii 7 of] off *1590*

Her light behauiour, and loose dalliaunce   viii
   Gaue wondrous great contentment to the knight,
   That of his way he had no souenaunce,
   Nor care of vow'd reuenge, and cruell fight,
   But to weake wench did yeeld his martiall might.
   So easie was to quench his flamed mind
   With one sweet drop of sensuall delight,
   So easie is, t'appease the stormie wind
Of malice in the calme of pleasant womankind.

Diuerse discourses in their way they spent,   ix
   Mongst which *Cymochles* of her questioned,
   Both what she was, and what that vsage ment,
   Which in her cot she daily practised.
   Vaine man (said she) that wouldest be reckoned
   A straunger in thy home, and ignoraunt
   Of *Phædria* (for so my name is red)
   Of *Phædria*, thine owne fellow seruaunt;
For thou to serue *Acrasia* thy selfe doest vaunt.

In this wide Inland sea, that hight by name   x
   The *Idle lake*, my wandring ship I row,
   That knowes her port, and thither sailes by ayme,
   Ne care, ne feare I, how the wind do blow,
   Or whether swift I wend, or whether slow:
   Both slow and swift a like do serue my tourne,
   Ne swelling *Neptune*, ne loud thundring *Ioue*
   Can chaunge my cheare, or make me euer mourne;
My litle boat can safely passe this perilous bourne.

Whiles thus she talked, and whiles thus she toyd,   xi
   They were farre past the passage, which he spake,
   And come vnto an Island, waste and voyd,
   That floted in the midst of that great lake,
   There her small Gondelay her port did make,
   And that gay paire issuing on the shore
   Disburdned her.   Their way they forward take
   Into the land, that lay them faire before,
Whose pleasaunce she him shew'd, and plentifull great store.

It was a chosen plot of fertile land,   xii
  Emongst wide waues set, like a litle nest,
  As if it had by Natures cunning hand
  Bene choisely picked out from all the rest,
  And laid forth for ensample of the best:
  No daintie flowre or herbe, that growes on ground,
  No arboret with painted blossomes drest,
  And smelling sweet, but there it might be found
To bud out faire, and her sweet smels throw all around.

No tree, whose braunches did not brauely spring;   xiii
  No braunch, whereon a fine bird did not sit:
  No bird, but did her shrill notes sweetly sing;
  No song but did containe a louely dit:
  Trees, braunches, birds, and songs were framed fit,
  For to allure fraile mind to carelesse ease.
  Carelesse the man soone woxe, and his weake wit
  Was ouercome of thing, that did him please;
So pleased, did his wrathfull purpose faire appease.

Thus when she had his eyes and senses fed   xiv
  With false delights, and fild with pleasures vaine,
  Into a shadie dale she soft him led,
  And laid him downe vpon a grassie plaine;
  And her sweet selfe without dread, or disdaine,
  She set beside, laying his head disarm'd
  In her loose lap, it softly to sustaine,
  Where soone he slumbred, fearing not be harm'd,
The whiles with a loud lay she thus him sweetly charm'd.

Behold, O man, that toilesome paines doest take,   xv
  The flowres, the fields, and all that pleasant growes,
  How they themselues doe thine ensample make,
  Whiles nothing enuious nature them forth throwes
  Out of her fruitfull lap; how, no man knowes,
  They spring, they bud, they blossome fresh and faire,
  And deck the world with their rich pompous showes;
  Yet no man for them taketh paines or care,
Yet no man to them can his carefull paines compare.

xii 3 hand, *1590 &c.*   9 her sweet smels throw] throwe her sweete smels *1590*
xiv 9 loud] loue *1590*   xv 1 take *1590, 1596*   5 no man] noman *1590*

The lilly, Ladie of the flowring field,   xvi
  The Flowre-deluce, her louely Paramoure,
  Bid thee to them thy fruitlesse labours yield,
  And soone leaue off this toylesome wearie stoure;
  Loe loe how braue she decks her bounteous boure,
  With silken curtens and gold couerlets,
  Therein to shrowd her sumptuous Belamoure,
  Yet neither spinnes nor cardes, ne cares nor frets,
But to her mother Nature all her care she lets.

Why then dost thou, O man, that of them all   xvii
  Art Lord, and eke of nature Soueraine,
  Wilfully make thy selfe a wretched thrall,
  And wast thy ioyous houres in needlesse paine,
  Seeking for daunger and aduentures vaine?
  What bootes it all to haue, and nothing vse?
  Who shall him rew, that swimming in the maine,
  Will die for thirst, and water doth refuse?
Refuse such fruitlesse toile, and present pleasures chuse.

By this she had him lulled fast a sleepe,   xviii
  That of no worldly thing he care did take;
  Then she with liquors strong his eyes did steepe,
  That nothing should him hastily awake:
  So she him left, and did her selfe betake
  Vnto her boat againe, with which she cleft
  The slouthfull waue of that great griesly lake;
  Soone she that Island farre behind her left,
And now is come to that same place, where first she weft.

By this time was the worthy *Guyon* brought   xix
  Vnto the other side of that wide strond,
  Where she was rowing, and for passage sought:
  Him needed not long call, she soone to hond
  Her ferry brought, where him she byding fond,
  With his sad guide; himselfe she tooke a boord,
  But the *Blacke Palmer* suffred still to stond,
  Ne would for price, or prayers once affoord,
To ferry that old man ouer the perlous foord.

    xvii 8 thirst] thrist *1590*   xviii 2 worldly] wordly *1590*   7 waue]
waues *1609*   griesly] griesy *1590*

Guyon was loath to leaue his guide behind,   xx
    Yet being entred, might not backe retyre;
    For the flit barke, obaying to her mind,
    Forth launched quickly, as she did desire,
    Ne gaue him leaue to bid that aged sire
    Adieu, but nimbly ran her wonted course
    Through the dull billowes thicke as troubled mire,
    Whom neither wind out of their seat could forse,
Nor timely tides did driue out of their sluggish sourse.

And by the way, as was her wonted guize,   xxi
    Her merry fit she freshly gan to reare,
    And did of ioy and iollitie deuize,
    Her selfe to cherish, and her guest to cheare:
    The knight was courteous, and did not forbeare
    Her honest merth and pleasaunce to partake;
    But when he saw her toy, and gibe, and geare,
    And passe the bonds of modest merimake,
Her dalliance he despisd, and follies did forsake.

Yet she still followed her former stile,   xxii
    And said, and did all that mote him delight,
    Till they arriued in that pleasant Ile,
    Where sleeping late she left her other knight.
    But when as *Guyon* of that land had sight,
    He wist himselfe amisse, and angry said;
    Ah Dame, perdie ye haue not doen me right,
    Thus to mislead me, whiles I you obaid.
Me litle needed from my right way to haue straid.

Faire Sir (quoth she) be not displeasd at all;   xxiii
    Who fares on sea, may not commaund his way,
    Ne wind and weather at his pleasure call:
    The sea is wide, and easie for to stray;
    The wind vnstable, and doth neuer stay.
    But here a while ye may in safety rest,
    Till season serue new passage to assay;
    Better safe port, then be in seas distrest.
Therewith she laught, and did her earnest end in iest.

xxi 8 bounds *1609*

But he halfe discontent, mote nathelesse   xxiv
   Himselfe appease, and issewd forth on shore:
   The ioyes whereof, and happie fruitfulnesse,
   Such as he saw, she gan him lay before,
   And all though pleasant, yet she made much more:
   The fields did laugh, the flowres did freshly spring,
   The trees did bud, and earely blossomes bore,
   And all the quire of birds did sweetly sing,
And told that gardins pleasures in their caroling.

And she more sweet, then any bird on bough,   xxv
   Would oftentimes emongst them beare a part,
   And striue to passe (as she could well enough)
   Their natiue musicke by her skilfull art:
   So did she all, that might his constant hart
   Withdraw from thought of warlike enterprize,
   And drowne in dissolute delights apart,
   Where noyse of armes, or vew of martiall guize
Might not reuiue desire of knightly exercize.

But he was wise, and warie of her will,   xxvi
   And euer held his hand vpon his hart:
   Yet would not seeme so rude, and thewed ill,
   As to despise so courteous seeming part,
   That gentle Ladie did to him impart,
   But fairely tempring fond desire subdewd,
   And euer her desired to depart.
   She list not heare, but her disports poursewd,
And euer bad him stay, till time the tide renewd.

And now by this, *Cymochles* howre was spent,   xxvii
   That he awoke out of his idle dreme,
   And shaking off his drowzie dreriment,
   Gan him auize, how ill did him beseeme,
   In slouthfull sleepe his molten hart to steme,
   And quench the brond of his conceiued ire.
   Tho vp he started, stird with shame extreme,
   Ne staied for his Damzell to inquire,
But marched to the strond, there passage to require.

And in the way he with Sir *Guyon* met,   xxviii
   Accompanyde with *Phædria* the faire,
   Eftsoones he gan to rage, and inly fret,
   Crying, Let be that Ladie debonaire,
   Thou recreant knight, and soone thy selfe prepare
   To battell, if thou meane her loue to gaine:
   Loe, loe alreadie, how the fowles in aire
   Doe flocke, awaiting shortly to obtaine
Thy carcasse for their pray, the guerdon of thy paine.

And therewithall he fiercely at him flew,   xxix
   And with importune outrage him assayld;
   Who soone prepard to field, his sword forth drew,
   And him with equall value counteruayld:
   Their mightie strokes their haberieons dismayld,
   And naked made each others manly spalles;
   The mortall steele despiteously entayld
   Deepe in their flesh, quite through the yron walles,
That a large purple streme adown their giambeux falles.

Cymochles, that had neuer met before   xxx
   So puissant foe, with enuious despight
   His proud presumed force increased more,
   Disdeigning to be held so long in fight;
   Sir *Guyon* grudging not so much his might,
   As those vnknightly raylings, which he spoke,
   With wrathfull fire his courage kindled bright,
   Thereof deuising shortly to be wroke,
And doubling all his powres, redoubled euery stroke.

Both of them high attonce their hands enhaunst,   xxxi
   And both attonce their huge blowes downe did sway;
   Cymochles sword on *Guyons* shield yglaunst,
   And thereof nigh one quarter sheard away;
   But *Guyons* angry blade so fierce did play
   On th'others helmet, which as *Titan* shone,
   That quite it cloue his plumed crest in tway,
   And bared all his head vnto the bone;
Wherewith astonisht, still he stood, as senselesse stone.

Still as he stood, faire *Phædria*, that beheld   xxxii
   That deadly daunger, soone atweene them ran;
   And at their feet her selfe most humbly feld,
   Crying with pitteous voice, and count'nance wan;
   Ah well away, most noble Lords, how can
   Your cruell eyes endure so pitteous sight,
   To shed your liues on ground? wo worth the man,
   That first did teach the cursed steele to bight
In his owne flesh, and make way to the liuing spright.

If euer loue of Ladie did empierce   xxxiii
   Your yron brestes, or pittie could find place,
   Withhold your bloudie hands from battell fierce,
   And sith for me ye fight, to me this grace
   Both yeeld, to stay your deadly strife a space.
   They stayd a while: and forth she gan proceed:
   Most wretched woman, and of wicked race,
   That am the author of this hainous deed,
And cause of death betweene two doughtie knights doe breed.

But if for me ye fight, or me will serue,   xxxiv
   Not this rude kind of battell, nor these armes
   Are meet, the which doe men in bale to sterue,
   And dolefull sorrow heape with deadly harmes:
   Such cruell game my scarmoges disarmes:
   Another warre, and other weapons I
   Doe loue, where loue does giue his sweet alarmes,
   Without bloudshed, and where the enemy
Does yeeld vnto his foe a pleasant victory.

Debatefull strife, and cruell enmitie   xxxv
   The famous name of knighthood fowly shend;
   But louely peace, and gentle amitie,
   And in Amours the passing houres to spend,
   The mightie martiall hands doe most commend;
   Of loue they euer greater glory bore,
   Then of their armes: *Mars* is *Cupidoes* frend,
   And is for *Venus* loues renowmed more,
Then all his wars and spoiles, the which he did of yore.

xxxv 2 shend] shent *1596*

Therewith she sweetly smyld.   They though full bent   xxxvi
  To proue extremities of bloudie fight,
  Yet at her speach their rages gan relent,
  And calme the sea of their tempestuous spight,
  Such powre haue pleasing words: such is the might
  Of courteous clemencie in gentle hart.
  Now after all was ceast, the Faery knight
  Besought that Damzell suffer him depart,
And yield him readie passage to that other part.

She no lesse glad, then he desirous was   xxxvii
  Of his departure thence; for of her ioy
  And vaine delight she saw he light did pas,
  A foe of folly and immodest toy,
  Still solemne sad, or still disdainfull coy,
  Delighting all in armes and cruell warre,
  That her sweet peace and pleasures did annoy,
  Troubled with terrour and vnquiet iarre,
That she well pleased was thence to amoue him farre.

Tho him she brought abord, and her swift bote   xxxviii
  Forthwith directed to that further strand;
  The which on the dull waues did lightly flote
  And soone arriued on the shallow sand,
  Where gladsome *Guyon* salied forth to land,
  And to that Damzell thankes gaue for reward.
  Vpon that shore he spied *Atin* stand,
  There by his maister left, when late he tar'd
In *Phædrias* flit barke ouer that perlous shard.

Well could he him remember, sith of late   xxxix
  He with *Pyrochles* sharp debatement made;
  Streight gan he him reuile, and bitter rate,
  As shepheards curre, that in darke euenings shade
  Hath tracted forth some saluage beastes trade;
  Vile Miscreant (said he) whither doest thou flie
  The shame and death, which will thee soone inuade?
  What coward hand shall doe thee next to die,
That art thus foully fled from famous enemie?

xxxvi 1 bent, *1590, 1596*   xxxviii 5 salied] sailed *1609*
8 Thereby *1590, 1596*   9 flit] fleet *1609*   xxxix 5 beastez *1609*

With that he stiffely shooke his steelehead dart: xl
  But sober *Guyon*, hearing him so raile,
  Though somewhat moued in his mightie hart,
  Yet with strong reason maistred passion fraile,
  And passed fairely forth.   He turning taile,
  Backe to the strond retyrd, and there still stayd,
  Awaiting passage, which him late did faile;
  The whiles *Cymochles* with that wanton mayd
The hastie heat of his auowd reuenge delayd.

Whylest there the varlet stood, he saw from farre   xli
  An armed knight, that towards him fast ran,
  He ran on foot, as if in lucklesse warre
  His forlorne steed from him the victour wan;
  He seemed breathlesse, hartlesse, faint, and wan,
  And all his armour sprinckled was with bloud,
  And soyld with durtie gore, that no man can
  Discerne the hew thereof.   He neuer stood,
But bent his hastie course towards the idle flood.

The varlet saw, when to the flood he came,   xlii
  How without stop or stay he fiercely lept,
  And deepe him selfe beducked in the same,
  That in the lake his loftie crest was steept,
  Ne of his safetie seemed care he kept,
  But with his raging armes he rudely flasht
  The waues about, and all his armour swept,
  That all the bloud and filth away was washt,
Yet still he bet the water, and the billowes dasht.

Atin drew nigh, to weet what it mote bee;   xliii
  For much he wondred at that vncouth sight;
  Whom should he, but his owne deare Lord, there see,
  His owne deare Lord *Pyrochles*, in sad plight,
  Readie to drowne himselfe for fell despight.
  Harrow now out, and well away, he cryde,
  What dismall day hath lent this cursed light,
  To see my Lord so deadly damnifyde?
Pyrochles, O *Pyrochles*, what is thee betyde?

  xli 1 Whiles *1609*   xlii 3 beduked *1596*   6 flasht, *1590 &c.*
  xliii 7 lent but this his cursed light, *1590*   8 damnifyde *1590, 1596*

I burne, I burne, I burne, then loud he cryde,   xliv
  O how I burne with implacable fire,
    Yet nought can quench mine inly flaming syde,
    Nor sea of licour cold, nor lake of mire,
    Nothing but death can doe me to respire.
  Ah be it (said he) from *Pyrochles* farre
    After pursewing death once to require,
    Or think, that ought those puissant hands may marre:
Death is for wretches borne vnder vnhappie starre.

Perdie, then is it fit for me (said he)   xlv
  That am, 1 weene, most wretched man aliue,
    Burning in flames, yet no flames can 1 see,
    And dying daily, daily yet reuiue:
    O *Atin*, helpe to me last death to giue.
  The varlet at his plaint was grieued so sore,
    That his deepe wounded hart in two did riue,
    And his owne health remembring now no more,
Did follow that ensample, which he blam'd afore.

Into the lake he lept, his Lord to ayd,   xlvi
  (So Loue the dread of daunger doth despise)
    And of him catching hold him strongly stayd
    From drowning.   But more happie he, then wise
    Of that seas nature did him not auise.
  The waues thereof so slow and sluggish were,
    Engrost with mud, which did them foule agriee,
    That euery weightie thing they did vpbeare,
Ne ought mote euer sinke downe to the bottome there.

Whiles thus they strugled in that idle waue,   xlvii
  And stroue in vaine, the one himselfe to drowne,
    The other both from drowning for to sauc,
    Lo, to that shore one in an aunccient gowne,
    Whose hoarie locks great grauitie did crowne,
  Holding in hand a goodly arming sword,
    By fortune came, led with the troublous sowne:
    Where drenched deepe he found in that dull ford
The carefull seruant, striuing with his raging Lord.

      xlv 1 is it] it is *1609*   3 Burning] But *1596*

Him *Atin* spying, knew right well of yore,   xlviii
   And loudly cald, Helpe helpe, O *Archimage*;
   To saue my Lord, in wretched plight forlore;
   Helpe with thy hand, or with thy counsell sage:
   Weake hands, but counsell is most strong in age.
   Him when the old man saw, he wondred sore,
   To see *Pyrochles* there so rudely rage:
   Yet sithens helpe, he saw, he needed more
Then pittie, he in hast approched to the shore.

And cald, *Pyrochles*, what is this, I see?   xlix
   What hellish furie hath at earst thee hent?
   Furious euer I thee knew to bee,
   Yet neuer in this straunge astonishment.
   These flames, these flames (he cryde) do me torment.
   What flames (quoth he) when I thee present see,
   In daunger rather to be drent, then brent?
   Harrow, the flames, which me consume (said hee)
Ne can be quencht, within my secret bowels bee.

That cursed man, that cruell feend of hell,   l
   Furor, oh *Furor* hath me thus bedight:
   His deadly wounds within my liuers swell,
   And his whot fire burnes in mine entrails bright,
   Kindled through his infernall brond of spight,
   Sith late with him I batteil vaine would boste;
   That now I weene *Ioues* dreaded thunder light
   Does scorch not halfe so sore, nor damned ghoste
In flaming *Phlegeton* does not so felly roste.

Which when as *Archimago* heard, his griefe   li
   He knew right well, and him attonce disarmd:
   Then searcht his secret wounds, and made a priefe
   Of euery place, that was with brusing harmd,
   Or with the hidden fire too inly warmd.
   Which done, he balmes and herbes thereto applyde,
   And euermore with mighty spels them charmd,
   That in short space he has them qualifyde,
And him restor'd to health, that would haue algates dyde.

xlviii 6 man, saw *1590* : *corr. F. E.*   l 3 liuer *1609*
    li 5 fire too] fier *1590*   7 euemore *1596*

Cant. VII.

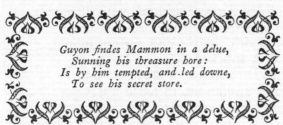

Guyon findes Mammon in a delue,
Sunning his threasure hore :
Is by him tempted, and.led downe,
To see his secret store.

AS Pilot well expert in perilous waue,   i
   That to a stedfast starre his course hath bent,
When foggy mistes, or cloudy tempests haue
The faithfull light of that faire lampe yblent,
And couer'd heauen with hideous dreriment,
Vpon his card and compas firmes his eye,
The maisters of his long experiment,
And to them does the steddy helme apply,
Bidding his winged vessell fairely forward fly :

So *Guyon* hauing lost his trusty guide,   ii
   Late left beyond that *Ydle lake,* proccedes
Yet on his way, of none accompanide ;
And euermore himselfe with comfort feedes,
Of his owne vertues, and prayse-worthy deedes.
So long he yode, yet no aduenture found,
Which fame of her shrill trompet worthy reedes :
For still he traueild through wide wastfull ground,
That nought but desert wildernesse shew'd all around.

At last he came vnto a gloomy glade,   iii
   Couer'd with boughes and shrubs from heauens light,
Whereas he sitting found in secret shade
An vncouth, saluage, and vnciuile wight,
Of griesly hew, and fowle ill fauour'd sight ;
His face with smoke was tand, and eyes were bleard,
His head and beard with sout were ill bedight,
His cole-blacke hands did seeme to haue beene seard
In smithes fire-spitting forge, and nayles like clawes appeard.

Arg. 1 *Mamon 1590, 1596*   i 9 fly. *1590, 1596*   iii 9 spetting *1609*

His yron coate all ouergrowne with rust,   iv
  Was vnderneath enueloped with gold,
  Whose glistring glosse darkned with filthy dust,
  Well yet appeared, to haue beene of old
  A worke of rich entayle, and curious mould,
  Wouen with antickes and wild Imagery:
  And in his lap a masse of coyne he told,
  And turned vpsidowne, to feede his eye
And couetous desire with his huge threasury.

And round about him lay on euery side   v
  Great heapes of gold, that neuer could be spent:
  Of which some were rude owre, not purifide
  Of *Mulcibers* deuouring element;
  Some others were new driuen, and distent
  Into great Ingoes, and to wedges square;
  Some in round plates withouten moniment;
  But most were stampt, and in their metall bare
The antique shapes of kings and kesars straunge and rare.

Soone as he *Guyon* saw, in great affright   vi
  And hast he rose, for to remoue aside
  Those pretious hils from straungers enuious sight,
  And downe them poured through an hole full wide,
  Into the hollow earth, them there to hide.
  But *Guyon* lightly to him leaping, stayd
  His hand, that trembled, as one terrifyde;
  And though him selfe were at the sight dismayd,
Yet him perforce restraynd, and to him doubtfull sayd.

What art thou man, (if man at all thou art)   vii
  That here in desert hast thine habitaunce,
  And these rich heapes of wealth doest hide apart
  From the worldes eye, and from her right vsaunce?
  Thereat with staring eyes fixed askaunce,
  In great disdaine, he answerd; Hardy Elfe,
  That darest vew my direfull countenaunce,
  I read thee rash, and heedlesse of thy selfe,
To trouble my still seate, and heapes of pretious pelfe.

iv 4 yet] it *1596, 1609*   8 vpside downe *1590*   9 And] A *1596*
    v 4 *Melcibers 1590*   vii 3 heapes] hils *1590*

God of the world and worldlings I me call,　　viii
　　Great *Mammon*, greatest god below the skye,
　　That of my plenty poure out vnto all,
　　And vnto none my graces do enuye:
　　Riches, renowme, and principality,
　　Honour, estate, and all this worldes good,
　　For which men swinck and sweat incessantly,
　　Fro me do flow into an ample flood,
And in the hollow earth haue their eternall brood.

Wherefore if me thou deigne to serue and sew,　　ix
　　At thy commaund lo all these mountaines bee;
　　Or if to thy great mind, or greedy vew
　　All these may not suffise, there shall to thee
　　Ten times so much be numbred francke and free.
　　Mammon (said he) thy godheades vaunt is vaine,
　　And idle offers of thy golden fee;
　　To them, that couet such eye-glutting gaine,
Proffer thy giftes, and fitter seruaunts entertaine.

Me ill besits, that in der-doing armes,　　x
　　And honours suit my vowed dayes do spend,
　　Vnto thy bounteous baytes, and pleasing charmes,
　　With which weake men thou witchest, to attend:
　　Regard of worldly mucke doth fowly blend,
　　And low abase the high heroicke spright,
　　That ioyes for crownes and kingdomes to contend;
　　Faire shields, gay steedes, bright armes be my delight:
Those be the riches fit for an aduent'rous knight.

Vaine glorious Elfe (said he) doest not thou weet,　　xi
　　That money can thy wantes at will supply?
　　Sheilds, steeds, and armes, and all things for thee meet
　　It can puruay in twinckling of an eye;
　　And crownes and kingdomes to thee multiply.
　　Do not I kings create, and throw the crowne
　　Sometimes to him, that low in dust doth ly?
　　And him that raignd, into his rowme thrust downe,
And whom I lust, do heape with glory and renowne?

x 1 besits] befits *1609*

R 2

All otherwise (said he) I riches read,   xii
  And deeme them roote of all disquietnesse;
  First got with guile, and then preseru'd with dread,
  And after spent with pride and lauishnesse,
  Leauing behind them griefe and heauinesse.
  Infinite mischiefes of them do arize,
  Strife, and debate, bloudshed, and bitternesse,
  Outrageous wrong, and hellish couetize,
That noble heart as great dishonour doth despize.

Ne thine be kingdomes, ne the scepters thine;   xiii
  But realmes and rulers thou doest both confound,
  And loyall truth to treason doest incline;
  Witnesse the guiltlesse bloud pourd oft on ground,
  The crowned often slaine, the slayer cround,
  The sacred Diademe in peeces rent,
  And purple robe gored with many a wound;
  Castles surprizd, great cities sackt and brent:
So mak'st thou kings, and gaynest wrongfull gouernement.

Long were to tell the troublous stormes, that tosse   xiv
  The priuate state, and make the life vnsweet:
  Who swelling sayles in Caspian sea doth crosse,
  And in frayle wood on *Adrian* gulfe doth fleet,
  Doth not, I weene, so many euils meet.
  Then *Mammon* wexing wroth, And why then, said,
  Are mortall men so fond and vndiscreet,
  So euill thing to seeke vnto their ayd,
And hauing not complaine, and hauing it vpbraid?

Indeede (quoth he) through fowle intemperaunce,   xv
  Frayle men are oft captiu'd to couetise:
  But would they thinke, with how small allowaunce
  Vntroubled Nature doth her selfe suffise,
  Such superfluities they would despise,
  Which with sad cares empeach our natiue ioyes:
  At the well head the purest streames arise:
  But mucky filth his braunching armes annoyes,
And with vncomely weedes the gentle waue accloyes.

The antique world, in his first flowring youth, xvi
  Found no defect in his Creatours grace,
  But with glad thankes, and vnreproued truth,
  The gifts of soueraigne bountie did embrace:
  Like Angels life was then mens happy cace;
  But later ages pride, like corn-fed steed,
  Abusd her plenty, and fat swolne encreace
  To all licentious lust, and gan exceed
The measure of her meane, and naturall first need.

Then gan a cursed hand the quiet wombe xvii
  Of his great Grandmother with steele to wound,
  And the hid treasures in her sacred tombe,
  With Sacriledge to dig. Therein he found
  Fountaines of gold and siluer to abound,
  Of which the matter of his huge desire
  And pompous pride eftsoones he did compound;
  Then auarice gan through his veines inspire
His greedy flames, and kindled life-deuouring fire.

Sonne (said he then) let be thy bitter scorne, xviii
  And leaue the rudenesse of that antique age
  To them, that liu'd therein in state forlorne;
  Thou that doest liue in later times, must wage
  Thy workes for wealth, and life for gold engage.
  If then thee list my offred grace to vse,
  Take what thou please of all this surplusage;
  If thee list not, leaue haue thou to refuse:
But thing refused, do not afterward accuse.

Me list not (said the Elfin knight) receaue xix
  Thing offred, till I know it well be got,
  Ne wote I, but thou didst these goods bereaue
  From rightfull owner by vnrighteous lot,
  Or that bloud guiltinesse or guile them blot.
  Perdy (quoth he) yet neuer eye did vew,
  Ne toung did tell, ne hand these handled not,
  But safe I haue them kept in secret mew,
From heauens sight, and powre of all which them pursew.

xviii 2 that *om. 1596*   xix 5 bloodguiltnesse *1590* : bloud guiltnesse *1596*

What secret place (quoth he) can safely hold   xx
  So huge a masse, and hide from heauens eye?
  Or where hast thou thy wonne, that so much gold
  Thou canst preserue from wrong and robbery?
  Come thou (quoth he) and see. So by and by
  Through that thicke couert he him led, and found
  A darkesome way, which no man could descry,
  That deepe descended through the hollow ground,
And was with dread and horrour compassed around.

At length they came into a larger space,   xxi
  That stretcht it selfe into an ample plaine,
  Through which a beaten broad high way did trace,
  That streight did lead to *Plutoes* griesly raine:
  By that wayes side, there sate infernall Payne,
  And fast beside him sat tumultuous Strife:
  The one in hand an yron whip did straine,
  The other brandished a bloudy knife,
And both did gnash their teeth, and both did threaten life.

On thother side in one consort there sate,   xxii
  Cruell Reuenge, and rancorous Despight,
  Disloyall Treason, and hart-burning Hate,
  But gnawing Gealosie out of their sight
  Sitting alone, his bitter lips did bight,
  And trembling Feare still to and fro did fly,
  And found no place, where safe he shroud him might,
  Lamenting Sorrow did in darknesse lye,
And Shame his vgly face did hide from liuing eye.

And ouer them sad Horrour with grim hew,   xxiii
  Did alwayes sore, beating his yron wings;
  And after him Owles and Night-rauens flew,
  The hatefull messengers of heauy things,
  Of death and dolour telling sad tidings;
  Whiles sad *Celeno*, sitting on a clift,
  A song of bale and bitter sorrow sings,
  That hart of flint a sunder could haue rift:
Which hauing ended, after him she flyeth swift.

xxi 5 infernall] internall *1590*   xxiii 1 horror *1590*: horrour *1596*

All these before the gates of *Pluto* lay,   xxiv
  By whom they passing, spake vnto them nought.
  But th'Elfin knight with wonder all the way
  Did feed his eyes, and fild his inner thought.
  At last him to a litle dore he brought,
  That to the gate of Hell, which gaped wide,
  Was next adioyning, ne them parted ought:
  Betwixt them both was but a litle stride,
That did the house of Richesse from hell-mouth diuide.

Before the dore sat selfe-consuming Care,   xxv
  Day and night keeping wary watch and ward,
  For feare least Force or Fraud should vnaware
  Breake in, and spoile the treasure there in gard:
  Ne would he suffer Sleepe once thither-ward
  Approch, albe his drowsie den were next;
  For next to death is Sleepe to be compard:
  Therefore his house is vnto his annext ;
Here Sleep, there Richesse, and Hel-gate them both betwext.

So soone as *Mammon* there arriu'd, the dore   xxvi
  To him did open, and affoorded way ;
  Him followed eke Sir *Guyon* euermore,
  Ne darkenesse him, ne daunger might dismay.
  Soone as he entred was, the dore streight way
  Did shut, and from behind it forth there lept
  An vgly feend, more fowle then dismall day,
  The which with monstrous stalke behind him stept,
And euer as he went, dew watch vpon him kept.

Well hoped he, ere long that hardy guest,   xxvii
  If euer couetous hand, or lustfull eye,
  Or lips he layd on thing, that likt him best,
  Or euer sleepe his eye-strings did vntye,
  Should be his pray.   And therefore still on hye
  He ouer him did hold his cruell clawes,
  Threatning with greedy gripe to do him dye
  And rend in peeces with his rauenous pawes,
If euer he transgrest the fatall *Stygian* lawes.

xxiv 7 ought] nought *1590*   xxv 9 betwixt *1609*

That houses forme within was rude and strong,   xxviii
  Like an huge caue, hewne out of rocky clift,
  From whose rough vaut the ragged breaches hong,
  Embost with massy gold of glorious gift,
  And with rich metall loaded euery rift,
  That heauy ruine they did seeme to threat;
  And ouer them *Arachne* high did lift
  Her cunning web, and spred her subtile net,
Enwrapped in fowle smoke and clouds more blacke then let.

Both roofe, and floore, and wals were all of gold,   xxix
  But ouergrowne with dust and old decay,
  And hid in darkenesse, that none could behold
  The hew thereof: for vew of chearefull day
  Did neuer in that house it selfe display,
  But a faint shadow of vncertain light;
  Such as a lamp, whose life does fade away:
  Or as the Moone cloathed with clowdy night,
Does shew to him, that walkes in feare and sad affright.

In all that rowme was nothing to be seene,   xxx
  But huge great yron chests and coffers strong,
  All bard with double bends, that none could weene
  Them to efforce by violence or wrong;
  On euery side they placed were along.
  But all the ground with sculs was scattered,
  And dead mens bones, which round about were flong,
  Whose liues, it seemed, whilome there were shed,
And their vile carcases now left vnburied.

They forward passe, ne *Guyon* yet spoke word,   xxxi
  Till that they came vnto an yron dore,
  Which to them opened of his owne accord,
  And shewd of richesse such exceeding store,
  As eye of man did neuer see before;
  Ne euer could within one place be found,
  Though all the wealth, which is, or was of yore,
  Could gathered be through all the world around,
And that aboue were added to that vnder ground.

xxxi 1 spake *1609*   3 his] it *1609*

The charge thereof vnto a couetous Spright
 Commaunded was, who thereby did attend,
 And warily awaited day and night,
 From other couetous feends it to defend,
 Who it to rob and ransacke did intend.
 Then *Mammon* turning to that warriour, said;
 Loe here the worldes blis, loe here the end,
 To which all men do ayme, rich to be made:
Such grace now to be happy, is before thee laid.

Certes (said he) I n'ill thine offred grace,
 Ne to be made so happy do intend:
 Another blis before mine eyes I place,
 Another happinesse, another end.
 To them, that list, these base regardes I lend:
 But I in armes, and in atchieuements braue,
 Do rather choose my flitting houres to spend,
 And to be Lord of those, that riches haue,
Then them to haue my selfe, and be their seruile sclaue.

Thereat the feend his gnashing teeth did grate,
 And grieu'd, so long to lacke his greedy pray;
 For well he weened, that so glorious bayte
 Would tempt his guest, to take thereof assay:
 Had he so doen, he had him snatcht away,
 More light then Culuer in the Faulcons fist.
 Eternall God thee saue from such decay.
 But whenas *Mammon* saw his purpose mist,
Him to entrap vnwares another way he wist.

Thence forward he him led, and shortly brought
 Vnto another rowme, whose dore forthright,
 To him did open, as it had beene taught:
 Therein an hundred raunges weren pight,
 And hundred fornaces all burning bright;
 By euery fornace many feends did bide,
 Deformed creatures, horrible in sight,
 And euery feend his busie paines applide,
To melt the golden metall, ready to be tride.

 xxxii 6 *Hammon 1590*: *corr. F. E.*   xxxiii 9 slaue *1609*

One with great bellowes gathered filling aire,   xxxvi
  And with forst wind the fewell did inflame;
  Another did the dying bronds repaire
  With yron toungs, and sprinckled oft the same
  With liquid waues, fiers *Vulcans* rage to tame,
  Who maistring them, renewd his former heat;
  Some scumd the drosse, that from the metall came;
  Some stird the molten owre with ladles great;
And euery one did swincke, and euery one did sweat.

But when as earthly wight they present saw,   xxxvii
  Glistring in armes and battailous aray,
  From their whot worke they did themselues withdraw
  To wonder at the sight : for till that day,
  They neuer creature saw, that camethat way.
  Their staring eyes sparckling with feruent fire,
  And vgly shapes did nigh the man dismay,
  That were it not for shame, he would retire,
Till that him thus bespake their soueraigne Lord and sire.

Behold, thou Faeries sonne, with mortall eye,   xxxviii
  That liuing eye before did neuer see:
  The thing, that thou didst craue so earnestly,
  To weet, whence all the wealth late shewd by mee,
  Proceeded, lo now is reueald to thee.
  Here is the fountaine of the worldes good:
  Now therefore, if thou wilt enriched bee,
  Auise thee well, and chaunge thy wilfull mood,
Least thou perhaps hereafter wish, and be withstood.

Suffise it then, thou Money God (quoth hee)   xxxix
  That all thine idle offers I refuse.
  All that I need I haue; what needeth mee
  To couet more, then I haue cause to vse?
  With such vaine shewes thy worldlings vile abuse :
  But giue me leaue to follow mine emprise.
  Mammon was much displeasd, yet no'te he chuse,
  But beare the rigour of his bold mesprise,
And thence him forward led, him further to entise.

xxxvi 4 yron] dying *1590*   xxxvii 1 as] an *1590*   5 cam *1590*
xxxix 8 mesprise] mespise *1596, 1609*

He brought him through a darksome narrow strait,   xl
  To a broad gate, all built of beaten gold :
  The gate was open, but therein did wait
  A sturdy villein, striding stiffe and bold,
  As if that highest God defie he would ;
  In his right hand an yron club he held,
  But he himselfe was all of golden mould,
  Yet had both life and sence, and well could weld
That cursed weapon, when his cruell foes he queld.

Disdayne he called was, and did disdaine   xli
  To be so cald, and who so did him call :
  Sterne was his looke, and full of stomacke vaine,
  His portaunce terrible, and stature tall,
  Far passing th'hight of men terrestriall ;
  Like an huge Gyant of the *Titans* race,
  That made him scorne all creatures great and small,
  And with his pride all others powre deface :
More fit amongst blacke fiendes, then men to haue his place.

Soone as those glitterand armes he did espye,   xlii
  That with their brightnesse made that darknesse light,
  His harmefull club he gan to hurtle hye,
  And threaten batteill to the Faery knight ;
  Who likewise gan himselfe to batteill dight,
  Till *Mammon* did his hasty hand withhold,
  And counseld him abstaine from perilous fight :
For nothing might abash the villein bold,
Ne mortall steele emperce his miscreated mould.

So hauing him with reason pacifide,   xliii
  And the fiers Carle commaunding to forbeare,
  He brought him in. The rowme was large and wide,
  As it some Gyeld or solemne Temple weare :
  Many great golden pillours did vpbeare
  The massy roofe, and riches huge sustayne,
  And euery pillour decked was full deare
  With crownes and Diademes, and titles vaine,
Which mortall Princes wore, whiles they on earth did rayne.

xl 5 if *om. 1596*   that] the *1590 &c.* : *corr. F. E.*   would *1596*
7 But] And *1590*   golden] yron *1590*   xli 3 his] to *1596, 1609*
5 terrestiall *1609*

A route of people there assembled were,   xliv
  Of euery sort and nation vnder skye,
  Which with great vprore preaced to draw nere
  To th'vpper part, where was aduaunced hye
  A stately siege of soueraigne maiestye ;
  And thereon sat a woman gorgeous gay,
  And richly clad in robes of royaltye,
  That neuer earthly Prince in such aray
His glory did enhaunce, and pompous pride display.

Her face right wondrous faire did seeme to bee,   xlv
  That her broad beauties beam great brightnes threw
  Through the dim shade, that all men might it see :
  Yet was not that same her owne natiue hew,
  But wrought by art and counterfetted shew,
  Thereby more louers vnto her to call ;
  Nath'lesse most heauenly faire in deed and vew
  She by creation was, till she did fall ;
Thenceforth she sought for helps, to cloke her crime withall.

There, as in glistring glory she did sit,   xlvi
  She held a great gold chaine ylincked well,
  Whose vpper end to highest heauen was knit,
  And lower part did reach to lowest Hell ;
  And all that preace did round about her swell,
  To catchen hold of that long chaine, thereby
  To clime aloft, and others to excell :
  That was *Ambition*, rash desire to sty,
And euery lincke thereof a step of dignity.

Some thought to raise themselues to high degree,   xlvii
  By riches and vnrighteous reward,
  Some by close shouldring, some by flatteree ;
  Others through friends, others for base regard ;
  And all by wrong wayes for themselues prepard.
  Those that were vp themselues, kept others low,
  Those that were low themselues, held others hard,
  Ne suffred them to rise or greater grow,
But euery one did striue his fellow downe to throw.

Which whenas *Guyon* saw, he gan inquire,   xlviii
 What meant that preace about that Ladies throne,
 And what she was that did so high aspire.
 Him *Mammon* answered; That goodly one,
 Whom all that folke with such contention,
 Do flocke about, my deare, my daughter is;
 Honour and dignitie from her alone
 Deriued are, and all this worldes blis
For which ye men do striue: few get, but many mis.

And faire *Philotime* she rightly hight,   xlix
 The fairest wight that wonneth vnder skye,
 But that this darksome neather world her light
 Doth dim with horrour and deformitie,
 Worthy of heauen and hye felicitie,
 From whence the gods haue her for enuy thrust:
 But sith thou hast found fauour in mine eye,
 Thy spouse I will her make, if that thou lust,
That she may thee aduance for workes and merites iust.

Gramercy *Mammon* (said the gentle knight)   l
 For so great grace and offred high estate;
 But I, that am fraile flesh and earthly wight,
 Vnworthy match for such immortall mate
 My selfe well wote, and mine vnequall fate;
 And were I not, yet is my trouth yplight,
 And loue auowd to other Lady late,
 That to remoue the same I haue no might:
To chaunge loue causelesse is reproch to warlike knight.

Mammon emmoued was with inward wrath;   li
 Yet forcing it to faine, him forth thence led
 Through griesly shadowes by a beaten path,
 Into a gardin goodly garnished
 With hearbs and fruits, whose kinds mote not be red:
 Not such, as earth out of her fruitfull woomb
 Throwes forth to men, sweet and well sauoured,
 But direfull deadly blacke both leafe and bloom,
Fit to adorne the dead, and decke the drery toombe.

xlviii 6 my deare my, *1596*   7 alone, *1590 &c.*   l 1 *Mammom 1590, 1596*

There mournfull *Cypresse* grew in greatest store,   lii
    And trees of bitter *Gall,* and *Heben* sad,
    Dead sleeping *Poppy,* and blacke *Hellebore,*
    Cold *Coloquintida,* and *Tetra* mad,
    Mortall *Samnitis,* and *Cicuta* bad,
    With which th'vniust *Atheniens* made to dy
    Wise *Socrates,* who thereof quaffing glad
    Pourd out his life, and last Philosophy
To the faire *Critias* his dearest Belamy.

The *Gardin* of *Proserpina* this hight;   liii
    And in the midst thereof a siluer seat,
    With a thicke Arber goodly ouer dight,
    In which she often vsd from open heat
    Her selfe to shroud, and pleasures to entreat.
    Next thereunto did grow a goodly tree,
    With braunches broad dispred and body great,
    Clothed with leaues, that none the wood mote see
And loaden all with fruit as thicke as it might bee.

Their fruit were golden apples glistring bright,   liv
    That goodly was their glory to behold,
    On earth like neuer grew, ne liuing wight
    Like euer saw, but they from hence were sold;
    For those, which *Hercules* with conquest bold
    Got from great *Atlas* daughters, hence began,
    And planted there, did bring forth fruit of gold:
    And those with which th'*Eubæan* young man wan
Swift *Atalanta,* when through craft he her out ran.

Here also sprong that goodly golden fruit,   lv
    With which *Acontius* got his louer trew,
    Whom he had long time sought with fruitlesse suit:
    Here eke that famous golden Apple grew,
    The which emongst the gods false *Ate* threw;
    For which th'*Idæan* Ladies disagreed,
    Till partiall *Paris* dempt it *Venus* dew,
    And had of her, faire *Helen* for his meed,
That many noble *Greekes* and *Troians* made to bleed.

lii 6 Which with *1590, 1596*: Which-with *1609*   liii 1 *Gordin 1596*
liv 8 th'] the *1590, 1596*: corr. *F. E.*

The warlike Elfe much wondred at this tree,   lvi
  So faire and great, that shadowed all the ground,
  And his broad braunches, laden with rich fee,
  Did stretch themselues without the vtmost bound
  Of this great gardin, compast with a mound,
  Which ouer-hanging, they themselues did steepe,
  In a blacke flood which flow'd about it round ;
    That is the riuer of *Cocytus* deepe,
In which full many soules do endlesse waile and weepe.

Which to behold, he clomb vp to the banke,   lvii
  And looking downe, saw many damned wights,
  In those sad waues, which direfull deadly stanke,
  Plonged continually of cruell Sprights,
  That with their pitteous cryes, and yelling shrights,
  They made the further shore resounden wide:
  Emongst the rest of those same ruefull sights,
    One cursed creature he by chaunce espide,
That drenched lay full deepe, vnder the Garden side.

Deepe was he drenched to the vpmost chin,   lviii
  Yet gaped still, as coueting to drinke
  Of the cold liquor, which he waded in,
  And stretching forth his hand, did often thinke
  To reach the fruit, which grew vpon the brincke:
  But both the fruit from hand, and floud from mouth
  Did flie abacke, and made him vainely swinke:
    The whiles he steru'd with hunger and with drouth
He daily dyde, yet neuer throughly dyen couth.

The knight him seeing labour so in vaine,   lix
  Askt who he was, and what he ment thereby:
  Who groning deepe, thus answerd him againe;
  Most cursed of all creatures vnder skye,
  Lo *Tantalus*, I here tormented lye:
  Of whom high *Ioue* wont whylome feasted bee,
  Lo here I now for want of food doe dye:
    But if that thou be such, as I thee see,
Of grace I pray thee, giue to eat and drinke to mee.

     lvi 1 Elfe, *1590, 1596*   lvii 8 creature, *1590, 1596*

Nay, nay, thou greedie *Tantalus* (quoth he)   lx
    Abide the fortune of thy present fate,
    And vnto all that liue in high degree,
    Ensample be of mind intemperate,
    To teach them how to vse their present state.
    Then gan the cursed wretch aloud to cry,
    Accusing highest *Ioue* and gods ingrate,
    And eke blaspheming heauen bitterly,
As authour of vniustice, there to let him dye.

He lookt a little further, and espyde   lxi
    Another wretch, whose carkasse deepe was drent
    Within the riuer, which the same did hyde:
    But both his hands most filthy feculent,
    Aboue the water were on high extent,
    And faynd to wash themselues incessantly;
    Yet nothing cleaner were for such intent,
    But rather fowler seemed to the eye;
So lost his labour vaine and idle industry.

The knight him calling, asked who he was,   lxii
    Who lifting vp his head, him answerd thus:
    I *Pilate* am the falsest Iudge, alas,
    And most vniust, that by vnrighteous
    And wicked doome, to Iewes despiteous
    Deliuered vp the Lord of life to die,
    And did acquite a murdrer felonous;
    The whiles my hands I washt in puritie,
The whiles my soule was soyld with foule iniquitie.

Infinite moe, tormented in like paine   lxiii
    He there beheld, too long here to be told:
    Ne *Mammon* would there let him long remaine,
    For terrour of the tortures manifold,
    In which the damned soules he did behold,
    But roughly him bespake. Thou fearefull foole,
    Why takest not of that same fruit of gold,
    Ne sittest downe on that same siluer stoole,
To rest thy wearie person, in the shadow coole.

lx 4 intemperate] more temperate *1590*

All which he did, to doe him deadly fall   lxiv
  In frayle intemperance through sinfull bayt;
  To which if he inclined had at all,
  That dreadfull feend, which did behind him wayt,
  Would him haue rent in thousand peeces strayt:
  But he was warie wise in all his way,
  And well perceiued his deceiptfull sleight,
  Ne suffred lust his safetie to betray ;
So goodly did beguile the Guyler of the pray.

And now he has so long remained there,   lxv
  That vitall powres gan wexe both weake and wan,
  For want of food, and sleepe, which two vpbeare,
  Like mightie pillours, this fraile life of man,
  That none without the same enduren can.
  For now three dayes of men were full outwrought,
  Since he this hardie enterprize began:
  For thy great *Mammon* fairely he besought,
Into the world to guide him backe, as he him brought.

The God, though loth, yet was constraind t'obay,   lxvi
  For lenger time, then that, no liuing wight
  Below the earth, might suffred be to stay:
  So backe againe, him brought to liuing light.
  But all so soone as his enfeebled spright
  Gan sucke this vitall aire into his brest,
  As ouercome with too exceeding might,
  The life did flit away out of her nest,
And all his senses were with deadly fit opprest.

lxiv 9 the pray] his pray *1590*

Cant. VIII.

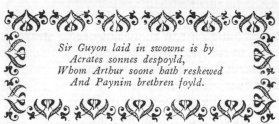

Sir Guyon laid in swowne is by
Acrates sonnes despoyld,
Whom Arthur soone hath reskewed
And Paynim brethren foyld.

ANd is there care in heauen? and is there loue   i
In heauenly spirits to these creatures bace,
That may compassion of their euils moue?
There is: else much more wretched were the cace
Of men, then beasts.   But O th'exceeding grace
Of highest God, that loues his creatures so,
And all his workes with mercy doth embrace,
That blessed Angels, he sends to and fro,
To serue to wicked man, to serue his wicked foe.

How oft do they, their siluer bowers leaue,   ii
To come to succour vs, that succour want?
How oft do they with golden pineons, cleaue
The flitting skyes, like flying Pursuiuant,
Against foule feends to aide vs millitant?
They for vs fight, they watch and dewly ward,
And their bright Squadrons round about vs plant,
And all for loue, and nothing for reward:
O why should heauenly God to men haue such regard?

During the while, that *Guyon* did abide   iii
In *Mammons* house, the Palmer, whom whyleare
That wanton Mayd of passage had denide,
By further search had passage found elsewhere,
And being on his way, approched neare,
Where *Guyon* lay in traunce, when suddenly
He heard a voice, that called loud and cleare,
Come hither, come hither, O come hastily;
That all the fields resounded with the ruefull cry.

iii 2 *Mamons 1590, 1596*   8 Come hither, hither *1609*

The Palmer lent his eare vnto the noyce,   iv
   To weet, who called so importunely :
   Againe he heard a more efforced voyce,
   That bad him come in haste.   He by and by
   His feeble feet directed to the cry ;
   Which to that shadie delue him brought at last,
   Where *Mammon* earst did sunne his threasury :
   There the good *Guyon* he found slumbring fast
In senselesse dreame ; which sight at first him sore aghast.

Beside his head there sate a faire young man,   v
   Of wondrous beautie, and of freshest yeares,
   Whose tender bud to blossome new began,
   And flourish faire aboue his equall peares ;
   His snowy front curled with golden heares,
   Like *Phœbus* face adornd with sunny rayes,
   Diuinely shone, and two sharpe winged sheares,
   Decked with diuerse plumes, like painted Iayes,
Were fixed at his backe, to cut his ayerie wayes.

Like as *Cupido* on *Idæan* hill,   vi
   When hauing laid his cruell bow away,
   And mortall arrowes, wherewith he doth fill
   The world with murdrous spoiles and bloudie pray,
   With his faire mother he him dights to play,
   And with his goodly sisters, *Graces* three ;
   The Goddesse pleased with his wanton play,
   Suffers her selfe through sleepe beguild to bee,
The whiles the other Ladies mind their merry glee.

Whom when the Palmer saw, abasht he was   vii
   Through fear and wonder, that he nought could say,
   Till him the child bespoke, Long lackt, alas,
   Hath bene thy faithfull aide in hard assay,
   Whiles deadly fit thy pupill doth dismay ;
   Behold this heauie sight, thou reuerend Sire,
   But dread of death and dolour doe away ;
   For life ere long shall to her home retire,
And he that breathlesse seemes, shal corage bold respire.

The charge, which God doth vnto me arret,   viii
  Of his deare safetie, I to thee commend;
  Yet will I not forgoe, ne yet forget
  The care thereof my selfe vnto the end,
  But euermore him succour, and defend
  Against his foe and mine: watch thou I pray;
  For euill is at hand him to offend.
  So hauing said, eftsoones he gan display
His painted nimble wings, and vanisht quite away.

The Palmer seeing his left empty place,   ix
  And his slow eyes beguiled of their sight,
  Woxe sore affraid, and standing still a space,
  Gaz'd after him, as fowle escapt by flight;
  At last him turning to his charge behight,
  With trembling hand his troubled pulse gan try;
  Where finding life not yet dislodged quight,
  He much reioyst, and courd it tenderly,
As chicken newly hatcht, from dreaded destiny.

At last he spide, where towards him did pace   x
  Two Paynim knights, all armd as bright as skie,
  And them beside an aged Sire did trace,
  And farre before a light-foot Page did flie,
  That breathed strife and troublous enmitie;
  Those were the two sonnes of *Acrates* old,
  Who meeting earst with *Archimago* slie,
  Foreby that idle strond, of him were told,
That he, which earst them combatted, was *Guyon* bold.

Which to auenge on him they dearely vowd,   xi
  Where euer that on ground they mote him fynd;
  False *Archimage* prouokt their courage prowd,
  And stryfull *Atin* in their stubborne mynd
  Coles of contention and whot vengeance tynd.
  Now bene they come, whereas the Palmer sate,
  Keeping that slombred corse to him assynd;
  Well knew they both his person, sith of late
With him in bloudie armes they rashly did debate.

xi 4 strife-full *1609*

Whom when *Pyrochles* saw, inflam'd with rage,   xii
   That sire he foule bespake, Thou dotard vile,
   That with thy brutenesse shendst thy comely age,
   Abandone soone, I read, the caitiue spoile
   Of that same outcast carkasse, that erewhile
   Made it selfe famous through false trechery,
   And crownd his coward crest with knightly stile;
   Loe where he now inglorious doth lye,
To proue he liued ill, that did thus foully dye.

To whom the Palmer fearelesse answered;   xiii
   Certes, Sir knight, ye bene too much to blame,
   Thus for to blot the honour of the dead,
   And with foule cowardize his carkasse shame,
   Whose liuing hands immortalizd his name.
   Vile is the vengeance on the ashes cold,
   And enuie base, to barke at sleeping fame:
   Was neuer wight, that treason of him told;
Your selfe his prowesse prou'd and found him fiers and bold.

Then said *Cymochles*; Palmer, thou doest dote,   xiv
   Ne canst of prowesse, ne of knighthood deeme,
   Saue as thou seest or hearst. But well I wote,
   That of his puissance tryall made extreeme;
   Yet gold all is not, that doth golden seeme,
   Ne all good knights, that shake well speare and shield:
   The worth of all men by their end esteeme,
   And then due praise, or due reproch them yield;
Bad therefore I him deeme, that thus lies dead on field.

Good or bad (gan his brother fierce reply)   xv
   What doe I recke, sith that he dyde entire?
   Or what doth his bad death now satisfy
   The greedy hunger of reuenging ire,
   Sith wrathfull hand wrought not her owne desire?
   Yet since no way is left to wreake my spight,
   I will him reaue of armes, the victors hire,
   And of that shield, more worthy of good knight;
For why should a dead dog be deckt in armour bright?

Faire Sir, said then the Palmer suppliaunt,   xvi
 For knighthoods loue, do not so foule a deed,
 Ne blame your honour with so shamefull vaunt
 Of vile reuenge.   To spoile the dead of weed
 Is sacrilege, and doth all sinnes exceed;
 But leaue these relicks of his liuing might,
 To decke his herce, and trap his tomb-blacke steed.
 What herce or steed (said he) should he haue dight,
But be entombed in the rauen or the kight?

With that, rude hand vpon his shield he laid,   xvii
 And th'other brother gan his helme vnlace,
 Both fiercely bent to haue him disaraid;
 Till that they spide, where towards them did pace
 An armed knight, of bold and bounteous grace,
 Whose squire bore after him an heben launce,
 And couerd shield.   Well kend him so farre space
 Th'enchaunter by his armes and amenaunce,
When vnder him he saw his Lybian steed to praunce.

And to those brethren said, Rise rise by liue,   xviii
 And vnto battell doe your selues addresse;
 For yonder comes the prowest knight aliue,
 Prince *Arthur*, flowre of grace and nobilesse,
 That hath to Paynim knights wrought great distresse,
 And thousand Sar'zins foully donne to dye.
 That word so deepe did in their harts impresse,
 That both eftsoones vpstarted furiously,
And gan themselues prepare to battell greedily.

But fierce *Pyrochles*, lacking his owne sword,   xix
 The want thereof now greatly gan to plaine,
 And *Archimage* besought, him that afford,
 Which he had brought for *Braggadocchio* vaine.
 So would I (said th'enchaunter) glad and faine
 Beteeme to you this sword, you to defend,
 Or ought that else your honour might maintaine,
 But that this weapons powre I well haue kend,
To be contrarie to the worke, which ye intend.

xix 6 this] his *1609*

For that same knights owne sword this is of yore,   xx
  Which *Merlin* made by his almightie art
  For that his noursling, when he knighthood swore,
  Therewith to doen his foes eternall smart.
  The metall first he mixt with *Medæwart*,
  That no enchauntment from his dint might saue ;
  Then it in flames of *Aetna* wrought apart,
  And seuen times dipped in the bitter waue
Of hellish *Styx*, which hidden vertue to it gaue.

The vertue is, that neither steele, nor stone   xxi
  The stroke thereof from entrance may defend ;
  Ne euer may be vsed by his fone,
  Ne forst his rightfull owner to offend,
  Ne euer will it breake, ne euer bend.
  Wherefore *Morddure* it rightfully is hight.
  In vaine therefore, *Pyrochles*, should I lend
  The same to thee, against his lord to fight,
For sure it would deceiue thy labour, and thy might.

Foolish old man, said then the Pagan wroth,   xxii
  That weenest words or charmes may force withstond :
  Soone shalt thou see, and then beleeue for troth,
  That I can carue with this inchaunted brond
  His Lords owne flesh. Therewith out of his hond
  That vertuous steele he rudely snatcht away,
  And *Guyons* shield about his wrest he bond ;
  So readie dight, fierce battaile to assay,
And match hio brother proud in battailous array.

By this that straunger knight in presence came,   xxiii
  And goodly salued them ; who nought againe
  Him answered, as courtesie became,
  But with sterne lookes, and stomachous disdaine,
  Gaue signes of grudge and discontentment vaine :
  Then turning to the Palmer, he gan spy
  Where at his feete, with sorrowfull demaine
  And deadly hew, an armed corse did lye,
In whose dead face he red great magnanimity.

xxii 7 wrist 1609

Said he then to the Palmer, Reuerend syre,   xxiv
    What great misfortune hath betidd this knight?
    Or did his life her fatall date expyre,
    Or did he fall by treason, or by fight?
    How euer, sure I rew his pitteous plight.
    Not one, nor other, (said the Palmer graue)
    Hath him befalne, but cloudes of deadly night
    A while his heauie eylids couer'd haue,
And all his senses drowned in deepe senselesse waue.

Which, those his cruell foes, that stand hereby,   xxv
    Making aduantage, to reuenge their spight,
    Would him disarme, and treaten shamefully,
    Vnworthy vsage of redoubted knight.
    But you, faire Sir, whose honorable sight
    Doth promise hope of helpe, and timely grace,
    Mote I beseech to succour his sad plight,
    And by your powre protect his feeble cace.
First praise of knighthood is, foule outrage to deface.

Palmer, (said he) no knight so rude, I weene,   xxvi
    As to doen outrage to a sleeping ghost:
    Ne was there euer noble courage seene,
    That in aduauntage would his puissance bost:
    Honour is least, where oddes appeareth most.
    May be, that better reason will asswage
    The rash reuengers heat.   Words well dispost
    Haue secret powre, t'appease inflamed rage:
If not, leaue vnto me thy knights last patronage.

Tho turning to those brethren, thus bespoke,   xxvii
    Ye warlike payre, whose valorous great might
    It seemes, iust wrongs to vengeance doe prouoke,
    To wreake your wrath on this dead seeming knight,
    Mote ought allay the storme of your despight,
    And settle patience in so furious heat?
    Not to debate the chalenge of your right,
    But for this carkasse pardon I entreat,
Whom fortune hath alreadie laid in lowest seat.

     xxv 1 his cruell] same *1590, 1596*: *corr. F. E.*: Which those same foes that
doen awaite hereby *1609*   xxvi 6 asswage, *1590, 1596*   9 patonage *1596*
xxvii 3 doe] doth *1609*

To whom *Cymochles* said; For what art thou,
  That mak'st thy selfe his dayes-man, to prolong
  The vengeance prest? Or who shall let me now,
  On this vile bodie from to wreake my wrong,
  And make his carkasse as the outcast dong?
  Why should not that dead carrion satisfie
  The guilt, which if he liued had thus long,
  His life for due reuenge should deare abie?
The trespasse still doth liue, albe the person die.

Indeed (then said the Prince) the euill donne
  Dyes not, when breath the bodie first doth leaue,
  But from the grandsyre to the Nephewes sonne,
  And all his seed the curse doth often cleaue,
  Till vengeance vtterly the guilt bereaue:
  So streightly God doth iudge. But gentle knight,
  That doth against the dead his hand vpreare,
  His honour staines with rancour and despight,
And great disparagment makes to his former might.

Pyrochles gan reply the second time,
  And to him said, Now felon sure I read,
  How that thou art partaker of his crime:
  Therefore by *Termagaunt* thou shalt be dead.
  With that his hand, more sad then lomp of lead,
  Vplifting high, he weened with *Morddure*,
  His owne good sword *Morddure*, to cleaue his head.
  The faithfull steele such treason no'uld endure,
But swaruing from the marke, his Lords life did assure.

Yet was the force so furious and so fell,
  That horse and man it made to reele aside;
  Nath'lesse the Prince would not forsake his sell:
  For well of yore he learned had to ride,
  But full of anger fiercely to him cride;
  False traitour miscreant, thou broken hast
  The law of armes, to strike foe vndefide.
  But thou thy treasons fruit, I hope, shalt taste
Right sowre, and feele the law, the which thou hast defast.

xxix 7 vpreare] vpheaue *MS. corr. in Malone* 615. *But cf.* II iii 28,
l. 7 *and note there.*

With that his balefull speare he fiercely bent   xxxii
  Against the Pagans brest, and therewith thought
  His cursed life out of her lodge haue rent:
  But ere the point arriued, where it ought,
  That seuen-fold shield, which he from *Guyon* brought
  He cast betwene to ward the bitter stound:
  Through all those foldes the steelehead passage wrought
  And through his shoulder pierst; wherwith to ground
He groueling fell, all gored in his gushing wound.

Which when his brother saw, fraught with great griefe   xxxiii
  And wrath, he to him leaped furiously,
  And fowly said, By *Mahoune*, cursed thiefe,
  That direfull stroke thou dearely shalt aby.
  Then hurling vp his harmefull blade on hye,
  Smote him so hugely on his haughtie crest,
  That from his saddle forced him to fly:
  Else mote it needes downe to his manly brest
Haue cleft his head in twaine, and life thence dispossest.

Now was the Prince in daungerous distresse,   xxxiv
  Wanting his sword, when he on foot should fight:
  His single speare could doe him small redresse,
  Against two foes of so exceeding might,
  The least of which was match for any knight.
  And now the other, whom he earst did daunt,
  Had reard himselfe againe to cruell fight,
  Three times more furious, and more puissaunt,
Vnmindfull of his wound, of his fate ignoraunt.

So both attonce him charge on either side,   xxxv
  With hideous strokes, and importable powre,
  That forced him his ground to trauerse wide,
  And wisely watch to ward that deadly stowre:
  For in his shield, as thicke as stormie showre,
  Their strokes did raine, yet did he neuer quaile,
  Ne backward shrinke, but as a stedfast towre,
  Whom foe with double battry doth assaile,
Them on her bulwarke beares, and bids them nought auaile.

So stoutly he withstood their strong assay,   xxxvi
   Till that at last, when he aduantage spyde,
   His poinant speare he thrust with puissant sway
   At proud *Cymochles*, whiles his shield was wyde,
   That through his thigh the mortall steele did gryde:
   He swaruing with the force, within his flesh
   Did breake the launce, and let the head abyde:
   Out of the wound the red bloud flowed fresh,
That vnderneath his feet soone made a purple plesh.

Horribly then he gan to rage, and rayle,   xxxvii
   Cursing his Gods, and himselfe damning deepe:
   Als when his brother saw the red bloud rayle
   Adowne so fast, and all his armour steepe,
   For very felnesse lowd he gan to weepe,
   And said, Caytiue, cursse on thy cruell hond,
   That twise hath sped; yet shall it not thee keepe
   From the third brunt of this my fatall brond:
Loe where the dreadfull Death behind thy backe doth stond.

With that he strooke, and th'other strooke withall,   xxxviii
   That nothing seem'd mote beare so monstrous might:
   The one vpon his coucred shield did fall,
   And glauncing downe would not his owner byte:
   But th'other did vpon his troncheon smyte,
   Which hewing quite a sunder, further way
   It made, and on his hacqueton did lyte,
   The which diuiding with importune sway,
It seizd in his right side, and there the dint did stay.

Wyde was the wound, and a large lukewarme flood,   xxxix
   Red as the Rose, thence gushed grieuously;
   That when the Paynim spyde the streaming blood,
   Gaue him great hart, and hope of victory.
   On th'other side, in huge perplexity,
   The Prince now stood, hauing his weapon broke;
   Nought could he hurt, but still at ward did ly:
   Yet with his troncheon he so rudely stroke
Cymochles twise, that twise him forst his foot reuoke.

xxxvii 3 rayle] traile *1609*

Whom when the Palmer saw in such distresse,   xl
  Sir *Guyons* sword he lightly to him raught,
  And said; Faire Son, great God thy right hand blesse,
  To vse that sword so wisely as it ought.
  Glad was the knight, and with fresh courage fraught,
  When as againe he armed felt his hond;
  Then like a Lion, which hath long time saught
  His robbed whelpes, and at the last them fond
Emongst the shepheard swaynes, then wexeth wood and yond.

So fierce he laid about him, and dealt blowes   xli
  On either side, that neither mayle could hold,
  Ne shield defend the thunder of his throwes:
  Now to *Pyrochles* many strokes he told;
  Eft to *Cymochles* twise so many fold:
  Then backe againe turning his busie hond,
  Them both attonce compeld with courage bold,
  To yield wide way to his hart-thrilling brond;
And though they both stood stiffe, yet could not both withstond.

As saluage Bull, whom two fierce mastiues bayt,   xlii
  When rancour doth with rage him once engore,
  Forgets with warie ward them to awayt,
  But with his dreadfull hornes them driues afore,
  Or flings aloft, or treads downe in the flore,
  Breathing out wrath, and bellowing disdaine,
  That all the forrest quakes to heare him rore:
  So rag'd Prince *Arthur* twixt his foemen twaine,
That neither could his mightie puissance sustaine.

But euer at *Pyrochles* when he smit,   xliii
  Who *Guyons* shield cast euer him before,
  Whereon the Faery Queenes pourtract was writ,
  His hand relented, and the stroke forbore,
  And his deare hart the picture gan adore,
  Which oft the Paynim sau'd from deadly stowre.
  But him henceforth the same can saue no more;
  For now arriued is his fatall howre,
That no'te auoyded be by earthly skill or powre.

    xl 3 fayre *1590*: faire *1596*   4 so wisely as] so well, as he *1590*

For when *Cymochles* saw the fowle reproch,   xliv
  Which them appeached, prickt with guilty shame,
  And inward griefe, he fiercely gan approch,
  Resolu'd to put away that loathly blame,
  Or dye with honour and desert of fame;
  And on the hauberk stroke the Prince so sore,
  That quite disparted all the linked frame,
  And pierced to the skin, but bit no more,
Yet made him twise to reele, that neuer moou'd afore.

Whereat renfierst with wrath and sharpe regret,   xlv
  He stroke so hugely with his borrowd blade,
  That it empierst the Pagans burganet,
  And cleauing the hard steele, did deepe inuade
  Into his head, and cruell passage made
  Quite through his braine. He tombling downe on ground,
  Breathd out his ghost, which to th'infernall shade
  Fast flying, there eternall torment found,
For all the sinnes, wherewith his lewd life did abound.

Which when his german saw, the stony feare   xlvi
  Ran to his hart, and all his sence dismayd,
  Ne thenceforth life ne courage did appeare,
  But as a man, whom hellish feends haue frayd,
  Long trembling still he stood: at last thus sayd;
  Traytour what hast thou doen? how euer may
  Thy cursed hand so cruelly haue swayd
  Against that knight: Harrow and well away,
Aftei so wicked deed why liu'st thou lenger day?

With that all desperate as loathing light,   xlvii
  And with reuenge desiring soone to dye,
  Assembling all his force and vtmost might,
  With his owne sword he fierce at him did flye,
  And strooke, and foynd, and lasht outrageously,
  Withouten reason or regard. Well knew
  The Prince, with patience and sufferaunce sly
  So hasty heat soone cooled to subdew:
Tho when this breathlesse woxe, that batteil gan renew.

xliv 2 guiltie *1590*: gulty *1596*   8 no more] not thore *1590*   xlv 3
empiest *1590*: *corr. F. E.*   xlvi 1 feare, *1590, 1596*   8 Horrow *1590*,
1596: *corr. F. E.*   weal-away! *1609*   xlvii 4 swerd *1590*

As when a windy tempest bloweth hye,   xlviii
　　That nothing may withstand his stormy stowre,
　　The cloudes, as things affrayd, before him flye;
　　But all so soone as his outrageous powre
　　Is layd, they fiercely then begin to shoure,
　　And as in scorne of his spent stormy spight,
　　Now all attonce their malice forth do poure;
　　So did Prince *Arthur* beare himselfe in fight,
And suffred rash *Pyrochles* wast his idle might.

At last when as the Sarazin perceiu'd,   xlix
　　How that straunge sword refusd, to serue his need,
　　But when he stroke most strong, the dint deceiu'd,
　　He flong it from him, and deuoyd of dreed,
　　Vpon him lightly leaping without heed,
　　Twixt his two mighty armes engrasped fast,
　　Thinking to ouerthrow and downe him tred:
　　But him in strength and skill the Prince surpast,
And through his nimble sleight did vnder him down cast.

Nought booted it the Paynim then to striue;   l
　　For as a Bittur in the Eagles claw,
　　That may not hope by flight to scape aliue,
　　Still waites for death with dread and trembling aw;
　　So he now subiect to the victours law,
　　Did not once moue, nor vpward cast his eye,
　　For vile disdaine and rancour, which did gnaw
　　His hart in twaine with sad melancholy,
As one that loathed life, and yet despisd to dye.

But full of Princely bounty and great mind,   li
　　The Conquerour nought cared him to slay,
　　But casting wrongs and all reuenge behind,
　　More glory thought to giue life, then decay,
　　And said, Paynim, this is thy dismall day;
　　Yet if thou wilt renounce thy miscreaunce,
　　And my trew liegeman yield thy selfe for ay,
　　Life will I graunt thee for thy valiaunce,
And all thy wrongs will wipe out of my souenaunce.

xlviii 8 Prince *Arthur*] Sir *Guyon 1590, 1596: corr. 1609*

Foole (said the Pagan) I thy gift defye,
   But vse thy fortune, as it doth befall,
   And say, that I not ouercome do dye,
   But in despight of life, for death do call.
   Wroth was the Prince, and sory yet withall,
   That he so wilfully refused grace;
   Yet sith his fate so cruelly did fall,
   His shining Helmet he gan soone vnlace,
And left his headlesse body bleeding all the place.

By this Sir *Guyon* from his traunce awakt,   liii
   Life hauing maistered her sencelesse foe;
   And looking vp, when as his shield he lakt,
   And sword saw not, he wexed wondrous woe:
   But when the Palmer, whom he long ygoe
   Had lost, he by him spide, right glad he grew,
   And said, Deare sir, whom wandring to and fro
   I long haue lackt, I ioy thy face to vew;
Firme is thy faith, whom daunger neuer fro me drew.

But read what wicked hand hath robbed mee   liv
   Of my good sword and shield? The Palmer glad,
   With so fresh hew vprising him to see,
   Him answered; Faire sonne, be no whit sad
   For want of weapons, they shall soone be had.
   So gan he to discourse the whole debate,
   Which that straunge knight for him sustained had,
   And those two Sarazins confounded late,
Whose carcases on ground were horribly prostrate.

Which when he heard, and saw the tokens trew,   lv
   His hart with great affection was embayd,
   And to the Prince bowing with reuerence dew,
   As to the Patrone of his life, thus sayd;
   My Lord, my liege, by whose most gratious ayd
   I liue this day, and see my foes subdewd,
   What may suffise, to be for meede repayd
   Of so great graces, as ye haue me shewd,
But to be euer bound

    liii 6 Had] Hast *1596*   liv 4 fayre *1590*: faire *1596*
      lv 3 with bowing *1590 &c.*: bowing *F. E.*

To whom the Infant thus, Faire Sir, what need   lvi
    Good turnes be counted, as a seruile bond,
    To bind their doers, to receiue their meede?
    Are not all knights by oath bound, to withstond
    Oppressours powre by armes and puissant hond?
    Suffise, that I haue done my dew in place.
    So goodly purpose they together fond,
    Of kindnesse and of curteous aggrace;
The whiles false *Archimage* and *Atin* fled apace.

Cant. IX.

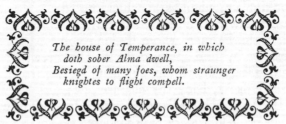

The house of Temperance, in which
doth sober Alma dwell,
Besiegd of many foes, whom straunger
knightes to flight compell.

O F all Gods workes, which do this world adorne,   i
    There is no one more faire and excellent,
    Then is mans body both for powre and forme,
    Whiles it is kept in sober gouernment;
    But none then it, more fowle and indecent,
    Distempred through misrule and passions bace:
    It growes a Monster, and incontinent
    Doth loose his dignitie and natiue grace.
Behold, who list, both one and other in this place.

After the Paynim brethren conquer'd were,   ii
    The *Briton* Prince recou'ring his stolne sword,
    And *Guyon* his lost shield, they both yfere
    Forth passed on their way in faire accord,
    Till him the Prince with gentle court did bord;
    Sir knight, mote I of you this curt'sie read,
    To weet why on your shield so goodly scord
    Beare ye the picture of that Ladies head?
Full liuely is the semblaunt, though the substance dead.

Arg. 4 *fight 1596, 1609*   i 5 incedent *1590: corr. F. E.*

Faire Sir (said he) if in that picture dead   iii
  Such life ye read, and vertue in vaine shew,
  What mote ye weene, if the trew liuely-head
  Of that most glorious visage ye did vew?
  But if the beautie of her mind ye knew,
  That is her bountie, and imperiall powre,
  Thousand times fairer then her mortall hew,
  O how great wonder would your thoughts deuoure,
And infinite desire into your spirite poure!

She is the mighty Queene of *Faerie*,   iv
  Whose faire retrait I in my shield do beare;
  She is the flowre of grace and chastitie,
  Throughout the world renowmed far and neare,
  My liefe, my liege, my Soueraigne, my deare,
  Whose glory shineth as the morning starre,
  And with her light the earth enlumines cleare;
  Far reach her mercies, and her prayses farre,
As well in state of peace, as puissaunce in warre.

Thrise happy man, (said then the *Briton* knight)   v
  Whom gracious lot, and thy great valiaunce
  Haue made thee souldier of that Princesse bright,
  Which with her bounty and glad countenance
  Doth blesse her seruaunts, and them high aduaunce.
  How may straunge knight hope euer to aspire,
  By faithfull seruice, and meet amenance,
  Vnto such blisse? sufficient were that hire
For losse of thousand liues, to dye at her desire.

Said *Guyon*, Noble Lord, what meed so great,   vi
  Or grace of earthly Prince so soueraine,
  But by your wondrous worth and warlike feat
  Ye well may hope, and easely attaine?
  But were your will, her sold to entertaine,
  And numbred be mongst knights of *Maydenhed*,
  Great guerdon, well I wote, should you remaine,
  And in her fauour high be reckoned,
As *Arthegall*, and *Sophy* now beene honored.

      v 3 thee] a *1609*   vi 9 *Arthogall, 1590*

Certes (then said the Prince) I God auow,   vii
    That sith I armes and knighthood first did plight,
    My whole desire hath beene, and yet is now,
    To serue that Queene with all my powre and might.
    Now hath the Sunne with his lamp-burning light,
    Walkt round about the world, and I no lesse,
    Sith of that Goddesse I haue sought the sight,
    Yet no where can her find: such happinesse
Heauen doth to me enuy, and fortune fauourlesse.

Fortune, the foe of famous cheuisaunce   viii
    Seldome (said *Guyon*) yields to vertue aide,
    But in her way throwes mischiefe and mischaunce,
    Whereby her course is stopt, and passage staid.
    But you, faire Sir, be not herewith dismaid,
    But constant keepe the way, in which ye stand;
    Which were it not, that I am else delaid
    With hard aduenture, which I haue in hand,
I labour would to guide you through all Faery land.

Gramercy Sir (said he) but mote I weete,   ix
    What straunge aduenture do ye now pursew?
    Perhaps my succour, or aduizement meete
    Mote stead you much your purpose to subdew.
    Then gan Sir *Guyon* all the story shew
    Of false *Acrasia*, and her wicked wiles,
    Which to auenge, the Palmer him forth drew
    From Faery court. So talked they, the whiles
They wasted had much way, and measurd many miles.

And now faire *Phœbus* gan decline in hast   x
    His weary wagon to the Westerne vale,
    Whenas they spide a goodly castle, plast
    Foreby a riuer in a pleasaunt dale,
    Which choosing for that euenings hospitale,
    They thither marcht: but when they came in sight,
    And from their sweaty Coursers did auale,
    They found the gates fast barred long ere night,
And euery loup fast lockt, as fearing foes despight.

    vii 5 Now hath] Seuen times *1590*   6 Walkt round] Hath walkte *1590*.
Cf. I ix 15   7 Since *1609*   viii 5 you *1596*   ix 1 weete,] wote,
1590 &c. MS. corr. in Malone 615

Which when they saw, they weened fowle reproch   xi
   Was to them doen, their entrance to forstall,
   Till that the Squire gan nigher to approch;
   And wind his horne vnder the castle wall,
   That with the noise it shooke, as it would fall:
   Eftsoones forth looked from the highest spire
   The watch, and lowd vnto the knights did call,
   To weete, what they so rudely did require.
Who gently answered, They entrance did desire.

Fly fly, good knights, (said he) fly fast away   xii
   If that your liues ye loue, as mecte ye should;
   Fly fast, and saue your selues from neare decay,
   Here may ye not haue entraunce, though we would:
   We would and would againe, if that we could;
   But thousand enemies about vs raue,
   And with long siege vs in this castle hould:
   Seuen yeares this wize they vs besieged haue,
And many good knights slaine, that haue vs sought to saue.

Thus as he spoke, loe with outragious cry   xiii
   A thousand villeins round about them swarmd
   Out of the rockes and caues adioyning nye,
   Vile caytiue wretches, ragged, rude, deformd,
   All threatning death, all in straunge manner armd,
   Some with vnweldy clubs, some with long speares,
   Some rusty kniues, some staues in fire warmd.
   Sterne was their looke, like wild amazed stearcs,
Staring with hollow eyes, and stiffe vpstanding heares.

Fiersly at first those knights they did assaile,   xiv
   And droue them to recoile: but when againe
   They gaue fresh charge, their forces gan to faile,
   Vnhable their encounter to sustaine;
   For with such puissaunce and impetuous maine
   Those Champions broke on them, that forst them fly,
   Like scattered Sheepe, whenas the Shepheards swaine
   A Lyon and a Tigre doth espye,
With greedy pace forth rushing from the forest nye.

xiii 1 spake *1609*

T 2

A while they fled, but soone returnd againe   xv
　　With greater fury, then before was found;
　　And euermore their cruell Capitaine
　　Sought with his raskall routs t'enclose them round,
　　And ouerrun to tread them to the ground.
　　But soone the knights with their bright-burning blades
　　Broke their rude troupes, and orders did confound,
　　Hewing and slashing at their idle shades;
For though they bodies seeme, yet substance from them fades.

As when a swarme of Gnats at euentide   xvi
　　Out of the fennes of Allan do arise,
　　Their murmuring small trompets sounden wide,
　　Whiles in the aire their clustring army flies,
　　That as a cloud doth seeme to dim the skies;
　　Ne man nor beast may rest, or take repast,
　　For their sharpe wounds, and noyous iniuries,
　　Till the fierce Northerne wind with blustring blast
Doth blow them quite away, and in the *Ocean* cast.

Thus when they had that troublous rout disperst,   xvii
　　Vnto the castle gate they come againe,
　　And entraunce crau'd, which was denied erst.
　　Now when report of that their perilous paine,
　　And combrous conflict, which they did sustaine,
　　Came to the Ladies eare, which there did dwell,
　　She forth issewed with a goodly traine
　　Of Squires and Ladies equipaged well,
And entertained them right fairely, as befell.

Alma she called was, a virgin bright;   xviii
　　That had not yet felt *Cupides* wanton rage,
　　Yet was she woo'd of many a gentle knight,
　　And many a Lord of noble parentage,
　　That sought with her to lincke in marriage:
　　For she was faire, as faire mote euer bee,
　　And in the flowre now of her freshest age;
　　Yet full of grace and goodly modestee,
That euen heauen reioyced her sweete face to see.

xv 3 Captaine *1590, 1596*   xvi 8 with *om. 1596*
　　xvii 4 perlous *1590*   5 comflict *1596*

In robe of lilly white she was arayd,   xix
　　That from her shoulder to her heele downe raught,
　　The traine whereof loose far behind her strayd,
　　Braunched with gold and pearle, most richly wrought,
　　And borne of two faire Damsels, which were taught
　　That seruice well.   Her yellow golden heare
　　Was trimly wouen, and in tresses wrought,
　　Ne other tyre she on her head did weare,
But crowned with a garland of sweete Rosiere.

Goodly she entertaind those noble knights,   xx
　　And brought them vp into her castle hall;
　　Where gentle court and gracious delight
　　She to them made, with mildnesse virginall,
　　Shewing her selfe both wise and liberall:
　　There when they rested had a season dew,
　　They her besought of fauour speciall,
　　Of that faire Castle to affoord them vew;
She graunted, and them leading forth, the same did shew.

First she them led vp to the Castle wall,   xxi
　　That was so high, as foe might not it clime,
　　And all so faire, and fensible withall,
　　Not built of bricke, ne yet of stone and lime,
　　But of thing like to that *Ægyptian* slime,
　　Whereof king *Nine* whilome built *Babell* towre;
　　But O great pitty, that no lenger time
　　So goodly workemanship should not endure:
Soone it must turne to earth; no earthly thing is sure.

The frame thereof seemd partly circulare,   xxii
　　And part triangulare, O worke diuine;
　　Those two the first and last proportions are,
　　The one imperfect, mortall, fœminine;
　　Th'other immortall, perfect, masculine,
　　And twixt them both a quadrate was the base,
　　Proportioned equally by seuen and nine;
　　Nine was the circle set in heauens place,
All which compacted made a goodly diapase.

　　xix 9 crownd *1590*: *corr. F. E.*   xx 6 There] Then *1590*   xxi 1
them] him *1590*   3 sensible *1596, 1609*   7 lenger a time *1590*: *corr.*
F. E.   xxii 9 *Dyapase 1590 &c.*: *corr. F. E.*

Therein two gates were placed seemly well: xxiii
  The one before, by which all in did pas,
  Did th'other far in workmanship excell;
  For not of wood, nor of enduring bras,
  But of more worthy substance fram'd it was;
  Doubly disparted, it did locke and close,
  That when it locked, none might thorough pas,
  And when it opened, no man might it close,
Still open to their friends, and closed to their foes.

Of hewen stone the porch was fairely wrought,   xxiv
  Stone more of valew, and more smooth and fine,
  Then Iet or Marble far from Ireland brought;
  Ouer the which was cast a wandring vine,
  Enchaced with a wanton yuie twine.
  And ouer it a faire Portcullis hong,
  Which to the gate directly did incline,
  With comely compasse, and compacture strong,
Neither vnseemely short, nor yet exceeding long.

Within the Barbican a Porter sate,   xxv
  Day and night duely keeping watch and ward,
  Nor wight, nor word mote passe out of the gate,
  But in good order, and with dew regard;
  Vtterers of secrets he from thence debard,
  Bablers of folly, and blazers of crime.
  His larumbell might lowd and wide be hard,
  When cause requird, but neuer out of time;
Early and late it rong, at euening and at prime.

And round about the porch on euery side   xxvi
  Twise sixteen warders sat, all armed bright
  In glistring steele, and strongly fortifide:
  Tall yeomen seemed they, and of great might,
  And were enraunged ready, still for fight.
  By them as *Alma* passed with her guestes,
  They did obeysaunce, as beseemed right,
  And then againe returned to their restes:
The Porter eke to her did lout with humble gestes.

Thence she them brought into a stately Hall,   xxvii
  Wherein were many tables faire dispred,
  And ready dight with drapets festiuall,
  Against the viaundes should be ministred.
  At th'upper end there sate, yclad in red
  Downe to the ground, a comely personage,
  That in his hand a white rod menaged,
  He Steward was hight *Diet*; rype of age,
And in demeanure sober, and in counsell sage.

And through the Hall there walked to and fro   xxviii
  A iolly yeoman, Marshall of the same,
  Whose name was *Appetite* ; he did bestow
  Both guestes and meate, when euer in they came,
  And knew them how to order without blame,
  As him the Steward bad. They both attone
  Did dewty to their Lady, as became;
  Who passing by, forth led her guestes anone
Into the kitchin rowme, ne spard for nicenesse none.

It was a vaut ybuilt for great dispence,   xxix
  With many raunges reard along the wall;
  And one great chimney, whose long tonnell thence
  The smoke forth threw. And in the midst of all
  There placed was a caudron wide and tall,
  Vpon a mighty furnace, burning whot,
  More whot, then *Aetn'*, or flaming *Mongiball*:
  For day and night it brent, ne ceased not,
So long as any thing it in the caudron got.

But to delay the heat, least by mischaunce   xxx
  It might breake out, and set the whole on fire,
  There added was by goodly ordinaunce,
  An huge great paire of bellowes, which did styre
  Continually, and cooling breath inspyre.
  About the Caudron many Cookes accoyld,
  With hookes and ladles, as need did require;
  The whiles the viandes in the vessell boyld
They did about their businesse sweat, and sorely toyld.

The maister Cooke was cald *Concoction*,   xxxi
    A carefull man, and full of comely guise:
    The kitchin Clerke, that hight *Digestion*,
    Did order all th'Achates in seemely wise,
    And set them forth, as well he could deuise.
    The rest had seuerall offices assind,
    Some to remoue the scum, as it did rise;
    Others to beare the same away did mind;
And others it to vse according to his kind.

But all the liquour, which was fowle and wast,   xxxii
    Not good nor seruiceable else for ought,
    They in another great round vessell plast,
    Till by a conduit pipe it thence were brought:
    And all the rest, that noyous was, and nought,
    By secret wayes, that none might it espy,
    Was close conuaid, and to the back-gate brought,
    That cleped was *Port Esquiline*, whereby
It was auoided quite, and throwne out priuily.

Which goodly order, and great workmans skill   xxxiii
    Whenas those knights beheld, with rare delight,
    And gazing wonder they their minds did fill;
    For neuer had they seene so straunge a sight.
    Thence backe againe faire *Alma* led them right,
    And soone into a goodly Parlour brought,
    That was with royall arras richly dight,
    In which was nothing pourtrahed, nor wrought,
Not wrought, nor pourtrahed, but easie to be thought.

And in the midst thereof vpon the floure,   xxxiv
    A louely beuy of faire Ladies sate,
    Courted of many a iolly Paramoure,
    The which them did in modest wise amate,
    And eachone sought his Lady to aggrate:
    And eke emongst them litle *Cupid* playd
    His wanton sports, being returned late
    From his fierce warres, and hauing from him layd
His cruell bow, wherewith he thousands hath dismayd.

    xxxi 4 th'Achates] the cates *1609*

Diuerse delights they found them selues to please;   xxxv
  Some song in sweet consort, some laught for ioy,
  Some plaid with strawes, some idly sat at ease;
  But other some could not abide to toy,
  All pleasaunce was to them griefe and annoy:
  This frownd, that faund, the third for shame did blush,
  Another seemed enuious, or coy,
  Another in her teeth did gnaw a rush:
But at these straungers presence euery one did hush.

Soone as the gracious *Alma* came in place,   xxxvi
  They all attonce out of their seates arose,
  And to her homage made, with humble grace:
  Whom when the knights beheld, they gan dispose
  Themselues to court, and each a Damsell chose:
  The Prince by chaunce did on a Lady light,
  That was right faire and fresh as morning rose,
  But somwhat sad, and solemne eke in sight,
As if some pensiue thought constraind her gentle spright.

In a long purple pall, whose skirt with gold   xxxvii
  Was fretted all about, she was arayd;
  And in her hand a Poplar braunch did hold:
  To whom the Prince in curteous manner said;
  Gentle Madame, why beene ye thus dismaid,
  And your faire beautie do with sadnesse spill?
  Liues any, that you hath thus ill apaid?
  Or doen you loue, or doen you lacke your will?
What euer be the cause, it sure bescemes you ill.

Faire Sir, (said she halfe in disdainefull wise,)   xxxviii
  How is it, that this mood in me ye blame,
  And in your selfe do not the same aduise?
  Him ill beseemes, anothers fault to name,
  That may vnwares be blotted with the same:
  Pensiue I yeeld I am, and sad in mind,
  Through great desire of glory and of fame;
  Ne ought I weene are ye therein behind,   (find.
That haue twelue moneths sought one, yet no where can her

   xxxvii 1 gold, *1590, 1596*   8 you loue,] your loue, *1590, 1596*: *corr.*
1609   xxxviii 2 mood] word *1590 &c.*: *corr. Morris*   9 twelue
moneths] three years *1590*

The Prince was inly moued at her speach,   xxxix
  Well weeting trew, what she had rashly told;
  Yet with faire semblaunt sought to hide the breach,
  Which chaunge of colour did perforce vnfold,
  Now seeming flaming whot, now stony cold.
  Tho turning soft aside, he did inquire,
  What wight she was, that Poplar braunch did hold:
  It answered was, her name was *Prays-desire*,
That by well doing sought to honour to aspire.

The whiles, the *Faerie* knight did entertaine   xl
  Another Damsell of that gentle crew,
  That was right faire, and modest of demaine,
  But that too oft she chaung'd her natiue hew:
  Straunge was her tyre, and all her garment blew,
  Close round about her tuckt with many a plight:
  Vpon her fist the bird, which shonneth vew,
  And keepes in couerts close from liuing wight,
Did sit, as yet ashamd, how rude *Pan* did her dight.

So long as *Guyon* with her commoned,   xli
  Vnto the ground she cast her modest eye,
  And euer and anone with rosie red
  The bashfull bloud her snowy cheekes did dye,
  That her became, as polisht yuory,
  Which cunning Craftesmans hand hath ouerlayd
  With faire vermilion or pure Castory.
  Great wonder had the knight, to see the mayd
So straungely passioned, and to her gently sayd,

Faire Damzell, seemeth, by your troubled cheare,   xlii
  That either me too bold ye weene, this wise
  You to molest, or other ill to feare
  That in the secret of your hart close lyes,
  From whence it doth, as cloud from sea arise.
  If it be I, of pardon I you pray;
  But if ought else that I mote not deuise,
  I will, if please you it discure, assay,
To ease you of that ill, so wisely as I may.

xxxix 3 samblaunt *1596*   xli 1 communed *1609* 6 Craftesman *1590, 1596*
7 Castory] lastery *1590 &c.: corr. F. E.*   xlii 1 cheare] cleare *1590*

She answerd nought, but more abasht for shame,　　xliii
　Held downe her head, the whiles her louely face
　The flashing bloud with blushing did inflame,
　And the strong passion mard her modest grace,
　That *Guyon* meruayld at her vncouth cace:
　Till *Alma* him bespake, Why wonder yee
　Faire Sir at that, which ye so much embrace?
　She is the fountaine of your modestee;
You shamefast are, but *Shamefastnesse* it selfe is shee.

Thereat the Elfe did blush in priuitee,　　xliv
　And turnd his face away; but she the same
　Dissembled faire, and faynd to ouersee.
　Thus they awhile with court and goodly game,
　Themselues did solace each one with his Dame,
　Till that great Ladie thence away them sought,
　To vew her castles other wondrous frame.
　Vp to a stately Turret she them brought,
Ascending by ten steps of Alablaster wrought.

That Turrets frame most admirable was,　　xlv
　Like highest heauen compassed around,
　And lifted high aboue this earthly masse,
　Which it suruew'd, as hils doen lower ground;
　But not on ground mote like to this be found,
　Not that, which antique *Cadmus* whylome built
　In *Thebes*, which *Alexander* did confound;
　Nor that proud towre of *Troy*, though richly guilt,
From which young *Hectors* bloud by cruell *Greekes* was spilt.

The roofe hereof was arched ouer head,　　xlvi
　And deckt with flowers and herbars daintily;
　Two goodly Beacons, set in watches stead,
　Therein gaue light, and flam'd continually:
　For they of liuing fire most subtilly
　Were made, and set in siluer sockets bright,
　Couer'd with lids deuiz'd of substance sly,
　That readily they shut and open might.
O who can tell the prayses of that makers might!

Ne can I tell, ne can I stay to tell xlvii
  This parts great workmanship, and wondrous powre,
  That all this other worlds worke doth excell,
  And likest is vnto that heauenly towre,
  That God hath built for his owne blessed bowre.
  Therein were diuerse roomes, and diuerse stages,
  But three the chiefest, and of greatest powre,
  In which there dwelt three honorable sages,
The wisest men, I weene, that liued in their ages.

Not he, whom *Greece*, the Nourse of all good arts, xlviii
  By *Phœbus* doome, the wisest thought aliue,
  Might be compar'd to these by many parts:
  Nor that sage *Pylian* syre, which did suruiue
  Three ages, such as mortall men contriue,
  By whose aduise old *Priams* cittie fell,
  With these in praise of pollicies mote striue.
  These three in these three roomes did sundry dwell,
And counselled faire *Alma*, how to gouerne well.

The first of them could things to come foresee: xlix
  The next could of things present best aduize;
  The third things past could keepe in memoree,
  So that no time, nor reason could arize,
  But that the same could one of these comprize.
  For thy the first did in the forepart sit,
  That nought mote hinder his quicke preiudize:
  He had a sharpe foresight, and working wit,
That neuer idle was, ne once could rest a whit.

His chamber was dispainted all within, l
  With sundry colours, in the which were writ
  Infinite shapes of things dispersed thin;
  Some such as in the world were neuer yit,
  Ne can deuized be of mortall wit;
  Some daily seene, and knowen by their names,
  Such as in idle fantasies doe flit:
  Infernall Hags, *Centaurs*, feendes, *Hippodames*,
Apes, Lions, Ægles, Owles, fooles, louers, children, Dames.

xlviii 3 these] this *1590*   xlix 4 reason] season *Drayton (teste Collier)*
9 would *1590*

And all the chamber filled was with flyes,   li
    Which buzzed all about, and made such sound,
    That they encombred all mens eares and eyes,
    Like many swarmes of Bees assembled round,
    After their hiues with honny do abound :
    All those were idle thoughts and fantasies,
    Deuices, dreames, opinions vnsound,
    Shewes, visions, sooth-sayes, and prophesies;
And all that fained is, as leasings, tales, and lies.

Emongst them all sate he, which wonned there,   lii
    That hight *Phantastes* by his nature trew;
    A man of yeares yet fresh, as mote apperc,
    Of swarth complexion, and of crabbed hew,
    That him full of melancholy did shew;
    Bent hollow beetle browes, sharpe staring eyes,
    That mad or foolish seemd: one by his vew
    Mote deeme him borne with ill disposed skyes,
When oblique *Saturne* sate in the house of agonyes.

Whom *Alma* hauing shewed to her guestes,   liii
    Thence brought them to the second roome, whose wals
    Were painted faire with memorable gestes,
    Of famous Wisards, and with picturals
    Of Magistrates, of courts, of tribunals,
    Of commen wealthes, of states, of pollicy,
    Of lawes, of iudgements, and of decretals;
    All artes, all science, all Philosophy,
And all that in the world was aye thought wittily.

Of those that roome was full, and them among   liv
    There sate a man of ripe and perfect age,
    Who did them meditate all his life long,
    That through continuall practise and vsage,
    He now was growne right wise, and wondrous sage.
    Great pleasure had those stranger knights, to see
    His goodly reason, and graue personage,
    That his disciples both desir'd to bee;
But *Alma* thence them led to th'hindmost roome of three.

That chamber seemed ruinous and old,   lv
  And therefore was remoued farre behind,
  Yet were the wals, that did the same vphold,
  Right firme and strong, though somewhat they declind;
  And therein sate an old oldman, halfe blind,
  And all decrepit in his feeble corse,
  Yet liuely vigour rested in his mind,
  And recompenst him with a better scorse:
Weake body well is chang'd for minds redoubled forse.

This man of infinite remembrance was,   lvi
  And things foregone through many ages held,
  Which he recorded still, as they did pas,
  Ne suffred them to perish through long eld,
  As all things else, the which this world doth weld,
  But laid them vp in his immortall scrine,
  Where they for euer incorrupted dweld:
  The warres he well remembred of king *Nine*,
Of old *Assaracus*, and *Inachus* diuine.

The yeares of *Nestor* nothing were to his,   lvii
  Ne yet *Mathusalem*, though longest liu'd;
  For he remembred both their infancies:
  Ne wonder then, if that he were depriu'd
  Of natiue strength now, that he them suruiu'd.
  His chamber all was hangd about with rolles,
  And old records from auncient times deriu'd,
  Some made in books, some in long parchment scrolles,
That were all worme-eaten, and full of canker holes.

Amidst them all he in a chaire was set,   lviii
  Tossing and turning them withouten end;
  But for he was vnhable them to fet,
  A litle boy did on him still attend,
  To reach, when euer he for ought did send;
  And oft when things were lost, or laid amis,
  That boy them sought, and vnto him did lend.
  Therefore he *Anamnestes* cleped is,
And that old man *Eumnestes*, by their propertis.

lv 9 welis *1590*: *corr. F. E.*   lvii 1 to] so *1590*

The knights there entring, did him reuerence dew   lix
  And wondred at his endlesse exercise,
  Then as they gan his Librarie to vew,
  And antique Registers for to auise,
  There chaunced to the Princes hand to rize,
  An auncient booke, hight *Briton moniments,*
  That of this lands first conquest did deuize,
  And old diuision into Regiments,
Till it reduced was to one mans gouernments.

Sir *Guyon* chaunst eke on another booke,   lx
  That hight *Antiquitie* of *Faerie* lond,
  In which when as he greedily did looke,
  Th'off-spring of Elues and Faries there he fond,
  As it deliuered was from hond to hond:
  Whereat they burning both with feruent fire,
  Their countries auncestry to vnderstond,
  Crau'd leaue of *Alma,* and that aged sire,
To read those bookes; who gladly graunted their desire.

Cant. X.

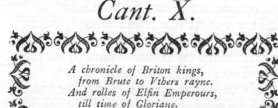

A chronicle of Briton kings,
from Brute to Vthers rayne.
And rolles of Elfin Emperours,
till time of Gloriane.

WHo now shall giue vnto me words and sound,   1
  Equall vnto this haughtie enterprise?
Or who shall lend me wings, with which from ground
My lowly verse may loftily arise,
And lift it selfe vnto the highest skies?
More ample spirit, then hitherto was wcount,
Here needes me, whiles the famous auncestries
Of my most dreaded Soueraigne I recount,
By which all earthly Princes she doth farre surmount.

lx 2 lond. *1596*   3 looke; *1596, 1609*

Ne vnder Sunne, that shines so wide and faire,   ii
  Whence all that liues, does borrow life and light,
  Liues ought, that to her linage may compaire,
  Which though from earth it be deriued right,
  Yet doth it selfe stretch forth to heauens hight,
  And all the world with wonder ouerspred;
  A labour huge, exceeding farre my might:
  How shall fraile pen, with feare disparaged,
Conceiue such soueraine glory, and great bountihed?

Argument worthy of *Mæonian* quill,   iii
  Or rather worthy of great *Phœbus* rote,
  Whereon the ruines of great *Ossa* hill,
  And triumphes of *Phlegræan Ioue* he wrote,
  That all the Gods admird his loftie note.
  But if some relish of that heauenly lay
  His learned daughters would to me report,
  To decke my song withall, I would assay,
Thy name, O soueraine Queene, to blazon farre away.

Thy name O soueraine Queene, thy realme and race,   iv
  From this renowmed Prince deriued arre,
  Who mightily vpheld that royall mace,
  Which now thou bear'st, to thee descended farre
  From mightie kings and conquerours in warre,
  Thy fathers and great Grandfathers of old,
  Whose noble deedes aboue the Northerne starre
  Immortall fame for euer hath enrold;
As in that old mans booke they were in order told.

The land, which warlike Britons now possesse,   v
  And therein haue their mightie empire raysd,
  In antique times was saluage wildernesse,
  Vnpeopled, vnmanurd, vnprou'd, vnpraysd,
  Ne was it Island then, ne was it paysd
  Amid the *Ocean* waues, ne was it sought
  Of marchants farre, for profits therein praysd,
  But was all desolate, and of some thought
By sea to haue bene from the *Celticke* mayn-land brought.

iv 3 Whom *1590, 1596: corr. F. E.*   6 and thy great *1590: corr.*
F. E.   old] gold *1590: corr. F. E.*   v 7 Marchants *1609*

Ne did it then deserue a name to haue, vi
   Till that the venturous Mariner that way
   Learning his ship from those white rocks to saue,
   Which all along the Southerne sea-coast lay,
   Threatning vnheedie wrecke and rash decay,
   For safeties sake that same his sea-marke made,
   And namd it *Albion.* But later day
   Finding in it fit ports for fishers trade,
Gan more the same frequent, and further to inuade.

But farre in land a saluage nation dwelt, vii
   Of hidcous Giants, and halfe beastly men,
   That neuer tasted grace, nor goodnesse felt,
   But like wild beasts lurking in loathsome den,
   And flying fast as Roebucke through the fen,
   All naked without shame, or care of cold,
   By hunting and by spoiling liued then;
   Of stature huge, and eke of courage bold,
That sonnes of men amazd their sternnesse to behold.

But whence they sprong, or how they were begot, viii
   Vneath is to assure; vneath to wene
   That monstrous error, which doth some assot,
   That *Dioclesians* fiftie daughters shene
   Into this land by chaunce haue driuen bene,
   Where companing with feends and filthy Sprights,
   Through vaine illusion of their lust vnclene,
   They brought forth Giants and such dreadfull wights,
As farre exceeded men in their immeasurd mights.

They held this land, and with their filthinesse ix
   Polluted this same gentle soyle long time:
   That their owne mother loathd their beastlinesse,
   And gan abhorre her broods vnkindly crime,
   All were they borne of her owne natiue slime,
   Vntill that *Brutus* anciently deriu'd
   From royall stocke of old *Assaracs* line,
   Driuen by fatall error, here arriu'd,
And them of their vniust possession depriu'd.

vi 6 safeties sake] safety *1590*   vii 7 liued then] liueden *1590*
ix 7 *Assaraos 1596*

SPENSER II   U

But ere he had established his throne,   x
    And spred his empire to the vtmost shore,
    He fought great battels with his saluage fone;
    In which he them defeated euermore,
    And many Giants left on groning flore;
    That well can witnesse yet vnto this day
    The westerne Hogh, besprincled with the gore
    Of mightie *Goëmot*, whom in stout fray
Corineus conquered, and cruelly did slay.

And eke that ample Pit, yet farre renownd,   xi
    For the large leape, which *Debon* did compell
    Coulin to make, being eight lugs of grownd;
    Into the which returning backe, he fell,
    But those three monstrous stones doe most excell
    Which that huge sonne of hideous *Albion*,
    Whose father *Hercules* in Fraunce did quell,
    Great *Godmer* threw, in fierce contention,
At bold *Canutus*; but of him was slaine anon.

In meed of these great conquests by them got,   xii
    Corineus had that Prouince vtmost west,
    To him assigned for his worthy lot,
    Which of his name and memorable gest
    He called *Cornewaile*, yet so called best:
    And *Debons* shayre was, that is *Deuonshyre*:
    But *Canute* had his portion from the rest,
    The which he cald *Canutium*, for his hyre;
Now *Cantium*, which Kent we commenly inquire.

Thus *Brute* this Realme vnto his rule subdewd,   xiii
    And raigned long in great felicitie,
    Lou'd of his friends, and of his foes eschewd,
    He left three sonnes, his famous progeny,
    Borne of faire *Inogene* of *Italy*;
    Mongst whom he parted his imperiall state,
    And *Locrine* left chiefe Lord of *Britany*.
    At last ripe age bad him surrender late
His life, and long good fortune vnto finall fate.

xii 2 that] the *1609*

Locrine was left the soueraine Lord of all;   xiv
   But *Albanact* had all the Northrene part,
   Which of himselfe *Albania* he did call;
   And *Camber* did possesse the Westerne quart,
   Which *Seuerne* now from *Logris* doth depart:
   And each his portion peaceably enioyd,
   Ne was there outward breach, nor grudge in hart,
   That once their quiet gouernment annoyd,
But each his paines to others profit still employd.

Vntill a nation straung, with visage swart,   xv
   And courage fierce, that all men did affray,
   Which through the world then swarmd in euery part,
   And ouerflow'd all countries farre away,
   Like *Noyes* great flood, with their importune sway,
   This land inuaded with like violence,
   And did themselues through all the North display:
   Vntill that *Locrine* for his Realmes defence,
Did head against them make, and strong munifence.

He them encountred, a confused rout,   xvi
   Foreby the Riuer, that whylome was hight
   The auncient *Abus*, where with courage stout
   He them defeated in victorious fight,
   And chaste so fiercely after fearfull flight,
   That forst their Chieftaine, for his safeties sake,
   (Their Chieftaine *Humber* named was aright)
   Vnto the mightie streame him to betake,
Where he an end of battell, and of life did make.

The king returned proud of victorie,   xvii
   And insolent wox through vnwonted ease,
   That shortly he forgot the ieopardie,
   Which in his land he lately did appease,
   And fell to vaine voluptuous disease:
   He lou'd faire Ladie *Estrild*, lewdly lou'd,
   Whose wanton pleasures him too much did please,
   That quite his hart from *Guendolene* remou'd,
From *Guendolene* his wife, though alwaies faithfull prou'd.

xv 9 munificence *1590, 1609*

The noble daughter of *Corineus*   xviii
   Would not endure to be so vile disdaind,
   But gathering force, and courage valorous,
   Encountred him in battell well ordaind,
   In which him vanquisht she to fly constraind:
   But she so fast pursewd, that him she tooke,
   And threw in bands, where he till death remaind;
   Als his faire Leman, flying through a brooke,
She ouerhent, nought moued with her piteous looke.

But both her selfe, and eke her daughter deare,   xix
   Begotten by her kingly Paramoure,
   The faire *Sabrina* almost dead with feare,
   She there attached, farre from all succoure;
   The one she slew in that impatient stoure,
   But the sad virgin innocent of all,
   Adowne the rolling riuer she did poure,
   Which of her name now *Seuerne* men do call:
Such was the end, that to disloyall loue did fall.

Then for her sonne, which she to *Locrin* bore,   xx
   Madan was young, vnmeet the rule to sway,
   In her owne hand the crowne she kept in store,
   Till ryper yeares he raught, and stronger stay:
   During which time her powre she did display
   Through all this realme, the glorie of her sex,
   And first taught men a woman to obay:
   But when her sonne to mans estate did wex,
She it surrendred, ne her selfe would lenger vex.

Tho *Madan* raignd, vnworthie of his race: xxi
   For with all shame that sacred throne he fild:
   Next *Memprise*, as vnworthy of that place,
   In which being consorted with *Manild*,
   For thirst of single kingdome him he kild.
   But *Ebranck* salued both their infamies
   With noble deedes, and warreyd on *Brunchild*
   In *Henault*, where yet of his victories
Braue moniments remaine, which yet that land enuies.

      xix 5 in that impatient stoure] vpon the present floure *1590*
            xx 2 of sway *1596, 1609*

An happie man in his first dayes he was, xxii
   And happie father of faire progeny:
   For all so many weekes as the yeare has,
   So many children he did multiply;
   Of which were twentie sonnes, which did apply
   Their minds to praise, and cheualrous desire:
   Those germans did subdew all Germany,
   Of whom it hight; but in the end their Sire
With foule repulse from Fraunce was forced to retire.

Which blot his sonne succeeding in his seat, xxiii
   The second *Brute*, the second both in name,
   And eke in semblance of his puissance gieat,
   Right woll iccur'd, and did away that blame
   With recompence of euerlasting fame.
   He with his victour sword first opened
   The bowels of wide Fraunce, a forlorne Dame,
   And taught her first how to be conquered;
Since which, with sundrie spoiles she hath beene ransacked.

Let *Scaldis* tell, and let tell *Hania*, xxiv
   And let the marsh of *Estham bruges* tell,
   What colour were their waters that same day,
   And all the moore twixt *Eluersham* and *Dell*,
   With bloud of *Henalois*, which therein fell.
   How oft that day did sad *Brunchildis* see
   The greene shield dyde in dolorous vermell?
   That not *Scuith guiridh* it mote seeme to bee,
But rather *y Scuith gogh*, signe of sad crueltee.

His sonne king *Leill* by fathers labour long, xxv
   Enioyd an heritage of lasting peace,
   And built *Cairleill*, and built *Cairleon* strong.
   Next *Huddibras* his realme did not encrease,
   But taught the land from wearie warres to cease.
   Whose footsteps *Bladud* following, in arts
   Exceld at *Athens* all the learned preace,
   From whence he brought them to these saluage parts,
And with sweet science mollifide their stubborne harts.

  xxii 5 apply, *1590, 1596*   xxiii 6 opened, *1590, 1596*   xxiv 8 *Scuith
guiridh om. 1590* it] he *1590* 9 rather *y Scuith gogh*, signe of sad crueltee
om. 1590. But Seuith Scuith F. E.

Ensample of his wondrous faculty,   xxvi
  Behold the boyling Bathes at *Cairbadon*,
  Which seeth with secret fire eternally,
  And in their entrails, full of quicke Brimston,
  Nourish the flames, which they are warm'd vpon,
  That to their people wealth they forth do well,
  And health to euery forreine nation:
  Yet he at last contending to excell
The reach of men, through flight into fond mischief fell.

Next him king *Leyr* in happie peace long raind,   xxvii
  But had no issue male him to succeed,
  But three faire daughters, which were well vptraind,
  In all that seemed fit for kingly seed:
  Mongst whom his realme he equally decreed
  To haue diuided.   Tho when feeble age
  Nigh to his vtmost date he saw proceed,
  He cald his daughters; and with speeches sage
Inquyrd, which of them most did loue her parentage.

The eldest *Gonorill* gan to protest,   xxviii
  That she much more then her owne life him lou'd:
  And *Regan* greater loue to him profest,
  Then all the world, when euer it were proou'd;
  But *Cordeill* said she lou'd him, as behoou'd:
  Whose simple answere, wanting colours faire
  To paint it forth, him to displeasance moou'd,
  That in his crowne he counted her no haire,
But twixt the other twaine his kingdome whole did shaire.

So wedded th'one to *Maglan* king of Scots,   xxix
  And th'other to the king of *Cambria*,
  And twixt them shayrd his realme by equall lots:
  But without dowre the wise *Cordelia*
  Was sent to *Aganip* of *Celtica*.
  Their aged Syre, thus eased of his crowne,
  A priuate life led in *Albania*,
  With *Gonorill*, long had in great renowne,
That nought him grieu'd to bene from rule deposed downe.

    xxvi 6 their] her *1590 &c.*: *corr. F. E.*   xxviii 1 *Gonerill 1590*
         xxix 4 *Cordelia, 1590, 1596*

But true it is, that when the oyle is spent,   xxx
  The light goes out, and weeke is throwne away;
So when he had resigned his regiment,
His daughter gan despise his drouping day,
And wearie waxe of his continuall stay.
  Tho to his daughter *Regan* he repayrd,
  Who him at first well vsed euery way;
  But when of his departure she despayrd,
Her bountie she abated, and his cheare empayrd.

The wretched man gan then auise too late,   xxxi
  That loue is not, where most it is profest,
Too truely tryde in his extreamest state;
At last resolu'd likewise to proue the rest,
He to *Cordelia* him selfe addrest,
  Who with entire affection him receau'd,
  As for her Syre and king her seemed best;
  And after all an army strong she leau'd,
To war on those, which him had of his realme bereau'd.

So to his crowne she him restor'd againe,   xxxii
  In which he dyde, made ripe for death by eld,
And after wild, it should to her remaine:
Who peaceably the same long time did weld:
And all mens harts in dew obedience held:
  Till that her sisters children, woxen strong
  Through proud ambition, against her rebeld,
  And ouercommen kept in prison long,
Till wearie of that wretched life, her selfe she hong.

Then gan the bloudie brethren both to raine: xxxiii
  But fierce *Cundah* gan shortly to enuie
His brother *Morgan*, prickt with proud disdaine,
To haue a pere in part of soueraintie,
And kindling coles of cruell enmitie,
  Raisd warre, and him in battell ouerthrew:
  Whence as he to those woodie hils did flie,
  Which hight of him *Glamorgan*, there him slew:
Then did he raigne alone, when he none equall knew.

xxx 2 weeke] wike *1609*   5 waxe] wox *1609*   6 *Rigan 1596, 1609*

His sonne *Riuallo* his dead roome did supply,   xxxiv
  In whose sad time bloud did from heauen raine:
  Next great *Gurgustus*, then faire *Cæcily*
  In constant peace their kingdomes did containe,
  After whom *Lago*, and *Kinmarke* did raine,
  And *Gorbogud*, till farre in yeares he grew:
  Then his ambitious sonnes vnto them twaine
  Arraught the rule, and from their father drew,
Stout *Ferrex* and sterne *Porrex* him in prison threw.

But O, the greedy thirst of royall crowne,   xxxv
  That knowes no kinred, nor regardes no right,
  Stird *Porrex* vp to put his brother downe;
  Who vnto him assembling forreine might,
  Made warre on him, and fell him selfe in fight:
  Whose death t'auenge, his mother mercilesse,
  Most mercilesse of women, *Wyden* hight,
  Her other sonne fast sleeping did oppresse,
And with most cruell hand him murdred pittilesse.

Here ended *Brutus* sacred progenie,   xxxvi
  Which had seuen hundred yeares this scepter borne,
  With high renowme, and great felicitie;
  The noble braunch from th'antique stocke was torne
  Through discord, and the royall throne forlorne:
  Thenceforth this Realme was into factions rent,
  Whilest each of *Brutus* boasted to be borne,
  That in the end was left no moniment
Of *Brutus*, nor of Britons glory auncient.

Then vp arose a man of matchlesse might,   xxxvii
  And wondrous wit to menage high affaires,
  Who stird with pitty of the stressed plight
  Of this sad Realme, cut into sundry shaires
  By such, as claymd themselues *Brutes* rightfull haires,
  Gathered the Princes of the people loose,
  To taken counsell of their common cares;
  Who with his wisedom won, him streight did choose
Their king, and swore him fealty to win or loose.

   xxxiv 1 *Riuall' 1590*: *Rivall' 1609* 7 Then] Till *1596*: When *1609*
      xxxvi 3 felicitie? *1596*   xxxvii 3 with] vp *1596*

Then made he head against his enimies,   xxxviii
    And *Ymner* slew, of *Logris* miscreate;
    Then *Ruddoc* and proud *Stater*, both allyes,
    This of *Albanie* newly nominate,
    And that of *Cambry* king confirmed late,
    He ouerthrew through his owne valiaunce;
    Whose countreis he redus'd to quiet state,
    And shortly brought to ciuill gouernaunce,
Now one, which earst were many, made through variaunce.

Then made he sacred lawes, which some men say   xxxix
    Were vnto him reueald in vision,
    By which he freed the Traueilers high way,
    The Churches part, and Ploughmans portion,
    Restraining stealth, and strong extortion;
    The gracious *Numa* of great *Britanie*:
    For till his dayes, the chiefe dominion
    By strength was wielded without pollicie;
Therefore he first wore crowne of gold for dignitie.

Donwallo dyde (for what may liue for ay?)   xl
    And left two sonnes, of pearelesse prowesse both;
    That sacked *Rome* too dearely did assay,
    The recompence of their periured oth,
    And ransackt *Greece* well tryde, when they were wroth;
    Besides subiected *Fraunce*, and *Germany*,
    Which yet their prayses speake, all be they loth,
    And inly tremble at the memory
Of *Brennus* and *Bellinus*, kings of Britany.

Next them did *Gurgunt*, great *Bellinus* sonne   xli
    In rule succeede, and eke in fathers praysc;
    He Easterland subdewd, and Danmarke wonne,
    And of them both did foy and tribute raise,
    The which was dew in his dead fathers dayes:
    He also gaue to fugitiues of *Spayne*,
    Whom he at sea found wandring from their wayes,
    A seate in *Ireland* safely to remayne,
Which they should hold of him, as subiect to *Britayne*.

xxxviii 2 of] or *1596, 1609*   xli 1 *Gurgiunt 1590*   3 Denmarke *1590*

After him raigned *Guitheline* his hayre,   xlii
  The iustest man and trewest in his dayes,
  Who had to wife Dame *Mertia* the fayre,
  A woman worthy of immortall prayse,
  Which for this Realme found many goodly layes,
  And wholesome Statutes to her husband brought;
  Her many deemd to haue beene of the *Fayes*,
  As was *Aegerie*, that *Numa* tought;
Those yet of her be *Mertian* lawes both nam'd and thought.

Her sonne *Sisillus* after her did rayne,   xliii
  And then *Kimarus*, and then *Danius*;
  Next whom *Morindus* did the crowne sustaine,
  Who, had he not with wrath outrageous,
  And cruell rancour dim'd his valorous
  And mightie deeds, should matched haue the best:
  As well in that same field victorious
  Against the forreine *Morands* he exprest;
Yet liues his memorie, though carcas sleepe in rest.

Fiue sonnes he left begotten of one wife,   xliv
  All which successiuely by turnes did raine;
  First *Gorboman* a man of vertuous life;
  Next *Archigald*, who for his proud disdaine,
  Deposed was from Princedome soueraine,
  And pitteous *Elidure* put in his sted;
  Who shortly it to him restord againe,
  Till by his death he it recouered;
But *Peridure* and *Vigent* him disthronized.

In wretched prison long he did remaine,   xlv
  Till they outraigned had their vtmost date,
  And then therein reseized was againe,
  And ruled long with honorable state,
  Till he surrendred Realme and life to fate.
  Then all the sonnes of these fiue brethren raynd
  By dew successe, and all their Nephewes late,
  Euen thrise eleuen descents the crowne retaynd,
Till aged *Hely* by dew heritage it gaynd.

xliii 1 sonnes *1596, 1609*   Sifillus *1590 &c.*   xliv 1 sonne *1596*

He had two sonnes, whose eldest called *Lud* xlvi
　Left of his life most famous memory,
　And endlesse moniments of his great good:
　The ruin'd wals he did reædifye
　Of *Troynouant,* gainst force of enimy,
　And built that gate, which of his name is hight,
　By which he lyes entombed solemnly.
He left two sonnes, too young to rule aright,
Androgeus and *Tenantius,* pictures of his might.

Whilst they were young, *Cassibalane* their Eme xlvii
　Was by the people chosen in their sted,
　Who on him tooke the royall Diademe,
　And goodly well long time it gouerned,
　Till the prowd *Romanes* him disquieted,
　And warlike *Cæsar,* tempted with the name
　Of this sweet Island, neuer conquered,
　And enuying the Britons blazed fame,
(O hideous hunger of dominion) hither came.

Yet twise they were repulsed backe againe, xlviii
　And twise renforst, backe to their ships to fly,
　The whiles with bloud they all the shore did staine,
　And the gray *Ocean* into purple dy:
　Ne had they footing found at last perdie,
　Had not *Androgeus,* false to natiue soyle,
　And enuious of Vncles soueraintie,
　Betrayd his contrey vnto forreine spoyle:
Nought else, but treason, from the first this land did foyle.

So by him *Cæsar* got the victory, xlix
　Through great bloudshed, and many a sad assay,
　In which him selfe was charged heauily
　Of hardy *Nennius,* whom he yet did slay,
　But lost his sword, yet to be seene this day.
　Thenceforth this land was tributarie made
　T'ambitious *Rome,* and did their rule obay,
　Till *Arthur* all that reckoning defrayd;
Yet oft the Briton kings against them strongly swayd.

xlix 8 did defray 1596, 1609

Next him *Tenantius* raigned, then *Kimbeline*,   1
　　What time th'eternall Lord in fleshly slime.
　　Enwombed was, from wretched *Adams* line
　　To purge away the guilt of sinfull crime:
　　O ioyous memorie of happy time,
　　That heauenly grace so plenteously displayd;
　　(O too high ditty for my simple rime.)
　　Soone after this the *Romanes* him warrayd;
For that their tribute he refusd to let be payd.

Good *Claudius*, that next was Emperour,   li
　　An army brought, and with him battell fought,
　　In which the king was by a Treachetour
　　Disguised slaine, ere any thereof thought:
　　Yet ceased not the bloudy fight for ought;
　　For *Aruirage* his brothers place supplide,
　　Both in his armes, and crowne, and by that draught
　　Did driue the *Romanes* to the weaker side,
That they to peace agreed.　So all was pacifide.

Was neuer king more highly magnifide,   lii
　　Nor dred of *Romanes*, then was *Aruirage*,
　　For which the Emperour to him allide
　　His daughter *Genuiss'* in marriage:
　　Yet shortly he renounst the vassalage
　　Of *Rome* againe, who hither hastly sent
　　Vespasian, that with great spoile and rage
　　Forwasted all, till *Genuissa* gent
Perswaded him to ceasse, and her Lord to relent.

He dyde; and him succeeded *Marius*,   liii
　　Who ioyd his dayes in great tranquillity,
　　Then *Coyll*, and after him good *Lucius*,
　　That first receiued Christianitie,
　　The sacred pledge of Christes Euangely;
　　Yet true it is, that long before that day
　　Hither came *Ioseph* of *Arimathy*,
　　Who brought with him the holy grayle, (they say)
And preacht the truth, but since it greatly did decay.

l 8 wrrayd *1596*　　li 7 his *om. 1596*: In armes, and eke in crowne *1609*
liii 2 in] with *1609*

This good king shortly without issew dide,   liv
   Whereof great trouble in the kingdome grew,
   That did her selfe in sundry parts diuide,
   And with her powre her owne selfe ouerthrew,
   Whilest *Romanes* dayly did the weake subdew:
   Which seeing stout *Bunduca,* vp arose,
   And taking armes, the *Britons* to her drew;
   With whom she marched streight against her foes,
And them vnwares besides the *Seuerne* did enclose.

There she with them a cruell battell tride,   lv
   Not with so good successe, as she deseru'd ;
   By reason that the Captaines on her side,
   Corrupted by *Paulinus,* from her sweru'd:
   Yet such, as were through former flight preseru'd,
   Gathering againe, her Host she did renew,
   And with fresh courage on the victour seru'd:
   But being all defeated, saue a few,
Rather then fly, or be captiu'd her selfe she slew.

O famous moniment of womens prayse,   lvi
   Matchable either to *Semiramis,*
   Whom antique history so high doth raise,
   Or to *Hypsiphil'* or to *Thomiris* :
   Her Host two hundred thousand numbred is ;
   Who whiles good fortune fauoured her might,
   Triumphed oft against her enimis;
   And yet though ouercome in haplesse fight,
She triumphed on death, in enemies despight.

Her reliques *Fulgent* hauing gathered,   lvii
   Fought with *Seuerus,* and him ouerthrew;
   Yet in the chace was slaine of them, that fled:
   So made them victours, whom he did subdew.
   Then gan *Carausius* tirannize anew,
   And gainst the *Romanes* bent their proper powre,
   But him *Allectus* treacherously slew,
   And took on him the robe of Emperoure:
Nath'lesse the same enioyed but short happy howre:

lv 5 perseru'd *1596*

For *Asclepiodate* him ouercame,   lviii
  And left inglorious on the vanquisht playne,
  Without or robe, or rag, to hide his shame.
  Then afterwards he in his stead did rayne;
  But shortly was by *Coyll* in battell slaine:
  Who after long debate, since *Lucies* time,
  Was of the *Britons* first crownd Soueraine:
  Then gan this Realme renewe her passed prime:
He of his name *Coylchester* built of stone and lime.

Which when the *Romanes* heard, they hither sent   lix
  Constantius, a man of mickle might,
  With whom king *Coyll* made an agreement,
  And to him gaue for wife his daughter bright,
  Faire *Helena*, the fairest liuing wight;
  Who in all godly thewes, and goodly prayse
  Did far excell, but was most famous hight
  For skill in Musicke of all in her dayes,
Aswell in curious instruments, as cunning layes.

Of whom he did great *Constantine* beget,   lx
  Who afterward was Emperour of *Rome*;
  To which whiles absent he his mind did set,
  Octauius here lept into his roome,
  And it vsurped by vnrighteous doome:
  But he his title iustifide by might,
  Slaying *Traherne*, and hauing ouercome
  The *Romane* legion in dreadfull fight:
So settled he his kingdome, and confirmd his right.

But wanting issew male, his daughter deare   lxi
  He gaue in wedlocke to *Maximian*,
  And him with her made of his kingdome heyre,
  Who soone by meanes thereof the Empire wan,
  Till murdred by the friends of *Gratian*;
  Then gan the Hunnes and Picts inuade this land,
  During the raigne of *Maximinian*;
  Who dying left none heire them to withstand,
But that they ouerran all parts with easie hand.

lxi 1 deare, *1590, 1596*

The weary *Britons*, whose war-hable youth   lxii
    Was by *Maximian* lately led away,
    With wretched miseries, and woefull ruth,
    Were to those Pagans made an open pray,
    And dayly spectacle of sad decay :
    Whom *Romane* warres, which now foure hundred yeares,
    And more had wasted, could no whit dismay ;
    Till by consent of Commons and of Peares,
They crownd the second *Constantine* with ioyous teares,

Who hauing oft in battell vanquished   lxiii
    Those spoilefull Picts, and swarming Easterlings,
    Long time in peace his Realme established,
    Yet oft annoyd with sundry bordragings
    Of neighbour Scots, and forrein Scatterlings,
    With which the world did in those dayes abound :
    Which to outbarre, with painefull pyonings
    From sea to sea he heapt a mightie mound,
Which from *Alcluid* to *Panwelt* did that border bound.

Three sonnes he dying left, all vnder age ;   lxiv
    By meanes whereof, their vncle *Vortigere*
    Vsurpt the crowne, during their pupillage ;
    Which th'Infants tutors gathering to feare,
    Them closely into *Armorick* did beare :
    For dread of whom, and for those Picts annoyes,
    He sent to *Germanie*, straunge aid to reare,
    From whence eftsoones arriued here three hoyes
Of *Saxons*, whom he for his satetie imployes.

Two brethren were their Capitains, which hight   lxv
    Hengist and *Horsus*, well approu'd in warre,
    And both of them men of renowmed might ;
    Who making vantage of their ciuill iarre,
    And of those forreiners, which came from farre,
    Grew great, and got large portions of land,
    That in the Realme ere long they stronger arre,
    Then they which sought at first their helping hand,
And *Vortiger* enforst the kingdome to aband.

lxv 1 Capitayns *1590* : Captains *1596*   9 enforst] haue forst *1590*

But by the helpe of *Vortimere* his sonne,   lxvi
　　He is againe vnto his rule restord,
　　And *Hengist* seeming sad, for that was donne,
　　Receiued is to grace and new accord,
　　Through his faire daughters face, and flattring word;
　　Soone after which, three hundred Lordes he slew
　　Of British bloud, all sitting at his bord;
　　Whose dolefull moniments who list to rew,
Th'eternall markes of treason may at *Stonheng* vew.

By this the sonnes of *Constantine*, which fled,   lxvii
　　Ambrose and *Vther* did ripe years attaine,
　　And here arriuing, strongly challenged
　　The crowne, which *Vortiger* did long detaine:
　　Who flying from his guilt, by them was slaine,
　　And *Hengist* eke soone brought to shamefull death.
　　Thenceforth *Aurelius* peaceably did rayne,
　　Till that through poyson stopped was his breath;
So now entombed lyes at Stoneheng by the heath.

After him *Vther*, which *Pendragon* hight,   lxviii
　　Succeding There abruptly it did end,
　　Without full point, or other Cesure right,
　　As if the rest some wicked hand did rend,
　　Or th'Authour selfe could not at least attend
　　To finish it: that so vntimely breach
　　The Prince him selfe halfe seemeth to offend,
　　Yet secret pleasure did offence empeach,
And wonder of antiquitie long stopt his speach.

At last quite rauisht with delight, to heare   lxix
　　The royall Ofspring of his natiue land,
　　Cryde out, Deare countrey, O how dearely deare
　　Ought thy remembraunce, and perpetuall band
　　Be to thy foster Childe, that from thy hand
　　Did commun breath and nouriture receaue?
　　How brutish is it not to vnderstand,
　　How much to her we owe, that all vs gaue,
That gaue vnto vs all, what euer good we haue.

　　　　lxvii 2 *Ambrise 1596, 1609*　　　lxviii 7 seemed *1590*

But *Guyon* all this while his booke did read,   lxx
   Ne yet has ended: for it was a great
   And ample volume, that doth far excead
   My leasure, so long leaues here to repeat:
   It told, how first *Prometheus* did create
   A man, of many partes from beasts deriued,
   And then stole fire from heauen, to animate
   His worke, for which he was by *Ioue* depriued
Of life him selfe, and hart-strings of an Ægle riued.

That man so made, he called *Elfe*, to weet   lxxi
   Quick, the first authour of all Elfin kind:
   Who wandring through the world with wearie feet,
   Did in the gardins of *Adonis* find
   A goodly creature, whom he deemd in mind
   To be no earthly wight, but either Spright,
   Or Angell, th'authour of all woman kind;
   Therefore a *Fay* he her according hight,
Of whom all *Faeryes* spring, and fetch their lignage right.

Of these a mightie people shortly grew,   lxxii
   And puissaunt kings, which all the world warrayd,
   And to them selues all Nations did subdew:
   The first and eldest, which that scepter swayd,
   Was *Elfin*; him all *India* obayd,
   And all that now *America* men call:
   Next him was noble *Elfinan*, who layd
   Cleopolis foundation first of all:
But *Elfiline* enclosd it with a golden wall.

His sonne was *Elfinell*, who ouercame   lxxiii
   The wicked *Gobbelines* in bloudy field:
   But *Elfant* was of most renowmed fame,
   Who all of Christall did *Panthea* build:
   Then *Elfar*, who two brethren gyants kild,
   The one of which had two heads, th'other three:
   Then *Elfinor*, who was in Magick skild;
   He built by art vpon the glassy See
A bridge of bras, whose sound heauens thunder seem'd to bee.

He left three sonnes, the which in order raynd,   lxxiv
   And all their Ofspring, in their dew descents,
   Euen seuen hundred Princes, which maintaynd
   With mightie deedes their sundry gouernments;
   That were too long their infinite contents
   Here to record, nè much materiall:
   Yet should they be most famous moniments,
   And braue ensample, both of martiall,
And ciuill rule to kings and states imperiall.

After all these *Elficleos* did rayne,   lxxv
   The wise *Elficleos* in great Maiestie,
   Who mightily that scepter did sustayne,
   And with rich spoiles and famous victorie,
   Did high aduaunce the crowne of *Faery*:
   He left two sonnes, of which faire *Elferon*
   The eldest brother did vntimely dy;
   Whose emptie place the mightie *Oberon*
Doubly supplide, in spousall, and dominion.

Great was his power and glorie ouer all,   lxxvi
   Which him before, that sacred seate did fill,
   That yet remaines his wide memoriall:
   He dying left the fairest *Tanaquill*,
   Him to succeede therein, by his last will:
   Fairer and nobler liueth none this howre,
   Ne like in grace, ne like in learned skill;
   Therefore they *Glorian* call that glorious flowre,
Long mayst thou *Glorian* liue, in glory and great powre.

Beguild thus with delight of nouelties,   lxxvii
   And naturall desire of countreys state,
   So long they red in those antiquities,
   That how the time was fled, they quite forgate,
   Till gentle *Alma* seeing it so late,
   Perforce their studies broke, and them besought
   To thinke, how supper did them long awaite.
   So halfe vnwilling from their bookes them brought,
And fairely feasted, as so noble knights she ought.

Cant. XI.

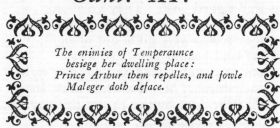

The enimies of Temperaunce
besiege her dwelling place:
Prince Arthur them repelles, and fowle
Maleger doth deface.

WHat warre so cruell, or what siege so sore,   i
    As that, which strong affections do apply
Against the fort of reason euermore
To bring the soule into captiuitie:
Their force is fiercer through infirmitie
Of the fraile flesh, relenting to their rage,
And exercise most bitter tyranny
Vpon the parts, brought into their bondage:
No wretchednesse is like to sinfull vellenage.

But in a body, which doth freely yeeld   ii
    His partes to reasons rule obedient,
And letteth her that ought the scepter weeld,
All happy peace and goodly gouernment
Is setled there in sure establishment;
There *Alma* like a virgin Queene most bright,
Doth florish in all beautie excellent:
And to her guestes doth bounteous banket dight,
Attempred goodly well for health and for delight.

Early before the Morne with cremosin ray,   iii
    The windowes of bright heauen opened had,
Through which into the world the dawning day
Might looke, that maketh euery creature glad,
Vprose Sir *Guyon*, in bright armour clad,
And to his purposd iourney him prepar'd:
With him the Palmer eke in habit sad,
Him selfe addrest to that aduenture hard:
So to the riuers side they both together far'd.

ii 9 and delight *1596*

X 2

Where them awaited ready at the ford   iv
   The *Ferriman,* as *Alma* had behight,
   With his well rigged boate: They go abord,
   And he eftsoones gan launch his barke forthright.
   Ere long they rowed were quite out of sight,
   And fast the land behind them fled away.
   But let them pas, whiles wind and weather right
   Do serue their turnes: here I a while must stay,
To see a cruell fight doen by the Prince this day.

For all so soone, as *Guyon* thence was gon   v
   Vpon his voyage with his trustie guide,
   That wicked band of villeins fresh begon
   That castle to assaile on euery side,
   And lay strong siege about it far and wide.
   So huge and infinite their numbers were,
   That all the land they vnder them did hide;
   So fowle and vgly, that exceeding feare
Their visages imprest, when they approched neare.

Them in twelue troupes their Captain did dispart   vi
   And round about in fittest steades did place,
   Where each might best offend his proper part,
   And his contrary obiect most deface,
   As euery one seem'd meetest in that cace.
   Seuen of the same against the Castle gate,
   In strong entrenchments he did closely place,
   Which with incessaunt force and endlesse hate,
They battred day and night, and entraunce did awate.

The other fiue, fiue sundry wayes he set,   vii
   Against the fiue great Bulwarkes of that pile,
   And vnto each a Bulwarke did arret,
   T'assayle with open force or hidden guile,
   In hope thereof to win victorious spoile.
   They all that charge did feruently apply,
   With greedie malice and importune toyle,
   And planted there their huge artillery,
With which they dayly made most dreadfull battery.

The first troupe was a monstrous rablement   viii
   Of fowle misshapen wights, of which some were
   Headed like Owles, with beckes vncomely bent,
   Others like Dogs, others like Gryphons dreare,
   And some had wings, and some had clawes to teare,
   And euery one of them had Lynces eyes,
   And euery one did bow and arrowes beare:
   All those were lawlesse lustes, corrupt enuies,
And couetous aspectes, all cruell enimies.

Those same against the bulwarke of the *Sight*   ix
   Did lay strong siege, and battailous assault,
   Ne once did yield it respit day nor night,
   But soone as *Titan* gan his head exault,
   And soone againe as he his light with hault,
   Their wicked engins they against it bent:
   That is each thing, by which the eyes may fault,
   But two then all more huge and violent,
Beautie, and money, they that Bulwarke sorely rent.

The second Bulwarke was the *Hearing* sence,   x
   Gainst which the second troupe dessignment makes;
   Deformed creatures, in straunge difference,
   Some hauing heads like Harts, some like to Snakes,
   Some like wild Bores late rouzd out of the brakes;
   Slaunderous reproches, and fowle infamies,
   Leasings, backbytings, and vaine-glorious crakes,
   Bad counsels, prayses, and faloe flatteries.
All those against that fort did bend their batteries.

Likewise that same third Fort, that is the *Smell*   xi
   Of that third troupe was cruelly assayd:
   Whose hideous shapes were like to feends of hell,
   Some like to hounds, some like to Apes, dismayd,
   Some like to Puttockes, all in plumes arayd:
   All shap't according their conditions,
   For by those vgly formes weren pourtrayd,
   Foolish delights and fond abusions,
Which do that sence besiege with light illusions.

   viii 3 beakes *1609*   ix 9 they against that Bulwarke lent *1590*
      x 2 assignment *1590*   xi 4 mismayd *conj. Jortin*

And that fourth band, which cruell battry bent,   xii
   Against the fourth Bulwarke, that is the *Tast*,
   Was as the rest, a grysie rablement,
   Some mouth'd like greedy Oystriges, some fast
   Like loathly Toades, some fashioned in the wast
   Like swine; for so deformd is luxury,
   Surfeat, misdiet, and vnthriftie wast,
   Vaine feasts, and idle superfluity:
All those this sences Fort assayle incessantly.

But the fift troupe most horrible of hew,   xiii
   And fierce of force, was dreadfull to report:
   For some like Snailes, some did like spyders shew,
   And some like vgly Vrchins thicke and short:
   Cruelly they assayled that fift Fort,
   Armed with darts of sensuall delight,
   With stings of carnall lust, and strong effort
   Of feeling pleasures, with which day and night
Against that same fift bulwarke they continued fight.

Thus these twelue troupes with dreadfull puissance   xiv
   Against that Castle restlesse siege did lay,
   And euermore their hideous Ordinance
   Vpon the Bulwarkes cruelly did play,
   That now it gan to threaten neare decay:
   And euermore their wicked Capitaine
   Prouoked them the breaches to assay,
   Somtimes with threats, somtimes with hope of gaine,
Which by the ransack of that peece they should attaine.

On th'other side, th'assieged Castles ward   xv
   Their stedfast stonds did mightily maintaine,
   And many bold repulse, and many hard
   Atchieuement wrought with perill and with paine,
   That goodly frame from ruine to sustaine:
   And those two brethren Giants did defend
   The walles so stoutly with their sturdie maine,
   That neuer entrance any durst pretend,
But they to direfull death their groning ghosts did send.

   xii 4 fac't *1609*   7 Surfait *1609*   xiii 2 was] is *1590*   5 They cruelly
1609   assayed *1590*

The noble virgin, Ladie of the place,   xvi
  Was much dismayed with that dreadfull sight:
  For neuer was she in so euill cace,
  Till that the Prince seeing her wofull plight,
  Gan her recomfort from so sad affright,
  Offring his seruice, and his dearest life
  For her defence, against that Carle to fight,
  Which was their chiefe and th'author of that strife:
She him remercied as the Patrone of her life.

Eftsoones himselfe in glitterand armes he dight,   xvii
  And his well proued weapons to him hent;
  So taking courteous conge he behight,
  Those gates to be vnbar'd, and forth he went.
  Faire mote he thee, the prowest and most gent,
  That euer brandished bright steele on hye:
  Whom soone as that vnruly rablement,
  With his gay Squire issuing did espy,
They reard a most outrageous dreadfull yelling cry.

And therewith all attonce at him let fly   xviii
  Their fluttring arrowes, thicke as flakes of snow,
  And round about him flocke impetuously,
  Like a great water flood, that tombling low
  From the high mountaines, threats to ouerflow
  With suddein fury all the fertile plaine,
  And the sad husbandmans long hope doth throw
  A downe the streame, and all his vowes make vaine,
Nor bounds nor banks his headlong ruine may sustaine.

Vpon his shield their heaped hayle he bore,   xix
  And with his sword disperst the raskall flockes,
  Which fled a sunder, and him fell before,
  As withered leaues drop from their dried stockes,
  When the wroth Western wind does reaue their locks;
  And vnder neath him his courageous steed,
  The fierce *Spumador* trode them downe like docks,
  The fierce *Spumador* borne of heauenly seed:
Such as *Laomedon* of *Phœbus* race did breed.

Which suddeine horrour and confused cry,   xx
      When as their Captaine heard, in haste he yode,
      The cause to weet, and fault to remedy;
      Vpon a Tygre swift and fierce he rode,
      That as the winde ran vnderneath his lode,
      Whiles his long legs nigh raught vnto the ground;
      Full large he was of limbe, and shoulders brode,
      But of such subtile substance and vnsound,
That like a ghost he seem'd, whose graue-clothes were vnbound.

And in his hand a bended bow was seene,   xxi
      And many arrowes vnder his right side,
      All deadly daungerous, all cruell keene,
      Headed with flint, and feathers bloudie dide,
      Such as the *Indians* in their quiuers hide;
      Those could he well direct and streight as line,
      And bid them strike the marke, which he had eyde,
      Ne was their salue, ne was their medicine,
That mote recure their wounds: so inly they did tine.

As pale and wan as ashes was his looke,   xxii
      His bodie leane and meagre as a rake,
      And skin all withered like a dryed rooke,
      Thereto as cold and drery as a Snake,
      That seem'd to tremble euermore, and quake:
      All in a canuas thin he was bedight,
      And girded with a belt of twisted brake,
      Vpon his head he wore an Helmet light,
Made of a dead mans skull, that seem'd a ghastly sight.

Maleger was his name, and after him,   xxiii
      There follow'd fast at hand two wicked Hags,
      With hoarie lockes all loose, and visage grim;
      Their feet vnshod, their bodies wrapt in rags,
      And both as swift on foot, as chased Stags;
      And yet the one her other legge had lame,
      Which with a staffe, all full of litle snags
      She did support, and *Impotence* her name:
But th'other was *Impatience*, arm'd with raging flame.

                    xxiii 8 disport *1596, 1609*

Soone as the Carle from farre the Prince espyde,   xxiv
   Glistring in armes and warlike ornament,
   His Beast he felly prickt on either syde,
   And his mischieuous bow full readie bent,
   With which at him a cruell shaft he sent:
   But he was warie, and it warded well
   Vpon his shield, that it no further went,
   But to the ground the idle quarrell fell:
Then he another and another did expell.

Which to preuent, the Prince his mortall speare   xxv
   Soone to him raught, and fierce at him did ride,
   To be auenged of that shot whyleare:
   But he was not so hardie to abide
   That bitter stownd, but turning quicke aside
   His light-foot beast, fled fast away for feare:
   Whom to pursue, the Infant after hide,
   So fast as his good Courser could him beare,
But labour lost it was, to weene approch him neare.

For as the winged wind his Tigre fled,   xxvi
   That vew of eye could scarse him ouertake,
   Ne scarse his feet on ground were seene to tred;
   Through hils and dales he speedie way did make,
   Ne hedge ne ditch his readie passage brake,
   And in his flight the villein turn'd his face,
   (As wonts the *Tartar* by the *Caspian* lake,
   When as the *Russian* him in fight does chace)
Vnto his Tygres taile, and shot at him apace.

Apace he shot, and yet he fled apace,   xxvii
   Still as the greedy knight nigh to him drew,
   And oftentimes he would relent his pace,
   That him his foe more fiercely should pursew:
   Who when his vncouth manner he did vew,
   He gan auize to follow him no more,
   But keepe his standing, and his shaftes eschew,
   Vntill he quite had spent his perlous store,
And then assayle him fresh, ere he could shift for more.

But that lame Hag, still as abroad he strew   xxviii
  His wicked arrowes, gathered them againe,
  And to him brought, fresh battell to renew:
  Which he espying, cast her to restraine
  From yielding succour to that cursed Swaine,
  And her attaching, thought her hands to tye;
  But soone as him dismounted on the plaine,
  That other Hag did farre away espy
Binding her sister, she to him ran hastily.

And catching hold of him, as downe he lent,   xxix
  Him backward ouerthrew, and downe him stayd
  With their rude hands and griesly graplement,
  Till that the villein comming to their ayd,
  Vpon him fell, and lode vpon him layd;
  Full litle wanted, but he had him slaine,
  And of the battell balefull end had made,
  Had not his gentle Squire beheld his paine,
And commen to his reskew, ere his bitter bane.

So greatest and most glorious thing on ground   xxx
  May often need the helpe of weaker hand;
  So feeble is mans state, and life vnsound,
  That in assurance it may neuer stand,
  Till it dissolued be from earthly band.
  Proofe be thou Prince, the prowest man aliue,
  And noblest borne of all in *Britayne* land;
  Yet thee fierce Fortune did so nearely driue,
That had not grace thee blest, thou shouldest not suruiue.

The Squire arriuing, fiercely in his armes   xxxi
  Snatcht first the one, and then the other Iade,
  His chiefest lets and authors of his harmes,
  And them perforce withheld with threatned blade,
  Least that his Lord they should behind inuade;
  The whiles the Prince prickt with reprochfull shame,
  As one awakt out of long slombring shade,
  Reuiuing thought of glorie and of fame,
Vnited all his powres to purge himselfe from blame.

  xxx 7 *Britom 1590*: *corr. F. E.*: *Briton 1596, 1609*   9 reuiue *1590*
&c.: *corr. F. E.*

Like as a fire, the which in hollow caue   xxxii
  Hath long bene vnderkept, and downe supprest,
  With murmurous disdaine doth inly raue,
  And grudge, in so streight prison to be prest,
  At last breakes forth with furious vnrest,
  And striues to mount vnto his natiue seat;
  All that did earst it hinder and molest,
  It now deuoures with flames and scorching heat,
And carries into smoake with rage and horror great.

So mightily the *Briton* Prince him rouzd   xxviii
  Out of his hold, and broke his caitiue bands,
  And as a Beare whom angry curres haue touzd,
  Hauing off-shakt them, and escapt their hands,
  Becomes more fell, and all that him withstands
  Treads downe and ouerthrowes.   Now had the Carle
  Alighted from his Tigre, and his hands
  Discharged of his bow and deadly quar'le,
To seize vpon his foe flat lying on the marle.

Which now him turnd to disauantage deare;   xxxiv
  For neither can he fly, nor other harme,
  But trust vnto his strength and manhood meare,
  Sith now he is farre from his monstrous swarme,
  And of his weapons did himselfe disarme.
  The knight yet wrothfull for his late disgrace,
  Fiercely aduaunst his valorous right arme,
  And him so sore smote with his yron mace,
That groueling to the ground he fell, and fild his place.

Well weened he, that field was then his owne,   xxxv
  And all his labour brought to happie end,
  When suddein vp the villein ouerthrowne,
  Out of his swowne arose, fresh to contend,
  And gan himselfe to second battell bend,
  As hurt he had not bene. Thereby there lay
  An huge great stone, which stood vpon one end,
  And had not bene remoued many a day;
Some land-marke seem'd to be, or signe of sundry way.

xxxii 5 vnrest] infest 1590

The same he snatcht, and with exceeding sway   xxxvi
   Threw at his foe, who was right well aware
   To shunne the engin of his meant decay;
   It booted not to thinke that throw to beare,
   But ground he gaue, and lightly leapt areare:
   Eft fierce returning, as a Faulcon faire
   That once hath failed of her souse full neare,
   Remounts againe into the open aire,
And vnto better fortune doth her selfe prepare.

So braue returning, with his brandisht blade,   xxxvii
   He to the Carle himselfe againe addrest,
   And strooke at him so sternely, that he made
   An open passage through his riuen brest,
   That halfe the steele behind his back did rest;
   Which drawing backe, he looked euermore
   When the hart bloud should gush out of his chest,
   Or his dead corse should fall vpon the flore;
But his dead corse vpon the flore fell nathemore.

Ne drop of bloud appeared shed to bee,   xxxviii
   All were the wounde so wide and wonderous,
   That through his carkasse one might plainely see:
   Halfe in a maze with horror hideous,
   And halfe in rage, to be deluded thus,
   Againe through both the sides he strooke him quight,
   That made his spright to grone full piteous:
   Yet nathemore forth fled his groning spright,
But freshly as at first, prepard himselfe to fight.

Thereat he smitten was with great affright,   xxxix
   And trembling terror did his hart apall,
   Ne wist he, what to thinke of that same sight,
   Ne what to say, ne what to doe at all;
   He doubted, least it were some magicall
   Illusion, that did beguile his sense,
   Or wandring ghost, that wanted funerall,
   Or aerie spirit vnder false pretence,
Or hellish feend raysd vp through diuelish science.

His wonder farre exceeded reasons reach,   xl
  That he began to doubt his dazeled sight,
  And oft of error did himselfe appeach:
  Flesh without bloud, a person without spright,
  Wounds without hurt, a bodie without might,
  That could doe harme, yet could not harmed bee,
  That could not die, yet seem'd a mortall wight,
  That was most strong in most infirmitee;
Like did he neuer heare, like did he neuer see.

A while he stood in this astonishment,   xli
  Yet would he not for all his great dismay
  Giue ouer to effect his first intent,
  And th'vtmost meanes of victorie assay,
  Or th'vtmost issew of his owne decay.
  His owne good sword *Morddure*, that neuer fayld
  At need, till now, he lightly threw away,
  And his bright shield, that nought him now auayld,
And with his naked hands him forcibly assayld.

Twixt his two mightie armes him vp he snatcht,   xlii
  And crusht his carkasse so against his brest,
  That the disdainfull soule he thence dispatcht,
  And th'idle breath all vtterly exprest:
  Tho when he felt him dead, a downe he kest
  The lumpish corse vnto the senselesse grownd;
  Adowne he kest it with so puissant wrest,
  That backe againe it did aloft rebownd,
And gaue against his mother earth a gronefull sownd.

As when *Ioues* harnesse-bearing Bird from hie   xliii
  Stoupes at a flying heron with proud disdaine,
  The stone-dead quarrey fals so forciblie,
  That it rebounds against the lowly plaine,
  A second fall redoubling backe againe.
  Then thought the Prince all perill sure was past,
  And that he victor onely did remaine;
  No sooner thought, then that the Carle as fast
Gan heap huge strokes on him, as ere he downe was cast.

xli 6 Mordure 1590, 1596

Nigh his wits end then woxe th'amazed knight,   xliv
    And thought his labour lost and trauell vaine,
    Against this lifelesse shadow so to fight:
    Yet life he saw, and felt his mightie maine,
    That whiles he marueild still, did still him paine:
    For thy he gan some other wayes aduize,
    How to take life from that dead-liuing swaine,
    Whom still he marked freshly to arize
From th'earth, and from her wombe new spirits to reprize.

He then remembred well, that had bene sayd,   xlv
    How th'Earth his mother was, and first him bore;
    She eke so often, as his life decayd,
    Did life with vsury to him restore,
    And raysd him vp much stronger then before,
    So soone as he vnto her wombe did fall;
    Therefore to ground he would him cast no more,
    Ne him commit to graue terrestriall,
But beare him farre from hope of succour vsuall.

Tho vp he caught him twixt his puissant hands,   xlvi
    And hauing scruzd out of his carrion corse
    The lothfull life, now loosd from sinfull bands,
    Vpon his shoulders carried him perforse
    Aboue three furlongs, taking his full course,
    Vntill he came vnto a standing lake;
    Him thereinto he threw without remorse,
    Ne stird, till hope of life did him forsake;
So end of that Carles dayes, and his owne paines did make.

Which when those wicked Hags from farre did spy,   xlvii
    Like two mad dogs they ran about the lands,
    And th'one of them with dreadfull yelling cry,
    Throwing away her broken chaines and bands,
    And hauing quencht her burning fier brands,
    Hedlong her selfe did cast into that lake;
    But *Impotence* with her owne wilfull hands,
    One of *Malegers* cursed darts did take,
So riu'd her trembling hart, and wicked end did make.

xliv 3 this] his *1590* : *corr. F. E.*

Thus now alone he conquerour remaines;   xlviii
  Tho comming to his Squire, that kept his steed,
  Thought to haue mounted, but his feeble vaines
  Him faild thereto, and serued not his need,
  Through losse of bloud, which from his wounds did bleed,
  That he began to faint, and life decay:
  But his good Squire him helping vp with speed,
  With stedfast hand vpon his horse did stay,
And led him to the Castle by the beaten way.

Where many Groomes and Squiers readie were,   xlix
  To take him from his steed full tenderly,
  And eke the fairest *Alma* met him there
  With balme and wine and costly spicery,
  To comfort him in his infirmity;
  Eftsoones she causd him vp to be conuayd,
  And of his armes despoyled easily,
  In sumptuous bed she made him to be layd,
And all the while his wounds were dressing, by him stayd.

Cant. XII.

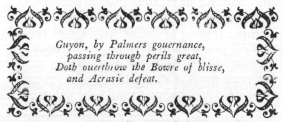

Guyon, by Palmers gouernance,
  passing through perils great,
Doth ouerthrow the Bowre of blisse,
  and Acrasie defeat.

N Ow gins this goodly frame of Temperance   i
  Fairely to rise, and her adorned hed
  To pricke of highest praise forth to aduance,
  Formerly grounded, and fast setteled
  On firme foundation of true bountihed;
  And this braue knight, that for that vertue fights,
  Now comes to point of that same perilous sted,
  Where Pleasure dwelles in sensuall delights,
Mongst thousand dangers, and ten thousand magick mights.

  Arg. 1 *by*] *through 1590*   2 *through passing 1590*   i 4 Formerly]
Formally   6 that] this *1590 &c.*: *corr. F. E.*

Two dayes now in that sea he sayled has,   ii
    Ne euer land beheld, ne liuing wight,
    Ne ought saue perill, still as he did pas:
    Tho when appeared the third *Morrow* bright,
    Vpon the waues to spred her trembling light,
    An hideous roaring farre away they heard,
    That all their senses filled with affright,
    And streight they saw the raging surges reard
Vp to the skyes, that them of drowning made affeard.

Said then the Boteman, Palmer stere aright,   iii
    And keepe an euen course; for yonder way
    We needes must passe (God do vs well acquight,)
    That is the *Gulfe of Greedinesse*, they say,
    That deepe engorgeth all this worldes pray:
    Which hauing swallowd vp excessiuely,
    He soone in vomit vp againe doth lay,
    And belcheth forth his superfluity,
That all the seas for feare do seeme away to fly.

On th'other side an hideous Rocke is pight,   iv
    Of mightie *Magnes* stone, whose craggie clift
    Depending from on high, dreadfull to sight,
    Ouer the waues his rugged armes doth lift,
    And threatneth downe to throw his ragged rift
    On who so commeth nigh; yet nigh it drawes
    All passengers, that none from it can shift:
    For whiles they fly that Gulfes deuouring iawes,
They on this rock are rent, and sunck in helplesse wawes.

Forward they passe, and strongly he them rowes,   v
    Vntill they nigh vnto that Gulfe arriue,
    Where streame more violent and greedy growes:
    Then he with all his puissance doth striue
    To strike his oares, and mightily doth driue
    The hollow vessell through the threatfull waue,
    Which gaping wide, to swallow them aliue,
    In th'huge abysse of his engulfing graue,
Doth rore at them in vaine, and with great terror raue.

        iii 9 do] did *1590*: *corr. F. E.*

They passing by, that griesly mouth did see,   vi
  Sucking the seas into his entralles deepe,
  That seem'd more horrible then hell to bee,
  Or that darke dreadfull hole of *Tartare* steepe,
  Through which the damned ghosts doen often creepe
  Backe to the world, bad liuers to torment:
  But nought that falles into this direfull deepe,
  Ne that approcheth nigh the wide descent,
May backe returne, but is condemned to be drent.

On th'other side, they saw that perilous Rocke,   vii
  Threatning it selfe on them to ruinate,
  On whose sharpe clifts the ribs of vessels broke,
  And shiuered ships, which had bene wrecked late,
  Yet stuck, with carkasses exanimate
  Of such, as hauing all their substance spent
  In wanton ioyes, and lustes intemperate,
  Did afterwards make shipwracke violent,
Both of their life, and fame for euer fowly blent.

For thy, this hight *The Rocke of* vile *Reproch*,   viii
  A daungerous and detestable place,
  To which nor fish nor fowle did once approch,
  But yelling Meawes, with Seagulles hoarse and bace,
  And Cormoyrants, with birds of rauenous race,
  Which still sate waiting on that wastfull clift,
  For spoyle of wretches, whose vnhappie cace,
  After lost credite and consumed thrift,
At last them driuen hath to this despairefull drift.

The Palmer seeing them in safetie past,   ix
  Thus said; Behold th'ensamples in our sights,
  Of lustfull luxurie and thriftlesse wast:
  What now is left of miserable wights,
  Which spent their looser daies in lewd delights,
  But shame and sad reproch, here to be red,
  By these rent reliques, speaking their ill plights?
  Let all that liue, hereby be counselled,
To shunne *Rocke of Reproch*, and it as death to dred.

viii 6 weiting *1590*: *corr. to* wayting *in F. E.*   ix 2 behold *1590. 1596*

So forth they rowed, and that *Ferryman*   x
  With his stiffe oares did brush the sea so strong,
  That the hoare waters from his frigot ran,
  And the light bubbles daunced all along,
  Whiles the salt brine out of the billowes sprong.
  At last farre off they many Islands spy,
  On euery side floting the floods emong:
  Then said the knight, Loe I the land descry,
Therefore old Syre thy course do thereunto apply.

That may not be, said then the *Ferryman*   xi
  Least we vnweeting hap to be fordonne:
  For those same Islands, seeming now and than,
  Are not firme lande, nor any certein wonne,
  But straggling plots, which to and fro do ronne
  In the wide waters: therefore are they hight
  The *wandring Islands.*   Therefore doe them shonne;
  For they haue oft drawne many a wandring wight
Into most deadly daunger and distressed plight.

Yet well they seeme to him, that farre doth vew,   xii
  Both faire and fruitfull, and the ground dispred
  With grassie greene of delectable hew,
  And the tall trees with leaues apparelled,
  Are deckt with blossomes dyde in white and red,
  That mote the passengers thereto allure;
  But whosoeuer once hath fastened
  His foot thereon, may neuer it recure,
But wandreth euer more vncertein and vnsure.

As th'Isle of *Delos* whylome men report   xiii
  Amid th' *Aegæan* sea long time did stray,
  Ne made for shipping any certaine port,
  Till that *Latona* traueiling that way,
  Flying from *Iunoes* wrath and hard assay,
  Of her faire twins was there deliuered,
  Which afterwards did rule the night and day;
  Thenceforth it firmely was established,
And for *Apolloes* honor highly herried.

          xii 2 disspred *1609*   xiii 9 honor] temple *1590*

They to him hearken, as beseemeth meete,   xiv
  And passe on forward: so their way does ly,
  That one of those same Islands, which doe fleet
  In the wide sea, they needes must passen by,
  Which seemd so sweet and pleasant to the eye,
  That it would tempt a man to touchen there:
  Vpon the banck they sitting did espy
  A daintie damzell, dressing of her heare,
By whom a litle skippet floting did appeare.

She them espying, loud to them can call,   xv
  Bidding them nigher draw vnto the shore;
  For she had cause to busie them withall;
  And therewith loudly laught: But nathemore
  Would they once turne, but kept on as afore:
  Which when she saw, she left her lockes vndight,
  And running to her boat withouten ore
  From the departing land it launched light,
And after them did driue with all her power and might.

Whom ouertaking, she in merry sort   xvi
  Them gan to bord, and purpose diuersly,
  Now faining dalliance and wanton sport,
  Now throwing forth lewd words immodestly;
  Till that the Palmer gan full bitterly
  Her to rebuke, for being loose and light:
  Which not abiding, but more scornefully
  Scoffing at him, that did her iustly wite,
She turnd her bote about, and from them rowed quite.

That was the wanton *Phædria*, which late   xvii
  Did ferry him ouer the *Idle lake*:
  Whom nought regarding, they kept on their gate,
  And all her vaine allurements did forsake,
  When them the wary Boateman thus bespake;
  Here now behoueth vs well to auyse,
  And of our safetie good heede to take;
  For here before a perlous passage lyes,
Where many Mermayds haunt, making false melodies.

xv 1 can] gan 1609

Y 2

But by the way, there is a great Quicksand,   xviii
  And a whirlepoole of hidden ieopardy,
  Therefore, Sir Palmer, keepe an euen hand;
  For twixt them both the narrow way doth ly.
  Scarse had he said, when hard at hand they spy
  That quicksand nigh with water couered;
  But by the checked waue they did descry
  It plaine, and by the sea discoloured:
It called was the quicksand of *Vnthriftyhed*.

They passing by, a goodly Ship did see,   xix
  Laden from far with precious merchandize,
  And brauely furnishęd, as ship might bee,
  Which through great disauenture, or mesprize,
  Her selfe had runne into that hazardize;
  Whose mariners and merchants with much toyle,
  Labour'd in vaine, to haue recur'd their prize,
  And the rich wares to saue from pitteous spoyle,
But neither toyle nor trauell might her backe recoyle.

On th'other side they see that perilous Poole,   xx
  That called was the *Whirlepoole of decay*,
  In which full many had with haplesse doole
  Beene suncke, of whom no memorie did stay:
  Whose circled waters rapt with whirling sway,
  Like to a restlesse wheele, still running round,
  Did couet, as they passed by that way,
  To draw their boate within the vtmost bound
Of his wide *Labyrinth*, and then to haue them dround.

But th'heedfull Boateman strongly forth did stretch   xxi
  His brawnie armes, and all his body straine,
  That th'vtmost sandy breach they shortly fetch,
  Whiles the dred daunger does behind remaine.
  Suddeine they see from midst of all the Maine,
  The surging waters like a mountaine rise,
  And the great sea puft vp with proud disdaine,
  To swell aboue the measure of his guise,
As threatning to deuoure all, that his powre despise.

xix 4 misprize *1609*   xx 8 their] the *1596. 1609*
xxi 1 heedfull] earnest *1590*

The waues come rolling, and the billowes rore
   Outragiously, as they enraged were,
   Or wrathfull *Neptune* did them driue before
   His whirling charet, for exceeding feare:
   For not one puffe of wind there did appeare,
   That all the three thereat woxe much afrayd,
   Vnweeting, what such horrour straunge did reare.
   Eftsoones they saw an hideous hoast arrayd,
Of huge Sea monsters, such as liuing sence dismayd.

Most vgly shapes, and horrible aspects,
   Such as Dame Nature selfe mote feare to see,
   Or shame, that euer should so fowle defects
   From her most cunning hand escaped bee;
   All dreadfull pourtraicts of deformitee:
   Spring-headed *Hydraes*, and sea-shouldring Whales,
   Great whirlpooles, which all fishes make to flee,
   Bright Scolopendraes, arm'd with siluer scales,
Mighty *Monoceroses*, with immeasured tayles.

The dreadfull Fish, that hath deseru'd the name
   Of Death, and like him lookes in dreadfull hew,
   The griesly Wasserman, that makes his game
   The flying ships with swiftnesse to pursew,
   The horrible Sea-satyre, that doth shew
   His fearefull face in time of greatest storme,
   Huge *Ziffius*, whom Mariners eschew
   No lesse, then rockes, (as trauellers informe,)
And greedy *Rosmarines* with visages deforme.

All these, and thousand thousands many more,
   And more deformed Monsters thousand fold,
   With dreadfull noise, and hollow rombling rore,
   Came rushing in the fomy waues enrold,
   Which seem'd to fly for feare, them to behold:
   Ne wonder, if these did the knight appall;
   For all that here on earth we dreadfull hold,
   Be but as bugs to fearen babes withall,
Compared to the creatures in the seas entrall.

     xxiii 9 *Monoceros 1590 &c.* : *corr. Child*

Feare nought, (then said the Palmer well auiz'd;)   xxvi
   For these same Monsters are not these in deed,
   But arc into these fearefull shapes disguiz'd
   By that same wicked witch, to worke vs dreed,
   And draw from on this iourney to proceede.
   Tho lifting vp his vertuous staffe on hye,
   He smote the sea, which calmed was with speed,
   And all that dreadfull Armie fast gan flye
Into great *Tethys* bosome, where they hidden lye.

Quit from that daunger, forth their course they kept,   xxvii
   And as they went, they heard a ruefull cry
   Of one, that wayld and pittifully wept,
   That through the sea the resounding plaints did fly:
   At last they in an Island did espy
   A seemely Maiden, sitting by the shore,
   That with great sorrow and sad agony,
   Seemed some great misfortune to deplore,
And lowd to them for succour called euermore.

Which *Guyon* hearing, streight his Palmer bad,   xxviii
   To stere the boate towards that dolefull Mayd,
   That he might know, and ease her sorrow sad:
   Who him auizing better, to him sayd;
   Faire Sir, be not displeasd, if disobayd:
   For ill it were to hearken to her cry;
   For she is inly nothing ill apayd,
   But onely womanish fine forgery,
Your stubborne hart t'affect with fraile infirmity.

To which when she your courage hath inclind   xxix
   Through foolish pitty, then her guilefull bayt
   She will embosome deeper in your mind,
   And for your ruine at the last awayt.
   The knight was ruled, and the Boateman strayt
   Held on his course with stayed stedfastnesse,
   Ne euer shruncke, ne euer sought to bayt
   His tyred armes for toylesome wearinesse,
But with his oares did sweepe the watry wildernesse.

xxvii 3 pittifull *1596*   4 sea resounding *1609*

And now they nigh approched to the sted,   xxx
  Where as those Mermayds dwelt: it was a still
  And calmy bay, on th'one side sheltered
  With the brode shadow of an hoarie hill,
  On th'other side an high rocke toured still,
  That twixt them both a pleasaunt port they made,
  And did like an halfe Theatre fulfill:
  There those fiue sisters had continuall trade,
And vsd to bath themselues in that deceiptfull shade.

They were faire Ladies, till they fondly striu'd   xxxi
  With th'*Heliconian* maides for maistery;
  Of whom they ouer-comen, were depriu'd
  Of their proud beautie, and th'one moyity
  Transform'd to fish, for their bold surquedry,
  But th'vpper halfe their hew retained still,
  And their sweet skill in wonted melody;
  Which euer after they abusd to ill,
T'allure weake trauellers, whom gotten they did kill.

So now to *Guyon*, as he passed by,   xxxii
  Their pleasaunt tunes they sweetly thus applide;
  O thou faire sonne of gentle Faery,
  That art in mighty armes most magnifide
  Aboue all knights, that euer battell tride,
  O turne thy rudder hither-ward a while:
  Here may thy storme-bet vessell safely ride;
  This is the Port of rest from troublous toyle,
The worlds sweet In, from paine and wearisome turmoyle.

With that the rolling sea resounding soft,   xxxiii
  In his big base them fitly answered,
  And on the rocke the waues breaking aloft,
  A solemne Meane vnto them measured,
  The whiles sweet *Zephirus* lowd whisteled
  His treble, a straunge kinde of harmony;
  Which *Guyons* senses softly tickeled,
  That he the boateman bad row easily,
And let him heare some part of their rare melody.

xxx 6 peasaunt *1596*   9 bathe *1609*   deceitfull *1609*
xxxii 4 That] Thou *1596*

But him the Palmer from that vanity,   xxxiv
    With temperate aduice discounselled,
    That they it past, and shortly gan descry
    The land, to which their course they leueled;
    When suddeinly a grosse fog ouer spred
    With his dull vapour all that desert has,
    And heauens chearefull face enueloped,
    That all things one, and one as nothing was,
And this great Vniuerse seemd one confused mas.

Thereat they greatly were dismayd, ne wist   xxxv
    How to direct their way in darkenesse wide,
    But feard to wander in that wastfull mist,
    For tombling into mischiefe vnespide.
    Worse is the daunger hidden, then descride.
    Suddeinly an innumerable flight
    Of harmefull fowles about them fluttering, cride,
    And with their wicked wings them oft did smight,
And sore annoyed, groping in that griesly night.

Euen all the nation of vnfortunate   xxxvi
    And fatall birds about them flocked were,
    Such as by nature men abhorre and hate,
    The ill-faste Owle, deaths dreadfull messengere,
    The hoars Night-rauen, trump of dolefull drere,
    The lether-winged Bat, dayes enimy,
    The ruefull Strich, still waiting on the bere,
    The Whistler shrill, that who so heares, doth dy,
The hellish Harpies, prophets of sad destiny.

All those, and all that else does horrour breed,   xxxvii
    About them flew, and fild their sayles with feare:
    Yet stayd they not, but forward did proceed,
    Whiles th'one did row, and th'other stifly steare;
    Till that at last the weather gan to cleare,
    And the faire land it selfe did plainly show.
    Said then the Palmer, Lo where does appeare
    The sacred soile, where all our perils grow;
Therefore, Sir knight, your ready armes about you throw.

                    xxxiv 1 the] that *1609*

He hearkned, and his armes about him tooke,   xxxviii
   The whiles the nimble boate so well her sped,
   That with her crooked keele the land she strooke,
   Then forth the noble *Guyon* sallied,
   And his sage Palmer, that him gouerned;
   But th'other by his boate behind did stay.
   They marched fairly forth, of nought ydred,
   Both firmely armd for euery hard assay,
With constancy and care, gainst daunger and dismay.

Ere long they heard an hideous bellowing   xxxix
   Of many beasts, that roard outrageously,
   As if that hungers point, or *Venus* sting
   Had them enraged with fell surquedry;
   Yet nought they feard, but past on hardily,
   Vntill they came in vew of those wild beasts:
   Who all attonce, gaping full greedily,
   And rearing fiercely their vpstarting crests,
Ran towards, to deuoure those vnexpected guests.

But soone as they approcht with deadly threat,   xl
   The Palmer ouer them his staffe vpheld,
   His mighty staffe, that could all charmes defeat:
   Eftsoones their stubborne courages were queld,
   And high aduaunced crests downe meekely feld,
   In stead of fraying, they them selues did feare,
   And trembled, as them passing they beheld:
   Such wondrous powre did in that staffe appeare,
All monsters to subdew to him, that did it beare.

Of that same wood it fram'd was cunningly,   xli
   Of which *Caduceus* whilome was made,
   Caduceus the rod of *Mercury*,
   With which he wonts the *Stygian* realmes inuade,
   Through ghastly horrour, and eternall shade;
   Th' infernall feends with it he can asswage,
   And *Orcus* tame, whom nothing can perswade,
   And rule the *Furyes*, when they most do rage:
Such vertue in his staffe had eke this Palmer sage.

xxxix 8 vpstarting] vpstaring *1590*   xl 1 approch't. *1609*   threat *1609*

Thence passing forth, they shortly do arriue,   xlii
  Whereas the Bowre of *Blisse* was situate;
  A place pickt out by choice of best aliue,
  That natures worke by art can imitate:
  In which what euer in this worldly state
  Is sweet, and pleasing vnto liuing sense,
  Or that may dayntiest fantasie aggrate,
  Was poured forth with plentifull dispence,
And made there to abound with lauish affluence.

Goodly it was enclosed round about,   xliii
  Aswell their entred guestes to keepe within,
  As those vnruly beasts to hold without;
  Yet was the fence thereof but weake and thin;
  Nought feard their force, that fortilage to win,
  But wisedomes powre, and temperaunces might,
  By which the mightiest things efforced bin:
  And eke the gate was wrought of substaunce light,
Rather for pleasure, then for battery or fight.

Yt framed was of precious yuory,   xliv
  That seemd a worke of admirable wit;
  And therein all the famous history
  Of *Iason* and *Medæa* was ywrit;
  Her mighty charmes, her furious louing fit,
  His goodly conquest of the golden fleece,
  His falsed faith, and loue too lightly flit,
  The wondred *Argo*, which in venturous peece
First through the *Euxine* seas bore all the flowr of *Greece*.

Ye might haue seene the frothy billowes fry   xlv
  Vnder the ship, as thorough them she went,
  That seemd the waues were into yuory,
  Or yuory into the waues were sent;
  And other where the snowy substaunce sprent
  With vermell, like the boyes bloud therein shed,
  A piteous spectacle did represent,
  And otherwhiles with gold besprinkeled;
Yt seemd th'enchaunted flame, which did *Creüsa* wed.

  xlii 7 dayntest *1590*   xliii 5 their] they *conj. ed.*   7 migtest *1590*

All this, and more might in that goodly gate   xlvi
  Be red; that euer open stood to all,
  Which thither came: but in the Porch there sate
  A comely personage of stature tall,
  And semblaunce pleasing, more then naturall,
  That trauellers to him seemd to entize;
  His looser garment to the ground did fall,
  And flew about his heeles in wanton wize,
Not fit for speedy pace, or manly exercize.

They in that place him *Genius* did call: xlvii
  Not that celestiall powre, to whom the care
  Of life, and generation of all
  That liues, pertaines in charge particulare,
  Who wondrous things concerning our welfare,
  And straunge phantomes doth let vs oft forsee,
  And oft of secret ill bids vs beware:
  That is our Selfe, whom though we do not see,
Yet each doth in him selfe it well perceiue to bee.

Therefore a God him sage Antiquity   xlviii
  Did wisely make, and good *Agdistes* call:
  But this same was to that quite contrary,
  The foe of life, that good enuyes to all,
  That secretly doth vs procure to fall,
  Through guilefull semblaunts, which he makes vs see.
  He of this Gardin had the gouernall,
  And Pleasures porter was deuizd to bee,
Holding a staffe in hand for more formalitee.

With diuerse flowres he daintily was deckt,   xlix
  And strowed round about, and by his side
  A mighty Mazer bowle of wine was set,
  As if it had to him bene sacrifide;
  Wherewith all new-come guests he gratifide:
  So did he eke Sir *Guyon* passing by:
  But he his idle curtesie defide,
  And ouerthrew his bowle disdainfully;
And broke his staffe, with which he charmed semblants sly.

Thus being entred, they behold around   i
  A large and spacious plaine, on euery side
  Strowed with pleasauns, whose faire grassy ground
  Mantled with greene, and goodly beautifide
  With all the ornaments of *Floraes* pride,
  Wherewith her mother Art, as halfe in scorne
  Of niggard Nature, like a pompous bride
  Did decke her, and too lauishly adorne,
When forth from virgin bowre she comes in th'early morne.

Thereto the Heauens alwayes Iouiall,   ii
  Lookt on them louely, still in stedfast state,
  Ne suffred storme nor frost on them to fall,
  Their tender buds or leaues to violate,
  Nor scorching heat, nor cold intemperate
  T'afflict the creatures, which therein did dwell,
  But the milde aire with season moderate
  Gently attempred, and disposd so well,
That still it breathed forth sweet spirit and holesome smell.

More sweet and holesome, then the pleasaunt hill   iii
  Of *Rhodope*, on which the Nimphe, that bore
  A gyaunt babe, her selfe for griefe did kill;
  Or the Thessalian *Tempe*, where of yore
  Faire *Daphne Phœbus* hart with loue did gore;
  Or *Ida*, where the Gods lou'd to repaire,
  When euer they their heauenly bowres forlore;
  Or sweet *Parnasse*, the haunt of Muses faire;
Or *Eden* selfe, if ought with *Eden* mote compaire.

Much wondred *Guyon* at the faire aspect   iiii
  Of that sweet place, yet suffred no delight
  To sincke into his sence, nor mind affect,
  But passed forth, and lookt still forward right,
  Bridling his will, and maistering his might:
  Till that he came vnto another gate;
  No gate, but like one, being goodly dight
  With boughes and braunches, which did broad dilate
Their clasping armes, in wanton wreathings intricate.

So fashioned a Porch with rare deuice,   liv
  Archt ouer head with an embracing vine,
  Whose bounches hanging downe, seemed to entice
  All passers by, to tast their lushious wine,
  And did themselues into their hands incline,
  As freely offering to be gathered :
  Some deepe empurpled as the *Hyacint*,
  Some as the Rubine, laughing sweetly red,
Some like faire Emeraudes, not yet well ripened.

And them amongst, some were of burnisht gold,   lv
  So made by art, to beautifie the rest,
  Which did themselues emongst the leaues enfold,
  As lurking from the vew of couetous guest,
  That the weake bowes, with so rich load opprest,
  Did bow adowne, as ouer-burdened.
  Vnder that Porch a comely dame did rest,
  Clad in faire weedes, but fowle disordered,
And garments loose, that seemd vnmeet for womanhed.

In her left hand a Cup of gold she held,   lvi
  And with her right the riper fruit did reach,
  Whose sappy liquor, that with fulnesse sweld,
  Into her cup she scruzd, with daintie breach
  Of her fine fingers, without fowle empeach,
  That so faire wine-presse made the wine more sweet :
  Thereof she vsd to giue to drinke to cach,
  Whom passing by she happened to meet :
It was her guise, all Straungers goodly so to greet.

So she to *Guyon* offred it to tast ;   lvii
  Who taking it out of her tender hond,
  The cup to ground did violently cast,
  That all in peeces it was broken fond,
  And with the liquor stained all the lond :
  Whereat *Excesse* exceedingly was wroth,
  Yet no'te the same amend, ne yet withstond,
  But suffered him to passe, all were she loth ;
Who nought regarding her displeasure forward goth.

There the most daintie Paradise on ground,　　　lviii
　　It selfe doth offer to his sober eye,
　　In which all pleasures plenteously abound,
　　And none does others happinesse enuye:
　　The painted flowres, the trees vpshooting hye,
　　The dales for shade, the hilles for breathing space,
　　The trembling groues, the Christall running by;
　　And that, which all faire workes doth most aggrace,
The art, which all that wrought, appeared in no place.

One would haue thought, (so cunningly, the rude,　　　lix
　　And scorned parts were mingled with the fine,)
　　That nature had for wantonesse ensude
　　Art, and that Art at nature did repine;
　　So striuing each th'other to vndermine,
　　Each did the others worke more beautifie;
　　So diff'ring both in willes, agreed in fine:
　　So all agreed through sweete diuersitie,
This Gardin to adorne with all varietie.

And in the midst of all, a fountaine stood,　　　lx
　　Of richest substaunce, that on earth might bee,
　　So pure and shiny, that the siluer flood
　　Through euery channell running one might see;
　　Most goodly it with curious imageree
　　Was ouer-wrought, and shapes of naked boyes,
　　Of which some seemd with liuely iollitee,
　　To fly about, playing their wanton toyes,
Whilest others did them selues embay in liquid ioyes.

And ouer all, of purest gold was spred,　　　lxi
　　A trayle of yuie in his natiue hew:
　　For the rich mettall was so coloured,
　　That wight, who did not well auis'd it vew,
　　Would surely deeme it to be yuie trew:
　　Low his lasciuious armes adown did creepe,
　　That themselues dipping in the siluer dew,
　　Their fleecy flowres they tenderly did steepe,
Which drops of Christall seemd for wantones to weepe.

　　　lx 5 curious] pure *1609*　　　lxi 8 tenderly] fearefully *1590*

Infinit streames continually did well   lxii
   Out of this fountaine, sweet and faire to see,
   The which into an ample lauer fell,
   And shortly grew to so great quantitie,
   That like a little lake it seemd to bee;
   Whose depth exceeded not three cubits hight,
   That through the waues one might the bottom see,
   All pau'd beneath with Iaspar shining bright,
That seemd the fountaine in that sea did sayle vpright.

And all the margent round about was set,   lxiii
   With shady Laurell trees, thence to defend
   The sunny beames, which on the billowes bet,
   And those which therein bathed, mote offend.
   As *Guyon* hapned by the same to wend,
   Two naked Damzelles he therein espyde,
   Which therein bathing, seemed to contend,
   And wrestle wantonly, ne car'd to hyde,
Their dainty parts from vew of any, which them eyde.

Sometimes the one would lift the other quight   lxiv
   Aboue the waters, and then downe againe
   Her plong, as ouer maistered by might,
   Where both awhile would couered remaine,
   And each the other from to rise restraine;
   The whiles their snowy limbes, as through a vele,
   So through the Christall waues appeared plaine:
   Then suddeinly both would themselues vnhele,
And th'amarous sweet spoiles to greedy eyes reuele.

As that faire Starre, the messenger of morne,   lxv
   His deawy face out of the sea doth reare:
   Or as the *Cyprian* goddesse, newly borne
   Of th'Oceans fruitfull froth, did first appeare:
   Such seemed they, and so their yellow heare
   Christalline humour dropped downe apace.
   Whom such when *Guyon* saw, he drew him neare,
   And somewhat gan relent his earnest pace,
His stubborne brest gan secret pleasaunce to embrace.

The wanton Maidens him espying, stood   lxvi
  Gazing a while at his vnwonted guise;
  Then th'one her selfe low ducked in the flood,
  Abasht, that her a straunger did a vise:
  But th'other rather higher did arise,
  And her two lilly paps aloft displayd,
  And all, that might his melting hart entise
  To her delights, she vnto him bewrayd:
The rest hid vnderneath, him more desirous made.

With that, the other likewise vp arose,   lxvii
  And her faire lockes, which formerly were bownd
  Vp in one knot, she low adowne did lose:
  Which flowing long and thick, her cloth'd arownd,
  And th'yuorie in golden mantle gownd:
  So that faire spectacle from him was reft,
  Yet that, which reft it, no lesse faire was fownd:
  So hid in lockes and waues from lookers theft,
Nought but her louely face she for his looking left.

Withall she laughed, and she blusht withall,   lxviii
  That blushing to her laughter gaue more grace,
  And laughter to her blushing, as did fall:
  Now when they spide the knight to slacke his pace,
  Them to behold, and in his sparkling face
  The secret signes of kindled lust appeare,
  Their wanton meriments they did encreace,
  And to him beckned, to approch more neare,
And shewd him many sights, that courage cold could reare.

On which when gazing him the Palmer saw,   lxix
  He much rebukt those wandring eyes of his,
  And counseld well, him forward thence did draw.
  Now are they come nigh to the *Bowre of blis*
  Of her fond fauorites so nam'd amis:
  When thus the Palmer; Now Sir, well auise;
  For here the end of all our trauell is:
  Here wonnes *Acrasia*, whom we must surprise,
Else she will slip away, and all our drift despise.

Eftsoones they heard a most melodious sound, lxx
  Of all that mote delight a daintie eare,
  Such as attonce might not on liuing ground,
  Saue in this Paradise, be heard elswhere:
  Right hard it was, for wight, which did it heare,
  To read, what manner musicke that mote bee:
  For all that pleasing is to liuing eare,
  Was there consorted in one harmonee,
Birdes, voyces, instruments, windes, waters, all agree.

The ioyous birdes shrouded in chearefull shade, lxxi
  Their notes vnto the voyce attempred sweet;
  Th'Angelicall soft trembling voyces made
  To th'instruments diuine respondence meet:
  The siluer sounding instruments did meet
  With the base murmure of the waters fall:
  The waters fall with difference discreet,
  Now soft, now loud, vnto the wind did call:
The gentle warbling wind low answered to all.

There, whence that Musick seemed heard to bee, lxxii
  Was the faire Witch her selfe now solacing,
  With a new Louer, whom through sorceree
  And witchcraft, she from farre did thither bring:
  There she had him now layd a slombering,
  In secret shade, after long wanton ioyes:
  Whilst round about them pleasauntly did sing
  Many faire Ladies, and lasciuious boyes,
That euer mixt their song with light licentious toyes.

And all that while, right ouer him she hong, lxxiii
  With her false eyes fast fixed in his sight,
  As seeking medicine, whence she was stong,
  Or greedily depasturing delight:
  And oft inclining downe with kisses light,
  For feare of waking him, his lips bedewd,
  And through his humid eyes did sucke his spright,
  Quite molten into lust and pleasure lewd;
Wherewith she sighed soft, as if his case she rewd.

lxxiii 1 that] the *1609*

The whiles some one did chaunt this louely lay;   lxxiv
  Ah see, who so faire thing doest faine to see,
  In springing flowre the image of thy day;
  Ah see the Virgin Rose, how sweetly shee
  Doth first peepe forth with bashfull modestee,
  That fairer seemes, the lesse ye see her may;
  Lo see soone after, how more bold and free
  Her bared bosome she doth broad display;
Loe see soone after, how she fades, and falles away.

So passeth, in the passing of a day,   lxxv
  Of mortall life the leafe, the bud, the flowre,
  Ne more doth flourish after first decay,
  That earst was sought to decke both bed and bowre,
  Of many a Ladie, and many a Paramowre:
  Gather therefore the Rose, whilest yet is prime,
  For soone comes age, that will her pride deflowre:
  Gather the Rose of loue, whilest yet is time,
Whilest louing thou mayst loued be with equall crime.

He ceast, and then gan all the quire of birdes   lxxvi
  Their diuerse notes t'attune vnto his lay,
  As in approuance of his pleasing words.
  The constant paire heard all, that he did say,
  Yet swarued not, but kept their forward way,
  Through many couert groues, and thickets close,
  In which they creeping did at last display
  That wanton Ladie, with her louer lose,
Whose sleepie head she in her lap did soft dispose.

Vpon a bed of Roses she was layd,   lxxvii
  As faint through heat, or dight to pleasant sin,
  And was arayd, or rather disarayd,
  All in a vele of silke and siluer thin,
  That hid no whit her alablaster skin,
  But rather shewd more white, if more might bee:
  More subtile web *Arachne* cannot spin,
  Nor the fine nets, which oft we wouen see
Of scorched deaw, do not in th'aire more lightly flee.

Her snowy brest was bare to readie spoyle   lxxviii
 Of hungry eies, which n'ote therewith be fild,
 And yet through languour of her late sweet toyle,
 Few drops, more cleare then Nectar, forth distild,
 That like pure Orient perles adowne it trild,
 And her faire eyes sweet smyling in delight,
 Moystened their fierie beames, with which she thrild
 Fraile harts, yet quenched not; like starry light
Which sparckling on the silent waues, does seeme more bright.

The young man sleeping by her, seemd to bee   lxxix
 Some goodly swayne of honorable place,
 That certes it great pittie was to see
 Him his nobilitie so foule deface;
 A sweet regard, and amiable grace,
 Mixed with manly sternnesse did appeare
 Yet sleeping, in his well proportiond face,
 And on his tender lips the downy heare
Did now but freshly spring, and silken blossomes beare.

His warlike armes, the idle instruments   lxxx
 Of sleeping praise, were hong vpon a tree,
 And his braue shield, full of old moniments,
 Was fowly ra'st, that none the signes might see;
 Ne for them, ne for honour cared hee,
 Ne ought, that did to his aduauncement tend,
 But in lewd loues, and wastfull luxuree,
 His dayes, his goods, his bodie he did spend:
O horrible enchantment, that him so did blend.

The noble Elfe, and carefull Palmer drew   lxxxi
 So nigh them, minding nought, but lustfull game,
 That suddein forth they on them rusht, and threw
 A subtile net, which onely for the same
 The skilfull Palmer formally did frame.
 So held them vnder fast, the whiles the rest
 Fled all away for feare of fowler shame.
 The faire Enchauntresse, so vnwares opprest,
Tryde all her arts, and all her sleights, thence out to wrest.

lxxxi 4 the] that 1590

z 2

And eke her louer stroue: but all in vaine;   lxxxii
   For that same net so cunningly was wound,
   That neither guile, nor force might it distraine.
   They tooke them both, and both them strongly bound
   In captiue bandes, which there they readie found:
   But her in chaines of adamant he tyde;
   For nothing else might keepe her safe and sound;
   But *Verdant* (so he hight) he soone vntyde,
And counsell sage in steed thereof to him applyde.

But all those pleasant bowres and Pallace braue,   lxxxiii
   Guyon broke downe, with rigour pittilesse;
   Ne ought their goodly workmanship might saue
   Them from the tempest of his wrathfulnesse,
   But that their blisse he turn'd to balefulnesse:
   Their groues he feld, their gardins did deface,
   Their arbers spoyle, their Cabinets suppresse,
   Their banket houses burne, their buildings race,
And of the fairest late, now made the fowlest place.

Then led they her away, and eke that knight   lxxxiv
   They with them led, both sorrowfull and sad:
   The way they came, the same retourn'd they right,
   Till they arriued, where they lately had
   Charm'd those wild-beasts, that rag'd with furie mad.
   Which now awaking, fierce at them gan fly,
   As in their mistresse reskew, whom they lad;
   But them the Palmer soone did pacify.
Then *Guyon* askt, what meant those beastes, which there did ly.

Said he, These seeming beasts are men indeed,   lxxxv
   Whom this Enchauntresse hath transformed thus,
   Whylome her louers, which her lusts did feed,
   Now turned into figures hideous,
   According to their mindes like monstruous.
   Sad end (quoth he) of life intemperate,
   And mournefull meed of ioyes delicious:
   But Palmer, if it mote thee so aggrate,
Let them returned be vnto their former state.

    lxxxiii 7 spoyle] spoyld *1596. 1609*   lxxxv 1 these *1590. 1596*

Streight way he with his vertuous staffe them strooke, lxxxvi
   And streight of beasts they comely men became ;
   Yet being men they did vnmanly looke,
   And stared ghastly, some for inward shame,
   And some for wrath, to see their captiue Dame :
   But one aboue the rest in speciall,
   That had an hog beene late, hight *Grille* by name,
   Repined greatly, and did him miscall,
That had from hoggish forme him brought to naturall.

Said *Guyon*, See the mind of beastly man, lxxxvii
   That hath so soone forgot the excellence
   Of his creation, when he life began,
   That now he chooseth, with vile difference,
   To be a beast, and lacke intelligence.
   To whom the Palmer thus, The donghill kind
   Delights in filth and foule incontinence :
   Let *Grill* be *Grill*, and haue his hoggish mind,
But let vs hence depart, whilest wether serues and wind.

THE THIRD
BOOKE OF THE
FAERIE QVEENE.
Contayning,

THE LEGEND OF BRITOMARTIS.
OR

Of Chastitie.

IT falls me here to write of Chastity,
That fairest vertue, farre aboue the rest;
For which what needs me fetch from *Faery*
Forreine ensamples, it to haue exprest?
Sith it is shrined in my Soueraines brest,
And form'd so liuely in each perfect part,
That to all Ladies, which haue it profest,
Need but behold the pourtraict of her hart,
If pourtrayd it might be by any liuing art.

But liuing art may not least part expresse,
Nor life-resembling pencill it can paint,
All were it *Zeuxis* or *Praxiteles*:
His dædale hand would faile, and greatly faint,
And her perfections with his error taint:
Ne Poets wit, that passeth Painter farre
In picturing the parts of beautie daint,
So hard a workmanship aduenture darre,
For fear through want of words her excellence to marre.

How then shall I, Apprentice of the skill,   iii
  That whylome in diuinest wits did raine,
  Presume so high to stretch mine humble quill?
  Yet now my lucklesse lot doth me constraine
  Hereto perforce. But O dred Soueraine
  Thus farre forth pardon, sith that choicest wit
  Cannot your glorious pourtraict figure plaine
  That I in colourd showes may shadow it,
And antique praises vnto present persons fit.

But if in liuing colours, and right hew,   iv
  Your selfe you couet to see pictured,
  Who can it doe more liuely, or more trew,
  Then that sweet verse, with *Nectar* sprinckeled,
  In which a gracious seruant pictured
  His *Cynthia,* his heauens fairest light?
  That with his melting sweetnesse rauished,
  And with the wonder of her beames bright,
My senses lulled are in slomber of delight.

But let that same delitious Poet lend   v
  A little leaue vnto a rusticke Muse
  To sing his mistresse prayse, and let him mend,
  If ought amis her liking may abuse:
  Ne let his fairest *Cynthia* refuse,
  In mirrours more then one her selfe to see,
  But either *Gloriana* let her chuse,
  Or in *Belphœbe* fashioned to bee:
In th'one her rule, in th'other her rare chastitee.

iv 2 Thy selfe thou *1590*

Cant. I.

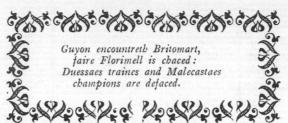

Guyon encountreth Britomart,
faire Florimell is chaced:
Duessaes traines and Malecastaes
champions are defaced.

THe famous Briton Prince and Faerie knight,   i
 After long wayes and perilous paines endured,
Hauing their wearie limbes to perfect plight
Restord, and sory wounds right well recured,
Of the faire *Alma* greatly were procured,
To make there lenger soiourne and abode;
But when thereto they might not be allured,
From seeking praise, and deeds of armes abrode,
They courteous conge tooke, and forth together yode.

But the captiu'd *Acrasia* he sent,   ii.
 Because of trauell long, a nigher way,
With a strong gard, all reskew to preuent,
And her to Faerie court safe to conuay,
That her for witnesse of his hard assay,
Vnto his *Faerie* Queene he might present:
But he him selfe betooke another way,
To make more triall of his hardiment,
And seeke aduentures, as he with Prince *Arthur* went.

Long so they trauelled through wastefull wayes,   iii
 Where daungers dwelt, and perils most did wonne,
To hunt for glorie and renowmed praise;
Full many Countries they did ouerronne,
From the vprising to the setting Sunne,
And many hard aduentures did atchieue;
Of all the which they honour euer wonne,
Seeking the weake oppressed to relieue,
And to recouer right for such, as wrong did grieue.

Arg. 3 *Malecastaes*] *Materastaes 1590 &c.*: *corr. F. E.*

At last as through an open plaine they yode,   iv
   They spide a knight, that towards pricked faire,
   And him beside an aged Squire there rode,
   That seem'd to couch vnder his shield three-square,
   As if that age bad him that burden spare,
   And yield it those, that stouter could it wield:
   He them espying, gan himselfe prepare,
   And on his arme addresse his goodly shield
That bore a Lion passant in a golden field.

Which seeing good Sir *Guyon*, deare besought   v
   The Prince of grace, to let him runne that turne.
   He graunted: then the Faery quickly raught
   His poinant speare, and sharpely gan to spurne
   His fomy steed, whose fierie feete did burne
   The verdant grasse, as he thereon did tread;
   Ne did the other backe his foot returne,
   But fiercely forward came withouten dread,
And bent his dreadfull speare against the others head.

They bene ymet, and both their points arriued,   vi
   But *Guyon* droue so furious and fell,
   That seem'd both shield and plate it would haue riued;
   Nathelesse it bore his foe not from his sell,
   But made him stagger, as he were not well:
   But *Guyon* selfe, ere well he was aware,
   Nigh a speares length behind his crouper fell,
   Yet in his fall so well him selfe he bare,
That mischieuous mischance his life and limbes did spare.

Great shame and sorrow of that fall he tooke;   vii
   For neuer yet, sith warlike armes he bore,
   And shiuering speare in bloudie field first shooke,
   He found himselfe dishonored so sore.
   Ah gentlest knight, that euer armour bore,
   Let not thee grieue dismounted to haue beene,
   And brought to ground, that neuer wast before;
   For not thy fault, but secret powre vnseene,
That speare enchaunted was, which layd thee on the greene.

vii 2 sith] since *1609*

But weenedst thou what wight thee ouerthrew,   viii
  Much greater griefe and shamefuller regret
  For thy hard fortune then thou wouldst renew,
  That of a single damzell thou wert met
  On equall plaine, and there so hard beset;
  Euen the famous *Britomart* it was,
  Whom straunge aduenture did from *Britaine* fet,
  To seeke her louer (loue farre sought alas,)
Whose image she had seene in *Venus* looking glas.

Full of disdainefull wrath, he fierce vprose,   ix
  For to reuenge that foule reprochfull shame,
  And snatching his bright sword began to close
  With her on foot, and stoutly forward came;
  Die rather would he, then endure that same.
  Which when his Palmer saw, he gan to feare
  His toward perill and vntoward blame,
  Which by that new rencounter he should reare:
For death sate on the point of that enchaunted speare.

And hasting towards him gan faire perswade,   x
  Not to prouoke misfortune, nor to weene
  His speares default to mend with cruell blade;
  For by his mightie Science he had seene
  The secret vertue of that weapon keene,
  That mortall puissance mote not withstond:
  Nothing on earth mote alwaies happie beene.
  Great hazard were it, and aduenture fond,
To loose long gotten honour with one euill hond.

By such good meanes he him discounselled,   xi
  From prosecuting his reuenging rage;
  And eke the Prince like treaty handeled,
  His wrathfull will with reason to asswage,
  And laid the blame, not to his carriage,
  But to his starting steed, that swaru'd asyde,
  And to the ill purueyance of his page,
  That had his furnitures not firmely tyde:
So is his angry courage fairely pacifyde.

Thus reconcilement was betweene them knit,　　　xii
　Through goodly temperance, and affection chaste,
　And either vowd with all their power and wit,
　To let not others honour be defaste,
　Of friend or foe, who euer it embaste,
　Ne armes to beare against the others syde:
　In which accord the Prince was also plaste,
　And with that golden chaine of concord tyde.
So goodly all agreed, they forth yfere did ryde.

O goodly vsage of those antique times,　　　xiii
　In which the sword was seruant vnto right;
　When not for malice and contentious crimes,
　But all for praise, and proofe of manly might,
　The martiall brood accustomed to fight:
　Then honour was the meed of victorie,
　And yet the vanquished had no despight:
　Let later age that noble vse enuie,
Vile rancour to auoid, and cruell surquedrie.

Long they thus trauelled in friendly wise,　　　xiv
　Through countries waste, and eke well edifyde,
　Seeking aduentures hard, to exercise
　Their puissance, whylome full dernely tryde:
　At length they came into a forrest wyde,
　Whose hideous horror and sad trembling sound
　Full griesly seem'd: Therein they long did ryde,
　Yet tract of liuing creatures none they found,
Saue Beares, Lions, and Buls, which romed them around.

All suddenly out of the thickest brush,　　　xv
　Vpon a milk-white Palfrey all alone,
　A goodly Ladie did foreby them rush,
　Whose face did seeme as cleare as Christall stone,
　And eke through feare as white as whales bone:
　Her garments all were wrought of beaten gold,
　And all her steed with tinsell trappings shone,
　Which fled so fast, that nothing mote him hold,
And scarse them leasure gaue, her passing to behold.

xiv 8 creature *1590*

Still as she fled, her eye she backward threw,   xvi
  As fearing euill, that pursewd her fast;
And her faire yellow locks behind her flew,
  Loosely disperst with puffe of euery blast:
  All as a blazing starre doth farre outcast
  His hearie beames, and flaming lockes dispred,
  At sight whereof the people stand aghast:
  But the sage wisard telles, as he has red,
That it importunes death and dolefull drerihed.

So as they gazed after her a while,   xvii
  Lo where a griesly Foster forth did rush,
  Breathing out beastly lust her to defile:
  His tyreling iade he fiercely forth did push,
  Through thicke and thin, both ouer banke and bush
  In hope her to attaine by hooke or crooke,
  That from his gorie sides the bloud did gush:
  Large were his limbes, and terrible his looke,
And in his clownish hand a sharp bore speare he shooke.

Which outrage when those gentle knights did see,   xviii
  Full of great enuie and fell gealosy,
  They stayd not to auise, who first should bee,
  But all spurd after fast, as they mote fly,
  To reskew her from shamefull villany.
  The Prince and *Guyon* equally byliue
  Her selfe pursewd, in hope to win thereby
  Most goodly meede, the fairest Dame aliue:
But after the foule foster *Timias* did striue.

The whiles faire *Britomart*, whose constant mind,   xix
  Would not so lightly follow beauties chace,
  Ne reckt of Ladies Loue, did stay behind,
  And them awayted there a certaine space,
  To weet if they would turne backe to that place:
  But when she saw them gone, she forward went,
  As lay her iourney, through that perlous Pace,
  With stedfast courage and stout hardiment;
Ne euill thing she fear'd, ne euill thing she ment.

At last as nigh out of the wood she came,   xx
  A stately Castle farre away she spyde,
  To which her steps directly she did frame.
  That Castle was most goodly edifyde,
  And plaste for pleasure nigh that forrest syde:
  But faire before the gate a spatious plaine,
  Mantled with greene, it selfe did spredden wyde,
  On which she saw sixe knights, that did darraine
Fierce battell against one, with cruell might and maine.

Mainly they all attonce vpon him laid,   xxi
  And sore beset on euery side around,
  That nigh he breathlesse grew, yet nought dismaid,
  Ne euer to them yielded foot of ground
  All had he lost much bloud through many a wound,
  But stoutly dealt his blowes, and euery way
  To which he turned in his wrathfull stound,
  Made them recoile, and fly from dred decay,
That none of all the sixe before, him durst assay.

Like dastard Curres, that hauing at a bay   xxii
  The saluage beast embost in wearie chace,
  Dare not aduenture on the stubborne pray,
  Ne byte before, but rome from place to place,
  To get a snatch, when turned is his face.
  In such distresse and doubtfull ieopardy,
  When *Britomart* him saw, she ran a pace
  Vnto his reskew, and with earnest cry,
Bad those same sixe forbeare that single enimy.

But to her cry they list not lenden eare,   xxiii
  Ne ought the more their mightie strokes surceasse,
  But gathering him round about more neare,
  Their direfull rancour rather did encreasse;
  Till that she rushing through the thickest preasse,
  Perforce disparted their compacted gyre,
  And soone compeld to hearken vnto peace:
  Tho gan she myldly of them to inquyre
The cause of their dissention and outrageous yre.

Whereto that single knight did answere frame;   xxiv
  These sixe would me enforce by oddes of might,
  To chaunge my liefe, and loue another Dame,
  That death me liefer were, then such despight,
  So vnto wrong to yield my wrested right:
  For I loue one, the truest one on ground,
  Ne list me chaunge; she th'*Errant Damzell* hight,
  For whose deare sake full many a bitter stownd,
I haue endur'd, and tasted many a bloudy wound.

Certes (said she) then bene ye sixe to blame,   xxv
  To weene your wrong by force to iustifie:
  For knight to leaue his Ladie were great shame,
  That faithfull is, and better were to die.
  All losse is lesse, and lesse the infamie,
  Then losse of loue to him, that loues but one;
  Ne may loue be compeld by maisterie;
  For soone as maisterie comes, sweet loue anone
Taketh his nimble wings, and soone away is gone.

Then spake one of those sixe, There dwelleth here   xxvi
  Within this castle wall a Ladie faire,
  Whose soueraine beautie hath no liuing pere,
  Thereto so bounteous and so debonaire,
  That neuer any mote with her compaire.
  She hath ordaind this law, which we approue,
  That euery knight, which doth this way repaire,
  In case he haue no Ladie, nor no loue,
Shall doe vnto her seruice neuer to remoue.

But if he haue a Ladie or a Loue,   xxvii
  Then must he her forgoe with foule defame,
  Or else with vs by dint of sword approue,
  That she is fairer, then our fairest Dame,
  As did this knight, before ye hither came.
  Perdie (said *Britomart*) the choise is hard:
  But what reward had he, that ouercame?
  He should aduaunced be to high regard,
(Said they) and haue our Ladies loue for his reward.

Therefore a read Sir, if thou haue a loue.
    Loue haue I sure, (quoth she) but Lady none;
    Yet will I not fro mine owne loue remoue,
    Ne to your Lady will I seruice done,
    But wreake your wrongs wrought to this knight alone,
    And proue his cause.   With that her mortall speare
    She mightily auentred towards one,
    And downe him smot, ere well aware he weare,
Then to the next she rode, and downe the next did beare.

Ne did she stay, till three on ground she layd,
    That none of them himselfe could reare againe;
    The fourth was by that other knight dismayd,
    All were he wearie of his former paine,
    That now there do but two of six remaine;
    Which two did yield, before she did them smight.
    Ah (said she then) now may ye all see plaine,
    That truth is strong, and trew loue most of might,
That for his trusty seruaunts doth so strongly fight.

Too well we see, (said they) and proue too well
    Our faulty weaknesse, and your matchlesse might:
    For thy, faire Sir, yours be the Damozell,
    Which by her owne law to your lot doth light,
    And we your liege men faith vnto you plight.
    So vnderneath her feet their swords they mard,
    And after her besought, well as they might,
    To enter in, and reape the dew reward:
She graunted, and then in they all together far'd.

Long were it to describe the goodly frame,
    And stately port of *Castle Ioyeous,*
    (For so that Castle hight by commune name)
    Where they were entertaind with curteous
    And comely glee of many gracious
    Faire Ladies, and of many a gentle knight,
    Who through a Chamber long and spacious,
    Eftsoones them brought vnto their Ladies sight,
That of them cleeped was the *Lady of delight.*

xxx 6 mard] shard *1590 &c.: corr. F. E.*   xxxi 6 of *om. 1596, 1609*
8 sight. *1596*

But for to tell the sumptuous aray   xxxii
  Of that great chamber, should be labour lost:
  For liuing wit, I weene, cannot display
  The royall riches and exceeding cost,
  Of euery pillour and of euery post;
  Which all of purest bullion framed were,
  And with great pearles and pretious stones embost,
  That the bright glister of their beames cleare
Did sparckle forth great light, and glorious did appeare.

These straunger knights through passing, forth were led xxxiii
  Into an inner rowme, whose royaltee
  And rich purueyance might vneath be red;
  Mote Princes place beseeme so deckt to bee.
  Which stately manner when as they did see,
  The image of superfluous riotize,
  Exceeding much the state of meane degree,
  They greatly wondred, whence so sumptuous guize
Might be maintaynd, and each gan diuersely deuize.

The wals were round about apparelled   xxxiv
  With costly clothes of *Arras* and of *Toure*,
  In which with cunning hand was pourtrahed
  The loue of *Venus* and her Paramoure
  The faire *Adonis*, turned to a flowre,
  A worke of rare deuice, and wondrous wit.
  First did it shew the bitter balefull stowre,
  Which her assayd with many a feruent fit,
When first her tender hart was with his beautie smit.

Then with what sleights and sweet allurements she   xxxv
  Entyst the Boy, as well that art she knew,
  And wooed him her Paramoure to be;
  Now making girlonds of each flowre that grew,
  To crowne his golden lockes with honour dew;
  Now leading him into a secret shade
  From his Beauperes, and from bright heauens vew,
  Where him to sleepe she gently would perswade,
Or bathe him in a fountaine by some couert glade.

xxxiii 4 be seeme *1596*

And whilst he slept, she ouer him would spred   xxxvi
    Her mantle, colour'd like the starry skyes,
    And her soft arme lay vnderneath his hed,
    And with ambrosiall kisses bathe his eyes;
    And whilest he bath'd, with her two crafty spyes,
    She secretly would search each daintie lim,
    And throw into the well sweet Rosemaryes,
    And fragrant violets, and Pances trim,
And euer with sweet Nectar she did sprinkle him.

So did she steale his heedelesse hart away,   xxxvii
    And ioyd his loue in secret vnespyde.
    But for she saw him bent to cruell play,
    To hunt the saluage beast in forrest wyde,
    Dreadfull of daunger, that mote him betyde,
    She oft and oft aduiz'd him to refraine
    From chase of greater beasts, whose brutish pryde
    Mote breede him scath vnwares: but all in vaine;
For who can shun the chaunce, that dest'ny doth ordaine?

Lo, where beyond he lyeth languishing,   xxxviii
    Deadly engored of a great wild Bore,
    And by his side the Goddesse groueling
    Makes for him endlesse mone, and euermore
    With her soft garment wipes away the gore,
    Which staines his snowy skin with hatefull hew:
    But when she saw no helpe might him restore,
    Him to a dainty flowre she did transmew,
Which in that cloth was wrought, as if it liuely grew.

So was that chamber clad in goodly wize,   xxxix
    And round about it many beds were dight,
    As whilome was the antique worldes guize,
    Some for vntimely ease, some for delight,
    As pleased them to vse, that vse it might:
    And all was full of Damzels, and of Squires,
    Dauncing and reueling both day and night,
    And swimming deepe in sensuall desires,
And *Cupid* still emongst them kindled lustfull fires.

xxxvii 8 scathe *1609*

And all the while sweet Musicke did diuide   xl
   Her looser notes with *Lydian* harmony;
   And all the while sweet birdes thereto applide
   Their daintie layes and dulcet melody,
   Ay caroling of loue and iollity,
   That wonder was to heare their trim consort.
   Which when those knights beheld, with scornefull eye,
   They sdeigned such lasciuious disport,
And loath'd the loose demeanure of that wanton sort.

Thence they were brought to that great Ladies vew,   xli
   Whom they found sitting on a sumptuous bed,
   That glistred all with gold and glorious shew,
   As the proud *Persian* Queenes accustomed :
   She seemd a woman of great bountihed,
   And of rare beautie, sauing that askaunce
   Her wanton eyes, ill signes of womanhed,
   Did roll too lightly, and too often glaunce,
Without regard of grace, or comely amenaunce.

Long worke it were, and needlesse to deuize   xlii
   Their goodly entertainement and great glee :
   She caused them be led in curteous wize
   Into a bowre, disarmed for to bee,
   And cheared well with wine and spiceree :
   The *Redcrosse* Knight was soone disarmed there,
   But the braue Mayd would not disarmed bee,
   But onely vented vp her vmbriere,
And so did let her goodly visage to appere.

As when faire *Cynthia*, in darkesome night,   xliii
   Is in a noyous cloud enueloped,
   Where she may find the substaunce thin and light,
   Breakes forth her siluer beames, and her bright hed
   Discouers to the world discomfited ;
   Of the poore traueller, that went astray,
   With thousand blessings she is heried ;
   Such was the beautie and the shining ray,
With which faire *Britomart* gaue light vnto the day.

xli 8 lightly] highly *1590, 1596*

And eke those six, which lately with her fought,   xliv
  Now were disarmd, and did them selues present
  Vnto her vew, and company vnsoght;
  For they all seemed curteous and gent,
  And all sixe brethren, borne of one parent,
  Which had them traynd in all ciuilitee,
  And goodly taught to tilt and turnament;
  Now were they liegemen to this Lady free,
And her knights seruice ought, to hold of her in fee.

The first of them by name *Gardante* hight,   xlv
  A iolly person, and of comely vew;
  The second was *Parlante*, a bold knight,
  And next to him *Iocante* did ensew;
  Basciante did him selfe most curteous shew;
  But fierce *Bacchante* seemd too fell and keene;
  And yet in armes *Noctante* greater grew:
  All were faire knights, and goodly well beseene,
But to faire *Britomart* they all but shadowes beene.

For she was full of amiable grace,   xlvi
  And manly terrour mixed therewithall,
  That as the one stird vp affections bace,
  So th'other did mens rash desires apall,
  And hold them backe, that would in errour fall;
  As he, that hath espide a vermeill Rose,
  To which sharpe thornes and breres the way forstall,
  Dare not for dread his hardy hand expose,
But wishing it far off, his idle wish doth lose.

Whom when the Lady saw so faire a wight,   xlvii
  All ignoraunt of her contrary sex,
  (For she her weend a fresh and lusty knight)
  She greatly gan enamoured to wex,
  And with vaine thoughts her falsed fancy vex:
  Her fickle hart conceiued hasty fire,
  Like sparkes of fire, which fall in sclender flex,
  That shortly brent into extreme desire,
And ransackt all her veines with passion entire.

xlvi 7 briers *1609*   xlvii 1 wight. *1596*   7 which] that *1590*
slender *1609*

Eftsoones she grew to great impatience   xlviii
    And into termes of open outrage brust,
    That plaine discouered her incontinence,
    Ne reckt she, who her meaning did mistrust;
    For she was giuen all to fleshly lust,
    And poured forth in sensuall delight,
    That all regard of shame she had discust,
    And meet respect of honour put to flight:
So shamelesse beauty soone becomes a loathly sight.

Faire Ladies, that to loue captiued arre,   xlix
    And chaste desires do nourish in your mind,
    Let not her fault your sweet affections marre,
    Ne blot the bounty of all womankind;
    'Mongst thousands good one wanton Dame to find:
    Emongst the Roses grow some wicked weeds;
    For this was not to loue, but lust inclind;
    For loue does alwayes bring forth bounteous deeds,
And in each gentle hart desire of honour breeds.

Nought so of loue this looser Dame did skill,   l
    But as a coale to kindle fleshly flame,
    Giuing the bridle to her wanton will,
    And treading vnder foote her honest name:
    Such loue is hate, and such desire is shame.
    Still did she roue at her with crafty glaunce
    Of her false eyes, that at her hart did ayme,
    And told her meaning in her countenaunce;
But *Britomart* dissembled it with ignoraunce.

Supper was shortly dight and downe they sat,   li
    Where they were serued with all sumptuous fare,
    Whiles fruitfull *Ceres*, and *Lyæus* fat
    Pourd out their plenty, without spight or spare:
    Nought wanted there, that dainty was and rare;
    And aye the cups their bancks did ouerflow,
    And aye betweene the cups, she did prepare
    Way to her loue, and secret darts did throw;
But *Britomart* would not such guilfull message know.

        xlviii 2 burst *1609*   9 loathy *1596, 1609*   sight, *1596*

So when they slaked had the feruent heat   lii
  Of appetite with meates of euery sort,
  The Lady did faire *Britomart* entreat,
  Her to disarme, and with delightfull sport
  To loose her warlike limbs and strong effort,
  But when she mote not thereunto be wonne,
  (For she her sexe vnder that straunge purport
  Did vse to hide, and plaine apparaunce shonne :)
In plainer wise to tell her grieuaunce she begonne.

And all attonce discouered her desire   liii
  With sighes, and sobs, and plaints, and piteous griefe,
  The outward sparkes of her in burning fire,
  Which spent in vaine, at last she told her briefe,
  That but if she did lend her short reliefe,
  And do her comfort, she mote algates dye.
  But the chaste damzell, that had neuer priefe
  Of such malengine and fine forgerie,
Did easily belceue her strong extremitie.

Full easie was for her to haue beliefe,   liv
  Who by self-feeling of her feeble sexe,
  And by long triall of the inward griefe,
  Wherewith imperious loue her hart did vexe,
  Could iudge what paines do louing harts perplexe.
  Who meanes no guile, be guiled soonest shall,
  And to faire semblaunce doth light faith annexe;
  The bird, that knowes not the false fowlers call,
Into his hidden net full easily doth fall.

For thy she would not in discourteise wise,   lv
  Scorne the faire offer of good will profest;
  For great rebuke it is, loue to despise,
  Or rudely sdeigne a gentle harts request;
  But with faire countenaunce, as beseemed best,
  Her entertaynd; nath'lesse she inly deemd
  Her loue too light, to wooe a wandring guest :
Which she misconstruing, thereby esteemd
That from like inward fire that outward smoke had steemd.

Therewith a while she her flit fancy fed,   lvi
  Till she mote winne fit time for her desire,
  But yet her wound still inward freshly bled,
  And through her bones the false instilled fire
  Did spred it selfe, and venime close inspire.
  Tho were the tables taken all away,
  And euery knight, and euery gentle Squire
  Gan choose his dame with *Basciomani* gay,
With whom he meant to make his sport and courtly play.

Some fell to daunce, some fell to hazardry,   lvii
  Some to make loue, some to make meriment,
  As diuerse wits to diuers things apply;
  And all the while faire *Malecasta* bent
  Her crafty engins to her close intent.
  By this th'eternall lampes, wherewith high *Ioue*
  Doth light the lower world, were halfe yspent,
  And the moist daughters of huge *Atlas* stroue
Into the *Ocean* deepe to driue their weary droue.

High time it seemed then for euery wight   lviii
  Them to betake vnto their kindly rest;
  Eftsoones long waxen torches weren light,
  Vnto their bowres to guiden euery guest:
  Tho when the Britonesse saw all the rest
  Auoided quite, she gan her selfe despoile,
  And safe commit to her soft fethered nest,
  Where through long watch, and late dayes weary toile,
She soundly slept, and carefull thoughts did quite assoile.

Now whenas all the world in silence deepe   lix
  Yshrowded was, and euery mortall wight
  Was drowned in the depth of deadly sleepe,
  Faire *Malecasta*, whose engrieued spright
  Could find no rest in such perplexed plight,
  Lightly arose out of her wearie bed,
  And vnder the blacke vele of guilty Night,
  Her with a scarlot mantle couered,
That was with gold and Ermines faire enueloped.

Then panting soft, and trembling euerie ioynt,   lx
  Her fearfull feete towards the bowre she moued;
  Where she for secret purpose did appoynt
  To lodge the warlike mayd vnwisely loued,
  And to her bed approching, first she prooued,
  Whether she slept or wakt, with her soft hand
  She softly felt, if any member mooued,
  And lent her wary eare to vnderstand,
If any puffe of breath, or signe of sence she fond.

Which whenas none she fond, with easie shift,   lxi
  For feare least her vnwares she should abrayd,
  Th'embroderd quilt she lightly vp did lift,
  And by her side her selfe she softly layd,
  Of euery finest fingers touch affrayd;
  Ne any noise she made, ne word she spake,
  But inly sigh'd. At last the royall Mayd
  Out of her quiet slomber did awake,
And chaungd her weary side, the better ease to take.

Where feeling one close couched by her side,   lxii
  She lightly lept out of her filed bed,
  And to her weapon ran, in minde to gride
  The loathed leachour. But the Dame halfe ded
  Through suddein feare and ghastly drerihed,
  Did shrieke alowd, that through the house it rong,
  And the whole family therewith adred,
  Rashly out of their rouzed couches sprong,
And to the troubled chamber all in armes did throng.

And those six Knights that Ladies Champions,   lxiii
  And eke the *Redcrosse* knight ran to the stownd,
  Halfe armd and halfe vnarmd, with them attons:
  Where when confusedly they came, they fownd
  Their Lady lying on the sencelesse grownd;
  On th'other side, they saw the warlike Mayd
  All in her snow-white smocke, with locks vnbownd,
  Threatning the point of her auenging blade,
That with so troublous terrour they were all dismayde.

      lx 8 weary *1590, 1596*   9 fand *1609*

About their Lady first they flockt arownd, lxiv
   Whom hauing laid in comfortable couch,
   Shortly they reard out of her frosen swownd;
   And afterwards they gan with fowle reproch
   To stirre vp strife, and troublous contecke broch:
   But by ensample of the last dayes losse,
   None of them rashly durst to her approch,
   Ne in so glorious spoile themselues embosse;
Her succourd eke the Champion of the bloudy Crosse.

But one of those sixe knights, *Gardante* hight, lxv
   Drew out a deadly bow and arrow keene,
   Which forth he sent with felonous despight,
   And fell intent against the virgin sheene:
   The mortall steele stayd not, till it was seene
   To gore her side, yet was the wound not deepe,
   But lightly rased her soft silken skin,
   That drops of purple bloud thereout did weepe,
Which did her lilly smock with staines of vermeil steepe.

Wherewith enrag'd she fiercely at them flew, lxvi
   And with her flaming sword about her layd,
   That none of them foule mischiefe could eschew,
   But with her dreadfull strokes were all dismayd:
   Here, there, and euery where about her swayd
   Her wrathfull steele, that none mote it abide;
   And eke the *Redcrosse* knight gaue her good aid,
   Ay ioyning foot to foot, and side to side,
That in short space their foes they haue quite terrifide.

Tho whenas all were put to shamefull flight, lxvii
   The noble *Britomartis* her arayd,
   And her bright armes about her body dight:
   For nothing would she lenger there be stayd,
   Where so loose life, and so vngentle trade
   Was vsd of Knights and Ladies seeming gent:
   So earely ere the grosse Earthes gryesy shade
   Was all disperst out of the firmament,
They tooke their steeds, and forth vpon their iourney went.

Cant. II.

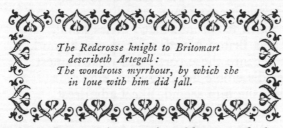

The Redcrosse knight to Britomart
describeth Artegall:
The wondrous myrrhour, by which she
in loue with him did fall.

HEre haue I cause, in men iust blame to find,   i
That in their proper prayse too partiall bee,
And not indifferent to woman kind,
To whom no share in armes and cheualrie
They do impart, ne maken memorie
Of their braue gestes and prowesse martiall;
Scarse do they spare to one or two or three,
Rowme in their writs; yet the same writing small
Does all their deeds deface, and dims their glories all.

But by record of antique times I find,   ii
That women wont in warres to beare most sway,
And to all great exploits them selues inclind:
Of which they still the girlond bore away,
Till enuious Men fearing their rules decay,
Gan coyne streight lawes to curb their liberty;
Yet sith they warlike armes haue layd away,
They haue exceld in artes and pollicy,
That now we foolish men that prayse gin eke t'enuy.

Of warlike puissaunce in ages spent,   iii
Be thou faire *Britomart*, whose prayse I write,
But of all wisedome be thou precedent,
O soueraigne Queene, whose prayse I would endite,
Endite I would as dewtie doth excite;
But ah my rimes too rude and rugged arre,
When in so high an obiect they do lite,
And striuing, fit to make, I feare do marre:
Thy selfe thy prayses tell, and make them knowen farre.

ii 2 wemen *1590*   7 away: *1596*

She trauelling with *Guyon* by the way,   iv
  Of sundry things faire purpose gan to find,
  T'abridg their iourney long, and lingring day;
  Mongst which it fell into that Faeries mind,
  To aske this Briton Mayd, what vncouth wind,
  Brought her into those parts, and what inquest
  Made her dissemble her disguised kind:
  Faire Lady she him seemd, like Lady drest,
But fairest knight aliue, when armed was her brest.

Thereat she sighing softly, had no powre   v
  To speake a while, ne ready answere make,
  But with hart-thrilling throbs and bitter stowre,
  As if she had a feuer fit, did quake,
  And euery daintie limbe with horrour shake;
  And euer and anone the rosy red,
  Flasht through her face, as it had been a flake
  Of lightning, through bright heauen fulmined;
At last the passion past she thus him answered.

Faire Sir, I let you weete, that from the howre   vi
  I taken was from nourses tender pap,
  I haue beene trained vp in warlike stowre,
  To tossen speare and shield, and to affrap
  The warlike ryder to his most mishap;
  Sithence I loathed haue my life to lead,
  As Ladies wont, in pleasures wanton lap,
  To finger the fine needle and nyce thread;
Me leuer were with point of foemans speare be dead.

All my delight on deedes of armes is set,   vii
  To hunt out perils and aduentures hard,
  By sea, by land, where so they may be met,
  Onely for honour and for high regard,
  Without respect of richesse or reward.
  For such intent into these parts I came,
  Withouten compasse, or withouten card,
  Far fro my natiue soyle, that is by name
The greater *Britaine*, here to seeke for prayse and fame.

iv 1 *Guyon*] Redcrosse   *MS. corr. in Malone 615*   vii 8 from *1609*

Fame blazed hath, that here in Faery lond   viii
  Do many famous Knightes and Ladies wonne,
  And many straunge aduentures to be fond,
  Of which great worth and worship may be wonne;
  Which I to proue, this voyage haue begonne.
  But mote I weet of you, right curteous knight,
  Tydings of one, that hath vnto me donne
  Late foule dishonour and reprochfull spight,
The which I seeke to wreake, and *Arthegall* he hight.

The word gone out, she backe againe would call,   ix
  As her repenting so to haue missayd,
  But that he it vp-taking ere the fall,
  Her shortly answered; Faire martiall Mayd
  Certes ye misauised beene, t'vpbrayd
  A gentle knight with so vnknightly blame:
  For weet ye well of all, that euer playd
  At tilt or tourney, or like warlike game,
The noble *Arthegall* hath euer borne the name.

For thy great wonder were it, if such shame   x
  Should euer enter in his bounteous thought,
  Or euer do, that mote deseruen blame:
  The noble courage neuer weeneth ought,
  That may vnworthy of it selfe be thought.
  Therefore, faire Damzell, be ye well aware,
  Least that too farre ye haue your sorrow sought:
  You and your countrey both I wish welfare,
And honour both; for each of other worthy are.

The royall Mayd woxe inly wondrous glad,   xi
  To heare her Loue so highly magnifide,
  And ioyd that euer she affixed had,
  Her hart on knight so goodly glorifide,
  How euer finely she it faind to hide:
  The louing mother, that nine monethes did beare,
  In the deare closet of her painefull side,
  Her tender babe, it seeing safe appeare,
Doth not so much reioyce, as she reioyced theare.

viii 5 Which to proue, I *1590*

But to occasion him to further talke,   xii
 To feed her humour with his pleasing stile,
 Her list in strifull termes with him to balke,
 And thus replide, How euer, Sir, ye file
 Your curteous tongue, his prayses to compile,
 It ill beseemes a knight of gentle sort,
 Such as ye haue him boasted, to beguile
 A simple mayd, and worke so haynous tort,
In shame of knighthood, as I largely can report.

Let be therefore my vengeaunce to disswade,   xiii
 And read, where I that faytour false may find.
 Ah, but if reason faire might you perswade,
 To slake your wrath, and mollifie your mind,
 (Said he) perhaps ye should it better find:
 For hardy thing it is, to weene by might,
 That man to hard conditions to bind,
 Or euer hope to match in equall fight,
Whose prowesse paragon saw neuer liuing wight.

Ne soothlich is it easie for to read,   xiv
 Where now on earth, or how he may be found;
 For he ne wonneth in one certaine stead,
 But restlesse walketh all the world around,
 Ay doing things, that to his fame redound,
 Defending Ladies cause, and Orphans right,
 Where so he heares, that any doth confound
 Them comfortlesse, through tyranny or might;
So is his soueraine honour raisde to heauens hight.

His feeling words her feeble sence much pleased,   xv
 And softly sunck into her molten hart;
 Hart that is inly hurt, is greatly eased
 With hope of thing, that may allegge his smart;
 For pleasing words are like to Magick art,
 That doth the charmed Snake in slomber lay:
 Such secret ease felt gentle *Britomart*,
 Yet list the same efforce with faind gainesay;
So dischord oft in Musick makes the sweeter lay.

xii 3 strife-full 1609

And said, Sir knight, these idle termes forbeare,   xvi
  And sith it is vneath to find his haunt,
  Tell me some markes, by which he may appeare,
  If chaunce I him encounter parauaunt;
  For perdie one shall other slay, or daunt:
  What shape, what shield, what armes, what steed, what sted,
  And what so else his person most may vaunt?
  All which the *Redcrosse* knight to point ared,
And him in euery part before her fashioned.

Yet him in euery part before she knew,   xvii
  How euer list her now her knowledge faine,
  Sith him whilome in *Britaine* she did vew,
  To her reuealed in a mirrhour plaine,
  Whereof did grow her first engraffed paine;
  Whose root and stalke so bitter yet did tast,
  That but the fruit more sweetnesse did containe,
  Her wretched dayes in dolour she mote wast,
And yield the pray of loue to lothsome death at last.

By strange occasion she did him behold,   xviii
  And much more strangely gan to loue his sight,
  As it in bookes hath written bene of old.
  In *Deheubarth* that now South-wales is hight,
  What time king *Ryence* raign'd, and dealed right,
  The great Magitian *Merlin* had deuiz'd,
  By his deepe science, and hell-dreaded might,
  A looking glasse, right wondrously aguiz'd,
Whose vertues through the wyde world soone were solemniz'd.

It vertue had, to shew in perfect sight,   xix
  What euer thing was in the world contaynd,
  Betwixt the lowest earth and heauens hight,
  So that it to the looker appertaynd;
  What euer foe had wrought, or frend had faynd,
  Therein discouered was, ne ought mote pas,
  Ne ought in secret from the same remaynd;
  For thy it round and hollow shaped was,
Like to the world it selfe, and seem'd a world of glas.

xvi 9 part] point 1609

Who wonders not, that reades so wonderous worke? xx
 But who does wonder, that has red the Towre,
 Wherein th'Ægyptian *Phao* long did lurke
 From all mens vew, that none might her discoure,
 Yet she might all men vew out of her bowre?
 Great *Ptolomæe* it for his lemans sake
 Ybuilded all of glasse, by Magicke powre,
 And also it impregnable did make;
Yet when his loue was false, he with a peaze it brake.

Such was the glassie globe that *Merlin* made, xxi
 And gaue vnto king *Ryence* for his gard,
 That neuer foes his kingdome might inuade,
 But he it knew at home before he hard
 Tydings thereof, and so them still debar'd.
 It was a famous Present for a Prince,
 And worthy worke of infinite reward,
 That treasons could bewray, and foes conuince;
Happie this Realme, had it remained euer since.

One day it fortuned, faire *Britomart* xxii
 Into her fathers closet to repayre;
 For nothing he from her reseru'd apart,
 Being his onely daughter and his hayre:
 Where when she had espyde that mirrhour fayre,
 Her selfe a while therein she vewd in vaine;
 Tho her auizing of the vertues rare,
 Which thereof spoken were, she gan againe
Her to bethinke of, that mote to her selfe pertaine.

But as it falleth, in the gentlest harts xxiii
 Imperious Loue hath highest set his throne,
 And tyrannizeth in the bitter smarts
 Of them, that to him buxome are and prone:
 So thought this Mayd (as maydens vse to done)
 Whom fortune for her husband would allot,
 Not that she lusted after any one;
 For she was pure from blame of sinfull blot,
Yet wist her life at last must lincke in that same knot.

Eftsoones there was presented to her eye   xxiv
   A comely knight, all arm'd in complete wize,
   Through whose bright ventayle lifted vp on hye
   His manly face, that did his foes agrize,
   And friends to termes of gentle truce entize,
   Lookt foorth, as *Phœbus* face out of the east,
   Betwixt two shadie mountaines doth arize;
   Portly his person was, and much increast
Through his Heroicke grace, and honorable gest.

His crest was couered with a couchant Hound,   xxv
   And all his armour seem'd of antique mould,
   But wondrous massie and assured sound,
   And round about yfretted all with gold,
   In which there written was with cyphers old,
   Achilles armes, which Arthegall did win.
   And on his shield enueloped scuenfold
   He bore a crowned litle Ermilin,
That deckt the azure field with her faire pouldred skin.

The Damzell well did vew his personage,   xxvi
   And liked well, ne further fastned not,
   But went her way; ne her vnguilty age
   Did weene, vnwares, that her vnlucky lot
   Lay hidden in the bottome of the pot;
   Of hurt vnwist most daunger doth redound:
   But the false Archer, which that arrow shot
   So slyly, that she did not feele the wound,
Did smyle full smoothly at her weetlesse wofull stound.

Thenceforth the feather in her loftie crest,   xxvii
   Ruffed of loue, gan lowly to auaile,
   And her proud portance, and her princely gest,
   With which she earst tryumphed, now did quaile:
   Sad, solemne, sowre, and full of fancies fraile
   She woxe; yet wist she neither how, nor why,
   She wist not, silly Mayd, what she did aile,
   Yet wist, she was not well at ease perdy,
Yet thought it was not loue, but some melancholy.

xxiv 2 complet *1596, 1609*

So soone as Night had with her pallid hew   xxviii
   Defast the beautie of the shining sky,
   And reft from men the worlds desired vew,
   She with her Nourse adowne to sleepe did lye;
   But sleepe full farre away from her did fly:
   In stead thereof sad sighes, and sorrowes deepe
   Kept watch and ward about her warily,
   That nought she did but wayle, and often steepe
Her daintie couch with teares, which closely she did weepe.

And if that any drop of slombring rest   xxix
   Did chaunce to still into her wearie spright,
   When feeble nature felt her selfe opprest,
   Streight way with dreames, and with fantasticke sight
   Of dreadfull things the same was put to flight,
   That oft out of her bed she did astart,
   As one with vew of ghastly feends affright:
   Tho gan she to renew her former smart,
And thinke of that faire visage, written in her hart.

One night, when she was tost with such vnrest,   xxx
   Her aged Nurse, whose name was *Glauce* hight,
   Feeling her leape out of her loathed nest,
   Betwixt her feeble armes her quickly keight,
   And downe againe in her warme bed her dight;
   Ah my deare daughter, ah my dearest dread,
   What vncouth fit (said she) what euill plight
   Hath thee opprest, and with sad drearyhead
Chaunged thy liuely cheare, and liuing made thee dead?

For not of nought these suddeine ghastly feares   xxxi
   All night afflict thy naturall repose,
   And all the day, when as thine equall peares
   Their fit disports with faire delight doe chose,
   Thou in dull corners doest thy selfe inclose,
   Ne tastest Princes pleasures, ne doest spred
   Abroad thy fresh youthes fairest flowre, but lose
   Both leafe and fruit, both too vntimely shed,
As one in wilfull bale for euer buried.

    xxviii 6 there of *1596*   xxx 5 her in her warme bed *1590*

The time, that mortall men their weary cares
  Do lay away, and all wilde beastes do rest,
  And euery riuer eke his course forbeares,
  Then doth this wicked euill thee infest,
  And riue with thousand throbs thy thrilled brest;
  Like an huge *Aetn'* of deepe engulfed griefe,
  Sorrow is heaped in thy hollow chest,
  Whence forth it breakes in sighes and anguish rife,
As smoke and sulphure mingled with confused strife.

Aye me, how much I feare, least loue it bee;
  But if that loue it be, as sure I read
  By knowen signes and passions, which I see,
  Be it worthy of thy race and royall sead,
  Then I auow by this most sacred head
  Of my deare foster child, to ease thy griefe,
  And win thy will: Therefore away doe dread;
  For death nor daunger from thy dew reliefe
Shall me debarre, tell me therefore my liefest liefe.

So hauing said, her twixt her armes twaine
  She straightly straynd, and colled tenderly,
  And euery trembling ioynt, and euery vaine
  She softly felt, and rubbed busily,
  To doe the frosen cold away to fly;
  And her faire deawy eies with kisses deare
  She oft did bath, and oft againe did dry;
  And euer her importund, not to feare
To let the secret of her hart to her appeare.

The Damzell pauzd, and then thus fearefully;
  Ah Nurse, what needeth thee to eke my paine?
  Is not enough, that I alone doe dye,
  But it must doubled be with death of twaine?
  For nought for me but death there doth remaine.
  O daughter deare (said she) despaire no whit;
  For neuer sore, but might a salue obtaine:
  That blinded God, which hath ye blindly smit,
Another arrow hath your louers hart to hit.

xxxii 3 forbeares *1596*

But mine is not (quoth she) like others wound;   xxxvi
  For which no reason can find remedy.
  Was neuer such, but mote the like be found,
  (Said she) and though no reason may apply
  Salue to your sore, yet loue can higher stye,
  Then reasons reach, and oft hath wonders donne.
  But neither God of loue, nor God of sky
  Can doe (said she) that, which cannot be donne.
Things oft impossible (quoth she) seeme, ere begonne.

These idle words (said she) doe nought asswage   xxxvii
  My stubborne smart, but more annoyance breed,
  For no no vsuall fire, no vsuall rage
  It is, O Nurse, which on my life doth feed,
  And suckes the bloud, which from my hart doth bleed.
  But since thy faithfull zeale lets me not hyde
  My crime, (if crime it be) I will it reed.
  Nor Prince, nor pere it is, whose loue hath gryde
My feeble brest of late, and launched this wound wyde.

Nor man it is, nor other liuing wight;   xxxviii
  For then some hope I might vnto me draw,
  But th'only shade and semblant of a knight,
  Whose shape or person yet I neuer saw,
  Hath me subiected to loues cruell law:
  The same one day, as me misfortune led,
  I in my fathers wondrous mirrhour saw,
  And pleased with that seeming goodly-hed,
Vnwares the hidden hooke with baite I swallowed.

Sithens it hath infixed faster hold   xxxix
  Within my bleeding bowels, and so sore
  Now ranckleth in this same fraile fleshly mould,
  That all mine entrailes flow with poysnous gore,
  And th'vlcer groweth daily more and more;
  Ne can my running sore find remedie,
  Other then my hard fortune to deplore,
  And languish as the leafe falne from the tree,
Till death make one end of my dayes and miserie.

       xxxvi 1 other *1590*   xxxvii 9 launced *1609*

Daughter (said she) what need ye be dismayd,   xl
   Or why make ye such Monster of your mind?
   Of much more vncouth thing I was affrayd;
   Of filthy lust, contrarie vnto kind:
   But this affection nothing straunge I find;
   For who with reason can you aye reproue,
   To loue the semblant pleasing most your mind,
   And yield your heart, whence ye cannot remoue?
No guilt in you, but in the tyranny of loue.

Not so th'*Arabian Myrrhe* did set her mind;   xli
   Nor so did *Biblis* spend her pining hart,
   But lou'd their natiue flesh against all kind,
   And to their purpose vsed wicked art:
   Yet playd *Pasiphaë* a more monstrous part,
   That lou'd a Bull, and learnd a beast to bee;
   Such shamefull lusts who loaths not, which depart
   From course of nature and of modestie?
Sweet loue such lewdnes bands from his faire companie.

But thine my Deare (welfare thy heart my deare)   xlii
   Though strange beginning had, yet fixed is
   On one, that worthy may perhaps appeare;
   And certes seemes bestowed not amis:
   Ioy thereof haue thou and eternall blis.
   With that vpleaning on her elbow weake,
   Her alablaster brest she soft did kis,
   Which all that while she felt to pant and quake,
As it an Earth-quake were; at last she thus bespake.

Beldame, your words doe worke me litle ease;   xliii
   For though my loue be not so lewdly bent,
   As those ye blame, yet may it nought appease
   My raging smart, ne ought my flame relent,
   But rather doth my helpelesse griefe augment.
   For they, how euer shamefull and vnkind,
   Yet did possesse their horrible intent:
   Short end of sorrowes they thereby did find;
So was their fortune good, though wicked were their mind.

xli 2 Not *1590* &c.: *corr. F. E.*   xlii 7 alablasted *1596*
xliii 3 nought] not *1609*
B b 2

But wicked fortune mine, though mind be good,
  Can haue no end, nor hope of my desire,
  But feed on shadowes, whiles I die for food,
  And like a shadow wexe, whiles with entire
  Affection, I doe languish and expire.
  I fonder, then *Cephisus* foolish child,
  Who hauing vewed in a fountaine shere
  His face, was with the loue thereof beguild;
I fonder loue a shade, the bodie farre exild.

Nought like (quoth she) for that same wretched boy
  Was of himselfe the idle Paramoure;
  Both loue and louer, without hope of ioy,
  For which he faded to a watry flowre.
  But better fortune thine, and better howre,
  Which lou'st the shadow of a warlike knight;
  No shadow, but a bodie hath in powre:
  That bodie, wheresoeuer that it light,
May learned be by cyphers, or by Magicke might.

But if thou may with reason yet represse
  The growing euill, ere it strength haue got,
  And thee abandond wholly doe possesse,
  Against it strongly striue, and yield thee not,
  Till thou in open field adowne be smot.
  But if the passion mayster thy fraile might,
  So that needs loue or death must be thy lot,
  Then I auow to thee, by wrong or right
To compasse thy desire, and find that loued knight.

Her chearefull words much cheard the feeble spright
  Of the sicke virgin, that her downe she layd
  In her warme bed to sleepe, if that she might;
  And the old-woman carefully displayd
  The clothes about her round with busie ayd;
  So that at last a little creeping sleepe
  Surprisd her sense: She therewith well apayd,
  The drunken lampe downe in the oyle did steepe,
And set her by to watch, and set her by to weepe.

xliv 1 mind] mine *1609*   xlvi 6 master *1609*

Earely the morrow next, before that day   xlviii
  His ioyous face did to the world reueale,
  They both vprose and tooke their readie way
  Vnto the Church, their prayers to appeale,
  With great deuotion, and with litle zeale:
  For the faire Damzell from the holy herse
  Her loue-sicke hart to other thoughts did steale;
  And that old Dame said many an idle verse,
Out of her daughters hart fond fancies to reuerse.

Returned home, the royall Infant fell   xlix
  Into her former fit; for why, no powre
  Nor guidance of her selfe in her did dwell.
  But th'aged Nurse her calling to her bowre,
  Had gathered Rew, and Sauine, and the flowre
  Of *Camphora*, and Calamint, and Dill,
  All which she in a earthen Pot did poure,
  And to the brim with Colt wood did it fill,
And many drops of milke and bloud through it did spill.

Then taking thrise three haires from off her head,   l
  Them trebly breaded in a threefold lace,
  And round about the pots mouth, bound the thread,
  And after hauing whispered a space
  Certaine sad words, with hollow voice and bace,
  She to the virgin said, thrise said she it;
  Come daughter come, come; spit vpon my face,
  Spit thrise vpon me, thrise vpon me spit;
Th'vneuen number for this businesse is most fit.

That sayd, her round about she from her turnd,   li
  She turned her contrarie to the Sunne,
  Thrise she her turnd contrary, and returnd,
  All contrary, for she the right did shunne,
  And euer what she did, was streight vndonne.
  So thought she to vndoe her daughters loue:
  But loue, that is in gentle brest begonne,
  No idle charmes so lightly may remoue,
That well can witnesse, who by triall it does proue.

xlix 6 *Camphara 1596, 1609*   7 a] an *1609*   l 2 Them] Then
1590: corr. F. E.   braided *1609*

Ne ought it mote the noble Mayd auayle,   iii
  Ne slake the furie of her cruell flame,
  But that she still did waste, and still did wayle,
  That through long languour, and hart-burning brame
  She shortly like a pyned ghost became,
  Which long hath waited by the Stygian strond.
  That when old *Glauce* saw, for feare least blame
  Of her miscarriage should in her be fond,
She wist not how t'amend, nor how it to withstond.

Cant. III.

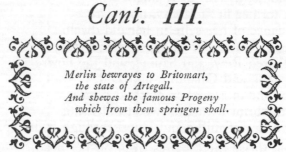

Merlin bewrayes to Britomart,
the state of Artegall.
And shewes the famous Progeny
which from them springen shall.

MOst sacred fire, that burnest mightily   i
  In liuing brests, ykindled first aboue,
  Emongst th'eternall spheres and lamping sky,
  And thence pourd into men, which men call Loue;
  Not that same, which doth base affections moue
  In brutish minds, and filthy lust inflame,
  But that sweet fit, that doth true beautie loue,
  And choseth vertue for his dearest Dame,
Whence spring all noble deeds and neuer dying fame:

Well did Antiquitie a God thee deeme,   ii
  That ouer mortall minds hast so great might,
  To order them, as best to thee doth seeme,
  And all their actions to direct aright;
  The fatall purpose of diuine foresight,
  Thou doest effect in destined descents,
  Through deepe impression of thy secret might,
  And stirredst vp th'Heroes high intents,
Which the late world admyres for wondrous moniments.

Arg. 2 *Arthegall 1590*   i 1 Most] Oh *1609*

But thy dread darts in none doe triumph more,   iii
  Ne brauer proofe in any, of thy powre
  Shew'dst thou, then in this royall Maid of yore,
  Making her seeke an vnknowne Paramoure,
  From the worlds end, through many a bitter stowre:
  From whose two loynes thou afterwards did rayse
  Most famous fruits of matrimoniall bowre,
  Which through the earth haue spred their liuing prayse,
That fame in trompe of gold eternally displayes.

Begin then, O my dearest sacred Dame,   iv
  Daughter of *Phœbus* and of *Memorie*,
  That doest ennoble with immortall name
  The warlike Worthies, from antiquitie,
  In thy great volume of Eternitie:
  Begin, O *Clio*, and recount from hence
  My glorious Soueraines goodly auncestrie,
  Till that by dew degrees and long protense,
Thou haue it lastly brought vnto her Excellence.

Full many wayes within her troubled mind,   v
  Old *Glauce* cast, to cure this Ladies griefe:
  Full many waies she sought, but none could find,
  Nor herbes, nor charmes, nor counsell, that is chiefe
  And choisest med'cine for sicke harts reliefe:
  For thy great care she tooke, and greater feare,
  Least that it should her turne to foule repriefe,
  And sore reproch, when so her father deare
Should of his dearest daughters hard misfortune heare.

At last she her auisd, that he, which made   vi
  That mirrhour, wherein the sicke Damosell
  So straungely vewed her straunge louers shade,
  To weet, the learned *Merlin*, well could tell,
  Vnder what coast of heauen the man did dwell,
  And by what meanes his loue might best be wrought:
  For though beyond the *Africk Ismaell*,
  Or th'Indian *Peru* he were, she thought
Him forth through infinite endeuour to haue sought.

    iv 3 Thou *1590*   7 auncestie *1596*   8 pretence *1596, 1609*

Forthwith themselues disguising both in straunge   vii
   And base attyre, that none might them bewray,
   To *Maridunum*, that is now by chaunge
   Of name *Cayr-Merdin* cald, they tooke their way:
   There the wise *Merlin* whylome wont (they say)
   To make his wonne, low vnderneath the ground,
   In a deepe delue, farre from the vew of day,
   That of no liuing wight he mote be found,
When so he counseld with his sprights encompast round.

And if thou euer happen that same way   viii
   To trauell, goe to see that dreadfull place:
   It is an hideous hollow caue (they say)
   Vnder a rocke that lyes a little space
   From the swift *Barry*, tombling downe apace,
   Emongst the woodie hilles of *Dyneuowre*:
   But dare thou not, I charge, in any cace,
   To enter into that same balefull Bowre,
For fear the cruell Feends should thee vnwares deuowre.

But standing high aloft, low lay thine eare,   ix
   And there such ghastly noise of yron chaines,
   And brasen Caudrons thou shalt rombling heare,
   Which thousand sprights with long enduring paines
   Doe tosse, that it will stonne thy feeble braines,
   And oftentimes great grones, and grieuous stounds,
   When too huge toile and labour them constraines:
   And oftentimes loud strokes, and ringing sounds
From vnder that deepe Rocke most horribly rebounds.

The cause some say is this: A litle while   x
   Before that *Merlin* dyde, he did intend,
   A brasen wall in compas to compile
   About *Cairmardin*, and did it commend
   Vnto these Sprights, to bring to perfect end.
   During which worke the Ladie of the Lake,
   Whom long he lou'd, for him in hast did send,
   Who thereby forst his workemen to forsake,
Them bound till his returne, their labour not to slake.

In the meane time through that false Ladies traine,   xi
  He was surprisd, and buried vnder beare,
  Ne euer to his worke returnd againe:
  Nath'lesse those feends may not their worke forbeare,
  So greatly his commaundement they feare,
  But there doe toyle and trauell day and night,
  Vntill that brasen wall they vp doe reare:
  For *Merlin* had in Magicke more insight,
Then euer him before or after liuing wight.

For he by words could call out of the sky   xii
  Both Sunne and Moone, and make them him obay:
  The land to sea, and sea to maineland dry,
  And darkesome night he eke could turne to day:
  Huge hostes of men he could alone dismay,
  And hostes of men of meanest things could frame,
  When so him list his enimies to fray:
  That to this day for terror of his fame,
The feends do quake, when any him to them does name.

And sooth, men say that he was not the sonne   xiii
  Of mortall Syre, or other liuing wight,
  But wondrously begotten, and begonne
  By false illusion of a guilefull Spright,
  On a faire Ladie Nonne, that whilome hight
  Matilda, daughter to *Pubidius*,
  Who was the Lord of *Mathrauall* by right,
  And coosen vnto king *Ambrosius*:
Whence he indued was with skill so maruellous.

They here ariuing, staid a while without,   xiv
  Ne durst aduenture rashly in to wend,
  But of their first intent gan make new dout
  For dread of daunger, which it might portend:
  Vntill the hardie Mayd (with loue to frend)
  First entering, the dreadfull Mage there found
  Deepe busied bout worke of wondrous end,
  And writing strange characters in the ground,
With which the stubborn feends he to his seruice bound.

He nought was moued at their entrance bold: xv
    For of their comming well he wist afore,
    Yet list them bid their businesse to vnfold,
    As if ought in this world in secret store
    Were from him hidden, or vnknowne of yore.
    Then *Glauce* thus, Let not it thee offend,
    That we thus rashly through thy darkesome dore,
    Vnwares haue prest: for either fatall end,
Or other mightie cause vs two did hither send.

He bad tell on; And then she thus began.   xvi
    Now haue three Moones with borrow'd brothers light,
    Thrice shined faire, and thrice seem'd dim and wan,
    Sith a sore euill, which this virgin bright
    Tormenteth, and doth plonge in dolefull plight,
    First rooting tooke; but what thing it mote bee,
    Or whence it sprong, I cannot read aright:
    But this I read, that but if remedee
Thou her afford, full shortly I her dead shall see.

Therewith th'Enchaunter softly gan to smyle   xvii
    At her smooth speeches, weeting inly well,
    That she to him dissembled womanish guyle,
    And to her said, Beldame, by that ye tell,
    More need of leach-craft hath your Damozell,
    Then of my skill: who helpe may haue elsewhere,
    In vaine seekes wonders out of Magicke spell.
    Th'old woman wox half blanck, those words to heare;
And yet was loth to let her purpose plaine appeare.

And to him said, If any leaches skill,   xviii
    Or other learned meanes could haue redrest
    This my deare daughters deepe engraffed ill,
    Certes I should be loth thee to molest:
    But this sad euill, which doth her infest,
    Doth course of naturall cause farre exceed,
    And housed is within her hollow brest,
    That either seemes some cursed witches deed,
Or euill spright, that in her doth such torment breed.

    xv 3 to *om. 1609*   6 let *1590, 1596*   xvi 8 remedee, *1590 &c.*

The wisard could no lenger beare her bord,   xix
   But brusting forth in laughter, to her sayd;
   Glauce, what needs this colourable word,
   To cloke the cause, that hath it selfe bewrayd?
   Ne ye faire *Britomartis*, thus arayd,
   More hidden are, then Sunne in cloudy vele;
   Whom thy good fortune, hauing fate obayd,
   Hath hither brought, for succour to appele:
The which the powres to thee are pleased to reuele.

The doubtfull Mayd, seeing her selfe descryde,   xx
   Was all abasht, and her pure yuory
   Into a cleare Carnation suddeine dyde;
   As faire *Aurora* rising hastily,
   Doth by her blushing tell, that she did lye
   All night in old *Tithonus* frosen bed,
   Whereof she seemes ashamed inwardly.
   But her old Nourse was nought dishartened,
But vauntage made of that, which *Merlin* had ared.

And sayd, Sith then thou knowest all our griefe,   xxi
   (For what doest not thou know?) of grace I pray,
   Pitty our plaint, and yield vs meet reliefe.
   With that the Prophet still awhile did stay,
   And then his spirite thus gan forth display;
   Most noble Virgin, that by fatall lore
   Hast learn'd to loue, let no whit thee dismay
   The hard begin, that meets thee in the dore,
And with sharpe fits thy tender hart oppresseth sore.

For so must all things excellent begin,   xxii
   And eke enrooted deepe must be that Tree,
   Whose big embodied braunches shall not lin,
   Till they to heauens hight forth stretched bee.
   For from thy wombe a famous Progenie
   Shall spring, out of the auncient *Troian* blood,
   Which shall reuiue the sleeping memorie
   Of those same antique Peres, the heauens brood,
Which *Greeke* and *Asian* riuers stained with their blood.

     xix 1 longer *1609*   xxii 9 *Greece 1596, 1609*

Renowmed kings, and sacred Emperours,   xxiii
   Thy fruitfull Ofspring, shall from thee descend;
   Braue Captaines, and most mighty warriours,
   That shall their conquests through all lands extend,
   And their decayed kingdomes shall amend:
   The feeble Britons, broken with long warre,
   They shall vpreare, and mightily defend
   Against their forrein foe, that comes from farre,
Till vniuersall peace compound all ciuill iarre.

It was not, *Britomart,* thy wandring eye,   xxiv
   Glauncing vnwares in charmed looking glas,
   But the streight course of heauenly destiny,
   Led with eternall prouidence, that has
   Guided thy glaunce, to bring his will to pas:
   Ne is thy fate, ne is thy fortune ill,
   To loue the prowest knight, that euer was.
   Therefore submit thy wayes vnto his will,
And do by all dew meanes thy destiny fulfill.

But read (said *Glauce*) thou Magitian   xxv
   What meanes shall she out seeke, or what wayes take?
   How shall she know, how shall she find the man?
   Or what needs her to toyle, sith fates can make
   Way for themselues, their purpose to partake?
   Then *Merlin* thus; Indeed the fates are firme,
   And may not shrinck, though all the world do shake:
   Yet ought mens good endeuours them confirme,
And guide the heauenly causes to their constant terme.

The man whom heauens haue ordaynd to bee   xxvi
   The spouse of *Britomart,* is *Arthegall*:
   He wonneth in the land of *Fayeree,*
   Yet is no *Fary* borne, ne sib at all
   To Elfes, but sprong of seed terrestriall,
   And whilome by false *Faries* stolne away,
   Whiles yet in infant cradle he did crall;
   Ne other to himselfe is knowne this day,
But that he by an Elfe was gotten of a *Fay.*

xxv 5 partake *1590*

But sooth he is the sonne of *Gorlois*,   xxvii
   And brother vnto *Cador* Cornish king,
   And for his warlike feates renowmed is,
   From where the day out of the sea doth spring,
   Vntill the closure of the Euening.
   From thence, him firmely bound with faithfull band,
   To this his natiue soyle thou backe shalt bring,
   Strongly to aide his countrey, to withstand
The powre of forrein Paynims, which inuade thy land.

Great aid thereto his mighty puissaunce,   xxviii
   And dreaded name shall giue in that sad day:
   Where also proofe of thy prow valiaunce
   Thou then shalt make, t'increase thy louers pray.
   Long time ye both in armes shall beare great sway,
   Till thy wombes burden thee from them do call,
   And his last fate him from thee take away,
   Too rathe cut off by practise criminall
Of secret foes, that him shall make in mischiefe fall.

With thee yet shall he leaue for memory   xxix
   Of his late puissaunce, his Image dead,
   That liuing him in all actiuity
   To thee shall represent.   He from the head
   Of his coosin *Constantius* without dread
   Shall take the crowne, that was his fathers right,
   And therewith crowne himselfe in th'others stead:
   Then shall he issew forth with dreadfull might,
Against his Saxon foes in bloudy field to fight.

Like as a Lyon, that in drowsie caue   xxx
   Hath long time slept, himselfe so shall he shake,
   And comming forth, shall spred his banner braue
   Ouer the troubled South, that it shall make
   The warlike *Mertians* for feare to quake:
   Thrise shall he fight with them, and twise shall win,
   But the third time shall faire accordaunce make:
   And if he then with victorie can lin,
He shall his dayes with peace bring to his earthly In.

xxix 1 With] Where *1596, 1609*

His sonne, hight *Vortipore*, shall him succeede xxxi
   In kingdome, but not in felicity;
   Yet shall he long time warre with happy speed,
   And with great honour many battels try:
   But at the last to th'importunity
   Of froward fortune shall be forst to yield.
   But his sonne *Malgo* shall full mightily
   Auenge his fathers losse, with speare and shield,
And his proud foes discomfit in victorious field.

Behold the man, and tell me *Britomart*, xxxii
   If ay more goodly creature thou didst see;
   How like a Gyaunt in each manly part
   Beares he himselfe with portly maiestee,
   That one of th'old *Heroes* seemes to bee:
   He the six Islands, comprouinciall
   In auncient times vnto great Britainee,
   Shall to the same reduce, and to him call
Their sundry kings to do their homage seuerall.

All which his sonne *Careticus* awhile xxxiii
   Shall well defend, and *Saxons* powre suppresse,
   Vntill a straunger king from vnknowne soyle
   Arriuing, him with multitude oppresse;
   Great *Gormond*, hauing with huge mightinesse
   Ireland subdewd, and therein fixt his throne,
   Like a swift Otter, fell through emptinesse,
   Shall ouerswim the sea with many one
Of his Norueyses, to assist the Britons fone.

He in his furie all shall ouerrunne, xxxiv
   And holy Church with faithlesse hands deface,
   That thy sad people vtterly fordonne,
   Shall to the vtmost mountaines fly apace:
   Was neuer so great wast in any place,
   Nor so fowle outrage doen by liuing men:
   For all thy Cities they shall sacke and race,
   And the greene grasse, that groweth, they shall bren,
That euen the wild beast shall dy in starued den.

xxxiv 6 autrage *1596*

Whiles thus thy Britons do in languour pine,   xxxv
    Proud *Etheldred* shall from the North arise,
    Seruing th'ambitious will of *Augustine*,
    And passing *Dee* with hardy enterprise,
    Shall backe repulse the valiaunt *Brockwell* twise,
    And *Bangor* with massacred Martyrs fill;
    But the third time shall rew his foolhardise:
    For *Cadwan* pittying his peoples ill,
Shall stoutly him defeat, and thousand *Saxons* kill.

But after him, *Cadwallin* mightily   xxxvi
    On his sonne *Edwin* all those wrongs shall wreake;
    Ne shall auaile the wicked sorcery
    Of false *Pellite*, his purposes to breake,
    But him shall slay, and on a gallowes bleake
    Shall giue th'enchaunter his vnhappy hire;
    Then shall the Britons, late dismayd and weake,
    From their long vassalage gin to respire,
And on their Paynim foes auenge their ranckled ire.

Ne shall he yet his wrath so mitigate,   xxxvii
    Till both the sonnes of *Edwin* he haue slaine,
    Offricke and *Osricke*, twinnes vnfortunate,
    Both slaine in battell vpon Layburne plaine,
    Together with the king of *Louthiane*,
    Hight *Adin*, and the king of *Orkeny*,
    Both ioynt partakers of their fatall paine:
    But *Penda*, fearefull of like desteny,
Shall yield him selfe his liegeman, and sweare fealty.

Him shall he make his fatall Instrument,   xxxviii
    T'afflict the other *Saxons* vnsubdewd;
    He marching forth with fury insolent
    Against the good king *Oswald*, who indewd
    With heauenly powre, and by Angels reskewd,
    All holding crosses in their hands on hye,
    Shall him defeate withouten bloud imbrewd:
    Of which, that field for endlesse memory,
Shall *Heuenfield* be cald to all posterity.

    xxxv 1 thy] the *1596, 1609*   xxxvi 6 hire *1596*
       xxxvii 7 their] the *1596, 1609*

Where at *Cadwallin* wroth, shall forth issew,   xxxix
  And an huge hoste into Northumber lead,
  With which he godly *Oswald* shall subdew,
  And crowne with martyrdome his sacred head.
  Whose brother *Oswin*, daunted with like dread,
  With price of siluer shall his kingdome buy,
  And *Penda*, seeking him adowne to tread,
  Shall tread adowne, and do him fowly dye,
But shall with gifts his Lord *Cadwallin* pacify.

Then shall *Cadwallin* dye, and then the raine   xl
  Of *Britons* eke with him attonce shall dye;
  Ne shall the good *Cadwallader* with paine,
  Or powre, be hable it to remedy,
  When the full time prefixt by destiny,
  Shalbe expird of *Britons* regiment.
  For heauen it selfe shall their successe enuy,
  And them with plagues and murrins pestilent
Consume, till all their warlike puissaunce be spent.

Yet after all these sorrowes, and huge hills   xli
  Of dying people, during eight yeares space,
  Cadwallader not yielding to his ills,
  From *Armoricke*, where long in wretched cace
  He liu'd, returning to his natiue place,
  Shalbe by vision staid from his intent:
  For th'heauens haue decreed, to displace
  The *Britons*, for their sinnes dew punishment,
And to the *Saxons* ouer-giue their gouernment.

Then woe, and woe, and euerlasting woe,   xlii
  Be to the Briton babe, that shalbe borne,
  To liue in thraldome of his fathers foe;
  Late King, now captiue, late Lord, now forlorne,
  The worlds reproch, the cruell victors scorne,
  Banisht from Princely bowre to wastfull wood:
  O who shall helpe me to lament, and mourne
  The royall seed, the antique *Troian* blood,
Whose Empire lenger here, then euer any stood.

The Damzell was full deepe empassioned,   xliii
   Both for his griefe, and for her peoples sake,
   Whose future woes so plaine he fashioned,
   And sighing sore, at length him thus bespake ;
   Ah but will heauens fury neuer slake,
   Nor vengeaunce huge relent it selfe at last ?
   Will not long misery late mercy make,
   But shall their name for euer be defast,
And quite from of the earth their memory be rast ?

Nay but the terme (said he) is limited,   xliv
   That in this thraldome *Britons* shall abide,
   And the iust reuolution measured,
   That they as Straungers shalbe notifide.
   For twise foure hundreth yeares shalbe supplide,
   Ere they to former rule restor'd shalbee,
   And their importune fates all satisfide :
   Yet during this their most obscuritee,   (see.
Their beames shall oft breake forth, that men them faire may

For *Rhodoricke*, whose surname shalbe Great,   xlv
   Shall of him selfe a braue ensample shew,
   That Saxon kings his friendship shall intreat ;
   And *Howell Dha* shall goodly well indew
   The saluage minds with skill of iust and trew ;
   Then *Griffyth Conan* also shall vp reare
   His dreaded head, and the old sparkes renew
   Of natiue courage, that his foen shall feare,
Least backe againe the kingdome he from them should beare.

Ne shall the Saxons selues all peaceably   xlvi
   Enioy the crowne, which they from Britons wonne
   First ill, and after ruled wickedly :
   For ere two hundred yeares be full outronne,
   There shall a Rauen far from rising Sunne,
   With his wide wings vpon them fiercely fly,
   And bid his faithlesse chickens ouerronne
   The fruitfull plaines, and with fell cruelty,
In their auenge, tread downe the victours surquedry.

    xliii 9 from th'earth *1590 &c.* : *corr. F. E.*   xliv 5 yeares *om. 1596,*
1609 : shall be full supplide *1609*   6 to] vnto their *1590*   xlv 7 th'olde
1609   xlvi 4 outronne] ouerronne *1596*

Yet shall a third both these, and thine subdew; xlvii
  There shall a Lyon from the sea-bord wood
  Of *Neustria* come roring, with a crew
  Of hungry whelpes, his battailous bold brood,
  Whose clawes were newly dipt in cruddy blood,
  That from the Daniske Tyrants head shall rend
  Th'vsurped crowne, as if that he were wood,
  And the spoile of the countrey conquered
Emongst his young ones shall diuide with bountyhed.

Tho when the terme is full accomplishid, xlviii
  There shall a sparke of fire, which hath long-while
  Bene in his ashes raked vp, and hid,
  Be freshly kindled in the fruitfull Ile
  Of *Mona*, where it lurked in exile;
  Which shall breake forth into bright burning flame,
  And reach into the house, that beares the stile
  Of royall maiesty and soueraigne name;
So shall the Briton bloud their crowne againe reclame.

Thenceforth eternall vnion shall be made xlix
  Betweene the nations different afore,
  And sacred Peace shall louingly perswade
  The warlike minds, to learne her goodly lore,
  And ciuile armes to exercise no more:
  Then shall a royall virgin raine, which shall
  Stretch her white rod ouer the *Belgicke* shore,
  And the great Castle smite so sore with all,
That it shall make him shake, and shortly learne to fall.

But yet the end is not. There *Merlin* stayd, l
  As ouercomen of the spirites powre,
  Or other ghastly spectacle dismayd,
  That secretly he saw, yet note discoure:
  Which suddein fit, and halfe extatick stoure
  When the two fearefull women saw, they grew
  Greatly confused in behauioure;
  At last the fury past, to former hew
Hee turnd againe, and chearefull looks ⟨as earst⟩ did shew.

  l 9 Shee *1590 &c.*: *corr. F. E.* ⟨as earst⟩ *om. 1590, 1596*: *add. 1609*

Then, when them selues they well instructed had   li
  Of all, that needed them to be inquird,
  They both conceiuing hope of comfort glad,
  With lighter hearts vnto their home retird;
  Where they in secret counsell close conspird,
  How to effect so hard an enterprize,
  And to possesse the purpose they desird:
  Now this, now that twixt them they did deuise,
And diuerse plots did frame, to maske in strange disguise.

At last the Nourse in her foolhardy wit   lii
  Conceiu'd a bold deuise, and thus bespake;
  Daughter, I deeme that counsell aye most fit,
  That of the time doth dew aduauntage take;
  Ye see that good king *Vther* now doth make
  Strong warre vpon the Paynim brethren, hight
  Octa and *Oza*, whom he lately brake
  Beside *Cayr Verolame*, in victorious fight,
That now all *Britanie* doth burne in armes bright.

That therefore nought our passage may empeach,   liii
  Let vs in feigned armes our selues disguize,
  And our weake hands (whom need new strength shall teach)
  The dreadfull speare and shield to exercize:
  Ne certes daughter that same warlike wize
  I weene, would you misseeme; for ye bene tall,
  And large of limbe, t'atchieue an hard emprize,
  Ne ought ye want, but skill, which practize small
Will bring, and shortly make you a mayd Martiall.

And sooth, it ought your courage much inflame,   liv
  To heare so often, in that royall hous,
  From whence to none inferiour ye came,
  Bards tell of many women valorous
  Which haue full many feats aduenturous
  Performd, in paragone of proudest men:
  The bold *Bunduca*, whose victorious
  Exploits made *Rome* to quake, stout *Guendolen*,
Renowmed *Martia*, and redoubted *Emmilen*.

  li 9 disguise] deuise *1596, 1609*   liii 3 (need makes good schollers)
teach *1590*   liv 3 came: *1590 &c.*

And that, which more then all the rest may sway,　　lv
　　Late dayes ensample, which these eyes beheld,
　　In the last field before *Meneuia*
　　Which *Vther* with those forrein Pagans held,
　　I saw a *Saxon* Virgin, the which feld
　　Great *Vlfin* thrise vpon the bloudy plaine,
　　And had not *Carados* her hand withheld
　　From rash reuenge, she had him surely slaine,
Yet *Carados* himselfe from her escapt with paine.

Ah read, (quoth *Britomart*) how is she hight?　　lvi
　　Faire *Angela* (quoth she) men do her call,
　　No whit lesse faire, then terrible in fight:
　　She hath the leading of a Martiall
　　And mighty people, dreaded more then all
　　The other *Saxons*, which do for her sake
　　And loue, themselues of her name *Angles* call.
　　Therefore faire Infant her ensample make
Vnto thy selfe, and equall courage to thee take.

Her harty words so deepe into the mynd　　lvii
　　Of the young Damzell sunke, that great desire
　　Of warlike armes in her forthwith they tynd,
　　And generous stout courage did inspire,
　　That she resolu'd, vnweeting to her Sire,
　　Aduent'rous knighthood on her selfe to don,
　　And counseld with her Nourse, her Maides attire
　　To turne into a massy habergeon,
And bad her all things put in readinesse anon.

Th'old woman nought, that needed, did omit;　　lviii
　　But all things did conueniently puruay:
　　It fortuned (so time their turne did fit)
　　A band of Britons ryding on forray
　　Few dayes before, had gotten a great pray
　　Of Saxon goods, emongst the which was seene
　　A goodly Armour, and full rich aray,
　　Which long'd to *Angela*, the Saxon Queene,
All fretted round with gold, and goodly well beseene.

　　lvii 5 vnmeeting *1596*　　lviii 2 conuiently *1596*　　5 dryes *1596*

The same, with all the other ornaments,　　lix
　　King *Ryence* caused to be hanged hy
　　In his chiefe Church, for endlesse moniments
　　Of his successe and gladfull victory:
　　Of which her selfe auising readily,
　　In th'euening late old *Glauce* thither led
　　Faire *Britomart*, and that same Armory
　　Downe taking, her therein appareled,
Well as she might, and with braue bauldrick garnished.

Beside those armes there stood a mighty speare,　　lx
　　Which *Bladud* made by Magick art of yore,
　　And vsd the same in battell ayo to beare;
　　Sith which it had bin here preseru'd in store,
　　For his great vertues proued long afore:
　　For neuer wight so fast in sell could sit,
　　But him perforce vnto the ground it bore:
　　Both speare she tooke, and shield, which hong by it:
Both speare and shield of great powre, for her purpose fit.

Thus when she had the virgin all arayd,　　lxi
　　Another harnesse, which did hang thereby,
　　About her selfe she dight, that the young Mayd
　　She might in equall armes accompany,
　　And as her Squire attend her carefully:
　　Tho to their ready Steedo they clombe full light,
　　And through back wayes, that none might them espy,
　　Couered with secret cloud of silent night,
Themselues they forth conuayd, and passed forward right.

Ne rested they, till that to Faery lond　　lxii
　　They came, as *Merlin* them directed late:
　　Where meeting with this *Redcrosse* knight, she fond
　　Of diuerse things discourses to dilate,
　　But most of *Arthegall*, and his estate.
　　At last their wayes so fell, that they mote part:
　　Then each to other well affectionate,
　　Friendship professed with vnfained hart,
The *Redcrosse* knight diuerst, but forth rode *Britomart*.

lxii 6 part *1596*

Cant. IIII.

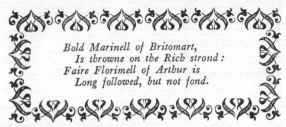

Bold Marinell of Britomart,
Is throwne on the Rich strond:
Faire Florimell of Arthur is
Long followed, but not fond.

Where is the Antique glory now become,   i
　　That whilome wont in women to appeare?
Where be the braue atchieuements doen by some?
Where be the battels, where the shield and speare,
And all the conquests, which them high did reare,
That matter made for famous Poets verse,
And boastfull men so oft abasht to heare?
Bene they all dead, and laid in dolefull herse?
Or doen they onely sleepe, and shall againe reuerse?

If they be dead, then woe is me therefore: ii
　　But if they sleepe, O let them soone awake:
For all too long I burne with enuy sore,
To heare the warlike feates, which *Homere* spake
Of bold *Penthesilee*, which made a lake
Of *Greekish* bloud so oft in *Troian* plaine;
But when I read, how stout *Debora* strake
Proud *Sisera*, and how *Camill'* hath slaine
The huge *Orsilochus*, I swell with great disdaine.

Yet these, and all that else had puissaunce,   iii
　　Cannot with noble *Britomart* compare,
Aswell for glory of great valiaunce,
As for pure chastitie and vertue rare,
That all her goodly deeds do well declare.
Well worthy stock, from which the branches sprong,
That in late yeares so faire a blossome bare,
As thee, O Queene, the matter of my song,
Whose lignage from this Lady I deriue along.

ii 5 *Panthesilee 1596, 1609*

Who when through speaches with the *Redcrosse* knight,   iv
  She learned had th'estate of *Arthegall*,
  And in each point her selfe informd aright,
  A friendly league of loue perpetuall
  She with him bound, and *Congé* tooke withall.
  Then he forth on his iourney did proceede,
  To seeke aduentures, which mote him befall,
  And win him worship through his warlike deed,
Which alwayes of his paines he made the chiefest meed.

But *Britomart* kept on her former course,   v
  Nc euer dofte her armes, but all the way
  Grew pensiue through that amorous discourse,
  By which the *Redcrosse* knight did earst display
  Her louers shape, and cheualrous aray;
  A thousand thoughts she fashioned in her mind,
  And in her feigning fancie did pourtray
  Him such, as fittest she for loue could find,
Wise, warlike, personable, curteous, and kind.

With such selfe-pleasing thoughts her wound she fed,   vi
  And thought so to beguile her grieuous smart;
  But so her smart was much more grieuous bred,
  And the deepe wound more deepe engord her hart,
  That nought but death her dolour mote depart.
  So forth she rode without repose or rest,
  Searching all lands and each remotest part,
  Following the guidaunce of her blinded guest,
Till that to the sea-coast at length she her addrest.

There she alighted from her light-foot beast,   vii
  And sitting downe vpon the rocky shore,
  Bad her old Squire vnlace her lofty creast;
  Tho hauing vewd a while the surges hore,
  That gainst the craggy clifts did loudly rore,
  And in their raging surquedry disdaynd,
  That the fast earth affronted them so sore,
  And their deuouring couetize restraynd,
Thereat she sighed deepe, and after thus complaynd.

    v 8 she] he *1590*   vi 9 her] had *1609*   vii 8 deuoring *1596*

Huge sea of sorrow, and tempestuous griefe,
    Wherein my feeble barke is tossed long,
    Far from the hoped hauen of reliefe,
    Why do thy cruell billowes beat so strong,
    And thy moyst mountaines each on others throng,
    Threatning to swallow vp my fearefull life?
    O do thy cruell wrath and spightfull wrong
    At length allay, and stint thy stormy strife,
Which in these troubled bowels raignes, and rageth rife.

For else my feeble vessell crazd, and crackt   ix
    Through thy strong buffets and outrageous blowes,
    Cannot endure, but needs it must be wrackt
    On the rough rocks, or on the sandy shallowes,
    The whiles that loue it steres, and fortune rowes;
    Loue my lewd Pilot hath a restlesse mind
    And fortune Boteswaine no assuraunce knowes,
    But saile withouten starres gainst tide and wind:
How can they other do, sith both are bold and blind?

Thou God of winds, that raignest in the seas,   x
    That raignest also in the Continent,
    At last blow vp some gentle gale of ease,
    The which may bring my ship, ere it be rent,
    Vnto the gladsome port of her intent:
    Then when I shall my selfe in safety see,
    A table for eternall moniment
    Of thy great grace, and my great ieopardee,
Great *Neptune,* I auow to hallow vnto thee.

Then sighing softly sore, and inly deepe,   xi
    She shut vp all her plaint in priuy griefe;
    For her great courage would not let her weepe,
    Till that old *Glauce* gan with sharpe repriefe,
    Her to restraine, and giue her good reliefe,
    Through hope of those, which *Merlin* had her told
    Should of her name and nation be chiefe,
    And fetch their being from the sacred mould
Of her immortall wombe, to be in heauen enrold.

viii 4 Why] Who *1609*   9 these] thy *1590*

Thus as she her recomforted, she spyde,   _{xii}
  Where farre away one all in armour bright,
  With hastie gallop towards her did ryde;
  Her dolour soone she ceast, and on her dight
  Her Helmet, to her Courser mounting light:
  Her former sorrow into suddein wrath,
  Both coosen passions of distroubled spright,
  Conuerting, forth she beates the dustie path ;
Loue and despight attonce her courage kindled hath.

As when a foggy mist hath ouercast   _{xiii}
  The face of heauen, and the cleare aire engrost,
  The world in darkenesse dwels, till that at last
  The watry Southwinde from the seabord cost
  Vpblowing, doth disperse the vapour lo'st,
  And poures it selfe forth in a stormy showre;
  So the faire *Britomart* hauing disclo'st
  Her clowdy care into a wrathfull stowre,
The mist of griefe dissolu'd, did into vengeance powre.

Eftsoones her goodly shield addressing faire,   _{xiv}
  That mortall speare she in her hand did take,
  And vnto battell did her selfe prepaire.
  The knight approching, sternely her bespake;
  Sir knight, that doest thy voyage rashly make
  By this forbidden way in my despight,
  Ne doest by others death ensample take,
  I read thee soone retyre, whiles thou hast might,
Least afterwards it be too late to take thy flight.

Ythrild with deepe disdaine of his proud threat,   _{xv}
  She shortly thus; Fly they, that need to fly;
  Words fearen babes. 1 meane not thee entreat
  To passe; but maugre thee will passe or dy.
  Ne lenger stayd for th'other to reply,
  But with sharpe speare the rest made dearly knowne.
  Strongly the straunge knight ran, and sturdily
  Strooke her full on the brest, that made her downe
Decline her head, and touch her crouper with her crowne.

    xiii 9 did *om. 1596*   powre, *1596*   xv 6 speares *1590, 1596*

But she againe him in the shield did smite   xvi
   With so fierce furie and great puissaunce,
   That through his threesquare scuchin percing quite,
   And through his mayled hauberque, by mischaunce
   The wicked steele through his left side did glaunce;
   Him so transfixed she before her bore
   Beyond his croupe, the length of all her launce,
   Till sadly soucing on the sandie shore,
He tombled on an heape, and wallowd in his gore.

Like as the sacred Oxe, that carelesse stands,   xvii
   With gilden hornes, and flowry girlonds crownd,
   Proud of his dying honor and deare bands,
   Whiles th'altars fume with frankincense arownd,
   All suddenly with mortall stroke astownd,
   Doth groueling fall, and with his streaming gore
   Distaines the pillours, and the holy grownd,
   And the faire flowres, that decked him afore;
So fell proud *Marinell* vpon the pretious shore.

The martiall Mayd stayd not him to lament,   xviii
   But forward rode, and kept her readie way
   Along the strond, which as she ouer-went,
   She saw bestrowed all with rich aray
   Of pearles and pretious stones of great assay,
   And all the grauell mixt with golden owre;
   Whereat she wondred much, but would not stay
   For gold, or perles, or pretious stones an howre,
But them despised all; for all was in her powre.

Whiles thus he lay in deadly stonishment,   xix
   Tydings hereof came to his mothers eare;
   His mother was the blacke-browd *Cymoent*,
   The daughter of great *Nereus*, which did beare
   This warlike sonne vnto an earthly peare,
   The famous *Dumarin*; who on a day
   Finding the Nymph a sleepe in secret wheare,
   As he by chaunce did wander that same way,
Was taken with her loue, and by her closely lay.

There he this knight of her begot, whom borne   xx
    She of his father *Marinell* did name,
    And in a rocky caue as wight forlorne,
    Long time she fostred vp, till he became
    A mightie man at armes, and mickle fame
    Did get through great aduentures by him donne:
    For neuer man he suffred by that same
    Rich strond to trauell, whereas he did wonne,
But that he must do battell with the Sea-nymphes sonne.

An hundred knights of honorable name   xxi
    He had subdew'd, and them his vassals made,
    That through all Farie lond his noble fame
    Now blazed was, and feare did all inuade,
    That none durst passen through that perilous glade.
    And to aduance his name and glorie more,
    Her Sea-god syre she dearely did perswade,
    T"endow her sonne with threasure and rich store,
Boue all the sonnes, that were of earthly wombes ybore.

The God did graunt his daughters deare demaund,   xxii
    To doen his Nephew in all riches flow;
    Eftsoones his heaped waues he did commaund,
    Out of their hollow bosome forth to throw
    All the huge threasure, which the sea below
    Had in his greedie gulfe deuoured deepe,
    And him enriched through the ouerthrow
    And wreckes of many wretches, which did weepe,
And often waile their wealth, which he from them did keepe.

Shortly vpon that shore there heaped was,   xxiii
    Exceeding riches and all pretious things,
    The spoyle of all the world, that it did pas
    The wealth of th'East, and pompe of *Persian* kings;
    Gold, amber, yuorie, perles, owches, rings,
    And all that else was pretious and deare,
    The sea vnto him voluntary brings,
    That shortly he a great Lord did appeare,
As was in all the lond of Faery, or elsewheare.

Thereto he was a doughtie dreaded knight,   xxiv
   Tryde often to the scath of many deare,
   That none in equall armes him matchen might,
   The which his mother seeing, gan to feare
   Least his too haughtie hardines might reare
   Some hard mishap, in hazard of his life:
   For thy she oft him counseld to forbeare
   The bloudie battell, and to stirre vp strife,
But after all his warre, to rest his wearie knife.

And for his more assurance, she inquir'd   xxv
   One day of *Proteus* by his mightie spell,
   (For *Proteus* was with prophecie inspir'd)
   Her deare sonnes destinie to her to tell,
   And the sad end of her sweet *Marinell.*
   Who through foresight of his eternall skill,
   Bad her from womankind to keepe him well:
   For of a woman he should haue much ill,
A virgin strange and stout him should dismay, or kill.

For thy she gaue him warning euery day,   xxvi
   The loue of women not to entertaine;
   A lesson too too hard for liuing clay,
   From loue in course of nature to refraine:
   Yet he his mothers lore did well retaine,
   And euer from faire Ladies loue did fly;
   Yet many Ladies faire did oft complaine,
   That they for loue of him would algates dy:
Dy, who so list for him, he was loues enimy.

But ah, who can deceiue his destiny,   xxvii
   Or weene by warning to auoyd his fate?
   That when he sleepes in most security,
   And safest seemes, him soonest doth amate,
   And findeth dew effect or soone or late.
   So feeble is the powre of fleshly arme.
   His mother bad him womens loue to hate,
   For she of womans force did feare no harme;
So weening to haue arm'd him, she did quite disarme.

xxiv 2 scathe *1609*   xxvii 6 fleshy *1590*

This was that woman, this that deadly wound,   xxviii
   That *Proteus* prophecide should him dismay,
   The which his mother vainely did expound,
   To be hart-wounding loue, which should assay
   To bring her sonne vnto his last decay.
   So tickle be the termes of mortall state,
   And full of subtile sophismes, which do play
   With double senses, and with false debate,
T'approue the vnknowen purpose of eternall fate.

Too true the famous *Marinell* it fownd,   xxix
   Who through late triall, on that wealthy Strond
   Inglorious now lies in senselesse swownd,
   Through heauy stroke of *Britomartis* hond.
   Which when his mother deare did vnderstond,
   And heauy tydings heard, whereas she playd
   Amongst her watry sisters by a pond,
   Gathering sweet daffadillyes, to haue made
Gay girlonds, from the Sun their forheads faire to shade;

Eftsoones both flowres and girlonds farre away   xxx
   She flong, and her faire deawy lockes yrent,
   To sorrow huge she turnd her former play,
   And gamesom merth to grieuous dreriment:
   She threw her selfe downe on the Continent,
   Ne word did speake, but lay as in a swowne,
   Whiles all her sisters did for her lament,
   With yelling outcries, and with shrieking sowne;
And euery one did teare her girlond from her crowne.

Soone as she vp out of her deadly fit   xxxi
   Arose, she bad her charet to be brought,
   And all her sisters, that with her did sit,
   Bad eke attonce their charets to be sought;
   Tho full of bitter griefe and pensiue thought,
   She to her wagon clombe; clombe all the rest,
   And forth together went, with sorrow fraught.
   The waues obedient to their beheast,
Them yielded readie passage, and their rage surceast.

  xxix 9 shade. *1590, 1596*   xxx 4 gameson *1590, 1596* : gamesome
1609   6 swownd *1590*   xxxi 5 pensife *1590*

Great *Neptune* stood amazed at their sight,   xxxii
　　Whiles on his broad round backe they softly slid
　　And eke himselfe mournd at their mournfull plight,
　　Yet wist not what their wailing ment, yet did
　　For great compassion of their sorrow, bid
　　His mightie waters to them buxome bee:
　　Eftsoones the roaring billowes still abid,
　　And all the griesly Monsters of the See
Stood gaping at their gate, and wondred them to see.

A teme of Dolphins raunged in aray,   xxxiii
　　Drew the smooth charet of sad *Cymoent* ;
　　They were all taught by *Triton*, to obay
　　To the long raynes, at her commaundement:
　　As swift as swallowes, on the waues they went,
　　That their broad flaggie finnes no fome did reare,
　　Ne bubbling roundell they behind them sent ;
　　The rest of other fishes drawen weare,
Which with their finny oars the swelling sea did sheare.

Soone as they bene arriu'd vpon the brim   xxxiv
　　Of the *Rich strond*, their charets they forlore,
　　And let their temed fishes softly swim
　　Along the margent of the fomy shore,
　　Least they their finnes should bruze, and surbate sore
　　Their tender feet vpon the stony ground:
　　And comming to the place, where all in gore
　　And cruddy bloud enwallowed they found
The lucklesse *Marinell*, lying in deadly swound;

His mother swowned thrise, and the third time   xxxv
　　Could scarce recouered be out of her paine ;
　　Had she not bene deuoyd of mortall slime,
　　She should not then haue bene reliu'd againe,
　　But soone as life recouered had the raine,
　　She made so piteous mone and deare wayment,
　　That the hard rocks could scarse from teares refraine,
　　And all her sister Nymphes with one consent
Supplide her sobbing breaches with sad complement.

xxxiii 4 raynes] traines *1596, 1609*

Deare image of my selfe (she said) that is,   <small>xxxvi</small>
   The wretched sonne of wretched mother borne,
   Is this thine high aduauncement, O is this
   Th'immortall name, with which thee yet vnborne
   Thy Gransire *Nereus* promist to adorne?
   Now lyest thou of life and honor reft;
   Now lyest thou a lumpe of earth forlorne,
   Ne of thy late life memory is left,
Ne can thy irreuocable destiny be weft?

Fond *Proteus*, father of false prophecis,   <small>xxxvii</small>
   And they more fond, that credit to thee giue,
   Not this the worke of womans hand ywis,
   That so deepe wound through these deare members driue.
   I feared loue: but they that loue do liue,
   But they that die, doe neither loue nor hate.
   Nath'lesse to thee thy folly I forgiue,
   And to my selfe, and to accursed fate
The guilt I doe ascribe: deare wisedome bought too late.

O what auailes it of immortall seed   <small>xxxviii</small>
   To beene ybred and neuer borne to die?
   Farre better I it deeme to die with speed,
   Then waste in woe and wailefull miserie.
   Who dyes the vtmost dolour doth abye,
   But who that liues, is left to waile his losse:
   So life is losse, and death felicitie.
   Sad life worse then glad death : and greater crosse
To see friends graue, then dead the graue selfe to engrosse.

But if the heauens did his dayes enuie,   <small>xxxix</small>
   And my short blisse maligne, yet mote they well
   Thus much afford me, ere that he did die
   That the dim eyes of my deare *Marinell*
   I mote haue closed, and him bed farewell,
   Sith other offices for mother meet
   They would not graunt.
    Yet maulgre them farewell, my sweetest sweet;
Farewell my sweetest sonne, sith we no more shall meet.

  xxxix 5 bid *1609*   9 sith we no more shall meet] till we againe may
meet *1590*

Thus when they all had sorrowed their fill,   xl
   They softly gan to search his griesly wound:
   And that they might him handle more at will,
   They him disarm'd, and spredding on the ground
   Their watchet mantles frindgd with siluer round,
   They softly wipt away the gelly blood
   From th'orifice; which hauing well vpbound,
   They pourd in soueraine balme, and Nectar good,
Good both for earthly med'cine, and for heauenly food.

Tho when the lilly handed *Liagore*,   xli
   (This *Liagore* whylome had learned skill
   In leaches craft, by great *Appolloes* lore,
   Sith her whylome vpon high *Pindus* hill,
   He loued, and at last her wombe did fill
   With heauenly seed, whereof wise *Pæon* sprong)
   Did feele his pulse, she knew their staied still
   Some litle life his feeble sprites emong;
Which to his mother told, despeire she from her flong.

Tho vp him taking in their tender hands,   xlii
   They easily vnto her charet beare:
   Her teme at her commaundement quiet stands,
   Whiles they the corse into her wagon reare,
   And strow with flowres the lamentable beare:
   Then all the rest into their coches clim,
   And through the brackish waues their passage sheare;
   Vpon great *Neptunes* necke they softly swim,
And to her watry chamber swiftly carry him.

Deepe in the bottome of the sea, her bowre   xliii
   Is built of hollow billowes heaped hye,
   Like to thicke cloudes, that threat a stormy showre,
   And vauted all within, like to the sky,
   In which the Gods do dwell eternally:
   There they him laid in easie couch well dight;
   And sent in haste for *Tryphon*, to apply
   Salues to his wounds, and medicines of might:
For *Tryphon* of sea gods the soueraine leach is hight.

xlii 1 vp him] him vp *1609*   xliii 4 vaulted *1609*

The whiles the *Nymphes* sit all about him round,   xliv
  Lamenting his mishap and heauy plight;
  And oft his mother vewing his wide wound,
  Cursed the hand, that did so deadly smight
  Her dearest sonne, her dearest harts delight.
  But none of all those curses ouertooke
  The warlike Maid, th'ensample of that might,
  But fairely well she thriu'd, and well did brooke
Her noble deeds, ne her right course for ought forsooke.

Yet did false *Archimage* her still pursew,   xlv
  To bring to passe his mischieuous intent,
  Now that he had her singled from the crew
  Of courteous knights, the Prince, and Faery gent,
  Whom late in chace of beautie excellent
  She left, pursewing that same foster strong;
  Of whose foule outrage they impatient,
  And full of fiery zeale, him followed long,
To reskew her from shame, and to reuenge her wrong.

Through thick and thin, through mountaines and through xlvi
  Those two great champions did attonce pursew   (plains,
  The fearefull damzell, with incessant paines :
  Who from them fled, as light-foot hare from vew
  Of hunter swift, and sent of houndes trew.
  At last they came vnto a double way,
  Where, doubtfull which to take, her to reskew,
  Themselues they did dispart, each to assay,
Whether more happie were, to win so goodly pray.

But *Timias*, the Princes gentle Squire,   xlvii
  That Ladies loue vnto his Lord forlent,
  And with proud enuy, and indignant ire,
  After that wicked foster fiercely went.
  So beene they three three sundry wayes ybent.
  But fairest fortune to the Prince befell,
  Whose chaunce it was, that soone he did repent,
  To take that way, in which that Damozell
Was fled afore, affraid of him, as feend of hell.

        xlvi 5 hunters *1609*   xlvii 7 repent *1609*

At last of her farre off he gained vew: xlviii
  Then gan he freshly pricke his fomy steed,
  And euer as he nigher to her drew,
  So euermore he did increase his speed,
  And of each turning still kept warie heed:
  Aloud to her he oftentimes did call,
  To doe away vaine doubt, and needlesse dreed:
  Full myld to her he spake, and oft let fall
Many meeke wordes, to stay and comfort her withall.

But nothing might relent her hastie flight;   xlix
  So deepe the deadly feare of that foule swaine
  Was earst impressed in her gentle spright:
  Like as a fearefull Doue, which through the raine,
  Of the wide aire her way does cut amaine,
  Hauing farre off espyde a Tassell gent,
  Which after her his nimble wings doth straine,
  Doubleth her haste for feare to be for-hent,
And with her pineons cleaues the liquid firmament.

With no lesse haste, and eke with no lesse dreed,   l
  That fearefull Ladie fled from him, that ment
  To her no euill thought, nor euill deed;
  Yet former feare of being fowly shent,
  Carried her forward with her first intent:
  And though oft looking backward, well she vewd,
  Her selfe freed from that foster insolent,
  And that it was a knight, which now her sewd,
Yet she no lesse the knight feard, then that villein rude.

His vncouth shield and straunge armes her dismayd,   li
  Whose like in Faery lond were seldome seene,
  That fast she from him fled, no lesse affrayd,
  Then of wilde beastes if she had chased beene:
  Yet he her followd still with courage keene,
  So long that now the golden *Hesperus*
  Was mounted high in top of heauen sheene,
  And warnd his other brethren ioyeous,
To light their blessed lamps in *Ioues* eternall hous.

xlix 8 fore-hent 1609   li 2 sildome 1609

All suddenly dim woxe the dampish ayre,   lii
    And griesly shadowes couered heauen bright,
    That now with thousand starres was decked fayre;
    Which when the Prince beheld, a lothfull sight,
    And that perforce, for want of lenger light,
    He mote surcease his suit, and lose the hope
    Of his long labour, he gan fowly wyte
    His wicked fortune, that had turnd aslope,
And cursed night, that reft from him so goodly scope.

Tho when her wayes he could no more descry,   liii
    But to and fro at disauenture strayd;
    Like as a ship, whose Lodestarre suddenly
    Couered with cloudes, her Pilot hath dismayd;
    His wearisome pursuit perforce he stayd,
    And from his loftie steed dismounting low,
    Did let him forage.   Downe himselfe he layd
    Vpon the grassie ground, to sleepe a throw;
The cold earth was his couch, the hard steele his pillow.

But gentle Sleepe enuyde him any rest;   liv
    In stead thereof sad sorrow, and disdaine
    Of his hard hap did vexe his noble brest,
    And thousand fancies bet his idle braine
    With their light wings, the sights of semblants vaine:
    Oft did he wish, that Lady faire mote bee
    His Faery Queene, for whom he did complaine:
    Or that his Faery Queene were such, as shee:
And euer hastie Night he blamed bitterlie.

Night thou foule Mother of annoyance sad,   lv
    Sister of heauie death, and nourse of woe,
    Which wast begot in heauen, but for thy bad
    And brutish shape thrust downe to hell below,
    Where by the grim floud of *Cocytus* slow
    Thy dwelling is, in *Herebus* blacke hous,
    (Blacke *Herebus* thy husband is the foe
    Of all the Gods) where thou vngratious,
Halfe of thy dayes doest lead in horrour hideous.

What had th'eternall Maker need of thee,   lvi
  The world in his continuall course to keepe,
  That doest all things deface, ne lettest see
  The beautie of his worke ?   Indeed in sleepe
  The slouthfull bodie, that doth loue to steepe
  His lustlesse limbes, and drowne his baser mind,
  Doth praise thee oft, and oft from *Stygian* deepe
  Calles thee, his goddesse in his error blind,
And great Dame Natures handmaide, chearing euery kind.

But well I wote, that to an heauy hart   lvii
  Thou art the root and nurse of bitter cares,
  Breeder of new, renewer of old smarts :
  In stead of rest thou lendest rayling teares,
  In stead of sleepe thou sendest troublous feares,
  And dreadfull visions, in the which aliue
  The drearie image of sad death appeares :
  So from the wearie spirit thou doest driue
Desired rest, and men of happinesse depriue.

Vnder thy mantle blacke there hidden lye,   lviii
  Light-shonning theft, and traiterous intent,
  Abhorred bloudshed, and vile felony,
  Shamefull deceipt, and daunger imminent ;
  Foule horror, and eke hellish dreriment :
  All these I wote in thy protection bee,
  And light doe shonne, for feare of being shent :
  For light ylike is loth'd of them and thee,
And all that lewdnesse loue, doe hate the light to see.

For day discouers all dishonest wayes,   lix
  And sheweth each thing, as it is indeed :
  The prayses of high God he faire displayes,
  And his large bountie rightly doth areed.
  Dayes dearest children be the blessed seed,
  Which darknesse shall subdew, and heauen win :
  Truth is his daughter ; he her first did breed,
  Most sacred virgin, without spot of sin.
Our life is day, but death with darknesse doth begin.

    lix 5 Dayes dearest children] The children of day *1590*

O when will day then turne to me againe,   lx
  And bring with him his long expected light?
  O *Titan*, haste to reare thy ioyous waine:
  Speed thee to spred abroad thy beames bright,
  And chase away this too long lingring night,
  Chase her away, from whence she came, to hell.
  She, she it is, that hath me done despight:
  There let her with the damned spirits dwell,
And yeeld her roome to day, that can it gouerne well.

Thus did the Prince that wearie night outweare,   lxi
  In restlesse anguish and vnquiet paine;
  And earely, ere the morrow did vpreare
  His deawy head out of the *Ocean* maine,
  He vp arose, as halfe in great disdaine,
  And clombe vnto his steed.   So forth he went,
  With heauie looke and lumpish pace, that plaine
  In him bewraid great grudge and maltalent:
His steed eke seem'd t'apply his steps to his intent.

Cant. V.

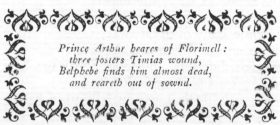

Prince *Arthur* heares of *Florimell*:
three fosters *Timias* wound,
Belphebe finds him almost dead,
and reareth out of sownd.

WOnder it is to see, in diuerse minds,   i
  How diuersly loue doth his pageants play,
And shewes his powre in variable kinds:
The baser wit, whose idle thoughts alway
Are wont to cleaue vnto the lowly clay,
It stirreth vp to sensuall desire,
And in lewd slouth to wast his carelesse day:
But in braue sprite it kindles goodly fire,
That to all high desert and honour doth aspire.

lx 4 bright? *1590, 1596*   Arg. 4 *swound 1609*

Ne suffereth it vncomely idlenesse,   ii
     In his free thought to build her sluggish nest:
     Ne suffereth it thought of vngentlenesse,
     Euer to creepe into his noble brest,
     But to the highest and the worthiest
     Lifteth it vp, that else would lowly fall:
     It lets not fall, it lets it not to rest:
     It lets not scarse this Prince to breath at all,
But to his first poursuit him forward still doth call.

Who long time wandred through the forrest wyde,   iii
     To finde some issue thence, till that at last
     He met a Dwarfe, that seemed terrifyde
     With some late perill, which he hardly past,
     Or other accident, which him aghast;
     Of whom he asked, whence he lately came,
     And whither now he trauelled so fast:
     For sore he swat, and running through that same
Thicke forest, was bescratcht, and both his feet nigh lame.

Panting for breath, and almost out of hart,   iv
     The Dwarfe him answerd, Sir, ill mote I stay
     To tell the same.   I lately did depart
     From Faery court, where I haue many a day
     Serued a gentle Lady of great sway,
     And high accompt through out all Elfin land,
     Who lately left the same, and tooke this way:
     Her now I seeke, and if ye vnderstand
Which way she fared hath, good Sir tell out of hand.

What mister wight (said he) and how arayd?   v
     Royally clad (quoth he) in cloth of gold,
     As meetest may beseeme a noble mayd;
     Her faire lockes in rich circlet be enrold,
     A fairer wight did neuer Sunne behold,
     And on a Palfrey rides more white then snow,
     Yet she her selfe is whiter manifold:
     The surest signe, whereby ye may her know,
Is, that she is the fairest wight aliue, I trow.

ii 8 breathe *1609*   iii 2 till at the last *1609*   iv 6 account *1609*
v 5 A] And *1596, 1609*

Now certes swaine (said he) such one I weene,   vi
  Fast flying through this forest from her fo,
  A foule ill fauoured foster, I haue seene;
  Her selfe, well as I might, I reskewd tho,
  But could not stay; so fast she did foregoe,
  Carried away with wings of speedy feare.
  Ah dearest God (quoth he) that is great woe,
  And wondrous ruth to all, that shall it heare.
But can ye read Sir, how I may her find, or where?

Perdy me leuer were to weeten that,   vii
  (Said he) then ransome of the richest knight,
  Or all the good that euer yet I gat:
  But froward fortune, and too forward Night
  Such happinesse did, maulgre, to me spight,
  And fro me reft both life and light attone.
  But Dwarfe aread, what is that Lady bright,
  That through this forest wandreth thus alone;
For of her errour straunge I haue great ruth and mone.

That Lady is (quoth he) where so she bee,   viii
  The bountiest virgin, and most debonaire,
  That euer liuing eye I weene did see;
  Liues none this day, that may with her compare
  In stedfast chastitie and vertue rare,
  The goodly ornaments of beautie bright;
  And is ycleped *Florimell* the faire,
  Faire *Florimell* belou'd of many a knight,
Yet she loues none but one, that *Marinell* is hight.

A Sea-nymphes sonne, that *Marinell* is hight,   ix
  Of my deare Dame is loued dearely well;
  In other none, but him, she sets delight,
  All her delight is set on *Marinell*;
  But he sets nought at all by *Florimell*:
  For Ladies loue his mother long ygoe
  Did him, they say, forwarne through sacred spell.
  But fame now flies, that of a forreine foe
He is yslaine, which is the ground of all our woe.

      vi 9 where. *1590, 1596*   viii 8 belou'd of a *1596*

Fiue dayes there be, since he (they say) was slaine,   x
    And foure, since *Florimell* the Court for-went,
    And vowed neuer to returne againe,
    Till him aliue or dead she did inuent.
    Therefore, faire·Sir, for loue of knighthood gent,
    And honour of trew Ladies, if ye may
    By your good counsell, or bold hardiment,
    Or succour her, or me direct the way;
Do one, or other good, I you most humbly pray.

So may ye gaine to you full great renowme,   xi
    Of all good Ladies through the world so wide,
    And haply in her hart find highest rowme,
    Of whom ye seeke to be most magnifide:
    At least eternall meede shall you abide.
    To whom the Prince; Dwarfe, comfort to thee take,
    For till thou tidings learne, what her betide,
    I here auow thee neuer to forsake.
Ill weares he armes, that nill them vse for Ladies sake.

So with the Dwarfe he backe return'd againe,   xii
    To seeke his Lady, where he mote her find;
    But by the way he greatly gan complaine
    The want of his good Squire late left behind,
    For whom he wondrous pensiue grew in mind,
    For doubt of daunger, which mote him betide;
    For him he loued aboue all mankind,
    Hauing him trew and faithfull euer tride,
And bold, as euer Squire that waited by knights side.

Who all this while full hardly was assayd   xiii
    Of deadly daunger, which to him betid;
    For whiles his Lord pursewd that noble Mayd,
    After that foster fowle he fiercely rid,
    To bene auenged of the shame, he did
    To that faire Damzell: Him he chaced long
    Through the thicke woods, wherein he would haue hid
    His shamefull head from his auengement strong,
And oft him threatned death for his outrageous wrong.

Nathlesse the villen sped him selfe so well,   xiv
   Whether through swiftnesse of his speedy beast,
   Or knowledge of those woods, where he did dwell,
   That shortly he from daunger was releast,
   And out of sight escaped at the least;
   Yet not escaped from the dew reward
   Of his bad deeds, which dayly he increast,
   Ne ceased not, till him oppressed hard
The heauy plague, that for such leachours is prepard.

For soone as he was vanisht out of sight,   xv
   His coward courage gan emboldned bee,
   And cast t'auenge him of that fowle despight,
   Which he had borne of his bold enimee.
   Tho to his brethren came: for they were three
   Vngratious children of one gracelesse sire,
   And vnto them complained, how that he
   Had vsed bene of that foolehardy Squire;
So them with bitter words he stird to bloudy ire.

Forthwith themselues with their sad instruments   xvi
   Of spoyle and murder they gan arme byliue,
   And with him forth into the forest went,
   To wreake the wrath, which he did earst reuiue
   In their sterne brests, on him which late did driue
   Their brother to reproch and shamefull flight:
   For they had vow'd, that neuer he aliue
   Out of that forest should escape their might;
Vile rancour their rude harts had fild with such despight.

Within that wood there was a couert glade,   xvii
   Foreby a narrow foord, to them well knowne,
   Through which it was vneath for wight to wade;
   And now by fortune it was ouerflowne:
   By that same way they knew that Squire vnknowne
   Mote algates passe; for thy themselues they set
   There in await, with thicke woods ouer growne,
   And all the while their malice they did whet
With cruell threats, his passage through the ford to let.

    xiv 2 beast; *1590, 1596*   xvii 3 wade] made *1590: corr. F. E.*

It fortuned, as they deuized had,   xviii
  The gentle Squire came ryding that same way,
  Vnweeting of their wile and treason bad,
  And through the ford to passen did assay;
  But that fierce foster, which late fled away,
  Stoutly forth stepping on the further shore,
  Him boldly bad his passage there to stay,
  Till he had made amends, and full restore
For all the damage, which he had him doen afore.

With that at him a quiu'ring dart he threw,   xix
  With so fell force and villeinous despighte,
  That through his haberieon the forkehead flew,
  And through the linked mayles empierced quite,
  But had no powre in his soft flesh to bite:
  That stroke the hardy Squire did sore displease,
  But more that him he could not come to smite;
  For by no meanes the high banke he could sease,
But labour'd long in that deepe ford with vaine disease.

And still the foster with his long bore-speare   xx
  Him kept from landing at his wished will;
  Anone one sent out of the thicket neare
  A cruell shaft, headed with deadly ill,
  And fethered with an vnlucky quill;
  The wicked steele stayd not, till it did light
  In his left thigh, and deepely did it thrill:
  Exceeding griefe that wound in him empight,
But more that with his foes he could not come to fight.

At last through wrath and vengeaunce making way,   xxi
  He on the bancke arriu'd with mickle paine,
  Where the third brother him did sore assay,
  And droue at him with all his might and maine
  A forrest bill, which both his hands did straine;
  But warily he did auoide the blow,
  And with his speare requited him againe,
  That both his sides were thrilled with the throw,
And a large streame of bloud out of the wound did flow.

  xix 3 habericon *1590*   5 no] now *1590*   xxi 9 bloud] flood *1590*

He tombling downe, with gnashing teeth did bite   xxii
   The bitter earth, and bad to let him in
   Into the balefull house of endlesse night,
   Where wicked ghosts do waile their former sin.
   Tho gan the battell freshly to begin;
   For nathemore for that spectacle bad,
   Did th'other two their cruell vengeaunce blin,
   But both attonce on both sides him bestad,
And load vpon him layd, his life for to haue had.

Tho when that villain he auiz'd, which late   xxiii
   Affrighted had the fairest *Florimell*,
   Full of fiers fury, and indignant hate,
   To him he turned, and with rigour fell
   Smote him so rudely on the Pannikell,
   That to the chin he cleft his head in twaine:
   Downe on the ground his carkas groueling fell;
   His sinfull soule with desperate disdaine,
Out of her fleshly ferme fled to the place of paine.

That seeing now the onely last of three,   xxiv
   Who with that wicked shaft him wounded had,
   Trembling with horrour, as that did foresee
   The fearefull end of his auengement sad,
   Through which he follow should his brethren bad,
   His bootelesse bow in feeble hand vpcaught,
   And therewith shot an arrow at the lad;
   Which faintly fluttring, scarce his helmet raught,
And glauncing fell to ground, but him annoyed naught.

With that he would haue fled into the wood;   xxv
   But *Timias* him lightly ouerhent,
   Right as he entring was into the flood,
   And strooke at him with force so violent,
   That headlesse him into the foord he sent:
   The carkas with the streame was carried downe,
   But th'head fell backeward on the Continent.
   So mischief fel vpon the meaners crowne;
They three be dead with shame, the Squire liues with renowne.

He liues, but takes small ioy of his renowne;   xxvi
  For of that cruell wound he bled so sore,
  That from his steed he fell in deadly swowne;
  Yet still the bloud forth gusht in so great store,
  That he lay wallowd all in his owne gore.
  Now God thee keepe, thou gentlest Squire aliue,
  Else shall thy louing Lord thee see no more,
  But both of comfort him thou shalt depriue,
And eke thy selfe of honour, which thou didst atchiue.

Prouidence heauenly passeth liuing thought,   xxvii
  And doth for wretched mens reliefe make way;
  For loe great grace or fortune thither brought
  Comfort to him, that comfortlesse now lay.
  In those same woods, ye well remember may,
  How that a noble hunteresse did wonne,
  She, that base *Braggadochio* did affray,
  And made him fast out of the forrest runne;
Belphœbe was her name, as faire as *Phœbus* sunne.

She on a day, as she pursewd the chace   xxviii
  Of some wild beast, which with her arrowes keene
  She wounded had, the same along did trace
  By tract of bloud, which she had freshly seene,
  To haue besprinckled all the grassy greene;
  By the great persue, which she there perceau'd,
  Well hoped she the beast engor'd had beene,
  And made more hast, the life to haue bereau'd:
But ah, her expectation greatly was deceau'd.

Shortly she came, whereas that woefull Squire   xxix
  With bloud deformed, lay in deadly swownd:
  In whose faire eyes, like lamps of quenched fire,
  The Christall humour stood congealed rownd;
  His locks, like faded leaues fallen to grownd,
  Knotted with bloud, in bounches rudely ran,
  And his sweete lips, on which before that stownd
  The bud of youth to blossome faire began,
Spoild of their rosie red, were woxen pale and wan.

Saw neuer liuing eye more heauy sight,   xxx
    That could haue made a rocke of stone to rew,
    Or riue in twaine: which when that Lady bright
    Besides all hope with melting eyes did vew,
    All suddeinly abasht she chaunged hew,
    And with sterne horrour backward gan to start:
    But when she better him beheld, she grew
    Full of soft passion and vnwonted smart:
The point of pitty perced through her tender hart.

Meekely she bowed downe, to weete if life   xxxi
    Yet in his frosen members did remaine,
    And feeling by his pulses beating rife,
    That the weake soule her seat did yet retaine,
    She cast to comfort him with busie paine:
    His double folded necke she reard vpright,
    And rubd his temples, and each trembling vaine;
    His mayled haberieon she did vndight,
And from his head his heauy burganet did light.

Into the woods thenceforth in hast she went,   xxxii
    To seeke for hearbes, that mote him remedy;
    For she of hearbes had great intendiment,
    Taught of the Nymphe, which from her infancy
    Her nourced had in trew Nobility:
    There, whether it diuine *Tobacco* were,
    Or *Panachæa*, or *Polygony*,
    She found, and brought it to her patient deare
Who al this while lay bleeding out his hart-bloud neare.

The soueraigne weede betwixt two marbles plaine   xxxiii
    She pownded small, and did in peeces bruze,
    And then atweene her lilly handes twaine,
    Into his wound the iuyce thereof did scruze,
    And round about, as she could well it vze,
    The flesh therewith she suppled and did steepe,
    T'abate all spasme, and soke the swelling bruze,
    And after hauing searcht the intuse deepe,
She with her scarfe did bind the wound from cold to keepe.

        xxx 7 better] bitter *1590*   xxxii 5 nursed *1609*

By this he had sweete life recur'd againe,   xxxiv
   And groning inly deepe, at last his eyes,
   His watry eyes, drizling like deawy raine,
   He vp gan lift toward the azure skies,
   From whence descend all hopelesse remedies:
   Therewith he sigh'd, and turning him aside,
   The goodly Mayd full of diuinities,
   And gifts of heauenly grace he by him spide,
Her bow and gilden quiuer lying him beside.

Mercy deare Lord (said he) what grace is this,   xxxv
   That thou hast shewed to me sinfull wight,
   To send thine Angell from her bowre of blis,
   To comfort me in my distressed plight?
   Angell, or Goddesse do I call thee right?
   What seruice may I do vnto thee meete,
   That hast from darkenesse me returnd to light,
   And with thy heauenly salues and med'cines sweete,
Hast drest my sinfull wounds?   I kisse thy blessed feete.

Thereat she blushing said, Ah gentle Squire,   xxxvi
   Nor Goddesse I, nor Angell, but the Mayd,
   And daughter of a woody Nymphe, desire
   No seruice, but thy safety and ayd;
   Which if thou gaine, I shalbe well apayd.
   We mortall wights, whose liues and fortunes bee
   To commun accidents still open layd,
   Are bound with commun bond of frailtee,
To succour wretched wights, whom we captiued see.

By this her Damzels, which the former chace   xxxvii
   Had vndertaken after her, arriu'd,
   As did *Belphœbe*, in the bloudy place,
   And thereby deemd the beast had bene depriu'd
   Of life, whom late their Ladies arrow ryu'd:
   For thy the bloudy tract they follow fast,
   And euery one to runne the swiftest stryu'd;
   But two of them the rest far ouerpast,
And where their Lady was, arriued at the last.

    xxxvi 7, 8 common *1609*   xxxvii 2 undertaken after her arriu'd
1596: undertaken, after her arriu'd *1609*

Where when they saw that goodly boy, with blood   xxxviii
  Defowled, and their Lady dresse his wownd,
  They wondred much, and shortly vnderstood,
  How him in deadly case their Lady fownd,
  And reskewed out of the heauy stownd.
  Eftsoones his warlike courser, which was strayd
  Farre in the woods, whiles that he lay in swownd,
  She made those Damzels search, which being stayd,
They did him set thereon, and forth with them conuayd.

Into that forest farre they thence him led,   xxxix
  Where was their dwelling, in a pleasant glade,
  With mountaines round about enuironed,
  And mighty woods, which did the valley shade,
  And like a stately Theatre it made,
  Spreading it selfe into a spatious plaine.
  And in the midst a little riuer plaide
  Emongst the pumy stones, which seemd to plaine
With gentle murmure, that his course they did restraine.

Beside the same a dainty place there lay,   xl
  Planted with mirtle trees and laurels greene,
  In which the birds song many a louely lay
  Of gods high prayse, and of their loues sweet terne,
  As it an earthly Paradize had beene:
  In whose enclosed shadow there was pight
  A faire Pauilion, scarcely to be seene,
  The which was all within most richly dight,
That greatest Princes liuing it mote well delight.

Thither they brought that wounded Squire, and layd   xli
  In easie couch his feeble limbes to rest,
  He rested him a while, and then the Mayd
  His ready wound with better salues new drest;
  Dayly she dressed him, and did the best
  His grieuous hurt to garish, that she might,
  That shortly she his dolour hath redrest,
  And his foule sore reduced to faire plight:
It she reduced, but himselfe destroyed quight.

  xxxviii 9 forthwith *1596*   xxxix 9 his] their *1590*   xl 4 loues
sweet] sweet loues *1590*   9 liuing] liking *1590*   xli 6 guarish *1590*

O foolish Physick, and vnfruitfull paine,   xlii
    That heales vp one and makes another wound:
    She his hurt thigh to him recur'd againe,
    But hurt his hart, the which before was sound,
    Through an vnwary dart, which did rebound
    From her faire eyes and gracious countenaunce.
    What bootes it him from death to be vnbound,
    To be captiued in endlesse duraunce
Of sorrow and despaire without aleggeaunce?

Still as his wound did gather, and grow hole,   xliii
    So still his hart woxe sore, and health decayd:
    Madnesse to saue a part, and lose the whole.
    Still whenas he beheld the heauenly Mayd,
    Whiles dayly plaisters to his wound she layd,
    So still his Malady the more increast,
    The whiles her matchlesse beautie him dismayd.
    Ah God, what other could he do at least,
But loue so faire a Lady, that his life releast?

Long while he stroue in his courageous brest,   xliv
    With reason dew the passion to subdew,
    And loue for to dislodge out of his nest:
    Still when her excellencies he did vew,
    Her soueraigne bounty, and celestiall hew,
    The same to loue he strongly was constraind:
    But when his meane estate he did reuew,
    He from such hardy boldnesse was restraind,
And of his lucklesse lot and cruell loue thus plaind.

Vnthankfull wretch (said he) is this the meed,   xlv
    With which her soueraigne mercy thou doest quight?
    Thy life she saued by her gracious deed,
    But thou doest weene with villeinous despight,
    To blot her honour, and her heauenly light.
    Dye rather, dye, then so disloyally
    Deeme of her high desert, or seeme so light:
    Faire death it is to shonne more shame, to dy:
Dye rather, dy, then euer loue disloyally.

But if to loue disloyalty it bee,   xlvi
  Shall I then hate her, that from deathes dore
  Me brought? ah farre be such reproch fro mee.
  What can I lesse do, then her loue therefore,
  Sith I her dew reward cannot restore?
  Dye rather, dye, and dying do her serue,
  Dying her serue, and liuing her adore;
  Thy life she gaue, thy life she doth deserue:
Dye rather, dye, then euer from her seruice swerue.

But foolish boy, what bootes thy seruice bace   xlvii
  To her, to whom the heauens do serue and sew?
  Thou a meane Squire, of meeke and lowly place,
  She heauenly borne, and of celestiall hew.
  How then? of all loue taketh equall vew:
  And doth not highest God vouchsafe to take
  The loue and seruice of the basest crew?
  If she will not, dye meekly for her sake;
Dye rather, dye, then euer so faire loue forsake.

Thus warreid he long time against his will,   xlviii
  Till that through weaknesse he was forst at last,
  To yield himselfe vnto the mighty ill:
  Which as a victour proud, gan ransack fast
  His inward parts, and all his entrayles wast,
  That neither blond in face, nor life in hart
  It left, but both did quite drye vp, and blast;
  As percing leuin, which the inner part
Of euery thing consumes, and calcineth by art.

Which seeing faire *Belphœbe*, gan to feare,   xlix
  Least that his wound were inly well not healed,
  Or that the wicked steele empoysned were:
  Litle she weend, that loue he close concealed;
  Yet still he wasted, as the snow congealed,
  When the bright sunne his beams thereon doth beat;
  Yet neuer he his hart to her reuealed,
  But rather chose to dye for sorrow great,
Then with dishonorable termes her to entreat.

xlvi 5 restore : 1590 &c.

She gracious Lady, yet no paines did spare,
  To do him ease, or do him remedy:
  Many Restoratiues of vertues rare,
  And costly Cordialles she did apply,
  To mitigate his stubborne mallady:
  But that sweet Cordiall, which can restore
  A loue-sick hart, she did to him enuy;
  To him, and to all th'vnworthy world forlore
She did enuy that soueraigne salue, in secret store.

That dainty Rose, the daughter of her Morne,
  More deare then life she tendered, whose flowre
  The girlond of her honour did adorne:
  Ne suffred she the Middayes scorching powre,
  Ne the sharp Northerne wind thereon to showre,
  But lapped vp her silken leaues most chaire,
  When so the froward skye began to lowre:
  But soone as calmed was the Christall aire,
She did it faire dispred, and let to florish faire.

Eternall God in his almighty powre,
  To make ensample of his heauenly grace,
  In Paradize whilome did plant this flowre,
  Whence he it fetcht out of her natiue place,
  And did in stocke of earthly flesh enrace,
  That mortall men her glory should admire:
  In gentle Ladies brest, and bounteous race
  Of woman kind it fairest flowre doth spire,
And beareth fruit of honour and all chast desire.

Faire ympes of beautie, whose bright shining beames
  Adorne the world with like to heauenly light,
  And to your willes both royalties and Realmes
  Subdew, through conquest of your wondrous might,
  With this faire flowre your goodly girlonds dight,
  Of chastity and vertue virginall,
  That shall embellish more your beautie bright,
  And crowne your heades with heauenly coronall,
Such as the Angels weare before Gods tribunall.

l
li
lii
liii

1 8 To him and all *1609*   lii 6 admire *1590, 1596*
liii 3 Reames *1590*   9 weare] were *1590*

To youre faire selues a faire ensample frame,   liv
   Of this faire virgin, this *Belphœbe* faire,
   To whom in perfect loue, and spotlesse fame
   Of chastitie, none liuing may compaire :
   Ne poysnous Enuy iustly can empaire
   The prayse of her fresh flowring Maidenhead ;
   For thy she standeth on the highest staire
   Of th'honorable stage of womanhead,
That Ladies all may follow her ensample dead.

In so great prayse of stedfast chastity,   lv
   Nathlesse she was so curteous and kind,
   Tempred with grace, and goodly modesty,
   That seemed those two vertues stroue to find
   The higher place in her Heroick mind :
   So striuing each did other more augment,
   And both encreast the prayse of woman kind,
   And both encreast her beautie excellent ;
So all did make in her a perfect complement.

Cant. VI.

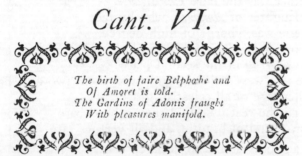

The birth of faire Belphœbe and
Of Amoret is told.
The Gardins of Adonis fraught
With pleasures manifold.

WEll may I weene, faire Ladies, all this while   i
   Ye wonder, how this noble Damozell
So great perfections did in her compile,
Sith that in saluage forests she did dwell,
So farre from court and royall Citadell,
The great schoolmistresse of all curtesy :
Seemeth that such wild woods should far expell
All ciuill vsage and gentility,
And gentle sprite deforme with rude rusticity.

i 6 schoolmaistresse *1590*

But to this faire *Belphœbe* in her berth   ii
   The heauens so fauourable were and free,
   Looking with myld aspect vpon the earth,
   In th'*Horoscope* of her natiuitee,
   That all the gifts of grace and chastitee
   On her they poured forth of plenteous horne;
   Ioue laught on *Venus* from his soueraigne see,
   And *Phœbus* with faire beames did her adorne,
And all the *Graces* rockt her cradle being borne.

Her berth was of the wombe of Morning dew,   iii
   And her conception of the ioyous Prime,
   And all her whole creation did her shew
   Pure and vnspotted from all loathly crime,
   That is ingenerate in fleshly slime.
   So was this virgin borne, so was she bred,
   So was she trayned vp from time to time,
   In all chast vertue, and true bounti-hed
Till to her dew perfection she was ripened.

Her mother was the faire *Chrysogonee*,   iv
   The daughter of *Amphisa*, who by race
   A Faerie was, yborne of high degree,
   She bore *Belphœbe*, she bore in like cace
   Faire *Amoretta* in the second place:
   These two were twinnes, and twixt them two did share
   The heritage of all celestiall grace.
   That all the rest it seem'd they robbed bare
Of bountie, and of beautie, and all vertues rare.

It were a goodly storie, to declare,   v
   By what straunge accident faire *Chrysogone*
   Conceiu'd these infants, and how them she bare,
   In this wild forrest wandring all alone,
   After she had nine moneths fulfild and gone:
   For not as other wemens commune brood,
   They were enwombed in the sacred throne
   Of her chaste bodie, nor with commune food,
As other wemens babes, they sucked vitall blood.

     iii 9 was] were *1590*   v 3 bare] bore *1590*

But wondrously they were begot, and bred   vi
    Through influence of th'heauens fruitfull ray,
    As it in antique bookes is mentioned.
    It was vpon a Sommers shynie day,
    When *Titan* faire his beames did display,
    In a fresh fountaine, farre from all mens vew,
    She bath'd her brest, the boyling heat t'allay;
    She bath'd with roses red, and violets blew,
And all the sweetest flowres, that in the forrest grew.

Till faint through irkesome wearinesse, adowne   vii
    Vpon the grassie ground her selfe she layd
    To sleepe, the whiles a gentle slombring swowne
    Vpon her fell all naked bare displayd;
    The sunne-beames bright vpon her body playd,
    Being through former bathing mollifide,
    And pierst into her wombe, where they embayd
    With so sweet sence and secret power vnspide,
That in her pregnant flesh they shortly fructifide.

Miraculous may seeme to him, that reades   viii
    So straunge ensample of conception ;
    But reason teacheth that the fruitfull seades
    Of all things liuing, through impression
    Of the sunbeames in moyst complexion,
    Doe life conceiue and quickned are by kynd:
    So after *Nilus* invndation,
    Infinite shapes of creatures men do fynd,
Informed in the mud, on which the Sunne hath shynd.

Great father he of generation   ix
    Is rightly cald, th'author of life and light;
    And his faire sister for creation
    Ministreth matter fit, which tempred right
    With heate and humour, breedes the liuing wight.
    So sprong these twinnes in wombe of *Chrysogone*,
    Yet wist she nought thereof, but sore affright,
    Wondred to see her belly so vpblone,
Which still increast, till she her terme had full outgone.

    vi 5 his hot beames *1609*   viii 8 creatures] creature *1596*

Whereof conceiuing shame and foule disgrace, x
   Albe her guiltlesse conscience her cleard,
   She fled into the wildernesse a space,
   Till that vnweeldy burden she had reard,
   And shund dishonor, which as death she feard:
   Where wearie of long trauell, downe to rest
   Her selfe she set, and comfortably cheard;
   There a sad cloud of sleepe her ouerkest,
And seized euery sense with sorrow sore opprest.

It fortuned, faire *Venus* hauing lost xi
   Her little sonne, the winged god of loue,
   Who for some light displeasure, which him crost,
   Was from her fled, as flit as ayerie Doue,
   And left her blisfull bowre of ioy aboue,
   (So from her often he had fled away,
   When she for ought him sharpely did reproue,
   And wandred in the world in strange aray,
Disguiz'd in thousand shapes, that none might him bewray.)

Him for to seeke, she left her heauenly hous, xii
   The house of goodly formes and faire aspects,
   Whence all the world deriues the glorious
   Features of beautie, and all shapes select,
   With which high God his workmanship hath deckt;
   And searched euery way, through which his wings
   Had borne him, or his tract she mote detect:
   She promist kisses sweet, and sweeter things
Vnto the man, that of him tydings to her brings.

First she him sought in Court, where most he vsed xiii
   Whylome to haunt, but there she found him not;
   But many there she found, which sore accused
   His falsehood, and with foule infamous blot
   His cruell deedes and wicked wyles did spot:
   Ladies and Lords she euery where mote heare
   Complayning, how with his empoysned shot
   Their wofull harts he wounded had whyleare,
And so had left them languishing twixt hope and feare.

xii 4 beauties *1596, 1609*

She then the Citties sought from gate to gate,   xiv
  And euery one did aske, did he him see;
  And euery one her answerd, that too late
  He had him seene, and felt the crueltie
  Of his sharpe darts and whot artillerie ;
  And euery one threw forth reproches rife
  Of his mischieuous deedes, and said, That hee
  Was the disturber of all ciuill life,
The enimy of peace, and author of all strife.

Then in the countrey she abroad him sought,   xv
  And in the rurall cottages inquired,
  Where also many plaints to her were brought,
  How he their heedlesse harts with loue had fyred,
  And his false venim through their veines inspyred;
  And eke the gentle shepheard swaynes, which sat
  Keeping their fleecie flockes, as they were hyred,
  She sweetly heard complaine, both how and what
Her sonne had to them doen; yet she did smile thereat.

But when in none of all these she him got,   xvi
  She gan auize, where else he mote him hyde:
  At last she her bethought, that she had not
  Yet sought the saluage woods and forrests wyde,
  In which full many louely Nymphes abyde,
  Mongst whom might be, that he did closely lye,
  Or that the loue of some of them him tyde:
  For thy she thither cast her course t'apply,
To search the secret haunts of *Dianes* company.

Shortly vnto the wastefull woods she came,   xvii
  Whereas she found the Goddesse with her crew,
  After late chace of their embrewed game,
  Sitting beside a fountaine in a rew,
  Some of them washing with the liquid dew
  From off their dainty limbes the dustie sweat,
  And soyle which did deforme their liuely hew;
  Others lay shaded from the scorching heat;
The rest vpon her person gaue attendance great.

xvii 6 off] of *1590*   8 Other *1609*

She hauing hong vpon a bough on high   xviii
  Her bow and painted quiuer, had vnlaste
  Her siluer buskins from her nimble thigh,
  And her lancke loynes vngirt, and brests vnbraste,
  After her heat the breathing cold to taste;
  Her golden lockes, that late in tresses bright
  Embreaded were for hindring of her haste,
  Now loose about her shoulders hong vndight,
And were with sweet *Ambrosia* all besprinckled light.

Soone as she *Venus* saw behind her backe,   xix
  She was asham'd to be so loose surprized,
  And woxe halfe wroth against her damzels slacke,
  That had not her thereof before auized,
  But suffred her so carelesly disguized
  Be ouertaken. Soone her garments loose
  Vpgath'ring, in her bosome she comprized,
  Well as she might, and to the Goddesse rose,
Whiles all her Nymphes did like a girlond her enclose.

Goodly she gan faire *Cytherea* greet,   xx
  And shortly asked her, what cause her brought
  Into that wildernesse for her vnmeet,
  From her sweete bowres, and beds with pleasures fraught:
  That suddein change she strange aduenture thought.
  To whom halfe weeping, she thus answered,
  That she her dearest sonne *Cupido* sought,
  Who in his frowardnesse from her was fled;
That she repented sore, to haue him angered.

Thereat *Diana* gan to smile, in scorne   xxi
  Of her vaine plaint, and to her scoffing sayd;
  Great pittie sure, that ye be so forlorne
  Of your gay sonne, that giues ye so good ayd
  To your disports: ill mote ye bene apayd.
  But she was more engrieued, and replide;
  Faire sister, ill beseemes it to vpbrayd
  A dolefull heart with so disdainfull pride;
The like that mine, may be your paine another tide.

As you in woods and wanton wildernesse   xxii
  Your glory set, to chace the saluage beasts,
  So my delight is all in ioyfulnesse,
  In beds, in bowres, in banckets, and in feasts:
  And ill becomes you with your loftie creasts,
  To scorne the ioy, that *Ioue* is glad to seeke;
  We both are bound to follow heauens beheasts,
  And tend our charges with obeisance meeke:
Spare, gentle sister, with reproch my paine to eeke.

And tell me, if that ye my sonne haue heard,   xxiii
  To lurke emongst your Nymphes in secret wize;
  Or keepe their cabins: much I am affeard,
  Least he like one of them him selfe disguize,
  And turne his arrowes to their exercize:
  So may he long himselfe full easie hide:
  For he is faire and fresh in face and guize,
  As any Nymph (let not it be enuyde.)
So saying euery Nymph full narrowly she eyde.

But *Phœbe* therewith sore was angered,   xxiv
  And sharply said; Goe Dame, goe seeke your boy,
  Where you him lately left, in *Mars* his bed;
  He comes not here, we scorne his foolish ioy,
  Ne lend we leisure to his idle toy:
  But if I catch him in this company,
  By *Stygian* lake I vow, whose sad annoy
  The Gods doe dread, he dearely shall abye:
Ile clip his wanton wings, that he no more shall fly.

Whom when as *Venus* saw so sore displeased,   xxv
  She inly sory was, and gan relent,
  What she had said: so her she soone appeased,
  With sugred words and gentle blandishment,
  Which as a fountaine from her sweet lips went,
  And welled goodly forth, that in short space
  She was well pleasd, and forth her damzels sent,
  Through all the woods, to search from place to place,
If any tract of him or tydings they mote trace.

xxv 5 Which as] From which *1590, 1596*: *corr. 1609.* Of which *conj.* *Church.*

To search the God of loue, her Nymphes she sent   xxvi
  Throughout the wandring forrest euery where :
  And after them her selfe eke with her went
  To seeke the fugitiue, both farre and nere,
  So long they sought, till they arriued were
  In that same shadie couert, whereas lay
  Faire *Crysogone* in slombry traunce whilere :
  Who in her sleepe (a wondrous thing to say)
Vnwares had borne two babes, as faire as springing day.

Vnwares she them conceiu'd, vnwares she bore :   xxvii
  She bore withouten paine, that she conceiued
  Withouten pleasure : ne her need implore
  Lucinaes aide : which when they both perceiued,
  They were through wonder nigh of sense bereaued,
  And gazing each on other, nought bespake :
  At last they both agreed, her seeming grieued
  Out of her heauy swowne not to awake,
But from her louing side the tender babes to take.

Vp they them tooke, each one a babe vptooke,   xxviii
  And with them carried, to be fostered ;
  Dame *Phœbe* to a Nymph her babe betooke,
  To be vpbrought in perfect Maydenhed,
  And of her selfe her name *Belphœbe* red :
  But *Venus* hers thence farre away conuayd,
  To be vpbrought in goodly womanhed,
  And in her litle loues stead, which was strayd,
Her *Amoretta* cald, to comfort her dismayd.

She brought her to her ioyous Paradize,   xxix
  Where most she wonnes, when she on earth does dwel.
  So faire a place, as Nature can deuize :
  Whether in *Paphos*, or *Cytheron* hill,
  Or it in *Gnidus* be, I wote not well ;
  But well I wote by tryall, that this same
  All other pleasant places doth excell,
  And called is by her lost louers name,
The *Gardin* of *Adonis*, farre renowmd by fame.

xxvi 4 both farre and nere *om. 1590*   xxviii 6 thence] hence *1596, 1609*
xxix 5 *Gnidus 1590*

In that same Gardin all the goodly flowres, xxx
    Wherewith dame Nature doth her beautifie,
    And decks the girlonds of her paramoures,
    Are fetcht : there is the first seminarie
    Of all things, that are borne to liue and die,
    According to their kindes. Long worke it were,
    Here to account the endlesse progenie
    Of all the weedes, that bud and blossome there;
But so much as doth need, must needs be counted here.

It sited was in fruitfull soyle of old, xxxi
    And girt in with two walles on either side;
    The one of yron, the other of bright gold,
    That none might thorough breake, nor ouer-stride:
    And double gates it had, which opened wide,
    By which both in and out men moten pas;
    Th'one faire and fresh, the other old and dride :
    Old *Genius* the porter of them was,
Old *Genius*, the which a double nature has.

He letteth in, he letteth out to wend, xxxii
    All that to come into the world desire;
    A thousand thousand naked babes attend
    About him day and night, which doe require,
    That he with fleshly weedes would them attire:
    Such as him list, such as eternall fate
    Ordained hath, he clothes with sinfull mire,
    And sendeth forth to liue in mortall state,
Till they againe returne backe by the hinder gate.

After that they againe returned beene, xxxiii
    They in that Gardin planted be againe;
    And grow afresh, as they had neuer seene
    Fleshly corruption, nor mortall paine.
    Some thousand yeares so doen they there remaine;
    And then of him are clad with other hew,
    Or sent into the chaungefull world againe,
    Till thither they returne, where first they grew:
So like a wheele around they runne from old to new.

xxxiii 5 remaire ; 1596

Ne needs there Gardiner to set, or sow,   xxxiv
   To plant or prune: for of their owne accord
   All things, as they created were, doe grow,
   And yet remember well the mightie word,
   Which first was spoken by th'Almightie lord,
   That bad them to increase and multiply:
   Ne doe they need with water of the ford,
   Or of the clouds to moysten their roots dry;
For in themselues eternall moisture they imply.

Infinite shapes of creatures there are bred,   xxxv
   And vncouth formes, which none yet euer knew,
   And euery sort is in a sundry bed
   Set by it selfe, and ranckt in comely rew:
   Some fit for reasonable soules t'indew,
   Some made for beasts, some made for birds to weare,
   And all the fruitfull spawne of fishes hew
   In endlesse rancks along enraunged were,
That seem'd the *Ocean* could not containe them there.

Daily they grow, and daily forth are sent   xxxvi
   Into the world, it to replenish more;
   Yet is the stocke not lessened, nor spent,
   But still remaines in euerlasting store,
   As it at first created was of yore.
   For in the wide wombe of the world there lyes,
   In hatefull darkenesse and in deepe horrore,
   An huge eternall *Chaos*, which supplyes
The substances of natures fruitfull progenyes.

All things from thence doe their first being fetch,   xxxvii
   And borrow matter, whereof they are made,
   Which when as forme and feature it does ketch,
   Becomes a bodie, and doth then inuade
   The state of life, out of the griesly shade.
   That substance is eterne, and bideth so,
   Ne when the life decayes, and forme does fade,
   Doth it consume, and into nothing go,
But chaunged is, and often altred to and fro.

xxxiv 2 of prune *1596*

The substance is not chaunged, nor altered,
  But th'only forme and outward fashion;
  For euery substance is conditioned
  To change her hew, and sundry formes to don,
  Meet for her temper and complexion:
  For formes are variable and decay,
  By course of kind, and by occasion;
  And that faire flowre of beautie fades away,
As doth the lilly fresh before the sunny ray.

Great enimy to it, and to all the rest,
  That in the *Gardin* of *Adonis* springs,
  Is wicked *Time*, who with his scyth addrest,
  Does mow the flowring herbes and goodly things,
  And all their glory to the ground downe flings,
  Where they doe wither, and are fowly mard:
  He flyes about, and with his flaggy wings
  Beates downe both leaues and buds without regard,
Ne euer pittie may relent his malice hard.

Yet pittie often did the gods relent,
  To see so faire things mard, and spoyled quight:
  And their great mother *Venus* did lament
  The losse of her deare brood, her deare delight:
  Her hart was pierst with pittie at the sight,
  When walking through the Gardin, them she spyde,
  Yet no'te she find redresse for such despight.
  For all that liues, is subiect to that law:
All things decay in time, and to their end do draw.

But were it not, that *Time* their troubler is,
  All that in this delightfull Gardin growes,
  Should happie be, and haue immortall blis:
  For here all plentie, and all pleasure flowes,
  And sweet loue gentle fits emongst them throwes,
  Without fell rancor, or fond gealosie;
  Franckly each paramour his leman knowes,
  Each bird his mate, ne any does enuie
Their goodly meriment, and gay felicitie.

xl 6 spyde] saw *corr. edd. But cf.* II viii 29 l. 7 &c.

There is continuall spring, and haruest there   xlii
   Continuall, both meeting at one time:
   For both the boughes doe laughing blossomes beare,
   And with fresh colours decke the wanton Prime,
   And eke attonce the heauy trees they clime,
   Which seeme to labour vnder their fruits lode:
   The whiles the ioyous birdes make their pastime
   Emongst the shadie leaues, their sweet abode,
And their true loues without suspition tell abrode.

Right in the middest of that Paradise,   xliii
   There stood a stately Mount, on whose round top
   A gloomy groue of mirtle trees did rise,
   Whose shadie boughes sharpe steele did neuer lop,
   Nor wicked beasts their tender buds did crop,
   But like a girlond compassed the hight,
   And from their fruitfull sides sweet gum did drop,
   That all the ground with precious deaw bedight,
Threw forth most dainty odours, and most sweet delight.

And in the thickest couert of that shade,   xliv
   There was a pleasant arbour, not by art,
   But of the trees owne inclination made,
   Which knitting their rancke braunches part to part,
   With wanton yuie twyne entrayld athwart,
   And Eglantine, and Caprifole emong,
   Fashiond aboue within their inmost part,
   That nether *Phœbus* beams could through them throng,
Nor *Aeolus* sharp blast could worke them any wrong.

And all about grew euery sort of flowre,   xlv
   To which sad louers were transformd of yore;
   Fresh *Hyacinthus*, *Phœbus* paramoure,
   And dearest loue,
   Foolish *Narcisse*, that likes the watry shore,
   Sad *Amaranthus*, made a flowre but late,
   Sad *Amaranthus*, in whose purple gore
   Me seemes I see *Amintas* wretched fate,
To whom sweet Poets verse hath giuen endlesse date.

   xlii 5 heauy] heauenly *1590*   xlv 4 And dearest loue, *om. 1590, 1596:*
add. 1609   5 *Marcisse 1590*

There wont faire *Venus* often to enioy   xlvi
  Her deare *Adonis* ioyous company,
  And reape sweet pleasure of the wanton boy;
  There yet, some say, in secret he does ly,
  Lapped in flowres and pretious spycery,
  By her hid from the world, and from the skill
  Of *Stygian* Gods, which doe her loue enuy;
  But she her selfe, when euer that she will,
Possesseth him, and of his sweetnesse takes her fill.

And sooth it seemes they say: for he may not   xlvii
  For euer die, and euer buried bee
  In balefull night, where all things are forgot;
  All be he subiect to mortalitie,
  Yet is eterne in mutabilitie,
  And by succession made perpetuall,
  Transformed oft, and chaunged diuerslie:
  For him the Father of all formes they call;
Therefore needs mote he liue, that liuing giues to all.

There now he liueth in eternall blis,   xlviii
  Ioying his goddesse, and of her enioyd:
  Ne feareth he henceforth that foe of his,
  Which with his cruell tuske him deadly cloyd:
  For that wilde Bore, the which him once annoyd,
  She firmely hath emprisoned for ay,
  That her sweet loue his malice mote auoyd,
  In a strong rocky Caue, which is they say,
Hewen vnderneath that Mount, that none him losen may.

There now he liues in euerlasting ioy,   xlix
  With many of the Gods in company,
  Which thither haunt, and with the winged boy
  Sporting himselfe in safe felicity:
  Who when he hath with spoiles and cruelty
  Ransackt the world, and in the wofull harts
  Of many wretches set his triumphes hye,
  Thither resorts, and laying his sad darts
Aside, with faire *Adonis* playes his wanton parts.

And his true loue faire *Psyche* with him playes,   I
  Faire *Psyche* to him lately reconcyld,
  After long troubles and vnmeet vpbrayes,
  With which his mother *Venus* her reuyld,
  And eke himselfe her cruelly exyld :
  But now in stedfast loue and happy state
  She with him liues, and hath him borne a chyld,
  Pleasure, that doth both gods and men aggrate,
Pleasure, the daughter of *Cupid* and *Psyche* late.

Hither great *Venus* brought this infant faire,   li
  The younger daughter of *Chrysogonee*,
  And vnto *Psyche* with great trust and care
  Committed her, yfostered to bee,
  And trained vp in true feminitee :
  Who no lesse carefully her tendered,
  Then her owne daughter *Pleasure*, to whom shee
  Made her companion, and her lessoned
In all the lore of loue, and goodly womanhead.

In which when she to perfect ripenesse grew,   lii
  Of grace and beautie noble Paragone,
  She brought her forth into the worldes vew,
  To be th'ensample of true loue alone,
  And Lodestarre of all chaste affectione,
  To all faire Ladies, that doe liue on ground.
  To Faery court she came, where many one
  Admyrd her goodly haueour, and found
His feeble hart wide launched with loues cruell wound.

But she to none of them her loue did cast,   liii
  Saue to the noble knight Sir *Scudamore*,
  To whom her louing hart she linked fast
  In faithfull loue, t'abide for euermore,
  And for his dearest sake endured sore,
  Sore trouble of an hainous enimy ;
  Who her would forced haue to haue forlore
  Her former loue, and stedfast loialty,
As ye may elsewhere read that ruefull history.

    lii 9 launched] launch *1590* : launced *1609*   liii 4 fathful *1596*

But well I weene, ye first desire to learne,   liv
   What end vnto that fearefull Damozell,
   Which fled so fast from that same foster stearne,
   Whom with his brethren *Timias* slew, befell:
   That was to weet, the goodly *Florimell*;
   Who wandring for to seeke her louer deare,
   Her louer deare, her dearest *Marinell*,
   Into misfortune fell, as ye did heare,
And from Prince *Arthur* fled with wings of idle feare.

Cant. VII.

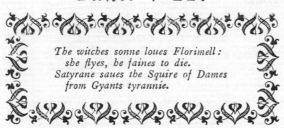

The witches sonne loues Florimell:
she flyes, he faines to die.
Satyrane saues the Squire of Dames
from Gyants tyrannie.

Like as an Hynd forth singled from the heard,   i
   That hath escaped from a rauenous beast,
   Yet flyes away of her owne feet affeard,
   And euery leafe, that shaketh with the least
   Murmure of winde, her terror hath encreast;
   So fled faire *Florimell* from her vaine feare,
   Long after she from perill was releast:
   Each shade she saw, and each noyse she did heare,
Did seeme to be the same, which she escapt whyleare.

All that same euening she in flying spent,   ii
   And all that night her course continewed:
   Ne did she let dull sleepe once to relent,
   Nor wearinesse to slacke her hast, but fled
   Euer alike, as if her former dred
   Were hard behind, her readie to arrest:
   And her white Palfrey hauing conquered
   The maistring raines out of her weary wrest,
Perforce her carried, where euer he thought best.

Arg. 4 *Gynunt, 1590*   i 8 she did] he did *1590*

So long as breath, and hable puissance   iii
　　Did natiue courage vnto him supply,
　　His pace he freshly forward did aduaunce,
　　And carried her beyond all ieopardy,
　　But nought that wanteth rest, can long aby.
　　He hauing through incessant trauell spent
　　His force, at last perforce a downe did ly,
　　Ne foot could further moue: The Lady gent
Thereat was suddein strooke with great astonishment.

And forst t'alight, on foot mote algates fare,   iv
　　A traueller vnwonted to such way:
　　Need teacheth her this lesson hard and rare,
　　That fortune all in equall launce doth sway,
　　And mortall miseries doth make her play.
　　So long she trauelled, till at length she came
　　To an hilles side, which did to her bewray
　　A little valley, subiect to the same,
All couerd with thick woods, that quite it ouercame.

Through the tops of the high trees she did descry   v
　　A litle smoke, whose vapour thin and light,
　　Reeking aloft, vprolled to the sky:
　　Which, chearefull signe did send vnto her sight,
　　That in the same did wonne some liuing wight.
　　Eftsoones her steps she thereunto applyde,
　　And came at last in weary wretched plight
　　Vnto the place, to which her hope did guyde,
To find some refuge there, and rest her weary syde.

There in a gloomy hollow glen she found   vi
　　A little cottage, built of stickes and reedes
　　In homely wize, and wald with sods around,
　　In which a witch did dwell, in loathly weedes,
　　And wilfull want, all carelesse of her needes;
　　So choosing solitarie to abide,
　　Far from all neighbours, that her deuilish deedes
　　And hellish arts from people she might hide,
And hurt far off vnknowne, whom euer she enuide.

v 1 th'tops *1609*

The Damzell there arriuing entred in;   vii
   Where sitting on the flore the Hag she found,
   Busie (as seem'd) about some wicked gin :
   Who soone as she beheld that suddein stound,
   Lightly vpstarted from the dustie ground,
   And with fell looke and hollow deadly gaze
   Stared on her awhile, as one astound,
   Ne had one word to speake, for great amaze,
But shewd by outward signes, that dread her sence did daze.

At last turning her feare to foolish wrath,   viii
   She askt, what deuill had her thither brought,
   And who she was, and what vnwonted path
   Had guided her, vnwelcomed, vnsought?
   To which the Damzell full of doubtfull thought,
   Her mildly answer'd; Beldame be not wroth
   With silly Virgin by aduenture brought
   Vnto your dwelling, ignorant and loth,
That craue but rowme to rest, while tempest ouerblo'th.

With that adowne out of her Christall eyne   ix
   Few trickling teares she softly forth let fall,
   That like two Orient pearles, did purely shyne
   Vpon her snowy cheeke ; and therewithall
   She sighed soft, that none so bestiall,
   Nor saluage hart, but ruth of her sad plight
   Would make to melt, or pitteously appall ;
   And that vile Hag, all were her whole delight
In mischiefe, was much moued at so pitteous sight.

And gan recomfort her in her rude wyse,   x
   With womanish compassion of her plaint,
   Wiping the teares from her suffused eyes,
   And bidding her sit downe, to rest her faint
   And wearie limbs a while.   She nothing quaint
   Nor s'deignfull of so homely fashion,
   Sith brought she was now to so hard constraint,
   Sate downe vpon the dusty ground anon,
As glad of that small rest, as Bird of tempest gon.

vii 8 amaze. *1596*   ix 3 two] to *conj. Hughes*

Tho gan she gather vp her garments rent,   xi
    And her loose lockes to dight in order dew,
    With golden wreath and gorgeous ornament;
    Whom such whenas the wicked Hag did vew,
    She was astonisht at her heauenly hew,
    And doubted her to deeme an earthly wight,
    But or some Goddesse, or of *Dianes* crew,
    And thought her to adore with humble spright;
T'adore thing so diuine as beauty, were but right.

This wicked woman had a wicked sonne,   xii
    The comfort of her age and weary dayes,
    A laesie loord, for nothing good to donne,
    But stretched forth in idlenesse alwayes,
    Ne euer cast his mind to couet prayse,
    Or ply him selfe to any honest trade,
    But all the day before the sunny rayes
    He vs'd to slug, or sleepe in slothfull shade:
Such laesinesse both lewd and poore attonce him made.

He comming home at vndertime, there found   xiii
    The fairest creature, that he euer saw,
    Sitting beside his mother on the ground;
    The sight whereof did greatly him adaw,
    And his base thought with terrour and with aw
    So inly smot, that as one, which had gazed
    On the bright Sunne vnwares, doth soone withdraw
    His feeble eyne, with too much brightnesse dazed,
So stared he on her, and stood long while amazed.

Softly at last he gan his mother aske,   xiv
    What mister wight that was, and whence deriued,
    That in so straunge disguizement there did maske,
    And by what accident she there arriued:
    But she, as one nigh of her wits depriued,
    With nought but ghastly lookes him answered,
    Like to a ghost, that lately is reuiued
    From *Stygian* shores, where late it wandered;
So both at her, and each at other wondered.

But the faire Virgin was so meeke and mild,   xv
    That she to them vouchsafed to embace
    Her goodly port, and to their senses vild,
    Her gentle speach applide, that in short space
    She grew familiare in that desert place.
    During which time, the Chorle through her so kind
    And curteise vse conceiu'd affection bace,
    And cast to loue her in his brutish mind;
No loue, but brutish lust, that was so beastly tind.

Closely the wicked flame his bowels brent,   xvi
    And shortly grew into outrageous fire;
    Yet had he not the hart, nor hardiment,
    As vnto her to vtter his desire;
    His caytiue thought durst not so high aspire,
    But with soft sighes, and louely semblaunces,
    He ween'd that his affection entire
    She should aread; many resemblaunces
To her he made, and many kind remembraunces.

Oft from the forrest wildings he did bring,   xvii
    Whose sides empurpled were with smiling red,
    And oft young birds, which he had taught to sing
    His mistresse prayses, sweetly caroled,
    Girlonds of flowres sometimes for her faire hed
    He fine would dight; sometimes the squirell wild
    He brought to her in bands, as conquered
    To be her thrall, his fellow seruant vild;
All which, she of him tooke with countenance meeke and mild.

But past awhile, when she fit season saw   xviii
    To leaue that desert mansion, she cast
    In secret wize her selfe thence to withdraw,
    For feare of mischiefe, which she did forecast
    Might be by the witch or that her sonne compast:
    Her wearie Palfrey closely, as she might,
    Now well recouered after long repast,
    In his proud furnitures she freshly dight,
His late miswandred wayes now to remeasure right.

xvii 4 maistresse *1590*   xviii 5 be by] by *1590*: be *1596, 1609*
that] by *1590*

And earely ere the dawning day appeard,   **xix**
    She forth issewed, and on her iourney went;
    She went in perill, of each noyse affeard,
    And of each shade, that did it selfe present;
    For still she feared to be ouerhent,
    Of that vile hag, or her vnciuile sonne:
    Who when too late awaking, well they kent,
    That their faire guest was gone, they both begonne
To make exceeding mone, as they had bene vndonne.

But that lewd louer did the most lament   **xx**
    For her depart, that euer man did heare;
    He knockt his brest with desperate intent,
    And scratcht his face, and with his teeth did teare
    His rugged flesh, and rent his ragged heare:
    That his sad mother seeing his sore plight,
    Was greatly woe begon, and gan to feare,
    Least his fraile senses were emperisht quight,
And loue to frenzy turnd, sith loue is franticke hight.

All wayes she sought, him to restore to plight,   **xxi**
    With herbs, with charms, with counsell, and with teares,
    But tears, nor charms, nor herbs, nor counsell might
    Asswage the fury, which his entrails teares:
    So strong is passion, that no reason heares.
    Tho when all other helpes she saw to faile,
    She turnd her selfe backe to her wicked leares
    And by her deuilish arts thought to preuaile,
To bring her backe againe, or worke her finall bale.

Eftsoones out of her hidden caue she cald   **xxii**
    An hideous beast, of horrible aspect,
    That could the stoutest courage haue appald;
    Monstrous mishapt, and all his backe was spect
    With thousand spots of colours queint elect,
    Thereto so swift, that it all beasts did pas:
    Like neuer yet did liuing eye detect;
    But likest it to an *Hyena* was,
That feeds on womens flesh, as others feede on gras.

xix 6 her] that *1609*   xxii 4 Monstrous, *1590*

It forth she cald, and gaue it streight in charge,
  Through thicke and thin her to pursew apace, ·
  Ne once to stay to rest, or breath at large,
  Till her he had attaind, and brought in place,
  Or quite deuourd her beauties scornefull grace.
  The Monster swift as word, that from her went,
  Went forth in hast, and did her footing trace
  So sure and swiftly, through his perfect sent,
And passing speede, that shortly he her ouerhent.

Whom when the fearefull Damzell nigh espide,
  No need to bid her fast away to flie;
  That vgly shape so sore her terrifide,
  That it she shund no lesse, then dread to die,
  And her flit Palfrey did so well apply
  His nimble feet to her conceiued feare,
  That whilest his breath did strength to him supply,
  From perill free he her away did beare:
But when his force gan faile, his pace gan wex areare.

Which whenas she perceiu'd, she was dismayd
  At that same last extremitie full sore,
  And of her safetie greatly grew afrayd;
  And now she gan approch to the sea shore,
  As it befell, that she could flie no more,
  But yield her selfe to spoile of greedinesse.
  Lightly she leaped, as a wight forlore,
  From her dull horse, in desperate distresse,
And to her feet betooke her doubtfull sickernesse.

Not halfe so fast the wicked *Myrrha* fled
  From dread of her reuenging fathers hond:
  Nor halfe so fast to saue her maidenhed,
  Fled fearefull *Daphne* on th'*Ægæan* strond,
  As *Florimell* fled from that Monster yond,
  To reach the sea, ere she of him were raught:
  For in the sea to drowne her selfe she fond,
  Rather then of the tyrant to be caught:
Thereto feare gaue her wings, and neede her courage taught.

It fortuned (high God did so ordaine)
  As she arriued on the roring shore,
  In minde to leape into the mighty maine,
  A little boate lay houing her before,
  In which there slept a fisher old and pore,
  The whiles his nets were drying on the sand:
  Into the same she leapt, and with the ore
  Did thrust the shallop from the floting strand:
So safetie found at sea, which she found not at land.

The Monster ready on the pray to sease,
  Was of his forward hope deceiued quight;
  Ne durst assay to wade the perlous seas,
  But greedily long gaping at the sight,
  At last in vaine was forst to turne his flight,
  And tell the idle tidings to his Dame:
  Yet to auenge his deuilish despight,
  He set vpon her Palfrey tired lame,
And slew him cruelly, ere any reskew came.

And after hauing him embowelled,
  To fill his hellish gorge, it chaunst a knight
  To passe that way, as forth he trauelled;
  It was a goodly Swaine, and of great might,
  As euer man that bloudy field did fight;
  But in vaine sheows, that wont yong knights bewitch,
  And courtly seruices tooke no delight,
  But rather ioyd to be; then seemen sich:
For both to be and seeme to him was labour lich.

It was to weete the good Sir *Satyrane*,
  That raungd abroad to seeke aduentures wilde,
  As was his wont in forrest, and in plaine;
  He was all armd in rugged steele vnfilde,
  As in the smoky forge it was compilde,
  And in his Scutchin bore a Satyres hed:
  He comming present, where the Monster vilde
  Vpon that milke-white Palfreyes carkas fed,
Vnto his reskew ran, and greedily him sped.

xxix 2 bellish *1596*

There well perceiu'd he, that it was the horse,　　xxxi
　　Whereon faire *Florimell* was wont to ride,
　　That of that feend was rent without remorse:
　　Much feared he, least ought did ill betide
　　To that faire Mayd, the flowre of womens pride;
　　For her he dearely loued, and in all
　　His famous conquests highly magnifide:
　　Besides her golden girdle, which did fall
From her in flight, he found, that did him sore apall.

Full of sad feare, and doubtfull agony,　　xxxii
　　Fiercely he flew vpon that wicked feend,
　　And with huge strokes, and cruell battery
　　Him forst to leaue his pray, for to attend
　　Him selfe from deadly daunger to defend:
　　Full many wounds in his corrupted flesh
　　He did engraue, and muchell bloud did spend,
　　Yet might not do him dye, but aye more fresh
And fierce he still appeard, the more he did him thresh.

He wist not, how him to despoile of life,　　xxxiii
　　Ne how to win the wished victory,
　　Sith him he saw still stronger grow through strife,
　　And him selfe weaker through infirmity;
　　Greatly he grew enrag'd, and furiously
　　Hurling his sword away, he lightly lept
　　Vpon the beast, that with great cruelty
　　Rored, and raged to be vnder-kept:
Yet he perforce him held, and strokes vpon him hept.

As he that striues to stop a suddein flood,　　xxxiv
　　And in strong banckes his violence enclose,
　　Forceth it swell aboue his wonted mood,
　　And largely ouerflow the fruitfull plaine,
　　That all the countrey seemes to be a Maine,
　　And the rich furrowes flote, all quite fordonne:
　　The wofull husbandman doth lowd complaine,
　　To see his whole yeares labour lost so soone,
For which to God he made so many an idle boone.

　　xxxiv 2 enclose] containe *MS. corr. in Malone 615.*　　*But cf.* III vi
40 l. 6 *&c.*

So him he held, and did through might amate: xxxv
   So long he held him, and him bet so long,
   That at the last his fiercenesse gan abate,
   And meekely stoup vnto the victour strong:
   Who to auenge the implacable wrong,
   Which he supposed donne to *Florimell*,
   Sought by all meanes his dolour to prolong,
   Sith dint of steele his carcas could not quell:
His maker with her charmes had framed him so well.

The golden ribband, which that virgin wore   xxxvi
   About her sclender wast, he tooke in hand,
   And with it bound the beast, that lowd did rore
   For great despight of that vnwonted band,
   Yet dared not his victour to withstand,
   But trembled like a lambe, fled from the pray,
   And all the way him followd on the strand,
   As he had long bene learned to obay;
Yet neuer learned he such seruice, till that day.

Thus as he led the Beast along the way,   xxxvii
   He spide far off a mighty Giauntesse,
   Fast flying on a Courser dapled gray,
   From a bold knight, that with great hardinesse
   Her hard pursewd, and sought for to suppresse;
   She bore before her lap a dolefull Squire,
   Lying athwart her horse in great distresse,
   Fast bounden hand and foote with cords of wire,
Whom she did meane to make the thrall of her desire.

Which whenas *Satyrane* beheld, in hast   xxxviii
   He left his captiue Beast at liberty,
   And crost the nearest way, by which he cast
   Her to encounter, ere she passed by:
   But she the way shund nathemore for thy,
   But forward gallopt fast; which when he spyde,
   His mighty speare he couched warily,
   And at her ran: she hauing him descryde,
Her selfe to fight addrest, and threw her lode aside.

xxxvi 2 slender *1609*

Like as a Goshauke, that in foote doth beare   xxxix
  A trembling Culuer, hauing spide on hight
  An Egle, that with plumy wings doth sheare
  The subtile ayre, stouping with all his might,
  The quarrey throwes to ground with fell despight,
  And to the battell doth her selfe prepare:
  So ran the Geauntesse vnto the fight;
  Her firie eyes with furious sparkes did stare,
And with blasphemous bannes high God in peeces tare.

She caught in hand an huge great yron mace,   xl
  Wherewith she many had of life depriued,
  But ere the stroke could seize his aymed place,
  His speare amids her sun-broad shield arriued;
  Yet nathemore the steele a sunder riued,
  All were the beame in bignesse like a mast,
  Ne her out of the stedfast sadle driued,
  But glauncing on the tempred mettall, brast
In thousand shiuers, and so forth beside her past.

Her Steed did stagger with that puissaunt strooke;   xli
  But she no more was moued with that might,
  Then it had lighted on an aged Oke;
  Or on the marble Pillour, that is pight
  Vpon the top of Mount *Olympus* hight,
  For the braue youthly Champions to assay,
  With burning charet wheeles it nigh to smite:
  But who that smites it, mars his ioyous play,
And is the spectacle of ruinous decay.

Yet therewith sore enrag'd, with sterne regard   xlii
  Her dreadfull weapon she to him addrest,
  Which on his helmet martelled so hard,
  That made him low incline his lofty crest,
  And bowd his battred visour to his brest:
  Wherewith he was so stund, that he n'ote ryde,
  But reeled to and fro from East to West:
  Which when his cruell enimy espyde,
She lightly vnto him adioyned side to syde;

xlii 6 he was] she was *1590*: *corr. to* hee *F. E.*   stuned *1590*: *corr. F. E.*

And on his collar laying puissant hand,   xliii
   Out of his wauering seat him pluckt perforse,
   Perforse him pluckt, vnable to withstand,
   Or helpe himselfe, and laying thwart her horse,
   In loathly wise like to a carion corse,
   She bore him fast away. Which when the knight,
   That her pursewed, saw, with great remorse
   He neare was touched in his noble spright,
And gan encrease his speed, as she encreast her flight.

Whom when as nigh approching she espyde,   xliv
   She threw away her burden angrily;
   For she list not the battell to abide,
   But made her selfe more light, away to fly:
   Yet her the hardy knight pursewd so nye,
   That almost in the backe he oft her strake:
   But still when him at hand she did espy,
   She turnd, and semblaunce of faire fight did make;
But when he stayd, to flight againe she did her take.

By this the good Sir *Satyrane* gan wake   xlv
   Out of his dreame, that did him long entraunce,
   And seeing none in place, he gan to make
   Exceeding mone, and curst that cruell chaunce,
   Which reft from him so faire a cheuisaunce:
   At length he spide, whereas that wofull Squire,
   Whom he had reskewed from captiuaunce
   Of his strong foe, lay tombled in the myre,
Vnable to arise, or foot or hand to styre.

To whom approching, well he mote perceiue   xlvi
   In that foule plight a comely personage,
   And louely face, made fit for to deceiue
   Fraile Ladies hart with loues consuming rage,
   Now in the blossome of his freshest age :
   He reard him vp, and loosd his yron bands,
   And after gan inquire his parentage,
   And how he fell into that Gyaunts hands,
And who that was, which chaced her along the lands.

xliii 7 saw *1590, 1596*   remorse, *1590, 1596*   8 neare] were *1590* : *corr.*
to nere *F. E.*   xlv 1 the *om. 1596, 1609*   wake] awake *1609*
5 him from *1609*   xlvi 8 that] the *1590*

Then trembling yet through feare, the Squire bespake,   xlvii
 That Geauntesse *Argante* is behight,
 A daughter of the *Titans* which did make
 Warre against heauen, and heaped hils on hight,
 To scale the skyes, and put *Ioue* from his right:
 Her sire *Typhœus* was, who mad through merth,
 And drunke with bloud of men, slaine by his might,
 Through incest, her of his owne mother Earth
Whilome begot, being but halfe twin of that berth.

For at that berth another Babe she bore,   xlviii
 To weet the mighty *Ollyphant*, that wrought
 Great wreake to many errant knights of yore,
 And many hath to foule confusion brought.
 These twinnes, men say, (a thing far passing thought)
 Whiles in their mothers wombe enclosd they were,
 Ere they into the lightsome world were brought,
 In fleshly lust were mingled both yfere,
And in that monstrous wise did to the world appere.

So liu'd they euer after in like sin,   xlix
 Gainst natures law, and good behauioure :
 But greatest shame was to that maiden twin,
 Who not content so fowly to deuoure
 Her natiue flesh, and staine her brothers bowre,
 Did wallow in all other fleshly myre,
 And suffred beasts her body to deflowre :
 So whot she burned in that lustfull fyre,
Yet all that might not slake her sensuall desyre.

But ouer all the countrey she did raunge,   l
 To seeke young men, to quench her flaming thrust,
 And feed her fancy with delightfull chaunge :
 Whom so she fittest finds to serue her lust,
 Through her maine strength, in which she most doth trust,
 She with her brings into a secret Ile,
 Where in eternall bondage dye he must,
 Or be the vassall of her pleasures vile,
And in all shamefull sort him selfe with her defile.

Me seely wretch she so at vauntage caught,   li
    After she long in waite for me did lye,
    And meant vnto her prison to haue brought,
    Her lothsome pleasure there to satisfye;
    That thousand deathes me leuer were to dye,
    Then breake the vow, that to faire *Columbell*
    I plighted haue, and yet keepe stedfastly:
    As for my name, it mistreth not to tell;
Call me the *Squyre of Dames*, that me beseemeth well.

But that bold knight, whom ye pursuing saw   lii
    That Geauntesse, is not such, as she seemed,
    But a faire virgin, that in martiall law,
    And deedes of armes aboue all Dames is deemed,
    And aboue many knights is eke esteemed,
    For her great worth; She *Palladine* is hight:
    She you from death, you me from dread redeemed.
    Ne any may that Monster match in fight,
But she, or such as she, that is so chaste a wight.

Her well beseemes that Quest (quoth *Satyrane*)   liii
    But read, thou *Squyre of Dames*, what vow is this,
    Which thou vpon thy selfe hast lately ta'ne?
    That shall I you recount (quoth he) ywis,
    So be ye pleasd to pardon all amis.
    That gentle Lady, whom I loue and serue,
    After long suit and weary seruicis,
    Did aske me, how I could her loue deserue,
And how she might be sure, that I would neuer swerue.

I glad by any meanes her grace to gaine,   liv
    Bad her commaund my life to saue, or spill.
    Eftsoones she bad me, with incessaunt paine
    To wander through the world abroad at will,
    And euery where, where with my power or skill
    I might do seruice vnto gentle Dames,
    That I the same should faithfully fulfill,
    And at the twelue monethes end should bring their names
And pledges; as the spoiles of my victorious games.

lii 4 is] it *1590*

So well I to faire Ladies seruice did,   lv
   And found such fauour in their louing hartes,
   That ere the yeare his course had compassid,
   Three hundred pledges for my good desartes,
   And thrise three hundred thanks for my good partes
   I with me brought, and did to her present:
   Which when she saw, more bent to eke my smartes,
   Then to reward my trusty true intent,
She gan for me deuise a grieuous punishment.

To weet, that I my trauell should resume,   lvi
   And with like labour walke the world around,
   Ne euer to her presence should presume,
   Till I so many other Dames had found,
   The which, for all the suit I could propound,
   Would me refuse their pledges to afford,
   But did abide for euer chast and sound.
   Ah gentle Squire (quoth he) tell at one word,
How many foundst thou such to put in thy record?

In deed Sir knight (said he) one word may tell   lvii
   All, that I euer found so wisely stayd;
   For onely three they were disposd so well,
   And yet three yeares I now abroad haue strayd,
   To find them out. Mote I (then laughing sayd
   The knight) inquire of thee, what were those three,
   The which thy proffred curtesie denayd?
   Or ill they seemed sure auizd to bee,
Or brutishly brought vp, that neu'r did fashions see.

The first which then refused me (said hee)   lviii
   Certes was but a common Courtisane,
   Yet flat refusd to haue a do with mee,
   Because I could not giue her many a Iane.
   (Thereat full hartely laughed *Satyrane*)
   The second was an holy Nunne to chose,
   Which would not let me be her Chappellane,
   Because she knew, she said, I would disclose
Her counsell, if she should her trust in me repose.

The third a Damzell was of low degree,   lix
   Whom I in countrey cottage found by chaunce;
   Full little weened I, that chastitee
   Had lodging in so meane a maintenaunce,
   Yet was she faire, and in her countenance
   Dwelt simple truth in seemely fashion.
   Long thus I woo'd her with dew obseruance,
   In hope vnto my pleasure to haue won;
But was as farre at last, as when I first begon.

Safe her, I neuer any woman found,   lx
   That chastity did for it selfe embrace,
   But were for other causes firme and sound;
   Either for want of handsome time and place,
   Or else for feare of shame and fowle disgrace.
   Thus am I hopelesse euer to attaine
   My Ladies loue, in such a desperate case,
   But all my dayes am like to wast in vaine,
Seeking to match the chaste with th'vnchaste Ladies traine.

Perdy, (said *Satyrane*) thou *Squire of Dames*,   lxi
   Great labour fondly hast thou hent in hand,
   To get small thankes, and therewith many blames,
   That may emongst *Alcides* labours stand.
   Thence backe returning to the former land,
   Where late he left the Beast, he ouercame,
   He found him not; for he had broke his band,
   And was return'd againe vnto his Dame,
To tell what tydings of faire *Florimell* became.

        lxi 4 emongst] among *1609*   5 backe] bace *1590*

Cant. VIII.

*The Witch creates a snowy Lady,
like to Florimell,
Who wrongd by Carle ·by Proteus sau'd,
is sought by Paridell.*

SO oft as I this history record,   i
  My hart doth melt with meere compassion,
  To thinke, how causelesse of her owne accord
  This gentle Damzell, whom I write vpon,
  Should plonged be in such affliction,
  Without all hope of comfort or reliefe,
  That sure I weene, the hardest hart of stone,
  Would hardly find to aggrauate her griefe;
For misery craues rather mercie, then repriefe.

But that accursed Hag, her hostesse late,   ii
  Had so enranckled her malitious hart,
  That she desyrd th'abridgement of her fate,
  Or long enlargement of her painefull smart.
  Now when the Beast, which by her wicked art
  Late forth she sent, she backe returning spyde,
  Tyde with her broken girdle, it a part
  Of her rich spoyles, whom he had earst destroyd,
She weend, and wondrous gladnesse to her hart applyde.

And with it running hast'ly to her sonne,   iii
  Thought with that sight him much to haue reliued;
  Who thereby deeming sure the thing as donne,
  His former griefe with furie fresh reuiued,
  Much more then earst, and would haue algates riued
  The hart out of his brest: for sith her ded
  He surely dempt, himselfe he thought depriued
  Quite of all hope, wherewith he long had fed
His foolish maladie, and long time had misled.

     ii 7 broken] golden *1590*   iii 2 relieued *1609*

With thought whereof, exceeding mad he grew,   iv
  And in his rage his mother would haue slaine,
  Had she not fled into a secret mew,
  Where she was wont her Sprights to entertaine
  The maisters of her art: there was she faine
  To call them all in order to her ayde,
  And them coniure vpon eternall paine,
  To counsell her so carefully dismayd,
How she might heale her sonne, whose senses were decayd.

By their aduise, and her owne wicked wit,   v
  She there deuiz'd a wondrous worke to frame,
  Whose like on earth was neuer framed yit,
  That euen Nature selfe enuide the same,
  And grudg'd to see the counterfet should shame
  The thing it selfe.   In hand she boldly tooke
  To make another like the former Dame,
  Another *Florimell*, in shape and looke
So liuely and so like, that many it mistooke.

The substance, whereof she the bodie made,   vi
  Was purest snow in massie mould congeald,
  Which she had gathered in a shadie glade
  Of the *Riphœan* hils, to her reueald
  By errant Sprights, but from all men conceald:
  The same she tempred with fine Mercury,
  And virgin wex, that neuer yet was seald,
  And mingled them with perfect vermily,
That like a liuely sanguine it seem'd to the eye.

In stead of eyes two burning lampes she set   vii
  In siluer sockets, shyning like the skyes,
  And a quicke mouing Spirit did arret
  To stirre and roll them, like a womans eyes;
  In stead of yellow lockes she did deuise,
  With golden wyre to weaue her curled head;
  Yet golden wyre was not so yellow thrise
  As *Florimells* faire haire: and in the stead
Of life, she put a Spright to rule the carkasse dead.

A wicked Spright yfraught with fawning guile,   viii
  And faire resemblance aboue all the rest,
  Which with the Prince of Darknesse fell somewhile,
  From heauens blisse and euerlasting rest;
  Him needed not instruct, which way were best
  Himselfe to fashion likest *Florimell,*
  Ne how to speake, ne how to vse his gest,
  For he in counterfeisance did excell,
And all the wyles of wemens wits knew passing well.

Him shaped thus, she deckt in garments gay,   ix
  Which *Florimell* had left behind her late,
  That who so then her saw, would surely say,
  It was her selfe, whom it did imitate,
  Or fairer then her selfe, if ought algate
  Might fairer be. And then she forth her brought
  Vnto her sonne, that lay in feeble state;
  Who seeing her gan streight vpstart, and thought
She was the Lady selfe, whom he so long had sought.

Tho fast her clipping twixt his armes twaine,   x
  Extremely ioyed in so happie sight,
  And soone forgot his former sickly paine;
  But she, the more to seeme such as she hight,
  Coyly rebutted his embracement light;
  Yet still with gentle countenaunce retained,
  Enough to hold a foole in vaine delight:
  Him long she so with shadowes entertained,
As her Creatresse had in charge to her ordained.

Till on a day, as he disposed was   xi
  To walke the woods with that his Idole faire,
  Her to disport, and idle time to pas,
  In th'open freshnesse of the gentle aire,
  A knight that way there chaunced to repaire;
  Yet knight he was not, but a boastfull swaine,
  That deedes of armes had euer in despaire,
  Proud *Braggadocchio,* that in vaunting vaine
His glory did repose, and credit did maintaine.

viii 3 lomewhyle *1590*: lomewhile *1596*   ix 9 whom] who *1590, 1596*
     x 6 countenaunce] countenant *1596*   xi 6 he *om. 1596*
        G g 2

He seeing with that Chorle so faire a wight,   xii
  Decked with many a costly ornament,
  Much merueiled thereat, as well he might,
  And thought that match a fowle disparagement:
  His bloudie speare eftsoones he boldly bent
  Against the silly clowne, who dead through feare,
  Fell streight to ground in great astonishment;
  Villein (said he) this Ladie is my deare,
Dy, if thou it gainesay: I will away her beare.

The fearefull Chorle durst not gainesay, nor dooe,   xiii
  But trembling stood, and yielded him the pray;
  Who finding litle leasure her to wooe,
  On *Tromparts* steed her mounted without stay,
  And without reskew led her quite away.
  Proud man himselfe then *Braggadocchio* deemed,
  And next to none, after that happie day,
  Being possessed of that spoyle, which seemed
The fairest wight on ground, and most of men esteemed.

But when he saw himselfe free from poursute,   xiv
  He gan make gentle purpose to his Dame,
  With termes of loue and lewdnesse dissolute;
  For he could well his glozing speaches frame
  To such vaine vses, that him best became:
  But she thereto would lend but light regard,
  As seeming sory, that she euer came
  Into his powre, that vsed her so hard,
To reaue her honor, which she more then life prefard.

Thus as they two of kindnesse treated long,   xv
  There them by chaunce encountred on the way
  An armed knight, vpon a courser strong,
  Whose trampling feet vpon the hollow lay
  Seemed to thunder, and did nigh affray
  That Capons courage: yet he looked grim,
  And fain'd to cheare his Ladie in dismay;
  Who seem'd for feare to quake in euery lim,
And her to saue from outrage, meekely prayed him.

Fiercely that stranger forward came, and nigh   xvi
  Approching, with bold words and bitter threat,
  Bad that same boaster, as he mote, on high
  To leaue to him that Lady for excheat,
  Or bide him battell without further treat.
  That challenge did too peremptory seeme,
  And fild his senses with abashment great;
  Yet seeing nigh him ieopardy extreme,
He it dissembled well, and light seem'd to esteeme.

Saying, Thou foolish knight, that weenst with words   xvii
  To steale away, that I with blowes hauc wonne,
  And brought throgh points of many perilous swords:
  But if thee list to see thy Courser ronne,
  Or proue thy selfe, this sad encounter shonne,
  And seeke else without hazard of thy hed.
  At those proud words that other knight begonne
  To wexe exceeding wroth, and him ared
To turne his steede about, or sure he should be ded.

Sith then (said *Braggadocchio*) needes thou wilt   xviii
  Thy dayes abridge, through proofe of puissance,
  Turne we our steedes, that both in equall tilt
  May meet againe, and each take happie chance.
  This said, they both a furlongs mountenance
  Retyrd their steeds, to ronne in euen race:
  But *Braggadocchio* with his bloudie lance
  Once hauing turnd, no more returnd his face,
But left his loue to losse, and fled himselfe apace.

The knight him seeing fly, had no regard   xix
  Him to poursew, but to the Ladie rode,
  And hauing her from *Trompart* lightly reard,
  Vpon his Courser set the louely lode,
  And with her fled away without abode.
  Well weened he, that fairest *Florimell*
  It was, with whom in company he yode,
  And so her selfe did alwaies to him tell;
So made him thinke him selfe in heauen, that was in hell.

But *Florimell* her selfe was farre away,   xx
  Driuen to great distresse by Fortune straunge,
  And taught the carefull Mariner to play,
  Sith late mischaunce had her compeld to chaunge
  The land for sea, at randon there to raunge:
  Yet there that cruell Queene auengeresse,
  Not satisfide so farre her to estraunge
  From courtly blisse and wonted happinesse,
Did heape on her new waues of weary wretchednesse.

For being fled into the fishers bote,   xxi
  For refuge from the Monsters crueltie,
  Long so she on the mightie maine did flote,
  And with the tide droue forward careleslie;
  For th'aire was milde, and cleared was the skie,
  And all his windes *Dan Aeolus* did keepe,
  From stirring vp their stormy enmitie,
  As pittying to see her waile and weepe;
But all the while the fisher did securely sleepe.

At last when droncke with drowsinesse, he woke,   xxii
  And saw his drouer driue along the streame,
  He was dismayd, and thrise his breast he stroke,
  For maruell of that accident extreame;
  But when he saw that blazing beauties beame,
  Which with rare light his bote did beautifie,
  He marueild more, and thought he yet did dreame
  Not well awakt, or that some extasie
Assotted had his sense, or dazed was his eie.

But when her well auizing, he perceiued   xxiii
  To be no vision, nor fantasticke sight,
  Great comfort of her presence he conceiued,
  And felt in his old courage new delight
  To gin awake, and stirre his frozen spright:
  Tho rudely askt her, how she thither came.
  Ah (said she) father, I note read aright,
  What hard misfortune brought me to the same;
Yet am I glad that here I now in safety am.

  xxii 5 saw, *1590, 1596*   xxiii 8 the] this *1590*   9 ame. 1590

But thou good man, sith farre in sea we bee,   xxiv
   And the great waters gin apace to swell,
   That now no more we can the maine-land see,
   Haue care, I pray, to guide the cock-bote well,
   Least worse on sea then vs on land befell.
   Thereat th'old man did nought but fondly grin,
   And said, his boat the way could wisely tell:
   But his deceiptfull eyes did neuer lin,
To looke on her faire face, and marke her snowy skin.

The sight whereof in his congealed flesh,   xxv
   Infixt such secret sting of greedy lust,
   That the drie withered stocke it gan refresh,
   And kindled heat, that soone in flame forth brust:
   The driest wood is soonest burnt to dust.
   Rudely to her he lept, and his rough hand
   Where ill became him, rashly would haue thrust,
   But she with angry scorne him did withstond,
And shamefully reproued for his rudenesse fond.

But he, that neuer good nor maners knew,   xxvi
   Her sharpe rebuke full litle did esteeme;
   Hard is to teach an old horse amble trew.
   The inward smoke, that did before but steeme,
   Broke into open fire and rage extreme,
   And now he strength gan adde vnto his will,
   Forcing to due, that did him fowle misseeme:
   Beastly he threw her downe, ne car'd to spill
Her garments gay with scales of fish, that all did fill.

The silly virgin stroue him to withstand,   xxvii
   All that she might, and him in vaine reuild:
   She struggled strongly both with foot and hand,
   To saue her honor from that villaine vild,
   And cride to heauen, from humane helpe exild.
   O ye braue knights, that boast this Ladies loue,
   Where be ye now, when she is nigh defild
   Of filthy wretch? well may shee you reproue
Of falshood or of slouth, when most it may behoue.

But if that thou, Sir *Satyran*, didst weete,   xxviii
  Or thou, Sir *Peridure*, her sorie state,
  How soone would yee assemble many a fleete,
  To fetch from sea, that ye at land lost late;
  Towres, Cities, Kingdomes ye would ruinate,
  In your auengement and dispiteous rage,
  Ne ought your burning fury mote abate;
  But if Sir *Calidore* could it presage,
No liuing creature could his cruelty asswage.

But sith that none of all her knights is nye,   xxix
  See how the heauens of voluntary grace,
  And soueraine fauour towards chastity,
  Doe succour send to her distressed cace:
  So much high God doth innocence embrace.
  It fortuned, whilest thus she stifly stroue,
  And the wide sea importuned long space
  With shrilling shriekes, *Proteus* abroad did roue,
Along the fomy waues driuing his finny droue.

Proteus is Shepheard of the seas of yore,   xxx
  And hath the charge of *Neptunes* mightie heard;
  An aged sire with head all frory hore,
  And sprinckled frost vpon his deawy beard:
  Who when those pittifull outcries he heard,
  Through all the seas so ruefully resound,
  His charet swift in haste he thither steard,
  Which with a teeme of scaly *Phocas* bound
Was drawne vpon the waues, that fomed him around.

And comming to that Fishers wandring bote,   xxxi
  That went at will, withouten carde or sayle,
  He therein saw that yrkesome sight, which smote
  Deepe indignation and compassion frayle
  Into his hart attonce: streight did he hayle
  The greedy villein from his hoped pray,
  Of which he now did very litle fayle,
  And with his staffe, that driues his Heard astray,
Him bet so sore, that life and sense did much dismay.

xxx 3 frory] frowy *1590, 1596*

The whiles the pitteous Ladie vp did ryse,   xxxii
  Ruffled and fowly raid with filthy soyle,
  And blubbred face with teares of her faire eyes:
  Her heart nigh broken was with weary toyle,
  To saue her selfe from that outrageous spoyle,
  But when she looked vp, to weet, what wight
  Had her from so infamous fact assoyld,
  For shame, but more for feare of his grim sight,
Downe in her lap she hid her face, and loudly shright.

Her selfe not saued yet from daunger dred   xxxiii
  She thought, but chaung'd from one to other feare;
  Like as a fearefull Partridge, that is fled
  From the sharpe Hauke, which her attached neare,
  And fals to ground, to seeke for succour theare,
  Whereas the hungry Spaniels she does spy,
  With greedy iawes her readie for to teare;
  In such distresse and sad perplexity
Was *Florimell*, when *Proteus* she did see thereby.

But he endeuoured with speeches milde   xxxiv
  Her to recomfort, and accourage bold,
  Bidding her feare no more her foeman vilde,
  Nor doubt himselfe; and who he was, her told.
  Yet all that could not from affright her hold,
  Ne to recomfort her at all preuayld;
  For her faint heart was with the frozen cold
  Benumbd so inly, that her wits nigh fayld,
And all her senses with abashment quite were quayld.

Her vp betwixt his rugged hands he reard,   xxxv
  And with his frory lips full softly kist,
  Whiles the cold ysickles from his rough beard,
  Dropped adowne vpon her yuorie brest:
  Yet he himselfe so busily addrest,
  That her out of astonishment he wrought,
  And out of that same fishers filthy nest
  Remouing her, into his charet brought,
And there with many gentle termes her faire besought.

                xxxiii 9 thereby] her by *1590*

But that old leachour, which with bold assault   xxxvi
   That beautie durst presume to violate,
   He cast to punish for his hainous fault;
   Then tooke he him yet trembling sith of late,
   And tyde behind his charet, to aggrate
   The virgin, whom he had abusde so sore:
   So drag'd him through the waues in scornefull state,
   And after cast him vp, vpon the shore;
But *Florimell* with him vnto his bowre he bore.

His bowre is in the bottome of the maine,   xxxvii
   Vnder a mightie rocke, gainst which do raue
   The roaring billowes in their proud disdaine,
   That with the angry working of the waue,
   Therein is eaten out an hollow caue,
   That seemes rough Masons hand with engines keene
   Had long while laboured it to engraue:
   There was his wonne, ne liuing wight was seene,
Saue one old *Nymph*, hight *Panope* to keepe it cleane.

Thither he brought the sory *Florimell*,   xxxviii
   And entertained her the best he might
   And *Panope* her entertaind eke well,
   As an immortall mote a mortall wight,
   To winne her liking vnto his delight:
   With flattering words he sweetly wooed her,
   And offered faire gifts t'allure her sight,
   But she both offers and the offerer
Despysde, and all the fawning of the flatterer.

Daily he tempted her with this or that,   xxxix
   And neuer suffred her to be at rest:
   But euermore she him refused flat,
   And all his fained kindnesse did detest,
   So firmely she had sealed vp her brest.
   Sometimes he boasted, that a God he hight:
   But she a mortall creature loued best:
   Then he would make himselfe a mortall wight;
But then she said she lou'd none, but a Faerie knight.

xxxvii 9 hight] high *1590*

Then like a Faerie knight himselfe he drest; xl
  For euery shape on him he could endew:
  Then like a king he was to her exprest,
  And offred kingdomes vnto her in vew,
  To be his Leman and his Ladie trew:
  But when all this he nothing saw preuaile,
  With harder meanes he cast her to subdew,
  And with sharpe threates her often did assaile,
So thinking for to make her stubborne courage quaile.

To dreadfull shapes he did himselfe transforme, xli
  Now like a Gyant, now like to a feend,
  Then like a Centaure, then like to a storme,
  Raging within the waues: thereby he weend
  Her will to win vnto his wished end.
  But when with feare, nor fauour, nor with all
  He else could doe, he saw himselfe esteemd,
  Downe in a Dongeon deepe he let her fall,
And threatned there to make her his eternall thrall.

Eternall thraldome was to her more liefe, xlii
  Then losse of chastitie, or chaunge of loue:
  Die had she rather in tormenting griefe,
  Then any should of falsenesse her reproue,
  Or loosenesse, that she lightly did remoue.
  Most vertuous virgin, glory be thy mee ¹,
  And crowne of heauenly praise with Saints aboue,
  Where most sweet hymmes of this thy famous deed
Are still emongst them song, that far my rymes exceed.

Fit song of Angels caroled to bee; xliii
  But yet what so my feeble Muse can frame,
  Shall be t'aduance thy goodly chastitee,
  And to enroll thy memorable name,
  In th'heart of euery honourable Dame,
  That they thy vertuous deedes may imitate,
  And be partakers of thy endlesse fame.
  It yrkes me, leaue thee in this wofull state,
To tell of *Satyrane,* where I him left of late.

xli 5 end.] eend. 1590

Who hauing ended with that *Squire of Dames*   xliv
  A long discourse of his aduentures vaine,
  The which himselfe, then Ladies more defames,
  And finding not th' *Hyena* to be slaine,
  With that same *Squire*, returned backe againe
  To his first way.   And as they forward went,
  They spyde a knight faire pricking on the plaine,
  As if he were on some aduenture bent,
And in his port appeared manly hardiment.

Sir *Satyrane* him towards did addresse,   xlv
  To weet, what wight he was, and what his quest:
  And comming nigh, eftsoones he gan to gesse
  Both by the burning hart, which on his brest
  He bare, and by the colours in his crest,
  That *Paridell* it was.   Tho to him yode,
  And him saluting, as beseemed best,
  Gan first inquire of tydings farre abrode;
And afterwardes, on what aduenture now he rode.

Who thereto answering, said; The tydings bad,   xlvi
  Which now in Faerie court all men do tell,
  Which turned hath great mirth, to mourning sad,
  Is the late ruine of proud *Marinell*,
  And suddein parture of faire *Florimell*,
  To find him forth: and after her are gone
  All the braue knights, that doen in armes excell,
  To sauegard her, ywandred all alone;
Emongst the rest my lot (vnworthy) is to be one.

Ah gentle knight (said then Sir *Satyrane*)   xlvii
  Thy labour all is lost, I greatly dread,
  That hast a thanklesse seruice on thee ta'ne,
  And offrest sacrifice vnto the dead:
  For dead, I surely doubt, thou maist aread
  Henceforth for euer *Florimell* to be,
  That all the noble knights of *Maydenhead*,
  Which her ador'd, may sore repent with me,
And all faire Ladies may for euer sory be.

    xliv 2 his] hir *1609*   xlv 3 ghesse *1609*   xlvi 9 vnworthy' *1590*

Which words when *Paridell* had heard, his hew   xlviii
  Gan greatly chaunge, and seem'd dismayd to bee;
  Then said, Faire Sir, how may I weene it trew,
  That ye doe tell in such vncertaintee?
  Or speake ye of report, or did ye see
  Iust cause of dread, that makes ye doubt so sore?
  For perdie else how mote it euer bee,
  That euer hand should dare for to engore
Her noble bloud? the heauens such crueltie abhore.

These eyes did see, that they will euer rew   xlix
  T'haue seene, (quoth he) when as a monstrous beast
  The Palfrey, whereon she did trauell, slew,
  And of his bowels made his bloudie feast:
  Which speaking token sheweth at the least
  Her certaine losse, if not her sure decay:
  Besides, that more suspition encreast,
  I found her golden girdle cast astray,
Distaynd with durt and bloud, as relique of the pray.

Aye me, (said *Paridell*) the signes be sad,   l
  And but God turne the same to good soothsay,
  That Ladies safetie is sore to be drad:
  Yet will I not forsake my forward way,
  Till triall doe more certaine truth bewray.
  Faire Sir (quoth he) well may it you succeed,
  Ne long shall *Satyrane* behind you stay,
  But to the rest, which in this Quest proceed
My labour adde, and be partaker of their speed.

Ye noble knights (said then the *Squire of Dames*)   li
  Well may ye speed in so praiseworthy paine:
  But sith the Sunne now ginnes to slake his beames,
  In deawy vapours of the westerne maine,
  And lose the teme out of his weary waine,
  Mote not mislike you also to abate
  Your zealous hast, till morrow next againe
  Both light of heauen, and strength of men relate:
Which if ye please, to yonder castle turne your gate.

      xlix 2 To haue *1590*   4 his bloudie] a bloudy *1609*

That counsell pleased well ; so all yfere   lii
    Forth marched to a Castle them before,
    Where soone arriuing, they restrained were
    Of readie entrance, which ought euermore
    To errant knights be commun : wondrous sore
    Thereat displeasd they were, till that young Squire
    Gan them informe the cause, why that same dore
    Was shut to all, which lodging did desire:
The which to let you weet, will further time require.

Cant. IX.

Malbecco will no straunge knights host,
*   For peeuish gealosie:*
Paridell giusts with Britomart:
*   Both shew their auncestrie.*

R Edoubted knights, and honorable Dames,   i
    To whom I leuell all my labours end,
    Right sore I feare, least with vnworthy blames
    This odious argument my rimes should shend,
    Or ought your goodly patience offend,
    Whiles of a wanton Lady I do write,
    Which with her loose incontinence doth blend
    The shyning glory of your soueraigne light,
And knighthood fowle defaced by a faithlesse knight.

But neuer let th'ensample of the bad   ii
    Offend the good: for good by paragone
    Of euill, may more notably be rad,
    As white seemes fairer, macht with blacke attone ;
    Ne all are shamed by the fault of one:
    For lo in heauen, whereas all goodnesse is,
    Emongst the Angels, a whole legione
    Of wicked Sprights did fall from happy blis;
What wonder then, if one of women all did mis ?

lii 5 commune *1590*   ii 4 attonce *1590*

Then listen Lordings, if ye list to weet   iii
    The cause, why *Satyrane* and *Paridell*
    Mote not be entertaynd, as seemed meet,
    Into that Castle (as that Squire does tell.)
    Therein a cancred crabbed Carle does dwell,
    That has no skill of Court nor courtesie,
    Ne cares, what men say of him ill or well;
    For all his dayes he drownes in priuitie,
Yet has full large to liue, and spend at libertie.

But all his mind is set on mucky pelfe,   iv
    To hoord vp heapes of euill gotten masse,
    For which he others wrongs, and wreckes himselfe;
    Yet is he lincked to a louely lasse,
    Whose beauty doth her bounty far surpasse,
    The which to him both far vnequall yeares,
    And also far vnlike conditions has;
    For she does ioy to play emongst her peares,
And to be free from hard restraint and gealous feares.

But he is old, and withered like hay,   v
    Vnfit faire Ladies seruice to supply;
    The priuie guilt whereof makes him alway
    Suspect her truth, and keepe continuall spy
    Vpon her with his other blincked eye;
    Ne suffreth he resort of liuing wight
    Approch to her, ne keepe her company,
    But in close bowre her mewes from all mens sight,
Depriu'd of kindly ioy and naturall delight.

Malbecco he, and *Hellenore* she hight,   vi
    Vnfitly yokt together in one teeme,
    That is the cause, why neuer any knight
    Is suffred here to enter, but he seeme
    Such, as no doubt of him he neede misdeeme.
    Thereat Sir *Satyrane* gan smile, and say;
    Extremely mad the man I surely deeme,
    That weenes with watch and hard restraint to stay
A womans will, which is disposd to go astray.

In vaine he feares that, which he cannot shonne: vii
  For who wotes not, that womans subtiltyes
  Can guilen *Argus*, when she list misdonne?
  It is not yron bandes, nor hundred eyes,
  Nor brasen walls, nor many wakefull spyes,
  That can withhold her wilfull wandring feet;
  But fast good will with gentle curtesyes,
  And timely seruice to her pleasures meet
May her perhaps containe, that else would algates fleet.

Then is he not more mad (said *Paridell*)   viii
  That hath himselfe vnto such seruice sold,
  In dolefull thraldome all his dayes to dwell?
  For sure a foole I do him firmely hold,
  That loues his fetters, though they were of gold.
  But why do we deuise of others ill,
  Whiles thus we suffer this same dotard old,
  To keepe vs out, in scorne of his owne will,
And rather do not ransack all, and him selfe kill?

Nay let vs first (said *Satyrane*) entreat   ix
  The man by gentle meanes, to let vs in,
  And afterwardes affray with cruell threat,
  Ere that we to efforce it do begin:
  Then if all fayle, we will by force it win,
  And eke reward the wretch for his mesprise,
  As may be worthy of his haynous sin.
  That counsell pleasd: then *Paridell* did rise,
And to the Castle gate approcht in quiet wise.

Whereat soft knocking, entrance he desyrd.   x
  The good man selfe, which then the Porter playd,
  Him answered, that all were now retyrd
  Vnto their rest, and all the keyes conuayd
  Vnto their maister, who in bed was layd,
  That none him durst awake out of his dreme;
  And therefore them of patience gently prayd.
  Then *Paridell* began to chaunge his theme,
And threatned him with force and punishment extreme.

But all in vaine; for nought mote him relent,   xi
　And now so long before the wicket fast
　They wayted, that the night was forward spent,
　And the faire welkin fowly ouercast,
　Gan blowen vp a bitter stormy blast,
　With shoure and hayle so horrible and dred,
　That this faire many were compeld at last,
　To fly for succour to a little shed,
The which beside the gate for swine was ordered.

It fortuned, soone after they were gone,   xii
　Another knight, whom tempest thither brought,
　Came to that Castle, and with carnest mone,
　Like as the rest, late entrance deare besought;
　But like so as the rest he prayd for nought,
　For flatly he of entrance was refusd,
　Sorely thereat he was displeasd, and thought
　How to auenge himselfe so sore abusd,
And euermore the Carle of curtesie accusd.

But to auoyde th'intollerable stowre,   xiii
　He was compeld to seeke some refuge neare,
　And to that shed, to shrowd him from the showre,
　He came, which full of guests he found whyleare,
　So as he was not let to enter there:
　Whereat he gan to wex exceeding wroth,
　And swore, that he would lodge with them yfere,
　Or them dislodge, all were they liefe or loth;
And so defide them each, and so defide them both.

Both were full loth to leaue that needfull tent,   xiv
　And both full loth in darkenesse to debate;
　Yet both full liefe him lodging to haue lent,
　And both full liefe his boasting to abate;
　But chiefly *Paridell* his hart did grate,
　To heare him threaten so despightfully,
　As if he did a dogge to kenell rate,
　That durst not barke; and rather had he dy,
Then when he was defide, in coward corner ly.

　　xiii 9 And defide them each *1596* : And them defied each *1609*
　　　　　　　xiv 7 to] in *1590*

Tho hastily remounting to his steed,   xv
  He forth issew'd; like as a boistrous wind,
  Which in th'earthes hollow caues hath long bin hid,
  And shut vp fast within her prisons blind,
  Makes the huge element against her kind
  To moue, and tremble as it were agast,
  Vntill that it an issew forth may find;
  Then forth it breakes, and with his furious blast
Confounds both land and seas, and skyes doth ouercast.

Their steel-hed speares they strongly coucht, and met   xvi
  Together with impetuous rage and forse,
  That with the terrour of their fierce affret,
  They rudely droue to ground both man and horse,
  That each awhile lay like a sencelesse corse.
  But *Paridell* sore brused with the blow,
  Could not arise, the counterchaunge to scorse,
  Till that young Squire him reared from below;
Then drew he his bright sword, and gan about him throw.

But *Satyrane* forth stepping, did them stay   xvii
  And with faire treatie pacifide their ire,
  Then when they were accorded from the fray,
  Against that Castles Lord they gan conspire,
  To heape on him dew vengeaunce for his hire.
  They bene agreed, and to the gates they goe
  To burne the same with vnquenchable fire,
  And that vncurteous Carle their commune foe
To do fowle death to dye, or wrap in grieuous woe.

Malbecco seeing them resolu'd in deed   xviii
  To flame the gates, and hearing them to call
  For fire in earnest, ran with fearefull speed,
  And to them calling from the castle wall,
  Besought them humbly, him to beare with all,
  As ignoraunt of seruants bad abuse,
  And slacke attendaunce vnto straungers call.
  The knights were willing all things to excuse,
Though nought beleu'd, and entraunce late did not refuse.

xv 3 bin] ben *1590*

They bene ybrought into a comely bowre, xix
  And seru'd of all things that mote needfull bee;
  Yet secretly their hoste did on them lowre,
  And welcomde more for feare, then charitee;
  But they dissembled, what they did not see,
  And welcomed themselues. Each gan vndight
  Their garments wet, and weary armour free,
  To dry them selues by *Vulcanes* flaming light,
And eke their lately bruzed parts to bring in plight.

And eke that straunger knight emongst the rest xx
  Was for like need enforst to disaray:
  Tho whenas vailed was her loftie crest,
  Her golden locks, that were in tramels gay
  Vpbounden, did them selues adowne display,
  And raught vnto her heeles; like sunny beames,
  That in a cloud their light did long time stay,
  Their vapour vaded, shew their golden gleames,
And through the persant aire shoote forth their azure streames.

She also dofte her heauy haberieon, xxi
  Which the faire feature of her limbs did hyde,
  And her well plighted frock, which she did won
  To tucke about her short, when she did ryde,
  She low let fall, that flowd from her lanck syde
  Downe to her foot, with carelesse modestee.
  Then of them all she plainly was espyde,
  To be a woman wight, vnwist to bee,
The fairest woman wight, that euer eye did see.

Like as *Minerua*, being late returnd xxii
  From slaughter of the Giaunts conquered;
  Where proud *Encelade*, whose wide nosethrils burnd
  With breathed flames, like to a furnace red,
  Transfixed with the speare, downe tombled ded
  From top of *Hemus*, by him heaped hye;
  Hath loosd her helmet from her lofty hed,
  And her *Gorgonian* shield gins to vntye
From her left arme, to rest in glorious victorye.

xx 1 rest; *1590, 1596* 9 persent *1609* xxii 1 *Minerua*] *Bellona 1590*
5 the] her *1590*

Which whenas they beheld, they smitten were xxiii
　　With great amazement of so wondrous sight,
　　And each on other, and they all on her
　　Stood gazing, as if suddein great affright
　　Had them surprised.　At last auizing right,
　　Her goodly personage and glorious hew,
　　Which they so much mistooke, they tooke delight
　　In their first errour, and yet still anew
With wonder of her beauty fed their hungry vew.

Yet note their hungry vew be satisfide, xxiv
　　But seeing still the more desir'd to see,
　　And euer firmely fixed did abide
　　In contemplation of diuinitie:
　　But most they meruaild at her cheualree,
　　And noble prowesse, which they had approued,
　　That much they faynd to know, who she mote bee;
　　Yet none of all them her thereof amoued,
Yet euery one her likte, and euery one her loued.

And *Paridell* though partly discontent xxv
　　With his late fall, and fowle indignity,
　　Yet was soone wonne his malice to relent,
　　Through gracious regard of her faire eye,
　　And knightly worth, which he too late did try,
　　Yet tried did adore.　Supper was dight;
　　Then they *Malbecco* prayd of curtesy,
　　That of his Lady they might haue the sight,
And company at meat, to do them more delight.

But he to shift their curious request, xxvi
　　Gan causen, why she could not come in place;
　　Her crased health, her late recourse to rest,
　　And humid euening ill for sicke folkes cace:
　　But none of those excuses could take place;
　　Ne would they eate, till she in presence came.
　　She came in presence with right comely grace,
　　And fairely them saluted, as became,
And shewd her selfe in all a gentle curteous Dame.

xxiii 9 hongry *1590*　　xxiv 5 most *om. 1596*

They sate to meat, and *Satyrane* his chaunce   xxvii
   Was her before, and *Paridell* besyde;
   But he him selfe sate looking still askaunce,
   Gainst *Britomart*, and euer closely eyde
   Sir *Satyrane*, that glaunces might not glyde:
   But his blind eye, that syded *Paridell*,
   All his demeasnure from his sight did hyde:
   On her faire face so did he feede his fill,
And sent close messages of loue to her at will.

And euer and anone, when none was ware,   xxviii
   With speaking lookes, that close embassage bore,
   He rou'd at her, and told his secret care:
   For all that art he learned had of yore.
   Ne was she ignoraunt of that lewd lore,
   But in his eye his meaning wisely red,
   And with the like him answerd euermore:
   She sent at him one firie dart, whose hed
Empoisned was with priuy lust, and gealous dred.

He from that deadly throw made no defence,   xxix
   But to the wound his weake hart opened wyde;
   The wicked engine through false influence,
   Past through his eyes, and secretly did glyde
   Into his hart, which it did sorely gryde.
   But nothing new to him was that same paine,
   Ne paine at all; for he so oft had tryde
   The powre thereof, and lou'd so oft in vaine,
That thing of course he counted, loue to entertaine.

Thenceforth to her he sought to intimate   xxx
   His inward griefe, by meanes to him well knowne,
   Now *Bacchus* fruit out of the siluer plate
   He on the table dasht, as ouerthrowne,
   Or of the fruitfull liquor ouerflowne,
   And by the dauncing bubbles did diuine,
   Or therein write to let his loue be showne;
   Which well she red out of the learned line,
A sacrament prophane in mistery of wine.

xxvii 5 that] with *1590*   7 demeanure *160*

And when so of his hand the pledge she raught,   xxxi
    The guilty cup she fained to mistake,
    And in her lap did shed her idle draught,
    Shewing desire her inward flame to slake:
    By such close signes they secret way did make
    Vnto their wils, and one eyes watch escape;
    Two eyes him needeth, for to watch and wake,
    Who louers will deceiue.   Thus was the ape,
By their faire handling, put into *Malbeccoes* cape.

Now when of meats and drinks they had their fill,   xxxii
    Purpose was moued by that gentle Dame,
    Vnto those knights aduenturous, to tell
    Of deeds of armes, which vnto them became,
    And euery one his kindred, and his name.
    Then *Paridell*, in whom a kindly pryde
    Of gracious speach, and skill his words to frame
    Abounded, being glad of so fit tyde
Him to commend to her, thus spake, of all well eyde.

Troy, that art now nought, but an idle name,   xxxiii
    And in thine ashes buried low dost lie,
    Though whilome far much greater then thy fame,
    Before that angry Gods, and cruell skye
    Vpon thee heapt a direfull destinie,
    What boots it boast thy glorious descent,
    And fetch from heauen thy great Genealogie,
    Sith all thy worthy prayses being blent,
Their of-spring hath embaste, and later glory shent.

Most famous Worthy of the world, by whome   xxxiv
    That warre was kindled, which did *Troy* inflame,
    And stately towres of *Ilion* whilome
    Brought vnto balefull ruine, was by name
    Sir *Paris* far renowmd through noble fame,
    Who through great prowesse and bold hardinesse,
    From *Lacedæmon* fetcht the fairest Dame,
    That euer *Greece* did boast, or knight possesse,
Whom *Venus* to him gaue for meed of worthinesse.

xxxii 8 yglad *1590*

Faire *Helene,* flowre of beautie excellent,   xxxv
  And girlond of the mighty Conquerours,
  That madest many Ladies deare lament
  The heauie losse of their braue Paramours,
  Which they far off beheld from *Troian* toures,
  And saw the fieldes of faire *Scamander* strowne
  With carcases of noble warrioures,
  Whose fruitlesse liues were vnder furrow sowne,
And *Xanthus* sandy bankes with bloud all ouerflowne.

From him my linage I deriue aright,   xxxvi
  Who long before the ten yeares siege of *Troy,*
  Whiles yet on *Ida* he a shepheard hight,
  On faire *Oenone* got a louely boy,
  Whom for remembraunce of her passed ioy,
  She of his Father *Parius* did name;
  Who, after *Greekes* did *Priams* realme destroy,
  Gathred the *Troian* reliques sau'd from flame,
And with them sayling thence, to th'Isle of *Paros* came.

That was by him cald *Paros,* which before   xxxvii
  Hight *Nausa,* there he many yeares did raine,
  And built *Nausicle* by the *Pontick* shore,
  The which he dying left next in remaine
  To *Paridas* his sonne.
  From whom I *Paridell* by kin descend;
  But for faire Ladies loue, and glories gaine,
  My natiue soile haue left, my dayes to spend
In sewing deeds of armes, my liues and labours end.

Whenas the noble *Britomart* heard tell   xxxviii
  Of *Troian* warres, and *Priams* Citie sackt,
  The ruefull story of Sir *Paridell,*
  She was empassiond at that piteous act,
  With zelous enuy of Greekes cruell fact,
  Against that nation, from whose race of old
  She heard, that she was lineally extract:
  For noble *Britons* sprong from *Troians* bold,
And *Troynouant* was built of old *Troyes* ashes cold.

xxxvii 9 seewing *1590, 1596*

Then sighing soft awhile, at last she thus: xxxix
  O lamentable fall of famous towne,
  Which raignd so many yeares victorious,
  And of all *Asie* bore the soueraigne crowne,
  In one sad night consumd, and throwen downe:
  What stony hart, that heares thy haplesse fate,
  Is not empierst with deepe compassiowne,
  And makes ensample of mans wretched state,
That floures so fresh at morne, and fades at euening late?

Behold, Sir, how your pitifull complaint   xl
  Hath found another partner of your payne:
  For nothing may impresse so deare constraint,
  As countries cause, and commune foes disdayne.
  But if it should not grieue you, backe agayne
  To turne your course, I would to heare desyre,
  What to *Aeneas* fell; sith that men sayne
  He was not in the Cities wofull fyre
Consum'd, but did him selfe to safetie retyre.

Anchyses sonne begot of *Venus* faire,   xli
  (Said he,) out of the flames for safegard fled,
  And with a remnant did to sea repaire,
  Where he through fatall errour long was led
  Full many yeares, and weetlesse wandered
  From shore to shore, emongst the Lybicke sands,
  Ere rest he found.   Much there he suffered,
  And many perils past in forreine lands,
To saue his people sad from victours vengefull hands.

At last in *Latium* he did arriue,   xlii
  Where he with cruell warre was entertaind
  Of th'inland folke, which sought him backe to driue,
  Till he with old *Latinus* was constraind,
  To contract wedlock: (so the fates ordaind.)
  Wedlock contract in bloud, and eke in blood
  Accomplished, that many deare complaind:
  The riuall slaine, the victour through the flood
Escaped hardly, hardly praisd his wedlock good.

xxxix 4 Asia 1609

Yet after all, he victour did suruiue,   xliii
   And with *Latinus* did the kingdome part.
   But after, when both nations gan to striue,
   Into their names the title to conuart,
   His sonne *Iülus* did from thence depart,
   With all the warlike youth of *Troians* bloud,
   And in long *Alba* plast his throne apart,
   Where faire it florished, and long time stoud,
Till *Romulus* renewing it, to *Rome* remoud.

There there (said *Britomart*) a fresh appeard   xliv
   The glory of the later world to spring,
   And *Troy* againe out of her dust was reard,
   To sit in second seat of soueraigne king,
   Of all the world vnder her gouerning.
   But a third kingdome yet is to arise,
   Out of the *Troians* scattered of-spring,
   That in all glory and great enterprise,
Both first and second *Troy* shall dare to equalise.

It *Troynouant* is hight, that with the waues   xlv
   Of wealthy *Thamis* washed is along,
   Vpon whose stubborne neck, whereat he raues
   With roring rage, and sore him selfe does throng,
   That all men feare to tempt his billowes strong,
   She fastned hath her foot, which standes so hy,
   That it a wonder of the world is song
   In forreine landes, and all which passen by,
Beholding it from far, do thinke it threates the skye.

The *Troian Brute* did first that Citie found,   xlvi
   And Hygate made the meare thereof by West,
   And *Ouert* gate by North: that is the bound
   Toward the land; two riuers bound the rest.
   So huge a scope at first him seemed best,
   To be the compasse of his kingdomes seat:
   So huge a mind could not in lesser rest,
   Ne in small meares containe his glory great,
That *Albion* had conquered first by warlike feat.

       xlv 3 necks *1590*   xlvi 2 Hygate gate *1596*

Ah fairest Lady knight, (said *Paridell*)   xlvii
   Pardon I pray my heedlesse ouersight,
   Who had forgot, that whilome I heard tell
   From aged *Mnemon*; for my wits bene light.
   Indeed he said (if I remember right,)
   That of the antique *Troian* stocke, there grew
   Another plant, that raught to wondrous hight,
   And far abroad his mighty branches threw,
Into the vtmost Angle of the world he knew.

For that same *Brute*, whom much he did aduaunce   xlviii
   In all his speach, was *Syluius* his sonne,
   Whom hauing slaine, through luckles arrowes glaunce
   He fled for feare of that he had misdonne,
   Or else for shame, so fowle reproch to shonne,
   And with him led to sea an youthly trayne,
   Where wearie wandring they long time did wonne,
   And many fortunes prou'd in th'*Ocean* mayne,
And great aduentures found, that now were long to sayne.

At last by fatall course they driuen were   xlix
   Into an Island spatious and brode,
   The furthest North, that did to them appeare:
   Which after rest they seeking far abrode,
   Found it the fittest soyle for their abode,
   Fruitfull of all things fit for liuing foode,
   But wholy wast, and void of peoples trode,
   Saue an huge nation of the Geaunts broode,
That fed on liuing flesh, and druncke mens vitall blood.

Whom he through wearie wars and labours long,   l
   Subdewd with losse of many *Britons* bold:
   In which the great *Goemagot* of strong
   Corineus, and *Coulin* of *Debon* old
   Were ouerthrowne, and layd on th'earth full cold,
   Which quaked vnder their so hideous masse,
   A famous history to be enrold
   In euerlasting moniments of brasse,
That all the antique Worthies merits far did passe.

   xlvii 3 hard *1590*   xlviii 6 to the sea *1596*   xlix 4 Which] And *1609*

His worke great *Troynouant,* his worke is eke   ii
   Faire *Lincolne,* both renowmed far away,
   That who from East to West will endlong seeke,
   Cannot two fairer Cities find this day,
   Except *Cleopolis:* so heard I say
   Old *Mnemon.* Therefore Sir, I greet you well
   Your countrey kin, and you entirely pray
   Of pardon for the strife, which late befell
Betwixt vs both vnknowne. So ended *Paridell.*

But all the while, that he these speaches spent,   iii
   Vpon his lips hong faire Dame *Hellenore,*
   With vigilant regard, and dew attent,
   Fashioning worlds of fancies euermore
   In her fraile wit, that now her quite forlore:
   The whiles vnwares away her wondring eye,
   And greedy eares her weake hart from her bore:
   Which he perceiuing, euer priuily
In speaking, many false belgardes at her let fly.

So long these knights discoursed diuersly,   iiii
   Of straunge affaires, and noble hardiment,
   Which they had past with mickle ieopardy,
   That now the humid night was farforth spent,
   And heauenly lampes were halfendeale ybrent:
   Which th'old man seeing well, who too long thought
   Euery discourse and euery argument,
   Which by the houres he measured, besought
Them go to rest. So all vnto their bowres were brought.

Cant. X.

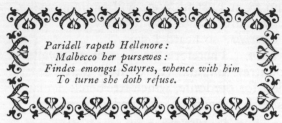

Paridell rapeth Hellenore:
Malbecco her pursewes:
Findes emongst Satyres, whence with him
To turne she doth refuse.

THe morow next, so soone as *Phœbus* Lamp   i
  Bewrayed had the world with early light,
And fresh *Aurora* had the shady damp
Out of the goodly heauen amoued quight,
Faire *Britomart* and that same *Faerie* knight
Vprose, forth on their iourney for to wend:
But *Paridell* complaynd, that his late fight
With *Britomart*, so sore did him offend,
That ryde he could not, till his hurts he did amend.

So forth they far'd, but he behind them stayd,   ii
  Maulgre his host, who grudged grieuously,
To house a guest, that would be needes obayd,
And of his owne him left not liberty:
Might wanting measure moueth surquedry.
Two things he feared, but the third was death;
That fierce youngmans vnruly maistery;
His money, which he lou'd as liuing breath;
And his faire wife, whom honest long he kept vneath.

But patience perforce he must abie,   iii
  What fortune and his fate on him will lay,
Fond is the feare, that findes no remedie;
Yet warily he watcheth euery way,
By which he feareth euill happen may:
So th'euill thinkes by watching to preuent;
Ne doth he suffer her, nor night, nor day,
Out of his sight her selfe once to absent.
So doth he punish her and eke himselfe torment.

ii 2 griuously *1590*

But *Paridell* kept better watch, then hee,   iv
   A fit occasion for his turne to find:
   False loue, why do men say, thou canst not see,
   And in their foolish fancie feigne thee blind,
   That with thy charmes the sharpest sight doest bind,
   And to thy will abuse? Thou walkest free,
   And seest euery secret of the mind;
   Thou seest all, yet none at all sees thee;
All that is by the working of thy Deitee.

So perfect in that art was *Paridell*,   v
   That he *Malbeccoes* halfen eye did wyle,
   His halfen eye he wiled wondrous well,
   And *Hellenors* both eyes did eke beguyle,
   Both eyes and hart attonce, during the whyle
   That he there soiourned his wounds to heale;
   That *Cupid* selfe it seeing, close did smyle,
   To weet how he her loue away did steale,
And bad, that none their ioyous treason should reueale.

The learned louer lost no time nor tyde,   vi
   That least auantage mote to him afford,
   Yet bore so faire a saile, that none espyde
   His secret drift, till he her layd abord.
   When so in open place, and commune bord,
   He fortun'd her to meet, with commune speach
   He courted her, yet bayted euery word,
   That his vngentle hoste n'ote him appeach
Of vile vngentlenesse, or hospitages breach.

But when apart (if euer her apart)   vii
   He found, then his false engins fast he plyde,
   And all the sleights vnbosomd in his hart ;
   He sigh'd, he sobd, he swownd, he perdy dyde,
   And cast himselfe on ground her fast besyde:
   Tho when againe he him bethought to liue,
   He wept, and wayld, and false laments belyde,
   Saying, but if she Mercie would him giue
That he mote algates dye, yet did his death forgiue.

And otherwhiles with amorous delights,   viii
  And pleasing toyes he would her entertaine,
  Now singing sweetly, to surprise her sprights,
  Now making layes of loue and louers paine,
  Bransles, Ballads, virelayes, and verses vaine;
  Oft purposes, oft riddles he deuysd,
  And thousands like, which flowed in his braine,
  With which he fed her fancie, and entysd
To take to his new loue, and leaue her old despysd.

And euery where he might, and euery while   ix
  He did her seruice dewtifull, and sewed
  At hand with humble pride, and pleasing guile,
  So closely yet, that none but she it vewed,
  Who well perceiued all, and all indewed.
  Thus finely did he his false nets dispred,
  With which he many weake harts had subdewed
  Of yore, and many had ylike misled:
What wonder then, if she were likewise carried?

No fort so fensible, no wals so strong,   x
  But that continuall battery will riue,
  Or daily siege through dispuruayance long,
  And lacke of reskewes will to parley driue;
  And Peece, that vnto parley eare will giue,
  Will shortly yeeld it selfe, and will be made
  The vassall of the victors will byliue:
  That stratageme had oftentimes assayd
This crafty Paramoure, and now it plaine displayd.

For through his traines he her intrapped hath,   xi
  That she her loue and hart hath wholy sold
  To him, without regard of gaine, or scath,
  Or care of credite, or of husband old,
  Whom she hath vow'd to dub a faire Cucquold.
  Nought wants but time and place, which shortly shee
  Deuized hath, and to her louer told.
  It pleased well.   So well they both agree ;
So readie rype to ill, ill wemens counsels bee.

Darke was the Euening, fit for louers stealth,   xii
   When chaunst *Malbecco* busie be elsewhere,
   She to his closet went, where all his wealth
   Lay hid: thereof she countlesse summes did reare,
   The which she meant away with her to beare;
   The rest she fyr'd for sport, or for despight;
   As *Hellene*, when she saw aloft appeare
   The *Troiane* flames, and reach to heauens hight
Did clap her hands, and ioyed at that dolefull sight.

This second *Hellene*, faire Dame *Hellenore*,   xiii
   The whiles her husband ranne with sory haste,
   To quench the flames, which she had tyn'd before,
   Laught at his foolish labour spent in waste;
   And ranne into her louers armes right fast;
   Where streight embraced, she to him did cry,
   And call aloud for helpe, ere helpe were past;
   For loe that Guest would beare her forcibly,
And meant to rauish her, that rather had to dy.

The wretched man hearing her call for ayd,   xiv
   And readie seeing him with her to fly,
   In his disquiet mind was much dismayd:
   But when againe he backward cast his eye,
   And saw the wicked fire so furiously
   Consume his hart, and scorch his Idoles face,
   He was therewith distressed diuersly,
   Ne wist he how to turne, nor to what place;
Was neuer wretched man in such a wofull cace.

Ay when to him she cryde, to her he turnd,   xv
   And left the fire; loue money ouercame:
   But when he marked, how his money burnd,
   He left his wife; money did loue disclame:
   Both was he loth to loose his loued Dame,
   And loth to leaue his liefest pelfe behind,
   Yet sith he n'ote saue both, he sau'd that same,
   Which was the dearest to his donghill mind,
The God of his desire, the ioy of misers blind.

xiii 8 would] did 1590

Thus whilest all things in troublous vprore were,   xvi
  And all men busie to suppresse the flame,
  The louing couple need no reskew feare,
  But leasure had, and libertie to frame
  Their purpost flight, free from all mens reclame;
  And Night, the patronesse of loue-stealth faire,
  Gaue them safe conduct, till to end they came:
  So bene they gone yfeare, a wanton paire
Of louers loosely knit, where list them to repaire.

Soone as the cruell flames yslaked were,   xvii
  Malbecco seeing, how his losse did lye,
  Out of the flames, which he had quencht whylere
  Into huge waues of griefe and gealosye
  Full deepe emplonged was, and drowned nye,
  Twixt inward doole and felonous despight;
  He rau'd, he wept, he stampt, he lowd did cry,
  And all the passions, that in man may light,
Did him attonce oppresse, and vex his caytiue spright.

Long thus he chawd the cud of inward griefe,   xviii
  And did consume his gall with anguish sore,
  Still when he mused on his late mischiefe,
  Then still the smart thereof increased more,
  And seem'd more grieuous, then it was before:
  At last when sorrow he saw booted nought,
  Ne griefe might not his loue to him restore,
  He gan deuise, how her he reskew mought,
Ten thousand wayes he cast in his confused thought.

At last resoluing, like a pilgrim pore,   xix
  To search her forth, where so she might be fond,
  And bearing with him treasure in close store,
  The rest he leaues in ground: So takes in hond
  To seeke her endlong, both by sea and lond.
  Long he her sought, he sought her farre and nere,
  And euery where that he mote vnderstond,
  Of knights and ladies any meetings were,
And of eachone he met, he tydings did inquere.

xviii 4 Then] So *1590*   xix 2 seach *1596*

But all in vaine, his woman was too wise,   xx
  Euer to come into his clouch againe,
  And he too simple euer to surprise
  The iolly *Paridell,* for all his paine.
  One day, as he forpassed by the plaine
  With weary pace, he farre away espide
  A couple, seeming well to be his twaine,
  Which houed close vnder a forrest side,
As if they lay in wait, or else themselues did hide.

Well weened he, that those the same mote bee,   xxi
  And as he better did their shape auize,
  Him seemed more their manner did agree;
  For th'one was armed all in warlike wize,
  Whom, to be *Paridell* he did deuize;
  And th'other all yclad in garments light,
  Discolour'd like to womanish disguise,
  He did resemble to his Ladie bright;
And euer his faint hart much earned at the sight.

And euer faine he towards them would goe,   xxii
  But yet durst not for dread approchen nie,
  But stood aloofe, vnweeting what to doe;
  Till that prickt forth with loues extremitie,
  That is the father of foule gealosy,
  He closely nearer crept, the truth to weet:
  But, as he nigher drew, he euoily
  Might scerne, that it was not his sweetest swcet,
Ne yet her Belamour, the partner of his sheet.

But it was scornefull *Braggadocchio,*   xxiii
  That with his seruant *Trompart* houerd there,
  Sith late he fled from his too earnest foe:
  Whom such when as *Malbecco* spyed clere,
  He turned backe, and would haue fled arere;
  Till *Trompart* ronning hastily, him did stay,
  And bad before his soueraine Lord appere:
  That was him loth, yet durst he not gainesay,
And comming him before, low louted on the lay.

xxi 9 yearned *1609*

The Boaster at him sterneiy bent his browe,   xxiv
  As if he could haue kild him with his looke,
  That to the ground him meekely made to bowe,
  And awfull terror deepe into him strooke,
  That euery member of his bodie quooke.
  Said he, Thou man of nought, what doest thou here,
  Vnfitly furnisht with thy bag and booke,
  Where I expected one with shield and spere,
To proue some deedes of armes vpon an equall pere.

The wretched man at his imperious speach,   xxv
  Was all abasht, and low prostrating, said;
  Good Sir, let not my rudenesse be no breach
  Vnto your patience, ne be ill ypaid;
  For I vnwares this way by fortune straid,
  A silly Pilgrim driuen to distresse,
  That seeke a Lady, There he suddein staid,
  And did the rest with grieuous sighes suppresse,
While teares stood in his eies, few drops of bitternesse.

What Ladie, man? (said *Trompart*) take good hart,   xxvi
  And tell thy griefe, if any hidden lye;
  Was neuer better time to shew thy smart,
  Then now, that noble succour is thee by,
  That is the whole worlds commune remedy.
  That cheareful word his weake hart much did cheare,
  And with vaine hope his spirits faint supply,
  That bold he said; O most redoubted Pere,
Vouchsafe with mild regard a wretches cace to heare.

Then sighing sore, It is not long (said hee)   xxvii
  Sith I enioyd the gentlest Dame aliue;
  Of whom a knight, no knight at all perdee,
  But shame of all, that doe for honor striue,
  By treacherous deceipt did me depriue;
  Through open outrage he her bore away,
  And with fowle force vnto his will did driue,
  Which all good knights, that armes do beare this day,
Are bound for to reuenge, and punish if they may.

      xxiv 6 thou *1590 &c.*   xxvii 2 Since *1609*

And you most noble Lord, that can and dare   xxviii
   Redresse the wrong of miserable wight,
   Cannot employ your most victorious speare
   In better quarrell, then defence of right,
   And for a Ladie gainst a faithlesse knight;
   So shall your glory be aduaunced much,
   And all faire Ladies magnifie your might,
   And eke my selfe, albe I simple such,
Your worthy paine shall well reward with guerdon rich.

With that out of his bouget forth he drew   xxix
   Great store of treasure, therewith him to tempt;
   But he on it lookt scornefully askew,
   As much disdeigning to be so misdempt,
   Or a war-monger to be basely nempt;
   And said; Thy offers base I greatly loth,
   And eke thy words vncourteous and vnkempt;
   I tread in dust thee and thy money both,
That, were it not for shame, So turned from him wroth.

But *Trompart*, that his maisters humor knew,   xxx
   In lofty lookes to hide an humble mind,
   Was inly tickled with that golden vew,
   And in his eare him rounded close behind:
   Yet stoupt he not, but lay still in the wind,
   Waiting aduauntage on the pray to sease;
   Till *Trompart* lowly to the ground inclind,
   Besought him his great courage to appease,
And pardon simple man, that rash did him displease.

Bigge looking like a doughtie Doucepere,   xxxi
   At last he thus; Thou clod of vilest clay,
   I pardon yield, and with thy rudenesse beare;
   But weete henceforth, that all that golden pray,
   And all that else the vaine world vaunten may,
   I loath as doung, ne deeme my dew reward:
   Fame is my meed, and glory vertues pray.
   But minds of mortall men are muchell mard,
And mou'd amisse with massie mucks vnmeet regard.

xxix 2 threasure *1609*   6 thy *1590, 1596*   xxx 4 grounded *1596*
xxxi 3 with thy] that with *1590*   7 vertues] vertuous *1590*   pray] pay *1609*

And more, I graunt to thy great miserie   xxxii
   Gratious respect, thy wife shall backe be sent,
   And that vile knight, who euer that he bee,
   Which hath thy Lady reft, and knighthood shent,
   By *Sanglamort* my sword, whose deadly dent
   The bloud hath of so many thousands shed,
   I sweare, ere long shall dearely it repent;
   Ne he twixt heauen and earth shall hide his hed,
But soone he shall be found, and shortly doen be ded.

The foolish man thereat woxe wondrous blith,   xxxiii
   As if the word so spoken, were halfe donne,
   And humbly thanked him a thousand sith,
   That had from death to life him newly wonne.
   Tho forth the Boaster marching, braue begonne
   His stolen steed to thunder furiously,
   As if he heauen and hell would ouerronne,
   And all the world confound with cruelty,
That much *Malbecco* ioyed in his iollity.

Thus long they three together traueiled,   xxxiv
   Through many a wood, and many an vncouth way,
   To seeke his wife, that was farre wandered:
   But those two sought nought, but the present pray,
   To weete the treasure, which he did bewray,
   On which their eies and harts were wholly set,
   With purpose, how they might it best betray;
   For sith the houre, that first he did them let
The same behold, therewith their keene desires were whet.

It fortuned as they together far'd,   xxxv
   They spide, where *Paridell* came pricking fast
   Vpon the plaine, the which himselfe prepar'd
   To giust with that braue straunger knight a cast,
   As on aduenture by the way he past:
   Alone he rode without his Paragone;
   For hauing filcht her bels, her vp he cast
   To the wide world, and let her fly alone,
He nould be clogd. So had he serued many one.

xxxii 1 more] mote *1590*

The gentle Lady, loose at randon left,   xxxvi
  The greene-wood long did walke, and wander wide
  At wilde aduenture, like a forlorne weft,
  Till on a day the *Satyres* her espide
  Straying alone withouten groome or guide;
  Her vp they tooke, and with them home her led,
  With them as housewife euer to abide,
  To milk their gotes, and make them cheese and bred,
And euery one as commune good her handeled.

That shortly she *Malbecco* has forgot,   xxxvii
  And eke Sir *Paridell,* all were he deare;
  Who from her went to seeke another lot,
  And now by fortune was arriued here,
  Where those two guilers with *Malbecco* were:
  Soone as the oldman saw Sir *Paridell,*
  He fainted, and was almost dead with feare,
  Ne word he had to speake, his griefe to tell,
But to him louted low, and greeted goodly well.

And after asked him for *Hellenore,*   xxxviii
  I take no keepe of her (said *Paridell*)
  She wonneth in the forrest there before.
  So forth he rode, as his aduenture fell;
  The whiles the Boaster from his loftie sell
  Faynd to alight, something amisse to mend;
  But the fresh Swayne would not his leasure dwell,
  But went his way; whom when he passed kend,
He vp remounted light, and after faind to wend.

Perdy nay (said *Malbecco*) shall ye not: xxxix
  But let him passe as lightly, as he came:
  For litle good of him is to be got,
  And mickle perill to be put to shame.
  But let vs go to seeke my dearest Dame,
  Whom he hath left in yonder forrest wyld:
  For of her safety in great doubt I am,
  Least saluage beastes her person haue despoyld:
Then all the world is lost, and we in vaine haue toyld.

They all agree, and forward them addrest: xl
  Ah but (said craftie *Trompart*) weete ye well,
  That yonder in that wastefull wildernesse
  Huge monsters haunt, and many dangers dwell;
  Dragons, and Minotaures, and feendes of hell,
  And many wilde woodmen, which robbe and rend
  All trauellers; therefore aduise ye well,
  Before ye enterprise that way to wend:
One may his iourney bring too soone to euill end.

Malbecco stopt in great astonishment,   xli
  And with pale eyes fast fixed on the rest,
  Their counsell crau'd, in daunger imminent.
  Said *Trompart*, You that are the most opprest
  With burden of great treasure, I thinke best
  Here for to stay in safetie behind;
  My Lord and I will search the wide forrest.
  That counsell pleased not *Malbeccoes* mind;
For he was much affraid, himselfe alone to find.

Then is it best (said he) that ye doe leaue   xlii
  Your treasure here in some securitie,
  Either fast closed in some hollow greaue,
  Or buried in the ground from ieopardie,
  Till we returne againe in safetie:
  As for vs two, least doubt of vs ye haue,
  Hence farre away we will blindfolded lie,
  Ne priuie be vnto your treasures graue.
It pleased: so he did.   Then they march forward braue.

Now when amid the thickest woods they were,   xliii
  They heard a noyse of many bagpipes shrill,
  And shrieking Hububs them approching nere,
  Which all the forrest did with horror fill:
  That dreadfull sound the boasters hart did thrill,
  With such amazement, that in haste he fled,
  Ne euer looked backe for good or ill,
  And after him eke fearefull *Trompart* sped;
The old man could not fly, but fell to ground halfe ded.

xl 1 They] The *1596*   3 wastefull] faithfull *1590*   7 avise *1609*
    xli 4 you *1590, 1596*   xlii 9 did, *1596*

Yet afterwards close creeping, as he might,
  He in a bush did hide his fearefull hed,
  The iolly *Satyres* full of fresh delight,
  Came dauncing forth, and with them nimbly led
  Faire *Hellenore*, with girlonds all bespred,
  Whom their May-lady they had newly made:
  She proud of that new honour, which they red,
  And of their louely fellowship full glade,
Daunst liuely, and her face did with a Lawrell shade.

The silly man that in the thicket lay
  Saw all this goodly sport, and grieued sore,
  Yet durst he not against it doe or say,
  But did his hart with bitter thoughts engore,
  To see th'vnkindnesse of his *Hellenore*.
  All day they daunced with great lustihed,
  And with their horned feet the greene grasse wore,
  The whiles their Gotes vpon the brouzes fed,
Till drouping *Phœbus* gan to hide his golden hed.

Tho vp they gan their merry pypes to trusse,
  And all their goodly heards did gather round,
  But euery *Satyre* first did giue a busse
  To *Hellenore*: so busses did abound.
  Now gan the humid vapour shed the ground
  With perly deaw, and th'Earthes gloomy shade
  Did dim the brightnesse of the welkin round,
  That euery bird and beast awarned made,
To shrowd themselues, whiles sleepe their senses did inuade.

Which when *Malbecco* saw, out of his bush
  Vpon his hands and feete he crept full light,
  And like a Gote emongst the Gotes did rush,
  That through the helpe of his faire hornes on hight,
  And misty dampe of misconceiuing night,
  And eke through likenesse of his gotish beard,
  He did the better counterfeite aright:
  So home he marcht emongst the horned heard,
That none of all the *Satyres* him espyde or heard.

xlv 8 fed. *1596*   xlvi 6 the Earthes *1609*
xlvii 1 his] the *1609*   2 hand *1596*

At night, when all they went to sleepe, he vewd,
  Whereas his louely wife emongst them lay,
  Embraced of a *Satyre* rough and rude,
  Who all the night did minde his ioyous play:
  Nine times he heard him come aloft ere day,
  That all his hart with gealosie did swell;
  But yet that nights ensample did bewray,
  That not for nought his wife them loued so well,
When one so oft a night did ring his matins bell.

So closely as he could, he to them crept,
  When wearie of their sport to sleepe they fell,
  And to his wife, that now full soundly slept,
  He whispered in her eare, and did her tell,
  That it was he, which by her side did dwell,
  And therefore prayd her wake, to heare him plaine.
  As one out of a dreame not waked well,
  She turned her, and returned backe againe:
Yet her for to awake he did the more constraine.

At last with irkesome trouble she abrayd;
  And then perceiuing, that it was indeed
  Her old *Malbecco*, which did her vpbrayd,
  With loosenesse of her loue, and loathly deed,
  She was astonisht with exceeding dreed,
  And would haue wakt the *Satyre* by her syde;
  But he her prayd, for mercy, or for meed,
  To saue his life, ne let him be descryde,
But hearken to his lore, and all his counsell hyde.

Tho gan he her perswade, to leaue that lewd
  And loathsome life, of God and man abhord,
  And home returne, where all should be renewd
  With perfect peace, and bandes of fresh accord,
  And she receiu'd againe to bed and bord,
  As if no trespasse euer had bene donne:
  But she it all refused at one word,
  And by no meanes would to his will be wonne,
But chose emongst the iolly *Satyres* still to wonne.

xlviii 9 oft] ought 1609

He wooed her, till day spring he espyde;   lii
    But all in vaine: and then turnd to the heard,
    Who butted him with hornes on euery syde,
    And trode downe in the durt, where his hore beard
    Was fowly dight, and he of death afeard.
    Early before the heauens fairest light
    Out of the ruddy East was fully reard,
    The heardes out of their foldes were loosed quight,
And he emongst the rest crept forth in sory plight.

So soone as he the Prison dore did pas,   liii
    He ran as fast, as both his feete could beare,
    And neuer looked, who behind him was,
    Ne scarsely who before: like as a Beare
    That creeping close, amongst the hiues to reare
    An hony combe, the wakefull dogs espy,
    And him assayling, sore his carkasse teare,
    That hardly he with life away does fly,
Ne stayes, till safe himselfe he see from ieopardy.

Ne stayd he, till he came vnto the place,   liv
    Where late his treasure he entombed had,
    Where when he found it not (for *Trompart* bace
    Had it purloyned for his maister bad:)
    With extreme fury he became quite mad,
    And ran away, ran with himselfe away:
    That who so straungely had him seene bestad,
    With vpstart haire, and staring eyes dismay,
From Limbo lake him late escaped sure would say.

High ouer hilles and ouer dales he fled,   lv
    As if the wind him on his winges had borne,
    Ne banck nor bush could stay him, when he sped
    His nimble feet, as treading still on thorne:
    Griefe, and despight, and gealosie, and scorne
    Did all the way him follow hard behind,
    And he himselfe himselfe loath'd so forlorne,
    So shamefully forlorne of womankind;
That as a Snake, still lurked in his wounded mind.

       lii 1 day springs *1596*   liii 5 emongst *1609*

Still fled he forward, looking backward still,　　lvi
　　Ne stayd his flight, nor fearefull agony,
　　Till that he came vnto a rockie hill,
　　Ouer the sea, suspended dreadfully,
　　That liuing creature it would terrify,
　　To looke adowne, or vpward to the hight:
　　From thence he threw himselfe dispiteously,
　　All desperate of his fore-damned spright,
That seem'd no helpe for him was left in liuing sight.

But through long anguish, and selfe-murdring thought　　lvii
　　He was so wasted and forpined quight,
　　That all his substance was consum'd to nought,
　　And nothing left, but like an aery Spright,
　　That on the rockes he fell so flit and light,
　　That he thereby receiu'd no hurt at all,
　　But chaunced on a craggy cliff to light;
　　Whence he with crooked clawes so long did crall,
That at the last he found a caue with entrance small.

Into the same he creepes, and thenceforth there　　lviii
　　Resolu'd to build his balefull mansion,
　　In drery darkenesse, and continuall feare
　　Of that rockes fall, which euer and anon
　　Threates with huge ruine him to fall vpon,
　　That he dare neuer sleepe, but that one eye
　　Still ope he keepes for that occasion;
　　Ne euer rests he in tranquillity,
The roring billowes beat his bowre so boystrously.

Ne euer is he wont on ought to feed,　　lix
　　But toades and frogs, his pasture poysonous,
　　Which in his cold complexion do breed
　　A filthy bloud, or humour rancorous,
　　Matter of doubt and dread suspitious,
　　That doth with curelesse care consume the hart,
　　Corrupts the stomacke with gall vitious,
　　Croscuts the liuer with internall smart,
And doth transfixe the soule with deathes eternall dart.

Yet can he neuer dye, but dying liues,   lx
    And doth himselfe with sorrow new sustaine,
    That death and life attonce vnto him giues.
    And painefull pleasure turnes to pleasing paine.
    There dwels he euer, miserable swaine,
    Hatefull both to him selfe, and euery wight;
    Where he through priuy griefe, and horrour vaine,
    Is woxen so deform'd, that he has quight
Forgot he was a man, and *Gealosie* is hight.

Cant. XI.

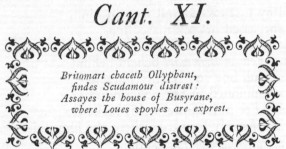

Britomart chaceth Ollyphant,
findes Scudamour distrest:
Assayes the house of Busyrane,
where Loues spoyles are exprest.

O Hatefull hellish Snake, what furie furst   i
  Brought thee from balefull house of *Proserpine*,
    Where in her bosome she thee long had nurst,
    And fostred vp with bitter milke of tine,
    Fowle Gealosie, that turnest loue diuine
    To ioylesse dread, and mak'st the louing hart
    With hatefull thoughts to languish and to pine,
    And feed it selfe with selfe-consuming smart?
Of all the passions in the mind thou vilest art.

O let him far be banished away,   ii
    And in his stead let Loue for euer dwell,
    Sweet Loue, that doth his golden wings embay
    In blessed Nectar, and pure Pleasures well,
    Vntroubled of vile feare, or bitter fell.
    And ye faire Ladies, that your kingdomes make
    In th'harts of men, them gouerne wisely well,
    And of faire *Britomart* ensample take,
That was as trew in loue, as Turtle to her make.

Who with Sir *Satyrane*, as earst ye red,   iii
   Forth ryding from *Malbeccoes* hostlesse hous,
   Far off aspyde a young man, the which fled
   From an huge Geaunt, that with hideous
   And hatefull outrage long him chaced thus;
   It was that *Ollyphant*, the brother deare
   Of that *Argante* vile and vitious,
   From whom the *Squire of Dames* was reft whylere;
This all as bad as she, and worse, if worse ought were.

For as the sister did in feminine   iv
   And filthy lust exceede all woman kind,
   So he surpassed his sex masculine,
   In beastly vse that I did euer find;
   Whom when as *Britomart* beheld behind
   The fearefull boy so greedily pursew,
   She was emmoued in her noble mind,
   T'employ her puissaunce to his reskew,
And pricked fiercely forward, where she him did vew.

Ne was Sir *Satyrane* her far behinde,   v
   But with like fiercenesse did ensew the chace:
   Whom when the Gyaunt saw, he soone resinde
   His former suit, and from them fled apace;
   They after both, and boldly bad him bace,
   And each did striue the other to out-goe,
   But he them both outran a wondrous space,
   For he was long, and swift as any Roe,
And now made better speed, t'escape his feared foe.

It was not *Satyrane*, whom he did feare,   vi
   But *Britomart* the flowre of chastity;
   For he the powre of chast hands might not beare,
   But alwayes did their dread encounter fly:
   And now so fast his feet he did apply,
   That he has gotten to a forrest neare,
   Where he is shrowded in security.
   The wood they enter, and search euery where,
They searched diuersely, so both diuided were.

   iii 3 espide *1609*   iv 4 that I did euer] all, that I euer *1590*   9 him
did] did him *1590*

Faire *Britomart* so long him followed,   vii
    That she at last came to a fountaine sheare,
    By which there lay a knight all wallowed
    Vpon the grassy ground, and by him neare
    His haberieon, his helmet, and his speare;
    A little off, his shield was rudely throwne,
    On which the winged boy in colours cleare
    Depeincted was, full easie to be knowne,
And he thereby, where euer it in field was showne.

His face vpon the ground did groueling ly,   viii
    As if he had bene slombring in the shade,
    That the braue Mayd would not for courtesy,
    Out of his quiet slomber him abrade,
    Nor seeme too suddeinly him to inuade:
    Still as she stood, she heard with grieuous throb
    Him grone, as if his hart were peeces made,
    And with most painefull pangs to sigh and sob,
That pitty did the Virgins hart of patience rob.

At last forth breaking into bitter plaintes   ix
    He said ; O soueraigne Lord that sit'st on hye,
    And raignst in blis emongst thy blessed Saintes,
    How suffrest thou such shamefull cruelty,
    So long vnwreaked of thine enimy?
    Or hast thou, Lord, of good mens cause no heed?
    Or doth thy iustice sleepe, and silent ly?
    What booteth then the good and righteous deed,
If goodnesse find no grace, nor righteousnesse no meed?

If good find grace, and righteousnesse reward,   x
    Why then is *Amoret* in caytiue band,
    Sith that more bounteous creature neuer far'd
    On foot, vpon the face of liuing land?
    Or if that heauenly iustice may withstand
    The wrongfull outrage of vnrighteous men,
    Why then is *Busirane* with wicked hand
    Suffred, these seuen monethes day in secret den
My Lady and my loue so cruelly to pen ?

      vii 6 off,] of *1590*   ix 6 hast, thou Lord, *1590, 1596*

My Lady and my loue is cruelly pend   xi
  In dolefull darkenesse from the vew of day,
  Whilest deadly' torments do her chast brest rend,
  And the sharpe steele doth riue her hart in tway,
  All for she *Scudamore* will not denay.
  Yet thou vile man, vile *Scudamore* art sound,
  Ne canst her ayde, ne canst her foe dismay;
  Vnworthy wretch to tread vpon the ground,
For whom so faire a Lady feeles so sore a wound.

There an huge heape of singultes did oppresse   xii
  His strugling soule, and swelling throbs empeach
  His foltring toung with pangs of drerinesse,
  Choking the remnant of his plaintife speach,
  As if his dayes were come to their last reach.
  Which when she heard, and saw the ghastly fit,
  Threatning into his life to make a breach,
  Both with great ruth and terrour she was smit,
Fearing least from her cage the wearie soule would flit.

Tho stooping downe she him amoued light;   xiii
  Who therewith somewhat starting, vp gan looke,
  And seeing him behind a straunger knight,
  Whereas no liuing creature he mistooke,
  With great indignaunce he that sight forsooke,
  And downe againe himselfe disdainefully
  Abiecting, th'earth with his faire forhead strooke:
  Which the bold Virgin seeing, gan apply
Fit medcine to his griefe, and spake thus courtesly.

Ah gentle knight, whose deepe conceiued griefe   xiv
  Well seemes t'exceede the powre of patience,
  Yet if that heauenly grace some good reliefe
  You send, submit you to high prouidence,
  And euer in your noble hart prepense,
  That all the sorrow in the world is lesse,
  Then vertues might, and values confidence,
  For who nill bide the burden of distresse,
Must not here thinke to liue: for life is wretchednesse.

Therefore, faire Sir, do comfort to you take,   xv
  And freely read, what wicked felon so
  Hath outrag'd you, and thrald your gentle make.
  Perhaps this hand may helpe to ease your woe,
  And wreake your sorrow on your cruell foe,
  At least it faire endeuour will apply.
  Those feeling wordes so neare the quicke did goe,
  That vp his head he reared easily,
And leaning on his elbow, these few wordes let fly.

What boots it plaine, that cannot be redrest,   xvi
  And sow vaine sorrow in a fruitlesse eare,
  Sith powre of hand, nor skill of learned broot,
  Ne worldly price cannot redeeme my deare,
  Out of her thraldome and continuall feare?
  For he the tyraunt, which her hath in ward
  By strong enchauntments and blacke Magicke Icare,
  Hath in a dungeon deepe her close embard,
And many dreadfull feends hath pointed to her gard.

There he tormenteth her most terribly,   xvii
  And day and night afflicts with mortall paine,
  Because to yield him loue she doth deny,
  Once to me yold, not to be yold againe:
  But yet by torture he would her constraine
  Loue to conceiue in her disdainfull brest;
  Till so she do, she must in doole remaine,
  Ne may by liuing meanes be thence relest:
What boots it then to plaine, that cannot be redrest?

With this sad hersall of his heauy stresse,   xviii
  The warlike Damzell was empassiond sore,
  And said ; Sir knight, your cause is nothing lesse,
  Then is your sorrow, certes if not more ;
  For nothing so much pitty doth implore,
  As gentle Ladies helplesse misery.
  But yet, if please ye listen to my lore,
  I will with proofe of last extremity,
Deliuer her fro thence, or with her for you dy.

xv 6 At] And 1596

Ah gentlest knight aliue, (said *Scudamore*)   xix
  What huge heroicke magnanimity
  Dwels in thy bounteous brest? what couldst thou more,
  If she were thine, and thou as now am I?
  O spare thy happy dayes, and them apply
  To better boot, but let me dye, that ought;
  More is more losse: one is enough to dy.
  Life is not lost, (said she) for which is bought
Endlesse renowm, that more then death is to be sought.

Thus she at length perswaded him to rise,   xx
  And with her wend, to see what new successe
  Mote him befall vpon new enterprise;
  His armes, which he had vowed to disprofesse,
  She gathered vp and did about him dresse,
  And his forwandred steed vnto him got:
  So forth they both yfere make their progresse,
  And march not past the mountenaunce of a shot,
Till they arriu'd, whereas their purpose they did plot.

There they dismounting, drew their weapons bold   xxi
  And stoutly came vnto the Castle gate;
  Whereas no gate they found, them to withhold,
  Nor ward to wait at morne and euening late,
  But in the Porch, that did them sore amate,
  A flaming fire, ymixt with smouldry smoke,
  And stinking Sulphure, that with griesly hate
  And dreadfull horrour did all entraunce choke,
Enforced them their forward footing to reuoke.

Greatly thereat was *Britomart* dismayd,   xxii
  Ne in that stownd wist, how her selfe to beare;
  For daunger vaine it were, to haue assayd
  That cruell element, which all things feare,
  Ne none can suffer to approchen neare:
  And turning backe to *Scudamour*, thus sayd;
  What monstrous enmity prouoke we heare,
  Foolhardy as th'Earthes children, the which made
Battell against the Gods? so we a God inuade.

    xix 9 death] life *conj. Jortin*   xx 6 for wandred *1596*
    xxii 8 th'Earthes] the Earthes *1590*   the which] which *1590*

Daunger without discretion to attempt,   xxiii
  Inglorious and beastlike is: therefore Sir knight,
  Aread what course of you is safest dempt,
  And how we with our foe may come to fight.
  This is (quoth he) the dolorous despight,
  Which earst to you I playnd: for neither may
  This fire be quencht by any wit or might,
  Ne yet by any meanes remou'd away,
So mighty be th'enchauntments, which the same do stay.

What is there else, but cease these fruitlesse paines,   xxiv
  And leaue me to my former languishing?
  Faire *Amoret* must dwell in wicked chaines,
  And *Scudamore* here dye with sorrowing.
  Perdy not so; (said she) for shamefull thing
  It were t'abandon noble cheuisaunce,
  For shew of perill, without venturing:
  Rather let try extremities of chaunce,
Then enterprised prayse for dread to disauaunce.

Therewith resolu'd to proue her vtmost might,   xxv
  Her ample shield she threw before her face,
  And her swords point directing forward right,
  Assayld the flame, the which eftsoones gaue place,
  And did it selfe diuide with equall space,
  That through she passed; as a thunder bolt
  Perceth the yielding ayre, and doth displace
  The soring clouds into sad showres ymolt;
So to her yold the flames, and did their force reuolt.

Whom whenas *Scudamour* saw past the fire,   xxvi
  Safe and vntoucht, he likewise gan assay,
  With greedy will, and enuious desire,
  And bad the stubborne flames to yield him way:
  But cruell *Mulciber* would not obay
  His threatfull pride, but did the more augment
  His mighty rage, and with imperious sway
  Him forst (maulgre) his fiercenesse to relent,
And backe retire, all scorcht and pitifully brent.

xxiii 3 dempt. *1590*   5 is *om. 1596*   xxiv 2 languishing; *1596*
   xxv 7 Pearceth *1609*   xxvi 7 with *om. 1596*: and his *1609*

With huge impatience he inly swelt,   xxvii
    More for great sorrow, that he could not pas,
    Then for the burning torment, which he felt,
    That with fell woodnesse he effierced was,
    And wilfully him throwing on the gras,
    Did beat and bounse his head and brest full sore;
    The whiles the Championesse now entred has
    The vtmost rowme, and past the formest dore,
The vtmost rowme, abounding with all precious store.

For round about, the wals yclothed were   xxviii
    With goodly arras of great maiesty,
    Wouen with gold and silke so close and nere,
    That the rich metall lurked priuily,
    As faining to be hid from enuious eye;
    Yet here, and there, and euery where vnwares
    It shewd it selfe, and shone vnwillingly;
    Like a discolourd Snake, whose hidden snares
Through the greene gras his long bright burnisht backe declares.

And in those Tapets weren fashioned   xxix
    Many faire pourtraicts, and many a faire feate,
    And all of loue, and all of lusty-hed,
    As seemed by their semblaunt did entreat;
    And eke all *Cupids* warres they did repeate,
    And cruell battels, which he whilome fought
    Gainst all the Gods, to make his empire great;
    Besides the huge massacres, which he wrought
On mighty kings and kesars, into thraldome brought.

Therein was writ, how often thundring *Ioue*   xxx
    Had felt the point of his hart-percing dart,
    And leauing heauens kingdome, here did roue
    In straunge disguize, to slake his scalding smart;
    Now like a Ram, faire *Helle* to peruart,
    Now like a Bull, *Europa* to withdraw:
    Ah, how the fearefull Ladies tender hart
    Did liuely seeme to tremble, when she saw
The huge seas vnder her t'obay her seruaunts law.

xxvii 7 entred] decked *1590*   8 formost *1609*   xxviii 8 Like] Like
to *1590*   9 Throgh *1609*

Soone after that into a golden showre   xxxi
  Him selfe he chaung'd faire *Danaë* to vew,
  And through the roofe of her strong brasen towre
  Did raine into her lap an hony dew,
  The whiles her foolish garde, that little knew
  Of such deceipt, kept th'yron dore fast bard,
  And watcht, that none should enter nor issew;
  Vaine was the watch, and bootlesse all the ward,
Whenas the God to golden hew him selfe transfard.

Then was he turnd into a snowy Swan,   xxxii
  To win faire *Leda* to his louely trade:
  O wondrous skill, and sweet wit of the man,
  That her in daffadillies sleeping made,
  From scorching heat her daintie limbes to shade:
  Whiles the proud Bird ruffing his fethers wyde,
  And brushing his faire brest, did her inuade;
  She slept, yet twixt her eyelids closely spyde,
How towards her he rusht, and smiled at his pryde.

Then shewd it, how the *Thebane Semelee*   xxxiii
  Deceiu'd of gealous *Iuno*, did require
  To see him in his soueraigne maiestee,
  Armd with his thunderbolts and lightning fire,
  Whence dearely she with death bought her desire.
  But faire *Alcmena* better match did make,
  Ioying his loue in likenesse more entire;
  Three nights in one, they say, that for her oake
He then did put, her pleasures lenger to partake.

Twise was he seene in soaring Eagles shape,   xxxiv
  And with wide wings to beat the buxome ayre,
  Once, when he with *Asterie* did scape,
  Againe, when as the *Troiane* boy so faire
  He snatcht from *Ida* hill, and with him bare:
  Wondrous delight it was, there to behould,
  How the rude Shepheards after him did stare,
  Trembling through feare, least down he fallen should,
And often to him calling, to take surer hould.

      xxxiii 9 her] his *1609*   xxxiv 8 should *1590. 1596*

In *Satyres* shape *Antiopa* he snatcht: xxxv
    And like a fire, when he *Aegin'* assayd:
    A shepheard, when *Mnemosyne* he catcht:
    And like a Serpent to the *Thracian* mayd.
    Whiles thus on earth great *Ioue* these pageaunts playd,
    The winged boy did thrust into his throne,
    And scoffing, thus vnto his mother sayd,
    Lo now the heauens obey to me alone,
And take me for their *Ioue*, whiles *Ioue* to earth is gone.

And thou, faire *Phœbus*, in thy colours bright   xxxvi
    Wast there enwouen, and the sad distresse,
    In which that boy thee plonged, for despight,
    That thou bewray'dst his mothers wantonnesse,
    When she with *Mars* was meynt in ioyfulnesse:
    For thy he thrild thee with a leaden dart,
    To loue faire *Daphne*, which thee loued lesse:
    Lesse she thee lou'd, then was thy iust desart,
Yet was thy loue her death, and her death was thy smart.

So louedst thou the lusty *Hyacinct*,   xxxvii
    So louedst thou the faire *Coronis* deare:
    Yet both are of thy haplesse hand extinct,
    Yet both in flowres do liue, and loue thee beare,
    The one a Paunce, the other a sweet breare:
    For griefe whereof, ye mote haue liuely seene
    The God himselfe rending his golden heare,
    And breaking quite his gyrlond euer greene,
With other signes of sorrow and impatient teene.

    Both for those two, and for his owne deare sonne,   xxxviii
    The sonne of *Climene* he did repent,
    Who bold to guide the charet of the Sunne,
    Himselfe in thousand peeces fondly rent,
    And all the world with flashing fier brent;
    So like, that all the walles did seeme to flame.
    Yet cruell *Cupid*, not herewith content,
    Forst him eftsoones to follow other game,
And loue a Shepheards daughter for his dearest Dame.

    xxxvii 4 beare] breare *1590*   5 breare] beare *1590*   8 garlond *1590*

He loued *Isse* for his dearest Dame,   xxxix
   And for her sake her cattell fed a while,
   And for her sake a cowheard vile became,
   The seruant of *Admetus* cowheard vile,
   Whiles that from heauen he suffered exile.
   Long were to tell each other louely fit,
   Now like a Lyon, hunting after spoile,
   Now like a Stag, now like a faulcon flit:
All which in that faire arras was most liuely writ.

Next vnto him was *Neptune* pictured,   xl
   In his diuine reoomblance wondrous lyke:
   His face was rugged, and his hoarie hed
   Dropped with brackish deaw; his three-forkt Pyke
   He stearnly shooke, and therewith fierce did stryke
   The raging billowes, that on euery syde
   They trembling stood, and made a long broad dyke,
   That his swift charet might haue passage wyde,
Which foure great *Hippodames* did draw in temewise tyde.

His sea-horses did seeme to snort amayne,   xli
   And from their nosethrilles blow the brynie streame,
   That made the sparckling waues to smoke agayne,
   And flame with gold, but the white fomy creame,
   Did shine with siluer, and shoot forth his beame.
   The God himselfe did pensiue seeme and sad,
   And hong adowne his head, as he did dreame:
   For priuy loue his brest empierced had,
Ne ought but deare *Bisaltis* ay could make him glad.

He loued eke *Iphimedia* deare,   xlii
   And *Aeolus* faire daughter *Arne* hight,
   For whom he turnd him selfe into a Steare,
   And fed on fodder, to beguile her sight.
   Also to win *Deucalions* daughter bright,
   He turnd him selfe into a Dolphin fayre;
   And like a winged horse he tooke his flight,
   To snaky-locke *Medusa* to repayre,
On whom he got faire *Pegasus*, that flitteth in the ayre.

xxxix 6 each] his *1590*   8 Stag *conj. Jortin* : Hag *1590 &c.*
    xlii 6 Her *1609*   8 snaly *1596*

Next *Saturne* was, (but who would euer weene,   xliii
    That sullein *Saturne* euer weend to loue?
    Yet loue is sullein, and *Saturnlike* seene,
    As he did for *Erigone* it proue,)
    That to a *Centaure* did him selfe transmoue.
    So proou'd it eke that gracious God of wine,
    When for to compasse *Philliras* hard loue,
    He turnd himselfe into a fruitfull vine,
And into her faire bosome made his grapes decline.

Long were to tell the amorous assayes,   xliv
    And gentle pangues, with which he maked meeke
    The mighty *Mars*, to learne his wanton playes:
    How oft for *Venus*, and how often eek
    For many other Nymphes he sore did shreek,
    With womanish teares, and with vnwarlike smarts,
    Priuily moystening his horrid cheek.
    There was he painted full of burning darts,
And many wide woundes launched through his inner parts.

Ne did he spare (so cruell was the Elfe)   xlv
    His owne deare mother, (ah why should he so?)
    Ne did he spare sometime to pricke himselfe,
    That he might tast the sweet consuming woe,
    Which he had wrought to many others moe.
    But to declare the mournfull Tragedyes,
    And spoiles, wherewith he all the ground did strow,
    More eath to number, with how many eyes
High heauen beholds sad louers nightly theeueryes.

Kings Queenes, Lords Ladies, Knights and Damzels gent   xlvi
    Were heap'd together with the vulgar sort,
    And mingled with the raskall rablement,
    Without respect of person or of port,
    To shew Dan *Cupids* powre and great effort:
    And round about a border was entrayld,
    Of broken bowes and arrowes shiuered short,
    And a long bloudy riuer through them rayld,
So liuely and so like, that liuing sence it fayld.

    xliii 4 proue.] *1596*   xliv 9 inner] i nward *1609*   parts, *1596*
               xlv 2 so! *1596*

And at the vpper end of that faire rowme,　　xlvii
　　There was an Altar built of pretious stone,
　　Of passing valew, and of great renowme,
　　On which there stood an Image all alone,
　　Of massy gold, which with his owne light shone;
　　And wings it had with sundry colours dight,
　　More sundry colours, then the proud *Pauone*
　　Beares in his boasted fan, or *Iris* bright,
When her discolourd bow she spreds through heauen bright.

Blindfold he was, and in his cruell fist　　xlviii
　　A mortall bow and arrowes keene did hold,
　　With which he shot at randon, when him list,
　　Some headed with sad lead, some with pure gold;
　　(Ah man beware, how thou those darts behold)
　　A wounded Dragon vnder him did ly,
　　Whose hideous tayle his left foot did enfold,
　　And with a shaft was shot through either eye,
That no man forth might draw, ne no man remedye.

And vnderneath his feet was written thus,　　xlix
　　Vnto the Victor of the Gods this bee:
　　And all the people in that ample hous
　　Did to that image bow their humble knee,
　　And oft committed fowle Idolatree.
　　That wondrous sight faire *Britomart* amazed,
　　Ne seeing could her wonder satisfie,
　　But euermore and more vpon it gazed,
The whiles the passing brightnes her fraile sences dazed.

Tho as she backward cast her busie eye,　　l
　　To search each secret of that goodly sted,
　　Ouer the dore thus written she did spye
　　Be bold: she oft and oft it ouer-red,
　　Yet could not find what sence it figured:
　　But what so were therein or writ or ment,
　　She was no whit thereby discouraged
　　From prosecuting of her first intent,
But forward with bold steps into the next roome went.

xlvii 9 heauens hight *conj. Church*　　xlviii 7 ensold *1596*　　xlix 8 euer
more *1609*　　l 2 sted *1590, 1596*

Much fairer, then the former, was that roome,   li
    And richlier by many partes arayd :
    For not with arras made in painefull loome,
    But with pure gold it all was ouerlayd,
    Wrought with wilde Antickes, which their follies playd,
    In the rich metall, as they liuing were:
    A thousand monstrous formes therein were made,
    Such as false loue doth oft vpon him weare,
For loue in thousand monstrous formes doth oft appeare.

And all about, the glistring walles were hong   lii
    With warlike spoiles, and with victorious prayes,
    Of mighty Conquerours and Captaines strong,
    Which were whilome captiued in their dayes
    To cruell loue, and wrought their owne decayes :
    Their swerds and speres were broke, and hauberques rent;
    And their proud girlonds of tryumphant bayes
    Troden in dust with fury insolent,
To shew the victors might and mercilesse intent.

The warlike Mayde beholding earnestly   liii
    The goodly ordinance of this rich place,
    Did greatly wonder, ne could satisfie
    Her greedy eyes with gazing a long space,
    But more she meruaild that no footings trace,
    Nor wight appear'd, but wastefull emptinesse,
    And solemne silence ouer all that place:
    Straunge thing it seem'd, that none was to possesse
So rich purueyance, ne them keepe with carefulnesse.

And as she lookt about, she did behold,   liv
    How ouer that same dore was likewise writ,
    Be bold, be bold, and euery where *Be bold,*
    That much she muz'd, yet could not construe it
    By any ridling skill, or commune wit.
    At last she spyde at that roomes vpper end,
    Another yron dore, on which was writ,
    Be not too bold; whereto though she did bend
Her earnest mind, yet wist not what it might intend.

    li 8 weare ? *1596*   lii 6 swords *1609*   liii 3 wonder *1596*

Thus she there waited vntill euentyde,   1v
  Yet liuing creature none she saw appeare :
  And now sad shadowes gan the world to hyde,
  From mortall vew, and wrap in darkenesse dreare;
  Yet nould she d'off her weary armes, for feare
  Of secret daunger, ne let sleepe oppresse
  Her heauy eyes with natures burdein deare,
  But drew her selfe aside in sickernesse,
And her welpointed weapons did about her dresse.

Cant. XII.

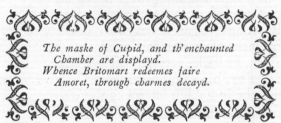

The maske of Cupid, and th'enchaunted
  Chamber are displayd.
Whence Britomart redeemes faire
  Amoret, through charmes decayd.

THo when as chearelesse Night ycouered had   i
  Faire heauen with an vniuersall cloud,
  That euery wight dismuyd with darknesse sad,
  In silence and in sleepe themselues did shroud,
  She heard a shrilling Trompet sound aloud,
  Signe of nigh battell, or got victory ;
  Nought therewith daunted was her courage proud,
  But rather stird to cruell enmity,
Expecting euer, when some foe she might descry.

With that, an hideous storme of winde arose,   ii
  With dreadfull thunder and lightning atwixt,
  And an earth-quake, as if it streight would lose
  The worlds foundations from his centre fixt;
  A direfull stench of smoke and sulphure mixt
  Ensewd, whose noyance fild the fearefull sted,
  From the fourth houre of night vntill the sixt;
  Yet the bold *Britonesse* was nought ydred,
Though much emmou'd, but stedfast still perseuered.

lv 1 she there] there she *1609*

All suddenly a stormy whirlwind blew   iii
   Throughout the house, that clapped euery dore,
   With which that yron wicket open flew,
   As it with mightie leuers had bene tore :
   And forth issewd, as on the ready flore
   Of some Theatre, a graue personage,
   That in his hand a branch of laurell bore,
   With comely haueour and count'nance sage,
Yclad in costly garments, fit for tragicke Stage.

Proceeding to the midst, he still did stand,   iv
   As if in mind he somewhat had to say,
   And to the vulgar beckning with his hand,
   In signe of silence, as to heare a play,
   By liuely actions he gan bewray
   Some argument of matter passioned ;
   Which doen, he backe retyred soft away,
   And passing by, his name discouered,
Ease, on his robe in golden letters cyphered.

The noble Mayd, still standing all this vewd,   v
   And merueild at his strange intendiment ;
   With that a ioyous fellowship issewd
   Of Minstrals, making goodly meriment,
   With wanton Bardes, and Rymers impudent,
   All which together sung full chearefully
   A lay of loues delight, with sweet concent :
   After whom marcht a iolly company,
In manner of a maske, enranged orderly.

The whiles a most delitious harmony,   vi
   In full straunge notes was sweetly heard to sound,
   That the rare sweetnesse of the melody
   The feeble senses wholly did confound,
   And the fraile soule in deepe delight nigh dround :
   And when it ceast, shrill trompets loud did bray,
   That their report did farre away rebound,
   And when they ceast, it gan againe to play,
The whiles the maskers marched forth in trim aray.

v 7 consent *1596*

The first was *Fancy*, like a louely boy, vii
 Of rare aspect, and beautie without peare;
 Matchable either to that ympe of *Troy*,
 Whom *Ioue* did loue, and chose his cup to beare,
 Or that same daintie lad, which was so deare
 To great *Alcides*, that when as he dyde,
 He wailed womanlike with many a teare,
 And·euery wood, and euery valley wyde
He fild with *Hylas* name; the Nymphes eke *Hylas* cryde.

His garment neither was of silke nor say, viii
 But painted plumes, in goodly order dight,
 Like as the sunburnt *Indians* do aray
 Their tawney bodies, in their proudest plight:
 As those same plumes, so seemd he vaine and light,
 That by his gate might easily appeare;
 For still he far'd as dauncing in delight,
 And in his hand a windy fan did beare,
That in the idle aire he mou'd still here and there.

And him beside marcht amorous *Desyre*, ix
 Who seemd of riper yeares, then th'other Swaine,
 Yet was that other swayne this elders syre,
 And gaue him being, commune to them twaine:
 His garment was disguised very vaine,
 And his embrodered Bonet sat awry;
 Twixt both his hands few sparkes he close did straine,
 Which still he blew, and kindled busily,
That soone they life conceiu'd, and forth in flames did fly.

Next after him went *Doubt*, who was yclad x
 In a discolour'd cote, of straunge disguyse,
 That at his backe a brode Capuccio had,
 And sleeues dependant *Albanese*-wyse:
 He lookt askew with his mistrustfull eyes,
 And nicely trode, as thornes lay in his way,
 Or that the flore to shrinke he did auyse,
 And on a broken reed he still did stay
His feeble steps, which shrunke, when hard theron he lay.

vii 3 ether *1590*   8 wood,] word, *1590*   viii 1 nether *1590*
         ix 3 other] others *1590, 1596*

With him went *Daunger*, cloth'd in ragged weed,   xi
   Made of Beares skin, that him more dreadfull made,
   Yet his owne face was dreadfull, ne did need
   Straunge horrour, to deforme his griesly shade;
   A net in th'one hand, and a rustie blade
   In th'other was, this Mischiefe, that Mishap;
   With th'one his foes he threatned to inuade,
   With th'other he his friends ment to enwrap:
For whom he could not kill, he practizd to entrap.

Next him was *Feare*, all arm'd from top to toe,   xii
   Yet thought himselfe not safe enough thereby,
   But feard each shadow mouing to and fro,
   And his owne armes when glittering he did spy,
   Or clashing heard, he fast away did fly,
   As ashes pale of hew, and wingyheeld;
   And euermore on daunger fixt his eye,
   Gainst whom he alwaies bent a brasen shield,
Which his right hand vnarmed fearefully did wield.

With him went *Hope* in rancke, a handsome Mayd,   xiii
   Of chearefull looke and louely to behold;
   In silken samite she was light arayd,
   And her faire lockes were wouen vp in gold;
   She alway smyld, and in her hand did hold
   An holy water Sprinckle, dipt in deowe,
   With which she sprinckled fauours manifold,
   On whom she list, and did great liking sheowe,
Great liking vnto many, but true loue to feowe.

And after them *Dissemblance*, and *Suspect*   xiv
   Marcht in one rancke, yet an vnequall paire:
   For she was gentle, and of milde aspect,
   Courteous to all, and seeming debonaire,
   Goodly adorned, and exceeding faire:
   Yet was that all but painted, and purloynd,
   And her bright browes were deckt with borrowed haire:
   Her deedes were forged, and her words false coynd,
And alwaies in her hand two clewes of silke she twynd.

    xi 1 cloth' *1596*   xii 3 and] or *1590*   6 winged heeld *1590*

But he was foule, ill fauoured, and grim,   xv
   Vnder his eyebrowes looking still askaunce;
   And euer as *Dissemblance* laught on him,
   He lowrd on her with daungerous eyeglaunce;
   Shewing his nature in his countenance;
   His rolling eyes did neuer rest in place,
   But walkt each where, for feare of hid mischaunce,
   Holding a lattice still before his face,
Through which he still did peepe, as forward he did pace.

Next him went *Griefe*, and *Fury* matcht yfere;   xvi
   Griefe all in sable sorrowfully clad,
   Downe hanging his dull head, with heauy chere,
   Yet inly being more, then seeming sad:
   A paire of Pincers in his hand he had,
   With which he pinched people to the hart,
   That from thenceforth a wretched life they lad,
   In wilfull languor and consuming smart,
Dying each day with inward wounds of dolours dart.

But *Fury* was full ill appareiled   xvii
   In rags, that naked nigh she did appeare,
   With ghastly lookes and dreadfull drerihed;
   For from her backe her garments she did teare,
   And from her head oft rent her snarled heare:
   In her right hand a firebrand she did tosse
   About her head, still roming here and there;
   As a dismayed Deare in chace embost,
Forgetfull of his safety, hath his right way lost.

After them went *Displeasure* and *Pleasance*,   xviii
   He looking lompish and full sullein sad,
   And hanging downe his heauy countenance;
   She chearefull fresh and full of ioyance glad,
   As if no sorrow she ne felt ne drad;
   That euill matched paire they seemd to bee:
   An angry Waspe th'one in a viall had
   Th'other in hers an hony-lady Bee;
Thus marched these six couples forth in faire degree.

xvii 6 a fierbrand she tost *conj. Church*   xviii 5 dread *1590*   8 hony-laden *Morris*

After all these there marcht a most faire Dame,   xix
  Led of two grysie villeins, th'one *Despight,*
  The other cleped *Cruelty* by name :
  She dolefull Lady, like a dreary Spright,
  Cald by strong charmes out of eternall night,
  Had deathes owne image figurd in her face,
  Full of sad signes, fearefull to liuing sight ;
  Yet in that horror shewd a seemely grace,
And with her feeble feet did moue a comely pace.

Her brest all naked, as net iuory,   xx
  Without adorne of gold or siluer bright,
  Wherewith the Craftesman wonts it beautify,
  Of her dew honour was despoyled quight,
  And a wide wound therein (O ruefull sight)
  Entrenched deepe with knife accursed keene,
  Yet freshly bleeding forth her fainting spright,
  (The worke of cruell hand) was to be seene,
That dyde in sanguine red her skin all snowy cleene.

At that wide orifice her trembling hart   xxi
  Was drawne forth, and in siluer basin layd,
  Quite through transfixed with a deadly dart,
  And in her bloud yet steeming fresh embayd :
  And those two villeins, which her steps vpstayd,
  When her weake feete could scarcely her sustaine,
  And fading vitall powers gan to fade,
  Her forward still with torture did constraine,
And euermore encreased her consuming paine.

Next after her the winged God himselfe   xxii
  Came riding on a Lion rauenous,
  Taught to obay the menage of that Elfe,
  That man and beast with powre imperious
  Subdeweth to his kingdome tyrannous :
  His blindfold eyes he bad a while vnbind,
  That his proud spoyle of that same dolorous
  Faire Dame he might behold in perfect kind ;
Which seene, he much reioyced in his cruell mind.

xxi 7 fading] failing *conj. Church*   8 still] skill *1590*
xxii 5 knigdome *1596*

Of which full proud, himselfe vp rearing hye,   xxiii
  He looked round about with sterne disdaine;
  And did suruay his goodly company:
  And marshalling the euill ordered traine,
  With that the darts which his right hand did straine,
  Full dreadfully he shooke that all did quake,
  And clapt on hie his coulourd winges twaine,
  That all his many it affraide did make:
Tho blinding him againe, his way he forth did take.

Behinde him was *Reproch, Repentance, Shame*;   xxiv
  Reproch the first, *Shame* next, *Repent* behind:
  Repentance feeble, sorrowfull, and lame:
  Reproch despightfull, carelesse, and vnkind;
  Shame most ill fauourd, bestiall, and blind:
  Shame lowrd, *Repentance* sigh'd, *Reproch* did scould;
  Reproch sharpe stings, *Repentance* whips entwind,
  Shame burning brond-yrons in her hand did hold:
All three to each vnlike, yet all made in one mould.

And after them a rude confused rout   xxv
  Of persons flockt, whose names is hard to read:
  Emongst them was sterne *Strife*, and *Anger* stout,
  Vnquiet *Care*, and fond *Vnthriftihead*,
  Lewd *Losse of Time*, and *Sorrow* seeming dead,
  Inconstant *Chaunge*, and false *Disloyaltie*,
  Consuming *Riotise*, and guilty *Dread*
  Of heauenly vengeance, faint *Infirmitie*,
Vile *Pouertie*, and lastly *Death* with infamie.

There were full many moe like maladies,   xxvi
  Whose names and natures I note readen well;
  So many moe, as there be phantasies
  In wauering wemens wit, that none can tell,
  Or paines in loue, or punishments in hell;
  All which disguized marcht in masking wise,
  About the chamber with that Damozell,
  And then returned, hauing marched thrise,.
Into the inner roome, from whence they first did rise.

  xxiii 5 right did *1590, 1596: corr. F. E.*   xxvi 6 All] And *1596,
1609*   7 with that] by the *1590*

So soone as they were in, the dore streight way   xxvii
   Fast locked, driuen with that stormy blast,
   Which first it opened; and bore all away.
   Then the braue Maid, which all this while was plast
   In secret shade, and saw both first and last,
   Issewed forth, and went vnto the dore,
   To enter in, but found it locked fast:
   It vaine she thought with rigorous vprore
For to efforce, when charmes had closed it afore.

Where force might not auaile, there sleights and art   xxviii
   She cast to vse, both fit for hard emprize;
   For thy from that same roome not to depart
   Till morrow next, she did her selfe auize,
   When that same Maske againe should forth arize.
   The morrow next appeard with ioyous cheare,
   Calling men to their daily exercize,
   Then she, as morrow fresh, her selfe did reare
Out of her secret stand, that day for to out weare.

All that day she outwore in wandering,   xxix
   And gazing on that Chambers ornament,
   Till that againe the second euening
   Her couered with her sable vestiment,
   Wherewith the worlds faire beautie she hath blent:
   Then when the second watch was almost past,
   That brasen dore flew open, and in went
   Bold *Britomart*, as she had late forecast,
Neither of idle shewes, nor of false charmes aghast.

So soone as she was entred, round about   xxx
   She cast her eies, to see what was become
   Of all those persons, which she saw without:
   But lo, they streight were vanisht all and some,
   Ne liuing wight she saw in all that roome,
   Saue that same woefull Ladie, both whose hands
   Were bounden fast, that did her ill become,
   And her small wast girt round with yron bands,
Vnto a brasen pillour, by the which she stands.

And her before the vile Enchaunter sate,   xxxi
   Figuring straunge characters of his art,
   With liuing bloud he those characters wrate,
   Dreadfully dropping from her dying hart,
   Seeming transfixed with a cruell dart,
   And all perforce to make her him to loue.
   Ah who can loue the worker of her smart?
   A thousand charmes he formerly did proue;
Yet thousand charmes could not her stedfast heart remoue.

Soone as that virgin knight he saw in place,   xxxii
   His wicked bookes in hast he ouerthrew,
   Not caring his long labours to deface,
   And fiercely ronning to that Lady trew,
   A murdrous knife out of his pocket drew,
   The which he thought, for villeinous despight,
   In her tormented bodie to embrew:
   But the stout Damzell to him leaping light,
His cursed hand withheld, and maistered his might.

From her, to whom his fury first he ment,   xxxiii
   The wicked weapon rashly he did wrest,
   And turning to her selfe his fell intent,
   Vnwares it strooke into her snowie chest,
   That little drops empurpled her faire brest.
   Exceeding wroth therewith the virgin grew,
   Albe the wound were nothing deepe imprest,
   And fiercely forth her mortall blade she drew,
To giue him the reward for such vile outrage dew.

So mightily she smote him, that to ground   xxxiv
   He fell halfe dead; next stroke him should haue slaine,
   Had not the Lady, which by him stood bound,
   Dernely vnto her called to abstaine,
   From doing him to dy.   For else her paine
   Should be remedilesse, sith none but hee,
   Which wrought it, could the same recure againe.
   Therewith she stayd her hand, loth stayd to bee;
For life she him enuyde, and long'd reuenge to see.

xxxi 3 wrote *1609*   xxxiii 3 her selfe] the next *1590*
xxxiv 4 her] him *1590, 1596*

And to him said, Thou wicked man, whose meed   xxxv
   For so huge mischiefe, and vile villany
   Is death, or if that ought do death exceed,
   Be sure, that nought may saue thee from to dy,
   But if that thou this Dame doe presently
   Restore vnto her health, and former state;
   This doe and liue, else die vndoubtedly.
   He glad of life, that lookt for death but late,
Did yield himselfe right willing to prolong his date.

And rising vp, gan streight to ouerlooke   xxxvi
   Those cursed leaues, his charmes backe to reuerse;
   Full dreadfull things out of that balefull booke
   He red, and measur'd many a sad verse,
   That horror gan the virgins hart to perse,
   And her faire locks vp stared stiffe on end,
   Hearing him those same bloudy lines reherse;
   And all the while he red, she did extend
Her sword high ouer him, if ought he did offend.

Anon she gan perceiue the house to quake,   xxxvii
   And all the dores to rattle round about;
   Yet all that did not her dismaied make,
   Nor slacke her threatfull hand for daungers dout,
   But still with stedfast eye and courage stout
   Abode, to weet what end would come of all.
   At last that mightie chaine, which round about
   Her tender waste was wound, adowne gan fall,
And that great brasen pillour broke in peeces small.

The cruell steele, which thrild her dying hart,   xxxviii
   Fell softly forth, as of his owne accord,
   And the wyde wound, which lately did dispart
   Her bleeding brest, and riuen bowels gor'd,
   Was closed vp, as it had not bene bor'd,
   And euery part to safety full sound,
   As she were neuer hurt, was soone restor'd:
   Tho when she felt her selfe to be vnbound,
And perfect hole, prostrate she fell vnto the ground.

xxxviii 5 bor'd] sor'd *1590*

Before faire *Britomart*, she fell prostrate,   xxxix
   Saying, Ah noble knight, what worthy meed
   Can wretched Lady, quit from wofull state,
   Yield you in liew of this your gratious deed?
   Your vertue selfe her owne reward shall breed,
   Euen immortall praise, and glory wyde,
   Which I your vassall, by your prowesse freed,
   Shall through the world make to be notifyde,
And goodly well aduance, that goodly well was tryde.

But *Britomart* vprearing her from ground,   xl
   Said, Gentle Dame, reward enough I weene
   For many labours more, then I haue found,
   This, that in safety now I haue you seene,
   And meane of your deliuerance haue beene:
   Henceforth faire Lady comfort to you take,
   And put away remembrance of late teene;
   In stead thereof know, that your louing Make,
Hath no lesse griefe endured for your gentle sake.

She much was cheard to heare him mentiond,   xli
   Whom of all liuing wights she loued best.
   Then laid the noble Championesse strong hond
   Vpon th'enchaunter, which had her distrest
   So sore, and with foule outrages opprest:
   With that great chaine, wherewith not long ygo
   He bound that pitteous Lady prisoner, now relest,
   Himselfe she bound, more worthy to be so,
And captiue with her led to wretchednesse and wo.

Returning backe, those goodly roomes, which erst   xlii
   She saw so rich and royally arayd,
   Now vanisht vtterly, and cleane subuerst
   She found, and all their glory quite decayd,
   That sight of such a chaunge her much dismayd.
   Thence forth descending to that perlous Porch,
   Those dreadfull flames she also found delayd,
   And quenched quite, like a consumed torch,
That erst all entrers wont so cruelly to scorch.

   xlii 2 She] He *1590*   4 She] He *1590*: *corr. F. E.*   5 her] him
1590: *corr. F. E.*

More easie issew now, then entrance late   xliii
   She found: for now that fained dreadfull flame,
   Which chokt the porch of that enchaunted gate,
   And passage bard to all, that thither came,
   Was vanisht quite, as it were not the same,
   And gaue her leaue at pleasure forth to passe.
   Th'Enchaunter selfe, which all that fraud did frame,
   To haue efforst the loue of that faire lasse,
Seeing his worke now wasted deepe engrieued was.

But when the victoresse arriued there,   xliv
   Where late she left the pensife *Scudamore*,
   With her owne trusty Squire, both full of feare,
   Neither of them she found where she them lore:
   Thereat her noble hart was stonisht sore;
   But most faire *Amoret*, whose gentle spright
   Now gan to feede on hope, which she before
   Conceiued had, to see her owne deare knight,
Being thereof beguyld was fild with new affright.

But he sad man, when he had long in drede   xlv
   Awayted there for *Britomarts* returne,
   Yet saw her not nor signe of her good speed,
   His expectation to despaire did turne,
   Misdeeming sure that her those flames did burne;
   And therefore gan aduize with her old Squire,
   Who her deare nourslings losse no lesse did mourne,
   Thence to depart for further aide t'enquire:
Where let them wend at will, whilest here I doe respire.

xliv 2 pensiue *1609*   xlv 7 Who with her *1596*

Stanzas xliii–xlv were first inserted in the 1596 quarto, displacing the
following stanzas which concluded Book III in the first edition.

At last she came vnto the place, where late
   She left Sir *Scudamour* in great distresse,
   Twixt dolour and despight halfe desperate,
   Of his loues succour, of his owne redresse,
   And of the hardie *Britomarts* successe:
   There on the cold earth him now thrown she found,
   In wilfull anguish, and dead heauinesse,
   And to him cald; whose voices knowen sound
Soone as he heard, himself he reared light from ground.

There did he see, that most on earth him ioyd,
   His dearest loue, the comfort of his dayes,
   Whose too long absence him had sore annoyd,
   And wearied his life with dull delayes:
   Straight he vpstarted from the loathed layes,
   And to her ran with hasty egernesse,
   Like as a Deare, that greedily embayes
   In the coole soile, after long thirstinesse,
Which he in chace endured hath, now nigh breathlesse.

Lightly he clipt her twixt his armes twaine,
   And streightly did embrace her body bright,
   Her body, late the prison of sad paine,
   Now the sweet lodge of loue and deare delight:
   But she faire Lady ouercommen quight
   Of huge affection, did in pleasure melt,
   And in sweete rauishment pourd out her spright:
   No word they spake, nor earthly thing they felt,
But like two senceles stocks in long embracement dwelt.

Had ye them seene, ye would haue surely thought,
   That they had beene that faire *Hermaphrodite*,
   Which that rich *Romane* of white marble wrought,
   And in his costly Bath causd to bee site:
   So seemd those two, as growne together quite,
   That *Britomart* halfe enuying their blesse,
   Was much empassiond in her gentle sprite,
   And to her selfe oft wisht like happinesse,
In vaine she wisht, that fate n'ould let her yet possesse.

Thus doe those louers with sweet counteruayle,
Each other of loues bitter fruit despoile.
But now my teme begins to faint and fayle,
All woxen weary of their iournall toyle:
Therefore I will their sweatie yokes assoyle
At this same furrowes end, till a new day:
And ye faire Swayns, after your long turmoyle,
Now cease your worke, and at your pleasure play;
Now cease your worke; to morrow is an holy day.

PRINTED IN GREAT BRITAIN
AT THE UNIVERSITY PRESS, OXFORD
BY VIVIAN RIDLER
PRINTER TO THE UNIVERSITY